New York Edition

The American Journey

Joyce Appleby, Ph.D.

Alan Brinkley, Ph.D.

Albert S. Broussard, Ph.D.

James M. McPherson, Ph.D.

Donald A. Ritchie, Ph.D.

NATIONAL GEOGRAPHIC

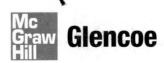

Mc Graw Hill Glencoe

Authors

Joyce Appleby, Ph.D., is Professor of History at UCLA. Dr. Appleby's published works include *Inheriting the Revolution: The First Generation of Americans; Capitalism and a New Social Order: The Jeffersonian Vision of the 1790s;* and *Economic Thought and Ideology in Seventeenth-Century England,* which won the Berkshire Prize. She served as president of both the Organization of American Historians and the American Historical Association, and chaired the Council of the Institute of Early American History and Culture at Williamsburg. Dr. Appleby has been elected to the American Philosophical Society and the American Academy of Arts and Sciences, and is a Corresponding Fellow of the British Academy.

Alan Brinkley, Ph.D., is Allan Nevins Professor of American History at Columbia University. His published works include *Voices of Protest: Huey Long, Father Coughlin, and the Great Depression,* which won the 1983 National Book Award; *The End of Reform: New Deal Liberalism in Recession and War; The Unfinished Nation: A Concise History of the American People;* and *Liberalism and Its Discontents.* He received the Levenson Memorial Teaching Prize at Harvard University.

Albert S. Broussard, Ph.D., is Professor of History and Graduate Coordinator at Texas A&M University. Before joining the Texas A&M faculty, Dr. Broussard was Assistant Professor of History and Director of the African American Studies Program at Southern Methodist University. Among his publications are the books *Black San Francisco: The Struggle for Racial Equality in the West, 1900–1954* and *African American Odyssey: The Stewarts, 1853–1963.* Dr. Broussard has also served as president of the Oral History Association.

Donald A. Ritchie, Ph.D., is Associate Historian of the United States Senate Historical Office. Dr. Ritchie received his doctorate in American history from the University of Maryland after service in the U.S. Marine Corps. He has taught American history at various levels, from high school to university. He edits the Historical Series of the Senate Foreign Relations Committee and is the author of several books, including *Doing Oral History, The Oxford Guide to the United States Government,* and *Press Gallery: Congress and the Washington Correspondents,* which received the Organization of American Historians Richard W. Leopold Prize. Dr. Ritchie has served as president of the Oral History Association and as a council member of the American Historical Association.

James M. McPherson, Ph.D., is George Henry Davis Professor of American History at Princeton University. Dr. McPherson is the author of 11 books about the Civil War era. These include *Battle Cry of Freedom: The Civil War Era,* for which he won the Pulitzer Prize in 1989, and *For Cause and Comrades: Why Men Fought in the Civil War,* for which he won the 1998 Lincoln Prize. He is a member of many professional historical associations, including the Civil War Preservation Trust.

The National Geographic Society, founded in 1888 for the increase and diffusion of geographic knowledge, is the world's largest nonprofit scientific and educational organization. Since its earliest days, the Society has used sophisticated communication technologies, from color photography to holography, to convey knowledge to a worldwide membership. The School Publishing Division supports the Society's mission by developing innovative educational programs—ranging from traditional print materials to multimedia programs including CD-ROMs, videodiscs, and software. "National Geographic Geography & History," featured in each unit of this textbook, was designed and developed by the National Geographic Society's School Publishing Division.

Contributing Author

Dinah Zike, M.Ed., is an award-winning author, educator, and inventor known for designing three-dimensional hands-on manipulatives and graphic organizers known as Foldables®. Foldables are used nationally and internationally by teachers, parents, and educational publishing companies. Dinah has developed over 150 supplemental educational books and materials. She is the author of *The Big Book of Books and Activities,* which was awarded Learning Magazine's Teachers' Choice Award. In 2004 Dinah was honored with the CESI Science Advocacy Award. Dinah received her M.Ed. from Texas A&M, College Station, Texas.

RFB&D learning through listening — Students with print disabilities may be eligible to obtain an accessible, audio version of the pupil edition of this textbook. Please call Recording for the Blind & Dyslexic at 1-800-221-4792 for complete information.

The McGraw·Hill Companies

Glencoe

Send all inquiries to:
Glencoe/McGraw-Hill
8787 Orion Place
Columbus, OH 43240-4027

ISBN: 978-0-07-881088-6
MHID: 0-07-881088-4

Printed in the United States of America.

2 3 4 5 6 7 8 9 10 071/043 12 11 10 09 08

Consultants & Reviewers

Academic Consultants

Laura Belmonte, Ph.D.
Associate Professor of
  History
Oklahoma State University
Stillwater, Oklahoma

David Berger, Ph.D.
Broeklundian Professor of
  History
Yeshiva University
New York, New York

Keith S. Bohannon, Ph.D.
Professor of History
University of West Georgia
Carrollton, Georgia

David Canton, Ph.D.
Jacob & Hilda Blaustein
  Assistant Professor of
  History
Connecticut College
New London, Connecticut

Jaime Cardenas, Jr., Ph.D.
Associate Professor of
  History
Seattle Central Community
  College
Seattle, Washington

Jeffrey A. Davis, Ph.D.
Associate Professor of
  History
Bloomsburg University of
  Pennsylvania
Bloomsburg, Pennsylvania

Allison Gough, Ph.D.
Assistant Professor of History
Hawaii Pacific University
Honolulu, Hawaii

Melissa Klapper, Ph.D.
Associate Professor of
  History
Rowan University
Glassboro, New Jersey

Daniel Lewis, Ph.D.
Professor of History
California State Polytechnic
  University
Pomona, California

Teacher Reviewers

Lysa Augustin
Davis Hills Middle School
Huntsville, Alabama

John Brandt
Cumberland County Middle
  School
Cumberland, Virginia

Joanne Cogan
Fairgrounds Middle School
Nashua, New Hampshire

Stephanie Doyle
Breckinridge Middle School
Roanoke, Virginia

Teresa Gallup
York Suburban Middle
  School
York, Pennsylvania

Tina Gersdorf
Jefferson Middle School
Champaign, Illinois

Michael Gordon
Barrington Middle School
Barrington, Illinois

Dawn Grindley
Westlake Middle School
Thornwood, New York

Chris Hartlieb
Highland Middle School
Highland, Illinois

Susan Hawes
Elm Middle School
Elmwood Park, Illinois

Thomas Joice
Clark Middle School
Vincennes, Indiana

Tom Kish
Zimmerman Middle School
Zimmerman, Minnesota

Steven Miller
Blue Ridge Middle School
Purcellville, Virginia

Lisa Ray
Chapin Middle School
Chapin, South Carolina

Terry Robinson
Alden Middle School
Alden, New York

Kathleen Shaeper
Allegany-Limestone Middle
  School
Allegany, New York

Karan Stubbs
Bixby Middle School
Bixby, Oklahoma

Stephanie Sumick
Thompson Middle School
Middletown, New Jersey

Laura Tabachnick
Academy School
Brattleboro, Vermont

Lynn Voorhees
Creekside Middle School
Carmel, Indiana

Marjorie White
Brentwood Middle School
North Charleston, South
  Carolina

Susan Yurkovic
Brownsburg West Middle
  School
Brownsburg, Indiana

Contents

NATIONAL GEOGRAPHIC Reference Atlas

Unit 1

The Americas: Worlds Meet 1

Unit 6

Reshaping the Nation.. 546

Unit 7

Reform and Empire. . . . 636

Contents

Features

LINKING PAST TO PRESENT

Navigation Tools 30
Women in War 154
The United States Flag 206
Roads: Tying the Nation Together 314
Roots of American Music 408
Battlefield Medicine 494
American Football 630

Conserving Wild Places. 658
Women in Government 796
Computers 862

NATIONAL GEOGRAPHIC GEOGRAPHY & HISTORY

Jamestown. 62
Battle of Yorktown. 180
Choosing the Location of Washington, D.C. 258
The Underground Railroad. 432
Southern Industry After the Civil War 542
Skin Houses, Sod Houses:
    Plains Indians and Homesteaders 572

World War I and Trench Warfare. 710
The Great Migration 748
Changing Settlement Patterns. 868
Immigration 1008

America's LITERATURE

The Witch of Blackbird Pond 70
The Journal of William Thomas Emerson 130
Fever 1793 310
Day of Tears 404
The Red Badge of Courage 488
Roughing It 558

Counting on Grace 648
"The Negro Speaks of Rivers" and
    "Mother to Son" 766
The Watsons Go to Birmingham—1963 892
Taking Sides. 964

Economics & History

Triangular Trade. 91
Purposes of Money. 192
Protective Tariffs 256

Imports and Exports 289
Productivity and Technology 402
Army Salaries. 477
Vertical and Horizontal Integration. 598
Federal Income Taxes 660
U.S. Auto Industry. 756
Food for a Year. 864
Average Gas Prices, 1950-2007. 960
Exporters, Importers, and Oil Reserves 1002

People IN HISTORY

YOU DECIDE

Features

Primary Sources
INTERPRETING
POLITICAL CARTOONS

TIME NOTEBOOK

Chance & Error in History

Skills Handbook

1 Learn It!

2 Practice It!

3 Apply It!

Critical Thinking Skills

Social Studies Skills

Documents of American History

Primary Source Quotes

Primary Source Quotes

Primary Source Quotes

NY18

Primary Source Quotes

Primary Source Quotes

Maps

Maps In Motion Maps, charts, and graphs with this logo have been enhanced by InMotion graphics in the StudentWorks™ Plus CD-ROM and the Presentation Plus! CD-ROM. These InMotion graphics allow students to interact with layers of data and listen to audio components.

Maps

Charts, Graphs, & Diagrams

Charts, Graphs, & Diagrams

Scavenger Hunt

The American Journey contains a wealth of information. The trick is to know where to look to access all the information in the book. If you complete this scavenger hunt exercise with your teachers or parents, you will see how the textbook is organized and how to get the most out of your reading and study time. Let's get started!

1. How many units and how many chapters are in this book?

2. Where would you look to quickly find facts about each state, including the capital and the year it was admitted into the Union?

3. You want to read the Declaration of Independence. How will you find it?

4. What time period does Chapter 16 cover?

5. In Chapter 4, what information will the Foldables activity help you organize?

6. What Reading History skill will you practice in Unit 2?

7. Where can you find the Essential Questions for each chapter?

8. What is the History Online Web Activity for Chapter 12?

9. Where in the back of the book can you quickly find the meaning of important vocabulary words such as sodbuster?

10. Where can you learn about and practice critical thinking and social studies skills?

Correlation to the New York Core Curriculum for U.S. and New York History

Standards	Student Edition Pages
UNIT ONE: THE GLOBAL HERITAGE OF THE AMERICAN PEOPLE PRIOR TO 1500	
I. History and the Social Sciences: The Study of People	
Objective 1: To understand the social scientific method and techniques used by social scientists to study human cultures	Ref18–Ref19, 6, 7, 9
Objective 2: To understand how the social scientific method and techniques can be applied to a variety of situations	Ref18–Ref19, 9
Objective 3: To formulate social science questions and define social science issues and problems	Ref18–Ref22
CONTENT OUTLINE	
A. History and the other social sciences provide a framework and methodology for a systematic study of human cultures	Ref18–Ref19, 7
1. The role of history and the historian	Ref18–Ref22, 6–7,
2. The other social sciences including anthropology, economics, geography, political science, psychology, and sociology	7, 9
B. The social scientific method as a technique for problem solving and decision making	Ref18–Ref22, 9
II. Geographic Factors Influence Culture	
Objective 1: To describe the relationships between people and environments and the connections between people and places	7, 8, 9, 10–15, 16–22, 25
Objective 2: To describe the reasons for periodizing history in different ways	Ref18–Ref22, 6–7
Objective 3: To map information about people, places, and environments	9, 10–15
Objective 4: To identify and compare the physical, human, and cultural characteristics of different regions and people	10–15
Objective 5: To understand the geography of settlement patterns and the development of cultural patterns	6, 7, 8, 9, 10–11, 12, 13, 14, 15
CONTENT OUTLINE	
A. Theories attempt to explain human settlement in the Americas	7, 8, 9, 25
1. Anthropologists theorize that Asians migrated across a land bridge between Asia and the Americas	7, 8, 9, 25
2. Native American Indians believe in indigenous development with migration patterns in both directions	NY56, NY57
B. Geographic factors affected the settlement patterns and living conditions of the earliest Americans	8, 9, 13, 17, 18, 19, 20, 21, 22, 24–25, NY56
C. Major Native American civilizations in Central and South America	5, 10–15
1. The Aztecs	5, 10, 13, 14, 15
2. The Mayas	5, 10, 11, 12, 13, 15
3. The Incas	5, 14, 15
III. Iroquoian and Algonquian Cultures on the Atlantic Coast of North America	
Objective 1: To know the social and economic characteristics such as customs, traditions, child-rearing practices, gender roles, foods, and religious and spiritual beliefs that distinguish different cultures and civilizations	16, NY56–NY58, NY59
Objective 2: To map information about people, places, and environments	16, 25
Objective 3: To understand the worldview held by native peoples of the Americas and how that worldview developed	21, 22, NY58
Objective 4: To understand the ways different people view the same event or issues from a variety of perspectives	NY58, NY59–NY60
CONTENT OUTLINE	
A. Iroquois (Haudenosaunee—People of the Longhouse) and Algonquian People adapted to the environment in which they settled	20, 21, 22, 25, NY56–NY58
1. Geographic regions of New York	21, NY56
2. Diversity of flora and fauna	NY56
3. Seasons and weather patterns	NY56
4. Kinds of settlements and settlement patterns	NY56–NY59

Standards	Student Edition Pages
B. The Iroquois (Haudenosaunee) developed cultural patterns that reflected their needs and values	NY56–NY58, NY59
1. Creation and religious beliefs	21, 22
2. Importance of the laws of nature and the wise use of natural resources	NY56, NY59
3. Patterns of time and space	NY58–NY59
4. Family and kinship	22, 24, NY56–NY58
5. Education	NY56–NY58
6. Government: Iroquois Confederacy and political organizations at the village level (tribal organization)	22
7. Conceptions of land ownership and use	NY59
8. Language	NY56–NY58
C. Algonquian Culture	NY56–NY58
1. Spiritual beliefs	NY56–NY58
2. Spatial patterns	NY56–NY59
IV. European Conceptions of the World in 1500	
Objective 1: To understand the worldview held by Europeans prior to 1500	29, 30, 31, 33, 34, 35, 40, NY58
Objective 2: To understand the ways different people view the same event or issues from a variety of perspectives	29, 30, 35, 38, 40, 41, NY58–NY59
CONTENT OUTLINE	
A. European knowledge was based on a variety of sources	28, 29, 31
1. Accounts of early travelers and explorers	28, 29, 31, 33
2. A variety of different maps	31, 33, 35
3. Writing of ancient scholars	38
4. Guesswork	38
5. Oral traditions and histories	38, 41
B. Different worldviews and ethnocentrism resulted in many misconceptions	35, 38, 39, 42
UNIT TWO: EUROPEAN EXPLORATION AND COLONIZATION OF THE AMERICAS	
I. European Exploration and Settlement	
Objective 1: To understand major turning points, such as the European exploration of and settlement in the Americas, by investigating the causes and other factors that brought about change and the results of these changes	31, 32, 39, 40, 41, 43, 44, 45, 47, 48, 49, 50, 51, 52, 59, 60, 61
Objective 2: To understand the impacts of European settlement on Native American Indians and Europeans	42, 43, 44, 47, 48, 104
Objective 3: To investigate why people and places are located where they are located and what patterns can be perceived in these locations	43, 45, 46, 48, 58, 59, 60
Objective 4: To understand the ways different people view the same event or issues from a variety of perspectives	28, 50, 51, 52, 58, 60
CONTENT OUTLINE	
A. Motivating factors	31, 32, 33, 41, 42
1. Technological improvements in navigation	31, 32, 33, 42
2. Consolidation of political power within certain countries in Europe	30, 31
3. Desire to break into the Eastern trade markets	29, 33, 34, 35, 36, 37, 41, 42
4. Missionary zeal	29, 46, 49, 50
B. Geographic factors influenced European exploration and settlement in North and South America	36, 37, 39, 42–43, 48, 59, 61
1. Effects of weather and natural hazards on the Atlantic crossings	36, 39, 45
2. Characteristics of different physical environments in the Americas and where different Europeans settled	41, 46, 59, 61
3. The development of "New England," "New France," "New Netherland," and "New Spain"	42–52, 72, 80–81
C. Effects of exploration and settlement in America and Europe—human-induced changes in the physical environment in the Americas caused changes in other places	44, 47, 49, 50, 51, 52, 68, 69, 79, 73
1. Introduction of new diseases to the Americas was devastating	44, 47, 51
2. The continued growth of population in the colonies resulted in the unjust acquisition of Native American lands	68, 69, NY59
3. New types of foods improved both European and Native American health and life spans	47, 74, 79
4. Economic and political changes in the balance of power in Europe and the Americas	49, 50, 52, 73
5. Introduction of African slaves into the Americas	47, 76–77, 79

Standards	Student Edition Pages
D. Exploration and settlement of the New York State area by the Dutch and English	50, 51, 52, 72–74
1. Relationships between the colonists and the Native American Indians	43–44, 46–47, 61, 66, 68, 75
2. Similarities between the Europeans and Native American Indians	NY59
a. The role of tradition	NY59
b. The importance of families and kinship ties	NY59
c. The hierarchical nature of the community and family	NY56, NY59
d. The need to be self-sufficient	NY59
3. Differences	NY59
a. Ideas about land ownership	47, 66–68, NY59
b. Roles of men and women	46–47, NY56–NY57
c. Beliefs about how people from different cultures should be addressed	46–47, NY59
4. Rivalry between the Dutch and English eventually resulted in English supremacy	72–73, NY59
II. Colonial Settlement: Geographic, Political, and Economic Factors	
Objective 1: To investigate the roles and contributions of individuals and groups in relation to key social, political, cultural, and religious practices throughout the colonial period	59, 61, NY58–NY60
Objective 2: To investigate why people and places are located where they are located and what patterns can be perceived in these locations	58, 72, 76, 77, 80, 81, 82, NY58–NY59
Objective 3: To explain how societies and nations attempt to satisfy their basic needs and wants by utilizing scarce capital and natural and human resources	60, 61, 73, 74, 76, 77, 78, 82, NY58–NY60
Objective 4: To analyze how the values of colonial powers affected the guarantee of civil rights and made provisions for human needs	61, 66, 67, 69, NY58–NY60
CONTENT OUTLINE	
A. English colonies: New England, Middle Atlantic, Southern	64–69, 72–75, 76–80, 82
1. Reviewed as a geographic region-criteria to define regions, types of regions	65, 74, 78
2. Settlement patterns: who? when? why?	65, 66, 67, 69, 73, 74, 75, 76, 77, 78, 79, 80
3. Economic patterns emerge to meet diverse needs: agricultural and urban settlements	74, 76, 77, 79
4. Political systems: the Mayflower Compact	66, 69
5. Social order	64, 74, 76, 77
B. New Netherland; French and Spanish colonies	72, 73, 74, 81, 82, NY58–NY60
1. Reviewed as a geographic region-types, connections between regions	73, 81, 82, NY58–NY60
2. Settlement patterns: who? when? why?	73, 74, 81, 82, NY58–NY60
3. Economic patterns emerge to meet diverse needs	73, 82, NY58–NY60
4. Political systems and social order	42–52, 72, 81–82, NY58–NY60
III. Life in Colonial Communities	
Objective 1: To understand how European and other settlers adapted to life in the American colonies	16, 61, 66, 69, 79, 80, 88–95, 98–103, NY58–NY60
Objective 2: To classify major developments in categories such as social, political, geographic, technological, scientific, cultural, or religious	66, 67, 68, 69, 72, 73, 75, NY58–NY61
Objective 3: To investigate the roles and contributions of individuals and groups in relation to key social, political, cultural, and religious practices throughout the American colonies	16, 66, 67, 68, 69, 72, 73, 74, 75, 76, 77, 78, 79, 80, 81, 82, 104, 105, 106, 107, NY57–NY58
Objective 4: To present geographical information in a variety of formats, including maps, tables, graphs, charts, diagrams, and computer-generated models	64, 74, 75, 78, 88, NY5
Objective 5: To investigate how people in colonial communities answered the three fundamental economic questions (What goods and services shall be produced and in what quantities? How shall goods and services be produced? For whom shall goods and services be produced?) and solved their economic problems	61, 74, 76, 77, 79, 90, 91, 92, 93, 94, NY58–NY60
Objective 6: To analyze how values of a people affect the guarantee of civil rights and make provision for human needs	65, 66, 67, 68, 69, NY59
CONTENT OUTLINE	
A. Colonial communities were the center of social, economic, and political life and tended to develop along European patterns	64–69, 72–75, 76–80, 82, NY58–NY61
1. Variations were found	61, 65, 67, 69, 75, 76, 79, 80
a. Religious-based	65, 67, 69, 75
b. Slave and free black communities	61, 76
c. Place of national origin	65, 67, 75, 79, 80, 92

Standards	Student Edition Pages
2. The social structure promoted interdependence	66, 75
3. Social goals promoted community consciousness over individual rights	66, 67, 68
4. Role of religions	64, 65, 67, 68, 69, 74, 75, 78, 80
a. Puritans	64, 65, 67, 69
b. Quakers	75
c. Catholics	78
d. Others	65, 68, 74, 80
5. Survival demanded cooperation and a strong work ethic	67, 68
6. Importance of waterways	68, 73, 79, 90, 94
7. A hierarchical social order created social inequity	73, 74, 79, 93, 95
B. Structure and roles of colonial families	64, 89, 90, 94, 95, 102
1. Nuclear families make up the basic social and economic unit	90, 102
2. Authority and obligation followed kinship lines	102
3. Roles of family members	64, 95, 102
C. Life in colonial communities was a reflection of geographic and social conditions	64–69, 72–75, 76–82, 89, 93
1. Impact of physical environments on	61, 66, 68, 77, 79, 89, 93, 95
a. Travel	89, 90
b. Communication	72, 77, 90, 92
c. Settlements	66, 68, 77
d. Resource use	61, 79, 89, 93
2. Social conditions led to	66, 67, 68, 73, 74, 75, 76, 77, 78, 79, 90, 93, 95
a. Different forms of government	66, 67, 68, 73, 74, 75, 78
b. Varying roles of religion	68, 69, 75
c. Inequalities of economic conditions	64, 72, 76, 90
d. Unequal treatment of blacks	76, 77, 79, 93, 95
3. The impact of geographic and social conditions could be seen in the divergent landholding systems that developed in:	64–69, 72–75, 76–80, 82, 89, 90, 92, 93, 95, NY58–NY59
a. New England	64–69, 89, 90, 95, NY59
b. New Netherland: patroonship system	73, 75, NY59
c. Southern colonies: plantation system	76–80, 82, 94
4. Life in French and Spanish colonies was both similar to and different from life in other colonies	81, 82
UNIT THREE: A NATION IS CREATED	
I. Background Causes of the American Revolution	
Objective 1: To understand the economic, political, and social causes of the American Revolution	106, 107, 108–112, 122–125, 126–129
Objective 2: To compare and contrast different interpretations of key events and issues in New York State and United States history and explain reasons for these different accounts	127, 128, 129
Objective 3: To investigate how people in the United States and throughout the world answer the three fundamental economic questions and solve basic economic problems	90, 91, 92, 93, 94, 112
Objective 4: To consider the nature and evolution of a constitutional democracy	99, 100, 101, 103
CONTENT OUTLINE	
A. Economic factors	89, 90, 91, 92, 93, 95, 99, 123
1. Growth of mercantilism: triangular trade	90, 91, 95, 99
2. Rise of an influential business community in the colonies	89, 92, 93
3. Cost of colonial wars against the French	123
B. Political factors	99, 100, 101, 103
1. The role of the British Civil War	99
2. Periods of political freedom in the colonies	100
3. Impact of the French and Indian War: Albany Plan of Union	107, 108–112
4. Political thought of the Enlightenment influenced prominent colonial leaders	103, 141
C. New social relationships between European powers and the American colonies: development of a new colonial identity	100, 101

Focus on New York

Standards	Student Edition Pages
II. The Shift From Protest to Separation	
Objective 1: To understand how colonists' concerns regarding political and economic issues resulted in the movement for independence	112, 122–126, 132–137
Objective 2: To compare and contrast different interpretations of key events and issues in New York State and United States history and explain reasons for these different accounts	126, 127, 128, 129
Objective 3: To consider the nature and evolution of constitutional democracies	122, 132–137
CONTENT OUTLINE	
A. New British attitude toward colonies following victory over France	122, 123, 124, 125
1. Colonies could not protect themselves	123
2. Colonies were not paying a fair amount toward their support	111, 123
B. New British policies antagonized many Americans	122, 123, 124
1. Various acts of Parliament such as the Quebec Act	129
2. New tax policies and taxes: Stamp Act and others	123, 124, 125
3. Other acts of repression: Zenger case and others	103
C. Public opinion was shaped in different forums	125, 127, 128, 129, 139, 140, 141
1. Political bodies	125, 139, 140, 141
2. Public display and demonstration	125, 127, 129
3. Print media	127, 128, 129, 140
D. Wide variety of viewpoints evolved	136, 137
1. Complete separation	136, 137, 140, 141
2. More autonomy for the colonies	136, 137
3. No change in status quo: the Loyalist position	137
III. Early Attempts to Govern the Newly Independent States	
Objective 1: To understand how the colonists attempted to establish new forms of self-government	98, 132–137, 138–142, NY61–NY62
Objective 2: To investigate key turning points in New York State and United States history and explain why these events or developments are significant	108, 138, 139, 140, 141, 142, 152–159, 160–165, NY60–NY62
Objective 3: To compare and contrast different interpretations of key events and issues in New York State and United States history and explain reasons for these different accounts	137, 140, 141
Objective 4: To describe how ordinary people and famous historic figures in the local community, State, and the United States have advanced the fundamental democratic values, beliefs, and traditions expressed in the Declaration of Independence, the New York State and United States constitutions, the Bill of Rights, and other important historic documents	132–137, 138–142, 155, 156, 157, 159, 162, 165, 170, 172, 173, 177
CONTENT OUTLINE	
A. The Revolution begins	132, 133, 134, 135, 136
1. Early confrontations	134, 135, 136
2. Important leaders	132, 133, 135, 136
3. First Continental Congress	132, 133, 137
B. The Second Continental Congress represented the first attempt to govern the colonies	138, 139, 149
1. "Republican" government	188
2. Request for state constitutions and political systems	187
3. Asserting independence	141, 142
C. A movement for independence evolved from the political debate of the day	139, 140, 141
D. Declaration of Independence	138, 141, 142
1. Origins	141, 142
2. Content	141, 142
3. Impact	141, 142
4. Ideals embodied	141, 142
E. Independence creates problems for New Yorkers	NY60–NY61
1. Organizing new State government	NY61–NY62
2. Economic problems	NY61–NY62
3. Political factions	NY61–NY62
4. Slavery	NY60
5. Recruiting soldiers for the war	155

Standards	Student Edition Pages
IV. Military and Political Aspects of the Revolution	
Objective 1: To understand how the colonists were able to unite against British power to win a major military and political victory	133, 134, 152–159, 160–165, 168–173, 174–178
Objective 2: To understand how events on the national level influenced and affected New Yorkers	156, 174, 186
Objective 3: To complete well-documented and historically accurate case studies about individuals and groups who represent different ethnic, national, and religious groups	161, 163, 170, 172, 173, 175
Objective 4: To explain how societies and nations attempt to satisfy their basic needs and wants by utilizing capital, natural, and human resources	170, 171, 172, 173, 174, 176
CONTENT OUTLINE	
A. Strategies of the principal military engagements	140, NY63
1. Washington's leadership	140, 153, 155, 157, 158
2. New York as the object of strategic planning	156
3. Evolution of the war from the North to the South: Lexington and Concord to Saratoga to Yorktown	134, 135, 136, 137, 159, 173, 174, 175, 176, 177, 178
B. Role of the Loyalists	154, 158, NY60–NY61
1. In New York City	NY60–NY61
2. Colonists of Nova Scotia, Quebec, and Prince Edward Island did not join the Revolution	154, NY61
a. Refuge for Loyalists	154, NY61
b. Staging ground for attacks on New York's patriots	158, NY61
C. The outcome of the war was influenced by many factors	153, 155, 157, 158, 159, 160, 161, 162, 163, 164, 165, 169, 170, 171, 172, 173, 175, 176, 177, 178
1. Personalities and leadership	153, 155, 159, 160, 161, 163, 169, 170, 172
2. Geography: importance of various physical features	158, 170, 171, 172, 178
3. Allocation of resources	153
4. Foreign aid: funds and volunteers	160, 161, 163, 164, 172, 173, 175, 178
5. Role of women, blacks, and Native American Indians	155, 157, 162, 164, 165, 169
6. Haphazard occurrences of events: the human factor	172, 175, 176, 178
7. Clash between colonial authority and Second Continental Congress	155, 177
V. Economic, Political, and Social Changes Brought About by the American Revolution	
Objective 1: To understand how a revolution can have a profound effect on the economic, political, and social fabric of a nation	177, 178, 186–193, 194–201, NY61
Objective 2: To analyze how the values of a Nation affect the guarantee of human rights and make provisions for human needs	178, 187, 204
Objective 3: To present information by using media and other appropriate visuals such as tables, charts, and graphs to communicate ideas and conclusions	185–185, 186, 190–191, 204
Objective 4: To understand how different experiences, beliefs, values, traditions, and motives cause individuals and groups to interpret historic events and issues from different perspectives	188, 196, 197, NY61
Objective 5: To explain how societies and nations attempt to satisfy their basic needs and wants by utilizing capital, natural, and human resources	191, 195–197
CONTENT OUTLINE	
A. On the national level	177, NY61
1. Britain gave up claims to govern	177, NY61
2. Slavery began to emerge as a divisive sectional issue because slaves did not receive their independence	196, 197
3. American economy was plagued by inflation and hurt by isolation from world markets	191, 195
B. In New York State	177, 178, 188
1. The effects of the American Revolution on the Iroquois Confederacy	NY61
2. Disposition of Loyalist property and resettlement of many Loyalists after the Revolution to Canada, thus changing the French/British balance	177, 178
3. A republican ideology developed which emphasized shared power and citizenship participation	188
C. In the Western Hemisphere	178, 192, 193
1. Britain did not accept the notion of American dominance of the hemisphere	192, 193
2. The remaining British colonies in Canada strengthened their ties to Great Britain	
3. Many leaders in South America drew inspiration from American ideas and actions in their struggle against Spanish rule	178

Standards	Student Edition Pages
UNIT FOUR: EXPERIMENTS IN GOVERNMENT	
I. The Articles of Confederation and the Critical Period	
Objective 1: To understand the earliest formal structure of the United States government as expressed in the Articles of Confederation	186–193, NY61–NY62
Objective 2: To consider the nature and evolution of constitutional democracies	186–193, 194–201, 204–210, NY61–NY62
CONTENT OUTLINE	
A. Need for a formal plan of union	107, 187, 188
1. Historical precedent: the Albany Plan of Union	107
2. Development of state constitutions	187, 188
3. Inadequacy of Continental Congress as a national government	188, 192, 193
B. Development of a formal plan of government	188, 189
1. Draft and debate in Congress, 1776–1777	188
2. Ratification by the states, 1778–1781; period of operation, 1781–1789	189
C. The structure of government under the Articles of Confederation	188, 189
1. Congress was the only branch of government	188
2. Each state had equal representation	189
3. Congress's power under the Articles included:	189
a. Making war and peace	189
b. Conducting foreign and Native American Indian affairs	189
c. The settlement of disputes between and among states	189
d. Issuance of currency and borrowing	189
D. The Articles suffered from many weaknesses	188, 189, 192, 193, 195, 196
1. Indirect representation	188
2. No coercive power: decisions more advisory than binding: e.g., Shays' Rebellion	193, 195, 196
3. Lack of national executive and judicial functions	189
4. Lack of taxing power	192, 193
5. Difficulty in passing legislation	189
E. The Articles did have several achievements and contributions	189, 190, 191, 193
1. Land Ordinance of 1785 and the Northwest Ordinance, 1787	190, 191, 193
2. Developed the privileges and immunities of citizenship	191
3. Developed the concept of limited government	193
II. The New York State Constitution of 1777	
Objective 1: To understand the earliest formal structure of the New York State government, as expressed in the first New York State Constitution	187
Objective 2: To compare and contrast the development and evolution of the United States and New York State constitutions	
Objective 3: To understand how the United States and New York State constitutions support majority rule but also protect the rights of the minority	214–223, 224–245
CONTENT OUTLINE	NY61–NY62
A. Adopted by convention without submission to popular vote	NY61–NY62
1. Included Declaration of Independence	NY61–NY62
2. Influence of leaders such as John Jay	NY61–NY62
B. Chronology of the document	NY61–NY62
1. Draft and debate in convention, 1776–1777	NY61–NY62
2. Period of operation, 1777–1822	NY61–NY62
C. Form of early State government	NY61–NY62
1. Similar to colonial government	NY61–NY62
2. Governor with limited authority and three-year term	NY61–NY62
3. Inclusion of rights and liberties	NY61–NY62
4. First system of State courts	NY61–NY62
5. Limited franchise	NY61–NY62
6. Bicameral legislature: Senate—four-year term; Assembly—one-year term	NY61–NY62

Standards	Student Edition Pages
D. Effectiveness	NY61–NY62
1. Smoother functioning than national government under the Articles of Confederation	NY61–NY62
2. Cumbersome administrative procedures	NY61–NY62
3. Excessive use of veto procedures	NY61–NY62
4. A model for the United States Constitution of 1787	NY61–NY62
III. The Writing, Structure, and Adoption of the United States Constitution	
Objective 1: To understand the importance of the events that took place during the writing and adoption of the United States Constitution and to recognize their significance beyond their time and place	194–201, 204–210
Objective 2: To explain what citizenship means in a democratic society, how citizenship is defined in the Constitution and other laws of the land, and how the definition of citizenship has changed in the United States and New York State over time	208, 214–223
Objective 3: To understand that the New York State Constitution, along with other documents, served as a model for the development of the United States Constitution	205, 206
Objective 4: To compare and contrast the development and evolution of the constitutions of the United States and New York State	NY61–NY62
Objective 5: To define federalism and describe the powers granted to the national and state governments by the United States Constitution	204, 206, 207
CONTENT OUTLINE	
A. Annapolis Convention, 1786	NY62
1. Impracticality of correcting weaknesses in Articles of Confederation	194, 195
2. Need for an improved form of government without losing key elements of a new philosophy of government	195, 197
3. Decision to write a constitution	198
B. Constitutional Convention: setting and composition	198, 199
C. Major issues	198, 199, 200, 201
1. Limits of power: national versus state	198, 199, 201
2. Representation: slaves and apportionment	200, 201
3. Electoral procedures: direct versus indirect election	199, 200
4. Rights of individuals	201
D. The need for compromise	200, 201
1. The issue of a "federal" or a "national" government	209
2. The Great Compromise on representation	200
3. The three-fifths compromise on slavery	201
4. The commerce compromises	201
E. The underlying legal and political principles of the Constitution	204, 206, 207, 208, 210
1. Federalism	206, 210
2. Separation of powers	207, 208, 210
3. Provisions for change	210
4. Protection of individual rights	208
F. The Constitution and the functioning of the federal government	207, 208
1. The Preamble states the purpose of the document	217, 224
2. The structure and function of the legislative, executive and judicial branches (Articles I, II, III)	207, 208, 224–230
3. The relation of states to the federal union (Article IV)	231–232
4. Assuming the responsibility for a federal system (Article VI)	220–223, 233
G. The Constitution as a living document	214–219
1. The elastic clause and delegated power facilitate action	227
2. Amendment procedure as a mechanism for change (Article V)	221, 232
3. The Bill of Rights	210, 221, 254, 255
4. Supreme Court decision (e.g., *Tinker v. DesMoines School district*, 1969)	279, 1045
H. The evolution of an "unwritten constitution"	253, 255, 257, 264–270
1. Political parties	264–270
2. The President's cabinet	253, 255
3. President's relation to Congress	255, 257
4. Committee system in Congress	223–226
5. Traditional limitations on Presidential term	263

Focus on New York

Standards	Student Edition Pages
I. The ratification process	209
1. The debates in the states, especially New York State	209
2. The Federalist Papers	209
3. Poughkeepsie convention	209, 210
a. Federalists—Hamilton	NY61–NY62
b. Anti-Federalists—Clinton	209, 210
4. Formal ratification of the Constitution and launching of the new government	210
5. The personal leadership of people like Washington, Franklin, Hamilton, Madison	132, 133, 135, 136, 198, 209
UNIT FIVE: LIFE IN THE NEW NATION	
I. New Government in Operation	
Objective 1: To understand how the new nation established itself and began to operate	252–257, 260–263, NY61–NY62
Objective 2: To understand how political parties emerged in response to concerns at the local, State, and national levels	264–270, 276, 277, 278, 320, 336
Objective 3: To understand how civic values reflected in the United States and New York State constitutions have been implemented through law and practice	264, 266, 270, 271, 279
Objective 4: To understand the relationship between and the relative importance of United States domestic and foreign policies over time	252–257, 260–263, 264–270, 278, 281, 282, 283, 289, 290, 291, 292, 293, 295, 296, 297, 298, 321, 322, 323, 325, 326
Objective 5: To analyze the role played by the United States in international politics, past and present	260, 262, 263, 269, 270, 281, 282, 283, 287, 288, 289, 290, 291, 292, 293, 295, 296, 297, 298, 325, 326
Objective 6: To explain how societies and nations attempt to satisfy their basic needs and wants by utilizing scarce capital, natural, and human resources	256, 257, 282, 283, 284, 285, 358
Objective 7: To investigate how people in the United States solve the three fundamental economic questions and solve basic economic problems	252, 255, 256, 257, 278, 281, 283, 285, 286, 304
Objective 8: To complete well-documented and historically correct case studies about individuals and groups who represent different ethnic, national, and religious groups, including Native American Indians in New York State and the United States	115, 145, 294
CONTENT OUTLINE	
A. Washington as President: Precedents	252, 253
B. Establishing stability	253
1. Hamilton's economic plan	256, 257
2. The Whiskey Rebellion	260, 261, 263
3. Preserving neutrality: the French Revolution, Citizen Genet, Jay, and Pinckney treaties	260, 262, 263
4. Political parties	264–270
5. Election of 1800	276, 277, 278
6. Judicial review: *Marbury v. Madison* (1803)	279
C. Expanding the nation's boundaries	260, 263, 280–285, 291, 292, 293, 294–298, 325, 326
1. Pinckney Treaty with Spain	260, 263
2. Louisiana Purchase	280–285
3. War of 1812: guaranteeing boundaries	294–298
4. Monroe Doctrine: sphere of influence	325, 326
5. Purchase of Florida	282
6. Native American Indian concessions and treaties	291, 292, 293, 296
D. Challenges to stability	289, 290, 291, 293, 294–298
1. French and English trade barriers and the Embargo Act	289, 290, 291
2. War of 1812: second war for independence	293, 294–298
E. The Era of Good Feelings	320, 321
1. Clay's American system	322
2. Internal expansion: new roads, canals, and railroads	313, 314, 315, 316, 317
3. Protective tariffs	323
4. National assertions: Marshall's decision, i.e., *Gibbons v. Ogden* (1824)	324
5. Extension of slavery by the Missouri Compromise	323
6. Threats to Latin America: the Monroe Doctrine	326
7. Disputed election of 1824	336, 337, 338

Standards	Student Edition Pages
II. The Age of Jackson	
Objective 1: To understand how an American consciousness began to develop during Jackson's administration	342, 348
Objective 2: To complete well-documented and historically accurate case studies about individuals and groups who represent different ethnic, national, and religious groups, including Native American Indians, in New York State and the United States at different times and in different locations	342, 346, 347
Objective 3: To describe how ordinary people and famous historic figures in the local community, the State, and the United States have advanced the fundamental democratic values, beliefs, and traditions expressed in the Declaration of Independence, the New York State and United States constitutions, the Bill of Rights, and other important historic documents	337, 339
Objective 4: To gather and organize information about the important achievements and contributions of individuals and groups living in New York State and the United States	339–340
Objective 5: To develop conclusions about economic issues and problems by creating broad statements that summarize findings and solutions	341, 348, 351, 352
CONTENT OUTLINE	
A. The age of the "common man"	336
1. Expansion of suffrage	339, 340
2. Citizenship	339
3. Election of 1828	336, 338, 339
4. Jackson: man, politician, President	338, 339
5. The "spoils system"	340, 341
6. New political parties	338
B. Jackson's Native American policy reflected frontier attitudes	342, 343, 347
1. Some Native Americans resisted government attempts to negotiate their removal by treaty	344, 346, 347
2. Government policy of forced removals (1820–1840) resulted in widespread suffering and death	345, 346, 347
3. Native American Indian territory	343, 344
C. Intensifying sectional differences	340, 341
1. Protective tariff, 1828	341
2. Nullification controversy, 1828, 1832	340, 341
3. Clay's compromise tariff, 1833	341
III. Preindustrial Age: 1790–1860s	
Objective 1: To understand the way of life of an agrarian society	305, 307, 312, 317, 342, 388, 400, 401, 402, 403, 406, 407, 408, 409, 410, 412
Objective 2: To understand the nature and effect of changes on society and individuals as the United States began to move from an agrarian to an industrial economy	304, 305, 309, 312, 389, 390, 391, 392, 393, 394, 395, 396, 397, 399, 434
Objective 3: To describe historic events through the eyes and experiences of those who were there	309, 363, 366, 378, 399, 434
Objective 4: To explore the meaning of American culture by identifying the key ideas, beliefs, patterns of behavior, and traditions that help define it and unite all Americans	320, 321, 366, 378, 394, 409, 411, 412
Objective 5: To define basic economic concepts such as scarcity, supply and demand, markets, resources, and economic systems	304–309, 401, 402, 403
Objective 6: To understand how scarcity requires people and nations to make choices that involve costs and future considerations	304–305, 323, 390–391 398
Objective 7: To develop conclusions about economic issues and problems by creating broad statements that summarize findings and solutions	400, 406, 448
Objective 8: To describe the relationships between people and environments and the connections between people and places	306, 307, 308, 309, 312, 313, 315, 316, 317, 359, 360, 361, 362, 372, 378, 379, 380, 381, 382, 390, 391, 392, 393, 395, 397, 401, 402, 403, 407, 408, 411, 412, 419, 426, 427, 428, 429, 430, 431, 448
Objective 9: To use a number of research skills (e.g., computer databases, periodicals, census reports, maps, standard reference works, interviews, surveys) to locate and gather geographical information about issues and problems	312, 316, 317, 362, 452, 462

Standards	Student Edition Pages
CONTENT OUTLINE	
A. Portrait of the United States, 1800	304, 305, 307, 308
1. Agriculturally based economy	305, 307, 308
2. Urban centers on the coast	305, 309
3. Poor communication and transportation systems	281, 313
4. Self-sufficiency	308
5. Regional differences	307, 308, 309
B. Patterns of community organization, work, and family life in agrarian America	305, 307, 308, 312, 400, 401
C. Technological changes altered the way people dealt with one another	306, 312, 313, 314, 315, 316, 317, 389, 390, 391
1. Improved transportation made travel and communication easier	312, 313, 314, 315, 317, 390, 391, 392
2. Greater ties between communities were possible	315, 316, 317, 389
3. The Erie Canal and its impact	315, 316, 317
a. Reasons for building the Erie Canal	315
b. Technology involved in its construction	315, 316
c. Types and sources of labor: ethnic and racial labor force	315
d. Results of building the Erie Canal	316, 317
D. The impact of early industrialization and technological changes on work and workers, the family, and the community	304, 305, 306, 307, 308, 317, 393, 395, 396, 397, 401, 402, 403
1. An increase in the production of goods for sale rather than personal use	307, 393
2. Increased purchasing of what was formerly produced at home	307, 393, 424
3. Emergence of a new work ethic	304
E. Family roles changed, affecting society in general	304
1. Changing role of women	304, 397, 421, 434–438
2. Childhood became a more distinct stage of life	304
3. Roles of private agencies	399, 420, 421, 437, 438
F. Slavery and abolition	401, 402, 407, 408, 409, 411, 424–431
1. Review the institution of slavery	401, 402, 407, 408, 409, 410, 425
2. The meaning and morality of slavery	402, 408, 409, 429
3. Abolition movement	411, 424–431, 453
a. Leadership (Harriet Tubman, Garrison, and others)	411, 424, 425, 426, 427, 428, 429, 431
b. Activities (e.g., freedom trail and the underground railroad)	411, 425, 430, 431, 453
4. Abolition in New York State	429
5. Canada's role	428, 432–433
6. Effects of abolition	430, 431
G. Social changes	418–421, 434–438
1. Religious revival	418, 419, 421
2. Women's rights	421, 434–438
3. Mental hospital and prison reform	420
4. Education	412, 420, 421, 437, 438
5. Temperance	419, 421, 437
H. An American culture begins to emerge	421, 630, 632
1. Literature	421, 630, 632
2. Art	632
I. Portrait of the United States, 1860	407, 412
1. Growth brought about many changes and regions-the spatial patterns of settlement in different regions in the United States	398, 412
a. The size and shape of communities	397, 398, 412
b. Environmental impacts due to development of natural resources and industry-human modification of the physical environment	392, 393
c. The diversity of people within the larger communities and regions	396, 398, 399, 412
d. The ability of the political system within communities to deal with deviance	410, 411
e. The Preindustrial Age took place at different times in different places	389, 390, 391, 395, 400–403

Standards	Student Edition Pages
2. The North	388–391, 397, 398, 399
a. Industrial base	389
b. Increasing population	391, 397, 398, 399
c. Urban centered-"causes and consequences of urbanization"	397, 398, 399
3. The South	400–403, 406–417
a. Agricultural base (cotton)	400, 401, 402
b. Impact of Industrial Revolution of agriculture	402
c. Increasing slave population	401, 402, 407, 408
UNIT SIX: DIVISION AND REUNION	
I. Underlying Causes of the Civil War	
Objective 1: To understand the series of events and resulting conditions that led to the American Civil War	372, 421, 424, 448–451, 452–455, 456–461, 462–466
Objective 2: To understand how different experiences, beliefs, values, traditions, and motives cause individuals and groups to interpret historic events and issues from different perspectives	367, 368, 369, 370, 374, 375, 376, 379, 380, 381, 382, 450, 451, 454, 455, 457, 458, 459, 460, 461, 463, 464, 468, 469
Objective 3: To participate in a negotiating and compromising role-playing activity that mirrors the attempts at political compromise in the 1850s	456
CONTENT OUTLINE	
A. Territorial expansion and slavery	368, 371, 381, 448–451
1. The secession of Texas, 1836	369, 370
2. The Mexican War, 1846–1848	372–377
3. Oregon Territory	358–363
4. The westward movement and its effects on the physical, social, and cultural environments	360, 361, 362, 367, 368, 369, 371, 374, 449, 450, 451
B. The emotional impact of slavery	451, 453, 455, 461
1. *Uncle Tom's Cabin*	421
2. John Brown's raid on Harper's Ferry	455, 461
3. Fugitive slave laws	451, 453, 455
C. Failure of political compromise	449, 450, 451, 454, 455, 464
1. Compromise of 1850	451
2. Kansas-Nebraska Act, 1854	454, 455
3. Founding of the Republican Party, 1854-1856	456, 457
4. *Dred Scott v. Sandford* (1857)	458, 459, 461
5. Lincoln-Douglas debate, 1858	460, 461
6. Election of 1860	462, 463
7. Firing on Fort Sumter, 1861	462, 466
II. The Civil War Breaks Out	
Objective 1: To understand the development and progress of the Civil War	462–466, 474–479, 480–487, 490–497, 498–505, 506–512
Objective 2: To investigate key turning points in the Civil War in New York State and United States history and explain why these events or developments are significant	481, 482, 483, 484, 485, 486, 499, 500, 501, 502, 503, 505, 507, 509, 510, 511, 512
Objective 3: To map information about people, places, and environments	482, 484, 487, 510, 511
Objective 4: To describe the relationships between people and environments and the connections between people and places	475, 476, 477, 479, 491, 492, 493, 494, 495, 496, 497, 499, 501, 503, 505
Objective 5: To identify and collect economic information related to the Civil War from standard reference works, newspapers, periodicals, computer databases, textbooks, and other primary and secondary sources	415–416, 477, 483, 485, 474, 511
CONTENT OUTLINE	
A. The Presidency of Lincoln	475
1. Personal leadership	475
2. Opposition	475
3. Emancipation Proclamation	486, 487

Standards	Student Edition Pages
B. Advantages and disadvantages of each side	475, 476, 477, 478, 479, 481, 485, 494, 495, 499, 500
1. Advantages	476, 485, 499
a. South	476, 485, 499
1) Military leadership	476, 499
2) Commitment of people to preserve their way of life	476
b. North	475, 476, 477, 479
1) Effective navy	477
2) Larger army	475, 479
3) Manufacturing	476
4) Agricultural production	476
5) Transportation system	476
2. Disadvantages	476, 478, 479, 481, 491, 494, 495
a. South	476
1) Lacked manufacturing	476
2) Lacked a navy	478–479
3) Not prepared for war	478, 479, 491, 494, 495
b. North	478, 479, 481, 499, 500
1) Lacked quality military leadership	481, 499, 500
2) Not prepared for war	478, 479
c. The military and political dimensions of the war	475, 476, 481, 482, 486, 487, 494, 495, 496, 502, 503, 505, 506, 508, 509, 510
3. Geographic factors influenced the war's progress and outcome-role of physical and other barriers	481, 482, 483, 484, 487, 499, 502, 503, 505, 508, 509, 510
4. Major campaigns evolved around a changing strategy on both sides	483, 484, 485, 498–505, 507, 508, 510, 511, 512
5. Wartime problems and political issues	486, 487, 494, 495, 496
6. Foreign policy maneuvering was crucial to the final outcome	486, 487, 503
a. Seward's concern with Mexico	508
b. Emancipation Proclamation as an element of foreign policy	486, 487
7. Technology of the war	481
C. New York State in the Civil War	496
1. Military role	NY61–63
2. Political opposition in New York City	NY61–63
3. Conscription laws and draft riots	496
a. Undemocratic nature of the draft	496
b. Conscription as a factor in racism	496
III. Results of the Civil War	
Objective 1: To understand how the Civil War affected the development of the postwar United States and influenced other countries	518–521, 522–527, 528–531, 534–540
Objective 2: To describe how ordinary people and famous historic figures in the local community, the State, and the United States have advanced fundamental democratic values, beliefs, and traditions expressed in the Declaration of Independence, the New York State and United States constitutions, the Bill of Rights, and other important historic documents	519, 520, 529, 531
Objective 3: To consider the sources of historic documents, narratives, or artifacts and evaluate their reliability	518, 522, 528, 534
Objective 4: To value the principles, ideals, and core values of the American democratic system based upon the premises of human dignity, liberty, justice, and equality	519, 520, 521, 523, 524, 527, 529, 531
Objective 5: To analyze the role played by the United States in international politics, past and present	674–677, 678–683, 684–689, 690–696
CONTENT OUTLINE	
A. Preservation of the Union	486, 487, 512
B. Abolition of slavery	486, 487, 521
1. The Emancipation Proclamation	486, 487
2. Civil Rights and the 13th Amendment	521, 524

Standards	Student Edition Pages
C. Political power and decision making	521, 526, 527
1. Secession	518-519, 521
2. States' rights	518-519, 521, 540
D. Reconstruction—theory, practice, and termination	518-521, 522-527, 528-531, 534-540
1. Lincoln's plan	519
2. Johnson's plan and congressional opposition resulted in his impeachment	521, 523
3. Congressional Reconstruction	520-523, 525
4. Constitutional Amendments 14 and 15 guarantee equal rights for all races except Native Americans	524, 525, 526, 527, 539
5. Problems of economic and social reconstruction led to sharecropping as a substitute for slavery	531, 539
6. The official end of Reconstruction in 1877	535
7. Segregation held legal: *Plessy v. Ferguson* (1896)	540
E. The enormous human suffering and loss of life caused by the war	511, 512, 518
UNIT SEVEN: AN INDUSTRIAL SOCIETY	
I. The Maturing of an Industrial Society in the Second Half of the 19th Century	
Objective 1: To understand how industrialization led to significant changes in the economic patterns for producing, distributing, and consuming goods and services	552-557, 574-578, 584-587, 588-593, 594-599, 602-606
Objective 2: To explain how societies and nations attempt to satisfy their basic needs and wants by utilizing scarce capital, natural, and human resources	534, 552-557, 560, 563-565, 594-599
Objective 3: To define basic economic concepts such as scarcity, supply and demand, markets, resources, and economic growth	534, 562, 574, 584-587, 588-593, 594-599
Objective 4: To understand how scarcity requires people and nations to make choices that involve costs and future considerations	574-578, 602-606
Objective 5: To understand how people in the United States and throughout the world are both producers and consumers of goods and services	561, 563-565, 574-578, 584
CONTENT OUTLINE	
A. Problems and progress in American politics: Framework for a changing United States	555, 556, 642, 643
1. New problems created a changing role for government and the political system	555, 556, 643
2. Scandals, depressions and limitations of traditional politics resulted in reluctant change, e.g., civil service	605, 644
3. National politics were dominated by the Democratic and Republican parties, but third parties occasionally arose to meet special interests	646
4. New York State and New York City in an era of machine politics, e.g., the Tweed Ring and Tammany Hall	642, 643, 644
5. Prevailing attitude of noninterference ("laissez-faire") as the appropriate role for government, with some regulations to meet excesses	587, 597-598, 699, 658
B. The United States developed as an industrial power	555, 556, 557, 561, 584-587, 589, 590, 591, 592, 593, 621, 625
1. Changes in the methods of production and distribution of manufactured goods	555, 557, 592, 593, 621
a. Transportation developments and their effects on economic developments, 1865-1900	555, 556, 557, 561, 584-587, 621, 625
b. Communication developments, 1865-1900	589, 590, 591, 592, 593
c. Industrial technology, 1865-1900	557, 584-587, 588-593, 594-599
d. Rise of banking and financial institutions	538, 596-597
2. Increase in the number and size of firms engaged in manufacture and distribution of goods	587, 588, 592, 593, 599, 621
3. Increase in the number and skill level of workers; new labor markets	602, 603
4. Expansion of markets for manufactured goods	556, 557, 588
5. The growth and emerging problems of the cities	598, 620-625
C. Growth of the corporation as a form of business organization: Case studies—oil, railroads, steel	585, 586, 587, 596, 597, 598, 599
1. One of several forms of business organization	585, 596, 597, 599
2. Many firms maintained traditional ways of doing business	585-587
3. Advantages and disadvantages of a corporation	585
D. Government response to industrial development and abuses	587, 599, 645
1. Laissez-faire versus regulation	587, 597-598, 599
2. Interstate commerce: state and national control	645
3. Sherman Antitrust Act: bigness as a threat	599, 645

Standards	Student Edition Pages
E. Changing patterns of agricultural organization and activity in the United States and New York State	565, 621
1. Unprecedented growth in agriculture	565, 621
2. Changes in the methods of production and distribution of farm products-spatial distribution of economic activities	565, 621
3. Efficient use of resources combined with competition and the profit motive to improve methods of production	563, 565
F. Occurrence of many significant and influential changes	556, 557, 564, 565, 587, 588–593, 598, 621, 624, 625, 643, 644
1. Communities grew in size and number	587, 598, 621
2. Interdependence increased	589, 590
3. Decision-making procedures changed	565, 585, 587, 625
4. Technology advanced	564, 587, 588–593, 624, 625
5. Adaptation of, rather than to, the environment-human modifications of the physical environment	556, 557, 565, 624, 625
6. Perceptions of time became more formal, e.g., railroad schedules	557, 587
7. Political machines influenced daily life	643, 644
G. The response of labor to industrialization	602–606
1. Industrialization created a larger workforce and more complex work	602, 603
2. Working conditions underwent extensive change, which often placed hardships on the workers; roles of women, children, minorities, disabled changed	602, 603, 615
3. Early attempts to unionize the workforce met with resistance and failure, e.g., the Knights of Labor and the Haymarket Riot, American Railway Union, the Industrial Workers of the World	604, 605, 606
4. Roots of modern labor unionism, e.g., the American Federation of Labor	604, 605
5. Labor as a reform movement in other aspects of society	605, 607
H. The response of the farmer to industrialization	575, 576, 577, 578
1. Expanding agricultural production and railroads	575, 585–586
2. Cheap money and high railroad rates	575, 578
3. The Grange and state reforms	575, 576
4. The Populist movement	577, 578
5. The closing of the frontier-limitations of physical environment	565, 576–578
II. Changes in the Social Structure Altered the American Scene	
Objective 1: To understand how industrialization altered the traditional social pattern of American society and created a need for reform	552–557, 602–606, 612–617, 620–625
Objective 2: To investigate key turning points in New York State and United States history and explain why these events or developments are significant	560–565, 566–571, 588–593, 612–617
Objective 3: To complete well-documented and historically accurate case studies about individuals and groups who represent different ethnic, national, and religious groups, including Native American Indians, in New York State and the United States at different times and in different locations	566–571
Objective 4: To consider the sources of historic documents, narratives, or artifacts and evaluate their reliability	612, 615, 620, 626
Objective 5: To describe historic events through the eyes and experiences of those who were there	566, 571, 625, 650
Objective 6: To understand how scarcity requires people and nations to make choices that involve costs and future considerations	560–565, 612–617
CONTENT OUTLINE	
A. The immigration experience	556, 564, 612–617, 621
1. Two distinct waves occurred, from the 1840s to the 1890s, and from the 1890s to the early 1920s; migration streams over time	556, 564, 612–617, 621
2. Differences were based on national origins, cultural patterns, and religion	556, 564, 612–617
3. Similarities included motivations for coming and patterns of community settlement	564, 565, 613
4. Initial clashes ended in varying degrees of acculturation	613, 616
5. Occupational and political experiences varied	613

Standards	Student Edition Pages
B. Case studies of the immigrant experience in the United States and New York State—population characteristics	615–161, 620. 623–623, 631
1. A comparison of European immigrants and the black slave experience-human migration's effects on the character of different places and regions	614
2. Immigrants as rural settlers in the Midwest	564
3. The Chinese experience in the Far West	556
4. Mexicans in the Southwest	613
5. New York City's ethnic neighborhoods	616
6. French-Canadian settlement in northern New York State	NY63
7. Immigration patterns and experiences throughout New York State	615, 616, 621
8. Irish immigration: Mass starvation in Ireland, 1845-1850	NY63
9. Immigrants in the local community	616
C. Legal basis for citizenship in the United States	NY61–NY63
1. Citizenship by the "law of the soil"	NY61–NY63
2. Citizenship by birth to an American parent	NY61–NY63
3. Citizenship through naturalization	NY61–NY63
D. Responsibilities of citizenship	NY61–NY63
1. Civic: A citizen should be:	NY61–NY63
a. Knowledgeable about the process of government	NY61–NY63
b. Informed about major issues	NY61–NY63
c. A participant in the political process	NY61–NY63
2. Legal: A citizen should:	NY61–NY63
a. Be knowledgeable about the law	NY61–NY63
b. Obey the laws	NY61–NY63
c. Respect the rights of others	NY61–NY63
d. Understand the importance of law in a democratic society	NY61–NY63
3. The changing role of the citizen	NY61–NY63
E. America becomes an increasingly mobile society	554, 560, 564, 565
1. Motivated by new economic opportunities	564
2. Changing patterns of movement, e.g., blacks begin to move North	564
3. Westward settlement	554, 560, 564, 565
4. The disappearance of the frontier- physical limits of geography	565
F. America developed as a consumer society	621, 622
1. Improved standard of living increased consumption	622
2. Greater variety of goods available	621
3. Continually rising expectations	622
G. Leisure activities reflected the prevailing attitudes and views of the Time	622, 630, 631, 632
1. Greater variety of leisure activities became available as less time was spent on work	622, 631, 632
2. Leisure activities reflected general characteristics of modern society, i.e., organized use of technology, emphasis on the individual role, and reliance on experts	622, 631, 632
III. The Progressive Movement, 1900–1920: Efforts to Reform the New Society	
Objective 1: To understand how industrialization led to a need for reevaluating and changing the traditional role of government in relation to the economy and social conditions	620–625, 626–632, 642–647, 650–655
Objective 2: To investigate key turning points in New York State and United States history and explain why these events or developments are significant	626–632, 642–647, 650–655, 656–661, 662–668
Objective 3: To gather and organize information about the important achievements and contributions of individuals and groups living in New York State and the United States	623, 624, 626–632, 642–647, 650–655, 656–661, 662–668
Objective 4: To classify major developments into categories such as social, political, economic, geographic, technological, scientific, cultural, or religious	627, 628, 629, 656–661, 662–668
Objective 5: To describe historic events through the eyes and experiences of those who were there	647, 655

Focus on New York

Standards	Student Edition Pages
CONTENT OUTLINE	
A. Social ills	623, 642-647
1. The Muckrakers—exposing corruption and abuses in industry, government, and urban living conditions	642, 646, 647
2. Fighting racial discrimination, e.g., the formation of the NAACP	663, 664, 665, 666, 667, 668
3. Temperance and prohibition	650, 655
4. Settlement houses	623, 625
B. Efforts to reform government and politics	642, 647
1. Need for responsive government, e.g., primary elections, the initiative, the referendum, the recall election	642, 647
2. Progressive leaders, e.g., LaFollette, Theodore Roosevelt, Taft, Debs	657, 659, 660
3. The Socialist Party challenges the political establishment	646
4. Direct election of Senators—the 17th Amendment	647
5. Women's suffrage—the 19th Amendment	651, 652, 653, 654
C. Economic reform efforts	656, 657, 658, 660, 661
1. Labor-related legislation, e.g., minimum wage laws, workmen's compensation insurance, safety regulations, child labor laws	658
2. Prosecuting trusts	657, 658, 661
3. Government regulation of the railroads	657
4. The Federal Reserve Act	656
5. Graduated income tax—the 16th Amendment	660
UNIT EIGHT: THE UNITED STATES AS AN INDEPENDENT NATION IN AN INCREASINGLY INTERDEPENDENT WORLD	
I. The United States Expands Its Territories and Builds an Overseas Empire	
Objective 1: To understand how and why the United States grew during the 19th century	674-677, 678-683
Objective 2: To recognize that American territorial and economic growth had widespread economic, political, and social impacts both at home and abroad	678-683, 690-696
Objective 3: To describe the reasons for periodizing history in different ways	642-647, 676, 685, 704
Objective 4: To understand the relative importance of U.S. domestic and foreign policies over time	674-677, 684-689, 690-696
Objective 5: To analyze the role played by the United States in international politics, past and present	674-677, 678-683, 684-689, 690-696
Objective 6: To compare and contrast different interpretations of key events and issues in New York State and United States history and offer reasons for these different accounts	684-689
CONTENT OUTLINE	
A. Growth of imperialist sentiment was caused by several factors	674-677
1. A belief that the nation had a right to the land, i.e., Manifest Destiny—"people's differing perceptions of places, people, and resources"	674-677, 689
2. Perceived moral obligations to extend America's way of life to others, i.e., ethnocentrism and racism	674-677, 689
3. American citizens were already migrating into new lands in North America—the effects of human migration on the characteristics of different places	675, 692-694
4. Increased foreign trade led to a growing interest in gaining control over some foreign markets	675, 677, 689, 692-694
5. Fear that other foreign nations would gain control of strategic locations at the expense of the United States	676, 677, 678, 679, 680, 683
6. Developing technology in transportation and communication contributed to American expansion potential—the importance of location and certain physical features	677, 678, 679, 680, 690, 691
B. The Spanish-American War signaled the emergence of the United States as a world power	684-689
1. The war's origins lay in Cuban attempts to gain freedom from Spain	684, 685, 686
2. Concerns of the United States, i.e., pro-expansionist sentiment, Cuba's location, Spanish tactics	686-687
3. Newspapers shaped public opinion over the Main incident—"yellow journalism"	686, 689
4. Conduct of the war created domestic and international problems	685, 688
5. Opposition to American imperialist movement	689
C. Victory in the Spanish-American War created a need for a new foreign policy	682, 683, 687, 688, 689
1. Acquisition of land far from America's shores-importance of resources and markets	688, 689
2. Emphasis on doing what the government felt was necessary and possible to protect American interests, i.e., maintaining a strong navy, gaining control of other strategic locations, advocating equal trading rights in Asia, e.g., the Open Door Policy	682, 683
3. Actions created conflict with Filipinos and Japanese	686, 687

Standards	Student Edition Pages
D. United States policies in Latin America	690–696
1. The United States attempted to control a number of locations in Latin America for economic and political reasons	691, 692, 694, 695, 696
2. The quest for Latin American stability through the Roosevelt Corollary to the Monroe Doctrine: Panama Canal	690, 692, 693, 694, 695, 696
3. Armed intervention in Latin America	691, 692, 694, 696
II. The United States Begins to Take a Role in Global Politics	
Objective 1: To understand how American relations with other nations developed between the end of the Civil War and the end of World War I	684, 712, 713, 714, 715, 716, 717, 718–723, 725, 728–732
Objective 2: To describe the reasons for periodizing history in different ways	704, 712, 718, 728, 742
Objective 3: To understand the relative importance of United States domestic and foreign policies over time	712–717, 718–723, 724–727, 728–732
Objective 4: To analyze the role played by the United States in international politics, past and present	704, 712–717, 718–723, 728–732
Objective 5: To describe the relationships between people and environments and the connections between people and places	705, 706, 724–727
CONTENT OUTLINE	
A. United States policy on noninvolvement in European political affairs was based on a number of factors	674, 675, 677
1. Tradition dating back to the earliest days of the country	674, 675
2. Focus on the international problems of the new nation	674, 675
3. Recognition of United States military unpreparedness	677
4. Impacts of geography (e.g., location, resources) on United States foreign policy	675
B. Pre-World War I involvements	677, 678, 682, 683, 685
1. Application of the Monroe Doctrine to the Western Hemisphere	677
2. Threats to American foreign trade	682, 685
3. Roosevelt's Treaty of Portsmouth	678, 683
C. World War I occurred as a result of international problems	704–709
1. Intense nationalism	705, 709
2. Power struggles among European nations	706, 707
3. A failure of leadership	704
4. European alliances	704, 705, 706, 707, 709
D. Events led to United States involvement in World War I	712–717, 718–723
1. The American people were divided in ways that made involvement difficult	713, 715
2. Fear that United States involvement would increase intolerance at home	713–714
3. Initial attempts to follow traditional policy of neutrality failed	715–716
4. Unwillingness of warring nations to accept President Wilson as a mediator	704
5. England was a major United States trade partner	714–715
6. Despite varied ethnic backgrounds in the United States, leaders felt closer to the English than to the Germans	714
7. While both sides attempted to restrict United States trade with their opponent, Germany did so by sinking American ships	714
8. Recognition that the United States would have no say at any peace conference if it remained neutral	716–717
E. The United States entered the war	718–723, 724–727
1. Combining new technology with old strategies e.g., chemical warfare led to the death of millions	709–710
2. The war was supported by the majority of Americans	717
3. The war effort created changes on the home front, e.g., economic controls, the role of women in the workforce, black migrations to the North, and attempts to organize labor to improve conditions	724–727
4. War promoted intolerance, e.g., the Espionage Act of 1917 and the Sedition Act of 1918; "hyphenated Americans" have their loyalty questioned	724, 727
F. The United States and the peace negotiations	728, 729, 730, 731, 732
1. Wilson's failed attempts to establish leadership with his Fourteen Points	729, 730, 732
2. Senate opposition to the League of Nations	731, 732
3. The Versailles Treaty	728, 729, 730, 731

Focus on New York

Standards	Student Edition Pages
G. The Bolshevik Revolution	719, 720, 723
1. Effect of World War I	720, 723
2. Civil war in Russia	719, 723, 729
3. Western intervention	730
4. Threat of international communism	730
UNIT NINE: THE UNITED STATES BETWEEN THE WARS	
I. The Roaring Twenties Reflected the Spirit of the Postwar Period	
Objective 1: To understand the economic, social, and political development of America in the period between World War I and World War II	744–747, 750–753, 754–757, 758–764, 772
Objective 2: To understand the relative importance of United States domestic and foreign policies over time	744, 750–753, 754–757
Objective 3: To analyze the role played by the United States in international politics, past and present	750, 753
Objective 4: To classify major developments into categories such as social, political, economic, geographic, technological, scientific, cultural, or religious	744–747, 754–757, 758–764
Objective 5: To understand how people in the United States and throughout the world are both producers and consumers of goods and services	754–757
CONTENT OUTLINE	
A. Prohibition and the 18th Amendment	761, 762
1. End of reform era	761, 762
2. The rise of organized crime	761, 762
3. Economic, social, political effects	761, 762
B. The Republican decade	750, 571, 752, 764
1. Political developments	747, 750, 751, 752, 764
a. Back to "normalcy"; the election of 1920	750
b. Scandals	751
c. Coolidge: austerity and integrity	747, 752
d. Government and business: laissez-faire and protection	752
e. Election of 1928	764
C. Relative isolation of the United States in world political affairs	731, 732, 753
1. General policy of noninvolvement in European affairs; the League of Nations controversy	731, 732
2. Limited participation in international activities	753–754
a. World Court	729, 832
b. Naval disarmament 1924	753
c. Efforts for peace; Kellogg-Briand Pact, 1928	753
d. Postwar reparation talks	730
e. Relief efforts in Europe	764
3. Expansion of international trade and tariffs	752
4. Restrictions on immigration, e.g., Quota Act, 1924	762, 763
D. A rising standard of living resulted in the growth of a consumer economy and the rise of the middle class	756, 757
1. Increase in single-family homes; move to nuclear families	755–757, 758
2. Emergence of suburbs	756–757
3. Spread of middle-class values	754, 756–757
4. Increased use of credit	756, 757
E. Changes in the workplace	754–755
1. Shift from agrarian to industrial workforce	754–755, 757
2. Lessened demand for skilled workers	754–755
3. Working conditions and wages improved	757
4. Increase in white-collar employees	754–755
5. Women continued to increase their presence in the workforce	759

Standards	Student Edition Pages
F. Problems developed in the midst of unprecedented prosperity	746–747, 755, 757
1. Not all groups benefited equally	757, 761, 762
a. Low farm prices	757
b. High black unemployment	746–747
c. Millions of poor	757
2. New trends conflicted with tradition	759, 764
3. Environmental balance was jeopardized	756
G. Foreign immigration and black migration resulted in a very diverse population and an increase in social tensions—the effects of human migrations on the nature and character of places and regions	746
1. Restrictions on immigration	762, 763
2. Black migration to Northern cities	787–788
3. Growth of organizations to fight discrimination; e.g., NAACP	747
4. Growth of black art, music, and cultural identity; e.g., the Harlem Renaissance	760
5. Generational conflicts	745, 746, 787–788
6. Widespread emergence of retired workers	755
7. Right-wing hate groups	745, 746
H. New ideas about the use of leisure time emerged	743, 756, 757, 758, 759, 760, 761
1. Impact of the automobile: Henry Ford	756, 757
2. Organized sports: Babe Ruth	743, 760
3. Search for heroes and heroines: Lindbergh, Amelia Earhart	758, 759
4. Motion pictures	759
5. Popular literature	760, 761
6. Fads and fashion	759, 760
7. Changes in social behavior	759, 760
I. The stock market crash marked the beginning of the worst economic time the country has ever known	774, 775, 776
1. National prosperity had been structured on the investments of the wealthy	773, 774, 775
2. There were problems with the economic structure	774, 775
3. People lost faith in the system	774, 775, 777
4. The government was unwilling or unable to correct the downturn	774, 776, 777
5. The economic depression that followed was the worst in our history	772, 775, 776, 777
II. The Great Depression	
Objective 1: To understand the economic, political, and social impacts of the Great Depression on the United States	772–777, 778–783, 786–791, 794–798
Objective 2: To understand the economic, political, and social changes that took place in the world during the 1930's	772–777, 778–783, 786–791, 794–798, 804–807
Objective 3: To explain how societies and nations attempt to satisfy their basic needs and wants by utilizing scarce capital, natural, and human resources	778–783, 786–791
Objective 4: To understand how scarcity requires people and nations to make choices that involve costs and future considerations	778–783, 794–798
Objective 5: To evaluate economic data by differentiating fact from opinion and identifying frames of reference	794–798
Objective 6: To develop conclusions about economic issues and problems by creating broad statements that summarize findings and solutions	772–777, 786
CONTENT OUTLINE	
A. Contributing factors	773, 774, 777
1. Economic growth declined during the late 1920s	773, 774
2. Stock purchases were made on margin/credit	772–773
3. Corporations and individuals became overextended	773, 774
4. The stock market crash led to a cycle of low demand and high unemployment	773, 774

Focus on New York

Standards	Student Edition Pages
B. Responses to deepening economic woes	774, 775, 776, 777
1. Hoover administration response: too little, too late	775, 776, 777
2. Local and State actions	775, 776
a. Soup kitchens and out-stretched hands	775, 776
b. A modified "new deal" in New York	781
3. Election of 1932; question of confidence	779, 780
C. The New Deal	780, 781, 782, 783
1. Psychological boost; FDR at the fireside	778, 781
2. Relieving human suffering; providing for dignity and jobs	780, 781, 782, 783, 794
3. Helping business and industry recover	781, 782, 783
4. Adjusting the economic system to prevent recurrence	781, 783, 796, 797
a. Government regulation of business and banking	781, 783
b. Instituting Social Security	796, 797
c. Providing a guaranteed labor voice: the Wagner Act	797
5. Other voices	794, 795, 798
a. Court-packing scheme	798
b. Alternative solutions: Father Coughlin, the Townsend Plan, Huey Long, socialism, communism	794, 795
1) The economics of war versus depression conditions; climbing out of depression and into war	798
D. Effects on work family, and communities	775, 776, 786, 789, 790, 791
1. Even though unemployment reached new heights, most people continued to hold jobs but at reduced hours and lower wages	775, 782
2. The loss of jobs fell unequally on women, blacks, and the unskilled	788, 789, 790, 791
3. The threat of possible job loss was a psychological strain on those who were employed	774, 787
4. Unemployment affected the traditional male role of provider, especially for those who equated success at work with success as a husband and father	776, 787
5. Charities' resources were inadequate	775, 776
6. Local communities attempted to meet the needs of their people	775, 776
7. The Dust Bowl and the Okies-human modification of the physical environment	787, 788
E. The cultural environment during the Great Depression	787, 791
1. The times were reflected in the arts and literature	787, 791
2. Escapism was popular in fiction and the cinema	791
3. Many works of social commentary and criticism appeared	791
4. Federal government supported the arts through the Works Project Administration (WPA)	782, 794, 796
F. Effects of the Great Depression on industrialized Europe	775, 776, 802
1. Trade and loans tied Western economies together	775, 803
2. The Great Depression followed similar patterns in affected nations	775, 803–804
a. Tighter credit	775, 803–804
b. Business failures	775, 803–804
c. Decreased money supply	775, 803
d. Lowered demand	775, 804
e. Lower production	775, 804
f. Widespread unemployment	776
3. Developing totalitarian responses: Germany, Italy, Spain, Japan; intensified communism characterized by:	790, 804–805
a. One-party governments headed by a strong individual	790, 804–805
b. Armies and police forces fostered national goals and eliminated opposition	790, 804–805
c. Use of propaganda in the media and schools to support national goals	791, 804–805
d. Art and literature were used to endorse official policies in totalitarian countries	791
G. European conflicts resulted in several basic problems for United States policy makers	804, 806, 811–812, 955, 959
1. The question of whether to shift focus from domestic problems to foreign policy	804, 811–812, 955, 959
2. Issue of neutrality versus the growing power of totalitarian states	803–806
3. Continued efforts to improve Latin American relations through the "Good Neighbor Policy" without losing influence in that area's affairs	812, 818, 945

Standards	Student Edition Pages
UNIT TEN: THE UNITED STATES ASSUMES WORLDWIDE RESPONSIBILITIES	
I. World War II	
Objective 1: To understand why World War II began and how it changed the lives of millions of people	804–807, 808–813, 814–819
Objective 2: To be aware of the much different world left as a legacy of World War II	832
Objective 3: To investigate key turning points in New York State and United States history and explain why these events or developments are significant	808–813, 820–827, 828–832
Objective 4: To understand the relative importance of United States domestic and foreign policies over time	804–807, 808–813, 814–819
Objective 5: To analyze the role played by the United States in international politics, past and present	820–827, 828–832
Objective 6: To describe historic events through the eyes and experiences of those who were there	813, 819, 827, 884
CONTENT OUTLINE	
A. Origins of the war	804–807
1. The Versailles Treaty	805
2. The Great Depression	803–806
3. Rise of totalitarianism; expansionism and persecution	804–807
4. The rearming of Germany	805–806
5. Isolationism	806, 810–811
6. Failure of the League of Nations	805
B. Prewar alliances	804–807, 808–813
1. Axis powers	804–807, 808–813
2. Allied powers	804–807, 808–813
3. Role of the United States	806–807
C. Failure of peace	804–807, 814–819, 820–827, 828–832
1. Aggression by Germany in Europe, Italy in Europe and Africa, and Japan in Asia	804–807
2. Appeasement; Chamberlain in Munich	807
3. German attack on Poland; World War II begins	807
4. United States role to 1941—guarded isolation, aid to allies	810–811, 814–819, 820–827, 828–832
D. The United States in World War II	810–813
1. Japanese attack on Pearl Harbor	812–813
2. A two-front war	820–827, 828–832
a. Europe—Eisenhower	820–827
b. Pacific—MacArthur	828–832
E. New aspects of the war	808–813
1. German blitzkrieg	808–809, 813
2. Aerial bombing	809, 810–813
3. New technology and its impact on people and the physical environment	808–813
4. Atomic bomb—the Manhattan Project	831, 832
5. The Nazi Holocaust	824–827
6. Concept of unconditional surrender	823, 832
F. The home front	814–819
1. Total mobilization of resources	814–819
2. Rationing	815–816
3. Role of women	817–818
4. War bonds	814–815
5. Internment to incarceration of Japanese-Americans	819
6. Limited progress toward economic, political, and social equality for black Americans, i.e., Roosevelt's Executive Order 8802	816–817
G. End of the war	820–827, 828–832
1. Allied agreement—Yalta Conference	842, 849
2. Defeat of Germany	820–827
3. Defeat of Japan	828–832

Focus on New York

Standards	Student Edition Pages
H. Impact of the war	826–827, 832
1. Entire countries were physically and demographically devastated-effects of physical and human geographic factors	826–827, 832
2. Millions of families suffered the loss of loved ones	832
3. The Nazi Holocaust-Hitler's "Final Solution"; worldwide horror; human rights violations	826–827
4. United States response to the Holocaust: Fort Ontario; Oswego, New York	824
5. The Nuremberg Trials	832
6. Global impact; rise of nationalism in Africa and Asia	874
7. Advent of the United Nations	750
8. Advent of the nuclear age	751
II. The United States as Leader of the Free World	
Objective 1: To understand why the United States assumed a leadership role in the post-World War II world	842–849, 852, 856–859, 894
Objective 2: To appreciate the historical background for the formation of U.S. foreign policy of this era	842–849, 894, 904–909, 910–915, 970
Objective 3: To understand the relative importance of United States domestic and foreign policies over time	856–859, 860–866, 884, 894, 904–909, 910–915, 918–923, 942
Objective 4: To analyze the role played by the United States in international politics, past and present	842–849, 856–859, 860–866, 904–909, 910–915
CONTENT OUTLINE	
A. Role of the United Nations	842, 944, 985
1. Human rights issues; United Nations Universal Declaration of Human Rights (1948)—role played by Eleanor Roosevelt on the United Nations Commission on Human Rights	842, 944, 985
2. Actions of the United Nations to promote peace	842, 944, 985
B. United States and the Soviet Union emerge as world leaders	842–849, 860, 863, 902–903, 904–909
1. The Cold War	844–849, 860, 862, 902–903
2. Truman Doctrine and Marshall Plan	842, 842, 844
3. Alliance systems: e.g., NATO, Warsaw Pact	842–843
C. Communist expansion leads to United States policy of containment	845, 847, 849, 856–859, 904–909, 910–915
1. In Europe: Berlin airlift, Berlin Wall	845, 849, 907
2. In Asia: Communist China, Korean War	847, 856–859
3. In Latin America: Cuban missile crisis	904–909
4. In Southeast Asia: Vietnam War	910–915
D. Superpower rivalry	861, 862, 902–903
1. The spread of nuclear weapons	861, 902-903
2. The arms race	861, 902-903
3. From Sputnik to astronauts on the Moon	862, 909
III. The United States in the Post-Cold War World	
Objective 1: To understand the historic, political, and social context in which United States foreign policy has evolved during the post-Cold War era	926–932, 942–947, 958–962, 970
Objective 2: To understand the relative importance of United States domestic and foreign policy over time	874, 926–932, 942–947, 948–955, 958–962, 976–981, 892–981
Objective 3: To analyze the role played by the United States in international politics, past and present	926–932, 942–947, 958–962, 976–981, 982–989
CONTENT OUTLINE	
A. Shifting foreign policies help lead to the end of the Cold War	862, 942–947
1. Détente and arms control beginning with President Nixon	926, 942–947, 975
2. Military buildup and treaties to bring about reductions	944, 972, 975
3. Fall of the Berlin Wall (1989) and the collapse of the Soviet Union	976–978
B. The United States seeks a new role in the world	942–947, 958–962
1. Arab-Israeli conflicts; Camp David Accord	945–956, 960–961
2. Persian Gulf War	979
3. Peacekeeping missions; Somalia, Bosnia	979, 985
C. Western Hemisphere relations	947, 972, 985 , 1003–1004
1. Economic competition and cooperation: NAFTA	985
2. Immigration patterns between the United States and Mexico, Latin America	1003–1004
3. Spread of democratic principles in Latin America	947, 972

Focus on New York

Standards	Student Edition Pages
UNIT ELEVEN: THE CHANGING NATURE OF THE AMERICAN PEOPLE FROM WORLD WAR II TO THE PRESENT	
I. Postwar Society Characterized by Prosperity and Optimism	
Objective 1: To understand that the period immediately following World War II was a prolonged period of prosperity with a high level of public confidence in the United States	860–866
Objective 2: To investigate key turning points in New York and United States history and explain why these events or developments are significant	874–879, 880–883, 884–891, 894–898, 906, 918–923, 926, 942–947, 948–955
Objective 3: To compare and contrast different interpretations of key events and issues in New York State and United States history and explain reasons for these different accounts	910, 948–955, 958, 990
CONTENT OUTLINE	
A. Changing patterns of production and consumption resulted in economic expansion	851, 860–866, 955, 959
1. Increased productivity, a result of improving technology and rising consumer demand, led to higher wages and declining unemployment	860–866
2. Number of service jobs, women in the workforce increased	817–818, 851, 864–865
3. Poverty continued to exist in the midst of plenty	865–866
B. Families and communities underwent significant changes	816, 862–866, 924
1. Postwar baby boom had major effects on social and economic decisions made by families	851, 862–863
2. Growth of suburbs paralleled by movement from major cities	816, 851, 924
3. Effect of automobiles reflected in interstate highway system, shopping centers, increased commuting to work	862–863, 866
C. Civil rights movement placed focus on equality and democracy	874–879, 884–891
1. Important executive and judicial decisions supported equal rights	874–875
2. *Brown v. Board of Education of Topeka* (1954) overturned legal basis of segregation	874–875
3. Activists and leaders such as Dr. Martin Luther King, Jr. developed strategies to secure civil rights for African-Americans	874–879, 884–891
4. Women, Native American Indians, and others also sought greater equality	894–898
5. Supreme Court moved to protect individual rights: *Miranda v. Arizona* (1966), *Tinker v. Des Moines Independent School District* (1969)	279, 1045
D. Self-confidence of early postwar years eroded by series of events	874–879, 880–883, 884–891, 894–898, 918–923, 926–932
1. Assassinations of major leaders: Kennedy, King	882, 891
2. Nation split over involvement in Vietnam War	918–923, 926–932, 954–955
3. Groups in society turn to violence to reach their goals	885, 886, 891
4. Resignation of President Nixon	948–955
5. Oil crisis and skyrocketing inflation	955
II. The United States Begins a New Century	
Objective 1: To understand the economic, social, and political trends that shaped the end of the 20th century and point to the 21st century	850, 880, 970–975, 976–981, 982–989, 990–997, 1000–1006
Objective 2: To investigate problems and opportunities the United States faces in its immediate future	990–997, 1000–1006
CONTENT OUTLINE	
A. The United States competes in a world economy	972–975, 1006
1. Competition from Europe, Asia, rest of Western Hemisphere	984, 1000–1001
2. Effects on economy of the United States	1000–1006
B. Federal and state governments reevaluate their roles	970–971, 983, 988–989, 1005
1. Fiscal and monetary policies: taxation, regulation, deregulation	970–971
2. Social programs: health, welfare, education	983, 988–989, 1005
C. Technology changes: the home and the workplace	1000, 1003
D. Old and new problems must be addressed	981, 1000–1006
1. Violent crime and substance abuse	981
2. Protection of the environment	1002–1003
3. Growing number of elderly Americans	1005
4. The continuing struggle for economic and social justice for all citizens	982, 989
5. Balancing the ideals of national unity with growing cultural diversity	983, 989
6. Civic and legal responsibilities of citizenship	146–149, 214–223

Symbols of New York

State Flower: Rose

The colorful, fragrant rose was chosen as the official state flower by a vote of New York's school children on Arbor Day 1891. However, the state legislature did not make their choice official until 1955.

State Animal: Beaver

Fur traders settled near present-day Albany in the 1600's so they could trade with Native Americans for much sought after beaver pelts. The beaver was officially adopted as the New York State animal in 1975. Adult beavers can measure three to four feet long and weigh 40 to 50 pounds. They build substantial dams on inland waterways by cutting down small trees with their sharp teeth and then using their long flat tails to pack the spaces between the branches with mud.

State Bird: Eastern Bluebird

The Eastern Bluebird, which became the official state bird of New York in 1970, is one of the first birds to return north each spring. Endangered in the 1950's, it has made a strong comeback thanks to the efforts of many people who built special nesting boxes for them to supplement dwindling natural nesting areas.

State Tree: Sugar Maple

Well known for its brilliant fall colors, the sugar maple became the official state tree in 1956. Also called hard maple or rock maple, it grows best in cool, moist climates and can reach heights of 100 feet. The sugar maple is valuable to the state's economy both for the production of maple syrup and for timber. It has been a favorite of American furniture makers since Colonial days.

State Gem: Garnet

The garnet, recognized as the state gem in 1969, has been popular in jewelry and as an abrasive since the Bronze Age. Although most frequently found in the color red, it also comes in a variety of earth tones as well as green, orange, and yellow. Barton Mines in the Adirondack Mountains is the world's largest garnet mine.

State Fruit: Apple

The apple, which was adopted as the state fruit in 1976, was introduced to New York by European settlers in the 1600's. Dried apples were a food staple for the colonists and apple cider was a popular drink. Today, apples are the third largest agricultural crop produced in New York.

State Flag

The state flag, a modern version of a Revolutionary War flag, displays the Great Seal of the State of New York on a dark blue background. The two figures on either side of the shield represent Liberty and Justice. Liberty holds a staff topped with a Phrygian cap, symbolic of the cap given to a Roman slave upon emancipation. The crown, thrown down at her feet, symbolizes the break with the British monarchy. Justice is blindfolded carrying a scale in one hand and a sword in the other to represent impartiality and fairness in handing out punishment and reward. The shield between them depicts navigation on the Hudson River with the mountains behind. The State Motto, Excelsior, which is Latin for "Ever Upward," appears at the bottom.

New York Counties

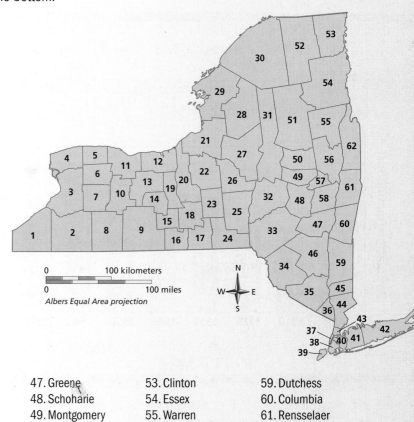

1. Chautauqua
2. Cattaraugus
3. Erie
4. Niagara
5. Orleans
6. Genesee
7. Wyoming
8. Allegany
9. Steuben
10. Livingston
11. Monroe
12. Wayne
13. Ontario
14. Yates
15. Schuyler
16. Chemung
17. Tioga
18. Tompkins
19. Seneca
20. Cayuga
21. Oswego
22. Onondaga
23. Cortland
24. Broome
25. Chenango
26. Madison
27. Oneida
28. Lewis
29. Jefferson
30. St. Lawrence
31. Herkimer
32. Otsego
33. Delaware
34. Sullivan
35. Orange
36. Rockland
37. New York
38. Kings
39. Richmond
40. Queens
41. Nassau
42. Suffolk
43. Bronx
44. Westchester
45. Putnam
46. Ulster
47. Greene
48. Schoharie
49. Montgomery
50. Fulton
51. Hamilton
52. Franklin
53. Clinton
54. Essex
55. Warren
56. Saratoga
57. Schenectady
58. Albany
59. Dutchess
60. Columbia
61. Rensselaer
62. Washington

New York's People

Comparing the Population of New York and the United States

	New York	United States
Population, 2006	19,306,183	299,398,484
Population, percent change, 2000 to 2005	1.7%	6.4%
Persons under 18 years old	23.6%	24.8%
Persons 65 years old and over	13.1%	12.4%
Females	51.6%	50.7%
Males	49.4%	49.3%
Whites	73.8%	80.2%
African Americans	17.4%	12.8%
Persons of Hispanic or Latino origins	16.1%	14.4%
Native Americans	0.1%	0.2%
Asian Americans	6.7%	4.3%

Note: Data on race are from those reporting only one race.
Source: *American Community Survey*, U.S. Census Bureau.

Population 1900–2010

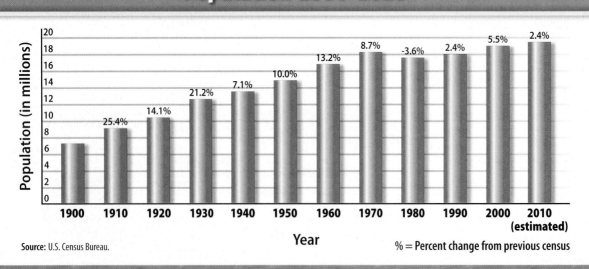

Source: U.S. Census Bureau.

Year

% = Percent change from previous census

New York's Economy

Employment by Industry, 2006

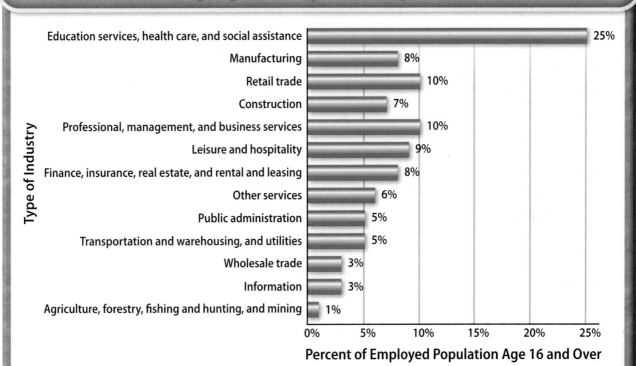

Type of Industry:
- Education services, health care, and social assistance — 25%
- Manufacturing — 8%
- Retail trade — 10%
- Construction — 7%
- Professional, management, and business services — 10%
- Leisure and hospitality — 9%
- Finance, insurance, real estate, and rental and leasing — 8%
- Other services — 6%
- Public administration — 5%
- Transportation and warehousing, and utilities — 5%
- Wholesale trade — 3%
- Information — 3%
- Agriculture, forestry, fishing and hunting, and mining — 1%

Percent of Employed Population Age 16 and Over

Source: American Community Survey, U.S. Census Bureau.

New York's Top 10 Leading Farm Products, 2006

Products	Total value (in millions of dollars)
Dairy Products	$1610
Greenhouse & Nursery	$403
Apples	$197
Cattle and Calves	$157
Hay	$109
Corn for Grain	$89
Sweet Corn	$84
Potatoes	$68
Cabbage	$64
Snap Beans	$63

Source: U.S. Department of Agriculture.

New York's Employers by Number of Employees, 2004

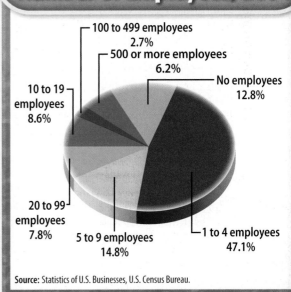

- 100 to 499 employees 2.7%
- 500 or more employees 6.2%
- No employees 12.8%
- 10 to 19 employees 8.6%
- 20 to 99 employees 7.8%
- 5 to 9 employees 14.8%
- 1 to 4 employees 47.1%

Source: Statistics of U.S. Businesses, U.S. Census Bureau.

New York State

Geography

The landforms, waterways, and climate of New York have shaped where people have lived in the state and how they have lived.

The state of New York has three large highland areas. They are the Adirondack Mountains in the northeast; the Allegheny Plateau and Catskill Mountains along the southern border; and low mountains—the Taconic range—along the eastern border.

Lowland areas form a sideways "T" that splits these highlands. The Hudson River valley and the Lake Champlain lowlands reach from the southeast corner north to Canada. The long body of the T stretches along the Mohawk River to the west, where it spreads out along Lake Ontario and Lake Erie. Another lowland area is found on Long Island, which is part of the Atlantic Coastal Plain.

The Hudson River and the Mohawk River have long been important waterways for New Yorkers, serving as centers of settlement, sources of water, and transportation and trade routes.

Climate New York has a temperate climate with four distinct seasons. Temperature ranges can vary greatly between New York City and Upstate New York. Rainfall is ample, allowing farmers to grow crops such as apples, grapes, corn, and soybeans. The Catskills receive the most rain while areas near Lake Erie and Lake Ontario often have heavy snowfalls in winter.

Early Peoples

Native Americans settled thousands of years ago in what is now New York. By around 1500, they had formed two large groups. The Mohican and Munsee peoples lived in the southeast. They spoke languages of the Algonquian family. Five groups of Iroquois lived in the center of the state. They were, from east to west, the Mohawks, Oneidas, Onondagas, Cayugas, and Senecas. These groups called themselves the Haudenosaunee, which means "the people of the longhouse."

How They Lived The Iroquois settled along freshwater rivers and lakes and lived by farming and hunting game. They grew three main crops—corn, beans, and squash—which they called "the Three Sisters." They also hunted deer in the fall and fished in the spring and summer.

Physical Regions
- St. Lawrence Lowland
- Adirondack Upland
- Tug Hill Plateau
- Erie-Ontario Lowland
- Appalachian Plateau
- Hudson-Mohawk Lowland
- New England Upland
- Atlantic Coastal Plain

0   100 kilometers
0   100 miles
Albers Equal Area projection

Iroquois villages consisted of several hundred people. As many as five families lived in each barn-shaped building called a longhouse. The Iroquois created curved roofs for the longhouses by bending the trunks of young trees to form an arch. Then they covered the frame with tree bark and carved chimney holes in the roofs.

Women, who did the farming, held the most important place in Iroquois society. Family relationships were traced through the mother. Families in the same village belonged to the same clan, meaning they were all descendants of the same woman. Iroquois men were known for their skill at hunting and for protecting their land from invaders.

Culture of Native Americans The culture of the Iroquois, especially their beliefs and art, came from the land and resources around them. At the center of Iroquois spiritual life was the belief that the Three Sisters had been a gift to them from the gods. Six times a year, they held festivals to give thanks for their crops.

The nations of the Iroquois Confederacy spoke related languages. The languages were close enough that people from the different groups could understand each other when groups met to discuss issues.

The arts of the Iroquois drew on their resources. They used the husks and silk of corn to make dolls and carved native wood to make ceremonial masks. Later, the Iroquois traded for glass beads and made beadwork objects of great beauty.

The Iroquois Confederacy

Frequent fighting over boundaries and hunting grounds plagued the five Iroquois groups for many years. Then, in the late 1500s, they joined together in a union called the League of Five Nations, or the Iroquois Confederacy. The Five Nations pledged peace to one another and promised to make all important decisions together. They also agreed that all decisions must be unanimous—each nation must agree with decisions.

The Iroquois had well-established cultures long before Europeans arrived in the Americas.

The female heads of each clan chose the *sachem,* or the men who sat on the nation's council. The women also had the power to reject group decisions. When important issues faced the Five Nations, the sachem would gather at the village of the main Onondaga leader. There they would discuss the issue and agree on a common solution. Even today, the Iroquois settle issues in the same way. In the early 1700s, another group—the Tuscaroras—joined the Confederacy, which became the Six Nations.

Europeans Arrive

The Native Americans' world changed dramatically in the 1600s when Europeans began to settle in North America.

The Spanish seized the southeastern and southwestern United States. The French took control of much of what is now eastern Canada, the Great Lakes region, and the Mississippi River. The British established colonies along the Atlantic coast. The Dutch settled in what is now New York. These groups often struggled with each other to control North America.

Europeans came to the Americas for several reasons. Governments sent explorers to look for shorter sea routes from Europe to Asia. They hoped to gain a greater share of the trade with Asia. When some explorers found gold and silver in the Americas, rulers sent more explorers, hoping to find some of this wealth.

Many of those who came to settle the Americas were hoping to start a new life. The large amount of land and good climate promised success at farming. Other Europeans came to escape being punished for their religious beliefs.

Founding of New Netherland

New York Harbor was originally discovered by an Italian, Giovanni da Verrazano, in 1524. In 1609, Henry Hudson sailed into the harbor and followed the river now named for him upstream, reaching

Henry Hudson and his crew, aboard the *Half Moon,* were met by Native Americans when he sailed into what is now New York Harbor.

near where Albany stands today. Because Hudson was sailing for the Netherlands, he claimed the river and the land along it for the Dutch.

The first Dutch settlement in New York was a fort built in 1624 at the site of present-day Albany. The next year, the Dutch bought Manhattan Island from a group of Native Americans. They built a new settlement there called New Amsterdam.

Life in the Dutch Colony The Dutch carried on trade along the Hudson River. From trading posts they exchanged cloth, tools, and weapons for the beaver furs Native Americans had trapped. In turn, the furs were sold for huge profits in Europe. Mainly interested in trade, the Dutch had few family settlements. New Amsterdam, with its excellent harbor became an important port for shipping goods back to Europe.

To encourage more settlement, the Dutch gave large areas of land to landowners called *patroons*. The role of the patroons was to encourage settlers to come to the area to farm the land and raise animals. The settlers would live on the land and pay a part of their earnings to the landowners.

Europeans and Native Americans

Europeans and Native Americans cooperated—and clashed. The two groups shared some characteristics, but they also had different ways of looking at the world. Europeans and many Native Americans were accustomed to farming and to trading for goods. Both had solid loyalties to their nations, and both had societies based on strong families.

The two peoples had differences, too. Many Europeans belonged to a Christian church. Strong in their faith, they wanted to convert Native Americans to their Christian religion. Some Native Americans did convert, but most wanted to follow their own beliefs.

Another key difference was the two groups' view of land ownership. Native Americans believed

that land belonged to the whole nation. Europeans thought that each person had the right to buy and control pieces of land. These differing attitudes produced tension and sometimes war.

There was other evidence of cooperation and conflict between the two groups. Europeans and Native Americans worked together to set up trade networks, and Native Americans helped Europeans learn how to grow corn, squash, and other native plants.

As time passed, though, Europeans took over more and more land. That often led to war with Native Americans who were trying to preserve their territory and way of life.

The French and the British

In 1664, New York saw a dramatic change. English ships sailed into New York Harbor to take control of the area. Overpowered, the governor of New Amsterdam surrendered. The Dutch colony was now in English hands and was given a new name—New York. Gaining New York gave the English several advantages that they would be able to use in their struggle against France for control of America.

In 1754, Britain—as England was now called—and France escalated their contest for control of American land into a war. With the help of the Iroquois, on whose land much of the war was fought, the British defeated the French. In the peace treaty ending the war, France gave up all its land in North America.

The Colonists and the British

Soon after winning this major victory, the British government faced a new problem. Many of its colonists in North America began to object to government actions and controls.

The British feared that if more colonists moved west, Native Americans there would revolt. Thus, in 1763 the British declared that white settlers could not move to the west of the Appalachian Mountains. This was one major control that angered many colonists.

The victorious George Washington and his troops rode through the heart of New York City in 1783.

The British also imposed new taxes on the Americans, such as the Stamp Act. The colonists called the taxes unfair and staged protests against them in many cities, including New York City.

Patriots and Loyalists The colonists who protested against the British came to be called *Patriots.* They insisted on basic freedoms for all Americans. Many New Yorkers formed small groups called the Sons of Liberty. *Loyalists,* on the other hand, argued that the colonists had a duty to obey British law. New York City was home to a great number of Loyalists.

In 1775 fighting broke out between American civilian-soldiers and British troops. Soon after, many colonies—including New York—sent representatives to a Continental Congress in Philadelphia. Some members urged the meeting attendees to declare the colonies independent of Britain. The Continental

Congress finally took that step in 1776. Soon after, Patriots in New York voted to agree with the decision.

New York in the Revolutionary War

Before and during the Revolutionary War, New York was a key battleground. Its strategic importance and the value of controlling New York Harbor made both sides want to control the state.

In 1776 the British invaded New York. They defeated the American forces and seized New York City. The British held the city for the rest of the war. The Americans controlled the rest of the state.

The next year, the British launched another attack on New York. A large force came down Lake Champlain to the Hudson River and fought the Americans at Saratoga. The British army lost the battle and was forced to surrender. This American

Workers such as these in an early 1900s General Electric plant moved to cities hoping to find jobs.

The Second Roosevelt Franklin Delano Roosevelt—a cousin of Theodore—helped lead New York state through the beginning of the Great Depression. He directed his efforts at trying to improve the state's economy. He was elected president of the United States in 1932.

In the White House, Roosevelt enacted several measures to rebuild the country's economy and help people hurt by the Depression. Though these measures were not completely successful, Americans re-elected him as president in 1936 and 1940. In 1944, while the country was in the midst of World War II, he ran a fourth time and won again. The next year, however, President Roosevelt died.

New York in the Late 1900s

In the first twenty years or so after World War II, the nation saw great economic growth. New York took part in the success of that era which historians call the postwar boom. In a major change, though, many people moved out of the cities into the suburbs. As a result, cities lost people who could pay taxes that were needed to fund services. The cities also became home to the poor.

Economic and Social Changes

In the 1970s, more economic problems arose. Many factories in New York closed as companies shifted operations to other parts of the country where labor costs were lower.

Racial tensions became a problem with regards to employment. African Americans protested that white Americans treated them unfairly, denying them jobs. Friction grew between African Americans and whites and between African Americans and the state's growing number of Latinos. New York experienced a changing workforce.

By the late 1900s, New York was rebounding, however. The number of new businesses increased, and increased the hiring from New York's well-educated population. Companies working in such fields as computers, communications, and research and engineering began to grow.

Another change was the growing share of women who worked outside the home during this time. Many of these well-educated women, too, helped make companies more productive and successful.

This theater was at the hub of African American culture in Harlem in the early 1900s.

New York Today

The People of New York

New York still ranks as one of the largest states in population as well as in size of its economy. It has a diverse population, skilled workforce, productive companies, and cultural and natural resources.

Today, New York has about 19 million people. Of the total population, nearly one in six are African Americans, and a similar share are Hispanic. About 7 percent of the population is Asian American.

New York City, nicknamed the "Big Apple" has long been one of the most diverse cities in the country. Today its people reflect more than 200 different ethnic groups. The city offers world-class restaurants, shops, museums, and entertainment. Tourism is a major industry in New York City and across the state.

New York faces some social concerns as do other states in the country. About 13 percent of the people—around one in eight—are 65 years old or older. Many rely for their income on payments they receive from the federal and state governments. The workforce will have to continue growing to meet these entitlement needs.

Poverty is another problem. More than 14 percent of the state's people live in poverty; many of these are children. The state has implemented plans to help with their daily needs and educations.

New York State Government

The current organization of New York government is established by its various constitutions. A bicameral legislature, made up of a 61-member Senate and an Assembly with 150 members, makes the laws. Each member is elected for a two-year term. The legislature makes public policy and works with the governor, who is elected to a four-year term, to maintain the welfare of the state. The New York governor holds a strong position with power over appointments and the state budget.

The state of New York has court justices that are both elected and appointed by the governor. The state is divided into 12 judicial districts. Several judges are elected from each district. They form the state's Supreme Court. The judges of the Court of Appeals are appointed by the governor from those elected to the Supreme Court. The Court of Claims hears cases against the state. Finally, there are a variety of lower courts from the county level down to local courts.

New York's Economy

New York produces about $822 billion worth of goods and services each year and ranks third among states in goods sold to other countries. If New York State were a country, it would have the eleventh-largest economy in the world.

High-technology industries are important in New York. These include industries that make computers and other electronic goods or that use biology to develop new foods and new treatments for health problems. The health care industry itself is one of the fastest growing sources of employment in the state.

Nearly 600,000 people in the state work in manufacturing. They make a range of products from computers to clothing and metals to machines. More than 1.5 million people work in health care and education. Others work in finance, insurance, scientific research, or similar fields. Many more sell goods in the state's stores or drive the trucks and fly the cargo planes that carry products across the state.

Agriculture remains strong in New York State with farmers producing dairy products, fruit, and some grains. Tourism consistently brings dollars to boost New York's economy as thousands visit the state each year. All parts of the state draw tourists, from Niagara Falls, to the Hudson River valley, to along the Atlantic coast, and of course, to New York City itself.

The Statue of Liberty at sunset

Preserving and Protecting the Empire State

Economic growth is important to New York to provide more and better jobs for its people in the future. Recent decades have shown that New Yorkers also have to work at preserving and protecting their environment. A significant problem that emerged in the late 1900s is pollution. The state's lakes and rivers were being poisoned by chemicals that killed fish and plants. Skies were polluted with smoke and dust, causing health problems and producing acid rain.

Since the 1970s, New York has made great progress in reducing the amount of pollution in the state. Dumping of harmful wastes in the waterways has been reduced, and new laws curtail air pollution. The state has acted to protect drinking water and reduce the release of harmful chemicals into the air.

Fighting Terrorism In 1993 and again in 2001, international terrorists attacked New York City. In both instances, they targeted the World Trade Center. In the second attack, thousands of people died and the twin towers of the Trade Center were destroyed. The eyes of the world focused on New York City as it dealt dramatically and successfully with these attacks. New York has since led the country in introducing stringent antiterrorism protections.

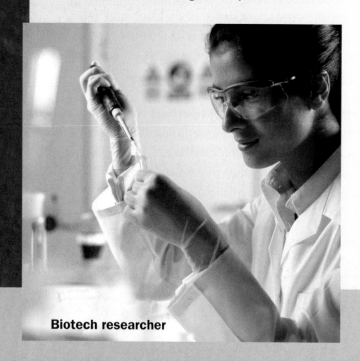

Biotech researcher

Agriculture is a vital part of New York's diverse and robust economy.

What Is a Document-Based Question?

A document-based question (DBQ) assesses your ability to understand, interpret, and analyze historical documents. You will be presented with a series of documents. These documents could appear in various forms. For example, they could be text excerpts, cartoons, or pictures. Questions will present a historical context and a task to help put the documents in perspective. The questions you answer about each document will help you write your essay in the second part of the question.

For the DBQ, you are often asked to:

1. Answer specific short-answer questions about each document.

2. Write an essay drawing upon your understanding of a group of the documents.

The following example is based on a sample short-answer DBQ reading.

DOCUMENT-BASED QUESTIONS

As you read the following document, note the source of the document as well as its author's point of view.

Historical Context: During the late 1800s and early 1900s, Progressive reformers worked to improve American society. Their goals included protecting consumers, regulating child labor, improving working conditions, and expanding democracy.

Short-Answer Questions
Directions: Analyze the document and answer the short-answer questions.

Document 1a

> . . . During the same winter three boys from a Hull-House club were injured at one machine in a neighboring factory for lack of a guard which would have cost but a few dollars. . . .
> . . . Florence Kelley . . . suggested to the Illinois State Bureau of Labor that they investigate the sweating system [sweatshops] in Chicago with its attendant [use of] child labor. . . . When the report was presented to the Illinois Legislature, a special committee was appointed to look into the Chicago conditions. . . .
>
> —Source: Jane Addams, *Twenty Years at Hull-House with Autobiographical Notes*, Macmillan, 1912

1a Based on this document, identify *one* social problem Jane Addams wanted to reform.

_____

2a According to Addams, who should take action to solve the problem?

_____

What Are Research Projects?

Preparing a research project can help you develop a more in-depth understanding of a historical topic. Read through the table of contents in your textbook and the New York Core Curriculum. Select a topic of interest related to American history, and then decide how you will structure the project to share your knowledge with others.

A research project has three main parts—the research, the writing, and the presentation. Most of the project is student-based, which means you have many choices, including the topic, the method of research, and the presentation format.

You should expect to spend two to six weeks preparing your project for presentation. Your teacher will help you along the way.

Choosing a Topic

Your first choice is identifying a topic that interests you. What do you enjoy learning about? What decade in the 20th century do you want to learn more about? What major events from the 18th or 19th century interest you? You may quickly scan the pages of your text, examining the photographs, headings, and features to get ideas. Make a list of all the topics that come to mind.

Your list may include diverse topics, such as the new technologies first used in World War I or the role of protest songs during the 1960s.

Once your list is complete, frame each of the topics as a question. For example, the new technologies first used in World War I could be written as a question: "What new technologies were introduced during World War I?" The role of protest songs during the 1960s could be phrased into the following question: "How did protest songs influence the political climate of the 1960s?"

Select the questions from your list that most interest you. Then consider whether the question is too large or too small to effectively research. The question of the new technologies introduced during World War I may be too broad. Instead, you could focus on the new weapons that were first used during World War I.

Show your selected topic to your teacher. Use your teacher's recommendations to help you make a topic selection. Once you have selected your topic, you can begin your research. As your research proceeds, you may find that you need to change your topic or expand or narrow its focus. Discuss these changes with your teacher so that you do not waste time.

Research Project Topics

Topic	Topic Question
World War I technology	What new technologies were introduced during World War I?
1960s protest songs	How did protest songs influence the political climate of the 1960s?

Beginning Your Research

The main goal of your research project is to demonstrate what you have learned about your topic and about American history. Your research may include your textbook, other books and printed materials, interviews with people who lived during the time period you are researching, and any electronic resources available to you.

To help you understand the research process, we will use a specific example. Assume that you and your teacher have agreed that your topic will address the question: "What weapons were first used in World War I?"

Using Your Textbook

Begin your research by learning more about the time period for the topic you have selected. Use your textbook to find out what was happening in American history at the time. Use the book's index to locate World War I, and find any entries related to weapons or technology. Turn to those pages and identify the information available to you.

If you think you will make use of the information, record the bibliographic information on an index card as shown below. Label the card "BC" to identify it as a bibliographic card.

BC #1
Title of Book: The American Journey
Authors: Appleby, Brinkley, and McPherson
Publisher: Glencoe
Date: 2008
Location of Company: Columbus, Ohio
Pages of chapter being used: 702-737

Take another index card and label it "Note Card #1." Read the textbook page or pages. Then, in your own words, write down the information you have learned. If you want to quote something, put the words in quotation marks, copying them exactly. Most of your presentation will be in your own words. However, you may use some quotations or primary source documents.

Taking Notes

Use the following three strategies for note taking:

1. Quote directly from the source. Be sure to cite your source completely to avoid plagiarism.
2. Paraphrase—rewrite the material in your own words.
3. Summarize—condense the main ideas from your reading.

Use these cards as examples of notes taken from the textbook. The label "BC #1" on the note card relates the content to the bibliographic card shown on the preceding page.

Using the Library

When you have completed taking notes from your textbook, search for additional resources in the library. Use the library's catalog to identify books and articles related to your topic. Scan these resources to select at least three (but not more than five) books for your research. For each source you have selected, create a bibliography card and corresponding note cards. Use the following examples as models.

Note Card #1   BC #1
Weapons like poison gas, the armored tank, and the airplane were first introduced in WW I.
Artillery fired bigger shells, and guns were more accurate than ever before.
Pages 709-710

Note Card #2   BC #1
Another new weapon was the submarine or U-boat. These boats were hard to locate and therefore were often able to sink ships and get away undetected. The British liner Lusitania and the French passenger ship Sussex were both sunk by submarines.   Pages 714-715

Note Card #3   BC #1
Poison gas was used for the first time. The wind would carry the gas into the trenches, "causing blindness, choking, damaged lungs, and death."
Page 719

Note Card #4   BC #2
Before WW I, most men thought of war as "an adventure," or just as a fight between nations or groups of men. This war was different; this war would be the first war where technology (meaning artillery, machine guns, and mustard gas) was a major factor.   Page 24

BC #2
Title of Book: The Century for Young People
Authors: Peter Jennings and Todd Brewster
Publisher: Random House
Date: 1999
Place of Publication: New York
Pages 22-26

Using the Internet

When you have completed your library research, search the Internet for additional information on your topic. Using a search engine like Google or Yahoo!, key in your search criteria. For example, you might key in "World War I," "World War I technology," or "World War I weapons." As you examine your search results, be sure to select sources that are current and reliable. As shown in the example below, take notes on information you find for your project.

Another method of accessing content on the Internet is through the Web links organized by topic at taj.glencoe.com.

Note Card #5   BC #3
The new machine guns used in WW I were called Weapons of Mass Destruction. These guns could fire up to 600 bullets at a time.

BC #3
World War I Weapons -- New Technology
Internet November 1, 2008
http://www.firstworldwar.com

Organizing Your Research

To ensure your project is completed by your deadline, prepare a time line that shows what you will do and when you will do it. Your time line will help you manage your time and check your progress. Following is an example of a time line containing important milestones:

Research Project Time Line

Research completed	Date: _____
Project outline completed	Date: _____
First draft completed	Date: _____
Revisions completed	Date: _____
Final project completed	Date: _____

Before you begin writing, you must determine how you will present your final project. What form will you use to communicate the results of your research? Ideas for presenting your final project follow. Regardless of the format you select, your goal is to clearly communicate the results of your research.

Designing a Project-Based Exhibit

Project-based exhibits are designed to display visual (graphic) and written information on your topic in an attractive, interesting, and understandable manner.

Use your research question to help you plan and design your display board. Clarity and organization are important. Select only the most important items to be displayed to explain, illustrate, and analyze your topic. Use labels, photographs, and graphics to provide information. Use color to add emphasis.

Planning a Performance-Based Project

Performance is another way to present the knowledge and understanding you have gained through your research. Choose a format that fits your personal talents and interests.

Are you comfortable with computer technology? Then you might want to present your research using a presentation program. Do you like to act or direct? You might write and present a skit. Do you like to give speeches? Then you could present a dramatic monologue in the character of a fictional or historic person. Are you artistic? Then you might create a visual display. Some ideas for performance-based projects are listed below. Review a complete list of possibilities with your teacher to make your final selection.

If you like music:
- Raps or songs
- Dances
- Musical montage

If you like art:
- Advertisements
- Annotated illustrations
- Annotated slides
- Book or compact disc covers

If you like technology:
- Video
- Presentation program

If you like math:
- Flowcharts
- Venn diagrams

If you like to write:
- Poetry
- Historic journal entries
- Historic markers
- Newscast
- Skit
- Dramatic monologue

Writing, Revising, and Editing

When you are ready to write, begin by considering how you will order your information. Prepare an outline for your project, and order your note cards accordingly. If you are creating a visual display, use a storyboard or diagram to organize your information.

Write a draft of the text for your project. Then consider what you can do to improve the draft. Will your presentation grab the attention of your audience? Is your writing logical, clear, and concise? Have you left out any important information? Are you wordy or redundant in places? Is the layout visually appealing? Revise your draft.

As you prepare your final draft, consider what visual aids might enhance your presentation. You might include overhead projection transparencies, slides within a presentation program, video, real objects, posters, handouts, or flip charts to add interest to your presentation.

Before your draft is complete, you must edit and proofread your work carefully. Check your work for errors in spelling, grammar, usage, structure, punctuation, and formatting. Check to be sure you have cited all your sources completely. Have at least one other person edit your work. Correct the errors and prepare to present your final product.

Presenting Your Project

The final step in your research project is the presentation. Organization, information, delivery, and visual aids will all play an important role in your final grade. Be sure to consider each of these points as you prepare to present your project.

To prepare, practice your presentation several times. With practice, your presentation will be more polished and you will be less nervous. Don't read directly from a script or report. Your presentation will be more interesting to your audience if you speak conversationally and maintain eye contact. If necessary, use note cards to remind you of your main points.

Remember that the style of your presentation is just as important as the content. Speak clearly and with enthusiasm. Monitor your volume so everyone can hear your voice. Use body language to reinforce your points, and use visual aids to add interest. When your presentation is completed, be prepared to answer questions that people might ask you about your topic.

REFERENCE ATLAS

NATIONAL GEOGRAPHIC

ATLAS KEY

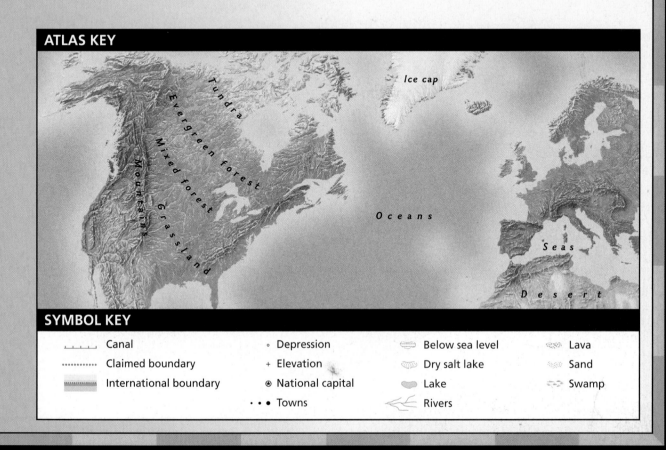

SYMBOL KEY

Canal		Depression		Below sea level		Lava	
Claimed boundary		Elevation		Dry salt lake		Sand	
International boundary		National capital		Lake		Swamp	
		Towns		Rivers			

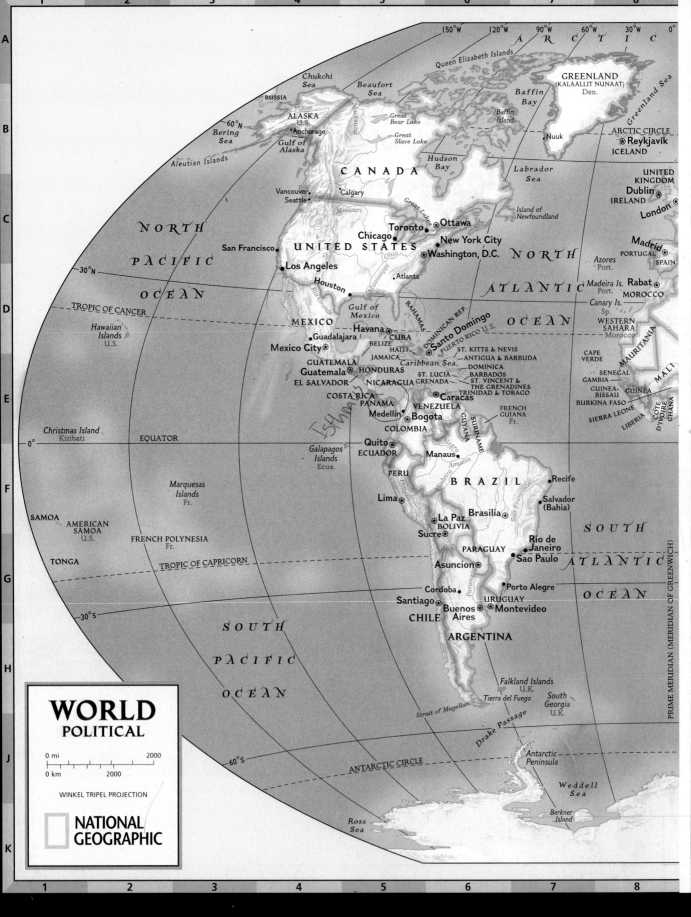

WORLD POLITICAL

0 mi 2000
0 km 2000

WINKEL TRIPEL PROJECTION

NATIONAL GEOGRAPHIC

ABBREVIATIONS

AUST. .... AUSTRIA
B.&H. .... BOSNIA & HERZEGOVINA
BELG. .... BELGIUM
CROAT. .... CROATIA
CZECH REP. .... CZECH REPUBLIC
DEM. REP. .... DEMOCRATIC
OF THE   REPUBLIC OF
CONGO   THE CONGO
EQ. GUINEA .... EQUATORIAL GUINEA
EST. .... ESTONIA
HUNG. .... HUNGARY
LITH. .... LITHUANIA
MACED. .... MACEDONIA
MOLD. .... MOLDOVA
NETH. .... NETHERLANDS
SERB. .... SERBIA
MONT. .... MONTENEGRO
SLOV. .... SLOVENIA
SWITZ. .... SWITZERLAND
U.A.E. .... UNITED ARAB EMIRATES

NORTH AMERICA
POLITICAL

0 mi 1000
0 km 1000

AZIMUTHAL EQUIDISTANT PROJECTION

NATIONAL GEOGRAPHIC

1. BAJA CALIFORNIA
2. BAJA CALIFORNIA SUR
3. SONORA
4. CHIHUAHUA
5. SINALOA
6. DURANGO
7. COAHUILA
8. NUEVO LEON
9. ZACATECAS
10. TAMAULIPAS
11. NAYARIT
12. AGUASCALIENTES
13. SAN LUIS POTOSI
14. JALISCO
15. GUANAJUATO
16. QUERETARO
17. HIDALGO
18. COLIMA
19. MICHOACAN
20. MEXICO
21. DISTRITO FEDERAL
22. TLAXCALA
23. MORELOS
24. PUEBLA
25. VERACRUZ
26. GUERRERO
27. OAXACA
28. TABASCO
29. CHIAPAS
30. CAMPECHE
31. QUINTANA ROO
32. YUCATAN

UNITED STATES PHYSICAL

ALBERS CONIC EQUAL-AREA PROJECTION

NATIONAL GEOGRAPHIC

PRINCIPAL HAWAIIAN ISLANDS

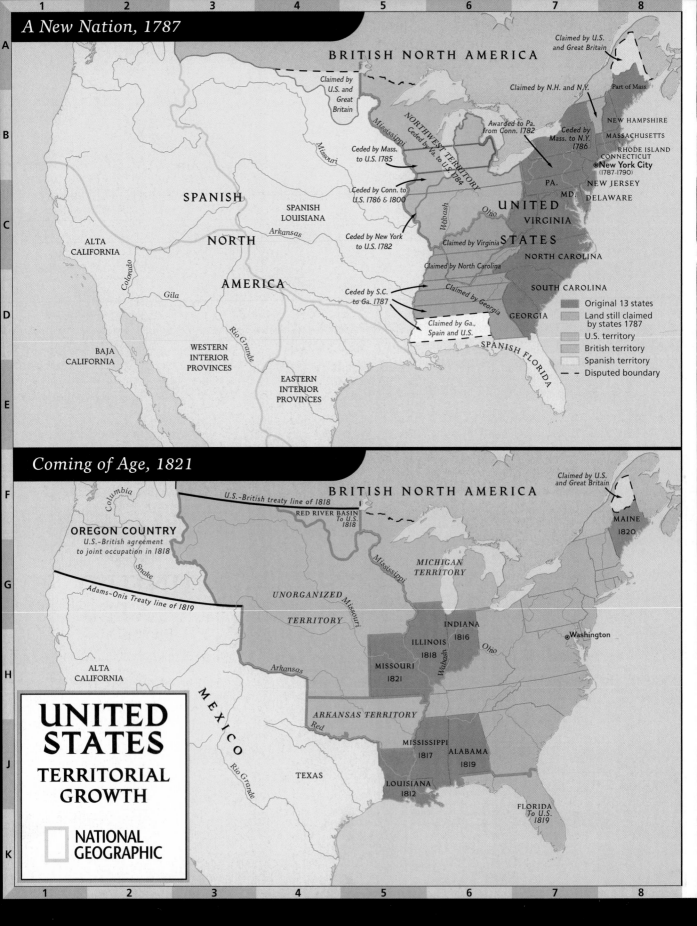

A New Nation, 1787

BRITISH NORTH AMERICA

Claimed by U.S. and Great Britain

Claimed by U.S. and Great Britain

Part of Mass.

Claimed by N.H. and N.Y.

NEW HAMPSHIRE

MASSACHUSETTS

RHODE ISLAND
CONNECTICUT

Awarded to Pa. from Conn. 1782

Ceded by Mass. to N.Y. 1786

⊙New York City
(1787-1790)

NEW JERSEY

DELAWARE

Ceded by Mass. to U.S. 1785

Ceded by Va. to U.S. 1784

NORTHWEST TERRITORY

PA.

MD.

Ceded by Conn. to U.S. 1786 & 1800

UNITED

VIRGINIA

STATES

Ceded by New York to U.S. 1782

Claimed by Virginia

NORTH CAROLINA

Claimed by North Carolina

SOUTH CAROLINA

Ceded by S.C. to Ga. 1787

Claimed by Georgia

GEORGIA

Claimed by Ga., Spain and U.S.

SPANISH FLORIDA

SPANISH

NORTH

AMERICA

SPANISH LOUISIANA

ALTA CALIFORNIA

BAJA CALIFORNIA

WESTERN INTERIOR PROVINCES

EASTERN INTERIOR PROVINCES

Mississippi · *Missouri* · *Arkansas* · *Colorado* · *Gila* · *Rio Grande* · *Wabash* · *Ohio*

Original 13 states
Land still claimed by states 1787
U.S. territory
British territory
Spanish territory
– – – Disputed boundary

Coming of Age, 1821

BRITISH NORTH AMERICA

Claimed by U.S. and Great Britain

U.S.-British treaty line of 1818

RED RIVER BASIN To U.S. 1818

MAINE 1820

OREGON COUNTRY
U.S.-British agreement to joint occupation in 1818

MICHIGAN TERRITORY

Adams-Onis Treaty line of 1819

UNORGANIZED TERRITORY

INDIANA 1816

ILLINOIS 1818

⊙Washington

ALTA CALIFORNIA

MISSOURI 1821

ARKANSAS TERRITORY

MISSISSIPPI 1817

ALABAMA 1819

LOUISIANA 1812

FLORIDA To U.S. 1819

MEXICO

TEXAS

Columbia · *Snake* · *Mississippi* · *Missouri* · *Arkansas* · *Red* · *Rio Grande* · *Wabash* · *Ohio*

UNITED STATES

TERRITORIAL GROWTH

NATIONAL GEOGRAPHIC

Expanding West of the Mississippi, 1803

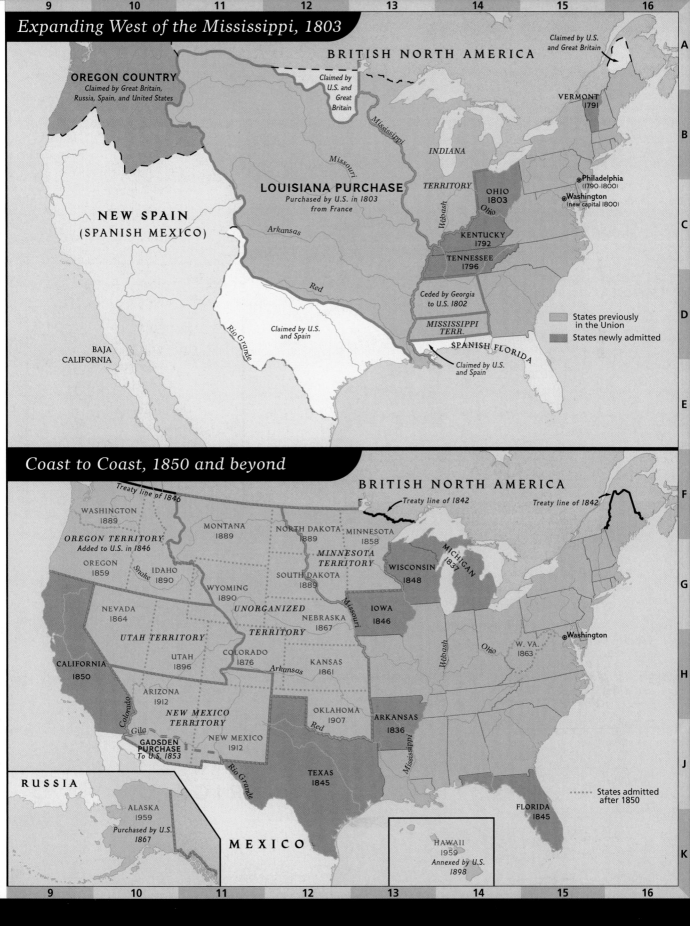

BRITISH NORTH AMERICA

Claimed by U.S. and Great Britain

OREGON COUNTRY
Claimed by Great Britain, Russia, Spain, and United States

Claimed by U.S. and Great Britain

VERMONT 1791

INDIANA

Mississippi

Missouri

LOUISIANA PURCHASE
Purchased by U.S. in 1803 from France

TERRITORY

OHIO 1803

Ohio

Wabash

Philadelphia (1790-1800)

Washington (new capital 1800)

NEW SPAIN (SPANISH MEXICO)

Arkansas

KENTUCKY 1792

TENNESSEE 1796

Red

Ceded by Georgia to U.S. 1802

Claimed by U.S. and Spain

Rio Grande

MISSISSIPPI TERR.

SPANISH FLORIDA

Claimed by U.S. and Spain

BAJA CALIFORNIA

States previously in the Union
States newly admitted

Coast to Coast, 1850 and beyond

BRITISH NORTH AMERICA

Treaty line of 1846

Treaty line of 1842

Treaty line of 1842

WASHINGTON 1889

MONTANA 1889

NORTH DAKOTA 1889

MINNESOTA 1858

OREGON TERRITORY
Added to U.S. in 1846

MINNESOTA TERRITORY

MICHIGAN 1837

OREGON 1859

Snake

IDAHO 1890

SOUTH DAKOTA 1889

WISCONSIN 1848

NEVADA 1864

WYOMING 1890

UNORGANIZED

Missouri

IOWA 1846

Washington

UTAH TERRITORY

NEBRASKA 1867

TERRITORY

Wabash

Ohio

W. VA. 1863

CALIFORNIA 1850

UTAH 1896

COLORADO 1876

KANSAS 1861

Arkansas

ARIZONA 1912

Colorado

NEW MEXICO TERRITORY

OKLAHOMA 1907

Red

ARKANSAS 1836

Gila

GADSDEN PURCHASE
To U.S. 1853

NEW MEXICO 1912

Mississippi

Rio Grande

TEXAS 1845

FLORIDA 1845

States admitted after 1850

RUSSIA

ALASKA 1959
Purchased by U.S. 1867

MEXICO

HAWAII 1959
Annexed by U.S. 1898

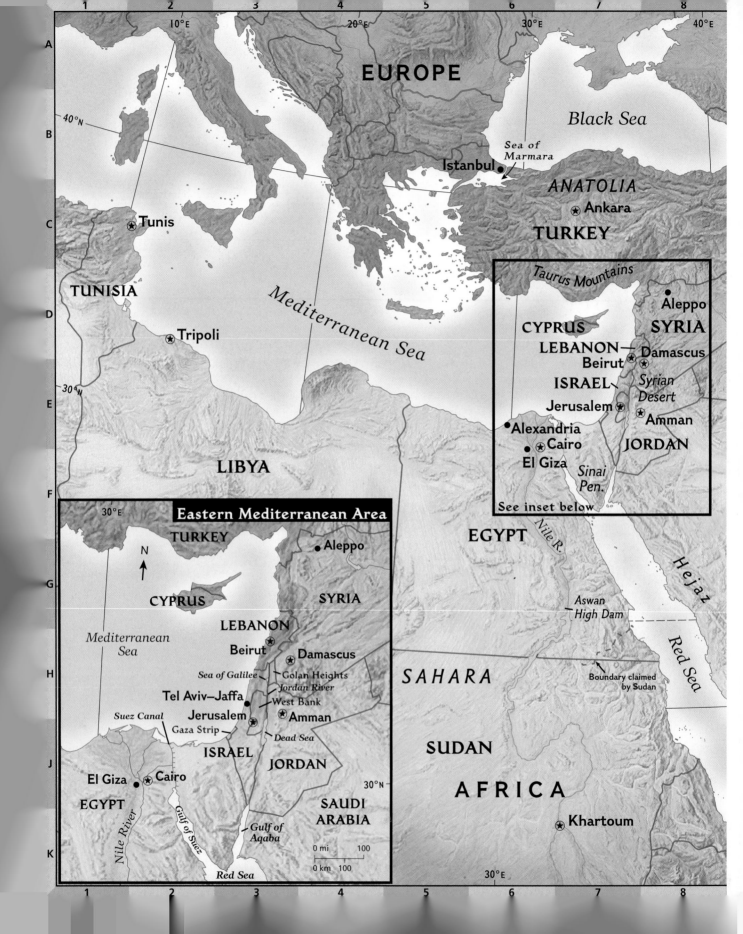

EUROPE

Black Sea

Sea of Marmara

Istanbul

ANATOLIA

Ankara

TURKEY

Tunis

TUNISIA

Tripoli

Mediterranean Sea

Taurus Mountains

CYPRUS

LEBANON

Beirut

ISRAEL

Jerusalem

Alexandria

Cairo

El Giza

Aleppo

SYRIA

Damascus

Syrian Desert

Amman

JORDAN

Sinai Pen.

See inset below

LIBYA

EGYPT

Nile R.

Hejaz

Aswan High Dam

Red Sea

Boundary claimed by Sudan

SAHARA

SUDAN

AFRICA

Khartoum

40°N

30°N

10°E

20°E

30°E

40°E

Eastern Mediterranean Area

30°E

N

TURKEY

Aleppo

CYPRUS

SYRIA

Mediterranean Sea

LEBANON

Beirut

Damascus

Sea of Galilee

Golan Heights

Jordan River

Tel Aviv–Jaffa

West Bank

Suez Canal

Jerusalem

Amman

Gaza Strip

Dead Sea

ISRAEL

JORDAN

El Giza

Cairo

EGYPT

Nile River

Gulf of Suez

Gulf of Aqaba

SAUDI ARABIA

30°N

0 mi   100

0 km   100

Red Sea

30°E

MIDDLE EAST

PHYSICAL / POLITICAL

0 mi ⸻ 500
0 km ⸻ 500

AZIMUTHAL EQUIDISTANT PROJECTION

NATIONAL GEOGRAPHIC

United States Facts

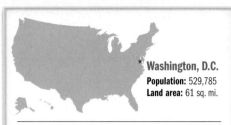

*Washington, D.C.
Population: 529,785
Land area: 61 sq. mi.

U.S. Territories

Puerto Rico
Population: 3,987,837
Land area: 3,425 sq. mi.

Guam
Population: 180,692
Land area: 209 sq. mi.

U.S. Virgin Islands
Population: 107,560
Land area: 134 sq. mi.

American Samoa
Population: 57,066
Land area: 77 sq. mi.

The states are listed in the order they were admitted to the Union.

Population figures are based on the U.S. Bureau of the Census projections for July 2010. House of Representatives figures from the 2000 census are from the Clerk of the House of Representatives. States are not drawn to scale.

1 Delaware
Year Admitted: 1787
Population: 884,342
Land area: 1,955 sq. mi.
Representatives: 1

*Dover

2 Pennsylvania
Year Admitted: 1787
Population: 12,584,487
Land area: 44,820 sq. mi.
Representatives: 19

Harrisburg *

3 New Jersey
Year Admitted: 1787
Population: 9,018,231
Land area: 7,419 sq. mi.
Representatives: 13

Trenton *

9 New Hampshire
Year Admitted: 1788
Population: 1,385,560
Land area: 8,969 sq. mi.
Representatives: 2

Concord

10 Virginia
Year Admitted: 1788
Population: 8,010,245
Land area: 39,598 sq. mi.
Representatives: 11

Richmond *

11 New York
Year Admitted: 1788
Population: 19,443,672
Land area: 47,224 sq. mi.
Representatives: 29

* Albany

17 Ohio
Year Admitted: 1803
Population: 11,576,181
Land area: 40,953 sq. mi.
Representatives: 18

* Columbus

18 Louisiana
Year Admitted: 1812
Population: 4,612,679
Land area: 43,566 sq. mi.
Representatives: 7

* Baton Rouge

19 Indiana
Year Admitted: 1816
Population: 6,392,139
Land area: 35,870 sq. mi.
Representatives: 9

Indianapolis

24 Missouri
Year Admitted: 1821
Population: 5,922,078
Land area: 68,898 sq. mi.
Representatives: 9

Jefferson City *

25 Arkansas
Year Admitted: 1836
Population: 2,875,039
Land area: 52,075 sq. mi.
Representatives: 4

Little Rock *

26 Michigan
Year Admitted: 1837
Population: 10,428,683
Land area: 56,809 sq. mi.
Representatives: 15

Lansing *

27 Florida
Year Admitted: 1845
Population: 19,251,691
Land area: 53,997 sq. mi.
Representatives: 25

* Tallahassee

28 Texas
Year Admitted: 1845
Population: 24,648,888
Land area: 261,914 sq. mi.
Representatives: 32

Austin *

33 Oregon
Year Admitted: 1859
Population: 3,790,996
Land area: 96,003 sq. mi.
Representatives: 5

* Salem

34 Kansas
Year Admitted: 1861
Population: 2,805,470
Land area: 81,823 sq. mi.
Representatives: 4

Topeka *

35 West Virginia
Year Admitted: 1863
Population: 1,829,141
Land area: 24,087 sq. mi.
Representatives: 3

* Charleston

36 Nevada
Year Admitted: 1864
Population: 2,690,531
Land area: 109,806 sq. mi.
Representatives: 3

* Carson City

37 Nebraska
Year Admitted: 1867
Population: 1,768,997
Land area: 76,878 sq. mi.
Representatives: 3

Lincoln *

42 Washington
Year Admitted: 1889
Population: 6,541,963
Land area: 66,582 sq. mi.
Representatives: 9

* Olympia

43 Idaho
Year Admitted: 1890
Population: 1,517,291
Land area: 82,751 sq. mi.
Representatives: 2

* Boise

44 Wyoming
Year Admitted: 1890
Population: 519,886
Land area: 97,105 sq. mi.
Representatives: 1

Cheyenne *

45 Utah
Year Admitted: 1896
Population: 2,595,013
Land area: 82,168 sq. mi.
Representatives: 3

* Salt Lake City

46 Oklahoma
Year Admitted: 1907
Population: 3,591,516
Land area: 68,679 sq. mi.
Representatives: 5

Oklahoma City *

4 Georgia
Year Admitted: 1788
Population: 9,589,080
Land area: 57,919 sq. mi.
Representatives: 13

★ Atlanta

5 Connecticut
Year Admitted: 1788
Population: 3,577,490
Land area: 4,845 sq. mi.
Representatives: 5

★ Hartford

6 Massachusetts
Year Admitted: 1788
Population: 6,649,441
Land area: 7,838 sq. mi.
Representatives: 10

Boston ★

7 Maryland
Year Admitted: 1788
Population: 5,904,970
Land area: 9,775 sq. mi.
Representatives: 8

Annapolis ★

8 South Carolina
Year Admitted: 1788
Population: 4,446,704
Land area: 30,111 sq. mi.
Representatives: 6

Columbia
★

12 North Carolina
Year Admitted: 1789
Population: 9,345,823
Land area: 48,718 sq. mi.
Representatives: 13

★
Raleigh

13 Rhode Island
Year Admitted: 1790
Population: 1,116,652
Land area: 1,045 sq. mi.
Representatives: 2

★ Providence

14 Vermont
Year Admitted: 1791
Population: 652,512
Land area: 9,249 sq. mi.
Representatives: 1

★ Montpelier

15 Kentucky
Year Admitted: 1792
Population: 4,265,117
Land area: 39,732 sq. mi.
Representatives: 6

Frankfort ★

16 Tennessee
Year Admitted: 1796
Population: 6,230,852
Land area: 41,220 sq. mi.
Representatives: 9

★ Nashville

20 Mississippi
Year Admitted: 1817
Population: 2,971,412
Land area: 46,914 sq. mi.
Representatives: 4

★ Jackson

21 Illinois
Year Admitted: 1818
Population: 12,916,894
Land area: 55,593 sq. mi.
Representatives: 19

★ Springfield

22 Alabama
Year Admitted: 1819
Population: 4,596,330
Land area: 50,750 sq. mi.
Representatives: 7

Montgomery
★

23 Maine
Year Admitted: 1820
Population: 1,357,134
Land area: 30,865 sq. mi.
Representatives: 2

★ Augusta

29 Iowa
Year Admitted: 1846
Population: 3,009,907
Land area: 55,875 sq. mi.
Representatives: 5

Des Moines
★

30 Wisconsin
Year Admitted: 1848
Population: 5,727,426
Land area: 54,314 sq. mi.
Representatives: 8

Madison
★

31 California
Year Admitted: 1850
Population: 38,067,134
Land area: 155,973 sq. mi.
Representatives: 53

Sacramento ★

32 Minnesota
Year Admitted: 1858
Population: 5,420,636
Land area: 79,617 sq. mi.
Representatives: 8

Saint Paul
★

38 Colorado
Year Admitted: 1876
Population: 4,831,554
Land area: 103,730 sq. mi.
Representatives: 7

Denver ★

39 North Dakota
Year Admitted: 1889
Population: 636,623
Land area: 68,994 sq. mi.
Representatives: 1

Bismarck
★

40 South Dakota
Year Admitted: 1889
Population: 786,399
Land area: 75,898 sq. mi.
Representatives: 1

Pierre
★

41 Montana
Year Admitted: 1889
Population: 968,598
Land area: 145,556 sq. mi.
Representatives: 1

★ Helena

47 New Mexico
Year Admitted: 1912
Population: 1,980,225
Land area: 121,365 sq. mi.
Representatives: 3

★
Santa Fe

48 Arizona
Year Admitted: 1912
Population: 6,637,381
Land area: 113,642 sq. mi.
Representatives: 8

★
Phoenix
★

49 Alaska
Year Admitted: 1959
Population: 694,109
Land area: 570,374 sq. mi.
Representatives: 1

Juneau ★

50 Hawaii
Year Admitted: 1959
Population: 1,340,674
Land area: 6,432 sq. mi.
Representatives: 2

Honolulu ★

Geography Skills Handbook

How Do I Study Geography?

Geographers have created these broad categories and standards as tools to help you understand the relationships among people, places, and environments.

- 🌐 5 Themes of Geography
- 🌐 6 Essential Elements
- 🌐 18 Geography Standards

5
Themes of Geography

1 Location

Location describes where something is. Absolute location describes a place's exact position on the Earth's surface. Relative location expresses where a place is in relation to another place.

2 Place

Place describes the physical and human characteristics that make a location unique.

3 Regions

Regions are areas that share common characteristics.

4 Movement

Movement explains how and why people and things move and are connected.

5 Human-Environment Interaction

Human-Environment Interaction describes the relationship between people and their environment.

Hemispheres

The Equator divides the Earth into Northern and Southern Hemispheres. Everything north of the Equator is in the Northern Hemisphere. Everything south of the Equator is in the Southern Hemisphere.

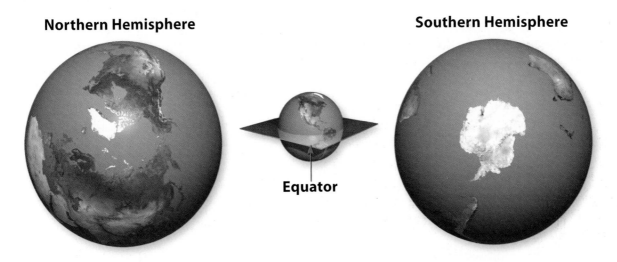

Northern Hemisphere

Southern Hemisphere

Equator

The Prime Meridian divides the Earth into Eastern and Western Hemispheres. Everything east of the Prime Meridian for 180 degrees is in the Eastern Hemisphere. Everything west of the Prime Meridian for 180 degrees is in the Western Hemisphere.

Western Hemisphere

Eastern Hemisphere

Prime Meridian

Skills Practice

1 **Identifying** What country is located at 30°S and 120°E?

2 **Analyzing Visuals** In which hemispheres is Europe located?

Parts of a Map

In addition to latitude and longitude, maps feature other important tools to help you interpret the information they contain.

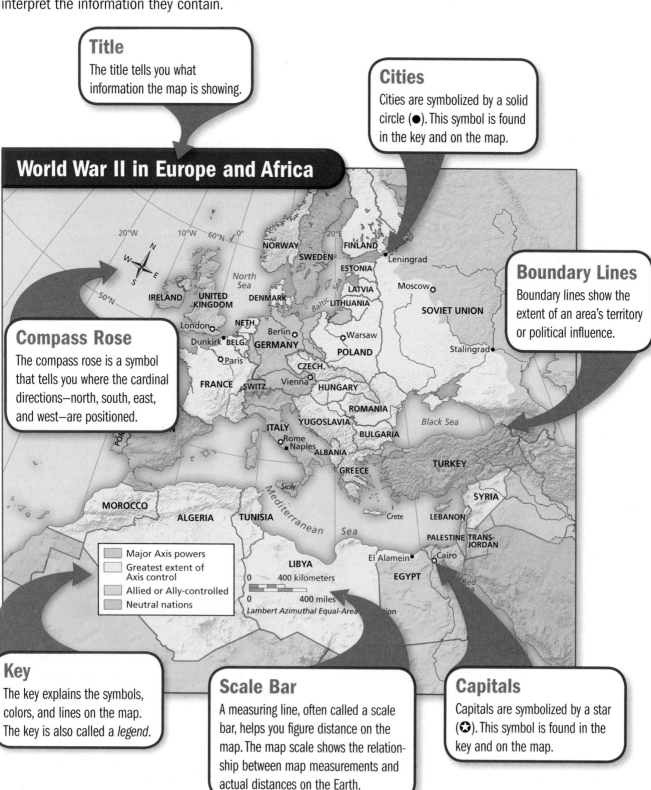

Title
The title tells you what information the map is showing.

Cities
Cities are symbolized by a solid circle (●). This symbol is found in the key and on the map.

World War II in Europe and Africa

Boundary Lines
Boundary lines show the extent of an area's territory or political influence.

Compass Rose
The compass rose is a symbol that tells you where the cardinal directions—north, south, east, and west—are positioned.

Key legend:
- Major Axis powers
- Greatest extent of Axis control
- Allied or Ally-controlled
- Neutral nations

0 400 kilometers
0 400 miles
Lambert Azimuthal Equal-Area

Key
The key explains the symbols, colors, and lines on the map. The key is also called a *legend*.

Scale Bar
A measuring line, often called a scale bar, helps you figure distance on the map. The map scale shows the relationship between map measurements and actual distances on the Earth.

Capitals
Capitals are symbolized by a star (✪). This symbol is found in the key and on the map.

Mountain range
Source of river
Channel
Glacier
Highland
Plateau
Lake
Hills
Mouth of river
Canyon
Desert
River
Upstream
Downstream
Plain
Lowland
Basin
Tributary

mesa broad, flat-topped landform with steep sides; smaller than a plateau

mountain land with steep sides that rises sharply (1,000 feet or more) from surrounding land; generally larger and more rugged than a hill

mountain peak pointed top of a mountain

mountain range a series of connected mountains

mouth (of a river) place where a stream or river flows into a larger body of water

ocean one of the four major bodies of salt water that surround the continents

ocean current stream of either cold or warm water that moves in a definite direction through an ocean

parallel one of many lines on the global grid that circle the Earth north and south of the Equator; used to measure degrees of latitude

peninsula body of land jutting into a lake or ocean, surrounded on three sides by water

physical feature characteristic of a place occurring naturally, such as a landform, body of water, climate pattern, or resource

plain area of level land, usually at a low elevation and often covered with grasses

plateau large area of flat or rolling land at a high elevation, about 300 to 3,000 feet (90 to 900 m) high

Prime Meridian line of the global grid running from the North Pole to the South Pole at Greenwich, England; starting point for measuring degrees of east and west longitude

relief changes in elevation over a given area of land

river large natural stream of water that runs through land

sea large body of water completely surrounded by land

seacoast land lying next to a sea or ocean

sea level position on land level with surface of nearby ocean or sea

sound body of water between a coastline and one or more islands off the coast

source (of a river) place where a river or stream begins, often in highlands

strait narrow stretch of water joining two larger bodies of water

tributary small river or stream that flows into a larger river or stream; a branch of the river

upstream direction opposite the flow of a river; toward the source of a river or stream

valley area of low land between hills or mountains

volcano mountain created as ash or liquid rock erupts from inside the Earth

Unit 1

The Americas: Worlds Meet
Beginnings to 1770

Chapter 1
The First Americans
Prehistory to 1492

Chapter 2
Exploring the Americas
1400–1625

Chapter 3
Colonial America
1587–1770

Chapter 4
Growth of the Thirteen Colonies
1607–1770

Walnut carved Pilgrim bowl, 1608

"All the land so far discovered is a bee-hive of people."
—Bartolomé de Las Casas

The Landing of the Pilgrims by Samuel Bartoll

1

Reading History

READING SKILL

Identifying the Main Idea

Learn It! Main ideas are the most important ideas in a paragraph, section, or chapter. Facts and examples that explain the main idea are the supporting details.

Main Idea
Maya traders transported goods along Mexico's coast.

Supporting Detail
The Maya traded many goods.

Supporting Detail
The traders visited a large area.

—*from Chapter 1, p. 12*

Maya traders also transported goods up and down Mexico's east coast. Their canoes carried jade statues, turquoise jewelry, cacao beans for making chocolate, and other goods to traders throughout a large area.

Practice It! Read the paragraph and write the main idea and details on another sheet of paper.

—*from Chapter 4, p. 89*

Most people in New England lived in well-organized towns. The meetinghouse stood in the center of the town. This building was used for both church services and town meetings. The meetinghouse faced a piece of land called the *green* or *common*. Here cows grazed and the citizen army trained. Farmers lived in the town and worked in fields on its outskirts.

Main Idea
_____

Supporting Detail
_____
_____

Supporting Detail
_____
_____

Academic Vocabulary Preview

Listed below are the academic vocabulary words and their definitions that you will come across as you study Unit 1. Practice It! will help you study the words and definitions.

Academic Vocabulary	Definition	Practice It!
Chapter 1 The First Americans		
source (SAWRS) *p. 8*	to supply	**Identify** *the term from Chapter 1 that best completes the sentences.* **1.** Ancient civilizations created _____ systems for communication. **2.** Scientific measures can provide an _____ on the age of artifacts. **3.** The Inca built paved roads to _____ outposts of their empire.
estimate (EHS · tuh · muht) *p. 9*	approximate number	
complex (KAHM · PLEHKS) *p. 11*	complicated; highly detailed	
link (LIHNK) *p. 13*	to join or connect	
channel (CHA · nuhl) *p. 17*	a trench	
structure (STRUHK · chuhr) *p. 17*	a building	
Chapter 2 Exploring the Americas		
acquire (uh · KWYUHR) *p. 31*	to come into possession of	**Identify** *the term from Chapter 2 that best matches the underlined term or terms.* **4.** Some empires became wealthy after choosing to <u>establish a tax</u> on traded goods. **5.** The <u>planet Earth</u> is divided into two hemispheres. **6.** Europeans sailed to North America to <u>map</u> its coastline.
impose (ihm · POHZ) *p. 32*	to establish or apply by authority	
devote (dih · VOHT) *p. 39*	to give time, money, or effort to a cause	
alter (AWL · tuhr) *p. 40*	to change	
grant (GRANT) *p. 43*	special privilege	
found (FAUND) *p. 46*	to establish or set up	
globe (GLOHB) *p. 51*	the planet Earth	
chart (CHAHRT) *p. 51*	to map	
Chapter 3 Colonial America		
expand (ihk · SPAND) *p. 61*	to increase or grow	**Choose** *the word that best matches the meaning of each vocabulary term from Chapter 3 listed below.* **7. expand** **8. function** **a.** end **a.** operate **b.** grow **b.** discuss **c.** give **c.** provide
policy (PAH · luh · see) *p. 68*	a plan of action	
ethnic (EHTH · nihk) *p. 74*	sharing a common culture	
function (FUHNK · shuhn) *p. 75*	to operate	
estate (ih · STAYT) *p. 77*	a piece of land	
Chapter 4 Growth of the Thirteen Colonies		
rely (rih · LY) *p. 89*	to depend on	**Choose** *terms from Chapter 4 to complete the paragraph.* Settlers in New England had to _____ on children to help grow food. In Southern Colonies, tobacco was a _____ crop. Farmers' _____ for success was greater in Southern Colonies due to a milder climate and rich soil.
principal (PRIHN · suh · puhl) *p. 93*	most important	
successor (suhk · SEH · suhr) *p. 99*	one who follows another in order	
convert (kuhn · VUHRT) *p. 105*	to change religious beliefs	
design (dih · ZYN) *p. 106*	to plan	
prospect (PRAH · SPEHKT) *p. 110*	a chance for success	

Chapter 1

The First Americans
Prehistory to 1492

Petroglyphs are carvings or inscriptions on rock. These petroglyphs in southern Utah were created by several cultures.

◀ Maya plaque

★ c. 28,000 B.C.
Asian hunters enter North America

★ c. 1500 B.C.
Olmec civilization develops in Mexico

★ c. A.D. 700
Maya Empire reaches its peak

c. A.D. 1000 ★
Leif Eriksson discovers Newfoundland

Americas

World

Prehistory

900

★ c. 10,000 B.C.
Last Ice Age ends

★ c. 215 B.C.
Great Wall of China built

Section 1: Migration to the Americas

Essential Question How did agriculture change the lives of early people?

Section 2: Cities and Empires

Essential Question How did the early civilizations of Mexico and Central America develop socially, politically, and economically?

Section 3: North American Peoples

Essential Question How was the way of life of the Native Americans of North America related to their environment?

FOLDABLES Study Organizer

Organizing Information Make this Foldable to help organize what you learn about the first Americans.

Step 1 Fold a sheet of paper in half from side to side.

Step 2 Turn the paper and fold it into thirds. Cut the top layer only to make three equal tabs.

Step 3 Draw and label your Foldable as shown.

Reading and Writing On the front of the Foldable, diagram early migratory routes; label sites of the Mound Builders; show the empires of the Aztec, Inca, and other ancient civilizations; and include other visual information about the people of the Americas.

Aztec serpent ▶

▼ Anasazi mortar, A.D. 1200

★ **c. A.D. 1130** Drought strikes Anasazi communities

★ **c. A.D. 1300** Hohokam civilization begins to decline

★ **A.D. 1325** Aztec establish Tenochtitlán

★ **c. A.D. 1400** Inca Empire begins to expand

1100 — **1300** — **1500**

★ **A.D. 1095** The Crusades begin

★ **A.D. 1215** England's King John signs Magna Carta

★ **A.D. 1312** Mansa Mūsā begins rule of West African kingdom of Mali

★ **A.D. 1368** Ming dynasty begins in China

Section 1 — Migration to the Americas

Essential Question ◄
How did agriculture change the lives of early people?

Reading Guide

Content Vocabulary
archaeology (p. 7)   maize (p. 9)
artifact (p. 7)   carbon dating (p. 9)
nomad (p. 8)   culture (p. 9)
migration (p. 8)

Academic Vocabulary
source (p. 8)   estimate (p. 9)

Key People and Events
Ice Age (p. 7)

Reading Strategy
Taking Notes As you read, identify reasons early peoples migrated from place to place.

Reasons Early Peoples Migrated
1.
2.

NEW YORK STANDARDS
The American Journey

U1.I.1 To understand the social scientific method and techniques used by social scientists to study human cultures

U1.II.1 To describe the relationships between people and environments and the connections between people and places

U1.II.5 To understand the geography of settlement patterns and the development of cultural patterns

American Diary

In 1974 at Meadowcroft, Pennsylvania, archaeologist James Adovasio and his team made an amazing discovery. Digging through soil and rock, they found fire pits, bones, shells, and stone tools. This evidence seemed to show that humans had been living there more than 14,000 years ago. For Adovasio, this "meant that people had been . . . in western Pennsylvania some four thousand years before any human being was supposed to have set foot anywhere in this hemisphere."

—*from* The First Americans

The Journey From Asia

Main Idea The first Americans were hunters and gatherers who came from Asia and spread throughout the Americas.

History and You Do you know if any prehistoric mammals, such as giant woolly mammoths or saber-toothed tigers, lived in your area? Read to find out why early peoples migrated to the Americas.

. . . .

Recent archaeological finds such as those in Meadowcroft suggest that the first Americans arrived thousands of years ago, much earlier than once believed. By A.D. 1500, millions of Native Americans, belonging to more than 2,000 different groups, lived on the two continents of North America and South America.

When Europeans arrived in the Americas in the late 1400s, they found Native Americans living there. The Europeans wondered where these peoples had come from and how they happened to settle in the Americas. Some believed the Native Americans had come from Atlantis, an island that supposedly sank beneath the Atlantic Ocean.

Modern scientists are still trying to determine how the first people came to the Americas. Experts in **archaeology,** the study of ancient peoples, continue to piece together the story of the first Americans.

Archaeologists learn about the past from **artifacts**—the tools, weapons, baskets, and carvings of early peoples. Their discoveries show that many early peoples may have come across a land that later sank into the sea. This land was not the mythical Atlantis, however, but a strip of land called Beringia that once joined Asia and the Americas.

Crossing the Land Bridge

During its long history, Earth has gone through several ice ages. These are periods of extreme cold. Huge ice sheets, or glaciers, formed and covered much of Earth in the ice ages. The most recent **Ice Age** began 100,000 years ago and ended about 12,000 years ago. The lower sea level during this period exposed a strip of land that would have run from Siberia in northeastern Asia to what is now Alaska, the westernmost part of the Americas. That land bridge, Beringia, now lies under the Bering Strait.

If You Were There / Early Toolmakers

A Way to Survive As an early American, you moved from place to place in search of food and shelter. One of your most important advances was creating tools, which made hunting, gathering, building shelter, and making clothing much easier. You may have made tools from bone or antler. Most tools were made from stone. As technology advanced, you began making specific tools, such as food choppers, meat scrapers, and spear points.

Antler or bone tool found at Meadowcroft ▼

◀ Spear point from Meadowcroft

Early Americans left evidence of their culture at Meadowcroft Rockshelter, near Pittsburgh, Pennsylvania.

Critical Thinking

Making Inferences Why do you think you would have chosen stones to make tools?

Prehistoric Migrations to the Americas

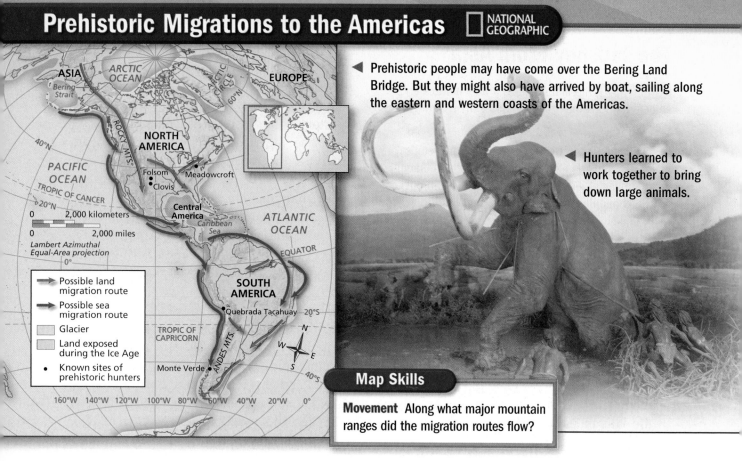

Prehistoric people may have come over the Bering Land Bridge. But they might also have arrived by boat, sailing along the eastern and western coasts of the Americas.

Hunters learned to work together to bring down large animals.

Map Skills

Movement Along what major mountain ranges did the migration routes flow?

Searching for Hunting Grounds

The early Americans were **nomads,** people who moved from place to place. They ate grains and fruits but depended on hunting for much of their food. While on a hunt, they crossed Beringia into what is now Alaska and Canada.

The crossing of the land bridge was a **migration,** a movement of a large number of people into a new homeland. As the centuries passed, many people traveled from Asia either on foot across the land bridge or in boats. They spread out across the Americas, going as far east as the Atlantic Ocean and as far south as the tip of South America.

Hunting for Food

Native American legends tell of giant beasts that roamed Earth in ancient times. When the first Americans arrived from Asia, they did indeed find huge mammals. There were the saber-toothed tiger, the woolly mammoth, and the mastodon. The mammoth and mastodon resembled modern elephants in shape but had shaggy fur and long tusks.

Early Americans were skilled at hunting these beasts. Armed with spears, bands of hunters stalked herds of bison, mastodons, or mammoths and then charged at the animals, hurling their weapons. A single mammoth provided tons of meat, enough to feed a group of people for months. The hunters and their families used every part of the animal. They made the skin into clothing, carved the bones into weapons and tools, and may have used the long ribs to build shelters.

About 15,000 years ago, the Earth's temperatures began to rise. As the great glaciers melted and the oceans rose, Beringia was submerged again. The Americas were cut off from Asia. At the same time, the hunters of America faced a new challenge. The mammoths and other large animals began to die out, either from being overhunted or because of changes in the environment. Early Americans had to find other **sources,** or supplies, of food.

Reading Check Explaining How do archaeologists learn about the past?

A.D. 300 Maya build large cities

300 B.C.

Maya

Aztec Calendar calendar sto[...] pictures to me[...] days and mont[...]

◀ **Maya Writing** Maya hieroglyphic writing was the only true system of writing developed in the Americas before the 1400s.

The Inca Empire

COLOMBIA
ECUADOR
PERU
EQUATOR
20°S

500 kilometers
500 miles
Lambert Azimuthal Equal-Area pro[...]

DBQ **Doc[...] [Que]stions**

Speculating Choose one of these pictures. Describe the image, and explain what you think was its purpose.

The Maya civilization collapsed, but descendants of the Maya still live in parts of Mexico and Central America today.

The Aztec

Centuries after the fall of the Maya, a group of hunters called the **Aztec** wandered through central Mexico, searching for a permanent home. In 1325 they came upon an island in Lake Texcoco (tehs•KOH•koh), today part of Mexico City. There the Aztec saw a sign: an eagle with a snake in its beak sitting on a cactus. According to Aztec legend, this sign from their god meant their journey had ended and that this island was to be their home.

Tenochtitlán

On this island emerged Tenochtitlán (tay•NAWCH•teet•LAHN), one of the greatest cities in the Americas. Its construction was a miracle of engineering and human labor. Directed by priests and nobles, workers toiled day and night. They pulled soil from the bottom of the lake to make causeways, or bridges

of earth, **linking**—or connecting—the island and the shore. They filled parts of the lake with earth so they could grow crops.

In time the Aztec capital expanded to the mainland around the lake. At its height Tenochtitlán was the largest city in the Americas and one of the largest in the world. Tenochtitlán was also a center of trade, attracting thousands of merchants to its outdoor marketplaces.

Aztec War and Religion

The Aztec civilization grew into a military empire. In the 1400s, the Aztec army marched through central and southern Mexico, conquering nearly all rival communities. Conquered people were forced to work as slaves in Aztec cities and villages.

Like the Maya, the Aztec organized their society around their religion. The Aztec believed that human sacrifices were necessary to keep the gods pleased and to ensure abundant harvests. They made sacrifices of thousands of prisoners of war.

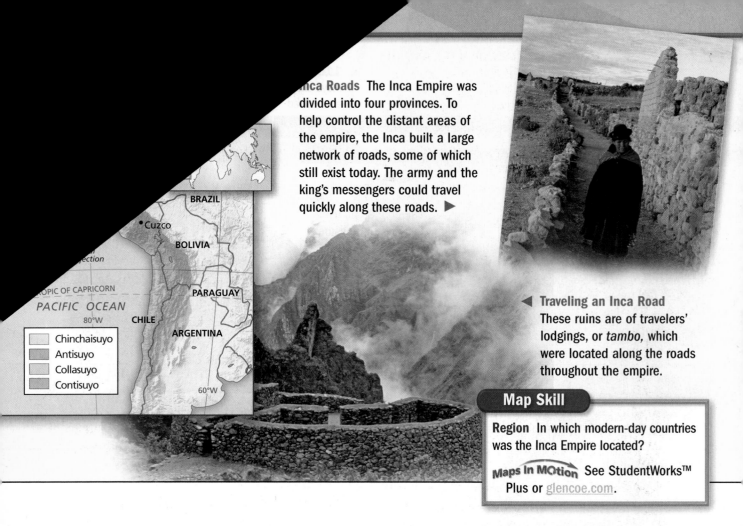

Inca Roads The Inca Empire was divided into four provinces. To help control the distant areas of the empire, the Inca built a large network of roads, some of which still exist today. The army and the king's messengers could travel quickly along these roads. ▶

Traveling an Inca Road These ruins are of travelers' lodgings, or *tambo*, which were located along the roads throughout the empire.

Map legend:
- Chinchaisuyo
- Antisuyo
- Collasuyo
- Contisuyo

Map Skill

Region In which modern-day countries was the Inca Empire located?

Maps In MOtion See StudentWorks™ Plus or glencoe.com.

A Great City Remembered

The first Europeans to see the Aztec capital were awed by its splendor. In 1519 Hernán Cortés led 550 Spanish soldiers into Tenochtitlán. Cortés wrote:

PRIMARY SOURCE

"There are forty towers at the least, all of stout construction and very lofty. . . . The workmanship both in wood and stone could not be bettered anywhere."
—Hernán Cortés, *Five Letters*

Bernal Díaz del Castillo, one of the soldiers, marveled at the "great stone towers and temples and buildings that rose straight up out of the water." Tenochtitlán, he explained, was a city of water. Some of the Spanish soldiers thought that Tenochtitlán was more magnificent than Rome and the other great European capitals of the time.

✔ Reading Check Describing Why was Tenochtitlán important?

The Inca

Main Idea The Inca in South America developed a well-organized empire with a structured society.

History and You How do you keep track of your school records? Read to learn about the Inca's record-keeping system.

Another great American civilization developed in the western highlands of South America. The empire of the Inca was the largest of the early American civilizations.

Around 1200, the **Inca** people founded their capital city of Cuzco (KOOS•koh). In 1438 the Inca emperor named Pachacuti (PAH•chah•KOO•tee) came to the throne. Through conquest, Pachacuti and his son, Topa Inca, built a large empire. It stretched from north to south for more than 3,000 miles (4,828 km), from present-day Colombia to northern Argentina and Chile.

The Inca state was built on war, and the Inca army was powerful. All men between 25 and 50 years old could be drafted to serve in the army for up to five years. Their weapons included clubs, spears, and spiked copper balls on ropes. Using slings, Inca soldiers could throw stones 30 yards (27 m).

Residents of conquered areas who did not resist were allowed to participate in the growing empire's government. Those who resisted or rebelled were dealt with harshly. Many people preferred to accept the terms offered by the Inca rather than go to war with the powerful Inca armies.

Life in the Empire

At its height, the Inca Empire had a population of more than 9 million, including many conquered peoples. To control this large empire, the Inca built at least 10,000 miles (16,093 km) of stone-paved roads that ran over rugged mountains, across deserts, and through dense jungles. Rope bridges, made from grass, crossed deep canyons and rivers.

Runners carried messages to and from the emperor and linked, or connected, outposts of the empire to Cuzco. The Inca language, **Quechua** (KEH•chuh•wuh), became the official language for the entire empire.

Although the Inca did not have a system of writing, they developed a system of record keeping with string called **quipus** (KEE•poos). Using various lengths and colors of string knotted in special patterns, the quipus were used to record information about resources such as grain supplies.

To farm their mountainous lands, the Inca cut **terraces,** or broad platforms, into steep slopes. They built stone walls on the terraces to hold the soil and plants in place. Inca farmers grew maize, squash, tomatoes, peanuts, chili peppers, cotton, and potatoes.

All Inca land belonged to the emperor, who was believed to be a descendant of the sun god. To please the sun god, the Inca made magnificent gold jewelry and temple ornaments. The Inca also built cities devoted to religious ceremonies, including Machu Picchu, a site hidden high up in the Andes.

Reading Check **Explaining** How did the Inca farm steep slopes?

Section 2 Review

History ONLINE
Study Central™ To review this section, go to glencoe.com.

Vocabulary

1. Write a short paragraph in which you use all of the following vocabulary terms: civilization, complex, theocracy, hieroglyphics, link, Quechua, quipu, terrace.

Main Ideas

2. Describing Describe the development of Tenochtitlán, and explain why the first Europeans to view the city were amazed by it.

3. Explaining How did the Inca build and govern their vast empire?

Critical Thinking

4. Making Inferences How does trade help enrich a civilization? Provide examples in your answer.

5. Categorizing Use a diagram like the one below to describe the role of religion in these early American civilizations.

Role of Religion

Maya: Aztec:

Inca:

6. Persuasive Writing Create a poster encouraging tourists to visit the ruins of an early American civilization. Use the images and text to describe the people and history of your chosen site.

Answer the
7. Essential Question
How did the early civilizations of Mexico and Central America develop socially, politically, and economically?

North American Peoples

Essential Question ◄

How was the way of life of the Native Americans of North America related to their environment?

Reading Guide

Content Vocabulary

pueblo (p. 17)   clan (p. 22)

federation (p. 21)

Academic Vocabulary

channel (p. 17)   structure (p. 17)

Key People and Events

Mound Builders (p. 18)

Iroquois (p. 21)

Reading Strategy

Taking Notes As you read, identify the Native American peoples who lived in the different areas of North America.

NEW YORK STANDARDS
The American Journey

U1.II.1 To describe the relationships between people and environments and the connections between people and places

U1.III.1 To know the social and economic characteristics such as customs, traditions, child-rearing practices, gender roles, foods, and religious and spiritual beliefs that distinguish different cultures and civilizations

U1.III.3 To understand the worldview held by native peoples of the Americas and how that worldview developed

American Diary

In a Comanche story, Humpback, a powerful being, kept all of the buffalo for himself in a corral. Coyote, an animal known for his tricks, changed himself into a little dog and befriended Humpback's son. At night, Coyote slipped into the corral, barking loudly and stampeding the buffalo away. Humpback's son cried, "'Where is my little dog?' 'That was no dog,' Humpback said sadly. 'That was Coyote the Trickster. He has turned loose all our buffalo.'"

—*from* Dee Brown's Folktales of The Native American

Early Native Americans

Main Idea The Hohokam, the Anasazi, and the Mound Builders were among the most advanced of early North American civilizations.

History and You Has your area ever experienced a drought? How did the drought affect you? Read to learn how droughts may have caused the decline of a Native American civilization in the Southwest.

. . . .

The Comanche were only one of many Native American cultures that rose and flourished in North America long before Europeans arrived in the 1500s. Among the most advanced of these earliest Native American cultures were the Hohokam and Anasazi of the Southwest and the Mound Builders of the Ohio River valley.

The Hohokam

The dry, hot desert of what is now Arizona was home to the Hohokam people. They may have come from Mexico about 300 B.C. The Hohokam culture flourished from about A.D. 300 to 1300 in an area bordered by the Gila and Salt River valleys.

The Hohokam were experts at squeezing every drop of available water from the sun-baked soil. Their way of life depended on the irrigation **channels,** or trenches, they dug to carry river water into their fields. In addition to hundreds of miles of irrigation channels, the Hohokam left behind pottery, carved stone, and shells etched with acid. The shells came from trade with coastal peoples.

The Anasazi

The Anasazi (AH•nuh•SAH•zee) lived around the same time as the Hohokam, roughly A.D. 1 to 1300, in the area known as the Four Corners. (This is the meeting place of the states currently known as Utah, Colorado, Arizona, and New Mexico.) There they built great stone dwellings that the Spanish explorers later called **pueblos** (PWEH•blohs), or villages. Pueblo Bonito, one of the most spectacular of the Anasazi pueblos, can still be seen in New Mexico. The huge semicircular **structure,** or building, of stone and sun-dried earth resembles an apartment building. It is four stories high and has hundreds of rooms. Archaeologists have found traces of a complex road system linking Pueblo Bonito with other villages. This suggests that Pueblo Bonito was an important trade or religious center for the Anasazi people.

Primary Source | **Buffalo Robe**

For centuries, the Comanche and other Native American groups hunted herds of buffalo that used to wander on the Great Plains in what is now the central United States.

Using the Buffalo Sacred to the Native American peoples of the Plains, the buffalo provided many of the people's basic needs. Buffalo meat served as food, bones were made into tools and weapons, and skins were used to make shelters and clothing. Painted buffalo skins were often made into robes.

Critical Thinking

Explaining How do you think Native Americans such as the Comanche depended on the environment?

The Anasazi also built dwellings in the walls of steep cliffs. Cliff dwellings were easy to defend and offered protection from winter weather. Mesa Verde (MAY•suh VUHR•dee) in Colorado, one of the largest cliff dwellings, held several thousand inhabitants.

In about 1300 the Anasazi began leaving the pueblos and cliff dwellings to settle in smaller communities. Their large villages may have been abandoned because of droughts, long periods of little rainfall, during which their crops died.

The Mound Builders

The early cultures of Mexico and Central America appear to have influenced people living in lands to the north. In central North America, prehistoric Native Americans built thousands of mounds of earth that resembled the stone pyramids of the Maya and the Aztec. Some of the mounds contained burial chambers. Some were topped with temples, as in the Maya and Aztec cultures.

The mounds dotted the landscape from what is now known as Pennsylvania to the Mississippi River valley. Archaeologists think that the first mounds were built about 1000 B.C. They were not the work of a single group but of many different peoples, who are referred to as the **Mound Builders.**

Among the earliest Mound Builders were the Adena, hunters and gatherers who flourished in the Ohio Valley by 800 B.C. They were followed by the Hopewell people, who lived between 200 B.C. and A.D. 500. Farmers and traders, the Hopewell built huge burial mounds in the shapes of birds, bears, and snakes. Archaeologists have found freshwater pearls, shells, cloth, and copper in the mounds, indicating a widespread pattern of trade.

Cahokia

The largest settlement of the Mound Builders was Cahokia (kuh•HOH•kee•uh) in what is today Illinois. A people called the

Selected Sites of the Mound Builders — NATIONAL GEOGRAPHIC

Adena Culture The Great Serpent Mound in southern Ohio (below) is an example of the earthen mounds built by the Adena people. At nearly a quarter mile long, it is the largest serpent effigy mound in the United States. An effigy mound is one made in the shape of a living creature. ▼

Mississippians built Cahokia after A.D. 900. The city may have had 16,000 or more residents. The largest mound in Cahokia, the Monks Mound, rises nearly 100 feet (30 m).

Cahokia resembled the great cities of Mexico, even though it was nearly 2,000 miles (3,200 km) away. The great pyramid-shaped mound dominated the city. A temple crowned the summit. Perhaps priests studied the heavens from the temple, or the priest-ruler may have lived there. A legend of the Natchez people, descendants of the Mississippians, hints of a direct link to Mexico:

PRIMARY SOURCE

"Before we came into this land, we lived yonder under the sun; [the speaker pointed southwest toward Mexico]. . . . Our nation extended itself along the great water [the Gulf of Mexico], where the large river [the Mississippi] loses itself."

—Natchez legend

Reading Check Explaining How did the Mound Builders appear to be related to the Maya and Aztec cultures?

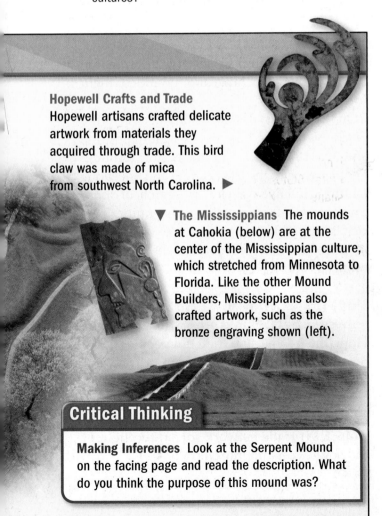

Hopewell Crafts and Trade
Hopewell artisans crafted delicate artwork from materials they acquired through trade. This bird claw was made of mica from southwest North Carolina. ▶

▼ **The Mississippians** The mounds at Cahokia (below) are at the center of the Mississippian culture, which stretched from Minnesota to Florida. Like the other Mound Builders, Mississippians also crafted artwork, such as the bronze engraving shown (left).

Critical Thinking

Making Inferences Look at the Serpent Mound on the facing page and read the description. What do you think the purpose of this mound was?

Other Native North Americans

Main Idea The early inhabitants of North America developed ways of life that were well suited to their environments.

History and You How has the climate in the area where you live affected the way that houses are built? Read to learn how Native Americans adapted to the climates of North America.

The civilizations of the Hohokam, the Anasazi, and the Mound Builders eventually faded away. A number of other Native American cultures arose to take their place. Around the time that Europeans began arriving, North America was home to many different societies.

Peoples of the North

The people who settled in the northernmost part of North America, in the lands around the Arctic Ocean, are called the Inuit. Some scientists think the Inuit were the last migrants to cross the land bridge that connected Asia with North America.

The Inuit had many skills that helped them survive in the cold Arctic climate. They may have brought some of these skills from Siberia, which was probably their original home. In the winter the Inuit built igloos, low-lying structures of snow blocks, which protected them from severe weather.

Their clothing of furs and sealskins was warm and waterproof. The Inuit were hunters and fishers. In the coastal waters, they pursued whales, seals, and walruses in small, skin-covered boats. On land they hunted caribou, large deerlike animals that lived in the far north. The Inuit made clothing from caribou skins and burned seal oil in lamps.

Peoples of the West

North America's West Coast had a mild climate and dependable food sources. These conditions created a favorable environment for many different groups.

Native American Cultures

NATIONAL GEOGRAPHIC

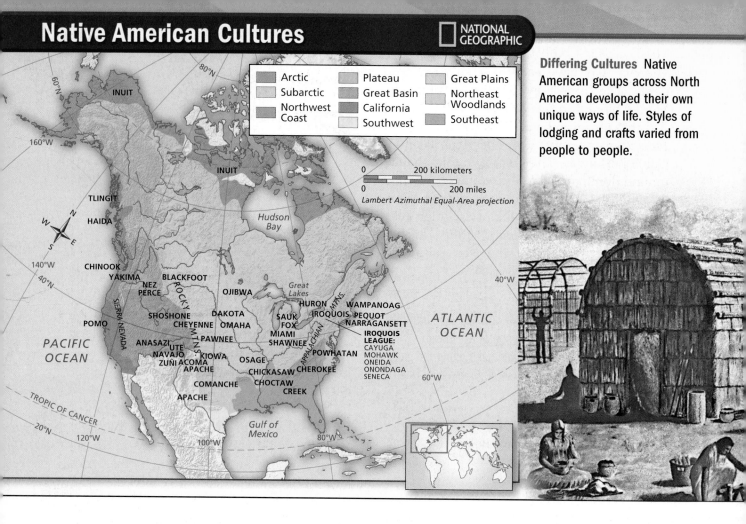

Differing Cultures Native American groups across North America developed their own unique ways of life. Styles of lodging and crafts varied from people to people.

The peoples of the northwestern coast, such as the Tlingit (TLIHNG•kuht), Haida, and Chinook, depended on the forest and the sea. They built wooden houses and made canoes, cloth, and baskets from tree bark. They fished for their main food, salmon, along the coast and in rivers such as the Columbia. They preserved the salmon by smoking it over fires.

Salmon was also important for the people of the plateau region, the area between the Cascade Mountains and the Rocky Mountains. The Nez Perce (NEHZ PUHRS) and Yakima peoples fished the rivers, hunted deer in forests, and gathered roots and berries. The Native Americans of the plateau region lived in earthen houses.

A great variety of cultures lived in what is now California. Along the northern coast, Native Americans fished for their food. In the more barren environment of the southern deserts, nomadic groups collected roots and

seeds. In the central valley of California, the Pomo gathered acorns and pounded them into flour.

In the Great Basin region, between the Sierra Nevada and the Rocky Mountains, the soil was too hard and rocky for farming. Peoples such as the Ute (YOOT) and Shoshone (shuh•SHOHN) traveled in search of food. They ate small game, pine nuts, juniper berries, roots, and some insects. The Great Basin peoples created temporary shelters from branches and reeds.

Peoples of the Southwest

Descendants of the Anasazi formed the Hopi, the Acoma, and the Zuni peoples of the Southwest. They built their homes from sun-dried mud bricks called adobe. They raised corn or maize as their basic food. They also grew beans, squash, melons, pumpkins, and fruit. Their trade network spread throughout the Southwest and into Mexico.

Southwest Pottery The peoples of the Southwest created beautiful pottery from the same clay with which they built their homes. Pots were used to store water and food. ▶

Buffalo Skin Bag The Native Americans of the Plains used the skins of the buffalo they hunted to make a number of everyday items. This buffalo skin bag shows a horse and rider. ▶

Northwest Artifact This ladle in the form of a bird was used by Native Americans in the Northwest at large parties called potlatches. Potlatches celebrated events such as births, deaths, and weddings. ▼

◀ **Longhouses** People of the East lived in bark-covered longhouses. Each building could shelter several families.

Map Skill

Region Identify some of the peoples who lived in the Great Plains region of North America.

Maps In MOtion See StudentWorks™ Plus or glencoe.com.

In the 1500s, two new peoples settled in the region—the Apache and the Navajo. Unlike other peoples of the Southwest, these new groups were hunters and gatherers. They hunted deer and other game. In time, the Navajo settled in villages and built square houses called hogans. In addition to hunting, they began to grow maize and beans. They also began raising sheep in the 1600s.

Peoples of the Plains

The peoples of the Great Plains were nomadic. Their villages were temporary, lasting only for a growing season or two. When the people moved from place to place, they dragged their homes—cone-shaped skin tents called tepees—behind them. The men hunted antelope, deer, and buffalo. The women planted maize, squash, and beans.

When the Spanish brought horses to Mexico in the 1500s, some got loose and made their way north. Native Americans captured and tamed the wild horses. The Comanche,

the Dakota, and other Plains peoples became skilled riders. They hunted and fought on horseback, using spears, bows and arrows, and clubs while riding.

Peoples of the East

The peoples who lived in the woodlands of eastern North America formed complex societies. The many Algonquian groups were linked by similar languages. The **Iroquois** (IHR•uh•KWAH) and Cherokee had formal law codes and formed **federations,** governments that linked different groups.

The Iroquois lived near Canada in what is now northern New York State. There were five Iroquois groups or nations: the Onondaga (AH•nuhn•DAW•guh), the Seneca, the Mohawk, the Oneida, and the Cayuga.

These groups often warred with each other. Finally, in the 1500s, these five groups established the Great Peace, an alliance that was joined in 1715 by the Tuscarora peoples. This alliance was called the Iroquois League.

The League created a constitution. At first the constitution was represented symbolically through art. Later, after the arrival of the Europeans, it was written down.

The Iroquois constitution established the Grand Council, a group of leaders who met regularly to settle disputes among the various peoples. Although Grand Council members were men, women played an important part in choosing delegates to the council. The different members of the Iroquois League were organized according to **clans,** or groups of related families. The women in each clan chose a clan mother. These clan mothers then chose the male members of the Grand Council.

The Iroquois constitution describes the Iroquois people's desire for peace:

PRIMARY SOURCE

"I am Dekanawidah and with the Five Nations' Confederate Lords I plant the Tree of Great Peace. . . . Roots have spread out from the Tree of the Great Peace, one to the north, one to the east, one to the south and one to the west."

—Dekanawidah, Iroquois Constitution

Peoples of the Southeast

The Southeast was also a woodlands area but with a warmer climate than the eastern woodlands. The Creek, Chickasaw, and Cherokee were among the region's Native American peoples.

The Creek lived in loosely knit farming communities in what is now Georgia and Alabama. There they grew corn, tobacco, squash, and other crops. The Chickasaw, most of whom lived farther west in what is now Mississippi, farmed the fertile river bottomlands. The Cherokee farmed in the mountains of Georgia and the Carolinas.

Wherever they lived in North America, the first Americans developed ways of life that were well suited to their environments. In the 1500s, however, the Native Americans would meet a new people with vastly different beliefs, cultures, and ways of life. These newcomers were the Europeans, and their arrival would change the Native Americans' world forever.

Reading Check **Describing** How did the peoples of the Great Plains use horses?

Section 3 Review

History ONLINE
Study Central™ To review this section, go to glencoe.com.

Vocabulary

1. Use each of these terms in a sentence that will help explain its meaning: channel, pueblo, structure, federation, clan.

Main Ideas

2. Describing Describe the cliff dwellings of the Anasazi and explain the advantages those dwellings offered.

3. Explaining What was the significance of the Iroquois League?

Critical Thinking

4. Making Connections What evidence suggests that the Mound Builders were influenced by other cultures?

5. Contrasting Use a diagram like the one below to show how the ways of life of Native American cultures differed by comparing their regions and forms of shelter.

Inuit	Hopi	Dakota
Region:	Region:	Region:
Shelter:	Shelter:	Shelter:

6. Descriptive Writing Choose one of the Native American peoples of North America and write two or three paragraphs describing a typical day in the life of a member of that group. Be sure to include details about the environment and the way of life of the group.

7. **Answer the Essential Question** How was the way of life of the Native Americans of North America related to their environment?

Prehistoric tool ▶

Prehistoric Migration to the Americas
(beginning c. 28,000 B.C.)

Nomadic hunter-gatherers arrived over a land bridge from Siberia or by boat and migrated throughout North and South America.

Temperatures rose; ocean waters submerged the land bridge, and large animals died out. Populations grew as people hunted smaller animals and began farming.

Cities and Empires in Central and South America
(beginning c. 1500 B.C.)

Civilizations developed large cities and empires; systems for writing, time keeping, and counting; farming and manufacturing; engineering; far-ranging trade; and religion-based societies.

▲ Aztec serpent

Olmec	Maya	Aztec	Inca

Native American Civilizations in North America
(beginning c. A.D. 300)

North and West adapted to Arctic, forest, ocean, and desert life

Plains nomadic hunters and farmers skilled at riding horses

East woodland dwellers; Iroquois developed a federation and a constitution

Southwest adapted farming to desert conditions

Southeast hunted and farmed in the fertile valleys of the Appalachian Mountains

◀ Buffalo skin bag

STUDY TO GO Study anywhere, anytime! Download quizzes and flash cards to your PDA from glencoe.com.

TEST-TAKING TIP

Answer the questions you know first, and go back to those for which you need more time.

Reviewing Main Ideas

Directions: Choose the best answer for each of the following questions.

1 Archaeologists believe that the Americas were first populated by people who

(1) sailed ships from Europe and landed in what is now Greenland.

(2) crossed into South America from Antarctica.

(3) crossed a land bridge that connected northeastern Asia to what is now Alaska.

(4) None of the above; evidence indicates that humans have always lived in the Americas.

2 The most important agricultural product grown by early Americans was probably

(1) wheat. **(3)** tobacco.

(2) maize. **(4)** rice.

3 Maya civilization can best be described as a society ruled by religious leaders, or a

(1) theocracy. **(3)** dictatorship.

(2) democracy. **(4)** kingdom.

4 The Creek, Chickasaw, and Cherokee peoples

(1) fished for salmon, their main food source, along North America's West Coast.

(2) are considered by most scientists to be the last migrants to cross Beringia into the Americas.

(3) lived in farming communities throughout southeastern North America.

(4) built thousands of mounds of earth, much like those of the Maya and the Aztec.

Short-Answer Question

Directions: Base your answers to question 5 on the excerpt below and on your knowledge of social studies.

> If a Lord of the Confederacy should seek to establish any authority independent of the jurisdiction of the Confederacy of the Great Peace, which is the Five Nations, he shall be warned three times in open council, first by the women relatives, second by the men relatives and finally by the Lords of the Confederacy of the Nation to which he belongs. If the offending Lord is still [unwilling to change] he shall be dismissed by the War Chief of his nation for refusing to conform to the laws of the Great Peace. His nation shall then install the candidate nominated by the female name holders of his family.
>
> —The Iroquois Constitution

5 What does this excerpt indicate about the role of women in Iroquois society?

Review the Essential Questions

6 Essay Compare the cultures of Native Americans of Mexico and Central America with the woodland Indians of eastern North America.

To help you write your essay, review your answers to the Essential Questions in the section reviews and the chapter Foldables Study Organizer. Your essay should include information about:

- the development of agriculture;
- the physical environment; and
- the customs and culture of various Native American peoples.

History ONLINE

For additional test practice, use **Self-Check Quizzes**—Chapter 1 at glencoe.com.

Document-Based Questions

Directions: Analyze the documents and answer the short-answer questions that follow.

Document 1

The following map shows two possible routes early Native Americans might have taken to move from Asia into the Americas.

Prehistoric Migrations

- → Possible land migration route
- ⇢ Possible sea migration route
- ▓ Glacier
- ☐ Land exposed during the Ice Age

0   2,000 kilometers
0   2,000 miles
Lambert Azimuthal Equal-Area projection

7 How might the information on this map help explain the presence of early Native Americans in South America before they arrived in what is now the United States?

Document 2

In this excerpt from *The Conquest of New Spain,* Spanish conquistador Bernal Díaz del Castillo describes the manner of Aztec sacrifices.

> They strike open the wretched Indian's chest with flint knives and hastily tear out the palpitating [beating] heart which, with the blood, they present to the idols in whose name they have performed the sacrifice.

Source: *The Conquest of New Spain*

8 What do you think was the author's feeling about this Aztec ritual? Explain.

Document 3

A Cacique chief expressed these thoughts to conquistador Hernando de Soto, who had summoned the chief to him.

> It is not my custom to visit any one, but rather all, of whom I have ever heard, have come to visit me, to serve and obey me, and pay me tribute, either voluntarily or by force: if you desire to see me, come where I am; if for peace, I will receive you with special goodwill; if for war, I will await you in my town; but neither for you, nor for any man, will I set back one foot.

Source: Edward Gaylord Bourne, "Account of Elvas"

9 Based on this document, describe the chief's position.

Document 4

The following illustration depicts a Pueblo Indian using a digging stick to plant corn seeds.

10 What might this illustration tell you about the lifestyle of the Pueblo Indians?

11 Expository Writing Using the information from the five documents and your knowledge of social studies, write an essay in which you:

- identify some ways Native Americans adapted to their environments; and

- explain why not all Native American cultures developed similarly.

Need Extra Help?											
If You Missed Questions. . .	1	2	3	4	5	6	7	8	9	10	11
Go to Page. . .	7–8	9	12	22	21–22	10–22	7–8	13	14–15	20–21	6–22

Exploring the Americas
1400–1625

Henry Hudson landing in North America

◀ Inca noble

Americas

c. 1438 ★		1492 ★	
The Inca leader		Christopher	★ 1497
Pachacuti begins to		Columbus	John Cabot
build an empire		reaches	sails to
		America	Newfoundland

1400   **1450**   **1500**

World

1429 ★	★ c. 1456	★ c. 1500
Joan of Arc	Johannes Gutenberg	Songhai
defeats the	uses movable metal	Empire rises
English at	type in printing	in Africa
Orléans		

Technology's Impact

Main Idea Technology produced better means of navigation and paved the way for European voyages of exploration.

History and You Have you ridden in a vehicle with an onboard navigation system? Read to learn how the astrolabe and compass improved navigation in the 1400s.

. . . .

Advances in **technology**—the use of scientific knowledge for practical purposes—paved the way for European voyages of exploration. In the 1450s the introduction of the printing press made it much easier to print books. Now more people had access to books and to new information. Many Europeans read Marco Polo's *Travels* when it appeared in printed form in 1477.

Better Maps and Instruments

Most early maps were inaccurate because they were drawn from the often-mistaken impressions of traders and travelers. Little by

little, cartographers, or mapmakers, improved their skills. Using reports of explorers and information from Arab geographers, mapmakers made more accurate land and sea maps. These maps showed the directions of ocean currents. They also showed lines of latitude, which measured the distance north and south of the Equator.

Better instruments were developed for navigating the seas. Sailors could determine their latitude while at sea with an **astrolabe.** This instrument measured the positions of stars. Europeans also **acquired** the magnetic compass. A Chinese invention, the compass began to be widely used in Europe and the Middle East in the 1200s. The compass allowed sailors to determine their direction when they were far from land.

Better Ships

Advances in ship design allowed shipbuilders to build sailing vessels that were capable of long ocean voyages. The stern rudder and the triangular sail made it possible for ships to sail into the wind. Both of these new features came from the Arabs.

Then, in the late 1400s, the Portuguese developed the three-masted caravel. It was the first and most famous ship of the European age of exploration. The caravel sailed faster than earlier ships and carried more cargo and food supplies. It also could float in shallow water. This feature allowed sailors to explore inlets and to sail their ships up to the beach if they needed to make repairs. A Venetian sailor called the caravels "the best ships that sailed the seas."

By the mid-1400s, the Italian ports faced increased competition for foreign trade. As a result, a new era of exploration was launched. Powerful countries such as Portugal and Spain began searching for sea routes to Asia. Portugal began its explorations by sending ships down the west coast of Africa, an area Europeans had never visited before.

Hikers can use a handheld GPS receiver to stay on course in the wilderness. ▶

Critical Thinking

1. **Explaining** How have the tools used for navigation changed since the late 1400s?
2. **Analyzing** What major technological advancements have allowed improvements in navigation?

✓ **Reading Check** Explaining How did the caravel affect overseas exploration in the 1400s?

Exploring the Americas **Chapter 2** **31**

African Trading Kingdoms

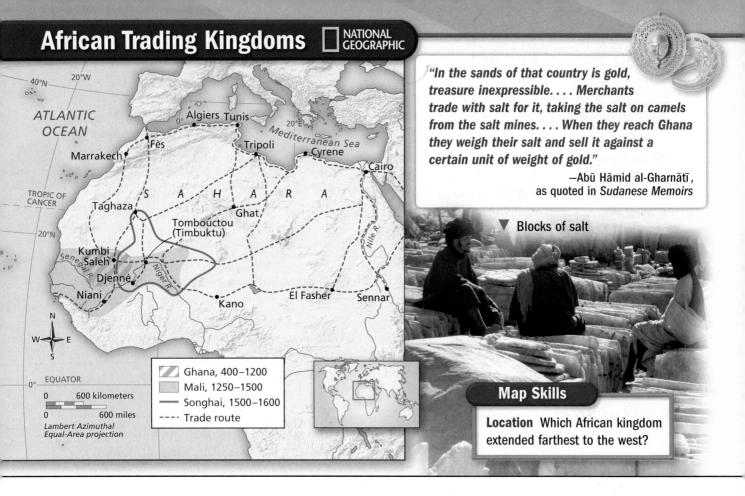

"In the sands of that country is gold, treasure inexpressible. . . . Merchants trade with salt for it, taking the salt on camels from the salt mines. . . . When they reach Ghana they weigh their salt and sell it against a certain unit of weight of gold."

—Abū Hāmid al-Gharnātī, as quoted in *Sudanese Memoirs*

▼ Blocks of salt

Map Skills

Location Which African kingdom extended farthest to the west?

Map legend:
- Ghana, 400–1200
- Mali, 1250–1500
- Songhai, 1500–1600
- --- Trade route

0 600 kilometers
0 600 miles
Lambert Azimuthal Equal-Area projection

African Kingdoms

Main Idea Ghana, Mali, and Songhai were among the most powerful empires in Africa.

History and You What items are valued today because they are rare? Read to find out how rare items, such as salt, drove the economies of early African kingdoms.

. . . .

Powerful kingdoms flourished in Africa south of the Sahara between A.D. 400 and A.D. 1600. Africans mined gold, copper, and iron ore. Trade with Islamic societies in North Africa brought wealth as well as Islamic ideas and customs to the West African kingdoms.

City-states on the east coast of Africa also benefited from trade. Arab traders from the Middle East brought cotton, silk, and porcelain from India and China. They exchanged these goods for ivory and metals from the African interior.

The Portuguese sailed south along the western coast of Africa in the mid-1400s. They set up trading posts along the coastline. From these posts, they traded for gold and for enslaved people.

Ghana—A Trading Empire

Between A.D. 400 and A.D. 1100, a vast trading empire called Ghana emerged in West Africa. Well located between the salt mines of the Sahara and the gold mines to the south, Ghana prospered from the taxes **imposed,** or placed, on trade.

Caravans with gold, ivory, and slaves from Ghana crossed the Sahara to North Africa, where Muslim traders loaded caravans with salt, cloth, and brass and headed back to Ghana. Trading contacts led many West Africans to become Muslims.

In 1076 people from North Africa, called Almoravids, attacked Ghana and disrupted its trade routes. While Ghana fought the Almoravids, new trade routes and gold mines opened up to the east, bypassing Ghana. Ghana then began to decline, and new states emerged in the region.

Social Classes

A class system developed in Spain's empire. At the top were people who were born in Spain, called *peninsulares*. The *peninsulares* owned the land, served in the Catholic Church, and ran the local government. Below them were the creoles, people who were born in the Americas to Spanish parents. Lower in order were the mestizos (meh•STEE•zohs), people with Spanish and Native American parents. Still lower were the Native Americans, most of whom lived in great poverty. At the bottom were enslaved Africans.

In the 1500s, the Spanish government granted conquistadors who settled in the Americas an *encomienda*, the right to demand taxes or labor from Native Americans living on the land. This system turned the Native Americans into slaves. Grueling labor took its toll. Many Native Americans died from malnutrition and disease.

A Spanish priest, Bartolomé de Las Casas, condemned the cruel treatment of the Native Americans. He pleaded for laws to protect them. Las Casas claimed that millions had died because the Spanish "made gold their ultimate aim, seeking to load themselves with riches in the shortest possible time."

Las Casas's reports influenced the Spanish government to pass the New Laws in 1542. These laws forbade making slaves of Native Americans. Although not always enforced, these laws did correct the worst abuses.

The Plantation System

Some Spanish settlers made large profits by exporting crops and raw materials to Spain. In the West Indies, the main exports were tobacco and sugarcane. To raise these crops, the Spanish developed the plantation system. A **plantation** is a large farm.

The Spanish used Native Americans to work their plantations. Las Casas suggested replacing them with enslaved Africans— a suggestion he bitterly regretted later. He thought the Africans could endure the labor better than the Native Americans. As a result, thousands of Africans from West Africa were brought to the Americas. The Africans who survived the brutal ocean voyage were sold to plantation owners. By the late 1500s, plantation slave labor was an essential part of the economy of the colonies.

Reading Check **Identifying** Whom did Las Casas try to protect?

Section 3 Review

History ONLINE
Study Central™ To review this section, go to glencoe.com.

Vocabulary

1. Write sentences or short paragraphs in which you define the following terms: conquistador, grant, pueblo, mission, found, *encomienda*, plantation.

Main Ideas

2. **Explaining** What were the first adventurers to explore North America looking for?

3. **Discussing** How did slavery begin in the Americas?

Critical Thinking

4. **Analyzing** Why were some Native Americans willing to form alliances with Cortés?

5. **Categorizing** Use a diagram like the one below to identify the explorers who went to each region.

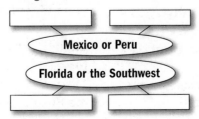

6. **Expository Writing** Write a short essay describing the Spanish exploration and settlement of the Americas.

Answer the
7. **Essential Question**
How did Spain's conquests affect the economic and social development of the Americas?

Section 4 — Exploring North America

Essential Question

Why did European nations establish colonies in North America?

Reading Guide

Content Vocabulary

mercantilism (p. 50)

Northwest Passage (p. 51)

Columbian Exchange (p. 51)

coureur de bois (p. 52)

Academic Vocabulary

globe (p. 51)

chart (p. 51)

Key People and Events

Martin Luther (p. 49)

Protestant Reformation (p. 49)

John Calvin (p. 49)

John Cabot (p. 51)

Jacques Cartier (p. 51)

Henry Hudson (p. 51)

Reading Strategy

Taking Notes As you read, use a diagram like the one below to list the explorers who tried to find the Northwest Passage.

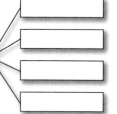

Search for the Northwest Passage

NEW YORK STANDARDS
The American Journey

U2.I.1 To understand major turning points, such as the European exploration of and settlement in the Americas, by investigating the causes and other factors that brought about change and the results of these changes

U2.I.4 To understand the ways different people view the same event or issues from a variety of perspectives

American Diary

In 1639 a French nun named Marie of the Incarnation arrived in Quebec, New France's first colony. To convert Native Americans, she learned their languages and wrote religious books in those languages. In a letter, she wrote:

"You will perhaps laugh that at the age of fifty years I am beginning to study a new tongue [language], but one must undertake all things for the service of God and the salvation of one's neighbour."

—from the book Word From New France

Sister Marie and other French nuns arrive in Quebec.

48

Motive for Exploration

Result

The Renaissance sparks an age of European exploration and discovery.

Technological advances in navigation and ship design allow long sea voyages.

European nations seek direct trade routes to Asia in order to bypass Arab traders.

Explorers sail to the Americas and along western Africa to India. West African gold and slave trade develops.

Queen Isabella of Spain ▶

Nation-states in Europe compete for power based on wealth.

Spain funds settlements in the Americas. Cortés defeats the Aztec, and Pizzaro conquers the Inca.

Portugal, Spain, England, France, and the Netherlands explore North America and set up colonies to provide raw materials, markets, and trade goods.

City of St. Augustine ▼

Catholics and Protestants clash after the Protestant Reformation.

Colonies in the Americas are established as bases for missionary work or areas where people can practice their religion freely.

STUDY TO GO Study anywhere, anytime! Download quizzes and flash cards to your PDA from glencoe.com.

GRADE 8 INTERMEDIATE TEST PRACTICE

TEST-TAKING TIP

For multiple-choice questions, think of answers in your head before looking at the possible answers on the test. Doing so will help you recognize a correct answer immediately.

Reviewing the Main Ideas

Directions: Choose the best answer for each of the following questions.

1 Why did Europeans seek trade routes to the East that bypassed Arab merchants?

(1) European rulers forbade trading with non-Christians.

(2) Arab merchants charged high prices for their goods.

(3) Arab merchants offered inferior goods.

(4) Arabs refused to trade with Europeans.

2 The Portuguese took the lead in exploring the boundaries of the known world because

(1) they were the best sailors in the world.

(2) their invention of the compass gave them an advantage in navigation.

(3) lack of a Mediterranean port prevented Portugal from joining in the profitable trade between Asia and Europe.

(4) they wanted to convert the entire world to Christianity.

3 Who conquerored the Aztec?

(1) Hernán Cortés

(2) Francisco Pizarro

(3) Christopher Columbus

(4) Hernando de Soto

4 The German priest Martin Luther

(1) helped strengthen Roman Catholicism.

(2) rejected the idea that good works alone would ensure a person's salvation.

(3) taught the doctrine of predestination, the idea that God had already chosen those who would be saved.

(4) believed the pope's authority should take precedence over the teachings of the Bible.

Short-Answer Question

Directions: Base your answer to question 5 on the excerpt below and on your knowledge of social studies.

> *All whom I saw were young, not above thirty years of age, well made, with fine shapes and faces; their hair short . . . combed toward the forehead, except a small portion which they suffer to hang down behind, and never cut. Some paint themselves with black, which makes them appear like those of the Canaries [Canary Islands], neither black nor white; others with white, others with red. . . . Some paint the face, and some the whole body; others only the eyes, and others the nose.*
>
> —Christopher Columbus, *The Log of Christopher Columbus*

5 Who was Columbus describing, and why did he include such detail?

Review the Essential Questions

6 Essay Explain how exploration brought about great change in Europe and the Americas.

To help you write your essay, review your answers to the Essential Questions in the section reviews and the chapter Foldables Study Organizer. Your essay should include:

- technological innovations of the 1300s and 1400s;
- growth of trade among Europe, Africa, and Asia;
- reasons behind European exploration and colonization of the Americas;
- treatment of Native Americans under the Spanish; and
- the influence of mercantilism and the impact of the Columbian Exchange.

Document-Based Questions

Directions: Analyze the documents and answer the short-answer questions that follow.

Document 1

This excerpt from *The Saga of Eric the Red* describes the Norsemen's encounters with the native peoples, whom the Norsemen called Skrellings, in Vinland.

> *The Skrellings put down their bundles then, and loosed them, and offered their wares [for barter], and were especially anxious to exchange these for weapons; but Karlsefni forbade his men to sell their weapons, and, taking counsel with himself, he bade the women carry out milk to the Skrellings, which they no sooner saw than they wanted to buy it, and nothing else.*

Source: *The Saga of Eric the Red*, 1387

7 Based on this document, describe the relations between the Norsemen and the native Vinlanders. What did the two peoples trade and why?

Document 2

This is an excerpt from *A Short Account of the Destruction of the Indies* (1542) by Bartolome de Las Casas.

> *The pattern established at the outset has remained unchanged to this day, and the Spaniards still do nothing save tear the native to shreds, murder them and inflict upon them untold misery, suffering and distress, tormenting . . . and persecuting them mercilessly.*

Source: *A Short Account of the Destruction of the Indies*

8 Based on the document, what was the view of Las Casas toward Spanish treatment of the native peoples they encountered? Explain.

Document 3

The following excerpt is from Thomas Mun's *England's Treasure By Forraign Trade* (1664).

> *The ordinary means therefore to increase our wealth and treasure is by Forraign Trade, wherein wee must ever observe this rule; to sell more to strangers yearly than wee consume of theirs in value.*

Source: *England's Treasure By Forraign Trade*, 1664

9 Based on the document, state the central belief of mercantilism.

Document 4

The Protestant Reformation spread a number of new Christian religions across Europe.

Religions of Western Europe

10 Which parts of Europe were predominantly Lutheran? Calvinist? Catholic?

11 **Expository Writing** Using the information from the four documents and your knowledge of social studies, write an essay in which you:

- explain how and why Europeans became leaders in world trade; and

- identify at least one consequence of the Protestant Reformation on the colonization of the Americas.

Need Extra Help?											
If you missed questions. . .	1	2	3	4	5	6	7	8	9	10	11
Go to page. . .	29	35	43	49	39–40	26–52	38	44–45	50–51	49–50	26–52

Chapter 3

Colonial America 1587–1770

William Penn meets with Native Americans in his colony of Pennsylvania.

1607 ★
English establish first permanent settlement at Jamestown

1612 ★
Tobacco planted in Virginia

★ **1620**
Pilgrims land at Plymouth Rock

★ **1630**
Puritans begin settling Massachusetts Bay

Americas

World

1550

1600

1650

1585 ★
Hideyoshi becomes dictator of Japan

★ **1588**
England defeats Spanish Armada

★ **c. 1605**
Shakespeare writes *King Lear*

★ **1609**
Tea from China arrives in Europe

Section 1: Early English Settlements
Essential Question Why did the English settle in North America?

Section 2: New England Colonies
Essential Question Why did the Separatists and Puritans leave England and settle in North America?

Section 3: Middle Colonies
Essential Question How did the Middle Colonies develop?

Section 4: Southern Colonies
Essential Question How and why did the Southern Colonies grow?

FOLDABLES
Study Organizer

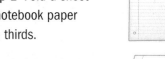

Summarizing Information

Make this Foldable to help you summarize what you learn about the early American colonies.

Step 1 Fold a sheet of notebook paper into thirds.

Step 2 Label the three sections as shown.

New England Colonies
Middle Colonies
Southern Colonies

Reading and Writing As you read the chapter, take notes about the important people and events in the American colonies under the correct headings.

◄ Mission church, San Diego, California

1697 ★
Spanish destroy last remains of Maya civilization in Yucatán

1718 ★
French establish port of New Orleans

1769 ★
Mission of San Diego founded

★ **1675**
King Philip's War begins

1700

1750

★ **1670**
Alafin Ajagbo founds Oyo empire in Nigeria

★ **1685**
All Chinese ports open to foreign trade

★ **1702**
England and France go to war

★ **1740**
Frederick the Great introduces freedom of press in Prussia

Chapter 3 57

Early English Settlements

Essential Question ◄
Why did the English settle in North America?

Reading Guide

Content Vocabulary

charter (p. 60)
joint-stock company (p. 60)
headright (p. 61)
burgesses (p. 61)

Academic Vocabulary

expand (p. 61)

Key People and Events

Sir Francis Drake (p. 59)
Sir Walter Raleigh (p. 59)
Captain John Smith (p. 61)
Pocahontas (p. 61)
House of Burgesses (p. 61)

Reading Strategy

Taking Notes As you read, use a diagram like the one below to list the hardships faced by the Jamestown settlers.

Hardships for Jamestown Settlers

NEW YORK STANDARDS
The American Journey

U2.II.1 To investigate the roles and contributions of individuals and groups in relation to key social, political, cultural, and religious practices throughout the colonial period

U2.II.3 To explain how societies and nations attempt to satisfy their basic needs and wants by utilizing scarce capital and natural and human resources

U2.II.4 To analyze how the values of colonial powers affected the guarantee of civil rights and made provisions for human needs

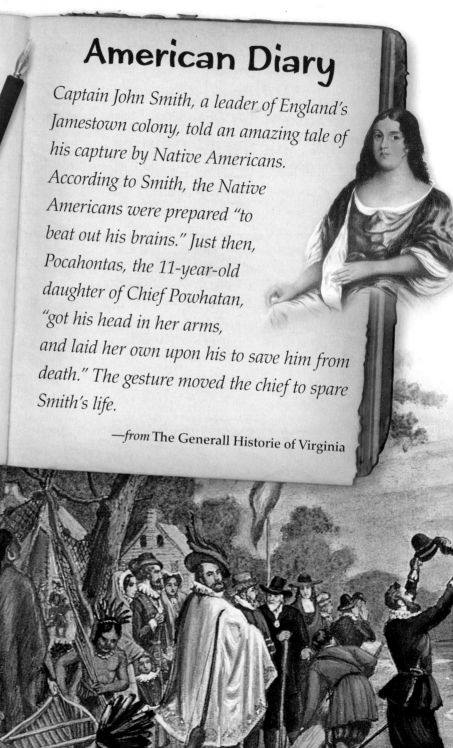

American Diary

Captain John Smith, a leader of England's Jamestown colony, told an amazing tale of his capture by Native Americans. According to Smith, the Native Americans were prepared "to beat out his brains." Just then, Pocahontas, the 11-year-old daughter of Chief Powhatan, "got his head in her arms, and laid her own upon his to save him from death." The gesture moved the chief to spare Smith's life.

—from The Generall Historie of Virginia

England in America

Main Idea After defeating the Spanish Armada, England became more interested in establishing colonies in North America.

History and You Do you like reading mystery novels? Read to learn about the disappearance of the English colonists on Roanoke Island.

The story of Smith and Pocahontas, whether true or not, comes from the earliest period of English settlement in America. Compared to the Spanish, who were their economic rivals, the English were slow to seek colonies.

The Spanish Armada

Trading rivalry and religious differences had been pushing England and Spain toward war for years. King Philip II, the powerful ruler of Spain, wanted to put a Catholic ruler on the throne of England. He did not consider Queen Elizabeth, a Protestant, the rightful ruler of England.

Also, English adventurers, such as **Sir Francis Drake,** had attacked Spanish ships and ports. Philip thought that Elizabeth should punish Drake for his raids. Instead, she honored Drake with knighthood. Philip sent the Spanish Armada, Spain's fleet of warships, to conquer England, but it failed completely. Although war between England and Spain continued until 1604, the defeat of the armada marked the end of Spanish control of the seas. The way was clear for England to start colonies in North America.

The Lost Colony of Roanoke

The English had made several attempts to establish a base in North America. Sir Humphrey Gilbert claimed Newfoundland for Queen Elizabeth in 1583. However, before he could find a place for a colony, Gilbert died at sea.

The following year, Queen Elizabeth gave **Sir Walter Raleigh** the right to claim land in North America. Raleigh sent an expedition to find a good place to settle. His scouts made an enthusiastic report of Roanoke Island, off the coast of present-day North Carolina.

The first settlers, 100 men, had a difficult winter on the island and returned to England. In 1587 Raleigh then sent 91 men, 17 women, and 9 children to Roanoke. John White, artist and mapmaker, led the group. Shortly after arriving on the island, White's daughter gave birth. Virginia Dare was the first English child born in North America.

Ships arrive at Jamestown, Virginia.

Time Line / Early English Settlements

Settling America Most of the early English settlements were founded by private investors who asked the English monarch for charters, or documents, that granted the right to establish colonies in America. Later, England's government placed direct controls on the American colonies.

★ **1590** Settlers at Roanoke vanish

★ **1583** Sir Humphrey Gilbert claims Newfoundland for Queen Elizabeth

★ **1607** Colonists settle at Jamestown

Critical Thinking

Theorizing Why do you think people in England invested in the founding of colonies in America?

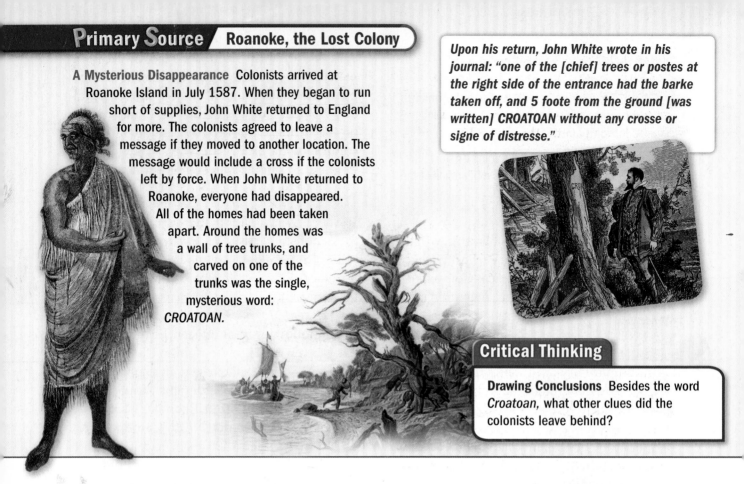

A Mysterious Disappearance Colonists arrived at Roanoke Island in July 1587. When they began to run short of supplies, John White returned to England for more. The colonists agreed to leave a message if they moved to another location. The message would include a cross if the colonists left by force. When John White returned to Roanoke, everyone had disappeared. All of the homes had been taken apart. Around the homes was a wall of tree trunks, and carved on one of the trunks was the single, mysterious word: *CROATOAN*.

Upon his return, John White wrote in his journal: "one of the [chief] trees or postes at the right side of the entrance had the barke taken off, and 5 foote from the ground [was written] CROATOAN without any crosse or signe of distresse."

Critical Thinking

Drawing Conclusions Besides the word *Croatoan*, what other clues did the colonists leave behind?

White explored the area and drew pictures of what he saw. In a book illustrated by White, another colonist described the Native American towns the settlers encountered:

PRIMARY SOURCE

"Their towns are small . . . a village may contain but ten or twelve houses—some . . . as many as twenty."
—from *A Brief and True Report of the New Found Land of Virginia*

Nine days after his granddaughter's birth, White returned to England for supplies. Although he had hoped to be back within a few months, the war with Spain delayed his return for nearly three years. When he returned to Roanoke, White found it deserted. Finding the word *Croatoan* carved on a gatepost, White believed the colonists had gone to Croatoan Island, about 50 miles to the south. Bad weather kept White from investigating, or examining further. The Roanoke colonists were never seen again.

Reading Check **Explaining** Why were England and Spain at war in the late 1500s?

Jamestown Settlement

Main Idea The first permanent English settlement in North America was at Jamestown.

History and You What obstacles would you have to overcome to create a home in the wilderness? Read to learn about the hardships of the Jamestown settlers.

For a time, the failure of the Roanoke colony discouraged others from planning English colonies in North America. However, the idea emerged again in 1606. Several groups of merchants sought **charters,** documents granting the right to organize settlements in an area, from King James I.

The Virginia Company

One group of merchants, the Virginia Company of London, received a charter. The Virginia Company was a **joint-stock company.** Investors bought stock, or part ownership, in the company in return for a share of its future profits. Settlers in America were to search for gold and establish trade in fish and furs.

In December 1606, the company sent 144 settlers in three ships to build a new colony in North America. In April 1607, the ships entered Chesapeake Bay and then sailed up a river flowing into the bay. The colonists named the river the James and their new settlement Jamestown to honor their king.

Jamestown Survives

The colonists faced hardships of disease and hunger. The colony survived its first two years because of 27-year-old **Captain John Smith,** an experienced explorer. Smith forced the settlers to work, explored the area, and sought corn from the local Native Americans led by Chief Powhatan. When John Smith returned to England, Jamestown lacked a strong leader. The winter of 1609–1610 became known as "the starving time." Fighting also broke out with the Native Americans.

The Virginia colonists finally discovered a way to make money for the investors by growing a type of tobacco using seeds from the West Indies. Soon planters all along the James River were raising tobacco.

The colony of Virginia began to prosper. Relations with the Native Americans improved after a colonist, John Rolfe, married **Pocahontas,** the daughter of Chief Powhatan. Land ownership was **expanded** when the Virginia Company gave a **headright,** or land grant, of 50 acres to settlers who paid their own way to the colony. Colonists also participated in government. The **House of Burgesses** first met in 1619. The **burgesses** were representatives of the colony's towns, and they could make local laws for the colony.

When the Virginia Company sent women to Jamestown, marriage and children became a part of life in Virginia. Another part of that life was slavery, first recognized in Virginia law in the 1660s.

By the 1620s, the Virginia Company faced financial troubles with Jamestown returning little profit. In 1624 King James canceled the company's charter and made Jamestown England's first royal colony in America.

Reading Check **Analyzing** Why was the House of Burgesses important?

Section 1 Review

History ONLINE
Study Central™ To review this section, go to glencoe.com.

Vocabulary

1. Use each of the following terms in a paragraph about the Jamestown settlement: charter, joint-stock company, expand, headright, burgesses.

Main Ideas

2. Making Connections Why was the defeat of the Spanish Armada important to England's quest for overseas colonies?

3. Explaining How did the Jamestown settlement survive the first two years?

Critical Thinking

4. Making Inferences Why do you think the king of England let a group of merchants try to establish a colony in North America?

5. Organizing Use a diagram like the one below to describe three attempts by the English to establish colonies in North America and the results.

Attempts to Colonize

Results

6. Descriptive Writing Imagine that you are a Native American who witnessed the arrival of the Jamestown colonists. Describe your first impression of these people in a report to Chief Powhatan.

Answer the
7. Essential Question
Why did the English settle in North America?

Colonial America **Chapter 3** **61**

Jamestown

On May 14, 1607, English colonists began work on a settlement near the James River. They built a triangular fort of upright logs, about an acre in size, in just 19 days. Made of a storehouse, a church, and a number of houses, the fort was near water deep enough for ships to anchor. It also was in a secure place, where enemy ships could not fire directly into the fort. Relations with the local Native Americans were often difficult, although at times the colonists were able to trade copper and iron goods for badly needed food.

How Did Geography Affect Jamestown?

The Jamestown settlers faced the hardships of an unfamiliar climate—colder winters and warmer, humid summers. They also discovered that they had built their fort beside the dirtiest part of the James River. River water was drinkable only part of the year; in the summer, it turned salty and slimy. By autumn, disease, salt poisoning, and starvation had killed almost half the colonists.

Powhatan's territory
Native American settlement

Rappahannock R.
Potomac R.
Chesapeake Bay
Toppahanock
Wighcocomoco
Mattaponi R.
Pamunkey R.
Chickahominy
Powhatan
Arrohateck
Chickahominy
Werowocomoco
Waenoc
York R.
James R.
Accomack
Jamestown
Nansemond
ATLANTIC OCEAN

39°N
37°N
77°W

0   40 kilometers
0   40 miles
Albers Equal-Area projection

Strategic Location Jamestown's upriver location, well inland from the Atlantic Ocean, was chosen in part because of its strategic position for defense of the river as well as to hide from Spanish ships that might be in the area.

Jamestown was built on a swampy, uninhabited site along the James River, which brought salty water from the ocean in the summer.

Jamestown Fort, 1607 The walls along the land sides were each 100 yards (91 meters) long. The wall along the river was 140 yards (128 meters) long.

The Scope of Suffering

Master George Percy was 27 years old when he helped establish the Jamestown Colony in 1607. He was one of the 38 aristocrats in the expedition and later served twice as the colony's governor before he returned to England.

"There were never Englishmen left in a foreign country in such misery as we were in this new-discovered Virginia."

Analyzing Geography

1. **Location** Why did the colonists choose Jamestown as their settlement site?

2. **Analyzing** In what ways was the fort's location a poor choice?

Section 2 New England Colonies

Essential Question ◄

Why did the Separatists and Puritans leave England and settle in North America?

Reading Guide

Content Vocabulary

dissent (p. 65)
Puritan (p. 65)
Separatist (p. 65)
Pilgrim (p. 65)
Mayflower Compact (p. 66)
Fundamental Orders of Connecticut (p. 68)

Academic Vocabulary

policy (p. 68)

Key People and Events

William Bradford (p. 66)
Squanto (p. 66)
John Winthrop (p. 67)
Roger Williams (p. 68)

Reading Strategy

Taking Notes As you read, use a diagram like the one below to list the colonies that the Separatists and Puritans formed in North America.

```
Colonies in North America
      /            \
Separatist      Puritan
```

NEW YORK STANDARDS
The American Journey

U2.III.1 To understand how European and other settlers adapted to life in the American colonies

U2.III.3 To investigate the roles and contributions of individuals and groups in relation to key social, political, cultural, and religious practices throughout the American colonies

U2.III.6 To analyze how values of a people affect the guarantee of civil rights and make provision for human needs

American Diary

Edward Winslow, a settler in New England, was thankful that the Pilgrims had survived their first year in America. Winslow wrote to a friend in England, "We have built seven-dwelling houses. . . . We set the last spring some twenty acres of Indian corn . . . and according to the manner of the Indians, we manured our ground. . . . God be praised, we had a good increase of Indian corn."

—from Pilgrim Edward Winslow to a friend in England

The Pilgrims built their colony, Plymouth, along Cape Cod Bay in what is today Massachusetts.

Religious Freedom

Main Idea To practice their religion more freely, a group of Separatists established the Plymouth colony in North America.

History and You Have you and a friend ever disagreed so much on an issue that you considered ending your friendship? Read about the reason why the Pilgrims settled in Plymouth.

Unlike the Jamestown settlers, the next wave of colonists arrived in search of religious freedom. England had been a Protestant country since 1534, when King Henry VIII broke away from the Roman Catholic Church and formed the Anglican Church. Not everyone in England was happy with the new church, however. Many people dissented; that is, they disagreed with the beliefs or practices of the Anglicans. English Catholics, for example, still considered the pope the head of the church. They were often persecuted, or treated harshly, for that reason.

Some Protestants wanted to change, or reform, the Anglican Church. Others wanted to break away from it altogether. The Protestants who wanted to reform the Anglican Church were called **Puritans.** Those who wanted to leave and set up their own churches were known as **Separatists.**

The Separatists were persecuted in England, and some fled to the Netherlands. Though they found religious freedom there, the Separatists had difficulty finding work. They also worried that their children were losing their religious values and their English way of life.

The Pilgrims' Journey

Some Separatists in the Netherlands made an arrangement with the Virginia Company. The Separatists could settle in Virginia and practice their religion freely. In return they would give the company a share of any profits they made.

The Separatists considered themselves **Pilgrims** because their journey had a religious purpose. Only 35 of the 102 passengers who boarded the *Mayflower* in September 1620 were Pilgrims. The others were called "strangers." They were common people—servants, craftspeople, and poor farmers—who hoped to find a better life in America. Because Pilgrim beliefs shaped life in the Plymouth colony, however, all the early settlers are usually called Pilgrims.

If You Were There / A Teenage Pilgrim Girl

Creating a Home As a teenage Pilgrim girl, you help your mother cook, keep house, do laundry, and raise the younger children. When the men and boys eat their meals, you stand quietly behind the table. At a church gathering, you cannot talk, and you must keep your head covered with a bonnet when in public. You are taught to read, but not to write. Your clothes are usually a full skirt, an apron, and an upper garment with long sleeves—much like your mother wears.

Critical Thinking

Making Connections How does the life of a Pilgrim teenager compare to your life today?

The Mayflower Compact

The *Mayflower's* passengers planned to settle in the Virginia colony. The first land they sighted was Cape Cod, well north of their target. It was November, and winter was fast approaching. The colonists decided to drop anchor in Cape Cod Bay. They went ashore on a cold, bleak day in December at a place called Plymouth. **William Bradford,** their leader and historian, reported that "all things stared upon them with a weather-beaten face."

Plymouth was outside the territory of the Virginia Company and its laws. Before going ashore, the Pilgrims drew up a formal document, the **Mayflower Compact.** The compact pledged their loyalty to England. It also declared their intention of forming "a civil body politic, for our better ordering and preservation." The signers also promised to obey the laws passed "for the general good of the colony." The Mayflower Compact was a necessary step in the development of representative government in the new American colonies.

Help From the Native Americans

During their first winter in America, almost half the Pilgrims died of malnutrition, disease, and cold. In the spring, two Native Americans, **Squanto** and Samoset, befriended the colonists.

Squanto and Samoset showed the Pilgrims how to grow corn, beans, and pumpkins and where to hunt and fish. Without their help, the Pilgrims might not have survived. Squanto and Samoset also helped the Pilgrims make peace with the Wampanoag people who lived in the area. Massasoit, a Wampanoag leader, signed a treaty with the Pilgrims in March 1621. The two groups lived in harmony.

Reading Check **Analyzing** What was the significance of the Mayflower Compact?

The *Mayflower*

The *Mayflower*
In September 1620, 102 passengers set off on the *Mayflower* on the journey across the Atlantic. The 2,750-mile trip took more than two months. In early November, the *Mayflower* reached the shores of America.

New Settlements

Main Idea To escape religious persecution in England, thousands of Puritans migrated to North America and set up new colonies.

History and You How would you react if someone set up camp in your backyard? Read about the conflict between Native Americans and the settlers in New England.

・・・・・・・・・・・・・・・・・・・・・・・・・・・・・・・

In 1625 Charles I became the king of England. Charles objected to the Puritans' calls for reform in the Anglican Church. Persecution of Puritans within the country increased again. As a result, some Puritans wanted to leave England.

In 1629 a group of Puritans formed the Massachusetts Bay Company. They received a royal charter to establish a colony north of Plymouth. This was the Puritans' chance to create a new society in America—a society based on the Bible.

The company chose **John Winthrop** to be the colony's governor. In 1630 Winthrop led about 900 men, women, and children to Massachusetts Bay. Most of them settled in a place they called Boston.

Growth and Government

During the 1630s, more than 15,000 Puritans journeyed to Massachusetts to escape religious persecution and economic hard times in England. This movement of people became known as the Great Migration.

At first John Winthrop and his assistants made the colony's laws. They were chosen by the General Court, which was made up of the colony's stockholders. In 1634 settlers demanded a larger role, or part, in the government. The General Court became an elected assembly. Adult male church members were allowed to vote for the governor and for their town's representatives to the General Court. In later years they also had to own property to vote.

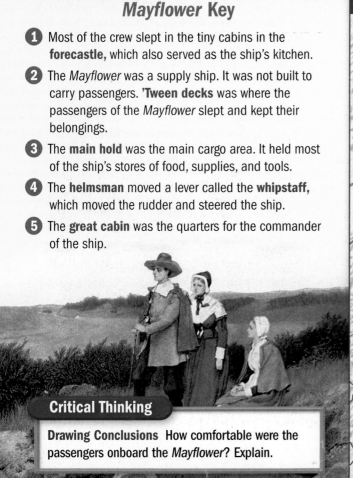

Mayflower Key

1. Most of the crew slept in the tiny cabins in the **forecastle,** which also served as the ship's kitchen.
2. The *Mayflower* was a supply ship. It was not built to carry passengers. **'Tween decks** was where the passengers of the *Mayflower* slept and kept their belongings.
3. The **main hold** was the main cargo area. It held most of the ship's stores of food, supplies, and tools.
4. The **helmsman** moved a lever called the **whipstaff,** which moved the rudder and steered the ship.
5. The **great cabin** was the quarters for the commander of the ship.

Critical Thinking

Drawing Conclusions How comfortable were the passengers onboard the *Mayflower*? Explain.

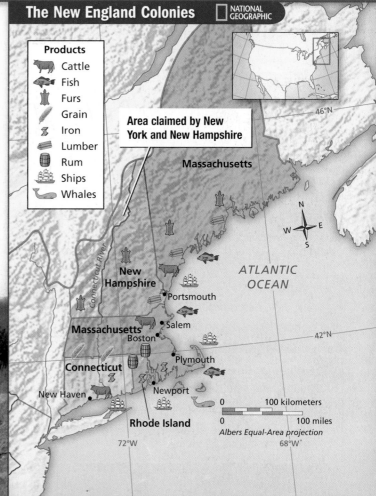

The New England Colonies

Products
- Cattle
- Fish
- Furs
- Grain
- Iron
- Lumber
- Rum
- Ships
- Whales

Area claimed by New York and New Hampshire

Massachusetts

New Hampshire

Portsmouth

Salem

Massachusetts

Boston

Plymouth

Connecticut

New Haven

Newport

Rhode Island

ATLANTIC OCEAN

0 · 100 kilometers
0 · 100 miles
Albers Equal-Area projection

46°N
42°N
72°W
68°W

YOU DECIDE

Should government be based on religion?

John Winthrop, a founder of the Massachusetts Bay Colony, believed that the colony should be governed on religious principles. Others, such as Roger Williams, disagreed and were banished from Massachusetts.

YES — JOHN WINTHROP

It is yourselves who have called us to this office, and, being called by you, we have our authority from God. . . . If you stand for your natural corrupt liberties . . . you will not endure the least weight of authority . . . but if you will be satisfied to enjoy such civil and lawful liberties, such as Christ allows you, then will you quietly and cheerfully submit unto that authority which is set over you . . . for your good.
—from "'Little Speech' on Liberty"

ROGER WILLIAMS — NO

I . . . only propose this case; There goes many a ship to sea, with many hundred souls in one ship, [which] is a true picture of a commonwealth. . . . It hath fallen out some times, that both Papists [Catholics] and Protestants, Jews and Turks, may be embarked in one ship; upon which supposal, I affirm . . . that none of the Papists, Protestants, Jews, or Turks, be forced to come to the ship's prayers or worship, or compelled from their own particular prayers or worship.
—from a letter to the town of Providence

DBQ Document-Based Questions

1. **Evaluating** How might Winthrop view people who held different religious views?
2. **Analyzing** Why might Williams have used the image of a ship at sea to make his case for religious freedom?

The Puritans came to America to put their religious beliefs into practice. They had little toleration for different beliefs, however. They criticized or persecuted people of other faiths. This lack of toleration led people to form new colonies in neighboring areas.

Connecticut and Rhode Island

The fertile Connecticut River valley, south of Massachusetts, was better for farming than was the stony soil around Boston. In the 1630s colonists began to settle in this area.

One such colonist, Massachusetts minister Thomas Hooker, grew dissatisfied with the way that Winthrop and other Puritan leaders ran the Massachusetts colony. In 1636 Hooker led his congregation through the wilderness to Connecticut where he founded the town of Hartford. Three years later Hartford and two other towns, Windsor and Wethersfield, formed a colony. They adopted a plan of government called the **Fundamental Orders of Connecticut.** This was the first written constitution in America. It described the organization of representative government in detail.

Good land drew colonists to Connecticut, but Rhode Island was settled by a minister named **Roger Williams** and other colonists who were forced out of Massachusetts. Williams felt that people should not be persecuted for their religious practices and that government should not force people to worship in a certain way. Williams also believed it was wrong for settlers to take land away from the Native Americans.

His ideas caused Massachusetts leaders to banish him in 1635. Williams took refuge with the Narraganset people. They later sold him land, where he founded the town of Providence. Williams received a charter in 1644 for a colony east of Connecticut called Rhode Island and Providence Plantations. With its **policy**—plan of action—of religious toleration, Rhode Island became a safe place for dissenters. It was the first place in America where people of all faiths could worship freely.

England and the Colonies

Main Idea After seizing the Dutch colony of New Netherland, the English renamed the colony New York and formed the New Jersey colony.

History and You Have you ever won a prize and then shared it with your friends? Read how the English seized the New Netherland colony and then formed the New Jersey colony.

In England, the Puritans who controlled Parliament struggled for power against King Charles I. In 1642 a civil war began. Led by Oliver Cromwell, a Puritan, the Parliamentary forces defeated the king. Many Puritans from New England returned to England to join in this struggle.

Charles I was beheaded in 1649 on charges of treason. A new government was established with Cromwell as Protector. After Cromwell died in 1658, Parliament restored the monarchy but with new limitations. When Charles II became king in 1660, his reign was known as the Restoration.

In 1660 England had two clusters of colonies in what is now the United States. In the north were Massachusetts, New Hampshire, Connecticut, and Rhode Island. Maryland and Virginia were in the south. Between the two groups of English colonies were lands that the Dutch controlled.

The main settlement of the New Netherland colony was New Amsterdam, located on Manhattan Island. Blessed with a good seaport, New Amsterdam became a center of shipping to and from the Americas.

The Dutch West India Company wanted to increase the number of settlers in its colony. It offered large estates to anyone who could bring at least 50 settlers to work the land. The landowners who acquired these estates were called **patroons.** The patroons ruled like kings. They had their own courts and laws. Settlers owed the patroons labor and a share of their crops.

England Takes Over

New Netherland had an excellent harbor and a thriving river trade. The English wanted to acquire this valuable Dutch colony. In 1664 the English sent a fleet to attack New Amsterdam. At that time Peter Stuyvesant was governor of the colony. He was unprepared for a battle and surrendered the colony to the English forces.

Primary Source / **New Netherland**

Colonial Dutch Crafts By the mid-1600s, New Netherland had a growing population and a prosperous economy. Immigrant artisans from the Netherlands and other parts of Europe settled in the Dutch colony. They produced outstanding furniture, silverware, and other household items, such as this finely crafted silver bowl.

Two-handed silver bowl ▶

Critical Thinking

Drawing Conclusions Why do you think New Netherland, later New York, was a valuable colony?

The Middle Colonies

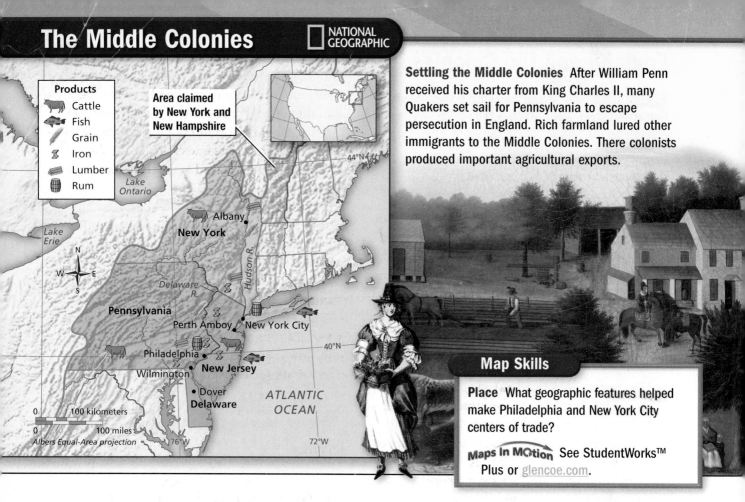

Products
- Cattle
- Fish
- Grain
- Iron
- Lumber
- Rum

Area claimed by New York and New Hampshire

Settling the Middle Colonies After William Penn received his charter from King Charles II, many Quakers set sail for Pennsylvania to escape persecution in England. Rich farmland lured other immigrants to the Middle Colonies. There colonists produced important agricultural exports.

Map Skills

Place What geographic features helped make Philadelphia and New York City centers of trade?

Maps In Motion See StudentWorks™ Plus or glencoe.com.

King Charles II gave the colony to his brother, the **Duke of York,** who renamed it New York. New York was a **proprietary colony,** a colony in which the owner, or proprietor, owned all the land and controlled the government. It differed from the New England colonies, where voters elected the governor and an assembly. Not until 1691 did the English government allow citizens of New York to elect their legislature.

New York continued to prosper under English control. It had a diverse population made up of Dutch, German, Swedish, and Native American people. Also among the population were Brazilian Jews, the first Jews to settle in North America.

In 1664 New York had about 8,000 inhabitants. That population also included at least 300 enslaved Africans. By 1683 the colony's population swelled to about 12,000 people. New York City, which was called New Amsterdam when it was controlled by the Dutch, was one of the fastest-growing locations in the colony.

New Jersey

The Duke of York gave the southern part of his colony, between the Hudson and Delaware Rivers, to Lord John Berkeley and Sir George Carteret. The proprietors named their colony New Jersey after the island of Jersey in the English Channel, where Carteret was born. To attract settlers, they offered large tracts of land and also promised freedom of religion, trial by jury, and a representative assembly. The assembly would make local laws and set tax rates.

Like New York, New Jersey was a place of **ethnic** and religious diversity. New Jersey had no natural harbors, so it did not develop a major port or city like New York, and New Jersey's proprietors made few profits. Both proprietors eventually sold their shares in the colony. By 1702 New Jersey had returned to the king, becoming a royal colony. However, the colonists continued to make local laws.

Reading Check **Explaining** Why did no major port develop in New Jersey?

Pennsylvania

Main Idea William Penn founded the colony of Pennsylvania and designed the city of Philadelphia.

History and You If given a choice, would you take land or money for a debt someone owed you? Read to learn how William Penn acquired Pennsylvania.

In 1681, **William Penn,** a wealthy English Quaker, received land as payment for a debt that King Charles II owed to Penn's father. The king gave Penn a tract of land in America stretching inland from the Delaware River. The new colony, named Pennsylvania, was nearly as large as England.

William Penn saw Pennsylvania as a "holy experiment," a chance to put his Quaker ideals into practice. The **Quakers,** or Society of Friends, believed that everyone was equal. People could follow their own "inner light" to salvation. They did not need clergy to guide them. Quakers were also **pacifists,** or people who refuse to use force or to fight in wars. They were considered a threat in England and were persecuted.

In 1682 Penn sailed to America to supervise the building of Philadelphia, the "city of brotherly love." Penn designed the city himself and wrote Pennsylvania's first constitution. Penn believed that the land belonged to the Native Americans and that settlers should pay for it. He negotiated several treaties with local Native Americans.

Penn advertised the colony throughout Europe. By 1683 more than 3,000 English, Welsh, Irish, Dutch, and German settlers had arrived. In 1701, in the Charter of Liberties, Penn granted colonists the right to elect representatives to the legislature.

Swedes had settled southern Pennsylvania before the Dutch and then the English took over the area. The Charter of Privileges allowed these lower counties to form their own legislature. The counties then **functioned,** or operated, as a separate colony known as Delaware under Pennsylvania's governor.

Reading Check **Inferring** What was William Penn's primary purpose for founding the colony of Pennsylvania?

Section 3 Review

History ONLINE
Study Central™ To review this section, go to glencoe.com.

Vocabulary

1. Define each of the following vocabulary terms and use each in a sentence: patroon, proprietary colony, ethnic, pacifist, function.

Main Ideas

2. Describing How were the colonies of New York and New Jersey governed?

3. Summarizing Describe three beliefs of the Quakers.

Critical Thinking

4. Making Connections Why do you think the Church of England might consider the Quakers a threat?

5. Contrasting Re-create the diagram below and describe how settlers in Pennsylvania and New England differed in the way they acquired land from Native Americans.

6. Persuasive Writing Take on the role of William Penn. Write an advertisement to persuade settlers to come to Pennsylvania. Include details about the Pennsylvania colony that people would find attractive.

Answer the
7. Essential Question
How did the Middle Colonies develop?

Southern Colonies

Essential Question ◄
How and why did the Southern Colonies grow?

Reading Guide

Content Vocabulary
indentured servant (p. 77)
constitution (p. 79)
debtor (p. 80)
tenant farmer (p. 81)
mission (p. 82)

Academic Vocabulary
estate (p. 77)

Key People and Events
Sir George Calvert, Lord Baltimore (p.77)
Nathaniel Bacon (p. 78)
James Oglethorpe (p. 80)
Louis Joliet (p. 81)
Jacques Marquette (p. 81)
René-Robert Cavelier, Sieur de La Salle (p. 81)

Reading Strategy
Taking Notes As you read, use a chart like the one below to identify the types of workers who came to the South and their reasons for coming.

Workers	Why They Came
indentured servants	

NEW YORK STANDARDS
The American Journey

U2.II.2 To investigate why people and places are located where they are located and what patterns can be perceived in these locations

U2.II.3 To explain how societies and nations attempt to satisfy their basic needs and wants by utilizing scarce capital and natural and human resources

U2.III.3 To investigate the roles and contributions of individuals and groups in relation to key social, political, cultural, and religious practices throughout the American colonies

American Diary

Anthony Johnson was one of the first Africans in colonial Virginia. Arriving in 1621, Johnson worked on a tobacco plantation along the James River. He and his wife, Mary, eventually bought their way out of bondage. They acquired their own land and raised livestock. After Johnson's death, however, a Virginia court ruled that because he was an African "and by consequence an alien [foreigner]," the land rightly belonged to the British Crown.

—quoted in Africans in America

A Virginia plantation owner oversees the packing of tobacco leaves to be shipped to England.

Maryland and Virginia

Main Idea While Maryland grew and dealt with Protestant-Catholic conflicts, Virginia settlers continued to push westward.

History and You Can you build a house wherever you want? Read about how Virginia settlers responded to restrictions placed on where they could live.

. . . .

Former enslaved Africans such as Anthony Johnson rarely owned land in colonial America. White males controlled most property, especially plantations which became important to the economic growth of the Southern Colonies. As the number of plantations grew, the need for workers increased.

Not all people came to work in the colonies of their own free will. English criminals and prisoners of war were shipped to the colonies. They could earn their release by working for a period of time—usually seven years. African rulers sold their prisoners of war to European slave traders, who took the enslaved prisoners to the colonies. Many people also came to the colonies as **indentured servants.** To pay for their passage to America, they agreed to work without pay for a ce[...] length of time.

Establishing Maryland

Maryland arose from the dream of **Sir George Calvert, Lord Baltimore.** Calvert wanted a safe place for his fellow Catholics who were being persecuted in England. King Charles I gave Calvert a proprietary colony north of Virginia. However, Calvert died before receiving the grant. His son, Cecilius, inherited the colony and named it Maryland. Cecilius sent two of his brothers to run the colony. They reached America in 1634.

Cecilius gave large **estates,** or pieces of land, to English aristocrats. He also granted land to other settlers. As the number of plantations grew and more workers were needed, the colony imported indentured servants and enslaved Africans.

For years the Calvert and Penn families argued over the boundary between Maryland and Pennsylvania. In the 1760s, they hired Charles Mason and Jeremiah Dixon to map the boundary and lay a line of stones bearing the Penn and Calvert crests—the Mason-Dixon line.

By the Numbers / Slavery in Colonial America

North and South Slavery was important to the economy of many of the American colonies. Most enslaved Africans lived in the Southern Colonies, where many worked on plantations, or large farms. The Northern Colonies had a smaller number of enslaved people but also profited from the international trade in Africans.

Enslaved People in the Colonies, 1650–1710

Source: The Gilder Lehrman Institute of American History

Enslaved People in the Colonies, 1650–1710

Year	North	South	Total
1650	880	720	1,600
1670	1,125	3,410	4,535
1690	3,340	13,389	16,729
1710	8,303	36,563	44,866

Critical Thinking

Speculating Why do you think more enslaved people lived in the Southern Colonies than in the Northern Colonies?

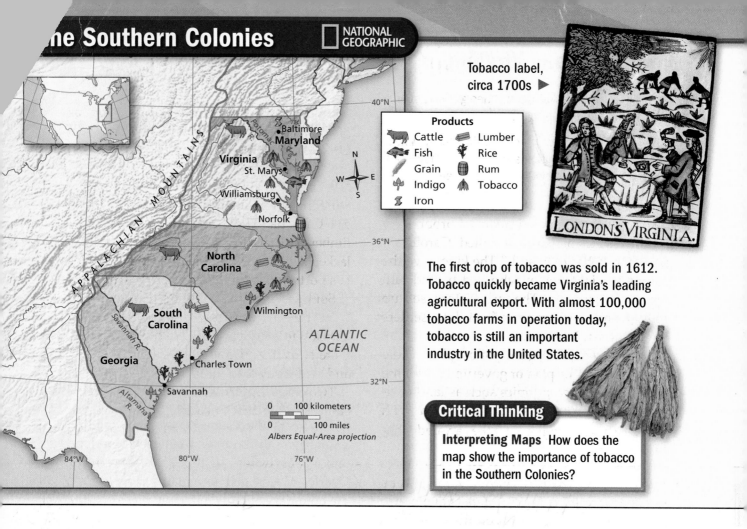

The Southern Colonies

NATIONAL GEOGRAPHIC

Tobacco label, circa 1700s ▶

Products
- 🐄 Cattle
- 🐟 Fish
- 🌾 Grain
- 🌿 Indigo
- Iron
- Lumber
- Rice
- Rum
- Tobacco

LONDON'S VIRGINIA.

The first crop of tobacco was sold in 1612. Tobacco quickly became Virginia's leading agricultural export. With almost 100,000 tobacco farms in operation today, tobacco is still an important industry in the United States.

Critical Thinking

Interpreting Maps How does the map show the importance of tobacco in the Southern Colonies?

Another conflict was harder to resolve. The Calverts had welcomed Protestants as well as Catholics in Maryland. Protestant settlers outnumbered Catholics. To protect the Catholics, the Act of Toleration was passed in 1649. The act granted Protestants and Catholics the right to worship freely. However, tensions continued. In 1692 the Protestant-controlled assembly made the Anglican Church the official church in Maryland. Catholics then faced the same restrictions as they had in England.

Bacon's Rebellion in Virginia

While other colonies were being founded, Virginia continued to grow. Settlers moved west and settled Native American lands. In the 1640s, to avoid conflicts, Virginia governor William Berkeley made a pledge to Native Americans. In exchange for a large piece of land, he agreed to keep settlers from pushing farther into their territory.

Nathaniel Bacon, a young planter in western Virginia, opposed the colonial government because it was dominated, or controlled, by easterners. Many westerners also resented Berkeley's pledge to stay out of Native American territory. Some settled in the forbidden areas. They then blamed the government for not protecting them.

In 1676 Bacon led attacks on Native American villages. His army also marched to Jamestown and drove Berkeley into exile. Only Bacon's sudden death kept him from governing Virginia. England then recalled Berkeley and sent troops to restore order.

Bacon's Rebellion showed that settlers would not be limited to the coast. The colonial government formed a militia to control Native Americans and opened up more land for settlement.

Reading Check Analyzing Why did Bacon oppose the colonial government?

The Carolinas and Georgia

Main Idea The Carolinas and Georgia developed into major Southern Colonies.

History and You Do you believe that people who are in debt should be given a fresh start in life? Read to learn the reasons why Georgia was created.

. . . .

In 1663 King Charles II created a proprietary colony south of Virginia called Carolina—Latin for "Charles's land." The king gave the colony to eight nobles who had helped him regain his throne. The proprietors set up estates and sold or rented land to settlers brought from England.

John Locke, an English philosopher, wrote a **constitution,** or plan of government, for the colony that covered topics such as land divisions and social ranking. Concerned with principles and rights, Locke argued that

"every man has a property in his own person. . . . The labour of his body, and the work of his hands . . . are properly his."

Carolina, however, did not develop as planned. It split into northern and southern Carolina, creating two colonies.

Northern and Southern Carolina

Farmers from inland Virginia settled northern Carolina. They grew tobacco and sold timber and tar. The northern Carolina coast lacked a good harbor, so farmers used Virginia's ports to conduct their trade.

Southern Carolina, however, prospered from fertile farmland and the harbor at Charles Town (later Charleston). Settlements there spread, and trade in deerskin, lumber, and beef thrived.

Two crops came to dominate Carolina agriculture. In the 1680s planters discovered that rice grew well in the wet coastal lowlands.

Founding the Thirteen Colonies

	Colony	1st Permanent Settlement	Reasons Founded	Founders or Leaders
New England Colonies	Massachusetts Plymouth Mass. Bay Colony	1620 1630	Religious freedom Religious freedom	John Carver, William Bradford John Winthrop
	New Hampshire	c. 1620	Profit from trade and fishing	Ferdinando Gorges, John Mason
	Rhode Island	1636	Religious freedom	Roger Williams
	Connecticut	1635	Profit from fur trade, farming; religious and political freedom	Thomas Hooker
Middle Colonies	New York	1624	Expand trade	Dutch settlers
	Delaware	1638	Expand trade	Swedish settlers
	New Jersey	1638	Profit from selling land	John Berkeley, George Carteret
	Pennsylvania	1682	Profit from selling land; religious freedom	William Penn
Southern Colonies	Virginia	1607	Expand trade	John Smith
	Maryland	1634	To sell land; religious freedom	Cecil Calvert
	North Carolina	c. 1660s	Profit from trade and selling land	Group of eight aristocrats
	South Carolina	1670	Profit from trade and selling land	Group of eight aristocrats
	Georgia	1733	Religious freedom; protection against Spanish Florida; safe home for debtors	James Oglethorpe

Chart Skills

Sequencing Which colony was the first to be settled? Which was the last?

Charts In MOtion See StudentWorks™ Plus or glencoe.com.

Growing rice required much labor, so the demand for slave labor rose. Another important crop, indigo, was developed in the 1740s by a young Englishwoman named Eliza Lucas. Indigo, a blue flowering plant, was used to dye textiles.

By the early 1700s, Carolina's settlers wanted political power. In 1719 settlers in southern Carolina seized control from its proprietors. In 1729 Carolina became two royal colonies—North Carolina and South Carolina.

Georgia

Georgia, founded in 1733, was the last British colony set up in America. **James Oglethorpe** received a charter for a colony where debtors and poor people could make a fresh start. In Britain, debtors—those who were not able to repay debts—were imprisoned.

British officials also had hoped that Georgia, located north of Spanish Florida, would protect the other colonies from Britain's enemy, Spain. Oglethorpe and the first group of settlers built the forts and town of Savannah as a barrier against Spanish expansion.

Georgia did not develop as Oglethorpe planned. Few debtors settled there. Instead, hundreds of poor people came from Britain. Religious refugees from Central Europe and a small group of Jews also arrived.

Many settlers complained about Oglethorpe's rules, especially the limits on landholding and the bans on slave labor and rum. A frustrated Oglethorpe finally agreed to their demands. Disappointed with the colony's slow growth, he gave up and turned Georgia back over to the king in 1751.

By that time, the British had been in eastern North America for almost 150 years. They had lined the Atlantic coast with colonies.

Reading Check **Explaining** Why was Georgia founded?

People IN HISTORY

Anne Hutchinson

Dissenter banished from Massachusetts Bay Colony

Hutchinson held meetings in her home in Boston to discuss and give her views on recent sermons. Puritan leaders charged her with *"dishonoring"* the commonwealth. In her trial, she defended herself by arguing, *"there lyes a clear rule in Titus [book in the Christian Bible New Testament], that the elder women should instruct the younger."* She was convicted and banished in 1637.

Margaret Brent

Landowner in Maryland

Brent, one of Maryland's largest landowners and most powerful citizens, requested a vote in the Maryland Assembly on January 21, 1648. When her request was denied because she was a woman, the Assembly noted in its minutes that, *"the s[ai]d Mrs Brent protested ag[ain]st all proceedings in this . . . Assembly, unlesse shee may . . . have [a] vote."* Brent was so angry that she moved to Virginia, where she spent the rest of her life.

History ONLINE

For additional test practice, use **Self-Check Quizzes**—Chapter 3 at glencoe.com.

Document-Based Questions

Directions: Analyze the documents and answer the short-answer questions that follow.

Document 1

Indian leader Powhatan expressed these thoughts to Captain John Smith in 1608.

> What will it availe [get] you to take . . . by force [what] you may quickly have by love, or to destroy them that provide you food. What can you get by [war], when we can hide our provisions [food supplies] and fly to the woods? whereby you must famish [starve] by wronging us your friends.

Source: John Smith, *The Generall Historie of Virginia*

7 Based on this document, describe why Powhatan believed that English settlers should establish peaceful relations with his people.

Document 2

This map shows when areas of the British colonies were settled.

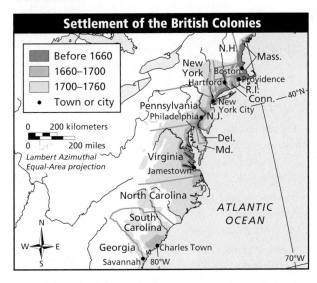

Settlement of the British Colonies

Legend: Before 1660; 1660–1700; 1700–1760; • Town or city

8 Based on the map, which colonies were most heavily settled before 1660?

Document 3

In this excerpt written in 1542, Cabeza de Vaca describes the people living on what is today Galveston Island, Texas.

> Their method of cure is to blow on the sick, the breath and the laying-on of hands supposedly casting out the infirmity [illness]. . . . We scoffed [laughed] at their cures and at the idea we knew how to heal. . . . An Indian told me I knew not whereof I spoke in saying their methods had no effect. Stones and other things growing about in the fields, he said, had a virtue whereby passing a pebble along the stomach could take away pain and heal; surely extraordinary men like us embodied such powers over nature.

Source: Cyclone Covey, translator, *Cabeza de Vaca's Adventures in the Unknown Interior of America*

9 Based on this document, why did the people de Vaca encountered believe that he and his men were healers?

Document 4

William Penn wrote this description of Pennsylvania to friends in England.

> The soil is good, air serene and sweet from the cedar, pine and sassafras, with wild myrtle of great fragrance. I have had better venison, bigger, more tender, as fat as in England. Turkeys of the wood I had of forty and fifty pounds weight. Fish in abundance, especially shad and rock. Oysters are monstrous for bigness. In the woods are divers [many different] fruits.

Source: M. Struthers Burt, *Philadelphia: Holy Experiment*

10 Explain how Penn's description of his colony might influence the people who read it.

11 Expository Writing Using the information from the four documents and your knowledge of social studies, write an essay in which you:
- identify major cultural differences between European settlers and Native Americans; and
- discuss the ways settlers dealt with these differences.

Need Extra Help?											
If you missed question. . .	1	2	3	4	5	6	7	8	9	10	11
Go to page. . .	59	68	73	82	81	56–82	61	67	82	75	56–82

Growth of the Thirteen Colonies 1607-1770

Colonial scene, 1701

◄ Iroquois mask

★ **c. 1570**
Iroquois
Confederacy
forms

★ **1651**
First
Navigation
Act regu-
lates colo-
nial trade

Americas

World

1550

1600

1650

Japanese samurai ►

1603 ★
Tokugawa
Shogunate
emerges
in Japan

★ **1610**
Galileo
observes plan-
ets and stars
with telescope

★ **1644**
Qing Dynasty
is estab-
lished in
China

Section 1: Life in the Colonies

Essential Question How did geography affect the economic development of the three colonial regions?

Section 2: Government, Religion, Culture

Essential Question In what ways was an American culture developing during the colonial period?

Section 3: France and Britain Clash

Essential Question Why did conflict arise in North America between France and Great Britain?

Section 4: The French and Indian War

Essential Question How did the outcome of the French and Indian War determine who controlled North America?

Great Awakening preacher, John Wesley ▶

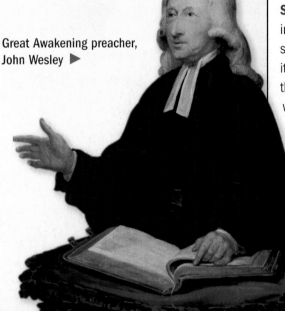

FOLDABLES Study Organizer

Organizing Information
Make this Foldable to help summarize what you learn about the growth of the colonies.

Step 1 Fold two sheets of paper in half and cut along the fold.

Step 2 Fold both sheets in half and then in half again.

Step 3 Cut tabs into three sheets so each sheet has its own tab. Leave the fourth sheet whole.

Step 4 Label your Foldable as shown.

Life in the Colonies | Government, Religion, and Culture | France and Britain Clash | The French and Indian War

Growth of the Thirteen Colonies

Reading and Writing As you read the chapter, list facts about life in the colonies and the challenges colonists faced.

★ **1676** Bacon's Rebellion

★ **1700s** Enslaved Africans brought to America

c. 1740 ★ Great Awakening peaks

1754 ★ French and Indian War begins

★ **1763** Proclamation of 1763

1700

1750

1689 ★ English Bill of Rights signed

English rulers William and Mary ▶

★ **1730** Emperor Yung Cheng reduces slavery in China

★ **1748** Montesquieu's The Spirit of Laws

★ **1765** Potato becomes most popular food in Europe

1767 ★ Burma invades Siam

Life in the Colonies

Essential Question ◄

How did geography affect the economic development of the three colonial regions?

Reading Guide

Content Vocabulary

subsistence farming (p. 89)	Tidewater (p. 94)
triangular trade (p. 90)	backcountry (p. 94)
Middle Passage (p. 91)	overseer (p. 94)
cash crop (p. 92)	slave code (p. 94)
surplus (p. 93)	

Academic Vocabulary

rely (p. 89)   principal (p. 93)

Key People and Events

Olaudah Equiano (p. 91)

Reading Strategy

Taking Notes As you read, use a diagram like the one below to describe the triangular trade route.

NEW YORK STANDARDS
The American Journey

U2.III.1 To understand how European and other settlers adapted to life in the American colonies

U2.III.5 To investigate how people in colonial communities answered the three fundamental economic questions (What goods and services shall be produced and in what quantities? How shall goods and services be produced? For whom shall goods and services be produced?) and solved their economic problems

U3.I.3 To investigate how people in the United States and throughout the world answer the three fundamental economic questions and solve basic economic problems

American Diary

In 1760 Englishman Andrew Burnaby traveled in the American colonies, observing daily life. He could not imagine that these colonies would ever unite for they were as different from one another as "fire and water," and each colony was jealous of the other. "In short, such is the difference of character, of manners, of religion, of interest, of the different colonies, that I think, . . . were they left to themselves, there would soon be a civil war, from one end of the continent to the other."

—from Travels Through the Middle Settlements in North America

Philadelphia, Pennsylvania, was one of the major seaports in colonial America.

The New England Colonies

Main Idea The economies of the New England Colonies focused on shipbuilding, fishing, and trade.

History and You Do people in your community manufacture products that are sold to other countries? Read to learn about how the economies of New England developed.

Although Burnaby believed the colonies would never unite, they continued to grow. The number of people living in the colonies rose from about 250,000 in 1700 to approximately 2.5 million by the mid-1770s. The population of African Americans increased at an even faster rate—from about 28,000 to more than 500,000.

Immigration was important to this growth. Between 1607 and 1775, almost a million people—an estimated 690,000 Europeans and 278,000 Africans—came to the colonies. By 1775, about 2,500 Jewish immigrants lived in the colonies. Most people lived in the cities of New York, Philadelphia, Charles Town, Savannah, and Newport, where they were allowed to worship as they pleased.

There was another reason for the growing population. Colonial women tended to marry early and have large families. In addition, America—especially New England—turned out to be a very healthy place to live.

Most people in New England lived in well-organized towns. The meetinghouse stood in the center of the town. This building was used for both church services and town meetings. The meetinghouse faced a piece of land called the *green* or *common*. Here cows grazed and the citizen army trained. Farmers lived in the town and worked in fields on its outskirts.

Farming was the main economic activity in all of the colonies. New England farms were smaller than those farther south. Long winters and thin, rocky soil made large-scale farming difficult. Farmers in New England practiced **subsistence farming.** This means that they generally produced just enough to meet their families' needs, with little left over to sell or exchange. Most Northern farmers **relied,** or depended, on their children for labor. Everyone in the family worked—spinning yarn, preserving fruit, milking cows, fencing in fields, and sowing and harvesting grain.

Commerce in New England

New England also had a large number of small businesses. Some people used the waterpower from the streams on their land to run mills for grinding grain or sawing lumber.

Primary Source / **Travel in Colonial America**

On the Road In colonial America, people traveled by land in a stagecoach, on horseback, or on foot. There were only a few roads, and they were unpaved and bumpy. Philip Mackenzie, a young colonial traveler, described a typical trip from Philadelphia to New York: "The Stage Wagon leaves Philadelphia Monday morning at Eight o'clock and [reaches] New York Tuesday afternoon late. We spent the Night at some Inn on the Road."

—from "Young Mackenzie Sees the World" in *The Way Our People Lived: An Intimate American History*

Critical Thinking

Making Connections How do you think geographic distance affected the unity of the American colonies?

Primary Source | Whaling in New England

American Whaling English colonists observed Native Americans hunting whales along the coast and took up the practice themselves. In the 1600s, whalers hunted right whales for their oil and bone. When the number of right whales began to decline in the early 1700s, the whalers started using ships to hunt the more profitable sperm whales that lived in the deep water.

Abundant wood from New England's forests allowed Americans to build excellent whaling vessels. ▶

◀ Whale oil lamps

◀ Oarsmen rowed boats within range, and whalers hurled harpoons with an attached line into the whale. Once the animal exhausted itself, it was killed and towed ashore. Whale bone was used to make corsets, collars, and other products.

Critical Thinking

Determining Cause and Effect What factors led to the development of a large whaling industry in New England?

Women made cloth, garments, candles, and soap for their families. They sometimes made enough of these products to sell or trade. Large towns attracted skilled craftspeople. These people were blacksmiths, shoemakers, furniture makers, gunsmiths, metalsmiths, and printers.

Shipbuilding was an important industry in New England. The lumber for building ships came from the nearby forests. Lumber was transported down rivers to the shipyards in coastal towns.

The region also relied on fishing. New Englanders fished for many types of seafood: cod, halibut, crabs, oysters, and lobsters. Some New Englanders ventured far out to sea to hunt whales for oil and whalebone.

Colonial Trade

Northern coastal cities were the center of the shipping trade. They linked the Northern Colonies with the Southern Colonies. They also linked America to other parts of the world. New England ships sailed south along the Atlantic coast. They traded with the colonies and with islands in the West Indies. Ships also traveled across the Atlantic Ocean, carrying fish, furs, and fruit to trade for manufactured goods in both England and Europe.

These colonial merchant ships followed many different trading routes. Some went directly to England and back. Others followed routes that came to be called the **triangular trade** because the routes formed a triangle.

On one leg of the route, ships brought sugar and molasses from the West Indies to New England. In New England, the molasses would be made into rum. Next, the rum and other goods were shipped to West Africa and traded for enslaved Africans.

Slavery was widely practiced throughout West Africa. Many West African kingdoms enslaved those they defeated in war. Some of the enslaved people were then sold to Arab slave traders. Others were forced to work in gold mines or farm fields. With the arrival of the Europeans, enslaved Africans also began to be shipped to America in exchange for goods.

The Middle Passage

For enslaved Africans, the voyage to America usually began with a march to a European fort on the West African coast. Tied together with ropes around their necks and hands, they were traded to Europeans, branded, and forced aboard a ship.

The cruelty continued when enslaved Africans were shipped to the West Indies. This part of the voyage was known as the **Middle Passage. Olaudah Equiano,** a young African, was forced onto a ship to America. He later described the journey:

PRIMARY SOURCE

"We were all put under deck. . . . The closeness . . . the heat . . . added to the number in the ship, which was so crowded that each had scarcely room to turn himself, almost suffocated us. . . . The shrieks . . . the groans of the dying, rendered [made] the whole a scene of horror."

—from *The Interesting Narrative and Other Writings*

Chained together for more than a month, prisoners such as Equiano could hardly sit or stand. They were given little food or water. Africans who died or became sick were thrown overboard. Those who refused to eat were whipped.

Africans who survived the Middle Passage faced another terror when they reached American ports—the slave market. Examined and prodded by plantation owners, most Africans were sold to work as laborers. Historians estimate that about 12 million Africans were forcibly transported to the Americas between the late 1400s and mid-1800s.

With its part in the triangular trade and its shipbuilding and fishing industries, New England flourished. Its population grew, and towns and cities developed.

Reading Check **Explaining** Where was the shipping center in America, and where did its trade extend?

Economics & History

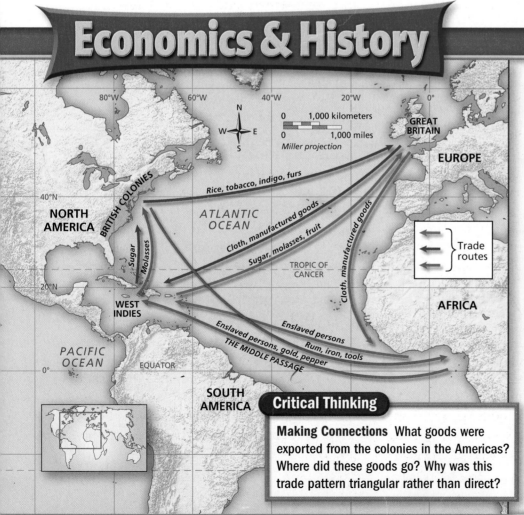

Triangular Trade During the colonial era, the desire for enslaved Africans to work plantations in the Americas led to a changed pattern of trade. Trade among Britain, Africa, and the American colonies formed a triangle. The trade in enslaved people formed one leg of the triangle—the terrible Middle Passage. Merchants sold British manufactured goods in Africa, bought enslaved Africans, and carried them to the West Indies to work on plantations. Plantation products, such as sugar, went to Europe, completing the triangle.

Critical Thinking

Making Connections What goods were exported from the colonies in the Americas? Where did these goods go? Why was this trade pattern triangular rather than direct?

The Middle Colonies

Main Idea The economies of the Middle Colonies depended on the sale of cash crops, such as wheat and corn.

History and You Have you ever visited a farm? What types of crops or animals were raised there? Read to learn about the effects farming had on the Middle Colonies.

* *

With more fertile soil and a milder climate than New England's, the farms in the Middle Colonies produced bigger harvests. In New York and Pennsylvania, farmers grew large quantities of wheat and other **cash crops.** These crops were used by the farmers' families, but they also were sold in colonial markets and overseas.

Farmers sent cargoes of wheat and livestock to New York City and Philadelphia for shipment. These cities became busy ports. By the 1760s New York City, with 18,000 people, and Philadelphia, with 24,000 people, were the largest cities in the American colonies.

Industries of the Middle Colonies

Like the New England Colonies, the Middle Colonies also had industries. Some were home-based crafts such as carpentry and flour making. Others were larger businesses, such as lumbering, mining, and small-scale manufacturing. One iron mill in northern New Jersey employed several hundred workers. Many of these workers were from Germany. Other, smaller ironworks operated in New Jersey and Pennsylvania.

German Immigrants

Nearly 100,000 German immigrants came to America in the colonial era. Most settled in Pennsylvania. They successfully farmed the land using European agricultural methods.

The Germans, Dutch, Swedish, and other non-English immigrants gave the Middle Colonies a cultural diversity, or variety, not found in New England. This diversity created a tolerance for the many cultural differences.

Reading Check **Explaining** What are cash crops?

Primary Source / The African Slave Trade

A Terrible Trade The transatlantic slave trade began in the 1500s when colonists needed a large labor force to work in their mines and plantations. West African slave traders sold captives acquired through wars and raids. Between 1520 and 1860, nearly 12 million Africans were enslaved. Many did not survive the march to the coastal trading sites or the voyage across the Atlantic. Between 9 and 10 million people faced a life of slavery in the Americas.

◀ Captains added platforms between decks to fit more captives onto their ships. Crowded slave compartments were covered with human waste, blood, and filth.

African slave traders set up road and river routes to move the captives to the coast. At the coastal trading sites, slaves were confined in wooden pens. ▶

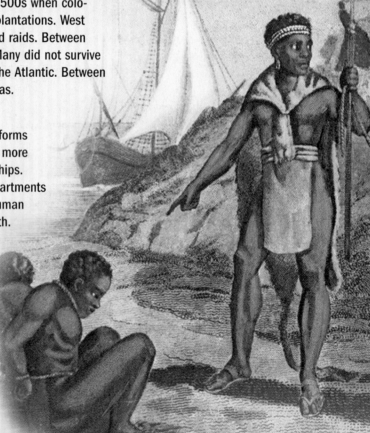

The Southern Colonies and Slavery

Main Idea Slavery played a role in the economic success of the Southern Colonies.

History and You Think about the types of resources that are needed to manage a large farm. Read to learn about how the economies of the Southern Colonies developed as a result of the physical features of the land and enslaved Africans.

. . . .

Rich soil and a warm climate made the Southern Colonies well suited to certain kinds of farming. Southern farmers could cultivate large areas of land and produce harvests of cash crops. Most settlers in the Southern Colonies made their living from farming, and little commerce or industry developed. For the most part, London merchants rather than local merchants managed Southern trade.

Tobacco and Rice

Tobacco was the **principal,** or most important, cash crop of Maryland and Virginia.

Most tobacco was sold in Europe, where the demand for it was strong. Growing tobacco and preparing it for sale required a good deal of labor. At first, planters used indentured servants to work in the fields. When indentured servants became scarce and expensive, Southern planters began using enslaved Africans instead.

Slaveholders with large farms grew wealthy from their tobacco crop. Sometimes, however, a **surplus,** or extra amounts, of tobacco on the market caused prices to fall. As a result, the growers' profits also fell. In time, some tobacco planters switched to growing other crops, such as corn and wheat.

The main cash crop in South Carolina and Georgia was rice. In low-lying areas along the coast, planters built dams to create rice fields, called paddies. These fields were flooded when the rice was young and drained when the rice was ready to harvest. Work in the rice paddies was extremely strenuous. It involved standing knee-deep in the mud all day with no protection from the blazing sun or biting insects.

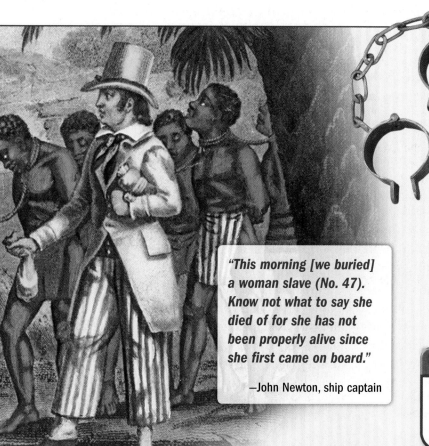

"This morning [we buried] a woman slave (No. 47). Know not what to say she died of for she has not been properly alive since she first came on board."

—John Newton, ship captain

◄ During the voyage, slaves were chained together in pairs—right leg to left leg. Crew members used whips and iron collars to punish the captives.

African Slave Trade 1450–1870

Destination	Total
British America/United States	427,000
Mexico and Central America	224,000
West Indies	4,040,000
Spanish South America	522,000
Guianas	531,000
Brazil	3,647,000
Europe	175,000

Critical Thinking

Explaining What did enslaved Africans experience on the journey from their homes to the Americas?

Primary Source / Plantation Life

Plantations—Large and Small Owners of small plantations—those of a few hundred acres—usually owned fewer than 50 slaves. Wealthy planters, in contrast, typically required 200 or more slaves to work their vast estates, which covered several thousand acres.

◄ Plantations often included a Big House, where the owner and his family lived, as well as slaves' cabins, stables, livestock pens, gardens, a kitchen, a sick house, and workshops for blacksmiths, weavers, and tanners.

"I rose at 5 o'clock this morning and . . . ate milk for breakfast. I said my prayers. Jenny and Eugene [two house slaves] were whipped. I danced my dance [physical exercises]. I read law in the morning and Italian in the afternoon. . . . I walked about the plantation."

—Virginia plantation owner, 1709

▼ Most slaves worked in the fields from dawn to sunset. The landowner or a hired worker supervised the enslaved Africans.

Critical Thinking

Theorizing What problems do you think a Southern plantation owner commonly faced in the 1700s?

Because rice harvesting required so much strenuous work, rice growers relied on slave labor. Rice proved to be an even more profitable crop than tobacco. As rice became popular in Europe, its price rose steadily. By the 1750s, South Carolina and Georgia had the fastest-growing economies in the colonies.

Tidewater and Backcountry

Most of the large Southern plantations were located in the **Tidewater,** a region of flat, low-lying plains along the seacoast. Plantations, or large farms, were often located on rivers so crops could be shipped to market by boat.

Each plantation was a self-contained community with fields stretching out around a cluster of buildings. The planter's wife supervised the main house and the household servants. A plantation included slave cabins, barns, and stables, as well as buildings that were used for carpenter and blacksmith shops, storerooms, and kitchens. A large plantation might also have its own chapel and school.

West of the Tidewater lay a region of hills and forests climbing up toward the Appalachian Mountains. This region was known as the **backcountry** and was settled in part by hardy newcomers to the colonies. The backcountry settlers grew corn and tobacco on small farms. They usually worked alone or with their families. Some of these families had one or two enslaved Africans to help them with their work.

In the Southern Colonies, the independent small farmers of the backcountry greatly outnumbered the large plantation owners. The plantation owners, however, were much wealthier and had more influence. They controlled the economic and political life of the region.

Slavery

Most enslaved Africans lived on plantations. Some did housework, but most worked in the fields and often suffered great cruelty. The large plantation owners hired **overseers,** or bosses, to keep the enslaved Africans working hard.

In 1705, the colony of Virginia created a **slave code.** These were strict rules that governed the behavior and punishment of enslaved Africans and helped define the relationship between enslaved people and free people. Many other colonies soon followed with their own slave codes.

Some codes did not allow slaves to leave the plantation without the slaveholder's written permission. Some made it illegal to teach enslaved people to read or write. Many of the codes made it illegal for enslaved people to move about freely or assemble in large groups. The codes usually allowed slaves to be whipped for minor offenses and hanged or burned to death for serious crimes. Slaves who ran away were punished severely when caught.

African Traditions

Enslaved Africans had strong family ties. Often, however, their families were torn apart when a slaveholder sold family members to other slaveholders. Slaves turned to their African roots as a source of strength. They developed a culture that drew on the languages, customs, and traditions of their homelands in West Africa.

Some enslaved Africans learned trades such as carpentry, blacksmithing, or weaving. Skilled workers could sometimes set up shops, sharing their profits with the slaveholders. Some slaves were able to buy their freedom and joined the small population of free African Americans.

Criticism of Slavery

The majority of white Southerners were not slaveholders. Slavery, however, played an important role in the economic success of the Southern Colonies. That success came to be built on the idea that one human being could own another. Some colonists did not believe in slavery. There was less support for slavery in the Northern Colonies. For example, many Puritans refused to own enslaved people. In Pennsylvania, Quakers and Mennonites condemned slavery. Eventually the debate over slavery would erupt in a bloody war, setting the North against the South.

✓ **Reading Check** **Describing** What was the purpose of slave codes?

Section 1 Review

History ONLINE
Study Central™ To review this section, go to glencoe.com.

Vocabulary

1. Define the following terms by using each one in a sentence: subsistence farming, rely, triangular trade, Middle Passage, cash crop, principal, surplus, Tidewater, backcountry, overseer, slave code.

Main Ideas

2. Discussing How did the coastal location of the New England colonies affect their prosperity?

3. Explaining Why were the Middle Colonies able to grow large quantities of crops?

4. Identifying How did cash crops affect the development of slavery?

Critical Thinking

5. Comparing and Contrasting Use a Venn diagram like the one below to compare and contrast characteristics of the Tidewater and the backcountry in Southern Colonies.

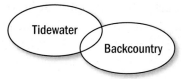

6. Expository Writing As a New England farmer, write a letter to relatives in Europe describing your family's daily life.

Answer the
7. Essential Question How did geography affect the economic development of the three colonial regions?

Growth of the Thirteen Colonies **Chapter 4** 95

TIME NOTEBOOK

What were people's lives like in the past?

These two pages will give you some clues to everyday life in the United States as you step back in time with TIME Notebook.

American Notes

FROM PRINCE TO ENSLAVEMENT TO LANDOWNER

In the 1700s, a formerly enslaved African, **VENTURE SMITH***, wrote about his life in a book titled* A Narrative of the Life and Adventures of Venture. *Here is an excerpt of his story.*

"I was born in Dukandarra, in Guinea [in Africa], about the year 1729. . . . My father's name was Saungm Furro, Prince of the tribe of Dukandarra."

At 6, Venture Smith was kidnapped by an enemy tribe and later sold to the crew of a slave ship. He wrote, "I was bought on board by one Robert Mumford . . . for four gallons of rum, and a piece of calico, and called Venture, on account of his having purchased me with his own private venture [property]. Thus I came by my name. All the slaves that were bought for that vessel's cargo were two hundred and sixty."

NORTH WIND PICTURE ARCHIVES / ALAMY

Venture was brought to Connecticut—where he was sold several times. When he was about 35 he was able to purchase his freedom for "seventy-one pounds, two shillings." He earned this money doing odd jobs, such as "cleaning . . . minks, raising potatoes and carrots, and by fishing in the night."

After years of more work—including sailing on a whaler—he was able to buy the freedom of his wife and children. In his book, Venture wrote, "My freedom is a privilege which nothing else can equal. Notwithstanding all the losses I have suffered . . . by the injustice of knaves. . . . I am now possessed of more than one hundred acres of land, and three habitable dwelling houses."

BOOM!

Bustling sea trade helped the populations of these port towns grow by leaps and bounds.

	1710	1730	1760
Boston	9,000	13,000	15,600
New York	5,700	8,600	18,000
Philadelphia	6,500	11,500	23,750
Charleston	3,000	4,500	8,000

MARY EVANS PICTURE LIBRARY / ALAMY

BOSTON HARBOR IN 1750

96

MANNERS

Oh, Behave!

George Washington, sometime before the age of 16, copied by hand a list of rules from a book called *Rules of Civility & Decent Behaviour in Company and Conversation: a Book of Etiquette.* It contains over 100 different things NOT to do in polite society. We have listed four of these tips below . . . and for fun we have added a fake. Can you spot the phony rule?

— Every action done in company ought to be with some sign of respect to those that are present.

— When in company, put not your radio on too loudly as it might congest the ears of others with noise.

— In the presence of others, sing not to yourself with a humming noise, nor drum with your fingers or feet.

— If you cough, sneeze, sigh, or yawn, do it not loud but privately; and speak not in your yawning, but put your handkerchief or hand before your face and turn aside.

— When you sit down, keep your feet firm and even, without putting one on the other or crossing them.

Answer: The second item is the fake—the radio had not been invented yet!

NORTH WIND PICTURE ARCHIVES / ALAMY

COLONIAL GAMES

Play Quoits

Do you feel left out of the fun when all your friends play quoits—the hot game of the 1700s? Just remember that quoits is a lot like horseshoes— only in this game you toss rings made of rope. Here is how to play one version:

JACK CAREY / ALAMY

1) Put two sets of four stakes in the ground—the sets should be 18 feet apart.

2) Standing next to one set, take turns with another player tossing two rings at the other set, while trying to loop them around the stakes.

3) Scoring:
   a. 2 points if your two rings land closer to a stake than either of your opponent's.
   b. 4 points if your ring goes around a stake—this is a "ringer."
   c. 3 points if your "ringer" lands on top of your opponent's ring.

4) Once a loop touches the ground, it's "dead." Even if it bounces up over a stake, it does not count.

5) After tossing their rings from one set, players start a new round by tossing from the other set.

6) The first player to score 21 points wins.

NUMBERS

UNITED STATES AT THE TIME

25 Percent of enslaved people who did not survive crossing the Atlantic from Africa to the Americas

0 Number of American political cartoons before Benjamin Franklin's first one appeared in the *Pennsylvania Gazette* in 1754; Franklin wanted the colonies to join together to defend themselves against a threat by the French and Native Americans

CORBIS

3 to 10 About the number of years indentured servants had to work in the 1700s to pay back the person who paid for their passage to the Americas

2 Number of tines, or points, on that new thing called the fork, which has just appeared on a table near you; talk is there will soon be three or four tines

CRITICAL THINKING

Comparing and Contrasting How are George Washington's etiquette rules similar to and different from today's rules of good manners?

Hypothesizing Does sea trade today affect cities in the same way it did in the 1700s? Explain your answer.

Section 2

Government, Religion, Culture

Essential Question ◄

In what ways was an American culture developing during the colonial period?

Reading Guide

Content Vocabulary

export (p. 99)

import (p. 99)

charter colony (p. 101)

proprietary colony (p. 101)

royal colony (p. 101)

Academic Vocabulary

successor (p. 99)

Key People and Events

Glorious Revolution (p. 99)

Navigation Acts (p. 100)

Great Awakening (p. 102)

Enlightenment (p. 103)

Reading Strategy

Taking Notes As you read, use a diagram like the one below to explain how the Great Awakening and the Enlightenment affected the colonists.

Great Awakening ▶ [ ]

Enlightenment ▶ [ ]

NEW YORK STANDARDS
The American Journey

U3.III.1 To understand how the colonists attempted to establish new forms of self-government

U2.III.3 To investigate the roles and contributions of individuals and groups in relation to key social, political, cultural, and religious practices throughout the American colonies

U3.I.4 To consider the nature and evolution of a constitutional democracy

American Diary

At 16 years old, Eliza Lucas Pinckney took over the family plantation when her father went to war. In 1741 she recorded: "Wrote to Mr. Murray to send down a boat load of white oak [strips], bacon and salted beef. . . . Sent up at the same time a barrel [of] salt." Eliza's major achievement, however, was finding a better way to make blue dye from the indigo plant. Used in military uniforms, the dye was in high demand. Eliza's success turned indigo into a very profitable crop.

—*from the* Journal of Eliza Lucas Pinckney

Drayton Hall, located near Charleston, South Carolina, was a rice plantation.

English Colonial Rule

Main Idea Although the American colonies developed some self-government, the British still set many laws, especially those concerning trade.

History and You How would you react if you were forced to buy clothes from only one store? Read to learn about the trade restrictions that England placed on its colonies.

. . . .

In her writings and activities, Eliza Lucas Pinckney celebrated a new American spirit. This spirit signaled that Americans were beginning to view themselves differently from the way Great Britain viewed them.

Trouble was brewing in England—and in the colonies—during the mid-1600s. England's monarchy was restored with Charles II on the throne. Many people, however, were not satisfied with his rule. James II, Charles's **successor**—the next king—attempted to take back the powers Parliament won during the English Civil War. He also tried to tighten royal control over the colonies.

In 1688 Parliament took action. It forced out James and placed his daughter Mary and her Dutch husband, William of Orange, on the throne. This change demonstrated the power of the elected representatives over the monarch. This period came to be known as the **Glorious Revolution.**

William and Mary signed an English Bill of Rights in 1689 guaranteeing certain basic rights to all citizens. This document became an important part of the heritage of English law that the American colonists shared. Some hundred years later, it inspired the people who created the American Bill of Rights.

England viewed its North American colonies as an economic resource. The colonies provided England with raw materials such as lumber. English manufacturers used these materials to produce finished goods, which they then sold to the colonists. This process followed an economic theory called mercantilism. As you learned earlier, this theory states that as a nation's trade grows, its gold reserves increase. The nation then becomes more powerful. To make money from its trade, England had to **export,** or sell abroad, more goods than it **imported,** or bought from foreign markets.

To ensure that only England benefited from trade with the colonies, Parliament passed several laws between 1651 and 1673.

If You Were There / Plantation Life

The Planter's Family As the son or daughter of a plantation owner, you enjoy great wealth and privilege. Your father serves in the colonial government, perhaps as a member of the royal governor's council. Your mother hosts elegant parties. If you are a planter's son, you are receiving the education of a British gentleman and learning business skills to run the plantation. If you are a daughter, you study art and music and are becoming skilled in managing a plantation household. Your home is decorated with the most fashionable furnishings imported from Britain.

Critical Thinking

Drawing Conclusions Do you think Eliza Lucas Pinckney's responsibilities were typical of a woman of the 1700s? Explain.

These **Navigation Acts** directed the trade between England and the colonies. Colonial merchants who had goods to send to England could not use foreign ships—even if those ships offered cheaper rates. The Navigation Acts also prevented the colonists from sending certain products, such as sugar or tobacco, outside the area that made up England's empire.

The colonists at first accepted the trade laws because they were guaranteed a place to sell their raw materials. Later, the colonists came to resent British restrictions. Merchants wanted to make their own manufactured goods and sell their products where they could get higher prices. Some colonists ignored these laws and began smuggling, or trading illegally, with other nations. Controls on trade would later cause even more conflict between the American colonies and England.

Reading Check **Identifying** What country strictly controlled shipping and trade with the colonies and why?

Colonial Government

Main Idea As the colonies grew, they developed some self-government.

History and You Does your school have a student council to represent students? Read to learn how colonists were represented in colonial governments.

The English colonists brought with them ideas about government and a respect for education that had been developing in England for centuries. By the 1600s, the English people had won political liberties, such as trial by jury, that were largely unknown elsewhere. At the heart of the English system were two principles of government—limited government and representative government. These two principles greatly influenced the development of the United States.

When the colonists reached North America, they believed that government was not all-powerful. This idea was already an accepted part of the English system of government.

Primary Source **Colonial Printing and Education**

An Educated Population Literacy rates were generally high in New England and the Middle Colonies. Education in the South was limited primarily to the wealthy. By the 1700s, many printed materials were available throughout the colonies. Colonists' ability to read and express ideas in print would play a major role in the later struggle for independence.

Massachusetts schoolmasters used *The New England Primer* to teach generations of students how to read and write. ▶

◀ The first printing press in the colonies was set up in Cambridge, Massachusetts, in 1639. By the mid-1700s, presses were found throughout the colonies.

Newspapers started appearing in colonial cities in the first half of the 1700s. ▶

It first appeared in the Magna Carta, or the Great Charter. The Magna Carta was signed by King John on June 15, 1215.

The Magna Carta established the principle of limited government. This means that the power of the king, or government, is limited. This document also provided for protection against unjust punishment. It protected against the loss of life, liberty, and property.

As the colonies grew, their town meetings developed into small governments, responsible for making local laws. By the 1760s, there were three types of colonies in America—charter colonies, proprietary colonies, and royal colonies.

Charter Colonies

Connecticut and Rhode Island were **charter colonies.** Settlers were given a charter, or a grant of rights and privileges, to establish charter colonies. These colonists elected their own governors and the members of the legislature. Great Britain had the right to approve the governor, but the governor could not veto the acts of the legislature.

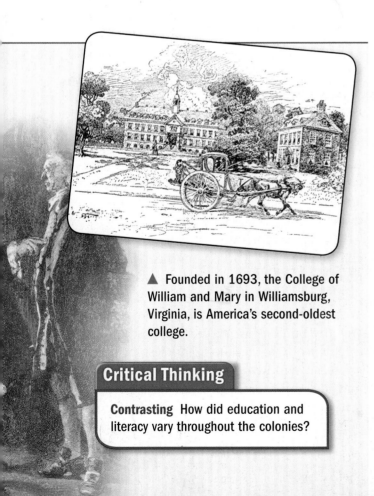

▲ Founded in 1693, the College of William and Mary in Williamsburg, Virginia, is America's second-oldest college.

Critical Thinking

Contrasting How did education and literacy vary throughout the colonies?

History ONLINE
Student Web Activity Visit glencoe.com and complete the Chapter 4 Web Activity about the Magna Carta.

Proprietary Colonies

The **proprietary colonies** of Delaware, Maryland, and Pennsylvania were ruled by proprietors. Proprietors were individuals or groups to whom Britain granted land. They were generally free to rule as they wished. Proprietors appointed the governor and members of the upper house of the legislature. The colonists elected the lower house.

Royal Colonies

By the 1760s, Georgia, Massachusetts, New Hampshire, New Jersey, New York, North Carolina, South Carolina, and Virginia were **royal colonies.** Britain directly ruled all royal colonies. In each, the king appointed a governor and council, known as the upper house, and the colonists elected an assembly called the lower house. The governor and the members of the council usually did what the British leaders told them to do. However, this often led to conflict with the colonists in the assembly. Most conflicts occurred when officials tried to enforce tax laws and trade restrictions.

Voting Rights

Colonial legislatures gave only some people a voice in government. Generally, white men who owned property had the right to vote. Most women, indentured servants, landless poor, and African Americans could not vote. In spite of these limits, the proportion of people involved in government was higher in the colonies, estimated at 80 to 90 percent, than anywhere in Europe. This strong participation in government gave Americans training that was valuable when the colonies became independent.

Reading Check **Drawing Inferences** How did the Magna Carta influence governments in the colonies?

People IN HISTORY

Benjamin Franklin

American Scientist and Revolutionary Leader

Although he was born in a poor family, Ben Franklin made a fortune as a printer in Philadelphia. By the age of 42, Franklin was one of the richest men in the colonies. He chose to retire from active business and become a "gentleman." He began to pursue "philosophical studies and amusements." He was especially curious about electricity, and his experiments made him famous. He wrote in his autobiography: *"What gave my book the more sudden and general celebrity, was the success of one of its proposed experiments, . . . drawing lightning from the clouds. . . . After [the experiments] were performed before the king and court, all the curious of Paris flocked to see them."*

CRITICAL Thinking

1. **Identifying** What does Franklin's autobiography tell you about the lives of gentlemen in the colonies?
2. **Analyzing** Why do you think Franklin's experiments with electricity made him famous?

An Emerging Culture

Main Idea An American culture, influenced by religion and education, began to develop in the colonies.

History and You What items or activities do you consider part of American culture? Grilled hamburgers? Playing baseball? Read to find out how the colonists began forming a culture that was different from European cultures.

From the 1720s through the 1740s, a religious revival called the **Great Awakening** swept through the colonies. In New England and the Middle Colonies, ministers called for "a new birth," a return to the strong faith of earlier days. One popular preacher was Jonathan Edwards of Massachusetts. People thought his sermons were powerful and convincing.

The English preacher George Whitefield started religious revivals beginning in 1739. Whitefield inspired worshipers throughout the colonies. The Great Awakening led to the formation of many new churches.

Family Roles

People adapted their traditions to the new conditions of life in America. Religion, education, and the arts contributed to a new American culture. The family, however, formed the basic foundation of colonial society.

Men were the formal heads of the households and represented the family in the community. Men worked in the fields and built barns, houses, and fences. Sons could work as indentured servants for local farmers. Young men also could be apprentices, or assistants, to workers who taught them a trade.

Women ran their households and cared for children. Many worked in the fields with their husbands. Married women were under their husbands' authority and had few rights. Young unmarried women might work for wealthy families as maids or cooks. Widows might work as teachers, nurses, or seamstresses. Widows and women who never married could run businesses and own property, but they could not vote.

Education

Most colonists valued education. Parents often taught their children to read and write at home. In New England and Pennsylvania, in particular, people set up schools to make sure everyone could read and study the Bible. In 1647 the Massachusetts Puritans passed a public education law. Each community with 50 or more homes was required to have a school.

By 1750, New England had a high level of literacy with about 85 percent of the men and about half of the women able to read. Many learned from *The New England Primer,* which combined lessons in good conduct with reading and writing.

Widows or unmarried women ran many colonial schools. Quakers and other religious groups in the Middle Colonies ran others. In towns and cities, craftspeople set up night schools for their apprentices.

The colonies' early colleges were founded to train ministers. The first was Harvard College, established in 1636 by the Puritans in Cambridge, Massachusetts. Anglicans founded William and Mary College in Virginia in 1693.

The Enlightenment

By the middle of the 1700s, many educated colonists were influenced by the **Enlightenment.** This movement began in Europe and was based upon the idea that knowledge, reason, and science could improve society. In the colonies, the Enlightenment increased interest in science. People observed nature, staged experiments, and published their findings. The best-known American scientist was Benjamin Franklin.

Freedom of the Press

In 1735 John Peter Zenger of the *New York Weekly Journal* faced charges of libel. He had printed a critical report about the royal governor of New York. Andrew Hamilton argued that free speech was a basic right of English people. He defended Zenger by asking the jury to base its decision on whether Zenger's article was true, not whether it was offensive. The jury found Zenger not guilty. Today the case is regarded as an important step in the development of a free press in America.

Reading Check **Analyzing** In what ways did the Great Awakening influence culture in the colonies?

Section 2 Review

History ONLINE
Study Central™ To review this section, go to glencoe.com.

Vocabulary

1. Define each of the following terms and use it in a sentence: successor, export, import, charter colony, proprietary colony, royal colony.

Main Ideas

2. **Explaining** How did the Navigation Acts affect colonial trade?

3. **Illustrating** Discuss how people in the charter colonies participated in government.

4. **Identifying** What was taught from *The New England Primer*?

Critical Thinking

5. **Summarizing** Use a diagram like the one below to identify and describe the three types of colonies in America.

6. **Persuasive Writing** Write a short speech that Andrew Hamilton might have used to defend John Peter Zenger.

Answer the
7. **Essential Question** In what ways was an American culture developing during the colonial period?

Section 3 — France and Britain Clash

Essential Question ◄

Why did conflict arise in North America between France and Great Britain?

Reading Guide

Content Vocabulary

Iroquois Confederacy *(p. 105)*   militia *(p. 107)*

Academic Vocabulary

convert *(p. 105)*   design *(p. 106)*

Key People and Events

George Washington *(p. 106)*

Albany Plan of Union *(p. 107)*

Reading Strategy

Taking Notes As you read, use a diagram like the one below to summarize why, in general, Native Americans had better relations with the French than with the British.

Native Americans
- Relations With the British
- Relations With the French

NEW YORK STANDARDS
The American Journey

U2.I.2 To understand the impacts of European settlement on Native American Indians and Europeans

U2.III.3 To investigate the roles and contributions of individuals and groups in relation to key social, political, cultural, and religious practices throughout the American colonies

U3.I.1 To understand the economic, political, and social causes of the American Revolution

American Diary

In 1754 a small force of colonial soldiers, led by a young George Washington, fought the French in what is today western Pennsylvania. Washington later stated that the French "kept up a constant . . . fire upon us; which was returned [until] . . . the most tremendous rain . . . filled our trenches with Water, [and] Wet . . . the Ammunition . . . in a small temporary [post] . . . called Fort Necessity . . . and left us nothing but a few . . . Bayonets for defence."

—quoted in An Eyewitness History: The Colonial Era

George Washington's colonial troops surrendering to the French outside Fort Necessity

British-French Rivalry

Main Idea Rivalry between Great Britain and France led to a war for control of North America.

History and You Is it sometimes difficult to stay out of a conflict when people around you are arguing? Read to learn how Native Americans became involved in the conflict between the British and French.

. . . .

As a young military officer, George Washington fought with British forces against the French. Both forces wanted control of lands west of the Appalachian Mountains. During the 1700s, Britain and France were two of the strongest powers in Europe. They competed for wealth and empire in different parts of the world. This rivalry caused bitter feelings between British and French colonists in North America.

This bitterness increased when British interests turned to the Ohio River valley. The French regarded this territory as their own. They did not want British colonists sharing in their profitable fur trade.

In the 1740s hostility between the two forces grew. British fur traders built a fort at a place called Pickawillany. Acting quickly, the French attacked Pickawillany and drove the British traders out of Ohio. French troops also began raiding towns in Maine and New York. In response, some New Englanders captured the important French fortress at Louisbourg on Cape Breton Island, north of Nova Scotia. Much to the disgust of the New Englanders, Britain returned Louisbourg to France.

Native Americans Take Sides

The French and British both knew that assistance from Native Americans could help them win control of North America. The French had an advantage over the British because they had many Native American allies.

Unlike the British, the French were interested mainly in fur trading. They did not want to take over Native American land. Also, French trappers and fur traders often married Native American women and followed their customs. French missionaries **converted**—changed the religious beliefs of—many Native Americans to Catholicism. For these reasons, Native Americans often helped the French and raided British settlements.

The Iroquois Confederacy

The most powerful group of Native Americans in the East was the **Iroquois Confederacy**, based in the New York area.

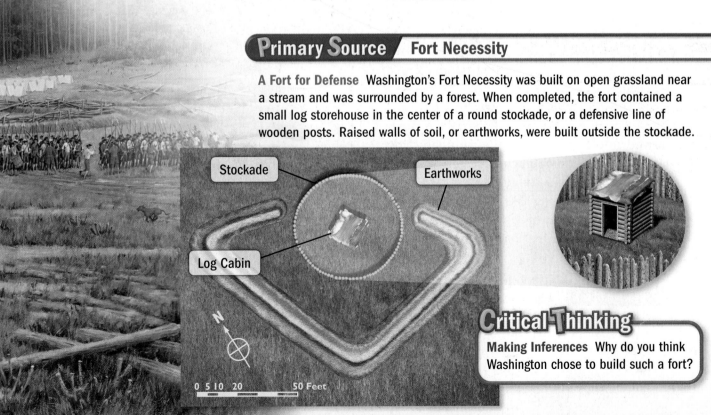

Primary Source / Fort Necessity

A Fort for Defense Washington's Fort Necessity was built on open grassland near a stream and was surrounded by a forest. When completed, the fort contained a small log storehouse in the center of a round stockade, or a defensive line of wooden posts. Raised walls of soil, or earthworks, were built outside the stockade.

Stockade

Earthworks

Log Cabin

0 5 10 20   50 Feet

Critical Thinking

Making Inferences Why do you think Washington chose to build such a fort?

America's first political cartoon, drawn by Benjamin Franklin in 1754, promoted his Albany Plan of Union. It reflects a popular superstition that a dead snake would come back to life if the pieces were placed next to each other. Each section represents a colony. The New England colonies are combined as one section.

1. **Identifying** The abbreviation *NE* stands for "New England." What colonies do the other sections represent?

2. **Interpreting** What warning does Franklin's cartoon convey about the approaching war with France?

The confederacy initially included five nations—the Mohawk, Seneca, Cayuga, Onondaga, and Oneida. Other groups of Native Americans later joined or were conquered by the Iroquois. After the Tuscarora joined in 1722, the English referred to the confederacy as the Six Nations.

The Iroquois managed to remain independent by trading with both the British and the French. By skillfully playing the British and French against each other, the Iroquois dominated the Great Lakes area.

By the mid-1700s, however, the Iroquois came under greater pressure as the British moved into the Ohio Valley. Eventually, the leaders of the confederacy gave certain trading rights to the British and reluctantly became their allies. By taking this step, the Iroquois upset the balance of power between the French and British that had been so difficult to establish.

Reading Check **Explaining** Why did hostilities between the French and British increase during the early 1740s?

American Colonists Take Action

Main Idea The American colonists prepared to defend themselves against the French and their Native American allies.

History and You Has anyone ever tried to take something that was yours? How did you react? Read to learn how the colonists responded to the growing conflict between France and Great Britain.

A group of Virginians had plans for settling the Ohio Valley. In the fall of 1753, Governor Robert Dinwiddie of Virginia sent a surveyor named **George Washington** into the Ohio country. Washington was 21 years old. His mission was to tell the French that they were trespassing on land that Great Britain claimed. He was to demand that they leave.

Washington delivered the message, but it did no good. "The French told me," Washington said later, "that it was their absolute **design**, or plan, to take possession of the Ohio, and by God they would do it."

Washington's First Command

In the spring of 1754, Dinwiddie made Washington a lieutenant colonel. He then sent Washington back to the Ohio country with a **militia**—a group of civilians trained to fight in emergencies—of 150 men. The militia had instructions to build a fort where the Allegheny and Monongahela Rivers meet to form the Ohio River—the site of present-day Pittsburgh. Washington and his troops arrived to find the French already building Fort Duquesne (doo•KAYN) on that spot.

Washington established a small post nearby, called Fort Necessity. Although greatly outnumbered, the troops of the inexperienced Washington attacked a French force. The French quickly forced Washington's soldiers to surrender. The British soldiers were later released, and they returned to Virginia. Washington's published account of the ordeal made him famous throughout the colonies and Europe. Washington had been defeated at Fort Necessity. The colonists, however, regarded him as a hero who struck the first blow against the French.

The Albany Plan of Union

Meanwhile, representatives from several colonies met in Albany, New York, in June 1754 to discuss the threat of war. They wanted to find a way to defend themselves against the French. They also hoped to persuade the Iroquois to support the British.

The representatives adopted Benjamin Franklin's **Albany Plan of Union** for a united colonial government. Franklin's plan called for "one general government" for eleven of the American colonies. Not a single colonial assembly, however, approved the plan. No colony was willing to give up any of its power. Disappointed, Franklin wrote: "Everybody cries, a Union is necessary; but when they come to the manner and form of the union, [they] are perfectly distracted."

The Albany meeting failed to unite the colonists in fighting the French. Soon, a full-scale war—the French and Indian War—erupted.

Reading Check **Describing** Describe Washington's expeditions into French territory.

Section 3 Review

History ONLINE
Study Central™ To review this section, go to glencoe.com.

Vocabulary

1. Define each of the following terms by using it in a complete sentence: convert, Iroquois Confederacy, design, militia.

Main Ideas

2. **Explaining** How did the Iroquois remain independent from both the British and the French? How did that change?

3. **Identifying** What happened as a result of Washington's defeat at Fort Necessity?

Critical Thinking

4. **Analyzing** Why did Benjamin Franklin propose the Albany Plan of Union?

5. **Determining Cause and Effect** Use a diagram like the one below to identify the causes of the increasing rivalry between the French and the British in North America.

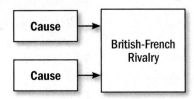

6. **Creative Writing** Write a short newspaper article describing the battle at Fort Necessity.

Answer the
7. **Essential Question**
Why did conflict arise in North America between France and Great Britain?

The French and Indian War

Essential Question ◀

How did the outcome of the French and Indian War determine who controlled North America?

Reading Guide

Content Vocabulary
alliance (p. 109)   speculator (p. 112)

Academic Vocabulary
prospect (p. 110)

Key People and Events
General Edward Braddock (p. 109)
Seven Years' War (p. 110)
William Pitt (p. 110)
Jeffrey Amherst (p. 111)
James Wolfe (p. 111)
Treaty of Paris (p. 111)
Pontiac's War (p. 112)
Proclamation of 1763 (p. 112)

Reading Strategy
Taking Notes As you read, use a diagram like the one below to list the lands that France lost when the Treaty of Paris of 1763 was signed.

French Lands → To Britain / To Spain

NEW YORK STANDARDS
The American Journey

U3.I.1 To understand the economic, political, and social causes of the American Revolution

U3.I.3 To investigate how people in the United States and throughout the world answer the three fundamental economic questions and solve basic economic problems

U3.II.1 To understand how colonists' concerns regarding political and economic issues resulted in the movement for independence

U3.III.2 To investigate key turning points in New York State and United States history and explain why these events or developments are significant

American Diary

Commanded by General James Wolfe, about 1,800 British troops landed "on the North Shore [of Quebec] . . . an Hour before Day Break." To get in position to attack, the soldiers had to climb a steep cliff. Scrambling up the slope, the British soldiers ran into "a little Firing" from French guards. They continued to climb until they "gained the top of the [cliff]." By the time the sun rose over Quebec, British and French soldiers were prepared to battle on the Plains of Abraham outside the city.

—from a letter by General George Townshend

In 1759 British troops climbed steep cliffs in order to attack the French stronghold of Quebec.

The British Take Action

Main Idea William Pitt helped turn the tide of the French and Indian War to the colonists' favor.

History and You Has a friend ever given you advice that you wished you had followed? Read to learn why one British general was defeated because of his failure to accept advice.

. . . .

The Battle of Quebec, fought in 1759, was a deciding moment in the conflict between Britain and France. That conflict was known as the French and Indian War. This war raged in North America through the late 1750s and early 1760s. The French and Indian War was part of a larger struggle between the British and the French. That struggle involved, or included, control of world trade and power on the seas.

In 1754 the governor of Massachusetts made an announcement to the colonial assembly. He told them that the French were on the way to "making themselves masters of this Continent."

The French were building well-armed forts throughout the Great Lakes region and the Ohio River valley. Their network of **alliances,** or unions, with Native Americans allowed the French to control large areas of land, stretching from the St. Lawrence River in Canada all the way south to New Orleans. The French and their Native American allies seemed to be winning control of the American frontier. The final showdown was about to begin.

During the early stages of the French and Indian War, the British colonists fought the French and the Native Americans with little help from Britain. In 1754, however, the government in London decided to intervene in the conflict. It was alarmed by the new forts the French were building and by Washington's defeat at Fort Necessity. In the fall of 1754, Great Britain appointed **General Edward Braddock** commander in chief of the British forces in America. Braddock's mission was to drive the French forces from the Ohio Valley region.

Braddock Marches to Duquesne

In June 1755, Braddock started out from Virginia with about 1,400 red-coated British soldiers and a smaller force of blue-coated colonial militia. George Washington served as an aide to Braddock during the campaign.

Primary Source / **Two Heroes: Wolfe and Montcalm**

Known as outstanding commanders, both the British General Wolfe and the French General Montcalm lost their lives in the Battle of Quebec. During the fighting, Wolfe was shot in the chest and was "carried off wounded to the rear of the front line." He reportedly heard cries of "they [the French] run." Told that the French lines had broken, Wolfe died peacefully, satisfied that the British had won. Montcalm also was wounded in battle. As he lay in bed, Montcalm asked how long he had to live. When told "about a dozen hours," the French general said, "So much the better. . . . I am happy I shall not live to see the surrender of Quebec."

—from *Historical Journal of the Campaigns in North America*

General James Wolfe ▼

◀ Marquis de Montcalm

Critical Thinking

Making Generalizations Why are Wolfe and Montcalm considered heroes? What qualities do you think make a person a hero?

On the march to Fort Duquesne, Washington reported that Braddock:

PRIMARY SOURCE

"[halted] to level every mole hill, and to erect bridges over every brook, by which means we were four days in getting twelve miles."

—from *Life of Washington*

Washington told Braddock that his army's style of marching was not well suited to fighting on the frontier. Lined up in columns and rows wearing bright-colored uniforms, the troops became easy targets. Braddock ignored Washington's advice.

Native Americans and French troops ambushed the British on July 9. The British were confused and frightened. They could not even see their attackers, who were hidden in the forest and shooting at them from behind trees. Braddock was killed. Defeated, the British lost nearly 1,000 men. Washington led the survivors back to Virginia.

Britain Declares War on France

The fighting in America helped start a new war in Europe. This war was known as the **Seven Years' War.** After arranging an alliance with Prussia, Britain declared war on France in 1756. Prussia fought France and its allies in Europe. Britain fought France in the Caribbean, India, and North America.

Early in the war, French troops captured several British forts, and their Native American allies began raiding frontier farms from New York to Pennsylvania. They killed settlers, burned farmhouses and crops, and drove many families back toward the coast. French forces from Canada captured British forts at Lake Ontario and at Lake George.

Pitt Takes Charge

Great Britain's **prospects,** or chances for success, in America improved after **William Pitt** came to power. Pitt served as secretary of state and then as prime minister of Great Britain and was a great military planner.

The French and Indian War, 1754–1763

NATIONAL GEOGRAPHIC

A War for North America During the French and Indian War, Great Britain and France each fought for control of the North American continent. Native American leaders, who had long played the European rivals against each other, were forced to choose sides.

To avoid arguments from the colonists about the cost of the war, Pitt decided that Great Britain would pay for the war supplies—no matter the cost. Pitt ran up an enormous debt. After the war the British raised the colonists' taxes to help pay this debt. Pitt had only delayed the moment when the colonists had to pay their share of the bill.

Pitt wanted more than just a clear path to the Western territories. He also intended to conquer French Canada. He sent British troops to North America under commanders **Jeffrey Amherst** and **James Wolfe.** In 1758 a British assault recaptured the fortress at Louisbourg. That same year a group of New Englanders, led by British officers, captured Fort Frontenac at Lake Ontario. Still another British force took Fort Duquesne in Pennsylvania, which was renamed Fort Pitt.

Reading Check **Describing** Why was William Pitt successful at managing the war for Britain?

"[Swords] and hatchets playing on every quarter with much . . . blood but our New Hampshire forces being fresh & courageous and the Enemy tired and much discouraged with the Defeat they met with, retreated and made their escape toward a Creek. . . . The day after ye battle three Frenchmen were taken up by the Guard of Fort Lymon who upon examination declared that their Army was entirely [defeated]."

—Colonist Robert Moses, diary entry, 1755

◀ Mohawk chief Joseph Brant was an important British ally.

Map Skills

Region Which country controlled the territory around the Great Lakes?

Maps In MOtion See StudentWorks™ Plus or glencoe.com.

The Fall of New France

Main Idea The fall of Quebec and Montreal ended the French and Indian War in North America.

History and You What factors lead to success or failure in battle? Read to learn how the British defeated the French in the French and Indian War.

. . . .

The British had so many victories in 1759 that people said the church bells of London wore thin with joyous ringing. The greatest victory of the war, though, took place in the heart of New France.

The Battle of Quebec

Quebec was the capital of New France and was located on top of a cliff overlooking the St. Lawrence River. Quebec was thought to be impossible to attack. In September 1759, British general James Wolfe's scouts spotted a poorly guarded path along the back of the cliff. During the night, Wolfe's soldiers overwhelmed the French guards and scrambled up the path. The British troops then surprised and defeated the French army on a field called the Plains of Abraham.

The Treaty of Paris

The fall of Quebec and General Amherst's capture of Montreal the following year brought an end to the fighting in North America. The **Treaty of Paris** of 1763 forced France to give Canada and most of its lands east of the Mississippi River to Great Britain. Great Britain also received Florida from France's ally, Spain. Spain acquired French lands west of the Mississippi River—the Louisiana Territory—as well as the port of New Orleans.

The Treaty of Paris marked the end of France as a power in North America. The continent was now divided between Great Britain and Spain.

Reading Check **Determining Cause and Effect** What happened to France's territory as a result of its defeat in the war?

Trouble on the Frontier

Main Idea Continued conflict between Native Americans and British settlers led to the Proclamation of 1763.

History and You How would you feel if a CD you ordered and paid for never arrived? Read to learn why some land investors were furious about the Proclamation of 1763.

The French loss dealt a blow to the Native Americans of the Ohio River valley. They had lost their French allies and trading partners. The British raised the prices of their goods and, unlike the French, refused to pay the Native Americans for the use of their land. Worst of all, more British settlers began moving west onto Native American lands.

Pontiac's War

Pontiac, chief of an Ottawa village near Detroit, regarded British settlers as a threat to his people's way of life. Just as Benjamin Franklin tried to bring the colonies together with his Albany Plan, Pontiac wanted Native American groups to unite to fight the British.

In the spring of 1763, Pontiac gathered forces and captured the British fort at Detroit and other British outposts. That summer, Native Americans killed settlers along the Pennsylvania and Virginia frontiers during **Pontiac's War.** The war finally ended in August 1765 after the British defeated Pontiac's allies. Pontiac signed a peace treaty, and the British pardoned him.

The Proclamation of 1763

To prevent more fighting, Britain called a halt to the settlers' westward expansion. The **Proclamation of 1763** set the Appalachian Mountains as the temporary western boundary for the colonies. The proclamation especially angered those who owned shares in land companies. These **speculators,** or investors, had already bought land west of the mountains. They were furious that Britain ignored their land claims. More conflicts would soon arise between Britain and the colonists.

Reading Check **Examining** Why were some colonists angered by the Proclamation of 1763?

Section 4 Review

History ONLINE
Study Central™ To review this section, go to glencoe.com.

Vocabulary

1. Using complete sentences, define the following terms: alliance, prospect, speculator.

Main Ideas

2. Identifying Before Pitt took charge, what advantages did the French have in North America?

3. Summarizing What effect did the Treaty of Paris have on France?

4. Discussing Why did Pontiac want the Native Americans to join forces?

Critical Thinking

5. Identifying Problems and Solutions Use a chart like the one below to list the problems of General Braddock's army. List actions he could have taken that might have brought about France's defeat.

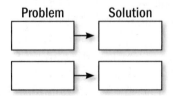

6. Creative Writing Write a conversation between two French fur trappers that describes how they might have felt about the Treaty of Paris.

Answer the
7. Essential Question How did the outcome of the French and Indian War determine who controlled North America?

Chapter 4

Visual Summary

Main Idea	Supporting Details
Geography affects the economic development of the American colonies.	• Regional geographic characteristics lead to: - subsistence farming and commerce in New England, - an economy based on cash crops and industry in the Middle Colonies, and - a farming economy dependent on slavery in the South.
A distinctly American culture begins to develop during the colonial period.	• Americans embrace religion, education, science and the arts, the family, and freedom of the press.
American ideas about government have their beginnings in both British law and colonial government.	• The colonists are inspired by the English Bill of Rights and by the English ideals of limited government and representative government.
Native Americans generally have better relations with French settlers than British settlers.	• The British want the support of Native Americans in fighting the French but seize Native American land without paying them for it. • The French receive more Native American help because they trade with them and do not try to take their land.
Worldwide competition between Britain and France for wealth and land leads to conflict in North America.	• Both Britain and France want control of North American resources. • Conflicts over fur trading in the Ohio River valley eventually lead to the French and Indian War.
The French and Indian War shifts the balance of power in North America.	• The Treaty of Paris divides North America between Britain and Spain. • Conflicts build between the settlers and the Native Americans, as well as between the colonists and Britain.

▲ Powder horn from the French and Indian War

◀ New England whalers

STUDY TO GO Study anywhere, anytime! Download quizzes and flash cards to your PDA from glencoe.com.

TEST-TAKING TIP

For a short-answer or essay question, take time to review what you have written. Does it completely answer the question? Do you need to add any more information?

Reviewing Main Ideas

Directions: Choose the best answer for each of the following questions.

1 Most German immigrants settled in

(1) Massachusetts. (3) Virginia.

(2) Pennsylvania. (4) New York.

2 Great Britain *directly* ruled

(1) charter colonies.

(2) proprietary colonies.

(3) royal colonies.

(4) all of the above.

3 The Albany Plan of Union was not approved by the colonies because

(1) it called for the colonies to declare their independence from Britain.

(2) most colonists did not consider the lands west of the Appalachian Mountains to be valuable.

(3) it diminished the strength of the united colonial government.

(4) colonies were not willing to give up any of their power.

4 How did the British victory over the French affect the Native Americans of the Ohio River valley?

(1) It helped them because the British, unlike the French, paid the Native Americans for the use of their land.

(2) It hurt them because it resulted in a huge rush of French refugees into Native American lands.

(3) It hurt them because they lost their French allies and trading partners.

(4) It helped them because the British lowered the prices of their goods.

Short-Answer Question

Directions: Base your answer to question 5 on the excerpt below and on your knowledge of social studies.

> "The concerns of this country are so closely connected and interwoven with Indian affairs, and not only a great branch of our trade, but even the safety of this province, do so much depend upon our continuing in Friendship with the Indians, that I thought it highly necessary to gain all the knowledge I could of them."
>
> —South Carolina Governor James Glen, 1763

5 Why did Glen's colony have a relationship with Native Americans?

Review the Essential Questions

6 Essay Identify three events in the mid-1700s that were most responsible for changing (a) life in colonial America and (b) the influence of the British Empire in North America. Explain your choices.

To help you write your essay, review your answers to the Essential Questions in the section reviews and the chapter Foldables Study Organizer. Your essay should include:

- the economies of the three colonial regions;
- the growth of slavery in the colonies;
- the impact of the Great Awakening and the Enlightenment; and
- the causes and effects of the French and Indian War and the outcome of the conflict.

GO ON ▶

Document-Based Questions

Directions: Analyze the documents and answer the short-answer questions that follow.

Document 1

This map illustrates trade and industry in the American colonies around 1750.

Colonial Trade and Industry, 1750

Legend:
- Cattle and grain
- Tobacco
- Rice and indigo
- Fur and skins
- Fishing
- Lumber
- Shipbuilding
- Ironworks

Source: *Historical Atlas of the United States*

7 Use the map to identify two differences between the economies of the New England and Middle Colonies and those of the Southern Colonies.

Document 2

"The Dutiful Child's Promises" is taken from the 1727 edition of *The New England Primer.*

> "I will fear GOD, and honour the KING.
> I will honour my Father & Mother.
> I will Obey my superiors.
> I will Submit to my Elders.
> I will Love my Friends.
> I will forgive my Enemies, and pray to God for them."

Source: *The New England Primer*

8 Identify at least two traits that reflect the culture of colonial America in the document.

Document 3

This is the introduction to the Albany Plan of Union (1754).

> "It is proposed that humble application be made for an act of Parliament of Great Britain, by virtue of which one general government may be formed in America, including all the said colonies, within and under which government each colony may retain its present constitution."

Source: Albany Plan of Union

9 Based on this document, what was the Albany Plan proposing? How would it have affected colonial constitutions?

Document 4

This is part of a 1755 British statement to the Acadians who were French settlers in Nova Scotia living in the region after Britain took control of it in 1710.

> "Your land and tenements [houses], cattle of all kinds and livestock of all sorts are forfeited [given over] to the Crown with all other effects saving your money and household goods and you are to be removed from this province."

Source: *Eyewitness to America*

10 What are the Acadians being told to do? Why would Britain have issued this statement?

11 Persuasive Writing Using the information from the four documents and your knowledge of social studies, write an essay in which you:
- compare and contrast cultural values of the colonial period with those of today; and
- explain how values from the colonial period influenced American values today.

Need Extra Help?											
If you missed questions...	1	2	3	4	5	6	7	8	9	10	11
Go to page...	92	101	107	112	109–112	88–112	88–95	102–103	105	108–111	88–112

Unit 2

Creating a Nation
1763–1790

Seven-dollar bill, U.S., 1776

116

"I only regret that I have but one life to lose for my country."
—Nathan Hale

Washington Enforces the Surrender at Yorktown by Eugene Hess

117

Unit 2 Reading History

Making Connections

Learn It!

When you make connections while reading, you connect the text with information you already know. This knowledge may be in math, science, geography, or any other subject area. You can also connect the text to personal experience.

Connect to Your Knowledge
What do you know about the Fourth of July?

1. The Fourth of July is the U.S. holiday celebrating the country's independence.

2. The Fourth of July is also known as Independence Day.

3. The term *freedom* also means "independence."

—*from Chapter 6, p. 153*

The Liberty Bell was rung every Fourth of July and for many public events until a crack appeared in about 1846. Today, the Liberty Bell is a symbol of freedom in the United States and throughout the world.

Practice It!

Read the paragraph below. On another sheet of paper, write three facts from your own knowledge that connect to the text.

—*from Chapter 6, p. 164*

To pay for the war, the Congress and the states printed hundreds of millions of dollars' worth of paper money. The bills quickly lost their value, though. The amount of bills in circulation grew faster than the supply of gold and silver backing them. This led to **inflation,** which means that it took more and more money to buy the same amount of goods. The Congress stopped issuing the paper money because no one would use it.

Connect to Your Knowledge
What do you know about inflation and paying higher prices for the same items?

1. _____
_____

2. _____
_____

3. _____
_____

Academic Vocabulary Preview

Listed below are the academic vocabulary words and their definitions that you will come across as you study Unit 2. Practice It! will help you study the words and definitions.

Academic Vocabulary	Definition	Practice It!
Chapter 5 The Spirit of Independence		
prohibit (proh · HIH · buht) *p. 123*	to stop; disallow	**Identify** *the term from Chapter 5 that best completes the sentences.*
violate (VY · uh · LAYT) *p. 124*	to disturb or disregard	1. The British created a proclamation to _____ colonists from western settlement.
occupy (AH · kyuh · PY) *p. 127*	to control	
encounter (ihn · KOWN · tuhr) *p. 127*	an unexpected meeting	2. During wartime, enemy soldiers sometimes _____ homes and cities.
approach (uh · PROHCH) *p. 135*	to move toward	3. Many soldiers _____ to serve in their country's military.
volunteer (VAH · luhn · TIHR) *p. 136*	to willingly step forward	
debate (dih · BAYT) *p. 141*	a discussion of opposing opinions	
status (STA · tus) *p. 142*	a rank or position	
Chapter 6 The American Revolution		
transfer (TRANS · FUHR) *p. 155*	to move from one place to another	**Choose** *the word that best matches the meaning of each vocabulary term from chapter 6 listed below.*
previous (PREE · vee · uhs) *p. 155*	earlier; coming before	
aid (AYD) *p. 161*	to help	4. **transfer** 6. **pursue**
issue (IH · shoo) *p. 165*	a point or matter of discussion	**a.** to move **a.** to continue
impact (IHM · PAKT) *p. 171*	an effect	**b.** to retain **b.** to retreat
sustain (suh · STAYN) *p. 173*	to suffer	**c.** to command **c.** to neglect
strategy (STRA · tuh · jee) *p. 175*	a plan of action	5. **issue** 7. **strategy**
pursue (puhr · SOO) *p. 177*	to continue	**a.** a story **a.** a game
		b. a paper **b.** a plan
		c. a matter **c.** a work
Chapter 7 A More Perfect Union		
abandon (uh · BAN · duhn) *p. 189*	to give up	**Choose** *terms from Chapter 7 to complete the paragraph.*
clause (KLAWZ) *p. 191*	a condition added to a document	A legal document may have a _____ that adds a condition to the document's terms. Leaders may hold a _____ to create legal documents. At these times, leaders may vote to _____ a document if they want it changed.
convention (kuhn · VEHN · shuhn) *p. 198*	a formal meeting	
amend (uh · MEHND) *p. 199*	to alter; improve	
tradition (truh · DIH · shuhn) *p. 205*	cultural beliefs and practices	
reside (rih · ZYD) *p. 208*	to exist or live within	

The Spirit of Independence
1763–1776

Colonial militia members, known as minutemen, left their homes on short notice to fight the British.

British tax stamp ►

United States

World

★ **1763**
Treaty of Paris signed

1763

★ **1764**
Mozart writes first symphony at age eight

★ **1765**
Colonists protest Stamp Act

1766

★ **1770**
British troops clash with civilians in Boston Massacre

1769

★ **1770**
Industrial Revolution begins in England

Section 1: Taxation Without Representation

Essential Question Following the French and Indian War, how did the British government anger the American colonists?

Section 2: Building Colonial Unity

Essential Question How did colonists react to British policies?

Section 3: A Call to Arms

Essential Question What brought about the clash between American colonists and British soldiers at Lexington and Concord?

Section 4: Moving Toward Independence

Essential Question Why did the American colonies choose to declare independence?

FOLDABLES
Study Organizer

Organizing Information

Make this four-tab Foldable to help you learn about the events that led to the American Revolution.

Step 1 Fold the top and bottom of a piece of paper into the middle.

Step 2 Fold the paper in half from side to side.

Step 3 Open and cut along the inside fold lines to form four tabs.

Step 4 Label the tabs as shown.

Reading and Writing

As you read the chapter, take notes about each section under the appropriate head. Use your Foldable to help you write a summary for each section.

Taxation Without Representation	Building Colonial Unity
A Call to Arms	Moving Toward Independence

Liberty Bell ▶

Statue of Minuteman, Concord, MA ▶

▲ Tea leaves from the Boston Tea Party

★ **1773**
Patriots carry out Boston Tea Party

★ **1774**
First Continental Congress meets

★ **1775**
Battles fought at Lexington and Concord

1772

1775

★ **1772**
Poland partitioned among Russia, Prussia, and Austria

★ **1774**
Louis XVI becomes king of France

◀ Chair owned by Louis XVI

Taxation Without Representation

Essential Question

Following the French and Indian War, how did the British government anger the American colonists?

Reading Guide

Content Vocabulary

revenue (p. 123)	writs of assistance (p. 123)
resolution (p. 125)	effigy (p. 125)
boycott (p. 125)	nonimportation (p. 125)
repeal (p. 125)	

Academic Vocabulary

prohibit (p. 123) violate (p. 124)

Key People and Events

Stamp Act (p. 124)

Patrick Henry (p. 125)

Samuel Adams (p. 125)

Reading Strategy

Taking Notes As you read, identify British policies that affected the colonists. Then describe the colonists' view of each policy.

British Policy		Colonists' View
	→	
	→	
	→	

NEW YORK STANDARDS
The American Journey

U3.I.1 To understand the economic, political, and social causes of the American Revolution

U3.II.1 To understand how colonists' concerns regarding political and economic issues resulted in the movement for independence

U3.II.3 To consider the nature and evolution of constitutional democracies

American Diary

In London, Benjamin Franklin stated the American view on British taxes: "They will oppose it to the last. They do not consider it as at all necessary for you to raise money . . . by your taxes. . . . America has been greatly misrepresented . . . [as] refusing to bear any part of [the war's] expense. The Colonies . . . paid and clothed near 25,000 men during the last war, a number equal to [that of] Britain."

—in an interview before the House of Commons, 1766

A SET of PLANS and FORTS in AMERICA. Reduced from Actual Surveys. 1765.

Relations With Britain

Main Idea After the French and Indian War, Great Britain passed laws to protect British interests in the colonies.

History and You How do you feel when someone treats you unfairly? Read to learn how the colonists felt about British laws that affected them.

. . . .

With victory in the French and Indian War, the British gained control of a vast territory in North America. However, they faced the challenge of protecting their interests in the colonies and new territory. With the Proclamation of 1763, the British government set up new provinces. The proclamation also **prohibited,** or prevented, colonists from moving west of the Appalachian Mountains.

Limiting western settlement provided several advantages for Britain. It allowed the British government to control westward movement and to avoid conflict with Native Americans. Also, keeping colonists near the East Coast ensured a market for British goods in the coastal cities, where trade flourished.

Finally, closing western settlement allowed Britain to control the fur trade in the frontier. Britain planned to station 10,000 troops in the colonies to protect these interests.

Britain needed new **revenue,** or incoming money, to pay troop expenses. Also, the French and Indian War left Britain with a huge debt. The king and Parliament believed that the colonists should pay part of the cost, so they issued new taxes on the colonies and began to enforce existing taxes more strictly.

Britain's Trade Laws

In 1763 George Grenville, prime minister of Britain, decided to act against smuggling. When the colonists smuggled goods to avoid taxes, Britain lost revenue.

Grenville knew that American juries often found smugglers innocent. He convinced Parliament to pass a law allowing smugglers to be sent to vice-admiralty courts, which were run by officers and did not have juries. In 1767 Parliament authorized **writs of assistance.** These legal documents allowed customs officers to enter any location to search for smuggled goods.

The Sugar Act

In 1764 Parliament passed the Sugar Act. This act lowered the tax on imported molasses. Grenville hoped the lower tax would convince colonists to pay the tax instead of smuggling. The act also let officers seize goods from smugglers without going to court.

During the colonial period, the British built a number of forts throughout their American colonies.

By the Numbers — Pounds and Shillings

Britain's Per-Capita War Debt, 1765

Share of the debt per person:

Britain: £ £ £ £ £ £ £ £ £
£ £ £ £ £ £ £ £

Colonies: S S S S S S S S S
S S S S S S S S

£ = 1 British pound   S = 1 British shilling

1 Pound (£) = 20 Shillings

Source: Don Cook. *The Long Fuse: How England Lost the American Colonies, 1760–1785.*

Britain's National Debt At the end of the French and Indian War, Great Britain's national debt soared to more than £140 million. British citizens paid far more on the debt per person than their counterparts in the colonies.

Critical Thinking

Analyzing How much more per-capita debt did residents of Britain have compared to residents of the colonies?

The Proclamation of 1763 NATIONAL GEOGRAPHIC

Map legend:
- Thirteen Colonies
- Other British Territory
- Spanish Territory
- - - Proclamation Line of 1763

"I can never look upon that Proclamation in any other light . . . than as a temporary expedient [solution] to quiet the Minds of the Indians and must fall . . . when those Indians are consenting to our Occupying the Lands."

—George Washington, 1767

Provisions of the Proclamation of 1763

- Created governments for the new North American territories won from France as a result of the French and Indian War
- Sought to prevent future conflicts with Native Americans
- Protected Native Americans by reserving the British Crown's right to enter into all land negotiations with them
- Forbade settlement of lands west of the Proclamation line
- Required settlers who had already moved west of the Proclamation line to move east of it
- Stated that the Native Americans were to govern the Proclamation territory under their own laws

Critical Thinking

Analyzing How did the Proclamation of 1763 attempt to protect Native American rights and lands?

The Sugar Act and the new laws to control smuggling angered colonists. They believed these British actions **violated,** or interfered with, their rights as English citizens. Writs of assistance violated their right to be secure in their homes. Vice-admiralty courts violated their right to a jury trial. Also, in vice-admiralty courts, defendants had to prove their innocence. This contradicted a British law stating "innocent until proved guilty."

These measures alarmed the colonists. James Otis, a lawyer in Boston, argued:

PRIMARY SOURCE

"No parts of [England's colonies] . . . can be taxed without their consent . . . every part has a right to be represented."

—from *The Rights of the British Colonies*

✓ **Reading Check** **Explaining** Why did George Grenville want smugglers sent to vice-admiralty courts?

New Taxes

Main Idea As the British government passed new tax laws, resistance by the colonists grew.

History and You Suppose everyone in your community refused to buy from a certain store. How would this decision affect the store? Read to learn how boycotts by the colonists affected British merchants.

In 1765 Parliament passed the **Stamp Act.** This law placed a tax on almost all printed material, including newspapers, wills, and playing cards. All printed material had to have a stamp. British officials applied the stamp after the tax was paid.

Opposition to the Stamp Act centered on two points. Parliament had interfered in colonial affairs by taxing the colonies directly. In addition, it taxed the colonists without their consent.

Protesting the Stamp Act

A member of the Virginia House of Burgesses, **Patrick Henry,** persuaded the burgesses to take action against the Stamp Act. The Virginia assembly passed a **resolution**—a formal expression of opinion—declaring it had "the only and sole exclusive right and power to lay taxes" on its citizens.

In Boston **Samuel Adams** helped start an organization called the Sons of Liberty to protest the Stamp Act. People in other cities also organized the Sons of Liberty groups. Protesters burned **effigies**—rag figures—representing tax collectors and destroyed houses belonging to royal officials.

In October delegates from nine colonies met in New York at the Stamp Act Congress. They drafted a petition to the king and Parliament declaring that the colonies could not be taxed except by their own assemblies.

In colonial cities, people refused to use the stamps. They urged merchants to **boycott**—refuse to buy—British and European goods in protest. Thousands of merchants signed **nonimportation** agreements—pledges not to buy or use goods imported from Britain. As the boycott spread, British merchants lost so much business that they begged Parliament to **repeal,** or cancel, the Stamp Act. In March 1766, Parliament repealed the law. However, on the same day, it passed the Declaratory Act. This law stated that Parliament had the right to tax and make decisions for the British colonies "in all cases."

The Townshend Acts

In 1767 Parliament passed a set of laws that came to be known as the Townshend Acts. British leaders knew from the Stamp Act that the colonists would resist internal taxes—those paid inside the colonies. As a result, the new taxes would apply only to imported goods such as glass, tea, and paper, with the tax being paid at the port of entry.

By this time, *any* British taxes angered the colonists. They believed that only their own representatives had the right to tax them. The colonists organized another boycott.

Throughout the colonies, women formed groups, sometimes called the Daughters of Liberty. They urged Americans to wear homemade fabrics and produce other goods they needed rather than buy British goods.

Reading Check **Describing** How did the Sons of Liberty attempt to influence British policy?

Section 1 Review

History ONLINE
Study Central™ To review this section, go to glencoe.com.

Vocabulary

1. Use each of these terms in a sentence that will help explain its meaning: prohibit, revenue, writs of assistance, violate, resolution, effigy, boycott, nonimportation, repeal.

Main Ideas

2. Specifying What advantages did the British gain by limiting westward settlement?

3. Explaining Why did some colonists smuggle goods?

4. Identifying Opposition to the Stamp Act centered on what two main points?

Critical Thinking

5. Contrasting How did the British and the colonists differ on the issue of taxes?

6. Determining Cause and Effect Describe the responses of the colonists to the Stamp Act and the result. Use a diagram like the one below.

Stamp Act → Responses → Result

7. Persuasive Writing Write a letter to the editor of a colonial newspaper. Your goal is to try to persuade fellow colonists to boycott British goods.

8. Answer the Essential Question
Following the French and Indian War, how did the British government anger the American colonists?

Building Colonial Unity

Essential Question

How did the colonists react to British policies?

Reading Guide

Content Vocabulary
propaganda (p. 127)
committee of correspondence (p. 128)

Academic Vocabulary
occupy (p. 127)   encounter (p. 127)

Key People and Events
Crispus Attucks (p. 127)
Boston Massacre (p. 127)
Tea Act (p. 128)
Boston Tea Party (p. 129)
George III (p. 129)
Coercive Acts (p. 129)

Reading Strategy
Taking Notes As you read, take notes on how the Intolerable Acts affected the colonists.

NEW YORK STANDARDS
The American Journey

U3.I.1 To understand the economic, political, and social causes of the American Revolution

U3.II.1 To understand how colonists' concerns regarding political and economic issues resulted in the movement for independence

U3.II.2 To compare and contrast different interpretations of key events and issues in New York State and United States history and explain reasons for these different accounts

American Diary

To enforce tax laws, British troops arrived in Boston. Conflict soon erupted. On March 5, 1770, a Boston merchant wrote: "The 29th [regiment] on duty. A quarrel between the soldiers and inhabitants; . . . A party of the 29th . . . fired on the people; they killed five, wounded several others. . . . The inhabitants are greatly enraged."

—from The Diary of John Rowe

British troops arrive in Boston to enforce British laws and keep the peace.

Trouble in Boston

Main Idea A violent clash between townspeople and British soldiers in Boston intensified anti-British feeling in the colonies.

History and You When someone taunts you, how do you react? Read to learn how British soldiers responded to the jeers of Bostonians.

By 1768, protests by the colonists were making British colonial officials nervous. They sent word to Britain that the colonies were on the brink of rebellion. Parliament sent troops to Boston. As angry Bostonians jeered, the "redcoats" set up camp in the center of the city.

Many colonists felt that the British had pushed them too far. First the British had passed laws that violated colonial rights. They also had sent an army to **occupy,** or control, colonial cities.

To make matters worse, the soldiers in Boston acted rudely and sometimes even violently toward the colonists. Mostly poor men, the redcoats earned little pay. Some stole goods from local shops or scuffled with boys who taunted them in the streets. The soldiers also competed off-hours for jobs that Bostonians wanted.

The Boston Massacre

On March 5, 1770, a fight broke out between Bostonians and the soldiers. While some British officers tried to calm the crowd, one man shouted, "We did not send for you. We will not have you here. We'll get rid of you, we'll drive you away!"

The angry townspeople moved toward the customhouse, where British taxes were collected, picking up sticks, stones, and clubs. As the crowd approached, the sentry panicked and called for help. The crowd threw sticks and stones at the soldiers. "Fire, you bloodybacks, you lobsters," the crowd screamed. "You dare not fire."

After one soldier was knocked down, the nervous redcoats did fire, killing five colonists. One Bostonian cried: "Are the inhabitants to be knocked down in the streets? Are they to be murdered . . . ?" Among the dead was **Crispus Attucks,** a dockworker who was part African, part Native American. The colonists called the tragic **encounter,** or unexpected meeting, the **Boston Massacre.**

The Word Spreads

Colonial leaders used the killings as **propaganda**—information made to influence public opinion. Samuel Adams put up posters that described the "Boston Massacre."

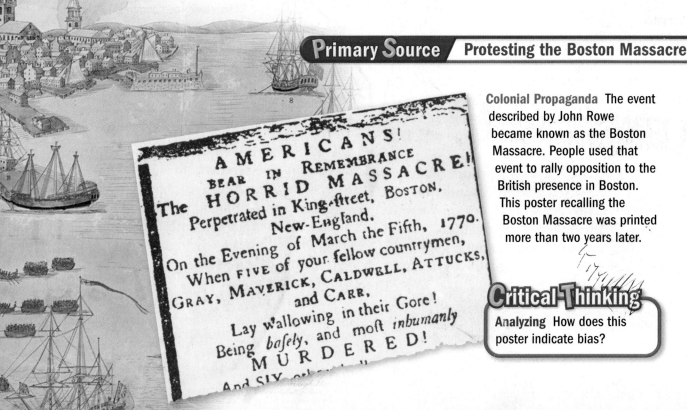

Primary Source / Protesting the Boston Massacre

AMERICANS!
BEAR IN REMEMBRANCE
The HORRID MASSACRE!
Perpetrated in King-ftreet, Boston,
New-England.
On the Evening of March the Fifth, 1770.
When FIVE of your fellow countrymen,
GRAY, MAVERICK, CALDWELL, ATTUCKS,
and CARR,
Lay wallowing in their Gore!
Being bafely, and moft inhumanly
MURDERED!
And SIX others...

Colonial Propaganda The event described by John Rowe became known as the Boston Massacre. People used that event to rally opposition to the British presence in Boston. This poster recalling the Boston Massacre was printed more than two years later.

Critical Thinking
Analyzing How does this poster indicate bias?

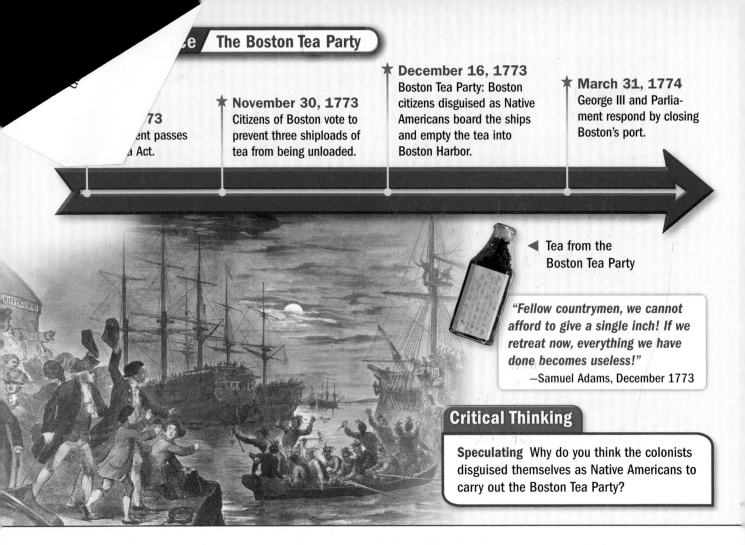

The Boston Tea Party

...73
...ent passes
...a Act.

★ **November 30, 1773**
Citizens of Boston vote to prevent three shiploads of tea from being unloaded.

★ **December 16, 1773**
Boston Tea Party: Boston citizens disguised as Native Americans board the ships and empty the tea into Boston Harbor.

★ **March 31, 1774**
George III and Parliament respond by closing Boston's port.

◀ Tea from the Boston Tea Party

"Fellow countrymen, we cannot afford to give a single inch! If we retreat now, everything we have done becomes useless!"
—Samuel Adams, December 1773

Critical Thinking

Speculating Why do you think the colonists disguised themselves as Native Americans to carry out the Boston Tea Party?

His posters showed a slaughter of innocent Americans by bloodthirsty redcoats. An engraving by Paul Revere showed British troops firing on an orderly crowd.

The Boston Massacre led many colonists to call for stronger boycotts on British goods. Aware of the opposition to its policies, Parliament repealed all the Townshend Acts taxes except the one on tea. The colonists ended their boycotts, except on tea. Trade with Britain resumed.

Some colonial leaders, however, continued to call for resistance to British rule. In 1772 Samuel Adams revived the Boston **committee of correspondence,** an organization used in earlier protests. Soon committees throughout the colonies were airing their grievances against Great Britain.

✓ Reading Check **Explaining** How did the colonists use the Boston Massacre to their advantage?

A Crisis Over Tea

Main Idea New British laws restricting colonial rights further enraged the colonists.

History and You If you destroyed someone else's property, would you expect to be punished for your actions? Read to find out about the consequences of the Boston Tea Party.

In 1773 the British East India Company faced ruin. To save the company, Parliament passed the **Tea Act.** This law allowed the company a virtual monopoly, or sole control, of the trade for tea in America. The act let the company sell tea directly to shopkeepers and bypass colonial merchants who normally distributed the tea.

Colonial merchants called for a new boycott. Colonists vowed to stop the East India Company's ships from unloading.

The Daughters of Liberty issued a pamphlet declaring that rather than part with freedom, "we'll part with our tea."

The Boston Tea Party

Despite warnings of a brewing crisis, the East India Company shipped tea to a number of colonial cities. The colonists forced the ships sent to New York and Philadelphia to turn back. Three tea ships arrived in Boston Harbor in late 1773. The royal governor refused to let the ships leave and ordered them to be unloaded. The Boston Sons of Liberty acted swiftly. On December 16, a group of men disguised as Mohawks boarded the ships at midnight. They threw 342 chests of tea overboard, an event that became known as the **Boston Tea Party.**

Word of this act of defiance spread. Colonists gathered to celebrate. Yet no one spoke of challenging British rule. Most colonists saw themselves as British citizens.

The Intolerable Acts

When news of the Boston Tea Party reached London, King **George III** realized that Britain was losing control of the colonies. He declared, "We must master them or totally leave them alone." The British government responded by passing the **Coercive Acts** in 1774. These harsh laws were intended to punish the people of Massachusetts for their resistance to British law.

The Coercive Acts closed Boston Harbor until the Massachusetts colonists paid for the ruined tea. This action prevented the arrival of food and other supplies that normally came by ship. Worse, the laws took away certain rights. For example, the laws banned most town meetings in New England.

The Coercive Acts also forced Bostonians to shelter soldiers in their own homes. Parliament planned to isolate Boston with these acts. Instead the other colonies sent food and clothing to support Boston. The colonists held that the Coercive Acts violated their rights as English citizens. These rights included no quartering of troops in private homes and no standing army in peacetime.

Parliament then passed the Quebec Act. This law set up a government for Quebec. It also gave Quebec the area west of the Appalachians and north of the Ohio River. This provision ignored colonial claims to the area. The colonists expressed their feelings in *their* name for the new laws—the Intolerable Acts.

Reading Check **Describing** How did the British react to the Boston Tea Party?

Section 2 Review

History ONLINE
Study Central™ To review this section, go to glencoe.com.

Vocabulary

1. Write a short paragraph in which you use all of the following vocabulary terms: occupy, encounter, propaganda, committee of correspondence.

Main Ideas

2. **Describing** Describe the events leading up to and following the Boston Massacre.

3. **Explaining** How did the Tea Act give an unfair advantage to the British East India Company?

Critical Thinking

4. **Evaluating** How did Samuel Adams and Paul Revere try to sway public opinion about the Boston Massacre?

5. **Organizing** Use a diagram like the one below to identify events and policies that led to rising tensions in the 1770s.

6. **Creative Writing** Write an account of the Boston Massacre from the point of view of a British soldier involved in the event.

Answer the
Essential Question
7. How did the colonists react to British policies?

The Spirit of Independence **Chapter 5** 129

America's LITERATURE

Meet the Author

Barry Denenberg (1946–) has said that the American Revolution is often presented to young people as a distant event. In writing *The Journal of William Thomas Emerson: A Revolutionary War Patriot,* Denenberg wanted to "bring the revolution to life by showing how it affected ordinary people and how they affected it."

Vocabulary

crown king

trampled crush

cowering crouching

feeble weak

soot ash

Building Background

In *The Journal of William Thomas Emerson: A Revolutionary War Patriot,* Barry Denenberg depicts life in Boston in the months leading up to the American Revolution as told by Will, a young orphan boy. Will works for Mr. Wilson, a tavern owner and member of the Committee, a group of colonists who oppose the British. As you read this excerpt, think about the actions of the Committee toward ordinary citizens and their effect on the political climate at the time.

THE JOURNAL OF WILLIAM THOMAS EMERSON: A REVOLUTIONARY WAR PATRIOT

Barry Denenberg

The Fitch Sisters and the Committee

Mrs. Thompson is still angry about the Fitch sisters, who have a shop on Milk Street. She never raises her voice like that.

"It's just like them to think they could bring in British goods and get away with it. You can count on the Fitch sisters to be concerned only about themselves, even in times like these. Imagine, claiming they are just trying to keep a roof

130

over their heads and food on the table. Isn't that all any of us are doing?"

The Fitch sisters say that if they didn't have British goods to sell they would find themselves poor in no time. But Mrs. Thompson says they're only making it harder on themselves by defending their actions and they should just admit their mistake. . . .

"They ought to get the same treatment as Mr. Carlisle," Mrs. Thompson said.

Henry told me all about Mr. Carlisle. We saw him one day walking down King Street dressed in lace and ruffles. Henry said he has long been suspected of being loyal to the **crown** and one night he finally got what he deserved. Some of the men from town marched out to his house. Mr. Carlisle is very rich, Henry said, "Almost as rich as Mr. Dudley. Mr. Carlisle's house was one of the grandest in Boston."

As soon as the crowd arrived they **trampled** the lawn, hacked down the trees, and overran the gate that surrounds the house. They smashed the big front doors with axes and then poured into the house, where they tore up the floorboards, ripped the curtains from the windows and, after finding Mr. Carlisle's portrait, tore the eyes out.

They dragged his finely carved furniture outside and smashed it to bits, ran off with his carpets and drank his wine cellar dry.

They found Mr. Carlisle **cowering** upstairs, trying to hide behind his bed curtains. They pulled him out despite his **feeble** efforts to hold on to the bedpost and then took his feather bed and threw it out the window. A ladder was put up and Mr. Carlisle was lowered to those waiting below.

Once they had him outside, they stripped off his nightclothes, smeared him with hot tar and covered him with the insides of the feather bed.

When the house caught fire someone wanted to call for the firemen, but the crowd shouted him down, yelling, "LET IT BURN, LET IT BURN," and so they did. The flames, Henry said, could be seen for miles by dawn. . . .

Most of the men pulled nightcaps over their heads or darkened their faces with chimney **soot** so they wouldn't be recognized. Some were armed with sticks and clubs and Henry said that Mr. Carlisle was lucky not to have suffered even greater injury to his person than to his pride.

Of course, Mrs. Thompson didn't say any of this to me. I overheard it when she was talking to Mr. Wilson right before he went into the regular Tuesday night meeting with the Committee.

That's why I stay put on Tuesday nights. I never go anywhere. They meet late, after the tavern closes, in the small room next to the big barroom. As soon as I hear them all coming in I just lie there quietly on my cot and listen. . . .

Analyzing Literature

1. **Respond** If asked to take sides in Mr. Carlisle's situation, which side would you take and why?

2. **Recall and Interpret**
   (a) Who tarred and feathered Mr. Carlisle? How do you know?
   (b) Why do you think the Committee acted so drastically?

3. **Evaluate**
   (a) What do you think will happen to the Fitch sisters?
   (b) Do you think the author does a good job in bringing the American Revolution to life for readers? Explain your answer.

Section 3

A Call to Arms

Essential Question ◄

What brought about the clash between American colonists and British soldiers at Lexington and Concord?

Reading Guide

Content Vocabulary

militia (p. 133)   Loyalist (p. 137)

minutemen (p. 134)   Patriot (p. 137)

Academic Vocabulary

approach (p. 135)   volunteer (p. 136)

Key People and Events

Continental Congress (p. 133)

John Adams (p. 133)

John Jay (p. 133)

Richard Henry Lee (p. 133)

George Washington (p. 133)

Paul Revere (p. 135)

Reading Strategy

Taking Notes As you read, list three key actions of the Continental Congress. Use a diagram like the one below.

NEW YORK STANDARDS
The American Journey

U3.III.1 To understand how the colonists attempted to establish new forms of self-government

U3.III.4 To describe how ordinary people and famous historic figures in the local community, State, and the United States have advanced the fundamental democratic values, beliefs, and traditions expressed in the Declaration of Independence, the New York State and United States constitutions, the Bill of Rights, and other important historic documents

U3.IV.1 To understand how the colonists were able to unite against British power to win a major, military and political victory

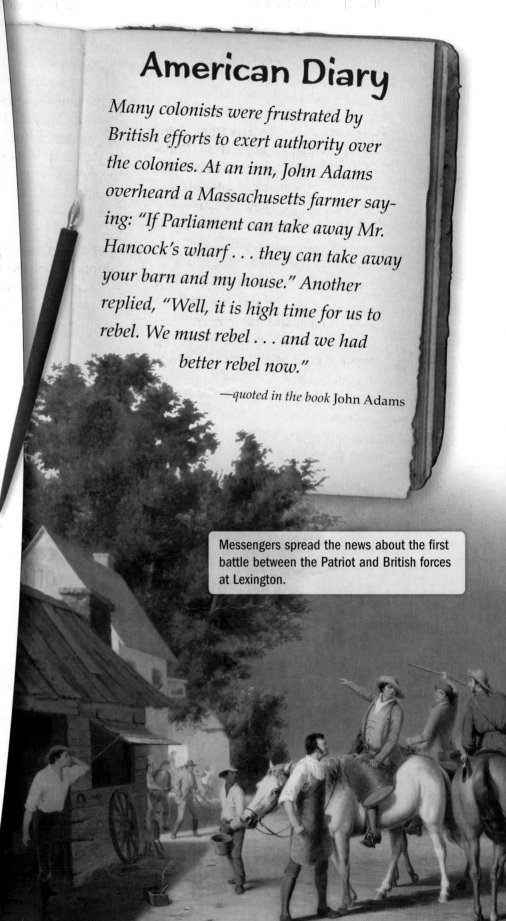

American Diary

Many colonists were frustrated by British efforts to exert authority over the colonies. At an inn, John Adams overheard a Massachusetts farmer saying: "If Parliament can take away Mr. Hancock's wharf . . . they can take away your barn and my house." Another replied, "Well, it is high time for us to rebel. We must rebel . . . and we had better rebel now."

—quoted in the book John Adams

Messengers spread the news about the first battle between the Patriot and British forces at Lexington.

The Continental Congress

Main Idea Colonial leaders met in Philadelphia to discuss their opposition to British policy.

History and You Have you ever worked with a group to accomplish a shared goal? Read to learn about the common goal that united the Continental Congress.

. . . .

In September 1774, 55 delegates from all the colonies except Georgia arrived in Philadelphia. They had come to establish a political body to represent American interests and challenge British control. They called the new organization the **Continental Congress.**

Delegates to the Congress

Political leaders from across the colonies attended the Congress. Massachusetts sent fiery Samuel Adams and his cousin **John Adams,** a lawyer. New York sent **John Jay,** another lawyer. From Virginia came **Richard Henry Lee** and Patrick Henry, two outspoken defenders of colonial rights, as well as **George Washington.** Patrick Henry summed up the meaning of the gathering:

PRIMARY SOURCE

"The distinctions between Virginians, Pennsylvanians, New Yorkers, and New Englanders, are no more. I am not a Virginian, but an American."
—Patrick Henry, at the Continental Congress

Decisions of the Congress

The delegates drafted a statement of grievances calling for the repeal of 13 acts of Parliament. They believed these laws violated the "laws of nature, the principles of the English constitution, and the several charters" of the colonies. The delegates voted to boycott British trade. No British goods could be brought in or used in the colonies. No colonial goods could be sold to Britain.

The Congress also decided to endorse the Suffolk Resolves, so named because they were prepared by the people of Suffolk County, Massachusetts. These resolutions called on the people of the county to arm themselves against the British. The people responded by forming **militias**—groups of citizen soldiers.

Reading Check **Explaining** What was the purpose of the Continental Congress?

If You Were There / Militias in the Colonies

Citizen Soldiers Even before the American Revolution, the American colonists had a long tradition of serving in the military. If you were a member of a militia, you were an important part of the defense of your town. You trained and drilled with the other soldiers. You practiced musket and cannon drills. You were required to provide your own weapons—usually a musket—and ammunition. As the break between Great Britain and the American colonies grew, town governments also supplied their militias. The chart to the left shows arms purchased by the town of Salem, Massachusetts.

Purchases authorized by Salem Provincial Congress, October 1774	
20 tons grape- and round shot, from 3 to 24 lb. @ £15	£300
10 tons bomb shells @ £20	£200
5 tons lead balls @ £33	£165
1,000 barrels of powder @ £8	£8,000
5,000 arms and bayonets @ £2	£10,000
And 75,000 flints	£100

Critical Thinking

Speculating What advantages would local militias have against British soldiers?

The First Battles

Main Idea America's fight for independence began when British troops clashed with minutemen at Lexington and Concord.

History and You Why would the element of surprise be a valuable weapon during a war? Read to learn how the minutemen used the element of surprise to their advantage.

Colonists expected that if fighting against the British broke out, it would begin in New England. Militia companies in Massachusetts held frequent training sessions, made bullets, and stockpiled rifles and muskets. Some companies, known as **minutemen,** boasted they would be ready to fight on a minute's notice. In the winter of 1774–1775, a British officer stationed in Boston noted in his diary:

PRIMARY SOURCE

"The people are evidently making every preparation for resistance. They are taking every means to provide themselves with Arms."

—from *Diary of Frederick Mackenzie*

Britain Sends Troops

The British also prepared for conflict. King George announced to Parliament that the New England Colonies were "in a state of rebellion" and said that "blows must decide" who would control America. By April 1775, several thousand British soldiers were in and around Boston, with many more on the way. Their general, Thomas Gage, had instructions to take away the weapons of the Massachusetts militia and arrest the leaders.

Gage learned that the militia was storing arms and ammunition at Concord, a town about 20 miles (32 km) northwest of Boston. He ordered 700 troops under Lieutenant Colonel Francis Smith to march "to Concord, where you will seize and destroy all the artillery and ammunition you can find."

Alerting the Colonists

On the night of April 18, 1775, Dr. Joseph Warren walked the streets of Boston looking for any unusual activity by the British army. He saw a regiment form ranks in Boston Common and begin to march out of the city.

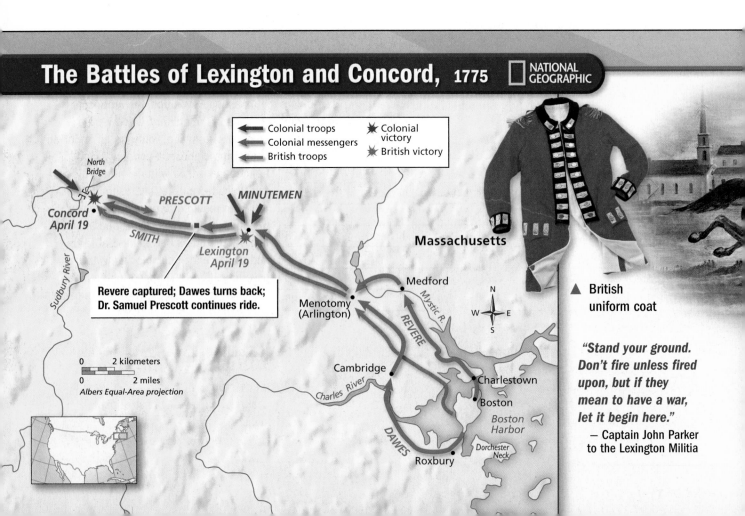

The Battles of Lexington and Concord, 1775 — NATIONAL GEOGRAPHIC

Colonial troops
Colonial messengers
British troops
Colonial victory
British victory

North Bridge

Concord April 19

PRESCOTT

MINUTEMEN

SMITH

Lexington April 19

Sudbury River

Revere captured; Dawes turns back; Dr. Samuel Prescott continues ride.

Menotomy (Arlington)

Medford

Mystic R.

REVERE

Massachusetts

0 — 2 kilometers
0 — 2 miles
Albers Equal-Area projection

Cambridge

Charles River

DAWES

Charlestown

Boston

Boston Harbor

Dorchester Neck

Roxbury

▲ British uniform coat

"Stand your ground. Don't fire unless fired upon, but if they mean to have a war, let it begin here."
— Captain John Parker to the Lexington Militia

Warren rushed to alert **Paul Revere** and William Dawes, members of the Sons of Liberty. Revere and Dawes rode to Lexington, a town east of Concord, to warn Samuel Adams and John Hancock that the British were coming. Revere galloped across the moonlit countryside, shouting, "The regulars are out!" to people along the way. Upon hearing the news, Adams exclaimed, "What a glorious morning this is!" Adams was ready to fight for independence.

Lexington and Concord

At dawn the redcoats **approached,** or moved closer to, Lexington. There they discovered about 70 minutemen who had been alerted by Revere and Dawes. Led by Captain John Parker, the minutemen stood on the town common with muskets in hand. A minuteman reported:

PRIMARY SOURCE

"There suddenly appeared a number of the king's troops . . . the foremost of which cried, 'Throw down your arms, ye villains, ye rebels!'"
—from *The Military Journals of Two Private Soldiers*

A shot was fired, and then both sides let loose an exchange of bullets. When the fighting ended, eight minutemen lay dead. The British troops continued their march to Concord. When they arrived, they found that most of the militia's gunpowder had already been removed. They destroyed the remaining supplies. At Concord's North Bridge, waiting minutemen turned back the British.

Messengers on horseback had spread word of the British movements. All along the road from Concord to Boston, farmers, blacksmiths, and clerks hid behind trees and stone fences. As the British marched down the road, the militia fired. By the time the redcoats reached Boston, at least 174 were wounded and 73 were dead.

Looking back, the poet Ralph Waldo Emerson wrote in "The Concord Hymn" that the Americans at Lexington and Concord had fired the "shot heard 'round the world." The battle for independence had begun.

Reading Check **Explaining** How were the colonists preparing for war with Britain?

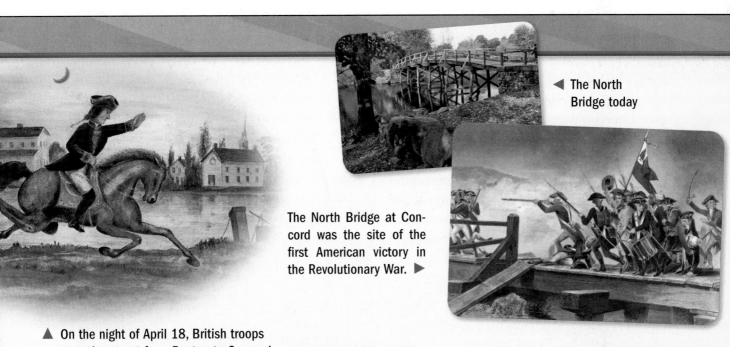

The North Bridge today

The North Bridge at Concord was the site of the first American victory in the Revolutionary War. ▶

▲ On the night of April 18, British troops secretly set out from Boston to Concord. Messengers, including Paul Revere (above), were sent to spread the alarm. When the British reached Lexington, Patriot minutemen were waiting.

Critical Thinking

Analyzing What happened after British forces reached Lexington?

Maps In Motion See StudentWorks™ Plus or glencoe.com.

The Spirit of Independence **Chapter 5** 135

People IN HISTORY

Patrick Henry

Lawyer and Revolutionary

Henry was one of the first members of the Virginia House of Burgesses to argue for independence from Britain. In a debate over whether the state should form a militia, he vowed, *"Give me liberty or give me death!"*

Samuel Adams

Patriot Leader in Boston

Adams argued that Massachusetts should be independent from Britain long before anyone else did. After the Townshend Acts were passed, he wrote that it was *"irreconcilable to . . . common sense and reason, that a British house of commons, should have a right . . . to give and grant the property of the Colonists."*

CRITICAL Thinking

1. **Synthesizing** What did Patrick Henry and Samuel Adams have in common?
2. **Analyzing** What do you think Patrick Henry meant when he said, "Give me liberty or give me death!"?

More Military Action

Main Idea As colonial militias formed and the fighting continued, American loyalties were split.

History and You Have you ever taken sides in a dispute between two friends? Read to learn how the issue of independence divided Americans.

Shortly after Lexington and Concord, Benedict Arnold, a captain in the Connecticut militia, was authorized to raise a force of 400 men to seize Fort Ticonderoga on Lake Champlain. Ticonderoga was not only strategically located but also rich in military supplies.

Arnold learned that Ethan Allen was also mounting an expedition in Vermont to attack the fort. Arnold joined his militia with Allen's force, known as the Green Mountain Boys. Together they caught the British by surprise. Fort Ticonderoga surrendered on May 10, 1775.

Later during the war, Arnold sold military information to the British. When he conspired to surrender the key fort of West Point to the British, his treason was discovered. Arnold fled to British-controlled New York City. He was given command of British troops and led raids against the Americans in Virginia and Connecticut.

Building Forces

After Lexington and Concord, the committees of correspondence sent out calls for **volunteers,** or helpers, to join the militias. Soon the colonial militia assembled around Boston was about 20,000 strong. For several weeks, the American and British armies waited nervously to see who would make the next move.

History ONLINE
Student Web Activity Visit glencoe.com and complete the Chapter 5 Web Activity about Benedict Arnold.

The Battle of Bunker Hill

On June 16, 1775, about 1,200 militiamen under the command of Colonel William Prescott set up fortifications at Bunker Hill and nearby Breed's Hill, across the harbor from Boston.

The British decided to drive the Americans from their strategic locations overlooking the city. The next day the redcoats assembled at the bottom of Breed's Hill. Bayonets drawn, they charged up the hill. With his forces low on ammunition, Colonel Prescott reportedly shouted the order, "Don't fire until you see the whites of their eyes." The Americans opened fire, forcing the British to retreat. The redcoats charged two more times, receiving furious fire. In the end the Americans ran out of gunpowder and had to withdraw.

The British won the Battle of Bunker Hill but suffered heavy losses—more than 1,000 dead and wounded. As one British officer wrote in his diary, "A dear bought victory, another such would have ruined us." The British had learned that defeating the Americans on the battlefield would not be quick or easy.

Choosing Sides

As American colonists heard about these battles, they faced a major decision. Should they join the rebels or remain loyal to Great Britain? Those who chose to stay with Britain, the **Loyalists,** did not consider unfair taxes and regulations good reasons for rebellion. Some Loyalists lived in relative isolation and had not been part of the wave of discontent that turned many Americans against Britain. Still others expected Britain to win the war and wanted to gain favor with the British.

The **Patriots,** on the other hand, were colonists who supported the war for independence. They believed that British rule had become unbearable. The Patriots were determined to fight the British until American independence was won.

The American Revolution was not just a war between the Americans and the British. It was also a civil war among colonists—Patriots against Loyalists.

Reading Check **Analyzing** What did the British learn from the Battle of Bunker Hill?

Section 3 Review

History ONLINE
Study Central™ To review this section, go to glencoe.com.

Vocabulary

1. Define each of the following terms and use them in a paragraph: militia, minutemen, approach, volunteer, Loyalist, Patriot.

Main Ideas

2. Explaining How did endorsement of the Suffolk Resolves by the Continental Congress push the colonies closer to war?

3. Describing What tactics did the colonists use against the British troops on their march back from Concord to Boston?

Critical Thinking

4. Interpreting Reread Patrick Henry's quote about the Continental Congress. What change was occurring in the way the colonists saw themselves?

5. Comparing and Contrasting Use a diagram like the one below to show the similarities and differences between Patriots and Loyalists.

Loyalists — Both — Patriots

6. Creative Writing Write a one-act play in which ordinary people in a small town react to the news of the Battle of Lexington. Remember that not all colonists wanted independence from Britain.

Answer the
7. Essential Question
What brought about the clash between American colonists and British soldiers at Lexington and Concord?

Moving Toward Independence

Essential Question

Why did the American colonies choose to declare independence?

Reading Guide

Content Vocabulary
petition (p. 140)   preamble (p. 142)

Academic Vocabulary
debate (p. 141)   status (p. 142)

Key People and Events
Second Continental Congress (p. 139)
Continental Army (p. 139)
Olive Branch Petition (p. 140)
Thomas Paine (p. 140)
Common Sense (p. 140)
Declaration of Independence (p. 141)

Reading Strategy
Taking Notes As you read, describe the parts of the Declaration of Independence. Use a diagram like the one below.

Declaration of Independence

Part 1:

↓

Part 2:

↓

Part 3:

↓

Part 4:

NEW YORK STANDARDS
The American Journey

U3.III.1 To understand how the colonists attempted to establish new forms of self-government

U3.III.2 To investigate key turning points in New York State and United States history and explain why these events or developments are significant

U3.III.4 To describe how ordinary people and famous historic figures in the local community, State, and the United States have advanced the fundamental democratic values, beliefs, and traditions expressed in the Declaration of Independence, the New York State and United States constitutions, the Bill of Rights, and other important historic documents

American Diary

Colonists debated the wisdom of pursuing peace or declaring independence from Britain. Thomas Paine wrote: "I have heard it asserted by some, that as America has flourished under her former connection with Great Britain, the same connection is necessary towards her future happiness. . . . Nothing can be more [false]. . . . We may as well assert that because a child has thrived upon milk, that it is never to have meat. . . . A government of our own is our natural right."

—*from* Common Sense

The Declaration of Independence is presented to the Second Continental Congress.

Colonial Leaders Emerge

Main Idea When the Second Continental Congress met for the first time, many leaders were not yet ready to call for independence.

History and You Do newspapers, books, or television news programs affect your opinion on important issues? Read to learn how a pamphlet by Thomas Paine influenced colonial opinion.

. . . .

On May 10, 1775, the **Second Continental Congress** assembled for the first time. However, many delegates were not yet prepared to break away from Great Britain. It would be another year before John Adams would ask Thomas Jefferson to write the Declaration of Independence.

The delegates to the Second Continental Congress included some of the greatest political leaders in America. Among those attending were John and Samuel Adams, Patrick Henry, Richard Henry Lee, and George Washington—all delegates to the First Continental Congress held in 1774. Several distinguished new delegates came as well.

Benjamin Franklin, one of the most respected men in the colonies, had been an influential member of the Pennsylvania legislature. In 1765, during the Stamp Act crisis, he represented the colonies in London and helped secure the repeal of the act.

John Hancock of Massachusetts was a wealthy merchant. He funded many Patriot groups, including the Sons of Liberty. The delegates chose Hancock as president of the Second Continental Congress.

Thomas Jefferson, only 32, had already earned a reputation as a brilliant thinker and writer. He served in the Virginia legislature.

The Second Continental Congress began to govern the colonies. It authorized the printing of money and set up a post office with Franklin in charge. It established committees to communicate with Native Americans and with other countries. Most important, the Congress created the **Continental Army** to fight against Britain in a more organized way than the colonial militias could. On John Adams's recommendation, the Congress unanimously chose George Washington to be the army's commander.

Primary Source | Creating the Declaration

Adams and Jefferson By June 1776, the Second Continental Congress was ready to separate from Britain. John Adams, Benjamin Franklin, Thomas Jefferson, Robert Livingston, and Roger Sherman formed the committee to draft a statement. Adams asked Jefferson to write the document because "he was so prompt, frank, explicit, and decisive upon committees and in conversation." Jefferson was reluctant, but Adams persuaded him, saying: "Reason first—You are a Virginian, and a Virginian ought to appear at the head of this business. Reason second—I am obnoxious, suspected, and unpopular. You are very much otherwise. Reason third—you can write ten times better than I can."

—from *The Writings of Thomas Jefferson*

◀ Early draft of the Declaration of Independence

Critical Thinking

Explaining What were Adams's reasons for wanting Jefferson to draft the Declaration of Independence?

YOU DECIDE

Independence: Yes or No?

Many Americans were uncertain whether independence was the correct course for the colonies. After Americans and British troops had fought, however, other colonists felt strongly that independence should be their goal.

In 1776 Thomas Paine made an impassioned appeal for independence in his pamphlet *Common Sense:*

THOMAS PAINE — **YES**

"Every thing that is right or natural pleads for separation. The blood of the slain, the weeping voice of nature cries, 'tis time to part.'"

Other Americans did not want to break away from Britain. Colonists who felt a strong sense of loyalty to the king were called Loyalists. They believed British law should be upheld.

Loyalist Charles Inglis argued against going to war with Britain, saying:

CHARLES INGLIS — **NO**

"Ruthless war, with all its aggravated horrors, will ravage our once happy land—our seacoasts and ports will be ruined, and our ships taken. Torrents of blood will be spilt, and thousands reduced to beggary and wretchedness."

DBQ Document-Based Questions

1. **Analyzing** What is Paine's argument in favor of independence?
2. **Identifying** What did Inglis believe would result from war with Britain?

After Washington left to take charge of the forces in Boston, the delegates offered Britain one last chance to avoid war. The Congress sent a **petition,** or formal request, to George III. Called the **Olive Branch Petition,** it assured the king of the colonists' desire for peace and asked him to protect the colonists' rights. George III refused to receive the Olive Branch Petition. Instead he prepared for war, hiring more than 30,000 German troops to fight beside British troops.

The Colonies Take the Offensive

Meanwhile the Congress learned that British troops in what is now Canada were planning to invade New York. The Americans decided to strike first. Marching north from Fort Ticonderoga, a Patriot force captured Montreal. An American attack on Quebec led by Benedict Arnold failed, however.

Washington reached Boston in July 1775, a few weeks after the Battle of Bunker Hill. While he found the size of the militia growing every day, Washington realized that the members lacked discipline, organization, and leadership. He began the hard work of shaping these armed civilians into an army.

By March 1776, Washington judged the Continental Army ready to fight. He positioned the army in a semicircle around Boston and gave the order for its cannons to bombard the British forces. The redcoats, under Sir William Howe, hurriedly withdrew from the city. On March 17, Washington led his jubilant troops into Boston. The British troops sailed to Halifax, Nova Scotia.

Moving Toward Independence

In early 1776, support for the position of absolute independence was growing. In January 1776, **Thomas Paine** published a pamphlet called ***Common Sense.*** In bold language, Paine called for complete independence. *Common Sense* greatly influenced opinion throughout the colonies.

Reading Check **Explaining** What was the significance of the Olive Branch Petition?

History ONLINE
Chapter Overview Visit glencoe.com
and click on **Chapter 6—Chapter Overviews**
to preview chapter information.

Section 1: The Early Years

Essential Question What challenges did the American revolutionaries face at the start of the war?

Section 2: The War Continues

Essential Question How did the United States gain allies and aid during the Revolutionary War?

Section 3: The War Moves West and South

Essential Question How did fighting in the West and South affect the course of the Revolutionary War?

Section 4: The War Is Won

Essential Question How did the Battle of Yorktown lead to American independence?

FOLDABLES
Study Organizer

Summarizing Information

Make this Foldable to help you summarize what you learn about the Revolutionary War.

Step 1 Begin with a 11" x 17" piece of paper.

Step 2 Fold the sides of the paper into the middle to make a shutter fold.

Step 3 Label the tabs as shown.

Reading and Writing As you read the chapter, list important battles, people, and other facts under the correct tabs.

Continental infantryman ▶

★ **1779**
Spain declares war on Britain

1780

★ **1780**
British forces capture Charles Town, South Carolina

★ **1780**
Britain declares war on Holland

★ **1781**
British surrender at Yorktown

1782

★ **1782**
Spain completes conquest of Florida

★ **1783**
Treaty of Paris

★ **1783**
Famine in Japan

The Early Years

Essential Question ◄

What challenges did the American revolutionaries face at the start of the war?

Reading Guide

Content Vocabulary

mercenary (p. 155)   recruit (p. 155)

Academic Vocabulary

transfer (p. 155)   previous (p. 155)

Key People and Events

Hessian (p. 155)

Molly Pitcher (p. 155)

General William Howe (p. 156)

Nathan Hale (p. 156)

Lemuel Hayes (p. 157)

Peter Salem (p. 157)

Benedict Arnold (p. 159)

General Horatio Gates (p. 159)

Reading Strategy

Taking Notes As you read, use a diagram like the one below to list the Patriot defeats and victories during the early years of the American Revolution.

Early Battles
- Defeats
- Victories

NEW YORK STANDARDS
The American Journey

U3.III.2 To investigate key turning points in New York State and United States history and explain why these events or developments are significant

U3.III.4 To describe how ordinary people and famous historic figures in the local community, State, and the United States have advanced the fundamental democratic values, beliefs, and traditions expressed in the Declaration of Independence, the New York State and United States constitutions, the Bill of Rights, and other important historic documents

U3.IV.1 To understand how the colonists were able to unite against British power to win a major military and political victory

American Diary

On the night of July 9, 1776, General George Washington asked that the Declaration of Independence be read to his assembled troops in New York City. Later that night, a crowd of American soldiers and civilians marched to a park, where they toppled a gold-leafed statue of Britain's king George III on horseback. "In it were 4,000 Pounds of Lead," a lieutenant in the Continental Army said, ". . . to be run up into Musquet Balls [bullets] for the use of the Yankies."

—*from the* Journal of Lieutenant Isaac Bangs

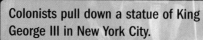

Colonists pull down a statue of King George III in New York City.

The Opposing Sides

Main Idea The British and American forces each had advantages and disadvantages during the war for American independence.

History and You What qualities should a leader have? Read to learn how George Washington's leadership qualities were an advantage for the Patriots.

As the toppling of the king's statue demonstrated, tensions between the colonies and Great Britain had reached a critical point after years of disagreement and negotiation. After the colonies declared independence from Britain in July 1776, the war for freedom was unavoidable.

Both sides expected the war for independence to be short. The British planned to crush the rebellion by force. Most of the Patriots—Americans who supported independence—believed the British would give up after losing one or two major battles. Few Patriots believed John Adams when he predicted in April 1776: "We shall have a long . . . and bloody war to go through."

At first glance the British had an overwhelming advantage in the war. They had the strongest navy in the world. They also had an experienced, well-trained army and the wealth of a worldwide empire. Great Britain also had a much larger population than the United States. More than 8 million people resided in Britain, compared with only 2.5 million in the United States.

The colonists suffered serious disadvantages. They lacked a regular army and a strong navy. American soldiers also lacked experience. Weapons and ammunition were in short supply. Many Patriots belonged to militia groups—local forces. However, they were volunteer soldiers who fought for short periods of time before returning home.

The Patriots faced another obstacle. Not all Americans supported the struggle for independence. Some people were neutral, taking neither side in the conflict. The Quakers, for example, would not participate in the war because they opposed all armed conflict. Still other Americans remained loyal to Britain.

The Loyalists

Those Americans who remained loyal to Britain and opposed the war for independence were called Loyalists or Tories. At least one American in five were thought to be Loyalists—perhaps as many as one in three. Some people changed sides during the war,

Primary Source / **The Liberty Bell**

Symbol of Freedom "Get us a good bell," wrote Isaac Norris, a Pennsylvania political leader to an aide in London in 1751. Arriving in 1752, the Liberty Bell was hung in the Pennsylvania State House (now Independence Hall). Its most famous ringing, on July 8, 1776, announced the first public reading of the Declaration of Independence. The Liberty Bell was rung every Fourth of July and for many public events until a crack appeared in about 1846. Today, the Liberty Bell is a symbol of freedom in the United States and throughout the world.

Critical Thinking

Speculating Why do you think symbols, such as statues, flags, and bells, are important to the people of a country?

THEN In 1776 women could not officially join the army. Yet their contributions proved critical to the war effort. Some women spied on British soldiers while others traveled with the troops, serving as cooks, seamstresses, and nurses. A few women even disguised themselves as men in order to become soldiers.

◄ Female Continental soldier

Colonist Lydia Darrah spied on the British and passed information to the Continental Army. ►

depending on which army was closer. Loyalist support varied from region to region throughout the war. In general, it was strongest in the Carolinas and Georgia and weakest in New England.

Loyalists supported Britain for different reasons. Some people remained loyal because they were members of the Anglican Church, headed by the British king. Others depended on the British for their jobs. Some Loyalists feared the disorder that might break out from challenging the established government. Others simply could not understand what all the commotion was about and why the colonies wanted independence. No other country, one Loyalist complained, "faced a rebellion arising from such trivial causes."

Friends and families were divided over their loyalty to Britain. For example, William Franklin, son of Patriot Benjamin Franklin, was a Loyalist who had served as a royal governor. As one Connecticut man observed:

PRIMARY SOURCE

"Neighbor [was] . . . against neighbor, father against son and son against father, and he that would not thrust his own blade through his brother's heart was called an infamous villain."

—from *Less Than Glory*, by Norman Gelb

African Americans in the War

Some African Americans also sided with the Loyalists. At the start of the war, the British appealed to enslaved Africans to join them. Lord Dunmore, the royal governor of Virginia, announced that enslaved people who fought on the British side would be freed. Many men answered his call. Eventually some of them ended up free in Canada. Others settled in the British colony of Sierra Leone in Africa.

Patriot Advantages

The Americans held some advantages. They were fighting on their own ground and fought with great determination to protect

NOW Today, women play a critical role in the U.S. military. By the mid-1990s, Congress had opened nearly all military jobs to women, including combat roles. Today, about one in every seven soldiers on active duty is a woman, and many women hold leadership positions throughout the armed forces.

Critical Thinking

Analyzing The Revolutionary War was fought on American soil. How do you think this fact influenced the role of women in the war?

it. The British, however, had to wage war in a faraway land. They were forced to ship soldiers and supplies thousands of miles across the Atlantic.

Another advantage for the Americans was the type of soldiers fighting for the British. The British relied on **mercenaries**—hired soldiers—to fight for them. The Americans called the mercenaries **Hessians,** after the region in Germany from where most of them came. The Patriots were fighting for the freedom of their own land. They believed they had a much greater stake in winning the war than the hired soldiers did, who were fighting for money. This belief gave the Americans an edge over the Hessians in battle.

The Americans' greatest advantage was probably their leader, George Washington. Few could match him for courage, honesty, and determination. The war might have taken a different turn without Washington.

Raising an Army

The Americans placed great value on liberty and personal freedom for citizens. After throwing off the rule of the British Parliament, they were unwilling to **transfer**—or move—power to their own Continental Congress. In some ways the American Revolution was really 13 separate wars, with each state pursuing its own interests. As a result, the Congress experienced difficulty enlisting soldiers and raising money to fight the war.

The militia played an essential role in the Patriots' forces. However, the Americans also needed well-trained soldiers who could fight anywhere in the colonies. The Congress established the Continental Army but depended on the states to **recruit,** or enlist, soldiers.

At first, soldiers signed up for one year of army service. General Washington appealed for longer terms. "If we ever hope for success," he said, "we must have men enlisted for the whole term of the war." Eventually the Continental Congress offered enlistments for three years or for the length of the war. Most soldiers, however, still signed up for only one year.

It was also difficult to recruit officers. The best officers in the Continental Army were veterans of **previous,** or earlier, wars or young men who were recruited from the ranks.

Women also fought with the Patriot forces. Margaret Corbin of Pennsylvania went with her husband when he joined the Continental Army. After he died in battle, she took his place. Mary Ludwig Hays McCauley also joined her husband in battle. The soldiers called her "Moll of the Pitcher," or **Molly Pitcher,** because she carried water pitchers to the soldiers. As a teenager, Deborah Sampson of Massachusetts watched her brothers and their friends go off to war. She then disguised herself as a boy and enlisted.

Reading Check **Summarizing** What disadvantages did the Patriots face?

Patriot Defeats and Victories

Main Idea After suffering defeat at the Battle of Long Island, the Americans rallied and won victories at Trenton and Princeton.

History and You Do you think a single victory can help a struggling sports team with a losing record? Read to learn how American troops rallied following a crushing defeat by the British.

$\bullet$ $\bullet$ $\bullet$ $\bullet$ $\bullet$ $\bullet$ $\bullet$ $\bullet$ $\bullet$ $\bullet$ $\bullet$ $\bullet$ $\bullet$ $\bullet$ $\bullet$ $\bullet$ $\bullet$

Most of the early battles in the war involved few troops. At Bunker Hill, for example, about 2,200 British soldiers fought 1,200 Americans. The British had not yet won a decisive victory over the Patriots, however. They realized they would need more troops to end the war quickly.

During the summer of 1776, Britain sent 32,000 troops across the Atlantic to New York. The British commander, **General William Howe,** hoped the sheer size of his army would convince the Patriots to give up. He was soon disappointed.

Defeat on Long Island

Although Washington and the Patriots had fewer than 20,000 troops, they were determined to fight. In late August the two sides clashed in the Battle of Long Island. Outnumbered and outmaneuvered, the Continental Army suffered a serious defeat at the hands of the British forces.

One Patriot, **Nathan Hale,** proved himself a hero at Long Island. A teacher from Connecticut, Hale volunteered to spy on British troops. He disguised himself as a Dutch schoolteacher. The British discovered his true identity, however, and hanged him. According to tradition, just before his hanging Hale said, "I only regret that I have but one life to lose for my country."

Although the Americans showed bravery, they ran short of supplies for the army. In the autumn of 1776, a British officer wrote that many of the Patriot soldiers killed on Long Island had not been wearing shoes, socks, or jackets. "They are also in great want of blankets," he said, predicting that the rebels would suffer during the winter.

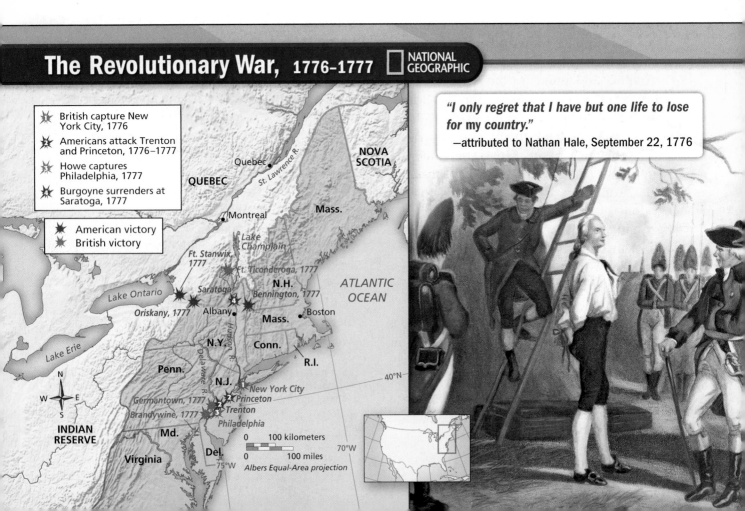

The Revolutionary War, 1776–1777 — NATIONAL GEOGRAPHIC

- British capture New York City, 1776
- Americans attack Trenton and Princeton, 1776–1777
- Howe captures Philadelphia, 1777
- Burgoyne surrenders at Saratoga, 1777

★ American victory
★ British victory

"I only regret that I have but one life to lose for my country."
—attributed to Nathan Hale, September 22, 1776

0 100 kilometers
0 100 miles
Albers Equal-Area projection

Independence

Main Idea The Patriots' spirit and resolve helped them win independence.

History and You What sort of influence do you think America's fight for independence had on the rest of the world? Read to find out how American ideals affected the world.

. . . .

The fighting did not end with Cornwallis's surrender at Yorktown. The British still held Savannah, Charles Town, and New York. A few more clashes took place on land and sea. The victory at Yorktown, however, convinced the British that the war was too costly to **pursue,** or continue.

The two sides sent delegates to Paris to work out a treaty. **Benjamin Franklin, John Adams,** and **John Jay** represented the United States. The American Congress **ratified,** or approved, the preliminary treaty in April 1783. The final **Treaty of Paris** was signed on September 3, 1783. By that time Britain had also made peace with France and Spain.

The Treaty of Paris was a triumph for the Americans. Great Britain recognized the United States as an independent nation. The British promised to withdraw all their troops from American territory. They also agreed to give Americans the right to fish in the waters off the coast of Canada.

The United States, in turn, agreed that British merchants could collect debts that Americans owed them. The treaty also stated that the Congress would advise the states to return to Loyalists the properties taken from them.

The Newburgh Conspiracy

Washington headquartered his strong army in Newburgh, New York, after the British surrendered. The Congress refused to fund the soldiers' pensions and failed to provide them with other pay. The soldiers' anger mounted. In disgust, some officers circulated a letter in March 1783. If their demands were not met, the letter said, the army should use force against Congress.

Washington realized that this threat of revolt was dangerous. The new nation could be destroyed. He persuaded the angry soldiers to be patient. Then Washington urged the Congress to meet their just demands. Washington's leadership ended the threat to the new nation. The Congress soon acted on the demands.

Washington Resigns

British troops left New York City in late November 1783. The war had truly ended. Washington could at last give up his command. On December 4, Washington said farewell to his troops. Three weeks later he formally resigned at a meeting of the Second Continental Congress. Washington said, "Having now finished the work assigned me I retire . . . and take my leave of all the employments of public life."

Washington returned home to Mount Vernon, Virginia, in time for Christmas. There he planned to remain and live quietly with his family.

Dr. Benjamin Rush ▶

Dr. Benjamin Rush, one of Washington's critics, served as surgeon general in the Continental Army. In a letter to John Adams, Rush compared Washington unfavorably to the hero of Saratoga, Horatio Gates.

"I have heard several officers who have served under General Gates compare his army to a well regulated family. . . . [They] have compared General Washington's imitation of an army to an unformed mob."

Critical Thinking

Analyzing What pressures did Washington face as a leader? Why do you think he did not quit?

Why the Americans Won

How did the Americans manage to win the Revolutionary War? How did they defeat Britain, the world's greatest power?

The Americans had several advantages in the war. First, they fought on their own land while the British had to bring troops and supplies from thousands of miles away. The siege of Yorktown showed how much the British depended on the sea. When their ships were blocked, the British troops had no support. Also, the Americans knew the local terrain and where to lay an **ambush**—a surprise attack. The British, in contrast, had much difficulty controlling the American countryside once they occupied the cities.

Second, help from other nations contributed to the American victory. The French supplied soldiers, ships, and loans. The Spanish gave aid when they attacked the British in the Mississippi Valley and along the Gulf of Mexico.

Perhaps most important, the American Revolution was a people's movement. Its outcome depended not on any one battle or event but on the determination and spirit of all Patriots. As Washington remarked about the patriotic crowds, "Here is an army they [the British] will never conquer."

Influence of the American Revolution

In 1776 the American colonists began a revolution. They made clear the principles of freedom and the rights outlined in the Declaration of Independence. These ideas bounded back across the Atlantic to influence the French Revolution. French rebels in 1789 fought in defense of "Liberty, Equality, and Fraternity." The French upheld these principles: "Men are born and remain free and equal in rights."

In 1791 the ideals of the American and French Revolutions traveled across the Caribbean and the Atlantic to the French colony of Saint Domingue. Inspired by talk of freedom, enslaved Africans took up arms. Led by Toussaint-Louverture, they shook off French rule. In 1804 Saint Domingue—present-day Haiti—became the second nation in the Americas to achieve independence from colonial rule. "We have asserted our rights," declared the revolutionaries. "We swear never to yield them to any power on earth."

 Reading Check **Explaining** Why did Washington take action to end the Newburgh Conspiracy?

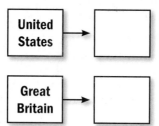

Section 4 Review

History ONLINE **Study Central™** To review this section, go to glencoe.com.

Vocabulary

1. Using complete sentences, define the following terms: strategy, pursue, ratify, ambush.

Main Ideas

2. Summarizing What role did the French play in the Patriot victory at Yorktown?

3. Explaining Why were the Americans successful in their fight for independence?

Critical Thinking

4. Categorizing Use a diagram like the one below to show what the United States and Great Britain agreed to in the Treaty of Paris.

```
┌──────────┐      ┌──────────┐
│ United   │ ───▶ │          │
│ States   │      │          │
└──────────┘      └──────────┘

┌──────────┐      ┌──────────┐
│ Great    │ ───▶ │          │
│ Britain  │      │          │
└──────────┘      └──────────┘
```

5. Expository Writing Write a paragraph comparing Washington's original plans to attack the British with his new secret strategy.

Answer the Essential Question

6. How did the Battle of Yorktown lead to American independence?

History ONLINE

For additional test practice, use **Self-Check Quizzes**–Chapter 6 at glencoe.com.

Document-Based Questions

Directions: Analyze the documents and answer the short-answer questions that follow.

Document 1

This is an excerpt from a document known as the Connecticut Slaves Petition for Freedom dated May 11, 1779.

> And we not only groan under our own burden, but with concern, & Horror, look forward, & contemplate, the miserable Condition of our Children, who are training up, and kept in Preparation, for a like State of Bondage, and Servitude. [We ask] your Honours serious Consideration, whether it is consistent with the present Claims, of the united States, to hold so many Thousands . . . in perpetual Slavery.

Source: Connecticut Slaves Petition for Freedom (1779)

7 What basic argument against slavery did the writers base their petition on?

Document 2

This is an excerpt from a letter from George Washington to John Hancock dated September 24, 1776.

> When Men are irritated, and the Passions inflamed, they fly hastely and chearfully to Arms; but after the first emotions are over, to expect, among such People, as compose the bulk of an Army, that they are influenced by any other principles than those of Interest, is to look for what never did, and I fear never will happen; the Congress will deceive themselves therefore if they expect it.

Source: *From Revolution to Reconstruction*

8 Based on the document, did Washington believe people could successfully be persuaded to join the Continental Army simply by appealing to their feelings of patriotism? Explain.

Document 3

In this document, Andrew Sherburne describes his experiences on a privateer ship during the Revolutionary War.

> I was not yet fourteen years of age. . . . The boys were employed in waiting on the officers, but in time of action a boy was quartered [assigned] to each gun to carry cartridges.

Source: "Andrew Sherburne's Experiences on a Privateer During the Revolutionary War (1828)"

9 How old was Sherburne and what were his duties aboard ship?

Document 4

The following map shows areas of Patriot and Loyalist strength during the Revolutionary Era.

10 According to the map, where was Loyalist sentiment the strongest?

11 **Expository Writing** Using the information from the four documents and your knowledge of social studies, write an essay in which you:
- explain how the war demonstrated the democratic ideals of the Patriots; and
- describe some ways those ideals were *not* upheld.

Need Extra Help?											
If You Missed Questions. . .	1	2	3	4	5	6	7	8	9	10	11
Go to Page. . .	158	163–164	172	177	155–157	153–176	154–157	155	170	153–154	164–165

Chapter 7

A More Perfect Union 1777–1790

Delegates to the Constitutional Convention, 1787

U.S. Events

World Events

1776

1779

1782

★ **1777**
Articles of
Confederation
written

1781 ★
Robert Morris
serves as superin-
tendent of finance
for the U.S.

★ **1783**
Treaty of
Paris

1778 ★
France goes
to war
against
Britain

1780 ★
League of
Armed
Neutrality
is formed

1782 ★
Rama I starts new
dynasty in Siam

Palace, Bangkok,
Thailand (Siam) ▶

Section 1: The Articles of Confederation
Essential Question How effective was government under the Articles of Confederation?

Section 2: Convention and Compromise
Essential Question Why is the Constitution a document of compromises?

Section 3: A New Plan of Government
Essential Question What ideas and features are found in the United States Constitution?

FOLDABLES Study Organizer

Organizing Information Make this Foldable to help you organize what you learn about the differences between the Articles of Confederation and the Constitution.

Step 1 Fold an 11" x 17" piece of paper lengthwise to create three equal sections.

Step 2 Then fold it into four equal columns.

Step 3 Label your Foldable as shown.

Reading and Writing As you read, describe each document by identifying its purpose and features, and evaluate how effective it was for governing.

E PLURIBUS UNUM

U.S. gold coin ▲

1787
- Shays's Rebellion is suppressed
- U.S. introduces dollar currency
- Northwest Ordinance is passed

1788 U.S. Constitution is ratified

1790 Philadelphia becomes federal capital of the U.S.

1785 **1788** **1791**

1784 Russians establish colony on Kodiak Island, Alaska

1785 First hot air balloon crosses English Channel

1788 British establish penal colony in Australia

1789 French Revolution begins

◄ Guillotine

The Articles of Confederation

Essential Question

How effective was government under the Articles of Confederation?

Reading Guide

Content Vocabulary

constitution (p. 187) petition (p. 190)

bicameral (p. 187) ordinance (p. 190)

republic (p. 188) depreciate (p. 191)

Academic Vocabulary

abandon (p. 189) clause (p. 191)

Key People and Events

Articles of Confederation (p. 188)

John Adams (p. 193)

Reading Strategy

Taking Notes As you read, use a diagram like the one below to identify the powers of the national government under the Articles of Confederation.

Powers of National Government

NEW YORK STANDARDS
The American Journey

U3.IV.2 To understand how events on the national level influenced and affected New Yorkers

U3.V.1 To understand how a revolution can have a profound effect on the economic, political, and social fabric of a nation

U4.I.1 To understand the earliest formal structure of the United States government as expressed in the Articles of Confederation

U4.I.2 To consider the nature and evolution of constitutional democracies

American Diary

As British forces approached Philadelphia on September 19, 1777, John Adams and members of the Second Continental Congress fled to York, Pennsylvania. Adams wrote to his wife: "War has no Charms for me. If I live much longer in Banishment I shall scarcely know my own Children. Tell my little ones, that if they will be very good, Pappa will come home."

—from Letters of Delegates to Congress

Congress Hall in Philadelphia (building in the left front) was the meeting place of the U.S. Congress from 1790 to 1800.

From Independent States to a Republic

Main Idea The Articles of Confederation created a weak central government and strong state governments.

History and You How hard is it to get a group of friends to agree on what type of movie to watch or game to play? Read about what was necessary for the new Congress to pass a law.

It was important for the Second Continental Congress to create a plan for government that would satisfy the needs of all 13 states. The states were united against the British, but would they be able to work together and still maintain their independence? How would each state's government be organized? After rejecting British rule, the states' first task was to establish their own political institutions.

State Constitutions

In May 1776, the Continental Congress asked the states to organize their governments. Each state moved quickly to adopt a state **constitution,** or plan of government. By the end of 1776, eight states had drafted constitutions. New York and Georgia followed in 1777 and Massachusetts in 1780. Connecticut and Rhode Island kept their colonial charters as state constitutions.

Their experience with British rule made Americans cautious about placing too much power in the hands of a single ruler. For that reason, the states adopted constitutions that limited the power of the governor. Pennsylvania even replaced the office of governor with an elected council of 12 members.

Limiting Power

States also divided government functions between the governor (or Pennsylvania's council) and the legislature. Most states established two-house, or **bicameral,** legislatures to divide the power even further.

The writers of the constitutions not only wanted to prevent abuses of power in the states, but they also wanted to keep power in the hands of the people. State legislators were popularly elected, and elections were frequent. In most states, only white males who were at least 21 years old could vote. These citizens also had to own a certain amount of property or pay a certain amount of taxes. Some states allowed free African American males to vote.

When and Where — Capitals of the United States

Capital Cities of the United States

City	Length of Time as U.S. Capital
Philadelphia, Pennsylvania	May 10, 1775 to December 12, 1776
Baltimore, Maryland	December 20, 1776 to February 27, 1777
Philadelphia, Pennsylvania	March 4, 1777 to September 18, 1777
Lancaster, Pennsylvania	September 27, 1777 (one day)
York, Pennsylvania	September 30, 1777 to June 27, 1778
Philadelphia, Pennsylvania	July 2, 1778 to June 21, 1781
Princeton, New Jersey	June 30, 1783 to November 4, 1783
Annapolis, Maryland	November 26, 1783 to August 19, 1784
Trenton, New Jersey	November 1, 1784 to December 24, 1784
New York City, New York	January 11, 1785 to August 12, 1790
Philadelphia, Pennsylvania	December 6, 1790 to May 14, 1800
Washington, D.C.	November 17, 1800 to present

Nine different cities have served as capitals, or seats of government, of the United States.

Critical Thinking

Making Inferences Why do you think the United States had numerous capital cities between 1775 and 1800? Do you think it is important for a country to have a permanent location for its seat of government? Explain.

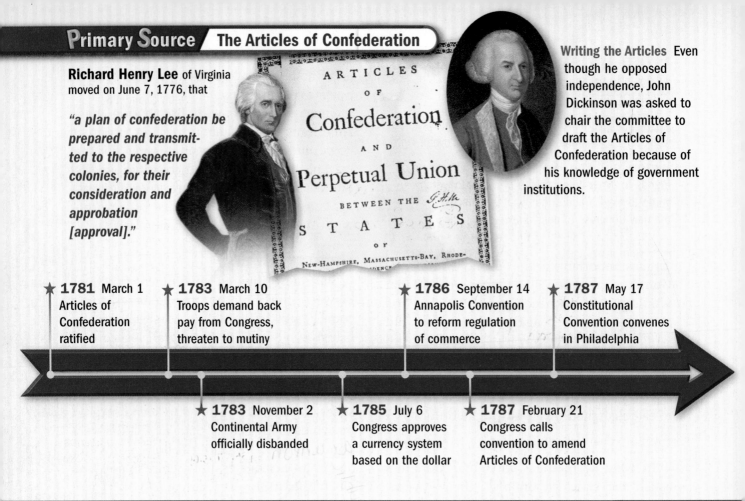

Richard Henry Lee of Virginia moved on June 7, 1776, that

"a plan of confederation be prepared and transmitted to the respective colonies, for their consideration and approbation [approval]."

Writing the Articles Even though he opposed independence, John Dickinson was asked to chair the committee to draft the Articles of Confederation because of his knowledge of government institutions.

ARTICLES OF Confederation AND Perpetual Union BETWEEN THE STATES OF NEW-HAMPSHIRE, MASSACHUSETTS-BAY, RHODE-...

1781 March 1 Articles of Confederation ratified

1783 March 10 Troops demand back pay from Congress, threaten to mutiny

1786 September 14 Annapolis Convention to reform regulation of commerce

1787 May 17 Constitutional Convention convenes in Philadelphia

1783 November 2 Continental Army officially disbanded

1785 July 6 Congress approves a currency system based on the dollar

1787 February 21 Congress calls convention to amend Articles of Confederation

State constitutions generally restricted the powers of the governors, which made the legislatures the most powerful branch of government. The state legislatures struggled to make taxes more fair, but disagreements arose. New challenges emerged as dependent colonies became self-governing states.

Forming a Republic

Americans agreed that their country should be a **republic,** a government in which citizens rule through elected representatives. They could not agree, however, on the organization and powers of their new republic. At first, most Americans favored a weak central government. They assumed the states would be like small, independent countries—similar to the way the colonies had been organized. The states would act independently on most issues, working together through a central government only to wage war and handle relations with other nations.

Planning a New Government

In 1776 the Second Continental Congress appointed a committee to draw up a plan for a new government. After much debate, the Congress adopted the **Articles of Confederation** in November 1777. The Articles, America's first constitution, provided for a new central government under which the states kept most of their power. For the states, the Articles of Confederation were "a firm league of friendship" in which each state retained "its sovereignty, freedom and independence." Under the Articles of Confederation, Congress had the authority to conduct foreign affairs, maintain armed forces, borrow money, and issue currency.

Congress, however, did not have the power to regulate trade, force citizens to join the army, or impose taxes. If Congress needed to raise money or troops, it had to ask the state legislatures—but they were not required to contribute.

Weaknesses of the Articles of Confederation

- Congress had no authority to raise money by collecting taxes
- Congress had no control over foreign trade

- Congress could not force states to carry out its laws
- All 13 states had to agree to any amendments, making it nearly impossible to correct problems

A Common Currency The national currency had little value. States issued their own money, and values varied from state to state.

According to George Washington, the Articles of Confederation were *"little more than the shadow without the substance."*

Regulating Trade Under the Articles of Confederation, the federal government did not have the authority to regulate commerce. In 1784 Congress wanted to take control of commerce for 15 years. The states, however, refused because they were afraid that Congress would then have too much power.

Critical Thinking

Predicting What economic problems might develop if a country uses different types of currency?

In addition, the government lacked a chief executive. The Confederation government carried on much of its business, such as selling western lands, through congressional committees.

The Articles of Confederation were not wholly supported by the states. Under the new plan, each state had one vote, regardless of its population, and all states had to approve the Articles and any amendments. States with large populations, however, believed they should have more votes. The states were also divided by whether or not they claimed land in the West. Maryland refused to approve the Articles until New York, Virginia, and other states **abandoned,** or gave up, land claims west of the Appalachian Mountains. Finally the states settled their differences. With Maryland's ratification, all 13 states approved the Articles. On March 1, 1781, the Confederation formally became the government of the United States of America.

The Confederation Government

The years between 1781 and 1789 were a critical period for the young American republic. The Articles of Confederation did not provide a government strong enough to handle the problems facing the United States. The Congress had limited authority. It could not pass a law unless 9 states voted in favor of it. Any attempt to change the Articles required the consent of all 13 states. This made it difficult for the Congress to pass laws when there was any opposition. Despite its weaknesses, the Confederation made some important achievements. Under the Confederation government, Americans won their independence from Britain and expanded the country's foreign trade. The Confederation also aided with settling and governing the nation's western territories.

Reading Check **Specifying** How many votes did each state have in the new Congress?

New Land Policies

Main Idea As people moved west, the country needed a process for new states joining the Union.

History and You Do you have to meet certain requirements to join some clubs or organizations? Read to learn the requirements for territories to become states.

⬤ ⬤

At the beginning of the Revolutionary War, only a few thousand settlers lived west of the Appalachian Mountains. By the 1790s, the number was approaching 120,000. These western settlers hoped to organize their lands as states and join the Union. The Articles of Confederation, however, did not contain a provision for adding new states. Congress realized that it had to extend its national authority over the frontier. During the 1780s, all of the states except Georgia gave up their claims to lands west of the Appalachians. The central government took control of these lands. In 1784 Congress divided the western territory into self-governing districts. When the number of people in a district reached the population of the smallest existing state, that district could **petition,** or apply to, Congress for statehood.

The Ordinance of 1785

In 1785 the Confederation Congress passed an **ordinance,** or law, that established a procedure for surveying and selling the western lands north of the Ohio River. The new law divided this massive territory into townships 6 miles long (9.7 km) and 6 miles wide (9.7 km). These townships were to be further divided into 36 sections of 640 acres (259 ha) each that would be sold at public auction for at least a dollar an acre. Land speculators viewed the law as an opportunity to accumulate large tracts of land cheaply. Concerned about lawless people moving into western lands, Richard Henry Lee, the president of the Congress, urged that "the rights of property be clearly defined" by the government. The Congress drafted another ordinance to protect the interests of hardworking settlers.

The Northwest Territory

NATIONAL GEOGRAPHIC

New Land The British gave up their claim to the Northwest Territory in the Treaty of Paris. After acquiring the land, Congress had to convince individual states to give up any claims they had on it. Then Congress had to negotiate treaties with Native Americans who were living in the Northwest Territory.

Legend:
- Northwest Territory
- Present-day state boundaries

Map labels: SPANISH LOUISIANA, Lake Superior, Mississippi River, Wisconsin, Lake Michigan, Lake Huron, Lake Ontario, Michigan, Lake Erie, Illinois, Indiana, Ohio, Ohio River, 40°N, 90°W, 80°W

0 200 kilometers
0 200 miles
Lambert Azimuthal Equal-Area projection

Township: American Building Block

Western lands north of the Ohio River were divided into townships 6 miles to a side. Each township contained 36 square miles, or "sections."

Township baseline 6 miles

Range line 6 miles

36	30	24	18	12	6
35	29	23	17	11	5
34	28	22	16	10	4
33	27	21	15	9	3
32	26	20	14	8	2
31	25	19	13	7	1

☐ Reserved for schools
☐ Reserved for federal government

Section 19
Half Section 320 acres
1 mile
Quarter Section 160 acres

The Northwest Ordinance

The Northwest Ordinance, passed in 1787, created a single Northwest Territory out of the lands north of the Ohio River and east of the Mississippi River. The lands were to be divided into three to five smaller territories. When the population of a territory reached 60,000, the people could petition for statehood. Each new state would have the same rights and privileges as the original 13 states. The Northwest Ordinance included a bill of rights for the settlers, guaranteeing freedom of religion and trial by jury. It also stated, "There shall be neither slavery nor involuntary servitude in said territory." This **clause,** or condition added to a document, marked the first attempt to stop the spread of slavery in the United States. The Ordinance of 1785 and the Northwest Ordinance opened the way for settlement of the Northwest Territory in a stable and orderly manner.

Reading Check **Explaining** What rule did the Northwest Ordinance have about slavery?

Trouble on Two Fronts

Main Idea Financial problems and disputes with Britain and Spain revealed serious weaknesses of the Confederation government.

History and You Imagine paying ten times the normal price for a gallon of milk or a loaf of bread. Read about the economic problems of the late 1700s.

. . . .

The Confederation government did not have enough power to deal with the country's financial problems and issues with other nations.

Financial Problems

By 1781, the money printed during the Revolutionary War **depreciated,** or fell in value, so far that it was almost worthless. Unable to collect taxes, the Continental Congress and the states printed their own paper money. No gold or silver backed up these bills, so they had no real value.

Paying Debts The government needed money to pay off the debt from the Revolutionary War. Much of the new territory's land was sold at auction to raise money to pay off that debt. The government did not have enough money to pay the Revolutionary War veterans' salaries. Instead, it gave veterans land in the Northwest Territory. ▼

▲ **New Settlements** Land speculators also bought large tracts of land in the Northwest Territory to sell to settlers for a profit. A group of land speculators built Campus Martius when they arrived in the Northwest Territory. Campus Martius served as a fort until the town of Marietta, in present-day Ohio, was established.

Critical Thinking

Analyzing How did settlers benefit from the Northwest Ordinance of 1787?

Economics & History

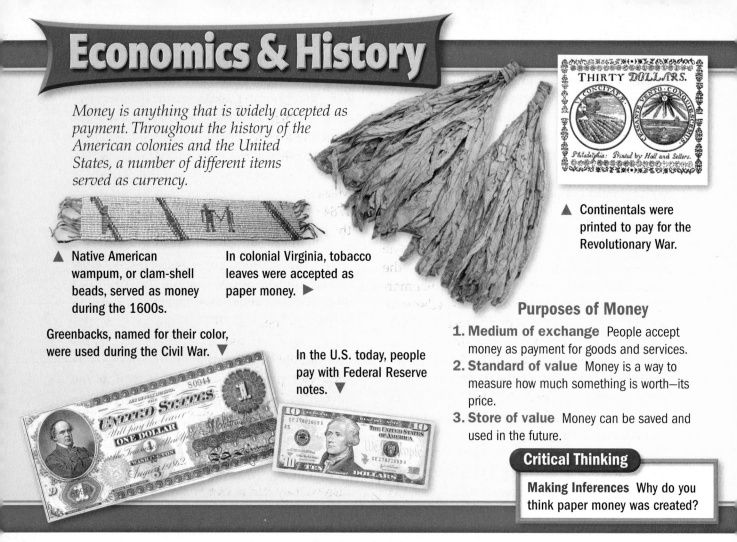

Money is anything that is widely accepted as payment. Throughout the history of the American colonies and the United States, a number of different items served as currency.

▲ Native American wampum, or clam-shell beads, served as money during the 1600s.

In colonial Virginia, tobacco leaves were accepted as paper money. ▶

▲ Continentals were printed to pay for the Revolutionary War.

Greenbacks, named for their color, were used during the Civil War. ▼

In the U.S. today, people pay with Federal Reserve notes. ▼

Purposes of Money

1. **Medium of exchange** People accept money as payment for goods and services.
2. **Standard of value** Money is a way to measure how much something is worth—its price.
3. **Store of value** Money can be saved and used in the future.

Critical Thinking

Making Inferences Why do you think paper money was created?

As more Continental dollars, or "Continentals," flowed into circulation, people realized that Congress could not redeem these bills for gold or silver. The public lost confidence in the money, and the value of the bills plummeted. Between 1779 and 1781, the number of Continental dollars required to buy one Spanish silver dollar rose from 40 to 146. "Not worth a Continental" became a common saying. At the same time, the price of food and other goods soared. In Boston and some other areas, high prices led to food riots.

The war for independence left the Continental Congress with a large debt. Congress had borrowed money from American citizens and foreign governments during the war. It still owed the Revolutionary soldiers their pay for their military service. Lacking the power to tax, the Confederation could not pay its debts. The Continental Congress requested funds from the states, but they were not required to contribute. The amount that was collected from the states amounted to only a small portion of the total money needed to pay off the debt.

Robert Morris's Import Tax

In 1781, faced with a total collapse of the country's finances, Congress created a department of finance led by Philadelphia merchant Robert Morris. While serving in Congress, Morris had proposed a 5 percent tax on imported goods to help pay the national debt. The plan required that the Articles of Confederation be changed to give Congress the power to levy the tax. Although 12 states approved the plan, Rhode Island's opposition killed it. A second effort in 1783 also failed to win unanimous approval by the states, and the financial crisis continued to worsen.

Problems With Britain

The weaknesses of the new American government became more evident as the United States encountered problems with other countries. In the Treaty of Paris of 1783, Britain promised to withdraw from the lands east of the Mississippi River. British troops, however, continued to occupy several strategic forts in the Great Lakes region.

British trade policy caused other problems. American merchants complained that the British were keeping Americans out of the West Indies and other profitable British markets. In 1785 Congress sent **John Adams** to London to discuss these difficulties. The British, however, were not willing to talk. They pointed to the failure of the United States to honor *its* promises made in the Treaty of Paris. The British claimed that Americans had agreed to pay Loyalists for the property taken from them during the Revolutionary War. The Congress had, in fact, recommended that the states pay the Loyalists. However, the states refused, and Congress could not require them to pay.

Problems With Spain

If American relations with Great Britain were poor, affairs with Spain were worse. Spain, which controlled Florida as well as lands west of the Mississippi River, was anxious to stop American expansion into its territory. As a result, Spain closed the lower Mississippi River to American shipping in 1784. Western settlers no longer had access to the Mississippi River, which they used for trade.

In 1786 American diplomats reached an agreement with Spain. Representatives from the Southern states, however, blocked the agreement because it did not include the right to use the Mississippi River. The weakness of the Confederation and its inability to deal with problems worried many leaders, including George Washington. Americans began to agree that the country needed a stronger government.

Reading Check **Analyzing** Why did Spain close the lower Mississippi River to American shipping in 1784?

Section 1 Review

History ONLINE
Study Central™ To review this section, go to glencoe.com.

Vocabulary

1. Define each of the following terms in a sentence: constitution, bicameral, republic, abandon, petition, ordinance, clause, depreciate.

Main Ideas

2. **Explaining** Why did most states limit the power of their governors and divide the legislature into two bodies?

3. **Specifying** According to the Northwest Ordinance, when might the people of a territory petition for statehood?

4. **Explaining** Why did the Continental Congress have difficulty raising money?

Critical Thinking

5. **Predicting** How do you think the Northwest Ordinance would affect Native Americans?

6. **Analyzing** Use a graphic organizer like the one below to summarize the strengths and weaknesses of the Confederation government.

7. **Persuasive Writing** You are a delegate to the Second Continental Congress. Congress is debating whether to allow the central government to impose taxes. Take a stand on this issue, and write a short essay defending your position. Give specific reasons for your opinion.

Answer the
8. **Essential Question**
How effective was government under the Articles of Confederation?

Convention and Compromise

Essential Question ◄

Why is the Constitution a document of compromises?

Reading Guide

Content Vocabulary

depression *(p. 195)*   proportional *(p. 199)*

manumission *(p. 197)*   compromise *(p. 200)*

Academic Vocabulary

convention *(p. 198)*   amend *(p. 199)*

Key People and Events

Shays's Rebellion *(p. 196)*

James Madison *(p. 197)*

Alexander Hamilton *(p. 197)*

Virginia Plan *(p. 199)*

New Jersey Plan *(p. 199)*

Great Compromise *(p. 200)*

Three-Fifths Compromise *(p. 201)*

Reading Strategy

Taking Notes As you read, use a graphic organizer like the one below to take notes about each individual's plan for creating a new government.

Leader	Role
Edmund Randolph	
James Madison	
Roger Sherman	
Gouverneur Morris	

NEW YORK STANDARDS
The American Journey

U3.V.2 To analyze how the values of a nation affect the guarantee of human rights and make provisions for human needs

U4.I.2 To consider the nature and evolution of constitutional democracies

U4.III.1 To understand the importance of the events that took place during the writing and adoption of the United States Constitution and to recognize their significance beyond their time and place

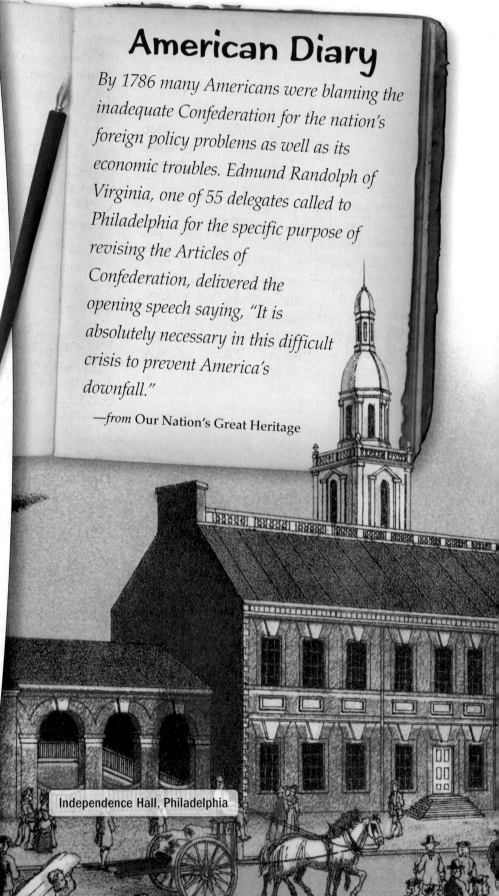

American Diary

By 1786 many Americans were blaming the inadequate Confederation for the nation's foreign policy problems as well as its economic troubles. Edmund Randolph of Virginia, one of 55 delegates called to Philadelphia for the specific purpose of revising the Articles of Confederation, delivered the opening speech saying, "It is absolutely necessary in this difficult crisis to prevent America's downfall."

—from **Our Nation's Great Heritage**

Independence Hall, Philadelphia

A Call for Change

Main Idea The government under the Articles of Confederation faced many problems.

History and You You make a plan, but the plan is not working—what do you do? Read to learn about the issues that challenged the government.

Many Americans called for the Articles of Confederation to be changed. They believed that the Confederation government was too weak to deal with the nation's problems. Those problems, however, were very difficult to solve. After the Revolutionary War, the United States experienced a **depression,** a period when economic activity slows and unemployment increases. Southern plantations were damaged during the war, and rice exports dropped sharply. Trade also decreased when the British closed the profitable West Indies market to American merchants. The little money that the government did have went to pay foreign debts, resulting in a serious currency shortage.

Shays's Rebellion

American farmers suffered because they could not sell their goods. They had trouble paying the money requested by the states to meet Revolutionary War debts. As a result state officials seized farmers' lands to pay their debts and threw many farmers in jail. Grumblings of protest soon grew into revolt. Resentment grew especially strong in Massachusetts. Farmers viewed the new government as just another form of tyranny. They wanted the government to issue paper money and make new policies to relieve debtors. In a petition to state officials, a number of farmers proclaimed:

PRIMARY SOURCE

"Surely your honours are not strangers to the distresses [problems] of the people but . . . know that many of our good inhabitants are now confined in [jail] for debt and taxes."
— "Petition from the Town of Greenwich, Massachusetts"

In 1786 angry farmers lashed out. Led by Daniel Shays, a former Continental Army captain, they forced courts in western Massachusetts to close so judges could not take away farmers' lands.

In January 1787, Shays led more than 1,000 farmers toward the federal arsenal in Springfield, Massachusetts, in search of guns and ammunition. The state militia ordered the advancing farmers to halt and then fired over their heads, but the farmers did not stop.

By the Numbers / Framers of the Constitution

Merchants 8

Lawyers 31

Politicians 4

Others 12

- Judges
- Physicians
- Planters
- Philosopher
- Professor
- Surveyor

Occupations of the Framers Edmund Randolph was a lawyer and a graduate of William and Mary College. Although he did not sign the United States Constitution, he had much in common with his fellow delegates at the Federal Convention of 1787. Of the 55 men designing and debating the Constitution, nearly half were college educated and almost two-thirds practiced law.

Source: *Fifty-Five Fathers: The Story of the Constitutional Convention*

Critical Thinking

Evaluating Do you think it is important for government leaders to have a college education? Why or why not?

Farmers Rebel in Massachusetts In 1787 Daniel Shays and rebellious farmers clashed with the state militia at the federal arsenal at Springfield.

"*Rebellion [against a king] may be pardoned, or lightly punished, but the man who dares to rebel against the laws of a republic ought to suffer death.*"

—Samuel Adams

◄ The federal arsenal at Springfield was used to store weapons and ammunition.

Shays and his followers attack the arsenal. ►

"*What country can preserve its liberties if their rulers are not warned from time to time that their people preserve the spirit of resistance?*"

—Thomas Jefferson, in a letter to William S. Smith, November 13, 1787

Critical Thinking

Evaluating In your opinion, is Jefferson or Adams correct in his thinking? Justify your answer.

The militia fired again, killing four farmers. Shays and his followers scattered, and the uprising was over. **Shays's Rebellion** frightened many Americans. They worried that the government could not control unrest and prevent violence. On hearing of the rebellion, George Washington wondered whether "mankind, when left to themselves, are unfit for their own government." Thomas Jefferson, minister to France at the time, had a different view. "A little rebellion, now and then," he wrote, "is a good thing."

The Issue of Slavery

The Revolutionary War brought attention to the contradiction between the American battle for liberty and the practice of slavery. Between 1776 and 1786, 11 states—all except South Carolina and Georgia—outlawed or heavily taxed the importation of enslaved people.

Although slavery was not a major source of labor in the North, it existed and was legal in all the Northern states. Many individuals and groups began to work to end the institution of slavery in America. In 1774 Quakers in Pennsylvania organized the first American antislavery society. Six years later Pennsylvania passed a law that provided for the gradual freeing of enslaved people. Between 1783 and 1804, Connecticut, Rhode Island, New York, and New Jersey passed laws that gradually ended slavery.

Still, free African Americans faced discrimination. They were barred from many public places, and few states gave free African Americans the right to vote. The children of most free blacks had to attend separate schools. Free African Americans established their own institutions—churches, schools, and mutual-aid societies—to seek social and economic opportunities.

The states south of Pennsylvania clung to the institution of slavery. The plantation system was built on slavery, and many Southerners feared that their economy could not survive without it.

History ONLINE

Student Web Activity Visit glencoe.com and complete the Chapter 7 Web Activity about Shays's Rebellion.

Nonetheless, an increasing number of slaveholders began freeing the enslaved people that they held after the war. Virginia passed a law that encouraged **manumission,** the freeing of individual enslaved persons, and the state's population of free African Americans grew.

The abolition of slavery in the North divided the new country on the critical issue of whether people should be allowed to keep other human beings in bondage. This division came at the time when many American leaders decided that the Articles of Confederation needed to be strengthened. In the summer of 1787, when state representatives assembled to plan a new government, they compromised on this issue. It would take a civil war to settle the slavery question.

Reading Check **Explaining** How did the North and South differ on slavery?

The Constitutional Convention

Main Idea National leaders reshape the government.

History and You When your family or group of friends faces a problem, does everyone agree to a solution right away? Read about how certain political views changed the United States government.

The American Revolution led to a union of 13 states, but it had not yet created a nation. Some leaders were satisfied with a system of independent state governments that resembled the old colonial governments. Others supported a strong national government. They demanded a reform of the Articles of Confederation. Two Americans who were active in the movement for change were **James Madison,** a Virginia planter, and **Alexander Hamilton,** a New York lawyer.

People IN HISTORY

George Washington
Presiding Officer of the Constitutional Convention

George Washington did not want to attend the Constitutional Convention, but he did because he worried that the nation would not survive under the weak Articles of Confederation. The delegates unanimously chose him as the presiding officer, or leader, of the Convention. Washington said very little during the debates but became one of the Constitution's strongest supporters. He argued that later generations could make any changes necessary: *"I think the people . . . can, as they will have the aid of experience on their side, decide . . . on the . . . amendments [which] shall be found necessary, . . . I do not conceive that we are more inspired—have more [wisdom]—or possess more virtue than those who will come after us."*

CRITICAL Thinking

1. **Evaluating** How did Washington contribute to the success of the Constitutional Convention?
2. **Analyzing** Why did Washington support the Constitution's ratification?

In September 1786, Hamilton proposed calling a **convention,** or meeting, in Philadelphia to discuss trade issues. He also suggested that this convention consider what possible changes were needed to make "the Constitution of the Federal Government adequate to the exigencies [needs] of the Union."

At first, George Washington was not enthusiastic about the movement to revise the Articles of Confederation. When Washington heard about Shays's Rebellion, however, he changed his mind. After Washington agreed to attend the Philadelphia convention, the meeting took on greater significance. The Philadelphia meeting began in May 1787 and continued through one of the hottest summers on record. The 55 delegates included planters, merchants, lawyers, physicians, generals, governors, and a college president. Three of the delegates were under 30 years of age, and one, Benjamin Franklin, was over 80. Many were well educated. At a time when only one white man in 1,000 went to college, 26 of the delegates had college degrees. Other groups, such as Native Americans, African Americans, and women, were not considered part of the political process, so they were not represented at the convention.

The presence of George Washington and Benjamin Franklin ensured that many people would trust the Convention's work. Two Philadelphians also played key roles. James Wilson often read Franklin's speeches and did important work on the details of the Constitution. Gouverneur Morris, a powerful speaker and writer, wrote the final draft of the Constitution. James Madison was a keen supporter of a strong national government. Madison's careful notes documented the Convention's work. Madison is often called the "Father of the Constitution" because he was the author of the basic plan of government that the Convention adopted.

Organization

The delegates chose George Washington to preside over the meetings. The delegates also decided that each state would have one vote on all questions. A simple majority vote of those states present would make decisions.

Primary Source / **Signing of the Constitution**

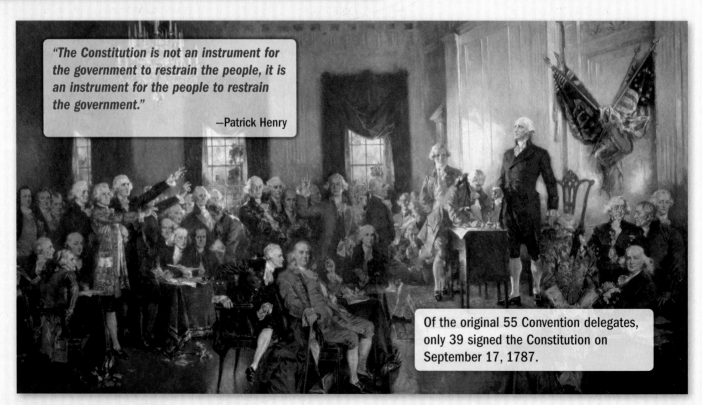

"The Constitution is not an instrument for the government to restrain the people, it is an instrument for the people to restrain the government."
—Patrick Henry

Of the original 55 Convention delegates, only 39 signed the Constitution on September 17, 1787.

History ONLINE

For additional test practice, use **Self-Check Quizzes**—Chapter 7 at glencoe.com.

Document-Based Questions

Directions: Analyze the documents and answer the short-answer questions that follow.

Document 1

This is Article 6 of the Northwest Ordinance (1787).

There shall be neither slavery nor involuntary servitude in the said territory. . . . Provided, always, That any person escaping into the same, from whom labor or service is lawfully claimed in any one of the original States, such fugitive may be lawfully reclaimed and conveyed [transferred] to the person claiming his or her labor or service as aforesaid.

Source: The Northwest Ordinance

7 Based on the document, what was the legal status of an enslaved person who escaped into the Northwest Territory?

Document 2

The following is from records of the Constitutional Convention discussion (1787) about the slave trade.

Mr. [Roger] Sherman [of Conn.] was for leaving the clause as it stands. He disapproved of the slave trade; yet, as the states were now possessed of the right to import slaves, as the public good did not require it to be taken from them, and as it was expedient [advantageous] to have as few objections as possible to the proposed scheme [plan] of government, he thought it best to leave the matter as we find it. He observed that the abolition of slavery seemed to be going on in the United States, and that the good sense of the several states would probably by degrees complete it.

Source: Records from a pro-slavery document

8 According to the document, identify two reasons Sherman had for not prohibiting the slave trade.

Document 3

This map of Massachusetts shows where support was located for the Federalists and Anti-Federalists when the state ratified the Constitution.

9 Based on the map, where were most of the Federalist supporters located?

Document 4

This is an excerpt from "On the Equality of the Sexes" by Judith Sargent Stevens Murray (1790).

Our souls are by nature equal to yours; the same breath of God animates, enlivens, and invigorates us.

Source: "On the Equality of the Sexes"

10 Using the document, identify the reason Murray believed women are equal to men.

11 **Persuasive Writing** Using the information from the documents and your knowledge of social studies, write an essay in which you:

- defend the Constitution as a great model of democracy; or

- express criticism of the Constitution based on differences between its ideals and the status of enslaved African Americans and women in the 1700s.

Need Extra Help?											
If you missed questions. . .	1	2	3	4	5	6	7	8	9	10	11
Go to page. . .	189	195–196	206	210	209–210	186–210	191	201	209–210	198	194–210

Constitution Handbook

For more than 200 years, the Constitution has provided the framework for the United States government and has helped preserve the basic rights of American citizens. It is the highest authority in the nation and the basic law of the United States. It is also a symbol of our nation, representing our system of government and our basic ideals, such as liberty and freedom.

Essential Question

Why is citizen participation essential to the preservation of the U.S. political system?

Reading Guide

Content Vocabulary

Preamble *(p. 215)*

popular sovereignty *(p. 215)*

republicanism *(p. 215)*

federalism *(p. 216)*

enumerated powers *(p. 216)*

reserved powers *(p. 216)*

concurrent powers *(p. 216)*

amend *(p. 218)*

implied powers *(p. 219)*

Academic Vocabulary

involve *(p. 221)*   diminish *(p. 223)*

Reading Strategy

Taking Notes As you read, use a diagram like the one below to identify the seven major principles on which the Constitution is based.

Federalism

Major Principles

The Constitution

Main Idea The Constitution sets forth the basic principles of government.

History and You What principles do you live by? Read to learn how the basic principles of the Constitution assure the rights of the people.

. . . .

The **Preamble,** or introduction, to the Constitution reflects the basic idea of American government—the right of the people to govern themselves. It also lists six goals for the United States government:

PRIMARY SOURCE

"to form a more perfect Union, establish Justice, insure domestic Tranquility [peace], provide for the common defence, promote the general Welfare, and secure the Blessings of Liberty to ourselves and our Posterity [descendents]."

—United States Constitution

Major Principles

The principles outlined in the Constitution were the Framers' solution to the problems of a representative government. The Constitution rests on seven major principles: (1) popular sovereignty, (2) republicanism, (3) limited government, (4) federalism, (5) separation of powers, (6) checks and balances, and (7) individual rights.

Popular Sovereignty The Declaration of Independence states that governments derive their powers from "the consent of the governed." The opening words of the Constitution, "We the People," reinforce this idea of **popular sovereignty**—or "authority of the people."

Republicanism Under **republicanism,** voters hold sovereign power. The people elect representatives and give them the responsibility to make laws and conduct government. For most Americans today, the terms *republic* and *representative democracy* mean the same thing: a system of limited government in which the people are the ultimate source of governmental power.

Limited Government The Framers saw both benefits and risks in creating a powerful national government. They agreed that the nation needed strong central authority but feared misuse of power. They wanted to prevent the government from using its power to give one group special advantages or to deprive another group of its rights. By creating a limited government, they made certain the government would have only those powers granted by the people.

Article I of the Constitution states the powers that the government has and the powers that it does not have. Other limits on government appear in the Bill of Rights, which guarantees certain rights and liberties to the people.

Limited government can be described as the "rule of law." No person or group of people is above the law. Government officials must obey the law.

Federalism When the states banded together under the Constitution, they gave up some independence. States could no longer print their own money or tax items imported from other states. Nevertheless, each state governed itself much as it had in the past.

This system, in which the power to govern is shared between the national government and the states, is called the federal system, or **federalism.** Our federal system allows the people of each state to deal with their needs in their own way. At the same time, it lets the states act together to deal with matters that affect all Americans.

The Constitution defines three types of government powers. **Enumerated powers** belong only to the federal government. These include the power to coin money, regulate interstate and foreign trade, maintain the armed forces, and create federal courts (Article I, Section 8).

The second kind of powers are those retained by the states, known as **reserved powers.** They include such rights as the power to establish schools, pass marriage and divorce laws, and regulate trade within a state. Although reserved powers are not listed specifically in the Constitution, the Tenth Amendment says that all powers not specifically granted to the federal government "are reserved to the States."

The third set of powers defined by the Constitution are **concurrent powers**—powers shared by the state and federal governments. Among these powers are the right to raise taxes, borrow money, provide for public welfare, and administer criminal justice.

When conflicts arise between state law and federal law, the Constitution declares that the Constitution is "the supreme Law of the Land." Conflicts between state law and federal law must be settled in a federal court.

Separation of Powers To prevent any single group or institution in government from gaining too much authority, the Framers divided the federal government into three branches: legislative, executive, and judicial. Each branch has its own functions and powers. The legislative branch, Congress, makes the laws. The executive branch, headed by the president, carries out the laws. The judicial branch, consisting of the Supreme Court and other federal courts, interprets and applies the laws.

Checks and Balances As an additional safeguard, the Framers established a system of checks and balances in which each branch of government can check, or limit, the power of the other branches. This system helps maintain a balance in the power of the three branches. For example, Congress can pass a

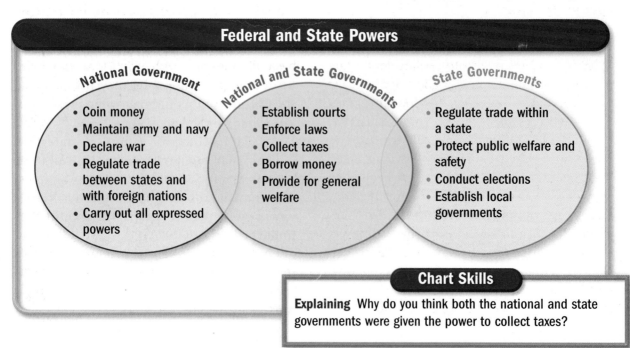

Federal and State Powers

National Government
- Coin money
- Maintain army and navy
- Declare war
- Regulate trade between states and with foreign nations
- Carry out all expressed powers

National and State Governments
- Establish courts
- Enforce laws
- Collect taxes
- Borrow money
- Provide for general welfare

State Governments
- Regulate trade within a state
- Protect public welfare and safety
- Conduct elections
- Establish local governments

Chart Skills

Explaining Why do you think both the national and state governments were given the power to collect taxes?

president no duties aside from presiding over the Senate. It is the president who determines what the vice president will do, such as working with Congress or making trips abroad.

The Judicial Branch

The Constitution calls for a Supreme Court and the creation of lower courts as Congress wishes. In 1789 Congress passed a Judiciary Act, which added a series of district courts to the federal court system. Appeals, or circuit courts, were added in 1891 to ease the workload of the Supreme Court.

Lower Federal Courts The duties of the lower federal courts are the following:

- **District Courts:** handle civil and criminal cases that come under federal authority; 91 district courts, with at least 1 in every state.

- **Appeals Courts:** review disctrict court decisions; overturn a verdict of the district court or order a retrial; 14 appeals courts in the United States.

The Supreme Court The Supreme Court stands at the top of the American legal system. It is one of the coequal branches of the national government, along with Congress and the president. The Supreme Court is comprised of nine justices: the chief justice of the United States and eight associate justices. Congress has the power to set this number and the power to change it.

The Constitution does not describe the duties of the justices, which have developed from laws and customs in response to national needs. The main duty of the justices is to hear and rule on cases. This duty **involves** them in three tasks: deciding which cases to hear from among thousands of appeals each year; deciding the case itself; and explaining the decision, called the Court's opinion.

The role of the judicial branch has grown as the powers implied in the Constitution have been put into practice. In the 1803 case *Marbury* v. *Madison,* Chief Justice John Marshall expanded Supreme Court powers by striking down an act of Congress. In that decision, the Court defined its right to determine whether a law violates the Constitution. Although not mentioned in the Constitution, this principle, known as judicial review, has become a major power of the judicial branch.

Reading Check **Describing** What is Congress's role in government spending?

The Supreme Court

◀ Seated left to right: Anthony Kennedy, John Paul Stevens, Chief Justice John G. Roberts, Jr., Antonin Scalia, David Souter. Standing left to right: Stephen Breyer, Clarence Thomas, Ruth Bader Ginsburg, Samuel Alito, Jr.

Critical Thinking

Describing Why do you think the number of justices is set an an uneven number?

Rights, Duties, and Responsibilities

Rights	Duties	Responsibilities
Security protection by government **Equality** equal treatment under the law **Liberty** rights guaranteed under the Constitution	• Obey the law • Pay taxes • Defend the nation • Serve in court • Attend school	• Be informed and vote • Participate in your community and government • Respect the rights and property of others • Respect different opinions and ways of life

Chart Skills

Contrasting How do duties differ from responsibilities?

Rights and Citizen Participation

Main Idea U.S. citizenship brings with it certain rights and responsibilities.

History and You Are you a good citizen? What are the rights and responsibilities of citizenship? Read to learn why American citizens have a responsibility to their community, the environment, and the law.

. . . .

All American citizens have certain basic rights, but they also have specific responsibilities. Living in a democracy means that every citizen is partly responsible for how society is governed and for the actions the government takes on each citizen's behalf.

The Rights of American Citizens

The rights of Americans fall into three broad categories: the right to be protected from unfair government actions, to have equal treatment under the law, and to enjoy basic freedoms.

Due Process The Fifth Amendment states that no person shall "be deprived of life, liberty, or property, without due process of law." Due process of law means that the government must follow procedures established by law and guaranteed by the Constitution, treating all people according to these principles.

Equal Protection All Americans, regardless of race, religion, or political beliefs, have the right to be treated the same under the law.

The Fourteenth Amendment requires every state to grant its citizens "equal protection of the laws."

Basic Freedoms The basic freedoms involve the liberties outlined in the First Amendment—freedom of speech, freedom of religion, freedom of the press, freedom of assembly, and the right to petition. In a democratic society, power exists in the hands of the people. Therefore, its citizens must be able to exchange ideas freely.

Limits on Rights Our rights are not unlimited. The government can establish laws or rules to protect the health, safety, security, and moral standards of a community. Moreover, rights may be limited to prevent one person's rights from interfering with the rights of others. The restrictions of rights, however, must be reasonable and must apply to everyone equally.

Citizen Participation

A citizen is a person who owes loyalty to and is entitled to the protection of a state or nation. How do you become an American citizen? Generally, citizenship is granted to anyone born within the borders of the United States. Citizenship is also granted to anyone born outside of the United States if one parent is a U.S. citizen. A person of foreign birth can become a citizen through the process of naturalization. Before being admitted citizenship, applicants must be willing to give up any foreign allegiance and must promise to

Section 5

[1.] Each House shall be the Judge of the Elections, Returns and Qualifications of its own Members, and a Majority of each shall constitute a **Quorum** to do Business; but a smaller Number may **adjourn** from day to day, and may be authorized to compel the Attendance of absent Members, in such Manner, and under such Penalties as each House may provide.

[2.] Each House may determine the Rules of its Proceedings, punish its Members for disorderly Behaviour, and, with the Concurrence of two thirds, expel a Member.

[3.] Each House shall keep a Journal of its Proceedings, and from time to time publish the same, excepting such Parts as may in their Judgment require Secrecy; and the Yeas and Nays of the Members of either House on any question shall, at the Desire of one fifth of those Present, be entered on the Journal.

[4.] Neither House, during the Session of Congress, shall, without the Consent of the other, adjourn for more than three days, nor to any other Place than that in which the two Houses shall be sitting.

Section 6

[1.] The Senators and Representatives shall receive a Compensation for their Services, to be ascertained by Law, and paid out of the Treasury of the United States. They shall in all Cases, except Treason, Felony and Breach of the Peace, be privileged from Arrest during their Attendance at the Session of their respective Houses, and in going to and returning from the same; and for any Speech or Debate in either House, they shall not be questioned in any other Place.

[2.] No Senator or Representative shall, during the Time for which he was elected, be appointed to any civil Office under the Authority of the United States, which shall have been created, or the **Emoluments** whereof shall have been encreased during such time; and no Person holding any Office under the United States, shall be a Member of either House during his Continuance in Office.

Section 7

[1.] All **Bills** for raising **Revenue** shall originate in the House of Representatives; but the Senate may propose or concur with Amendments as on other Bills,

[2.] Every Bill which shall have passed the House of Representatives and the Senate, shall, before it become a Law, be presented to the President of the United States: If he approve he shall sign it, but if not he shall return it, with his Objections to that House in which it shall have originated, who shall enter the Objections at large on their Journal, and proceed to reconsider it. If after such Reconsideration two thirds

▲ Congresswoman Nydia Velázquez represents New York's 12th District.

What It Means

Congressional Salaries To strengthen the federal government, the Founders set congressional salaries to be paid by the United States Treasury rather than by members' respective states. Originally, members were paid $6 per day. In 2006 all members of Congress received a base salary of $165,200.

What It Means

Where Tax Laws Begin All tax laws must originate in the House of Representatives. This ensures that the branch of Congress that is elected by the people every two years has the major role in determining taxes.

What It Means

How Bills Become Laws A bill may become a law only by passing both houses of Congress and by being signed by the president. The president can check Congress by rejecting— vetoing—its legislation. *How can Congress override the president's veto?*

The Constitution of the United States **227**

What It Means

Powers of Congress Expressed powers are those powers directly stated in the Constitution. Most of the expressed powers of Congress are listed in Article I, Section 8. These powers are also called enumerated powers because they are numbered 1–18. *Which clause gives Congress the power to declare war?*

▲ Civil War money

Vocabulary

resolution: legislature's formal expression of opinion

impost: tax

naturalization: procedure by which a citizen of a foreign nation becomes a citizen of the United States

tribunal: a court

letter of marque: authority given to a citizen to outfit an armed ship and use it to attack enemy ships in time of war

reprisal: taking by force property or territory belonging to another country or to its citizens

of that House shall agree to pass the Bill, it shall be sent, together with the Objections, to the other House, by which it shall likewise be reconsidered, and if approved by two thirds of that House, it shall become a Law. But in all such Cases the Votes of both Houses shall be determined by yeas and Nays, and the Names of the Persons voting for and against the Bill shall be entered on the Journal of each House respectively. If any Bill shall not be returned by the President within ten Days (Sundays excepted) after it shall have been presented to him, the Same shall be a Law, in like Manner as if he had signed it, unless the Congress by their Adjournment prevent its Return, in which Case it shall not be a Law.

[3.] Every Order, **Resolution,** or Vote to which the Concurrence of the Senate and House of Representatives may be necessary (except on a question of Adjournment) shall be presented to the President of the United States; and before the Same shall take Effect, shall be approved by him, or being disapproved by him, shall be repassed by two thirds of the Senate and House of Representatives, according to the Rules and Limitations prescribed in the Case of a Bill.

Section 8

[1.] The Congress shall have the Power To lay and collect Taxes, Duties, **Imposts** and Excises, to pay the Debts and provide for the common Defence and general Welfare of the United States; but all Duties, Imposts and Excises shall be uniform throughout the United States;

[2.] To borrow Money on the credit of the United States;

[3.] To regulate Commerce with foreign Nations, and among the several States, and with the Indian Tribes;

[4.] To establish an uniform Rule of **Naturalization,** and uniform Laws on the subject of Bankruptcies throughout the United States;

[5.] To coin Money, regulate the Value thereof, and of foreign Coin, and fix the Standard of Weights and Measures;

[6.] To provide for the Punishment of counterfeiting the Securities and current Coin of the United States;

[7.] To establish Post Offices and post Roads;

[8.] To promote the Progress of Science and useful Arts, by securing for limited Times to Authors and Inventors the exclusive Right to their respective Writings and Discoveries;

[9.] To constitute **Tribunals** inferior to the supreme Court;

[10.] To define and punish Piracies and Felonies committed on the high Seas, and Offences against the Law of Nations;

[11.] To declare War, grant **Letters of Marque** and **Reprisal,** and make Rules concerning Captures on Land and Water;

[12.] To raise and support Armies, but no Appropriation of Money to that Use shall be for a longer Term than two Years;

[13.] To provide and maintain a Navy;

[14.] To make Rules for the Government and Regulation of the land and naval Forces;

[15.] To provide for calling forth the Militia to execute the Laws of the Union, suppress **Insurrections** and repel Invasions;

[16.] To provide for organizing, arming, and disciplining, the Militia, and for governing such Part of them as may be employed in the Service of the United States, reserving to the States respectively, the Appointment of the Officers, and the Authority of training the Militia according to the discipline prescribed by Congress;

[17.] To exercise exclusive Legislation in all Cases whatsoever, over such District (not exceeding ten Miles square) as may, by Cession of particular States, and the Acceptance of Congress, become the Seat of Government of the United States, and to exercise like Authority over all Places purchased by the Consent of the Legislature of the State in which the Same shall be, for the Erection of Forts, Magazines, Arsenals, dock-Yards, and other needful Buildings;—And

[18.] To make all Laws which shall be necessary and proper for carrying into Execution the foregoing Powers, and all other Powers vested by this Constitution in the Government of the United States, or in any Department or Officer thereof.

Section 9

[1]. The Migration or Importation of such Persons as any of the States now existing shall think proper to admit, shall not be prohibited by the Congress prior to the Year one thousand eight hundred and eight, but a Tax or **duty** may be imposed on such Importation, not exceeding ten dollars for each Person.

[2.] The Privilege of the Writ of Habeas Corpus shall not be suspended, unless when in Cases of Rebellion or Invasion the public Safety may require it.

[3.] No Bill of Attainder or ex post facto Law shall be passed.

[4.] No Capitation, or other direct, Tax shall be laid, unless in Proportion to the Census or enumeration herein before directed to be taken.

[5.] No Tax or Duty shall be laid on Articles exported from any State.

[6.] No Preference shall be given by any Regulation of Commerce or Revenue to the Ports of one State over those of another; nor shall Vessels bound to, or from, one State, be obliged to enter, clear, or pay Duties in another.

[7.] No Money shall be drawn from the Treasury, but in Consequence of **Appropriations** made by Law; and a regular Statement and Account of the Receipts and Expenditures of all public Money shall be published from time to time.

[8.] No Title of Nobility shall be granted by the United States: And no Person holding any Office of Profit or Trust under them, shall, without the Consent of the Congress, accept of any present, Emolument, Office, or Title, of any kind whatever, from any King, Prince, or foreign State.

What It Means

Elastic Clause The final enumerated power is often called the "elastic clause." This clause gives Congress the right to make all laws "necessary and proper" to carry out the powers expressed in the other clauses of **Article I.** It is called the elastic clause because it lets Congress "stretch" its powers to meet situations the Founders could never have anticipated.

What does the phrase **"necessary and proper"** in the elastic clause mean? Almost from the beginning, this phrase was a subject of dispute. The issue was whether a strict or a broad interpretation of the Constitution should be applied. The dispute was first addressed in 1819, in the case of *McCulloch* v. *Maryland*, when the Supreme Court ruled in favor of a broad interpretation.

What It Means

Habeas Corpus A writ of habeas corpus issued by a judge requires a law official to bring a prisoner to court and show cause for holding the prisoner. A bill of attainder is a bill that punished a person without a jury trial. An "ex post facto" law is one that makes an act a crime after the act has been committed. *What does the Constitution say about bills of attainder?*

Vocabulary

insurrection: rebellion

duty: tax

appropriations: funds set aside for a specific use

The Constitution of the United States **229**

Section 10

[1.] No State shall enter into any Treaty, Alliance, or Confederation; grant Letters of Marque and Reprisal; coin Money; emit Bills of Credit; make any Thing but gold and silver Coin a Tender in Payment of Debts; pass any Bill of Attainder, ex post facto Law, or Law impairing the Obligation of Contracts, or grant any Title of Nobility.

[2.] No State shall, without the Consent of the Congress, lay any Imposts or Duties on Imports or Exports, except what may be absolutely necessary for executing its inspection Laws: and the net Produce of all Duties and Imposts, laid by any State on Imports or Exports, shall be for the Use of the Treasury of the United States; and all such Laws shall be subject to the Revision and Controul of the Congress.

[3.] No State shall, without the Consent of Congress, lay any Duty of Tonnage, keep Troops, or Ships of War in time of Peace, enter into any Agreement or Compact with another State, or with a foreign Power, or engage in War, unless actually invaded, or in such imminent Danger as will not admit of delay.

Article II

Section 1

[1.] The executive Power shall be vested in a President of the United States of America. He shall hold his Office during the Term of four Years, and, together with the Vice President, chosen for the same Term, be elected, as follows:

[2.] Each State shall appoint, in such Manner as the Legislature thereof may direct, a Number of Electors, equal to the whole Number of Senators and Representatives to which the State may be entitled in the Congress: but no Senator or Representative, or Person holding an Office of Trust or Profit under the United States, shall be appointed an Elector.

[3.] The Electors shall meet in their respective States, and vote by Ballot for two Persons, of whom one at least shall not be an Inhabitant of the same State with themselves. And they shall make a List of all the Persons voted for, and of the Number of Votes for each; which List they shall sign and certify, and transmit sealed to the Seat of the Government of the United States, directed to the President of the Senate. The President of the Senate shall, in the Presence of the Senate and House of Representatives, open all the Certificates, and the Votes shall then be counted. The Person having the greatest Number of Votes shall be the President, if such Number be a Majority of the whole Number of Electors appointed; and if there be more than one who have such Majority, and have an equal Number of Votes, then the House of Representatives shall immediately chuse by Ballot one of them for President; and if no person have a Majority,

▲ United States coins

then from the five highest on the List the said House shall in like Manner chuse the President. But in chusing the President, the Votes shall be taken by States, the Representation from each State having one Vote; A quorum for this Purpose shall consist of a Member or Members from two thirds of the States, and a Majority of all the States shall be necessary to a Choice. In every Case, after the Choice of the President, the Person having the greatest Number of Votes of the Electors shall be the Vice President. But if there should remain two or more who have equal Votes, the Senate shall chuse from them by Ballot the Vice President.

[4.] The Congress may determine the Time of chusing the Electors, and the Day on which they shall give their Votes; which Day shall be the same throughout the United States.

[5.] No Person except a natural born Citizen, or a Citizen of the United States, at the time of the Adoption of this Constitution, shall be eligible to the Office of President; neither shall any Person be eligible to that Office who shall not have attained to the Age of thirty five Years, and been fourteen Years a Resident within the United States.

[6.] In Case of the Removal of the President from Office, or of his Death, Resignation, or Inability to discharge the Powers and Duties of the said Office, the Same shall devolve on the Vice President, and the Congress may by Law provide for the Case of Removal, Death, Resignation or Inability, both of the President and Vice President, declaring what Officer shall then act as President, and such Officer shall act accordingly, until the Disability be removed, or a President shall be elected.

[7.] The President shall, at stated Times, receive for his Services, a Compensation, which shall neither be increased nor diminished during the Period for which he shall have been elected, and he shall not receive within that Period any other Emolument from the United States, or any of them.

[8.] Before he enter on the Execution of his Office, he shall take the following Oath or Affirmation:—"I do solemnly swear (or affirm) that I will faithfully execute the Office of President of the United States, and will to the best of my Ability, preserve, protect and defend the Constitution of the United States."

Section 2

[1.] The President shall be Commander in Chief of the Army and Navy of the United States, and of the Militia of the several States, when called into the actual Service of the United States; he may require the Opinion, in writing, of the principal Officer in each of the executive Departments, upon any Subject relating to the Duties of their respective Offices, and he shall have Power to grant Reprieves and Pardons for Offences against the United States, except in Cases of Impeachment.

What It Means

Previous Elections The Twelfth Amendment, added in 1804, changed the method of electing the president stated in Article II, Section 3. The Twelfth Amendment requires that the electors cast separate ballots for president and vice president.

What It Means

Qualifications The president must be a citizen of the United States by birth, at least 35 years of age, and a resident of the United States for 14 years.

What It Means

Vacancies If the president dies, resigns, is removed from office by impeachment, or is unable to carry out the duties of the office, the vice president becomes president. The Twenty-fifth Amendment sets procedures for presidential succession.

What It Means

Salary Originally, the president's salary was $25,000 per year. The president's current salary is $400,000 plus a $50,000 nontaxable expense account per year. The president also receives living accommodations in two residences—the White House and Camp David.

What It Means

The Cabinet Mention of "the principal officer in each of the executive departments" is the only suggestion of the president's cabinet to be found in the Constitution. The cabinet is an advisory body, and its power depends on the president. Section 2, Clause 1, also makes the president—a civilian—the head of the armed services. This established the principle of civilian control of the military.

What It Means

Presidential Powers An executive order is a command issued by a president to exercise a power which he or she has been given by the U.S. Constitution or by a federal statute. In times of emergency, presidents sometimes have used the executive order to override the Constitution of the United States and the Congress. During the Civil War, President Lincoln suspended many fundamental rights guaranteed in the Constitution and the Bill of Rights. He closed down newspapers that opposed his policies and imprisoned some who disagreed with him. Lincoln said that these actions were justified to preserve the Union.

What It Means

Article III. The Judicial Branch The term "judicial" refers to courts. The Constitution set up only the Supreme Court but provided for the establishment of other federal courts. The judiciary of the United States has two different systems of courts. One system consists of the federal courts, whose powers derive from the Constitution and federal laws. The other includes the courts of each of the 50 states, whose powers derive from state constitutions and laws.

What It Means

Statute Law Federal courts deal mostly with "statute law," or laws passed by Congress, treaties, and cases involving the Constitution itself.

[2.] He shall have Power, by and with the Advice and Consent of the Senate, to make Treaties, provided two thirds of the Senators present concur; and he shall nominate, and by and with the Advice and Consent of the Senate, shall appoint Ambassadors, other public Ministers and Consuls, Judges of the supreme Court, and all other Officers of the United States, whose Appointments are not herein otherwise provided for, and which shall be established by Law: but the Congress may by Law vest the Appointment of such inferior Officers, as they think proper, in the President alone, in the Courts of Law, or in the Heads of Departments.

[3.] The President shall have Power to fill up all Vacancies that may happen during the Recess of the Senate, by granting Commissions which shall expire at the End of their next Session.

Section 3

He shall from time to time give to the Congress Information of the State of the Union, and recommend to their Consideration such Measures as he shall judge necessary and expedient; he may, on extraordinary Occasions, convene both Houses, or either of them, and in Case of Disagreement between them, with Respect to the Time of Adjournment, he may adjourn them to such Time as he shall think proper; he shall receive Ambassadors and other public Ministers; he shall take Care that the Laws be faithfully executed, and shall Commission all the Officers of the United States.

Section 4

The President, Vice President and all civil Officers of the United States, shall be removed from Office on Impeachment for, and Conviction of, Treason, Bribery, or other high Crimes and Misdemeanors.

Article III

Section 1

The judicial Power of the United States shall be vested in one supreme Court, and in such inferior Courts as the Congress may from time to time ordain and establish. The Judges, both of the supreme and inferior Courts, shall hold their Offices during good Behaviour, and shall, at stated Times, receive for their Services a Compensation, which shall not be diminished during their Continuance in Office.

Section 2

[1.] The judicial Power shall extend to all Cases, in Law and Equity, arising under this Constitution, the Laws of the United States, and Treaties made, or which shall be made, under their Authority;—to all Cases affecting Ambassadors, other public Ministers and Consuls;—to all Cases of admiralty and maritime Jurisdiction;—to Controversies to which the United States shall be a Party;—to Controversies between two or more States;—between a State and Citizens of another State;—between Citizens of different States;—between Citizens of the same State claiming Lands under Grants of different States, and between a State, or the Citizens thereof, and foreign States, Citizens or Subjects.

[2.] In all Cases affecting Ambassadors, other public Ministers and Consuls, and those in which a State shall be Party, the supreme Court shall have **original Jurisdiction.** In all the other Cases before mentioned, the supreme Court shall have **appellate Jurisdiction,** both as to Law and Fact, with such Exceptions, and under such Regulations as the Congress shall make.

[3.] The Trial of all Crimes, except in Cases of Impeachment, shall be by Jury; and such Trial shall be held in the State where the said Crimes shall have been committed; but when not committed within any State, the Trial shall be at such Place or Places as the Congress may by Law have directed.

Section 3

[1.] **Treason** against the United States, shall consist only in levying War against them, or in adhering to their Enemies, giving them Aid and Comfort. No Person shall be convicted of Treason unless on the Testimony of two Witnesses to the same overt Act, or on Confession in open Court.

[2.] The Congress shall have Power to declare the Punishment of Treason, but no Attainder of Treason shall work Corruption of Blood, or Forfeiture except during the Life of the Person attainted.

Article IV

Section 1

Full Faith and Credit shall be given in each State to the public Acts, Records, and judicial Proceedings of every other State. And the Congress may by general Laws prescribe the Manner in which such Acts, Records and Proceedings shall be proved, and the Effect thereof.

Section 2

[1.] The Citizens of each State shall be entitled to all Privileges and Immunities of Citizens in the several States.

[2.] A Person charged in any State with Treason, Felony, or other Crime, who shall flee from Justice, and be found in another State, shall on Demand of the executive Authority of the State from which he fled, be delivered up, to be removed to the State having Jurisdiction of the Crime.

[3.] No Person held to Service of Labour in one State, under the Laws thereof, escaping into another, shall, in Consequence of any Law or Regulation therein, be discharged from such Service or Labour, but shall be delivered up on Claim of the Party to whom such Service or Labour may be due.

What It Means

The Supreme Court A court with "original jurisdiction" has the authority to be the first court to hear a case. The Supreme Court has "appellate jurisdiction" and mostly hears cases appealed from lower courts.

What It Means

Article IV. Relations Among the States Article IV explains the relationship of the states to one another and to the national government. This article requires each state to give citizens of other states the same rights as its own citizens, addresses admitting new states, and guarantees that the national government will protect the states.

Vocabulary

original jurisdiction: authority to be the first court to hear a case

appellate jurisdiction: authority to hear cases that have been appealed from lower courts

treason: violation of the allegiance owed by a person to his or her own country, for example, by aiding an enemy

Section 3

[1.] New States may be admitted by the Congress into this Union; but no new State shall be formed or erected within the Jurisdiction of any other State; nor any State be formed by the Junction of two or more States, or Parts of States, without the Consent of the Legislatures of the States concerned as well as of the Congress.

[2.] The Congress shall have Power to dispose of and make all needful Rules and Regulations respecting the Territory or other Property belonging to the United States; and nothing in this Constitution shall be so construed as to Prejudice any Claims of the United States, or of any particular State.

Section 4

The United States shall guarantee to every State in this Union a Republican Form of Government, and shall protect each of them against Invasion; and on Application of the Legislature, or of the Executive (when the Legislature cannot be convened), against domestic Violence.

Article V

The Congress, whenever two thirds of both Houses shall deem it necessary, shall propose **Amendments** to this Constitution, or, on the Application of the Legislatures of two thirds of the several States, shall call a Convention for proposing Amendments, which, in either Case, shall be valid to all Intents and Purposes, as Part of this Constitution, when ratified by the Legislatures of three fourths of the several States, or by Conventions in three fourths thereof, as the one or the other Mode of **Ratification** may be proposed by the Congress; Provided that no Amendment which may be made prior to the Year One thousand eight hundred and eight shall in any Manner affect the first and fourth Clauses in the Ninth Section of the first Article; and that no State, without its Consent, shall be deprived of its equal Suffrage in the Senate.

Article VI

[1.] All Debts contracted and Engagements entered into, before the Adoption of this Constitution, shall be as valid against the United States under this Constitution, as under the Confederation.

[2.] This Constitution, and the Laws of the United States which shall be made in Pursuance thereof; and all Treaties made, or which shall be made, under the Authority of the United States, shall be the supreme Law of the Land; and the Judges in every State shall be bound thereby, any Thing in the Constitution or Laws of any State to the Contrary notwithstanding.

[3.] The Senators and Representatives before mentioned, and the Members of the several State Legislatures, and all executive

Vocabulary

amendment: a change to the Constitution

ratification: the process by which an amendment is approved and judicial Officers, both of the United States and of the several States, shall be bound by Oath or Affirmation, to support this Constitution; but no religious Test shall ever be required as a Qualification to any Office or public Trust under the United States.

Article VII

The Ratification of the Conventions of nine States, shall be sufficient for the Establishment of this Constitution between the States so ratifying the Same.

Done in Convention by the Unanimous Consent of the States present the Seventeenth Day of September in the Year of our Lord one thousand seven hundred and Eighty seven and of the Independence of the United States of America the Twelfth. In witness whereof We have hereunto subscribed our Names,

What It Means

Article VII. Ratification Article VII addresses ratification and declares that the Constitution would take effect after it was ratified by nine states.

Signers

George Washington,
President and Deputy
from Virginia

New Hampshire
John Langdon
Nicholas Gilman

Massachusetts
Nathaniel Gorham
Rufus King

Connecticut
William Samuel Johnson
Roger Sherman

New York
Alexander Hamilton

New Jersey
William Livingston
David Brearley
William Paterson
Jonathan Dayton

Pennsylvania
Benjamin Franklin
Thomas Mifflin
Robert Morris
George Clymer
Thomas FitzSimons
Jared Ingersoll
James Wilson
Gouverneur Morris

Delaware
George Read
Gunning Bedford, Jr.
John Dickinson
Richard Bassett
Jacob Broom

Maryland
James McHenry
Daniel of
*   St. Thomas Jenifer*
Daniel Carroll

Virginia
John Blair
James Madison, Jr.

North Carolina
William Blount
Richard Dobbs Spaight
Hugh Williamson

South Carolina
John Rutledge
Charles Cotesworth
*   Pinckney*
Charles Pinckney
Pierce Butler

Georgia
William Few
Abraham Baldwin

Attest:
William Jackson, Secretary

The Amendments This part of the Constitution consists of amendments. The Constitution has been amended 27 times throughout the nation's history.

What It Means

The Bill of Rights The first 10 amendments are known as the Bill of Rights (1791). These amendments limit the powers of government. The First Amendment protects the civil liberties of individuals in the United States. The amendment freedoms are not absolute, however. They are limited by the rights of other individuals. *What freedoms does the First Amendment protect?*

Vocabulary

quarter: to provide living accommodations

warrant: a document that gives police particular rights or powers

probable cause: a reasonable basis to believe a person is linked to a crime

Amendment I

Congress shall make no law respecting an establishment of religion, or prohibiting the free exercise thereof; or abridging the freedom of speech, or of the press; or the right of the people peaceably to assemble, and to petition the Government for a redress of grievances.

Amendment II

A well regulated Militia, being necessary to the security of a free State, the right of the people to keep and bear Arms, shall not be infringed.

Amendment III

No Soldier shall, in time of peace be **quartered** in any house, without the consent of the Owner, nor in time of war, but in a manner to be prescribed by law.

Amendment IV

The right of the people to be secure in their persons, houses, papers, and effects, against unreasonable searches and seizures, shall not be violated, and no **Warrants** shall issue, but upon **probable cause,** supported by Oath or affirmation, and particularly describing the place to be searched, and the persons or things to be seized.

Amendment V

No person shall be held to answer for a capital, or otherwise infamous crime, unless on a presentment or indictment of a Grand Jury, except in cases arising in the land or naval forces, or in the Militia, when in actual service in time of War or public danger; nor shall any person be subject for the same offence to be twice put in jeopardy of life or limb; nor shall be compelled in any criminal case to be a witness against himself, nor be deprived of life, liberty, or property, without due process of law; nor shall private property be taken for public use, without just compensation.

Amendment VI

In all criminal prosecutions, the accused shall enjoy the right to a speedy and public trial, by an impartial jury of the State and district wherein the crime shall have been committed, which district shall have been previously ascertained by law, and to be informed of the nature and cause of the accusation; to be confronted with the witnesses against him; to have compulsory process for obtaining declaration, or, if Congress is not in session, within twenty-one days after Congress is required to assemble, determines by two-thirds vote of both Houses that the President is unable to discharge the powers and duties of his office, the Vice President shall continue to discharge the same as Acting President; otherwise, the President shall resume the power and duties of his office.

Amendment XXVI

Section 1

The right of citizens of the United States, who are eighteen years of age or older, to vote shall not be denied or abridged by the United States or by any State on account of age.

Section 2

The Congress shall have power to enforce this article by appropriate legislation.

Amendment XXVII

No law, varying the compensation for the services of Senators and Representatives, shall take effect, until an election of representatives shall have intervened.

What It Means

Eighteen-Year-Old Vote The Twenty-sixth Amendment (1971) guarantees the right to vote to all citizens 18 years of age and older.

What It Means

Restraint on Congressional Salaries The Twenty-seventh Amendment (1992) makes congressional pay raises effective during the term following their passage. James Madison offered the amendment in 1789, but it was never adopted. In 1982 Gregory Watson, then a student at the University of Texas, discovered the forgotten amendment while doing research for a school paper. Watson made the amendment's passage his crusade.

▼ **Joint meeting of Congress**

Unit 3

Launching the Republic
1789–1825

Chapter 8

The Federalist Era
1789–1800

Chapter 9

The Jefferson Era
1800–1816

Chapter 10

Growth and Expansion
1790–1825

Original limestone marker along National Road, 1806

246

"Peace, commerce, and honest friendship with all nations, entangling alliances with none ..."
—Thomas Jefferson

Ships of the Plains by Samuel Colman

Reading History

READING SKILL

Summarizing Information

Learn It!

When you summarize information, you recount key points from the text. As you read to summarize, stop occasionally to answer the 5W questions in your own words: *Who? What? Where? When? Why?*

Who?	Thomas Pinckney
What?	Negotiated Pinckney's Treaty
Where?	Spain
When?	1795
Why?	To settle differences between the U.S. and Spain

—from Chapter 8, p. 263

Spanish leaders feared that the United States and Great Britain would work together against them in North America. Thomas Pinckney was sent to Spain to settle the differences between the United States and Spain. In 1795 **Pinckney's Treaty** gave the Americans free navigation of the Mississippi River and the right to trade at New Orleans.

Practice It!

Read the paragraphs and answer the 5W questions on another sheet of paper.

—from Chapter 10, p. 306

In 1793 **Eli Whitney** of Massachusetts invented the cotton gin. The **cotton gin** was a simple machine that quickly and efficiently removed the seeds from the cotton fiber.

Whitney also started using **interchangeable parts.** These were identical machine parts that could be put together quickly to make a complete product. These parts also made machine repair easier. Interchangeable parts allowed for the production of different kinds of goods on a large scale. This reduced the price of the goods.

Who?	_____
What?	_____
Where?	_____
When?	_____
Why?	_____

President Washington

Main Idea President Washington and the new Congress had to make many decisions about the structure of the new government.

History and You If you were founding our nation's government, what do you think would be most important? Read about the choices that Washington and the new Congress had to make.

. . . .

On April 30, 1789, George Washington took the oath of office as the first president of the United States under the federal Constitution. (Several presidents served under the Articles of Confederation.) John Adams became vice president.

Washington knew that the **precedents,** or traditions, he established would shape the future of the United States. "No slip will pass unnoticed," he said. With Congress, Washington would create departments within the executive branch, set up the court system, and add the Bill of Rights to the Constitution.

The First Congress

During the summer of 1789, Congress set up three departments and two offices in the executive branch of government. Washington chose prominent political figures to head them. The State Department, led by **Thomas Jefferson,** handled relations with other nations. The Department of the Treasury, led by **Alexander Hamilton,** handled financial matters. Henry Knox provided for the nation's defense as the secretary of the Department of War. To handle the government's legal affairs, Washington chose Edmund Randolph as attorney general. The office of postmaster general also was established.

The three department heads and the attorney general became known as the **cabinet.** However, Congress debated how much power the president should have over the cabinet. Senators were evenly divided in voting on the issue.

Vice President John Adams broke the tie. He voted to allow the president the authority to dismiss cabinet officers without Senate approval. This decision strengthened the president's position and it established his authority over the executive branch.

Judiciary Act of 1789

The first Congress also had to decide how to set up the nation's judicial system.

The first president takes the oath of office at Federal Hall in New York City.

Primary Source / Customs and Traditions

Washington's Precedents

In a letter to James Madison, Washington noted that the actions of the new government would be "the first of every thing, in our situation." Washington knew that what he did as the first president would set the standard for later presidents. Washington did set many precedents for the presidency, including:

✔ the Inaugural Address
✔ two terms in office
✔ creation of the cabinet
✔ foreign policy of neutrality

—*The Writings of George Washington*

▲ President Bush's Inaugural Address

Critical Thinking

Analyzing Why are precedents important?

Primary Source

Bill of Rights

Ratified December 15, 1791, the first 10 amendments to the U.S. Constitution state specific guarantees of individual freedoms. These rights and protections help Americans define the meaning of liberty. Examples are given below.

▲ The Bill of Rights

I Congress shall make no law respecting an establishment of religion, or prohibiting the free exercise thereof; or **abridging** the freedom of speech, or of the press; or the right of the people peaceably to assemble, and to petition the Government for a **redress** of grievances.

IV The right of the people to be secure in their persons, houses, papers, and effects, against unreasonable searches and seizures, shall not be violated, and no **Warrants** shall issue, but upon probable cause, supported by Oath or affirmation, and particularly describing the place to be searched, and the persons or things to be seized.

VI In all criminal prosecutions, the accused shall enjoy the right to a speedy and public trial, by an impartial jury of the State and district wherein the crime shall have been committed, which district shall have been previously ascertained by law, and to be informed of the nature and cause of the accusation; to be confronted with the witnesses against him; to have compulsory process for obtaining witnesses in his favor, and to have the Assistance of Counsel for his defence.

X The powers not delegated to the United States by the Constitution, nor prohibited by it to the States, are reserved to the States respectively, or to the people.

I: The First Amendment combines the five separate freedoms of religion, speech, press, assembly, and petition, or formally requesting changes of the government.

IV: The Fourth Amendment protects Americans against "unreasonable searches and seizures." No soldier, government agent, or police officer can search your home or take your property without probable, or a valid, cause.

VI: In the United States of America, the government cannot imprison people without announcing a charge, keep them imprisoned without a trial, hold a trial in secret, or stop them from seeing a lawyer.

X: This amendment is meant to prevent the federal government from abusing its power by going beyond what the Constitution allows.

VOCABULARY

abridging (uh·BRIHJ·ing): reducing
redress (rih·DREHS): fair adjustment
warrants (WAWR·uhnts): documents granting authorization

Critical Thinking

1. **Differentiating** How is freedom of speech different from freedom of the press?

2. **Making Connections** Following the terrorist attacks of September 11, 2001, many have called for increased police powers. Do you think the rights listed in the Fourth and Sixth Amendments should apply to Americans suspected of terrorism?

3. **Evaluating** Why do you think the Tenth Amendment is important?

Disagreements arose between those favoring a **uniform,** or standard, national legal system and those favoring state courts. The two groups reached a compromise in the Judiciary Act of 1789 with which Congress established a federal court system with 13 district courts and three circuit courts to serve the nation. State laws remained, but the federal courts had the power to reverse state decisions.

The Supreme Court would be the final authority on many issues. President Washington nominated **John Jay** to lead the Supreme Court as chief justice. The Senate approved Jay's nomination. With the Judiciary Act, Congress took the first steps toward creating a strong and independent national judiciary.

The Bill of Rights

Americans had long feared strong central governments. They fought a revolution to get rid of one and did not want to replace it with another. Many people insisted that the Constitution needed to include guarantees of civil liberties. Some states supported the Constitution on the condition that a bill of rights be added in the near future to guarantee personal liberties.

To fulfill promises to these states, James Madison introduced a set of amendments during the first session of Congress. Congress passed 12 amendments, and the states ratified 10 of them. In December 1791, these 10 amendments, the **Bill of Rights,** were added to the Constitution.

The Bill of Rights limits the powers of government. Its purpose is to protect the rights of individual liberty, such as freedom of speech, and the rights of persons accused of crimes, including trial by jury. With the Tenth Amendment, Madison hoped to use the states as an important line of defense against a too-powerful national government. *(See the Appendix for the Bill of Rights.)*

 Reading Check **Identifying** What did the Judiciary Act do?

The New Country's Economy

Main Idea The new country's economy developed under the guidance of Alexander Hamilton.

History and You Have you ever borrowed money from a family member or one of your friends? By doing so, you acquired a debt and had to figure out how to pay it back. Hamilton faced a similar challenge with the nation's debt.

President Washington rarely proposed laws and almost always approved the bills that Congress passed. The first president concentrated mainly on foreign affairs and military matters. Washington left the government's economic policies to his dynamic secretary of the treasury, Alexander Hamilton. When Washington appointed him to the position, Hamilton was only 34 years old. Yet he had bold plans and definite policies to deal with the country's finances.

The new nation faced serious financial problems. The **national debt**—the amount of money owed by the nation's government—was growing. Hamilton tried to find a way to improve the government's financial reputation and strengthen the nation at the same time.

Hamilton's Plan

Days after he took office, Hamilton was asked by the House of Representatives to prepare a plan for the "adequate support of public credit." This meant that the United States needed a way to borrow money for its government, its industrial development, and its commercial activity. How good the government's credit would be in the future depended on how well it could pay back the money it currently owed.

In 1790 Hamilton made his proposal. He said the new government should pay off the millions of dollars in debts owed by the Confederation government to other countries and to individual American citizens. The states fought for the nation's independence, Hamilton argued, so the national government should pay for the cost of their help.

Economics & History

Protective Tariffs *In the late 1700s, American industries lacked the experience to make goods efficiently. As a result, their production costs were higher than those of their foreign competitors. A protective tariff would raise the price of imported products, helping American companies compete.*

Hat made in Britain $7   **Hat made in U.S.** $6

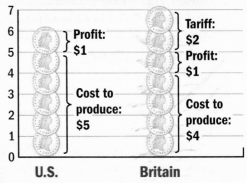

Breakdown of Cost

U.S.: Profit: $1; Cost to produce: $5
Britain: Tariff: $2; Profit: $1; Cost to produce: $4

▲ A British-made hat would cost $5 in Britain. The same hat made in America is $6. With a $2 tariff, Americans pay $7 for the imported British hat but only $6 for the American-made hat.

Critical Thinking

1. **Drawing Conclusions** Which hat would sell more with the tariff? Why?
2. **Speculating** How might the issue of tariffs impact U.S. relations with Britain?

Hamilton also believed that federal payment of state debts would give the states a strong interest in the success of the national government.

Opposition to the Plan

Congress agreed to pay money owed to other nations. However, Hamilton's plan to pay off the debt to American citizens unleashed a storm of protest. When borrowing money during the American Revolution, the government issued **bonds.** These are paper notes promising to repay the money in a certain length of time. While waiting for the payment, many of the original bond owners—shopkeepers, farmers, and soldiers—sold the bonds for less than their value. They were purchased by speculators, people who risk money in order to make a larger profit. Hamilton proposed that these bonds be paid off at their original value.

Opponents believed that Hamilton's plan would make speculators rich. They said his plan was "established at the expense of national justice, gratitude, and humanity." The original bond owners also felt betrayed by the government. They lost money on their bonds while new bond owners profited.

Even stronger opposition came from the Southern states, which **accumulated,** or collected, much less debt than the Northern states. Southern states complained that they would have to pay more than their share under Hamilton's plan.

Compromise Results in a Capital

To win support for his plan, Hamilton worked out a compromise with Southern leaders. If they voted for his plan to pay off the state debts, he would, in return, support locating the new nation's capital in the South.

A special district would be laid out between Virginia and Maryland along the banks of the Potomac River. This district became Washington, D.C. While workers prepared the new city, the nation's capital was moved from New York to Philadelphia.

The Fight Over the Bank

To help build a strong national economy, Hamilton also asked Congress to create a national bank—the Bank of the United States. Both private investors and the national government would own the Bank's stock, or shares of ownership.

In 1792 only eight other banks existed in the nation, all of them established by the states. Madison and Jefferson opposed a national bank, believing it would benefit the wealthy. They also charged that the Bank was **unconstitutional**—or inconsistent with the Constitution. Hamilton agreed that the Constitution did not specifically say a bank could be created. However, he argued, Congress still had the power to do so. Washington agreed, and a national bank was created.

Tariffs and Taxes

Hamilton believed that agricultural America would benefit from more manufacturing. He proposed a **tariff**—a tax on imports—to protect new American industries from foreign competition. The South, having little industry, opposed such tariffs. Hamilton, however, won support in Congress for low tariffs, which raised money rather than protected industry.

Hamilton's plan also called for national taxes to help the government pay off the national debt. At Hamilton's request, Congress approved a variety of taxes, including one on whiskey distilled in the United States.

Hamilton also planned to give the national government new financial powers. Opponents, such as Jefferson and Madison, however, feared a strong national government run by the wealthy. Their vision of America was very different.

✔ **Reading Check** Summarizing Summarize Hamilton's plan for building the nation's economy.

Section 1 Review

History ONLINE
Study Central™ To review this section, go to glencoe.com.

Vocabulary

1. Use each term in a sentence to help explain its meaning: precedent, cabinet, uniform, national debt, bond, accumulate, unconstitutional, tariff.

Main Ideas

2. Discussing How did the first Congress support President Washington in establishing the executive branch?

3. Summarizing Why did Madison and Jefferson disagree with Hamilton's proposal for a national bank? What was the outcome?

Critical Thinking

4. Diagramming Use a diagram like the one below to show the court system established by the Judiciary Act of 1789. List the two levels and explain their powers.

Level:
Power:

Level:
Power:

5. Contrasting Discuss the arguments of those in favor of and against Hamilton's plan to improve the economy.

6. Expository Writing Do you think the first Congress was right in giving the president the authority to dismiss cabinet members without the approval of the Senate? Write a paragraph explaining your point of view.

Answer the
7. Essential Question
What were the precedents that Washington established as the first president of the United States?

Choosing the Location of Washington, D.C.

Before 1790 the United States had no permanent capital city. Early Congresses met in various cities. A political compromise established the nation's capital along the Potomac River.

How Did Geography Affect the Early Development of Washington, D.C.?

The city's site was selected by George Washington. He may have chosen it for its natural scenery or his belief that the Potomac would become a great navigable waterway. Unfortunately, debris and silt were deposited in the shallow tidal areas around the developing city. Ships could not travel the length of the river. The stagnant water created unhealthy conditions and a rotten smell.

◄ French architect Pierre L'Enfant designed the plan for the city of Washington, D.C., in 1791.

▲ **Map of Washington, D.C., 1791** L'Enfant's basic plan included wide avenues and major streets radiating out from traffic circles. Modern Washington, D.C., still retains many of the elements of L'Enfant's plan.

◄ Mathematician and inventor Benjamin Banneker was hired in 1791 to help survey the land for the new national capital. In addition to his other talents, Banneker was also a farmer and a publisher of a well-known yearly almanac.

Benjamin Banneker
Black Heritage USA 15c

◄ **The City's Location** Straddling the Potomac River, Washington, D.C., was laid out on land handed over to the federal government from both Maryland and Virginia. The Virginia land was given back to Virginia in 1846. Thus, all of the city's current area was originally part of Maryland.

◄ Washington, D.C., is famous for its cherry blossoms. This scene shows blossoms along the Tidal Basin.

The Tidal Basin To help reduce the amount of stagnant water near the Potomac, an inlet called the Tidal Basin was created in the 1880s. The basin provides a means for draining the Washington Channel and flushing the channel with relatively clean water with each change of tide.

1 **Washington Monument**

2 **Jefferson Memorial**

3 **Franklin Delano Roosevelt Memorial**

4 **White House**

Washington, D.C., in 1801 The city was slowly rising from a marshy site on the Potomac River. The nation's capital had only two noteworthy buildings—the president's mansion (later called the White House) and the still-unfinished Capitol. Between them stretched about two miles of muddy streets. ►

MAIN·FLOOR·PLAN
PRESENT
EXECUTIVE·MANSION
James Hoban, Original Architect. 1792.

Analyzing Geography

1. **Human-Environment Interaction** One of the reasons that the site was chosen as the capital was that it was in the center of the country. What are the advantages of such a location?

2. **Location** How do you think the location of Washington, D.C., affected its early growth? Explain.

Section 2 ★ Early Challenges

Essential Question ◄

What challenges did the United States face during Washington's administration?

Reading Guide

Content Vocabulary

neutrality (p. 262)

impressment (p. 263)

Academic Vocabulary

challenge (p. 261)   maintain (p. 261)

Key People and Events

Whiskey Rebellion (p. 261)

Battle of Fallen Timbers (p. 262)

Treaty of Greenville (p. 262)

Edmond Genêt (p. 263)

Jay's Treaty (p. 263)

Pinckney's Treaty (p. 263)

Reading Strategy

Taking Notes As you read, use a diagram like the one below to summarize how the treaties described in this section affected the United States.

Treaty		Effect
Treaty of Greenville	→	
Jay's Treaty	→	
Pinckney's Treaty	→	

NEW YORK STANDARDS
The American Journey

U5.I.1 To understand how the new nation established itself and began to operate

U5.I.4 To understand the relationship between and the relative importance of United States domestic and foreign policies over time

U5.I.5 To analyze the role played by the United States in international politics, past and present

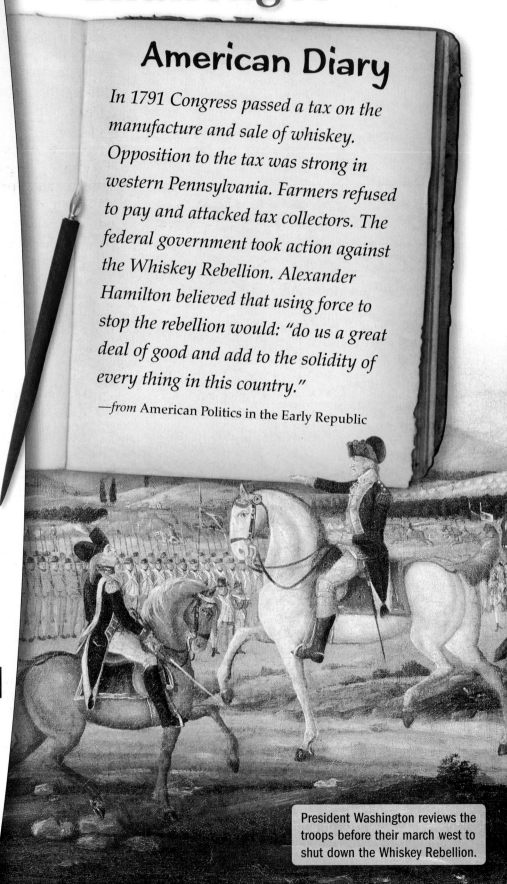

American Diary

In 1791 Congress passed a tax on the manufacture and sale of whiskey. Opposition to the tax was strong in western Pennsylvania. Farmers refused to pay and attacked tax collectors. The federal government took action against the Whiskey Rebellion. Alexander Hamilton believed that using force to stop the rebellion would: "do us a great deal of good and add to the solidity of every thing in this country."

—*from* American Politics in the Early Republic

President Washington reviews the troops before their march west to shut down the Whiskey Rebellion.

The Whiskey Rebellion and the West

Main Idea The new government was faced with challenges in Pennsylvania and on the frontier.

History and You Have you ever opposed a government action? Read to learn how the new government handled rebellious citizens.

The Whiskey Rebellion was only one **challenge,** or demanding situation, faced by the new government. Native Americans, aided by the British and Spanish, were resisting the American settlers' expansion westward. Britain and France were pressuring the United States to become more involved in their conflicts. President Washington stood firm by not involving the United States in foreign conflicts.

The Whiskey Rebellion

Washington was concerned about the growing resistance of western Pennsylvania farmers to the tax on whiskey. Their protest turned violent in July 1794. An armed mob attacked tax collectors and burned down buildings. This armed protest, called the **Whiskey Rebellion,** alarmed government leaders. Washington and his advisers decided to crush the challenge. This action sent messages that the government would use force when necessary to **maintain,** or keep, the social order.

Struggle Over the West

The new government also faced difficult problems in the West. Washington worried about European ambitions in the Northwest Territory. He signed treaties with the Native Americans, hoping to lessen the influence of the British and Spanish on them. American settlers ignored the treaties and moved onto lands promised to the Native Americans. Fighting broke out between the two groups.

Washington sent an army under General Arthur St. Clair to restore order in the Northwest Territory. In November 1791, St. Clair's forces were defeated by Little Turtle, chief of the Miami people. More than 600 American soldiers died in the battle by the Wabash River.

Many Americans believed an alliance with France would help them defeat the British, Spanish, and Native Americans in the West.

Primary Source | The Whiskey Rebellion

Thomas Jefferson accused Hamilton of orchestrating the rebellion: "an insurrection [rebellion] was announced & proclaimed & armed against, but could never be found."

▲ Rebels tar and feather a tax collector during the Whiskey Rebellion.

Critical Thinking

Explaining How did Alexander Hamilton want to respond to the rebellion?

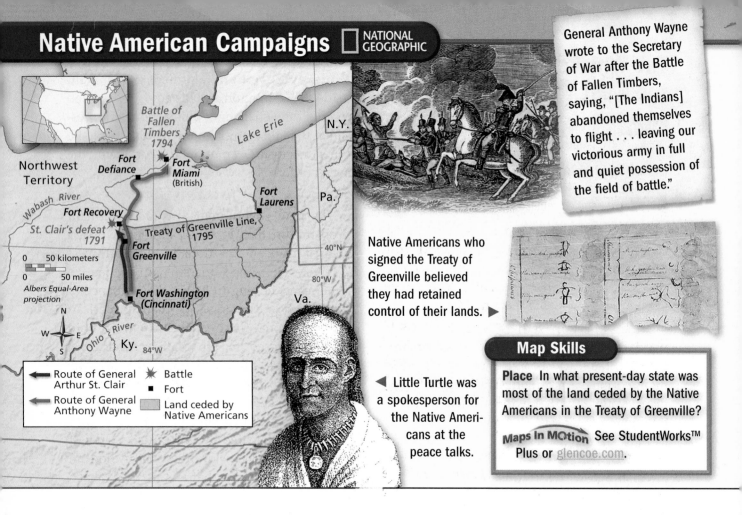

Native American Campaigns NATIONAL GEOGRAPHIC

General Anthony Wayne wrote to the Secretary of War after the Battle of Fallen Timbers, saying, "[The Indians] abandoned themselves to flight . . . leaving our victorious army in full and quiet possession of the field of battle."

Native Americans who signed the Treaty of Greenville believed they had retained control of their lands. ▶

◀ Little Turtle was a spokesperson for the Native Americans at the peace talks.

Map Skills

Place In what present-day state was most of the land ceded by the Native Americans in the Treaty of Greenville?

Maps In Motion See StudentWorks™ Plus or glencoe.com.

Map legend:
- Route of General Arthur St. Clair
- Route of General Anthony Wayne
- ✱ Battle
- ■ Fort
- Land ceded by Native Americans

The possibility of French involvement prompted Britain to take action in the West. In 1794 the British government urged Native Americans to destroy American settlements west of the Appalachians. The British also began building a new fort in Ohio.

The Native Americans demanded that all settlers north of the Ohio River leave the territory. Washington sent another army under Anthony Wayne, a former Revolutionary War general, to challenge their demands. In August 1794 his army defeated more than 1,000 Native Americans led by the Shawnee chief Blue Jacket at the **Battle of Fallen Timbers** (near present-day Toledo, Ohio). The Battle of Fallen Timbers crushed the Native Americans' hopes of keeping their land. In the **Treaty of Greenville** (1795), they agreed to surrender most of the land in what is now Ohio.

Reading Check **Analyzing** Why did some Americans want to form an alliance with France?

Problems With Europe

Main Idea President Washington wanted the nation to remain neutral in foreign conflicts.

History and You Have you ever been in the middle of a disagreement between two friends? Read why Washington looked for middle ground in a war between Britain and France.

Most Americans cheered the French Revolution of 1789 because of its similarity to America's own revolution. By 1793, however, the French Revolution turned bloody. Public opinion was now divided.

When Britain and France went to war in 1793, some Americans sympathized with France and others supported Britain. Washington hoped that the United States could maintain its **neutrality**—not taking sides in the conflict between France and Britain. As time passed, however, remaining neutral became more difficult.

Washington Proclaims Neutrality

The French tried to involve the United States in their conflict with Britain. They sent diplomat **Edmond Genêt** (zhuh•NAY) to recruit American volunteers to attack British ships. In response, President Washington issued a Proclamation of Neutrality, which prohibited American citizens from fighting in the war. It also barred French and British warships from American ports. The British captured American ships that traded with the French and forced the American crews into the British navy. This practice of **impressment** angered the Americans.

Washington sent John Jay, chief justice of the Supreme Court, to negotiate a peaceful solution with Britain. Few Americans approved of **Jay's Treaty.** In it, the British agreed to withdraw from American soil. However, the treaty did not deal with the issue of impressment or British interference with American trade. Washington found fault with the treaty but realized it would end the crisis. The Senate narrowly approved it after a fierce debate.

Treaty With Spain

Spanish leaders feared that the United States and Great Britain would work together against them in North America. Thomas Pinckney was sent to Spain to settle the differences between the United States and Spain. In 1795 **Pinckney's Treaty** gave the Americans free navigation of the Mississippi River and the right to trade at New Orleans.

Washington's Farewell

Washington decided not to seek a third term. In his Farewell Address, he attacked political parties and involvement in foreign affairs. He also urged his fellow citizens to:

PRIMARY SOURCE

"Observe good faith and justice toward all nations. . . . . . . It is our true policy to steer clear of permanent alliances."

—from *The Annals of America*

These parting words influenced the nation's foreign policy for more than 100 years.

Reading Check **Explaining** What was the significance of Jay's Treaty?

Section 2 Review

History ONLINE
Study Central™ To review this section, go to glencoe.com.

Vocabulary

1. Write headlines for newspaper stories about the U.S. role in the Britain-France conflict. Use and show understanding of the terms: challenge, maintain, neutrality, impressment.

Main Ideas

2. **Identifying** What did Washington's actions in crushing the Whiskey Rebellion signify to the country?

3. **Discussing** How did the British challenge U.S. neutrality in the war between France and Britain?

Critical Thinking

4. **Comparing and Contrasting** Compare and contrast U.S. attitudes and actions toward the Native Americans and U.S. actions in foreign affairs.

5. **Determining Cause and Effect** Use a diagram like the one below to show the causes and the effect of the Battle of Fallen Timbers.

6. **Persuasive Writing** Imagine that you disagree with Washington's policy of neutrality in the war between France and Britain. Write a letter to the president to persuade him to side with France.

Answer the Essential Question

7. What challenges did the United States face during Washington's administration?

The First Political Parties

Essential Question

How did the Federalist and Republican Parties form, and on what issues did they disagree?

Reading Guide

Content Vocabulary

partisan (p. 265)
implied powers (p. 266)
caucus (p. 268)
alien (p. 269)

sedition (p. 270)
nullify (p. 270)
states' rights (p. 270)

Academic Vocabulary

resolve (p. 269)   principle (p. 270)

Key People and Events

XYZ affair (p. 269)
Alien and Sedition Acts (p. 270)
Virginia and Kentucky Resolutions (p. 270)

Reading Strategy

Taking Notes As you read, create a diagram like the one below. Identify the differences between the Federalists and the Republicans on the role of the federal government.

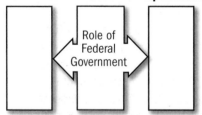

Federalists   Issue   Republicans

Role of Federal Government

NEW YORK STANDARDS
The American Journey

U5.I.2 To understand how political parties emerged in response to concerns at the local, State, and national levels

U5.I.3 To understand how civic values reflected in the United States and New York State constitutions have been implemented through law and practice

U5.I.4 To understand the relationship between and the relative importance of United States domestic and foreign policies over time

American Diary

Although many Americans hailed George Washington as a great leader, the president did not escape criticism. One critic was Ben Franklin's grandson, Benjamin Franklin Bache, a writer and publisher. Washington, Bache wrote, was "but a man, and certainly not a great man." Bache even criticized Washington's military leadership during the American Revolution, describing him as "ignorant of war both in theory and useful practice."

— *from* Remarks Occasioned by the Late Conduct of Mr. Washington

George and Martha Washington

History ONLINE

For additional test practice, use **Self-Check Quizzes**–Chapter 8 at glencoe.com.

Document-Based Questions

Directions: Analyze the documents and answer the short-answer questions that follow.

Document 1

The following passage is taken from the Treaty of Greenville, 1795.

> The Indian tribes who have a right to those lands, are quietly to enjoy them, hunting, planting, and dwelling thereon, so long as they please, without any [interference] from the United States; but when those tribes, or any of them, shall . . . sell their lands, or any part of them, they are to be sold only to the United States; and until such sale, the United States will protect all the said Indian tribes in the quiet enjoyment of their lands against all citizens of the United States. . . . And the said Indian tribes again acknowledge themselves to be under the protection of the said United States, and no other power whatever.

Source: The Treaty of Greenville

7 What does the United States government promise Native Americans in this document? What do Native Americans promise to do?

Document 2

In the following passage, Washington describes his feelings about political parties.

> I . . . warn you in the most solemn manner against the baneful [harmful] effects of the spirit of party generally.
>
> This spirit, unfortunately, is inseparable from our nature. . . . It exists under different shapes in all governments . . . but, in those of the popular form, it is seen in its greatest rankness, and is truly their worst enemy.

Source: George Washington's Farewell Address

8 According to Washington, why do political parties exist?

Document 3

This 1798 cartoon depicts a fight between two House members—Republican Matthew Lyon (center) and Federalist Roger Griswold (right)—over the Sedition Act.

Source: CORBIS

9 How are others reacting to the fight?

Document 4

Tenth Amendment to the U.S. Constitution:

> The powers not delegated to the United States by the Constitution, nor prohibited by it to the States, are reserved to the States respectively, or to the people.

Source: The Bill of Rights

10 Which political party—Federalists or Republicans—do you think supported this amendment more? Explain.

11 Persuasive Writing Using the information from the four documents and your knowledge of social studies, write an essay in which you:

- compare and contrast Federalist and Republican visions of America; and

- explain which of those visions is most closely related to the ideals on which the United States was founded.

Need Extra Help?											
If you missed questions. . .	1	2	3	4	5	6	7	8	9	10	11
Go to page. . .	253–255	266–267	261	270	266–267	260–268	261–262	264–268	269–270	264–268	252–270

The Jefferson Era 1800-1816

Monticello, located in Charlottesville, Virginia, was the home of Thomas Jefferson.

THOMAS JEFFERSON 1801–1809

PRESIDENTS

U.S. Events

★ **1801** Robert Fulton builds first submarine

★ **1803** Supreme Court establishes judicial review

1804 Lewis and Clark begin expedition

★ **1804** Alexander Hamilton duels with Aaron Burr

JAMES MADISON 1809–1817

World Events

1800

1805

Drawing of Fulton's submarine ▶

★ **1803** War begins again between France and Britain

1804 ★ Napoleon proclaims himself emperor of France

★ **1806** Holy Roman Empire officially ends

★ **1808** Extensive excavations begin at Pompeii

Section 1: The Republicans Take Power

Essential Question In what ways did Thomas Jefferson and the Republicans limit the powers of the government?

Section 2: The Louisiana Purchase

Essential Question How did the Louisiana Purchase affect the nation's economy and politics?

Section 3: A Time of Conflict

Essential Question What were the challenges to the nation's stability during the late 1700s and early 1800s?

Section 4: The War of 1812

Essential Question How did the United States benefit from its victory in the War of 1812?

FOLDABLES
Study Organizer

Organizing Information
Make this four-tab Foldable to help you learn about the events of the Jefferson era.

Step 1 Fold the sides of a piece of paper into the middle to make a shutter fold.

Step 2 Cut each tab at the midpoint to form four tabs.

Step 3 Label the tabs as shown.

Reading and Writing
As you read the chapter, take notes about each section under the appropriate head. Use your Foldable to help you write a summary for each section.

◀ The U.S. Capitol after it was burned by the British in 1814.

Tecumseh ▶

1811 Tecumseh joins British forces after the Battle of Tippecanoe

1812 U.S. declares war on Britain

1814 British forces burn Washington, D.C.

1815 Battle of New Orleans

1810

1812

1816

1809 Ecuador wins independence from Spain

1812 Napoleon invades Russia

1813 Simón Bolívar becomes dictator of Venezuela

1814 Congress of Vienna meets

1815 Napoleon defeated at Waterloo

Section 1

The Republicans Take Power

Essential Question ◄

In what ways did Thomas Jefferson and the Republicans limit the powers of the government?

Reading Guide

Content Vocabulary

laissez-faire *(p. 278)*

judicial review *(p. 279)*

customs duties *(p. 278)*

Academic Vocabulary

similar *(p. 278)*

conflict *(p. 279)*

Key People and Events

Thomas Jefferson *(p. 277)*

Aaron Burr *(p. 277)*

Judiciary Act of 1801 *(p. 279)*

Marbury v. Madison (p. 279)

Reading Strategy

Taking Notes As you read, use a diagram like the one below to identify how the Republicans reduced the role of government.

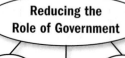

Reducing the Role of Government

NEW YORK STANDARDS
The American Journey

U5.I.1 To understand how the new nation established itself and began to operate

U5.I.2 To understand how political parties emerged in response to concerns at the local, State, and national levels

U5.I.3 To understand how civic values reflected in the United States and New York State constitutions have been implemented through law and practice

American Diary

For eight years, Thomas Jefferson opposed the Federalists and eventually won the presidency as a member of a new political party—the Democratic-Republicans. In his Inaugural Address, Jefferson tried to reach out to Federalists and bridge the gap that developed between the two parties. "We are all Republicans, we are all Federalists. . . . Let us, then, with courage and confidence pursue our own Federal and Republican principles, our attachment to union and representative government."

—from Jefferson's first Inaugural Address, 1801

The Capitol, Washington, D.C., 1800

276

The Election of 1800

Main Idea The election of 1800 showed that power could be peacefully transferred even when the political parties were in disagreement.

History and You Think about today's political campaigns. Are they based on emotional appeals or serious discussion of the issues? Read to find out how the presidential election campaign of 1800 was conducted.

- -

The Federalist and Republican Parties fought a bitter election campaign in 1800. Federalists supported President Adams for a second term and Charles Pinckney for vice president. Republicans nominated **Thomas Jefferson** for president and **Aaron Burr** as his running mate.

The election campaign of 1800 differed greatly from campaigns of today. Neither Adams nor Jefferson traveled around the country to gather support. This would have been considered inappropriate. Instead, the candidates and their supporters began a letter-writing campaign. They sent hundreds of letters to leading citizens and newspapers to make their views public. Federalists accused Jefferson, who believed in freedom of religion, of being "godless." Republicans warned that the Federalists favored the wealthy and would bring back monarchy.

Election Deadlock

Jefferson and Burr each received 73 electoral votes. Because of the tie vote, the House of Representatives had to decide the election. At this time, the electors voted for each candidate individually. The candidate with the majority of votes became president. The candidate with the next-largest number of votes became vice president.

In the House, Federalists saw a chance to prevent the election of Jefferson. They supported Burr. For 35 ballots, the election remained tied. Finally, at Alexander Hamilton's urging, one Federalist decided not to vote for Burr. Jefferson became president, and Burr became vice president.

To prevent another tie between a presidential and vice-presidential candidate, Congress passed the Twelfth Amendment to the Constitution in 1803. Electors now had to vote for the president and vice president on separate ballots.

By the Numbers — Election Results, 1800

Presidential Candidate
- Jefferson (Democratic-Republican)
- Adams (Federalist)
- 3 Electoral votes

Critical Thinking

Speculating Do you think a person's political views will always match those of his or her political party?

Invention and Design Thomas Jefferson was a passionate inventor and architect. He invented a plow that was easy to use on hills, a machine to make macaroni, and a device to encode secret messages. Jefferson also designed his Monticello home and the Rotunda on the campus of the University of Virginia.

"One new idea leads to another, that to a third, and so on through a course of time until some one, with whom no one of these ideas was original, combines all together, and produces what is justly called a new invention."

—The Writings of Thomas Jefferson

▲ Jefferson employed other people's inventions at his Monticello home. He used a copying machine, known as a "polygraph," invented by John Isaac Hawkins. This machine used two pens to copy words at the same time, allowing the writer to create automatic duplicates of documents.

◄ Thomas Jefferson and Charles-Louis Clerisseau were the architects for Virginia's State Capitol in Richmond. Jefferson's design was inspired by first-century Roman architecture.

Critical Thinking

Drawing Conclusions What characteristics do you think a person should have in order to be a successful inventor?

Jefferson's Inauguration

Jefferson, dressed in everyday clothes, walked from his boardinghouse to the Senate to be sworn in as president. President Adams chose not to attend the ceremony.

In his Inaugural Address, Jefferson tried to bridge the gap between the political parties. Then he outlined some of his goals. They included "a wise and frugal government" and "the support of state governments in all their rights." Jefferson believed a large federal government threatened liberty. The states, he believed, could better protect freedom.

Jefferson believed in reducing the power and size of the government. These ideas were **similar** to the French philosophy known as **laissez-faire** (LEH•SAY FEHR). This phrase means "let people do as they choose."

Reading Check **Describing** What does the Twelfth Amendment require?

Jefferson's Presidency

Main Idea Thomas Jefferson wanted to reduce the power of the federal government.

History and You How do you think government should balance individual liberty with national interests? Read about Jefferson's views.

Thomas Jefferson had strong ideas about how to make the United States a great nation. He surrounded himself with those who shared his views.

Cutting Costs

Jefferson and Albert Gallatin, secretary of the treasury, reduced the national debt. They scaled down military expenses. All federal internal taxes, including the whiskey tax, were repealed. Government funds would come only from **customs duties**—taxes on imported goods—and from the money raised from the sale of western lands. Jefferson also limited the number of federal government workers to a few hundred people.

Judiciary Act of 1801

Before Jefferson took office, the Federalists passed the **Judiciary Act of 1801.** This act set up regional courts for the United States with 16 judges and other judicial officials.

In his last days as president, John Adams made hundreds of appointments to these judicial positions with the approval of the Federalist-controlled Congress. Adams also asked John Marshall, secretary of state, to serve as chief justice. Thus, Adams shut Jefferson out of the appointment process and ensured Federalist control of the courts.

Adams and Marshall worked around the clock to process these judicial appointments. The appointments could not take effect, however, until the papers, also known as commissions, for these last-minute "midnight judges" were received. When Jefferson became president, a few of the commissions had not yet been delivered. He told his Secretary of State James Madison not to deliver them. One commission was to go to William Marbury.

Marbury v. Madison

To force the delivery of his commission, Marbury took his case directly to the Supreme Court. He claimed this court had jurisdiction. John Marshall wrote an opinion turning down Marbury's claim. He noted that the Constitution did not give the Court jurisdiction to decide Marbury's case.

In *Marbury v. Madison,* three principles of **judicial review** were established: (1) the Constitution is the supreme law; (2) the Constitution must be followed when there is a **conflict,** or disagreement, between it and any other law; and (3) the judicial branch must uphold the Constitution and nullify, or cancel, unconstitutional laws.

Marshall broadened federal power at the expense of the states. In *McCulloch* v. *Maryland* (1819), the Court held that Congress is allowed to do more than the Constitution expressly authorizes it to do. In *Gibbons* v. *Ogden* (1824), the Court held that federal law takes precedence over state law in interstate transportation.

✔ **Reading Check** **Summarizing** Summarize the three principles of judicial review.

Section 1 Review

History ONLINE
Study Central™ To review this section, go to glencoe.com.

Vocabulary

1. Use the following terms in sentences that show you understand their meanings: similar, laissez-faire, customs duties, judicial review, conflict.

Main Ideas

2. Discussing How did President Jefferson's Inaugural Address reflect his beliefs about government?

3. Explaining Explain how the Federalists benefited from the Judiciary Act of 1801.

Critical Thinking

4. Identifying Central Issues Use a diagram like the one below to show how the powers of the Supreme Court and federal law were extended.

Case	Decision
Marbury v. *Madison*	
McCulloch v. *Maryland*	
Gibbons v. *Ogden*	

5. Persuasive Writing You are a supporter of Thomas Jefferson in the 1800 election. Write a letter to voters that will appear in all the newspapers in your state.

Answer the
6. Essential Question
In what ways did Thomas Jefferson and the Republicans limit the powers of the government?

Section 2 ★ The Louisiana Purchase

Essential Question ◄

How did the Louisiana Purchase affect the nation's economy and politics?

Reading Guide

Content Vocabulary

Conestoga wagon *(p. 281)*

secede *(p. 285)*

Academic Vocabulary

purchase *(p. 283)*   authority *(p.283)*

Key People and Events

Napoleon Bonaparte *(p. 282)*

Meriwether Lewis *(p. 284)*

William Clark *(p. 284)*

Sacagawea *(p. 284)*

Zebulon Pike *(p. 285)*

Reading Strategy

Taking Notes As you read, use a diagram like the one below to describe the areas that Lewis and Clark and Zebulon Pike explored.

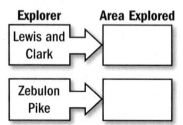

Explorer	Area Explored
Lewis and Clark →	
Zebulon Pike →	

NEW YORK STANDARDS
The American Journey

U5.I.4 To understand the relationship between and the relative importance of United States domestic and foreign policies over time

U5.I.5 To analyze the role played by the United States in international politics, past and present

U5.I.6 To explain how societies and nations attempt to satisfy their basic needs and wants by utilizing scarce capital, natural, and human resources

American Diary

In this journal entry from May 5, 1805, Meriwether Lewis describes America's bounty along the trail: "Buffalo Elk and goats or Antelopes feeding in every direction; we kill whatever we wish, the buffalo furnish us with fine veal and fat beef, we also have venison and beaver tails when we wish them; the flesh of the Elk and goat are less esteemed, and certainly are inferior. We have not been able to take any fish for some time past. The country is as yesterday beautiful in the extreme."

—from the journals of Lewis and Clark

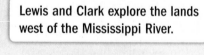

Lewis and Clark explore the lands west of the Mississippi River.

Western Territory

Main Idea As Americans moved west in the early 1800s, Spain and France made a secret agreement about land that affected American trade.

History and You If you have ever moved to a new city or state, what challenges did you face? How did you learn where grocery stores or your school were located? Read to learn about challenges that the pioneers experienced as they moved west.

• •

During the early 1800s, Americans moved west in search of land and adventure. Pioneers traveled over the mountains into Kentucky and Tennessee. Many also set out for the less settled areas of the Northwest Territory. Most of these pioneers were farmers. They made a long and exhausting journey over the Appalachian Mountains. Pioneers heading to the western lands had to trudge along crude, muddy roads or cut their way through dense forests.

Settlers loaded their household goods into **Conestoga wagons,** sturdy vehicles topped with white canvas. These westward-bound pioneers traveled with their two most valued possessions: rifles and axes. Rifles were carried for protection and for hunting animals for food. Axes helped the settlers cut through the dense forests so that their wagons could travel through them.

In 1800 the territory of the United States extended only as far west as the Mississippi River. The area to the west of the river was known as the Louisiana Territory. This region belonged to Spain. It was an enormous area of land, anchored to the south by the city of New Orleans and extending west to the Rocky Mountains. Its northern boundaries remained undefined.

Many of the pioneers established farms along rivers that fed into the upper Mississippi River. They used the river system to ship their crops to markets. The goods they sent downriver were unloaded in New Orleans. The goods were then loaded onto other ships and sent to markets on the East Coast. If the farmers did not have access to the Mississippi River, then there was no way to ship their goods.

Even though the Spanish controlled the region, they allowed the Americans to sail on the lower Mississippi and trade in New Orleans. For the western farmers, this agreement was vital to their economic survival.

Primary Source / The Journals

Exploring the West From 1804 to 1806, Meriwether Lewis and William Clark explored and mapped more than 7,000 miles (11,265 km) from St. Louis to the Pacific Ocean and back. During the journey, they met with many Native Americans and accumulated valuable information about the western frontier.

In addition to their travel supplies, the expedition also took along items that were used to trade or give as gifts to the Native Americans. These items included:

- 12 dozen pocket mirrors
- 144 small pairs of scissors
- 8 brass kettles
- 33 pounds (15 kg) of tiny beads of assorted colors

Critical Thinking

Speculating What challenges do you think the expedition might have faced?

Wagons to Go West Conestoga wagons were first built in the Conestoga Creek region of Lancaster, Pennsylvania. During the mid-1700s, these sturdy wagons transported settlers over the Appalachian Mountains. As people pushed even farther westward, Conestoga wagons could be seen rolling across the plains toward Oregon and California.

1 Six to eight draft horses or a dozen oxen pull the wagon. The driver rides or walks beside the animals.

2 The boat-shaped wagon's high front and back keep goods from falling out on steep mountain trails.

3 A **toolbox** attached to the side of the wagon holds spare parts for needed repairs.

4 A white canvas cloth stretches over the hoops, or **wagon bows.** This cover protects passengers and cargo from heat, rain, and snow.

5 Broad **wheels** help keep the heavy wagon from being mired in the mud.

The average Conestoga wagon was 21 feet (6 m) long and 11 feet (3 m) high. It could carry up to 12,000 pounds (5,443 kg) of cargo.

Critical Thinking

Listing List three things a family traveling by wagon will have to plan for.

The French Threat

In 1802, however, the Spanish suddenly changed their policy. They refused to allow American goods to move into or past New Orleans. President Jefferson confirmed that Spain and France had secretly agreed to transfer the Louisiana Territory to France.

Jefferson was alarmed. This agreement between Spain and France posed a serious diplomatic and economic threat to the United States. France's leader, **Napoleon Bonaparte,** had plans to create empires in Europe and the Americas. Jefferson believed French control would put American trade on the Mississippi River at risk. Jefferson authorized Robert Livingston, the new minister to France, to offer as much as $10 million for New Orleans and West Florida in order to gain control of the territory. Jefferson believed that France had gained Florida as well as Louisiana in its secret agreement with Spain.

Revolt in Santo Domingo

Napoleon saw Santo Domingo as an important Caribbean naval base from which he could control an American empire. Events in Santo Domingo, however, ended Napoleon's dream of a Western empire.

The ideas of the French Revolution inspired enslaved Africans and other laborers in Santo Domingo to revolt against the island's plantation owners. Toussaint-Louverture (TOO•SA LOO•vuhr•TYUR) led the rebels. After fierce fighting, the rebels won and declared the colony an independent republic. Toussaint-Louverture established a new government.

In 1802 Napoleon sent troops to regain control of Santo Domingo, but they were not successful. By 1804, the French were driven out of Santo Domingo. The country regained its original name of Haiti.

Reading Check **Explaining** Why did French control of the Louisiana Territory worry Jefferson?

The Nation Expands

Main Idea The Louisiana Purchase opened a vast area to exploration and settlement.

History and You Imagine you are preparing to lead an expedition to explore new lands. Who would you travel with? What would you like to research? Read about the exploration of the Louisiana Territory.

. . . .

Without Santo Domingo, Napoleon had little use for Louisiana. Napoleon, however, needed money to finance his plans for war against Britain. The French believed that it was time to sell the Louisiana Territory.

French foreign minister Charles de Talleyrand informed the American diplomats that the entire Louisiana Territory was for sale. Robert Livingston and James Monroe, who was Jefferson's new special representative, were taken completely by surprise. They were not authorized to accept such an offer. The deal, however, was too good to pass up. After a few days of negotiation, the parties agreed on a price of $15 million.

The new territory would provide cheap and abundant land for farmers for future generations and give the United States control of the Mississippi River. Jefferson worried, though, about whether the **purchase** was legal. The Constitution said nothing about acquiring new territory. By what **authority,** or power, could he justify the purchase? Livingston wrote from Paris. He urged Jefferson to accept the deal before Napoleon changed his mind. Jefferson decided the government's treaty-making powers allowed the purchase of the new territory. The Senate approved it in October 1803. The size of the United States doubled.

Lewis and Clark

Little was known about the newly acquired land west of the Mississippi. Even before the deal was complete, Jefferson had been making plans to learn more about the western territory. He persuaded Congress to sponsor an expedition to gather information about the new land. Jefferson was particularly interested in the expedition as a scientific venture.

Louisiana Purchase and Westward Expansion   NATIONAL GEOGRAPHIC

"The great objects in view . . . were to . . . acquire such geographical knowledge of the southwestern boundary of Louisiana as to enable our Government to enter into a definite arrangement for a line of demarcation between that territory and North Mexico."
—Lt. Zebulon Pike, 1806

▼ Zebulon Pike Expedition

Map Skills

Movement Why did the expedition travel so far north into the territory?

Maps In MOtion See StudentWorks™ Plus or glencoe.com.

People IN HISTORY

Sacagawea

Shoshone Interpreter

Sacagawea, the daughter of a Shoshone chief, was kidnapped by the Hidatsa when she was a young girl. Later, she was sold to a French Canadian fur trader who married her.

The couple brought along their infant son when they were hired as interpreters by Meriwether Lewis and William Clark for their expedition to the Pacific Ocean.

Sacagawea made herself invaluable. She negotiated the purchases of horses, found edible wild plants, and made moccasins and clothing. Clark wrote that her presence alone calmed fears among Native Americans:

"The sight of This Indian woman . . . confirmed those people of our friendly intentions, as no woman ever accompanies a war party of Indians in this quarter [region]."

—from the journals of Lewis and Clark

CRITICAL Thinking

Theorizing What challenges might the expedition have faced without Sacagawea?

The expedition would document findings about the territory's plants and animals and recommend sites for future forts.

The expedition was also responsible for finding and mapping the fabled "Northwest Passage." In order to trade with Asia, Europeans had to sail around Africa. The route was time-consuming and costly, so European explorers searched, unsuccessfully, for a more direct route. Once the Americas were colonized, Americans and Europeans continued to sail around Africa or around the tip of South America in order to reach Asia. It became more important than ever to find a water route across North America.

To head the expedition, Jefferson chose **Meriwether Lewis,** his 28-year-old private secretary. During the Whiskey Rebellion, Lewis joined the militia and had been in the army since that time. The expedition's coleader was **William Clark.** Clark was 32 years old and a friend of Lewis's.

Both Lewis and Clark were well-informed amateur scientists. They both had conducted business with Native Americans. Together they assembled a crew of expert river men, gunsmiths, carpenters, scouts, and a cook. Two men of mixed Native American and French heritage served as interpreters. An African American named York was also a member of the group.

The expedition left St. Louis in the spring of 1804 and worked its way up the Missouri River. Lewis and Clark kept a journal and made notes on what they saw and did.

Along their journey, the members of the expedition encountered many Native American groups. One young Shoshone woman named **Sacagawea** (SA•kuh•juh•WEE•uh) joined their group as a guide. After 18 months and nearly 4,000 miles (6,437 km), Lewis and Clark reached the Pacific Ocean. They spent the winter there, and then both explorers headed back east along separate routes.

War Fever

Main Idea Trade issues with Britain and France and tensions between Native Americans and settlers challenged James Madison.

History and You Why do you think tension between different groups occurs? Read about the conflicts among the various groups during the early 1800s.

. . . .

James Madison took office as president under unfavorable conditions. At home and abroad, the nation was involved in the embargo crisis. Meanwhile, Britain continued to halt American ships. Cries for war with Britain grew louder.

Closer to War

In 1810 Congress passed a law permitting direct trade with either France or Britain, depending on which country first lifted its trade **restrictions,** or limits, against America. Napoleon seized the opportunity and promised to end France's trade restrictions.

The French, however, continued to seize American ships, selling them and pocketing the proceeds. Americans were deeply divided. The nation was on the verge of war, but it was hard to decide whether the enemy was Britain or France. Madison believed that Britain was the bigger threat to the United States.

Frontier Conflicts

Madison also received news about problems in the West. Ohio became a state in 1803. White settlers wanted more land in the Ohio Valley. Native Americans already gave up many millions of acres. However, the settlers continued to move onto lands that were guaranteed to Native Americans by the treaty.

Tensions increased as some Native Americans renewed their contacts with British agents and fur traders in Canada.

Other Native Americans pursued a new strategy. **Tecumseh** (tuh•KUHM•suh), a powerful Shawnee chief, built a confederacy among Native American nations in the Northwest.

Territorial Expansion, 1800-1820

Map Skills

Place Describe the changes in French territory between 1800 and 1820.

Primary Source / Tecumseh

Tecumseh organized a confederation of 14 Native American nations to oppose white settlement on lands in the Northwest. He recognized that individual Native American groups had little power to negotiate with the United States government.

"The only way to stop this evil [white settlement of Indians' land], is for all the red men to unite in claiming a common and equal right in the land as it was at first, and should be now—for it never was divided, but belongs to all. . . . Sell a country! Why not sell the air, the clouds, and the great sea, as well as the earth?"
—Tecumseh in a letter to President Harrison, 1810

Tecumseh's brother Tenskwatawa, known as the Prophet, founded Prophetstown in Indiana. This village served as the spiritual, social, and political capital of the confederation of Native American nations.

▼ The Prophet

Tecumseh's pipe tomahawk ▶

When Tecumseh died at the Battle of the Thames, hopes for a lasting Native American confederacy ended.

Critical Thinking

Making Inferences Why do you think American leaders feared Tecumseh?

Tecumseh believed that a strong alliance—with the backing of the British in Canada—could halt white movement into Native American lands. A commanding speaker, Tecumseh had great political skills. He believed the U.S. government's treaties with separate Native American nations were worthless. "The Great Spirit gave this great island to his red children," he said. No one nation had the right to give it away.

Tecumseh had a powerful ally in his brother, Tenskwatawa, known as the Prophet. The Prophet urged Native Americans to return to their ancestors' customs. His message attracted a large following. The Prophet founded Prophetstown in northern Indiana, located near where the Tippecanoe and Wabash Rivers meet.

A Meeting With Harrison

William Henry Harrison, governor of the Indiana Territory, became alarmed by the growing power of the two Shawnee brothers.

He feared they would form an alliance with the British. Harrison warned Tecumseh in a letter that the United States had more warriors than all the Indian nations combined. Tecumseh replied to Harrison in person.

PRIMARY SOURCE

"Brother . . . Since the peace was made, you have killed some Shawnees, Delawares and Winnebagoes. . . . You have taken land from us and I do not see how we can remain at peace if you continue to do so. You try to force red people to do some injury. It is you that are pushing them on to some mischief. You endeavor [try] to make distinctions. You try to prevent the Indians from doing as they wish—to unite and let them consider their lands common property of the whole."
—from *Tecumseh, an Indian Moses*

The Battle of Tippecanoe

When Tecumseh went south to expand the confederacy, Harrison attacked Prophetstown on the Tippecanoe River. After more than two hours, the Prophet's forces fled in defeat.

The **Battle of Tippecanoe** was declared a glorious victory for the Americans. Harrison's victory, however, resulted in something the American people hoped to prevent. Tecumseh joined forces with the British, whom, settlers believed, had supplied his confederacy with guns.

War Hawks

In the meantime, President Madison faced demands for a more aggressive policy toward Britain. The most pressure came from a group of young Republicans known as the War Hawks. They wanted war with Britain. The leading War Hawks were Kentucky's **Henry Clay** and South Carolina's **John Calhoun.**

The War Hawks were mainly from the West and South. They supported increases in military spending and were driven by hunger for land. War Hawks from the West wanted the fertile forests of southern Canada, whereas Southerners desired Spanish Florida. The War Hawks also wanted to expand the nation's power. Their **nationalism**—or loyalty to their country—appealed to a renewed American patriotism.

Not everyone, however, wanted war. The Federalists in the Northeast remained strongly opposed to it.

Declaring War

By the spring of 1812, Madison knew that war with Britain was inevitable. In a message to Congress on June 1, he cited:

PRIMARY SOURCE

"Such is the spectacle of injuries and indignities which have been heaped on our country."
—from Madison's "War Message"

Madison asked for a declaration of war.

Meanwhile, the British had decided to end their policy of search and seizure of American ships. Unfortunately, it took much time for this news to travel across the Atlantic, and leaders in Washington, D.C., did not know about Britain's change in policy. Word of the policy change arrived too late. Once set in motion, the war machine could not be stopped.

✔ **Reading Check** **Summarizing** What factors led to the war with Britain?

Section 3 Review

History ONLINE
Study Central™ To review this section, go to glencoe.com.

Vocabulary

1. Define each of the following terms in a sentence: tribute, neutral rights, impressment, react, embargo, restriction, nationalism.

Main Ideas

2. **Discussing** How widespread was American trade by 1800? Include information about the types of goods that were traded.

3. **Explaining** Explain why U.S. security was threatened as a result of the war between Britain and France.

4. **Summarizing** How did conflict on the American frontier increase tensions between the United States and Britain?

Critical Thinking

5. **Drawing Conclusions** Use a diagram like the one below to identify how people from each region felt about going to war with Britain.

6. **Expository Writing** Take the role of William Henry Harrison. Write a letter to the president explaining why you plan to attack Prophetstown.

Answer the
7. **Essential Question**
What were the challenges to the nation's stability during the late 1700s and early 1800s?

The War of 1812

Essential Question ◄

How did the United States benefit from its victory in the War of 1812?

Reading Guide

Content Vocabulary
frigate (p. 296)   privateer (p. 296)

Academic Vocabulary
underestimate (p. 295)
goal (p. 297)

Key People and Events
Andrew Jackson (p. 296)
Battle of Horseshoe Bend (p. 296)
Francis Scott Key (p. 297)
Treaty of Ghent (p. 298)
Battle of New Orleans (p. 298)

Reading Strategy
Taking Notes As you read, re-create the diagram below and describe each battle's outcome.

Battle		Outcome
Lake Erie	➡	
Washington, D.C.	➡	
New Orleans	➡	

NEW YORK STANDARDS
The American Journey

U5.I.4 To understand the relationship between and the relative importance of United States domestic and foreign policies over time

U5.I.5 To analyze the role played by the United States in international politics, past and present

U5.I.8 To complete well-documented and historically correct case studies about individuals and groups who represent different ethnic, national and religious groups, including Native American Indians in New York State and the United States

American Diary

"When the detachment [small military unit], sent out to destroy Mr. Madison's house, entered his dining parlor, they found a dinner table spread. . . . You will readily imagine, that these preparations were beheld, by a party of hungry soldiers, with no indifferent eye. . . . They sat down to it, therefore, not indeed in the most orderly manner . . . and having satisfied their appetites . . . they finished by setting fire to the house which had so liberally entertained them."

—quoted from George Robert Gleig, a British soldier, in 1814

In August 1814, British troops burn Washington, D.C.

History ONLINE

For additional test practice, use **Self-Check Quizzes**—Chapter 9 at glencoe.com.

Document-Based Questions

Directions: Analyze the documents and answer the short-answer questions that follow.

Document 1

This passage describes a visit from a German baron to Jefferson's White House.

> As [the baron] sat by the table, among the newspapers that were scattered about, he perceived one that was always filled with the most virulent [hateful] abuse of Mr. Jefferson, calumnies [lies] the most offensive, personal as well as political. "Why are these libels [lies] allowed?" asked the Baron taking up the paper, 'Why is not this libelous journal suppressed, or its Editor at least, fined and imprisoned?'
>
> Mr. Jefferson smiled, saying, "Put that paper in your pocket Baron, and should you hear the reality of our liberty, the freedom of our press, questioned, show this paper, and tell where you found it."

Source: Margaret Bayard Smith, *Forty Years of Washington Society*, 1906

7 Why did Jefferson not stop the libels printed about him?

Document 2

Lewis and Clark presented these medals to Native Americans on their expedition.

8 Why do you think these medals were given to Native Americans?

Document 3

In October 1811, William Henry Harrison recorded his observations about Tecumseh after meeting with him at Vincennes, the capital of the Indiana Territory.

> If it is his [Tecumseh's] object to begin with the surprise of this place, it is impossible that a more favorable situation could have been chosen, than the one he occupies: it is just so far off as to be removed from immediate observation, and yet so near as to enable him to strike us, when the water is high, in twenty-four hours.

Source: David Colbert, *Eyewitness to America*

9 Based on the document, what strategic advantage did Tecumseh's forces have over Harrison's?

Document 4

In this passage, an unknown eyewitness describes an incident during the Battle of New Orleans.

> As the British Officer came in, Paleface [one of the American soldiers] demanded his sword. He hesitated about giving it to him, probably thinking it was derogatory to his dignity, to surrender to a private all over begrimed with dust and powder and that some Officer should show him the courtesy to receive it.

Source: Robert Vincent Remini, *The Battle of New Orleans*

10 Based on the document, why did the British officer not want to surrender his sword to Paleface?

11 **Persuasive Writing** Using the information from the four documents and your knowledge of social studies, write an essay in which you:
- agree with the belief of many historians that the election of 1800 was a "revolution"; or
- disagree with the viewpoint.

Need Extra Help?											
If you missed questions...	1	2	3	4	5	6	7	8	9	10	11
Go to page...	279	283	289	297	298	276–298	276–279	283–285	291–293	298	276–298

Growth and Expansion
1790–1825

The Erie Canal provided a new transportation route for merchants and travelers.

PRESIDENTS

U.S. Events

World Events

GEORGE WASHINGTON

★ **1790** Washington, D.C., founded

★ **1792** Russia invades Poland

1793 Eli Whitney invents cotton gin

JOHN ADAMS

THOMAS JEFFERSON

1807 ★ Robert Fulton designs first practical steamboat

1790

1800

◄ Russian general's uniform

★ **1804** Haiti claims independence from France

History ONLINE
Chapter Overview Visit glencoe.com
and click on Chapter 10—Chapter
Overviews to preview chapter information.

Section 1: Economic Growth

Essential Question What effects did the Industrial Revolution have on the U.S. economy?

Section 2: Westward Bound

Essential Question How did land and water transportation affect westward expansion?

Section 3: Unity and Sectionalism

Essential Question How were nation-building issues resolved in the early 1800s?

This flag from Fort McHenry inspired Key to write "The Star-Spangled Banner." ▶

FOLDABLES®
Study Organizer

Organizing Information
Make this Foldable to help organize what you learn about how transportation methods changed in the early 1800s.

Step 1 Place two sheets of paper on top of one another about one inch apart.

Step 2 Fold the papers to form four equal tabs.

Step 3 Staple the sheets, and label each tab as shown.

Transportation: Growth and Expansion
- Roads
- Rivers
- Canals

Reading and Writing As you read the chapter, list the inventors, inventions, and routes that changed transportation in the United States in the early 1800s.

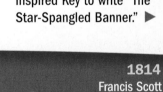

JAMES MADISON

1814 ★
Francis Scott Key writes poem that becomes national anthem

JAMES MONROE

★ **1820**
Missouri Compromise passed

JOHN Q. ADAMS

★ **1825**
Erie Canal completed

1810

1813 ★
Jane Austen writes *Pride and Prejudice*

★ **1815**
Napoleon defeated at Battle of Waterloo

1820

★ **1822**
Franz Liszt debuts as pianist in Vienna at age 11

★ **1823**
Mexico becomes a republic

1830

Section 1 ★ Economic Growth

Essential Question ◄
What effects did the Industrial Revolution have on the U.S. economy?

Reading Guide

Content Vocabulary

cotton gin (p. 306)   capitalism (p. 307)

interchangeable parts (p. 306)   capital (p. 307)

patent (p. 306)   free enterprise (p. 307)

factory system (p. 306)

Academic Vocabulary

contribute (p. 305)   element (p. 307)

Key People and Events

Industrial Revolution (p. 305)

Eli Whitney (p. 306)

Reading Strategy

Taking Notes As you read, use a diagram like the one below to identify the major elements of the free enterprise system.

Free Enterprise System

NEW YORK STANDARDS
The American Journey

U5.I.7 To investigate how people in the United States solve the three fundamental economic questions and solve basic economic problems

U5.III.2 To understand the nature and effect of changes on society and individuals as the United States began to move from an agrarian to an industrial economy

U5.III.5 To define basic economic concepts such as scarcity, supply and demand, markets, resources, and economic systems

U5.III.8 To describe the relationships between people and environments and the connections between people and places

Economic Growth

American Diary

Lucy Larcom started working in the textile mills of Lowell, Massachusetts, at 11 years of age. She later recalled her life in the factory. "I had learned to do a spinner's work, and I obtained permission to tend some frames that stood directly in front of the river-windows with only them and the wall behind me, extending half the length of the mill,—and one young woman beside me. . . . I was, when with strangers, rather a reserved girl; so I kept myself occupied with the river, my work, and my thoughts."

—from A New England Girlhood

Winslow Homer painted young women heading to work in the mills.

The Growth of Industry

Main Idea New technology changed the way things were made.

History and You Do you know someone who works in a factory? What is his or her job like? Read to learn how new technology spurred the Industrial Revolution in New England.

- -

Lucy Larcom was one of the many young women who worked in the new industries that developed in the Northeast during the early 1800s. Since colonial times, most people lived and worked on farms. Thus, workers were in short supply for jobs outside of the home. To make up for this lack of workers, Americans developed tools that made their jobs easier and more efficient.

People working in their homes or in workshops made cloth and most other goods. Using hand tools, they made furniture, farm equipment, household items, and clothing.

In the mid-1700s, however, the way goods were made began to change. These changes appeared first in Great Britain. British inventors created machinery to perform some of the work involved in cloth making, such as spinning. Because these machines ran on waterpower, British cloth makers built textile mills along rivers and installed the new machines in these mills. People left their homes and farms to work in the mills and earn wages. This historic development is so important that it is known as the **Industrial Revolution.**

Industrial Revolution in New England

The Industrial Revolution took root in the United States around 1800. The changes appeared first in New England. The region's geography **contributed,** or added, to the development of the Industrial Revolution.

First, farming was difficult with New England's poor soil. Many people willingly gave up farming to find work elsewhere. Second, New England had rivers and streams to provide the waterpower needed to run the machines in the new factories. Third, New England was close to other resources, including coal and iron deposits in Pennsylvania. Fourth, the area had many ports. Raw materials like cotton, as well as finished goods like cloth, were shipped through these ports.

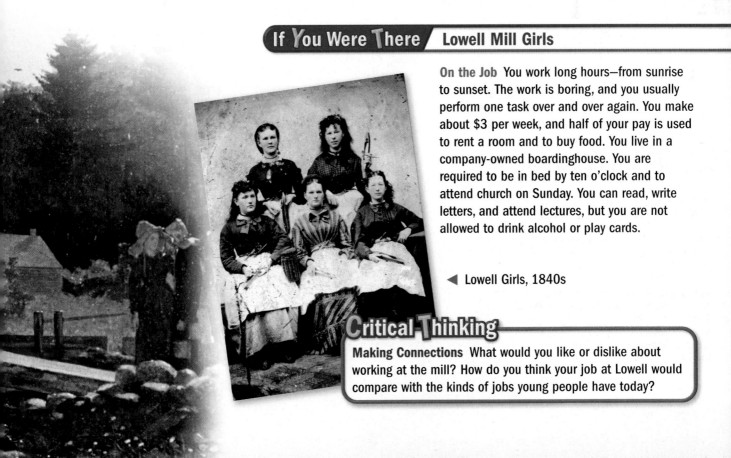

If You Were There / Lowell Mill Girls

On the Job You work long hours—from sunrise to sunset. The work is boring, and you usually perform one task over and over again. You make about $3 per week, and half of your pay is used to rent a room and to buy food. You live in a company-owned boardinghouse. You are required to be in bed by ten o'clock and to attend church on Sunday. You can read, write letters, and attend lectures, but you are not allowed to drink alcohol or play cards.

◀ Lowell Girls, 1840s

Critical Thinking

Making Connections What would you like or dislike about working at the mill? How do you think your job at Lowell would compare with the kinds of jobs young people have today?

New Technology

The invention of new machines and technology led to the Industrial Revolution. For example, the spinning jenny, the water frame—which spun thread—and the power loom—which wove the thread into cloth—allowed many steps in making cloth to be done by machine. These machines saved both time and money.

In 1793 **Eli Whitney** of Massachusetts invented the **cotton gin.** The cotton gin was a simple machine that quickly and efficiently removed the seeds from the cotton fiber.

Whitney also started using **interchangeable parts.** These were identical machine parts that could be put together quickly to make a complete product. These parts also made machine repair easier. Interchangeable parts allowed for the production of different kinds of goods on a large scale. This reduced the price of the goods.

Patents and Factories

In 1790 Congress passed a patent law to protect the rights of inventors. A **patent** gives an inventor the sole legal right to the invention and its profits for a certain period of time.

Although the British tried to keep their new industrial technology a secret, a few British workers brought their knowledge to the United States. One such worker was Samuel Slater. He memorized the design of the machines used in the British factory in which he worked.

Once in the United States, Slater took over the management of a cotton mill in Pawtucket, Rhode Island. There he duplicated the British machines that made cotton thread. Women working in their homes then wove the thread into cloth. Slater's mill marked an important step in the Industrial Revolution in the United States.

Francis Cabot Lowell improved on Slater's process in 1814. In Lowell's textile plant in Massachusetts, all the stages of cloth making were performed under one roof. Lowell began the **factory system,** where all manufacturing steps are brought together in one place to increase efficiency.

Primary Source / Technology and Industry

Growth of Industry New England was the perfect location for the Industrial Revolution to begin in the United States because its rushing rivers provided power to run the machinery. The industrial growth that began in New England spread to other areas of the country. By 1870, the nation's industrial cities were growing.

Slater Mill in Pawtucket, Rhode Island Because Britain prohibited the export of textile machinery, Slater had to design his factory and build the machines from memory. It was an immediate success. ▼

"If thou canst do this thing, I invite thee to come to Rhode Island, and have the credit of introducing cotton-manufacture into America."
—Moses Brown, in a letter to Samuel Slater in 1789

Growth of Industrial Cities

Free Enterprise

Industrial growth requires an economic system that allows competition to flourish with little government interference. **Capitalism** is the economic system of the United States. Under capitalism, individuals put their **capital,** or money, into a business, hoping that the business will be successful and make a profit.

Free enterprise is another term used to describe the American economy. In a free enterprise economy, people are free to buy, sell, and produce whatever they want. They can also work wherever they wish. The major **elements,** or parts, of free enterprise are competition, profit, private property, and economic freedom. Business owners have the freedom to produce the products that they think will sell the best and be the most profitable. In a free enterprise economy, buyers also compete to find the best products at the lowest prices.

Reading Check **Describing** How did New England's physical geography support the growth of industries?

Agriculture Expands

Main Idea Agriculture expanded and remained the leading occupation of most Americans in the 1800s.

History and You Do any of your relatives own and work on a farm? Read to learn how agriculture expanded in the 1800s.

Although many New Englanders went to work in factories during the first half of the 1800s, agriculture remained the country's leading economic activity. Most Americans still lived and worked on farms.

In the Northeast, farms were small and worked by families. Farmers in the Northeast usually marketed their produce locally. In the South, cotton production rose dramatically. The demand for cotton grew steadily with the development of the textile industries of New England and Europe.

History ONLINE
Student Web Activity Visit glencoe.com and complete the Chapter 10 Web Activity about the Industrial Revolution.

Textile Mill The Lowell factory system was designed to bring work and workers together. A typical Lowell textile mill in 1830 housed 4,500 spindles, 120 power looms, and more than 200 employees under one roof.

◀ A water frame was used to spin thread.

1 The first steps in textile production were to clean the raw cotton and turn loose cotton into crude yarn.

2 The spinning process transforms the yarn into thread.

3 At the weaving stage, power looms interlace the threads into coarse cloth or fabric.

4 Fabric is measured and batched for dyeing. Vegetable dyes were the earliest known dyes.

Critical Thinking

Determining Cause and Effect Did the increase of factories lead to better technology, or did better technology lead to more factories? Explain.

Population of the United States, 1820 NATIONAL GEOGRAPHIC

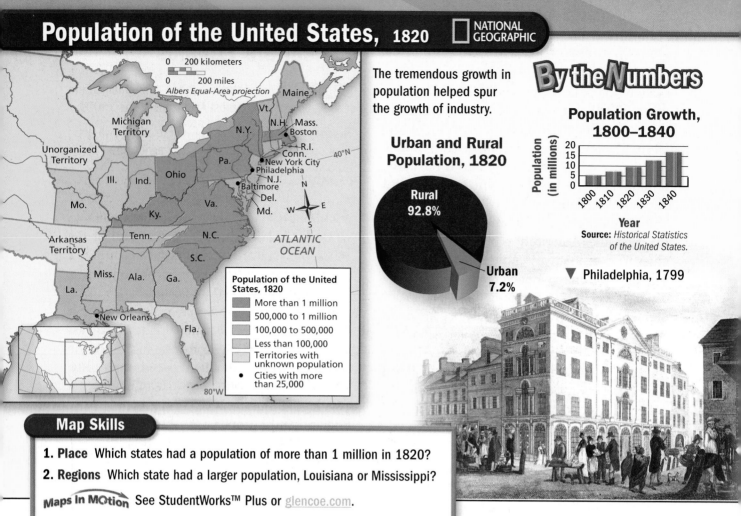

The tremendous growth in population helped spur the growth of industry.

Urban and Rural Population, 1820

Rural 92.8%

Urban 7.2%

By the Numbers

Population Growth, 1800–1840

Population (in millions) — 1800, 1810, 1820, 1830, 1840

Source: *Historical Statistics of the United States.*

▼ Philadelphia, 1799

Population of the United States, 1820
- More than 1 million
- 500,000 to 1 million
- 100,000 to 500,000
- Less than 100,000
- Territories with unknown population
- • Cities with more than 25,000

Map Skills

1. **Place** Which states had a population of more than 1 million in 1820?
2. **Regions** Which state had a larger population, Louisiana or Mississippi?

Maps In MOtion See StudentWorks™ Plus or glencoe.com.

Southern plantation owners used enslaved workers from Africa to plant, tend, and pick the cotton. The recently invented cotton gin encouraged the planters to raise even larger amounts of the crop. The new machine made it possible to clean cotton faster and more cheaply than could be done by hand. Between 1790 and 1820, cotton production soared from 3,000 bales produced per year to more than 300,000 bales produced per year in the South.

Agriculture also expanded in the West. Southern farmers seeking new land moved west to plant cotton. Western farmers in the region north of the Ohio River concentrated on raising pork and cash crops such as corn and wheat.

Reading Check **Contrasting** How was agriculture different in the Northeast than in the South?

Economic Independence

Main Idea The growth of factories and trade led to the development of corporations and cities.

History and You If you had your choice, would you prefer living in the city or in the country? Why? Read to learn about the growth of cities in the 1800s.

Small investors, such as shopkeepers, merchants, and farmers, financed most new businesses. These people invested their money in hopes of earning profits if the new businesses succeeded. Low taxes, minimum government regulations, and competition encouraged people to invest in new industries.

Corporations Develop

Large businesses called corporations began to develop rapidly in the 1830s when legal obstacles to their formation were removed.

from New York City to Albany in the unheard-of time of 32 hours. Using only sails, the trip would have taken four days.

About 140 feet (43 m) long and 14 feet (4 m) wide, the *Clermont* offered great comforts to its passengers. They could sit or stroll about on deck. At night they could relax in the sleeping compartments below deck. The engine was noisy, but its power provided a fairly smooth ride.

Steamboats ushered in a new age in river travel. They greatly improved the transport of goods and passengers along major inland rivers. Shipping goods became cheaper and faster. Regular steamboat service began along the Mississippi River, between New Orleans and Natchez, Mississippi, in 1812. Steamboats also contributed to the growth of other river cities like Cincinnati and St. Louis. By 1850, some 700 steamboats were carrying cargo and passengers within the United States.

Reading Check **Identifying** What advantages did river travel offer?

Canals

Main Idea Business and government officials developed a plan to build a canal to link the eastern and western parts of the country.

History and You Have you ever worked long and hard to build something? Read to learn about the accomplishment of thousands of laborers who constructed the Erie Canal.

Steamboats were a great improvement in transportation, but their routes depended on the existing river system. Because most major rivers in the eastern United States flowed north to south, steamboats could not effectively tie together the eastern and western parts of the country.

Business and government officials led by **De Witt Clinton** in New York developed a plan to link New York City with the Great Lakes region. They would build a **canal**—an artificial waterway—across New York state. The canal would connect Albany on the Hudson River with Buffalo on Lake Erie.

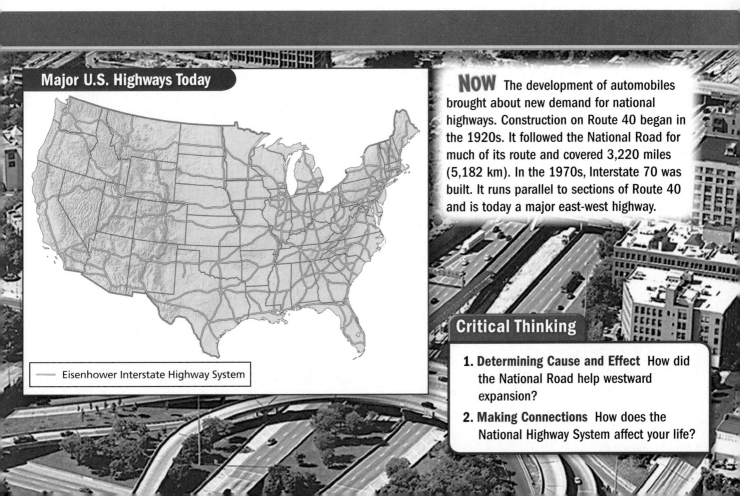

Major U.S. Highways Today

—— Eisenhower Interstate Highway System

NOW The development of automobiles brought about new demand for national highways. Construction on Route 40 began in the 1920s. It followed the National Road for much of its route and covered 3,220 miles (5,182 km). In the 1970s, Interstate 70 was built. It runs parallel to sections of Route 40 and is today a major east-west highway.

Critical Thinking

1. **Determining Cause and Effect** How did the National Road help westward expansion?

2. **Making Connections** How does the National Highway System affect your life?

Canals, 1820–1860

NATIONAL GEOGRAPHIC

"But when we consider that this canal will open a way into the great rivers that fall into the Mississippi . . . and that it will communicate with . . . the most productive regions of America; there can be no question respecting the blessings that it will produce [and] the riches that it will create."
—De Witt Clinton in a letter, November 1823

Canal Mileage, 1850

- OH, 792 miles
- IN, 214 miles
- IL, 100 miles
- Other states, 800 miles
- NY and PA, 1,757 miles

The Canal Boom The success of the Erie Canal sparked a wave of canal-building across the United States. Engineers who had worked on the Erie Canal spread out across the country to assist in numerous canal projects.

▲ To celebrate the opening of the Erie Canal, Governor Clinton pours water from Lake Erie into the Atlantic Ocean.

Map Skills

Location What bodies of water were connected by the Illinois and Michigan Canal?

Building the Erie Canal

Thousands of laborers, many of them Irish immigrants, worked on the construction of the 363-mile (584 km) Erie Canal. Along the canal they built a series of locks—separate compartments in which water levels were raised or lowered. Locks provided a way to raise and lower boats at places canal levels changed.

Construction of the canal proved dangerous for workers. Diggers were buried when canal beds collapsed and others died in blasting accidents. The swamps in which they toiled led to disease among the workers.

After more than two years of construction, the Erie Canal opened on October 26, 1825. Clinton boarded a barge in Buffalo and traveled on the canal to Albany. From there he sailed down the Hudson River to New York City. As crowds cheered, the officials poured water from Lake Erie into the Atlantic Ocean.

Improving Canal Travel

In its early years, the Erie Canal did not allow steamboats. Their powerful engines could damage the canal's earthen embankments. Instead, teams of mules or horses hauled the boats and barges. A two-horse team pulled a 100-ton (91 t) barge about 24 miles (39 km) in one day. This was fast compared with travel by wagon. In the 1840s, the canal banks were reinforced to accommodate steam tugboats that could pull the barges.

The success of the Erie Canal led to an explosion in canal building. By 1850, the United States had more than 3,600 miles (5,794 km) of canals. Canals lowered the cost of shipping goods and brought prosperity to the towns along their routes. Perhaps most important, they linked regions of a growing country.

 Reading Check **Finding the Main Idea** Why were canals built?

Western Settlement

Main Idea Americans continued to move westward, settling near rivers so they could ship their goods to markets.

History and You Think about what your life might be like if you could not watch TV or use the computer. Read to learn about the lives of Western families in the early 1800s.

. . . .

Americans moved westward in waves. The first wave began before the 1790s and led to the admission of four new states between 1791 and 1803—Vermont, Kentucky, Tennessee, and Ohio. A second wave of westward growth began between 1816 and 1821. Five new western states were created—Indiana, Illinois, Mississippi, Alabama, and Missouri.

The new states reflected the dramatic growth of the region west of the Appalachians. In 1800 only 387,000 white settlers lived west of the Appalachian Mountains. By 1820, that number had grown to more than 2.4 million people. Ohio, for example, had only 45,000 settlers in 1800. By 1820, it had 581,000 settlers.

Pioneer families tended to settle in communities along the great rivers, such as the Ohio and the Mississippi. They settled by rivers so they could ship their crops and other goods to markets. The canals, which crisscrossed the land in the 1820s and 1830s, allowed people to live farther away from the rivers.

People also often preferred to settle with others from their home communities. Indiana, for example, was settled mainly by people from Kentucky and Tennessee. Michigan's pioneers came mostly from the New England area.

Western families often gathered together for social events. Men took part in sports such as wrestling. Women met for quilting and sewing parties. Both men and women participated in cornhuskings. These were gatherings where farm families shared the work of stripping the outer layers from corn.

Life in the West did not include the conveniences of Eastern town life. However, the pioneers had not traveled to the West to live a pampered life. They wanted to make a new life for themselves and their families. America's population continued to spread westward in the years ahead.

Reading Check **Describing** What was life like for families on the western frontier?

Section 2 Review

History ONLINE
Study Central™ To review this section, go to glencoe.com.

Vocabulary

1. Define the following terms by using each one in a sentence: census, reveal, turnpike, region, canal, lock.

Main Ideas

2. Discussing How were the improvements in westward travel financed in the early 1800s?

3. Identifying What were the benefits of canal travel?

4. Listing What determined where people would settle as they moved westward?

Critical Thinking

5. Analyzing Use a chart like the one below to describe why each item was important to the nation's growth.

	Significance
National Road	
Clermont	
Erie Canal	

6. Persuasive Writing Would you have preferred Eastern city life or life in a western settlement in 1820? Write a paragraph to persuade people to join you in one of the two places.

Answer the
7. Essential Question
How did land and water transportation affect westward expansion?

TIME NOTEBOOK

What were people's lives like in the past?

These two pages will give you some clues to everyday life in the United States as you step back in time with TIME Notebook.

BETTMANN / CORBIS

American Voices

FULL STEAM AHEAD!

ROBERT FULTON *might not have invented the steamboat, but he does believe in its potential to turn waterways into business routes and transform America's economic future. In 1807 he's ready for his trial run of the first commercial passenger steamboat. The boat is 150 feet (46 m) long and only 13 feet (4 m) wide and will travel from New York City to Albany—and back again. People are terrified the engines that power the ship's two paddle wheels will explode, so he has a tough time getting passengers onboard. In this letter, Fulton describes what happens just as the ship leaves the dock in New York City.*

ROBERT FULTON

NORTH WIND PICTURE ARCHIVES / ALAMY

"The moment arrived in which the word was to be given for the boat to move. My friends were in groups on the deck. There was anxiety mixed with fear among them. They were silent, sad, and weary. I read in their looks nothing but disaster, and almost repented of my efforts. The signal was given and the boat moved on a short distance and then stopped and became immovable. To the silence of the preceding moment, now succeeded murmurs of discontent, and agitations, and whispers and shrugs. I could hear distinctly repeated, 'I told you it was so; it is a foolish scheme: I wish we were well out of it.'... I went below and examined the machinery, and discovered that the cause was a slight maladjustment...The boat was again put in motion."

VERBATIM

WHAT PEOPLE ARE SAYING

❝ If Uncle Sam needs, I'll be glad to assist him. ❞

POLITICAL CARTOON IN 1813
that makes the first-known use of the term "Uncle Sam"

❝ The land is ours. No one has a right to remove us, because we were the first owners. ❞

TECUMSEH,
chief of the Shawnees, in 1810, in response to a message sent by President Madison

❝ Let us bind the republic together with a perfect system of roads and canals. Let us conquer space. ❞

CONGRESSMAN JOHN C. CALHOUN,
from South Carolina, in 1816

Sea Talk

*The **U.S.S. CONSTITUTION,** the world's largest warship with its 54 cannons, was instrumental in helping the United States win the War of 1812. Want to join its crew of 450? If so, you'll have to learn some sea terms. Here's a seafaring glossary.*

1. **KEEL OVER:** Putting a ship in for repair

2. **TACK:** The course or direction boats take into the wind

3. **LET THE CAT OUT OF THE BAG:** Sailors who do wrong are disciplined with a cat-o'-nine-tails whip that's kept in a red sack

4. **SHIPSHAPE:** Good condition

BETTMANN / CORBIS

First Things First

Someone's got to be first—see if you can match up each name with the correct description.

1. Thomas Hopkins Gallaudet
2. Thomas Jefferson
3. James Madison
4. James Madison Randolph
5. Frederick Graff

ILLUSTRATION WORKS / GETTY IMAGES

a. First president to wear pants instead of knee breeches.

b. First child born in the White House (1806)—his grandfather was Thomas Jefferson.

c. Founder of first school for advanced education of hearing-impaired students.

d. First president to shake hands instead of bowing when meeting people.

e. Engineer for Philadelphia Water Works who installed the country's first fire hydrant in 1801.

Answers: 1. c; 2. d; 3. a; 4. b; 5. e

NUMBERS

UNITED STATES AT THE TIME

$15 million Price the United States pays for the Louisiana Purchase in 1803

16 Number of states in the Union in 1800—that number will grow to 23 by 1820

17 Age of Sacagawea when she started guiding Lewis and Clark on their famous expedition

BETTMANN / CORBIS

18 Months it takes Lewis and Clark to reach the Pacific in 1805

19th Date in August 1812 that the U.S.S. *Constitution* earns its nickname "Old Ironsides" after defeating the British warship, *Guerriere*

MILESTONES

EVENTS AND PEOPLE OF THE TIME

BORROWED. The music from the English song "To Anacreon in Heaven" by Francis Scott Key for his new poem "The Star-Spangled Banner," which he wrote in 1814.

STARVED. Many Vermont farmers and their families as snow falls all summer in 1816—a year some call "eighteen hundred and froze-to-death." Some think the bizarre weather is caused by last year's volcanic eruption in the Dutch East Indies that sent dust and ash far up into the air where it blocked out the sun.

DUG. First shovel of dirt as work on the proposed 363-mile-long Erie Canal begins in 1817. Many are labeling it "The Big Ditch."

BITTEN. United States officials, by insects in 1800 as the country's government moves from Philadelphia to Washington, D.C.—a place many complain is a bug-infested swamp.

NORTH WIND PICTURE ARCHIVES / ALAMY

RESCUED. Treasures, such as the original Declaration of Independence and a famous portrait of George Washington, by First Lady Dolley Madison after the British set fire to the White House in 1814.

CRITICAL THINKING

Describing What was the atmosphere like on board Fulton's steamboat on its first voyage?

Theorizing Was Tecumseh, the chief of the Shawnees, justified in his response to President Madison's message? Explain your answer.

Section 3 — Unity and Sectionalism

Essential Question ◄

How were nation-building issues resolved in the early 1800s?

Reading Guide

Content Vocabulary

sectionalism (p. 322)

state sovereignty (p. 322)

American System (p. 323)

Academic Vocabulary

intense (p. 322)   internal (p. 322)

Key People and Events

Missouri Compromise (p. 323)

McCulloch v. Maryland (p. 324)

Gibbons v. Ogden (p. 324)

Adams-Onís Treaty (p. 326)

Monroe Doctrine (p. 326)

Reading Strategy

Taking Notes As you read, create a diagram like the one below to list the three parts of Henry Clay's American System.

NEW YORK STANDARDS
The American Journey

U5.I.2 To understand how political parties emerged in response to concerns at local, state, and national levels

U5.I.4 To understand the relationship between and the relative importance of United States domestic and foreign policies over time

U5.I.5 To analyze the role played by the United States in international politics, past and present

U5.III.4 To explore the meaning of American culture by identifying the key ideas, beliefs, patterns of behavior, and traditions that help define it and unite all Americans

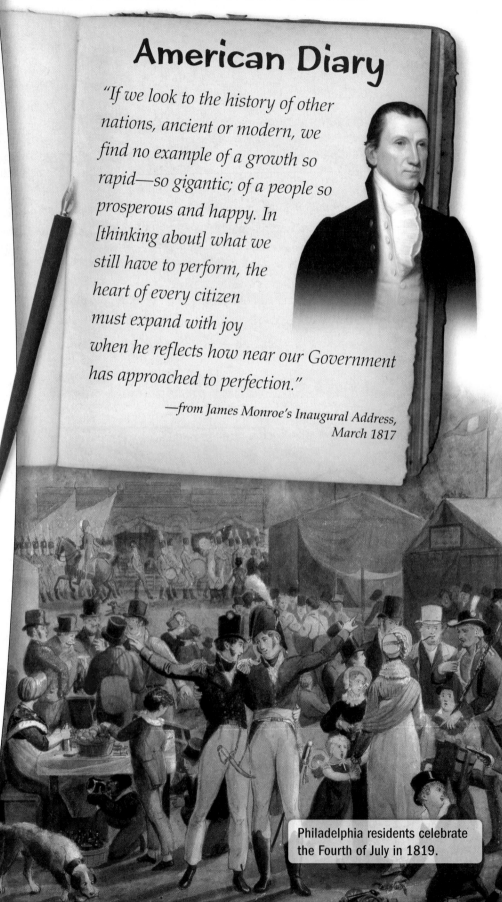

American Diary

"If we look to the history of other nations, ancient or modern, we find no example of a growth so rapid—so gigantic; of a people so prosperous and happy. In [thinking about] what we still have to perform, the heart of every citizen must expand with joy when he reflects how near our Government has approached to perfection."

—from James Monroe's Inaugural Address, March 1817

Philadelphia residents celebrate the Fourth of July in 1819.

The Era of Good Feelings

Main Idea After the War of 1812, a new spirit of nationalism spread throughout the United States.

History and You Do you believe your favorite sports team is better than any other team? Read on to find out about the national pride many Americans felt for their country.

- -

The absence of major political divisions after the War of 1812 helped forge a sense of national unity. In the 1816 presidential election, James Monroe, the Republican candidate, faced almost no opposition. The Federalists, weakened by doubts of their loyalty during the War of 1812, barely existed as a national party. Monroe won the election by an overwhelming margin.

Although the Federalist Party had almost disappeared, many of its programs had gained popularity. Support grew for tariffs to protect industries and a national bank.

Political differences among citizens, however, seemed to fade. A Boston newspaper called these years the Era of Good Feelings. President James Monroe symbolized these good feelings. Monroe had been involved in national politics since the American Revolution. He wore breeches, or short pants, and powdered wigs—styles no longer in fashion at that time. With his sense of dignity, Monroe represented a united America, free of political strife.

Early in his term, Monroe toured the nation. No president since George Washington had done so. Monroe even paid for the trip using his own expenses and tried to travel without an official escort. Local officials everywhere greeted the president and celebrated his visit.

Monroe arrived in Boston, the former Federalist stronghold, in the summer of 1817. About 40,000 well-wishers cheered him. John Adams, the second president, invited Monroe to his home. Abigail Adams praised the new president's "unassuming manner."

Monroe did not think the demonstrations were meant for him personally. He wrote James Madison that they revealed a "desire in the body of the people to show their attachment to the union."

Two years later Monroe continued his tour throughout the country. He traveled as far south as Savannah and as far west as Detroit. In 1820 President Monroe won reelection, receiving all but one electoral vote.

Reading Check **Summarizing** Why did James Monroe appeal to people?

Primary Source / **Celebrating Independence**

Fourth of July Independence Day was first observed on July 8, 1776. On that day in Philadelphia, the Declaration of Independence was read in public for the first time. The next year, Philadelphia honored the nation's independence on July 4—the day the Declaration of Independence was adopted by the Continental Congress. People celebrated the occasion with bonfires, parades, and fireworks. In 1826 Thomas Jefferson wrote: "Let the annual return of this day forever refresh our recollections of [our] rights, and an undiminished devotion to them."

Critical Thinking

Making Connections How do people express patriotism for the United States today?

Sectionalism and the American System

Main Idea Regional differences brought an end to the Era of Good Feelings.

History and You Why do people support certain political leaders? Read about three influential spokespeople in Congress during the early 1800s.

Regional differences soon brought an end to the Era of Good Feelings. Most Americans felt a strong allegiance to the region where they lived. They thought of themselves as Westerners or Southerners or Northerners. This **sectionalism,** or loyalty to their region, grew more **intense** over national policies.

Most white Southerners, for example, supported slavery. They argued that states were given the right in the Constitution to govern themselves. Southerners believed the federal government and people in the North were interfering with a state's right to maintain the institution of slavery.

The different regions also disagreed strongly on the need for tariffs, a national bank, and **internal** improvements. Internal improvements were federal, state, and privately funded projects, such as canals and roads, to develop the nation's transportation system. Three regional spokespersons emerged in Congress.

John C. Calhoun

John C. Calhoun, a planter from South Carolina, had called for war with Great Britain in 1812. He remained a nationalist for some time after the war. Calhoun supported internal improvements, the development of industries, and a national bank. He believed that these programs would benefit the South.

In the 1820s, however, Calhoun's views began to change. He emerged as a chief supporter of **state sovereignty,** the idea that states have autonomous power, or the right to govern themselves. Calhoun became a strong opponent of national programs.

People IN HISTORY

John C. Calhoun

Politician from South Carolina

Calhoun was a fierce supporter of states' rights. He believed that if the federal government passed a law where it overstepped its authority over states, then people had the right to refuse to obey it. *"Let it never be forgotten that, where the majority rules without restriction, the minority is the subject."*

Daniel Webster

Politician from New England

Webster argued against the right of states to declare laws invalid. He stated, *"I say, the right of a state to annul [declare invalid] a law of Congress, cannot be maintained, but on the ground of the unalienable right of man to resist [the cruel use of power]; that is to say, upon the ground of revolution."*

Calhoun and other Southerners opposed high tariffs. Calhoun argued that tariffs raised the prices of manufactured goods that they could not make for themselves and that high tariffs protected inefficient manufacturers.

Daniel Webster

Daniel Webster was first elected to Congress in 1812 to represent his home state of New Hampshire. He later represented Massachusetts in both the House and the Senate. Webster at first supported free trade and the shipping interests of New England. In time Webster came to favor the Tariff of 1816, which protected American industries from foreign competition. He also supported other policies that he thought would strengthen the nation and help the North.

Webster gained fame as one of the greatest public speakers of his day. As a U.S. senator, he spoke eloquently in defense of the nation as a whole against sectional interests. In one of his most memorable speeches, Webster declared, "Liberty and Union, now and forever, one and inseparable!"

Henry Clay

Henry Clay of Kentucky was another leading War Hawk. He became speaker of the House of Representatives in 1811 and a leader who represented the interests of the Western states. He also served as a member of the delegation that negotiated the Treaty of Ghent, ending the War of 1812. Above all, Henry Clay became known as the national leader who tried to resolve sectional disputes.

The Missouri Compromise

Sectional tension reached new heights in 1820. The issue was whether to allow slavery in states when they joined the Union. The South wanted Missouri admitted as a slave state, whereas Northerners wanted it to be free of slavery. The issue was further complicated when Maine, still a part of Massachusetts, also applied for statehood.

Eventually Henry Clay helped work out a compromise that preserved the balance between North and South. The **Missouri Compromise,** reached in March 1820, provided for the admission of Missouri as a slave state and Maine as a free state. Slavery was banned in the rest of the Louisiana Territory north of the 36°30'N parallel.

Henry Clay believed his policies would benefit all sections of the nation. In an 1824 speech, he called his program the "American System." The **American System** included three parts: (1) a protective tariff, (2) a program of internal improvements, and (3) a national bank. Not everyone saw Clay's program in such positive terms. Many Southerners did not see the benefits of the tariff or internal improvements.

In the end, little of Clay's American System went into effect. Congress eventually adopted some internal improvements, but they were not on the scale Clay hoped for. Congress created a Second National Bank in 1816, but it remained controversial.

Henry Clay

Politician from Kentucky

Clay's ability to resolve arguments earned him the nickname "The Great Compromiser." He was a strong nationalist. In a speech on the Senate floor, he said: *"If the . . . sad event of the dissolution [breaking up] of this Union is to happen, that I shall not survive to behold the sad and heart-rending [distressing] spectacle."*

CRITICAL Thinking

1. **Comprehending** According to Webster, when might a state declare the federal government's laws invalid?
2. **Contrasting** Describe the differences in the three men's views about the power of government.
3. **Analyzing** How does Clay's statement reflect nationalist views?

The Missouri Compromise

NATIONAL GEOGRAPHIC

A Compromise on Slavery Missouri's application for statehood sparked a national debate over the issue of slavery. Northern Congressional leaders sought to restrict the entry of Missouri as a slave state. Southern leaders retaliated by blocking Maine's application for statehood. The Missouri Compromise allowed for Missouri to be admitted as a slave state and Maine as a free state.

"All know that permitting the slaves of the South to spread in the West . . . will dilute [weaken] the evil everywhere . . . getting finally rid of it."
—Thomas Jefferson in a letter, December 1820

"Freedom and slavery are the parties which stand this day before the senate, and upon its decision the empire of the one or the other will be established in the new state which we are about to admit into the Union."
—Senator Rufus King, February 1820

Map Skills

Location Was the Unorganized Territory open or closed to slavery?

Maps in Motion See StudentWorks™ Plus or glencoe.com.

McCulloch v. Maryland

The Supreme Court also became involved in sectional and states' rights issues at this time. Its decisions strengthened the power of the national government. The state of Maryland imposed a tax on the Baltimore branch of the Second National Bank of the United States, a federal institution. The Bank refused to pay the state tax. The case, **McCulloch v. Maryland,** reached the Court in 1819.

Speaking for the Court, Chief Justice John Marshall ruled that Maryland had no right to tax the Bank. Marshall argued that the Constitution gave certain powers to the federal government, such as collecting taxes, borrowing money, and regulating commerce. Marshall claimed that the national bank helped the federal government carry out these powers.

Next, Marshall stated that the government could use any method that was necessary to carry out its powers, as long as it was not forbidden by the Constitution. Finally, Marshall claimed that a state government could not interfere with a federal agency that was using its constitutional powers in that state. The tax was interfering with the bank and its constitutional powers and was, thus, unconstitutional.

Gibbons v. Ogden

Another Supreme Court case, **Gibbons v. Ogden,** established that states could not enact legislation that would interfere with congressional power over interstate commerce. People who supported states' rights believed that the Court's decisions in these cases increased federal power at the expense of state power. Nationalists welcomed the rulings' support for federal power.

Reading Check **Explaining** Describe how the Supreme Court's decisions affected the power of the federal government.

Foreign Affairs

Main Idea The United States defined its role in the Americas with the Monroe Doctrine.

History and You Have you ever had to take a stand on an issue with a friend? Read about American foreign policies in the early 1800s.

. . . .

The War of 1812 heightened Americans' pride in their country. Americans also realized that the United States had to establish a new relationship with the "Old World."

Relations With Britain

In the 1817 Rush-Bagot Treaty, the United States and Britain agreed to limit the number of naval vessels on the Great Lakes and remove weapons located along the border of the United States and British Canada.

The Convention of 1818 set the boundary of the Louisiana Territory between the United States and Canada at the 49th parallel. The convention also created a secure and demilitarized border. In other words, each country agreed to maintain its border without armed forces. Through Secretary of State John Quincy Adams's efforts, Americans also gained the right to settle in the Oregon Country.

Relations With Spain

Spain owned East Florida and also claimed West Florida. The United States argued that West Florida was part of the Louisiana Purchase. In 1810 and 1812, Americans simply added parts of West Florida to Louisiana and Mississippi. Spain objected but took no action.

General Andrew Jackson was ordered to stop Seminole raids on America from Florida. In April 1818, Jackson invaded Spanish East Florida and seized two Spanish forts. Secretary of State Adams had not authorized Jackson's actions, but he did nothing about them.

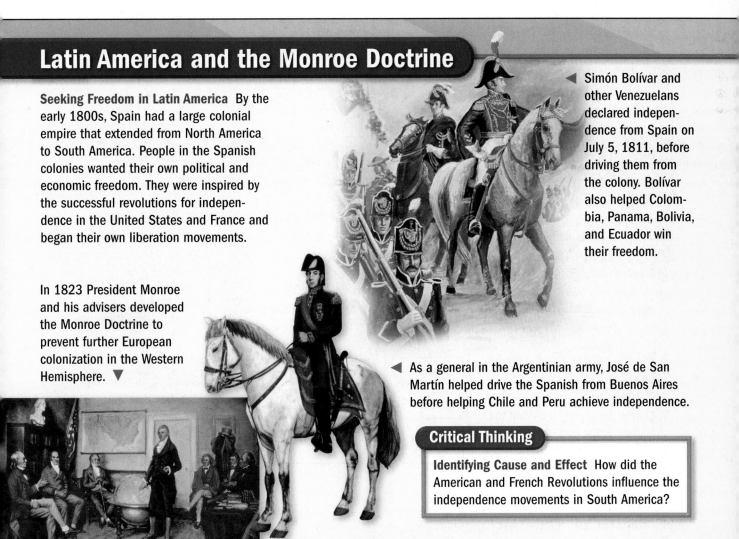

Latin America and the Monroe Doctrine

Seeking Freedom in Latin America By the early 1800s, Spain had a large colonial empire that extended from North America to South America. People in the Spanish colonies wanted their own political and economic freedom. They were inspired by the successful revolutions for independence in the United States and France and began their own liberation movements.

In 1823 President Monroe and his advisers developed the Monroe Doctrine to prevent further European colonization in the Western Hemisphere. ▼

◄ Simón Bolívar and other Venezuelans declared independence from Spain on July 5, 1811, before driving them from the colony. Bolívar also helped Colombia, Panama, Bolivia, and Ecuador win their freedom.

◄ As a general in the Argentinian army, José de San Martín helped drive the Spanish from Buenos Aires before helping Chile and Peru achieve independence.

Critical Thinking

Identifying Cause and Effect How did the American and French Revolutions influence the independence movements in South America?

Jackson's raid demonstrated American military strength. Secretary of State Adams believed that the Spanish did not want war and wanted to settle the dipute. His assumption was correct.

Adams-Onís Treaty and Mexico

With the **Adams-Onís Treaty** in 1819, the United States gained East Florida, and Spain also abandoned all claims to West Florida. In return the United States gave up its claims to Spanish Texas and agreed to border boundaries. As a result, the United States gained a territory in the Pacific Northwest.

Meanwhile Spain was losing power in its vast empire, especially in Mexico. In the fall of 1810 a priest, Miguel Hidalgo (ee•DAHL•goh), led a rebellion in Mexico. Hidalgo called for racial equality and the redistribution of land. The Spanish defeated the revolutionary forces and executed Hidalgo. In 1821 Mexico finally gained its independence.

Bolívar and San Martín

Simón Bolívar, also known as "the Liberator," led the independence movement that won freedom for the present-day countries of Venezuela, Colombia, Panama, Bolivia, and Ecuador. José de San Martín successfully achieved independence for Chile and Peru. By 1824, Spain lost control of most of South America.

The Monroe Doctrine

In 1822 the Quadruple Alliance—France, Austria, Russia, and Prussia—discussed a plan to help Spain regain its American holdings. The possibility of increased European involvement in North America led President Monroe to take action.

The president issued a statement, later known as the **Monroe Doctrine,** on December 2, 1823. The United States would not interfere with any existing European colonies in the Americas. However, North and South America "are henceforth not to be considered as subjects for future colonization by any European powers." The Monroe Doctrine became an important element in American foreign policy.

Reading Check **Making Inferences** Why was the Monroe Doctrine issued?

Section 3 Review

History ONLINE **Study Central™** To review this section, go to glencoe.com.

Vocabulary

1. Define the following terms using complete sentences: sectionalism, intense, internal, state sovereignty, American System.

Main Ideas

2. **Describing** Describe the overall feeling in the U.S. after the War of 1812.

3. **Listing** What issues divided the country at the end of the Era of Good Feelings?

4. **Explaining** Why was the Monroe Doctrine issued?

Critical Thinking

5. **Organizing** Use a diagram like the one below to show the effects of the Missouri Compromise.

Maine	⟹	
Missouri	⟹	
Louisiana Territory	⟹	

6. **Persuasive Writing** If you had been a congressperson at the time, do you think you would have supported the ideas of John C. Calhoun or Henry Clay? Write a paragraph explaining who you would support and why.

7. **Answer the Essential Question** How were nation-building issues resolved in the early 1800s?

Visual Summary

Growth and Expansion

The Economy Grows

- The Industrial Revolution and the factory system energize the U.S. economy.
- Free enterprise encourages economic growth.
- Agriculture expands in the South and West.
- Corporations emerge, and people invest in new industries.
- Towns and cities develop as a result of increased trade.

Westward Expansion Occurs

- Turnpikes are constructed to make it easier to travel and trade.
- Steamboats improve the transportation of goods and passengers along rivers.
- Canals are built to link the eastern and western parts of the U.S.
- America's population continues to move west.

▲ Corduroy road

Sectional Differences Emerge

- People living in different regions disagree about national policies.
- The issue of slavery continues to divide Southerners and Northerners.
- The Missouri Compromise attempts to resolve the issue of slavery in states being admitted in the Union.
- The Supreme Court supports federal power over states' rights.

▲ Slater Mill, Pawtucket, Rhode Island

The U.S. Defines Its Role With Europe

- Policy agreements are made peacefully with Britain.
- The U.S. acquires West and East Florida from Spain.
- Spain loses most of its colonies in South America as a result of independence movements.
- The U.S. issues the Monroe Doctrine to prevent the establishment of new European colonies in the Western Hemisphere.

▲ Water frame

◀ Discussing the Monroe Doctrine

STUDY TO GO Study anywhere, anytime! Download quizzes and flash cards to your PDA from glencoe.com.

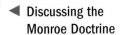

GRADE 8 INTERMEDIATE TEST PRACTICE

TEST-TAKING TIP

Eliminate answers that you know for certain are incorrect. Then choose the most likely answer from those remaining.

Reviewing Main Ideas

Directions: Choose the best answer for each of the following questions.

1 The invention of the cotton gin

(1) encouraged farmers in the Northeast to begin planting cotton.

(2) led to a dramatic increase in Southern cotton production.

(3) had no impact on the demand for cotton.

(4) encouraged many plantation owners to free their enslaved workers.

2 The system in which all manufacturing steps are brought together in one place to increase efficiency is called the

(1) factory system.

(2) patent system.

(3) capital system.

(4) corporation system.

3 Pioneer families tended to settle in communities along major rivers

(1) to gain greater protection from Native Americans.

(2) to make it easier for them to travel east.

(3) because they provided fresh drinking water.

(4) so that they could more easily ship their crops to market.

4 In the mid-1800s, by whom were tariffs *least* likely to be supported?

(1) Northeastern factory owners

(2) Southern planters

(3) Westerners living on the frontier

(4) free African Americans living in the North

Short-Answer Question

Directions: Base your answer to question 5 on the following excerpt and on your knowledge of social studies.

> With the existing colonies . . . of any European power we have not interfered and shall not interfere. But with the [Latin American] governments who have declared their independence and maintained it . . . we could not view any [involvement] for the purpose of oppressing them . . . by any European power in any other light than as the [showing] of an unfriendly disposition toward the United States.
>
> —James Monroe, Speech to Congress, December 1823

5 In this excerpt, what distinction does Monroe make between European involvement in their American colonies and in independent Latin American nations?

Review the Essential Questions

6 Essay Describe the forces that tended to unify Americans in the early 1800s. What were some important points of dispute?

To help you write your essay, review your answers to the Essential Questions in the section reviews and the chapter Foldables Study Organizer. Your essay should include:

- the Industrial Revolution and the growth of American cities;
- the Western settlement of the United States;
- transportation systems in early and mid-1800s in America;
- sectional conflicts and the American System; and
- America's relations with foreign nations.

GO ON

Document-Based Questions

Directions: Analyze the documents and answer the short-answer questions that follow.

Document 1

In this passage, Harriet Hanson Robinson recounts the 1836 strike of the mill girls of Lowell, Massachusetts.

> Cutting down their wages was not [the workers'] only grievance, nor the only cause of the strike. Hitherto the corporations had paid twenty-five cents a week toward the board of each operative, and now it was their purpose to have the girls pay the sum; and this, in addition to the cut in the wages, would make a difference of at least a dollar a week.

Source: *Loom and Spindle,* 1898

7 Based on the excerpt, why did the Lowell mill girls go on strike in 1836?

Document 2

In this excerpt, the English writer Frances Trollope records a conversation with a man in Cincinnati, Ohio.

> "You [Americans] spend a good deal of time in reading the newspapers."
>
> "And I'd like you to tell me how we can spend it better. How should freemen spend their time, but looking after their government, and watching that them fellers as we gives offices to, does their duty, and gives themselves no airs?"
>
> "But I sometimes think, sir, that your fences might be in more thorough repair, and your roads in better order, if less time was spent in politics."

Source: *Domestic Manners of the Americans,* 1832

8 According to the man, why do Americans spend so much time reading newspapers? What is the writer's opinion about this?

Document 3

This is a portion of the Missouri Compromise.

> Section 8. *And be it further enacted,* that in all that territory ceded by France to the United States, under the name of Louisiana, . . . slavery and involuntary servitude . . . shall be, and is hereby, forever prohibited.

Source: Missouri Compromise

9 What historical issue is addressed in the document?

Document 4

This map shows the sequence of the acquisition of Florida.

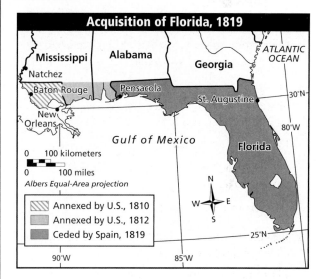

10 Based on the map, in which direction did the U.S. acquire the various parts of Florida?

11 **Expository Writing** Using the information from the four documents and your knowledge of social studies, write an essay in which you:

- describe how Americans generally felt about themselves and their place in the world in the early 1800s; and

- explain why they felt this way and which Americans might have thought differently.

Need Extra Help?											
If you missed questions. . .	1	2	3	4	5	6	7	8	9	10	11
Go to page. . .	306	306	317	322–323	326	302–326	304–307	313	323–324	325–326	302–326

Unit 4

Nationalism and Sectionalism
1820–1860

Child's sled from 1848

"We are the nation of human progress, and who will, what can, set limits to our onward march?"
—John L. O'Sullivan

Log cabin and farm site in Ohio, 1831

331

Reading History

Making Inferences

Learn It!

To comprehend some texts, you will need to make inferences. When you infer, you use clues from the text along with your own knowledge to figure out the author's meaning.

Question: Why do you think the Cherokees' journey west is called the Trail of Tears?

Inference Process

Text Clue:
Cherokee leaders were reluctant to relocate their people.

Text Clue:
Many Cherokee died on the journey.

Background Knowledge:
It is difficult to lose your home and experience the loss of family and friends.

—*from Chapter 11, p. 346*
Filled with sadness and anger, their leaders gave in, and the long march to the West began. . . . Around 2,000 Cherokee died in camps waiting for the move to begin. About another 2,000 died along the way from starvation, disease, and exposure to brutal weather.

Practice It!

Read the paragraph, and follow the inference process on another sheet of paper.

—*from Chapter 13, p. 412*
The South was behind other sections of the country in **literacy,** the number of people able to read and write. One reason . . . was the South's geography. The South had few people per square mile. Many families could not send their children great distances to attend school. In addition, many Southerners believed that education was a private matter, not a state function.

Question: How did the South's agricultural economy affect its children's education?

Inference Process

Text Clue:
_____

Text Clue:
_____

Background Knowledge:
_____

Academic Vocabulary Preview

Listed below are the academic vocabulary words and their definitions that you will come across as you study Unit 4. The activities in the Practice It! column will help you study the words and definitions.

Academic Vocabulary	Definition	Practice It!
Chapter 11 The Jackson Era		
select (suh · LEHKT) *p. 337*	to choose	**Choose** *terms from Chapter 11 to complete the paragraph.* The president of the United States is an elected member of the **1.** _____ government. In an election, if no presidential candidate receives a majority of electoral votes, members of the House of Representatives **2.** _____ the president. The House is an **3.** _____ of the U.S. legislative government.
participate (pahr · TIH · suh · PAYT) *p. 340*	to take part in	
federal (FEH · duh · ruhl) *p. 343*	the central governing authority	
survive (suhr · VYV) *p. 347*	to continue to live	
institution (IHN · stuh · TOO · shuhn) *p. 349*	an organization	
symbol (SIHM · buhl) *p. 352*	an object representing something else	
Chapter 12 Manifest Destiny		
access (AK · sehs) *p. 359*	the ability to get to	**Identify** *the term from Chapter 12 that best completes the sentence.* **4.** In the early 1800s, many Americans wanted _____ to the Pacific Ocean. **5.** Spain encouraged families to _____ a colony in Texas. **6.** Before earning statehood, California wrote a _____ that banned slavery.
establish (ihs · TA · blihsh) *p. 367*	to set up	
resource (REE · SOHRS) *p. 374*	an available source of wealth	
commence (kuh · MENTS) *p. 375*	to begin	
constitution (KAHNT · stuh · TOO · shuhn) *p. 380*	a list of fundamental laws to support a government	
incorporate (ihn · KAWR · puh · RAYT) *p. 382*	to include; to bring into	
Chapter 13 North and South		
innovation (IH · nuh · VAY · shuhn) *p. 389*	a new idea or method	**Identify** *the term from Chapter 13 that best matches the underlined word or phrase.* **7.** Canals and railways <u>changed</u> trade in the United States in the early 1800s. **8.** Many <u>towns</u> in the North did not allow enslaved people to attend school. **9.** Today, slavery is not <u>allowed by law</u> in the United States.
transform (trants · FAWRM) *p. 391*	to change	
community (kuh · MYOO · nuh · tee) *p. 396*	a group of people living in a particular place	
license (LY · suhnts) *p. 397*	to grant official authority	
consequence (KAHNT · suh · kwehnts) *p. 402*	a result	
legal (LEE · guhl) *p. 409*	permitted by law	
Chapter 14 The Age of Reform		

lecture (LEHK · chuhr) *p. 419*	a speech intended as a warning	**Choose** *the word that best matches the meaning of each vocabulary term listed below.*
		10. lecture **11. capable**
		  a. praise **a.** able
		  b. essay **b.** loud
		  c. speech **c.** unable

route (ROOT) *p. 430*	a line of travel	
capable (KAY · puh · buhl) *p. 437*	having the necessary abilities	
ministry (MIH · nuh · stree) *p. 438*	religious services	

Chapter 11

The Jackson Era 1824–1845

In the 1830s, many Native Americans were forced to move west along what became known as the Trail of Tears.

JAMES MONROE 1817–1825

★ 1823 Monroe Doctrine issued

JOHN Q. ADAMS 1825–1829

ANDREW JACKSON 1829–1837

1830 ★ Indian Removal Act

★ 1833 Force Bill passes

PRESIDENTS

U.S. Events

World Events

1820

1825

1830

★ 1822 Brazil gains independence from Portugal

1826 ★ French scientist Niépce produces first photograph

★ 1829 Louis Braille publishes reading system for the blind

calling the election a contest "between an honest patriotism, on the one side, and an unholy, selfish ambition, on the other." The National Republicans fought back. They created a vicious campaign song to play up embarrassing incidents in Jackson's life. One involved Jackson's order in the War of 1812 to execute soldiers who deserted.

Mudslinging was not the only new tactic introduced in the 1828 campaign. Election slogans, rallies, buttons, and events such as barbecues also were used to stir up enthusiasm. All of these new features became a permanent part of American political life.

In the election of 1828, Jackson received most of the votes cast in the frontier states. He also received many votes in the South, where his support for states' rights was popular. John C. Calhoun of South Carolina, who had been Adams's vice president, switched parties to run with Jackson. Calhoun also supported states' rights. Jackson won the election in an overwhelming victory, or landslide.

Reading Check **Identifying** What campaign practices of the 1828 election still are used today?

Philadelphia editor John Binns published several "coffin handbills" attacking Andrew Jackson. This cartoon shows Binns **A** struggling to carry a burden consisting of coffins for Secretary of State Henry Clay **B** and President John Quincy Adams **C**. Adams is clinging to the presidential chair that he was soon to lose.

Critical Thinking

Interpreting What is the cartoonist trying to say about the coffin handbills?

Jackson as President

Main Idea Andrew Jackson made the American political system more democratic.

History and You What are the requirements for today's citizens to be eligible to vote? Read on to learn how President Jackson expanded voting rights to include a larger number of people.

Andrew Jackson was everything most Americans admired—a patriot, a self-made man, and a war hero. Thousands of farmers and laborers arrived in Washington to hear Jackson's Inaugural Address. Later, a crowd attended the White House reception. They filled the elegant rooms, trampling carpets with muddy shoes and spilling food on chairs. They were there to shake the hand of the president who seemed just like them.

"Old Hickory"

Like many of his supporters, Andrew Jackson was born in a log cabin. During the War of 1812, he defeated the Creek Nation in the Battle of Horseshoe Bend and the British at the Battle of New Orleans. His troops called him "Old Hickory" because he was as tough as a hickory stick.

Small farmers, craftspeople, and others who felt left out of the expanding American economy loved Jackson. They felt that his rise from a log cabin to the White House demonstrated the American success story.

New Voters

President Andrew Jackson promised "equal protection and equal benefits" for all Americans—at least for all white American men. During his first term, a spirit of equality spread throughout American politics.

In the nation's early years, only men who owned property or paid taxes had suffrage, or the right to vote. By the 1820s, many states had loosened the property requirements. Democracy expanded as people who had not been allowed to vote became new voters.

In 1832 South Carolina called a state convention to declare the tariffs of 1828 and 1832 null and void. In addition, the state threatened to secede, or withdraw, from the Union if the federal government attempted to use force to collect those tariffs within its borders.

"It is hereby declared . . . that the . . . laws for the imposing of duties . . . on the importation of foreign commodities. . . are null, void, and no law, nor binding upon this State. . . .

Any act authorizing the employment of a military or naval force against the State of South Carolina, . . . [is] inconsistent with the . . . continuance of South Carolina in the Union."

—from the South Carolina Ordinance of Nullification

Vice President John C. Calhoun argued that any state had the authority to call a formal convention to declare null and void any federal law it considered unconstitutional. Tensions between Calhoun and President Jackson increased when Jackson sided with those opposing nullification.

The Nullification Proclamation declared that nullification was unconstitutional. It also stated that threatening to secede was an act of treason.

"I consider, then, the power to annul a law of the United States, assumed by one State, incompatible with the existence of the Union, . . . and destructive of the great object for which it was formed."

—President Andrew Jackson's proclamation from the nullification

President Andrew Jackson privately threatened to march an army into South Carolina to hang Calhoun. Instead, he issued a proclamation against nullification. Congress passed a bill to lower tariffs—along with a bill to enforce it.

Critical Thinking

Comparing and Contrasting How did each side in the nullification crisis defend its position?

For the first time, white male sharecroppers, factory workers, and others **participated,** or took part, in the political process. Women, however, could not vote, and African Americans and Native Americans had few rights of any kind.

Also, by 1828, 22 of the 24 states had changed their constitutions to allow the people, rather than the state legislatures, to choose presidential electors. This change further broadened democracy.

The Spoils System

Democrats wanted to open up government jobs to people from all walks of life. They argued that ordinary citizens could handle any government job. Many Democrats were disturbed that the federal government had become a bureaucracy, a system in which nonelected officials carry out laws.

President Jackson fired many federal workers and replaced them with his supporters. The fired employees protested.

They charged that Jackson was acting like a tyrant. Jackson responded that new federal employees would be good for democracy.

One Jackson supporter said: "To the victors belong the spoils." In other words, because the Jacksonians won the election, they had the right to the spoils, or the benefits of victory. The practice of replacing government employees with the winner's supporters is called the **spoils system.**

Electoral Changes

Jackson's supporters abandoned the unpopular **caucus** system, in which major candidates were chosen by members of Congress. The caucuses were replaced by **nominating conventions** in which delegates from the states chose the party's presidential candidate. This system allowed many people to participate in the selection of candidates.

Reading Check **Describing** What is a caucus system?

The Tariff Debate

Main Idea A fight over tariffs ignited a crisis on the question of states' rights versus the rights of the federal government.

History and You Can you ignore a school rule? Read how South Carolina rejected a federal law.

. . . .

A **tariff** is a fee paid on imported goods. The high tariff on European manufactured goods pleased Northeastern factory owners. Tariffs made European goods more expensive, prompting American consumers to buy American-made goods. Southerners hated the tariff, because tariffs meant higher prices.

John C. Calhoun of South Carolina argued that a state had the right to **nullify,** or cancel, a federal law if it was considered to be against state interests. Because the states created the federal government, he argued, the states are the final authority. Daniel Webster disagreed, claiming that nullification would destroy the Union.

Nobody knew Jackson's views. At a dinner, however, Jackson spoke directly to Calhoun: "Our federal union . . . must be preserved!" Answering the challenge, Calhoun said, "The Union—next to our liberty, most dear." He meant that the Union must take second place to a state's liberty to overrule the Constitution if its interests were threatened.

In 1832 Congress enacted a lower tariff, but it did not cool the protest. South Carolina passed the **Nullification Act,** declaring it would not pay the "illegal" tariffs of 1828 and 1832. The state threatened to **secede,** or break away, from the Union if the U.S. federal government interfered.

To ease the crisis, Jackson backed a bill that would gradually lower the tariff. Jackson, however, had Congress pass the Force Bill, allowing him to use the military to enforce acts of Congress. South Carolina accepted the new tariff but nullified the Force Bill.

Reading Check **Explaining** How would Northeastern factory owners react to a high tariff?

Section 1 Review

History ONLINE
Study Central™ To review this section, go to glencoe.com.

Vocabulary

1. Define each of the following words by using it in a sentence: majority, plurality, select, participate, spoils system, caucus, nominating convention, tariff, nullify, secede.

Main Ideas

2. **Specifying** What key issue split the Republican Party in the 1828 presidential election?

3. **Explaining** Why did Andrew Jackson fire many government employees?

4. **Summarizing** Why was the issue of states' rights versus federal authority serious?

Critical Thinking

5. **Making Inferences** Why do you think Speaker of the House Henry Clay was willing to make the "corrupt bargain"?

6. **Organizing** Use a diagram like the one below to describe the changes that took place in the political system under Andrew Jackson.

7. **Creative Writing** Write three questions you would ask President Andrew Jackson if you interviewed him. Then write answers to the questions as you think Jackson might have responded.

Answer the
8. **Essential Question**
How did political beliefs and events shape Andrew Jackson's presidency?

Conflicts Over Land

Essential Question ◄

How did Andrew Jackson's presidency affect Native Americans?

Reading Guide

Content Vocabulary

relocate (p. 343)

guerrilla tactics (p. 347)

Academic Vocabulary

federal (p. 343)

survive (p. 347)

Key People and Events

Indian Removal Act (p. 343)

Indian Territory (p. 344)

General Winfield Scott (p. 345)

Trail of Tears (p. 346)

Black Hawk (p. 346)

Osceola (p. 347)

Reading Strategy

Taking Notes As you read, use a diagram like the one below to describe how each group of Native Americans resisted removal and the result.

NEW YORK STANDARDS
The American Journey

U5.II.1 To understand how American consciousness began to develop during Jackson's administration

U5.II.2 To complete well-documented and historically accurate case studies about individuals and groups who represent different ethnic, national, and religious groups, including Native American Indians, in New York State and the United States at different times and in different locations

U5.III.1 To understand the way of life of an agrarian society

American Diary

As they moved west in 1838 during a forced removal from their lands, the Cherokee were said to be on a "Trail of Tears." A legend developed that a Cherokee rose appeared along the road wherever a Cherokee tear landed. Poet Rick Brown described the event:

"As wagons, weighted, marked their way, from New Echota to where they close; where each tear fell, as some will tell, will be seen a Cherokee rose."

—quoted from "A Cherokee Rose"

The Seminole people of Florida fought against being forced to abandon their homes and way of life.

Visual Summary

Main Idea	Supporting Details
The Election of 1828 transformed American political campaigns.	• Mudslinging, election slogans, rallies, buttons, and campaign events were first practiced in 1828.
President Andrew Jackson made changes to the American political system.	• Jackson established the spoils system (replacing government employees with supporters of the winning candidate). • His supporters created nominating conventions to select presidential candidates.
President Jackson supported the demands of western settlers for Native American land.	• In 1830 Jackson pushed the Indian Removal Act through Congress. This law forced Native Americans to move west.
Some Native American groups resisted relocation.	• The Cherokee Nation sued to keep its land. However, after a few Cherokee signed a treaty in 1835, thousands were forced to move west on the "Trail of Tears." • The Seminole resisted removal by using guerrilla tactics to attack white settlements on the Florida coast.
President Jackson opposed the Bank of the United States.	• Jackson believed the national bank was undemocratic and unconstitutional. He vetoed a bill extending the bank's charter, eventually forcing it to close.

Study anywhere, anytime! Download quizzes and flash cards to your PDA from glencoe.com.

GRADE 8 INTERMEDIATE TEST PRACTICE

TEST-TAKING **TIP**

Read an extended-response question carefully. Are you being asked to explain something or to demonstrate what you know about a subject? Be sure to understand what you are being asked.

Reviewing Main Ideas

Directions: Choose the best answer for each of the following questions.

1 In the 1828 presidential election, Andrew Jackson's Democratic-Republican Party

  (1) wanted a strong central government.

  (2) supported setting up a national bank.

  (3) favored states' rights.

  (4) was dominated by merchants and farmers.

2 In *Worcester* v. *Georgia* (1832), Chief Justice John Marshall ruled that

  (1) Georgia had no right to interfere with the Cherokee.

  (2) the "spoils system" was unconstitutional.

  (3) the federal government had no authority over Native Americans.

  (4) states had to support a national bank.

3 Jackson attacked the Bank of the United States because

  (1) it was being run by corrupt elected officials.

  (2) it provided loans to all citizens.

  (3) it financed foreign business deals that put Americans out of work.

  (4) it was controlled by wealthy Easterners.

4 One reason the Whigs won the presidential election of 1840 was that

  (1) they made a "corrupt bargain" with Henry Clay to steal the presidency.

  (2) the Democrats split over Van Buren.

  (3) they ended the Panic of 1837.

  (4) they gained support from laborers and farmers rather than the wealthy elite.

Short-Answer Question

Directions: Base your answer to question 5 on the excerpt below and on your knowledge of social studies.

> Carriages, wagons and carts all pursuing him [Jackson] to the President's house. . . . Ladies fainted, men were seen with bloody noses and such a scene of confusion took place as is impossible to describe. . . . This concourse [event] had not been anticipated and therefore not provided against. Ladies and gentlemen, only had been expected at this Levee [reception], not the people en masse [as a whole]. But it was the People's day, and the People's President and the People would rule.
>
> —a letter by Margaret Bayard Smith describing Jackson's inauguration in 1829

5 What is Smith's attitude toward Jackson and his enthusiastic supporters? Explain.

Review the Essential Questions

6 Essay Andrew Jackson is often considered by historians to be one of the 10 greatest presidents in American history. Write an essay in which you agree or disagree with this position.

To help you write your essay, review your answers to the Essential Questions in the section reviews and the chapter Foldables Study Organizer. Your essay should include:

- Jackson's campaign and the election of 1828;
- Jacksonian policies regarding suffrage, the spoils system, tariffs, and states' rights;
- the removal of Native Americans; and
- Jackson's war against the Bank.

GO ON

Document-Based Questions

Directions: Analyze the documents and answer the short-answer questions that follow.

Document 1

In the 1840 election campaign, the Whigs marched in parades, carrying miniature log cabins on poles.

Source: Smithsonian Institution

7 Based on the photo, explain why Harrison's supporters made the log cabin their symbol.

8 What political symbols do political parties use today?

Document 2

Massachusetts Senator Daniel Webster made these comments in 1830 regarding the nullification crisis.

> If anything be found in the national constitution, . . . which ought not to be in it, the people know how to get rid of it. If any construction . . . [is] unacceptable to them so as to become practically a part of the constitution, they will amend it.

Source: Daniel Webster, *The Writings and Speeches of Daniel Webster*

9 Based on the excerpt, what did Webster think was a better solution than nullification if the people disapproved of a law?

Document 3

This is a selection from William Coodey's account of the Cherokee removal to Indian Territory.

> I almost fancied a voice of divine indignation for the wrongs of my poor and unhappy countrymen, driven by brutal power from all they loved and cherished in the land of their fathers, to gratify the cravings of [greed].

Source: David Colbert, *Eyewitness to America*

10 Based on the document, does Coodey approve of the removal of the Cherokee?

11 What reasons does Coodey give for their removal?

Document 4

Frederick Marryat recorded these views about life in New York City during the Panic of 1837.

> Go to the theaters and places of public amusement, and, instead of change, you receive an IOU from the treasury.—It is the same every where. . . .The barbers give you tickets, good for so many shaves; and were there beggars in the streets, I presume they would give you tickets in change, good for so much philanthropy.

Source: Captain Frederick Marryat, *Diary in America*

12 Based on the excerpt, describe one effect the Panic of 1837 had on the economy.

13 Expository Writing Using the information from the four documents and your knowledge of social studies, write an essay in which you:

- discuss the economics and social climate of the United States during the Jackson era; and

- describe the Jackson presidency and any changes it brought to American politics.

Need Extra Help?												
If you missed questions. . .	1	2	3	4	5	6	7	8	9	10	11	12	13
Go to page. . .	338	344	349	351	336-340	336-350	351-352	336-350	341	350-351	343-347	350-351	336-350

Manifest Destiny 1818–1853

Traveling along the Oregon Trail

JAMES MADISON 1809–1817

1809 Elizabeth Ann Seton founds Sisters of Charity

JAMES MONROE 1817–1825

1824 Russia surrenders land south of Alaska

1824 U.S. House elects John Q. Adams president

JOHN Q. ADAMS 1825–1829

ANDREW JACKSON 1829–1837

PRESIDENTS

U.S. Events

World Events

1810

1820

1830

1821 Mexico declares independence from Spain

1826 First Burmese War ends

1830 France occupies Algeria

Section 1: The Oregon Country

Essential Question How did the belief in Manifest Destiny influence western settlement?

Section 2: Independence for Texas

Essential Question Why did Texans fight for their independence from Mexico?

Section 3: War With Mexico

Essential Question How did Mexican lands in the West become part of the United States?

Section 4: California and Utah

Essential Question What factors affected the settlement of California and Utah in the West?

Numerous Engravings....12½ cts.

Mexican Treacheries and Cruelties.

INCIDENTS AND SUFFERINGS
IN THE
MEXICAN WAR;
WITH
Accounts of Hardships endured; Treacheries of the Mexicans; Battles Fought, and Success of American Arms;

The "Heroine of Fort Brown."

Also, an Account of Valiant Soldiers Fallen,
AND THE PARTICULARS OF THE
Death and Funeral Services in honor of
Capt. George Lincoln, of Worcester.

BY A VOLUNTEER RETURNED FROM THE WAR.

BOSTON AND NEW YORK:
1847.

Entered according to Act of Congress, in the year 1847, by LIEUT. G. N. ALLEY.

FOLDABLES
Study Organizer

Organizing Information

Make this Foldable to help organize what you learn about the expansion of the United States.

Step 1 Fold four sheets of paper in half from top to bottom. Cut each paper in half along the folds.

Step 2 Fold each piece of paper in half from top to bottom again.

Step 3 On each folded paper, make a cut 1 inch from the side on the top flap.

Step 4 Place the folded papers one on top of the other, and staple the sections together.

Manifest Destiny

Reading and Writing As you read, note dates and events about new territories in Oregon, Texas, New Mexico, California, and Utah.

MARTIN VAN BUREN 1837–1841

★ **1839** Mutiny occurs on slave ship *Amistad*

WILLIAM HENRY HARRISON 1841

JOHN TYLER 1841–1845

1845 ★ U.S. annexes Texas

★ **1846** Congress declares war on Mexico

JAMES POLK 1845–1849

ZACHARY TAYLOR 1849–1850

1840

1850

1839 ★ Opium War begins between Britain and China

◀ A man pulls Chinese women in a rickshaw

★ **1842** Treaty of Nanking gives Hong Kong to Great Britain

★ **1846** Neptune discovered

The Oregon Country

Essential Question

How did the belief in Manifest Destiny influence western settlement?

Reading Guide

Content Vocabulary

joint occupation (p. 359)

mountain man (p. 360)

rendezvous (p. 360)

emigrant (p. 362)

prairie schooner (p. 362)

Manifest Destiny (p. 363)

Academic Vocabulary

plus (p. 359)   access (p. 359)

Key People and Events

Adams-Onís Treaty (p. 359)

Oregon Trail (p. 362)

Henry Clay (p. 363)

Reading Strategy

Taking Notes As you read, list key events in a time line like the one below.

1819   1825   1836   1846

NEW YORK STANDARDS
The American Journey

U5.I.6 To explain how societies and nations attempt to satisfy their basic needs and wants by utilizing scarce capital, natural and human resources

U5.III.3 To describe historic events through the eyes and experiences of those who were there

U5.III.8 To describe the relationships between people and environments and the connections between people and places

U5.III.9 To use a number of research skills (e.g., computer databases, periodicals, census reports, maps, standard reference works, interviews, surveys) to locate geographical information about issues and problems

American Diary

Families left everything familiar behind when they made the often uncomfortable and dangerous trip to the Western frontier. Martha Gay was a 13-year-old who, in 1851, left Springfield, Missouri, in a covered wagon. She later wrote about the experience of leaving loved ones and friends behind: "Farewell sermons were preached and prayers offered for our safety. . . . All places of business and the schools were closed . . . and everybody came to say goodbye to us."

—*from* One Woman's West

A mountain man gives advice to pioneers.

Manifest Destiny

Since colonial times many Americans had believed their nation had a special role to fulfill. For years people thought the nation's mission should be to serve as a model of freedom and democracy. In the 1800s that vision changed. Many believed that the mission of the United States was to spread freedom by occupying the entire continent. In 1819 John Quincy Adams expressed what many Americans were thinking when he said expansion to the Pacific was as inevitable "as that the Mississippi should flow to the sea."

In the 1840s, New York newspaper editor John O'Sullivan expressed the idea of a national mission in more specific words. O'Sullivan declared it was America's "**Manifest Destiny** to overspread and to possess the whole of the continent which Providence has given us." O'Sullivan meant that the United States was clearly destined—set apart for a special purpose—by God to extend its boundaries all the way to the Pacific Ocean.

"Fifty-Four Forty or Fight"

Many Americans wanted the United States to own all of Oregon. In the 1844 presidential election, James K. Polk, the Democratic nominee, supported this demand. Democrats used the slogan "Fifty-Four Forty or Fight," referring to the line of latitude they believed should be the nation's northern border in Oregon.

Polk's Whig opponent, **Henry Clay,** did not take a strong position on the Oregon issue. Polk won the election because Whig support was not united behind Clay.

A firm believer in Manifest Destiny, Polk was focused on making Oregon part of the United States. Britain, however, would not accept a border at "Fifty-Four Forty." This would mean giving up its land claim entirely. In 1846 the two countries finally compromised. They set the border between American and British parts of Oregon at latitude 49°N.

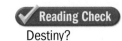 **Reading Check** **Defining** What is Manifest Destiny?

Section 1 Review

History ONLINE
Study Central™ To review this section, go to glencoe.com.

Vocabulary

1. Use each of these terms in a sentence that will help explain its meaning: plus, access, joint occupation, mountain man, rendezvous, emigrant, prairie schooner, Manifest Destiny.

Main Ideas

2. **Specifying** Which nations claimed the Oregon Country? How did John Quincy Adams help resolve the claims?

3. **Explaining** What was James K. Polk's campaign slogan in the 1844 election? What did the slogan mean?

Critical Thinking

4. **Analyzing** During the 1840s, many more Americans than British settled in the Oregon Country. How do you think this influenced negotiations over the territory?

5. **Summarizing** Create a diagram like the one below to list details about what life was like for a mountain man. Add more boxes to your diagram if necessary.

```
        Life of a Mountain Man
        ┌──────┴──────┐
    ┌───┐   ┌───┐   ┌───┐
    └───┘   └───┘   └───┘
```

6. **Creative Writing** Take the role of a pioneer about to travel to the Oregon Country. A friend asks why you are leaving. Write your answer in the voice of your character. Include details about who you are, your reasons for going, and your feelings about the journey ahead.

Answer the
7. **Essential Question** How did the belief in Manifest Destiny influence western settlement?

YOU DECIDE

Spanish mission in the Southwest

Was Manifest Destiny Justified?

Building Background

In 1845 a magazine editor named John L. O'Sullivan declared that it was the "manifest destiny" of Americans to expand westward to the Pacific Ocean. Many Americans believed in this concept of Manifest Destiny—the idea that God had given the continent to Americans and wanted them to settle western land. Manifest Destiny did have its opponents, however. Long-time public servant Albert Gallatin expressed his opposition to Manifest Destiny and to war with Mexico in an 1847 pamphlet *Peace with Mexico*.

NO

ALBERT GALLATIN

It is said, that the people of the United States have a hereditary superiority of race over the Mexicans, which gives them the right to subjugate[1] and keep in bondage the inferior nation. . . .

Is it compatible with the principle of Democracy, which rejects every hereditary claim of individuals, to admit a hereditary superiority of races? . . . Can you for a moment suppose, that a very doubtful descent from men, who lived one thousand years ago, has transmitted to you a superiority over your fellow-men? . . . At this time, the claim is but a pretext for covering and justifying unjust usurpation[2] and unbounded ambition. . . .

Among ourselves, the most ignorant, the most inferior, either in physical or mental faculties,[3] is recognized as having equal rights, and he has an equal vote with any one, however superior to him in all those respects. This is founded on the immutable[4] principle that no one man is born with the right of governing another man.

[1] **subjugate** conquer
[2] **usurpation** seizure
[3] **faculties** abilities
[4] **immutable** unchanging

The Struggle for Independence

Main Idea Texans fought for their independence from Mexico.

History and You Did you know that Texas was once a nation? Read why Texas remained independent before it became a state.

During 1835 unrest among Texans sometimes erupted in open conflict. Santa Anna sent an army into Texas to punish the rebels. In October some Mexican troops tried to seize a cannon held by Texans at the town of Gonzales. The Texans taunted the Mexicans. They put a white flag on the cannon, bearing the words "Come and Take It." After a brief battle, the Texans drove back the Mexican troops. Texans consider this to be the first fight of the Texan Revolution.

The Texans called for volunteers. Many answered, including African Americans and Tejanos. In December 1835, the Texans freed San Antonio from a larger Mexican force.

Santa Anna's Letter Explaining the Attack
"[Travis's] responses were insulting, which made it imperative to assault the fort before it could be reinforced by Samuel Houston. . . . The obstinancy [stubbornness] of Travis and his soldiers was the cause of the death of the whole of them, for not one would surrender."

Critical Thinking

1. **Identifying Cause and Effect** What effect did the defeat of the Alamo have on the Texas independence movement?
2. **Speculating** What do you think might have happened to the independence movement had the defenders of the Alamo abandoned the fort?

Despite these victories, problems arose. Various groups argued over who would lead and what actions to take. In early 1836, when Texas should have been preparing to face Santa Anna, plans had stalled.

The Battle of the Alamo

Santa Anna marched north, furious at the loss of San Antonio. When his army reached San Antonio in late February 1836, it found a small Texan force barricaded inside a nearby mission called the **Alamo.**

Although the Texans had cannons, they lacked gunpowder. The Texans were at a further disadvantage because they had only about 180 soldiers to take on Santa Anna's army of several thousand. The Texans had brave leaders, however, including Davy Crockett and a tough Texan named Jim Bowie. The commander, William B. Travis, who was only 26 years old, was determined to hold his position at the Alamo. Travis managed to send messages through Mexican lines. Several messages appealed to the people of Texas and the United States for aid.

For 12 long days, through several attacks, the defenders of the Alamo kept Santa Anna's army at bay with rifle fire. On March 6, 1836, Mexican cannon fire smashed the Alamo's walls.

The Mexicans were too numerous to hold back. They entered the fortress, killing all the defenders, including Travis, Crockett, and Bowie. Only a few women and children and some servants survived to tell of the battle.

Although the defenders at the Alamo had been defeated, they had bought the Texans time to gather troops and supplies.

Texas Declares Its Independence

During the siege at the Alamo, Texan leaders were meeting at Washington-on-the-Brazos, where they were writing a new constitution. There, on March 2, 1836—four days before the fall of the Alamo—American settlers and Tejanos declared independence from Mexico. They then established the Republic of Texas.

Texas War for Independence, 1835–1836

Legend:
- Mexican forces
- Mexican victory
- Texan forces
- Texan victory
- Austin's colony
- Disputed territory

From Independence to Statehood Texas remained independent for several years. At first the United States refused to annex Texas. To pressure the United States, Texas threatened to form an alliance with Great Britain. The United States did not want the British near its southern border, and in 1845 Texas was admitted to the Union as a slave state.

The Republic of Texas had a three-branch government. Its first Congress met in 1837 at this house in present-day Houston. ▼

▲ Texas banknote, 1838

"In my judgment it would be far better for this Country that Texas should remain an independent State if this were possible."
—Senator James Buchanan

Map Skills

Location What battle was fought northeast of Brazoria?

Maps In Motion See StudentWorks™ Plus or glencoe.com.

The Texas Declaration stated that the government of Santa Anna had violated the Mexican Constitution. It noted that the Texans' protests against these violations were met with force. The declaration proclaimed the following:

PRIMARY SOURCE

"The people of Texas, in solemn convention assembled, appealing to a candid world for the necessities of our condition, do hereby resolve and declare, that our political connection with the Mexican nation has forever ended, and that the people of Texas do now constitute a free, Sovereign, and independent republic."
—The Declaration of Independence of Texas

With Mexican troops in Texas, it was not possible to hold an election to ratify the constitution and vote for leaders. Texas leaders set up a temporary government.

The government named **Sam Houston** as commander in chief of the Texas forces. Houston wanted to prevent the Mexicans from overrunning other forts. He ordered the troops at Goliad to abandon their position. As they retreated, however, they came face to face with Mexican troops. After a fierce fight, several hundred Texans surrendered. On Santa Anna's orders, the Texans were executed. This action outraged Texans, who called it the "Goliad Massacre."

The Battle of San Jacinto

Houston gathered an army of about 900 at San Jacinto (SAN huh•SIHN•toh), near the site of present-day Houston. Santa Anna was camped nearby with an army of more than 1,300. On April 21, the Texans launched a surprise attack, shouting, "Remember the Alamo! Remember Goliad!" They killed more than 600 soldiers and captured about 700 more—including Santa Anna. On May 14, 1836, Santa Anna signed a treaty that recognized the independence of Texas.

The Lone Star Republic

In September 1836, Texans elected Sam Houston as their president. Mirabeau Lamar, who had fought at the Battle of San Jacinto, served as vice president. Houston sent a delegation to Washington, D.C., asking the United States to **annex,** or take control of, Texas.

Andrew Jackson, however, refused their request. An addition of another slave state would upset the balance of slave and free states in Congress. For the moment, Texas would remain an independent country.

The Road to Statehood

After winning independence, Texas still had difficulties with Mexico, and it faced a mounting debt. Many Texans wanted to join the United States. Southerners favored Texas annexation, but Northerners opposed admitting another slave state to the Union. President Martin Van Buren did not want to inflame the slavery issue or risk war with Mexico. He put off the question of annexing Texas. John Tyler, who became president in 1841, supported Texas annexation. The Senate, however, was still divided over the slavery issue and failed to ratify the annexation treaty.

The situation changed with the 1844 presidential campaign. Manifest Destiny was a popular idea at the time. The South wanted Texas. The North favored gaining all of Oregon. Candidate James K. Polk supported both actions. After Polk won, Congress passed a resolution to annex Texas. In 1845 Texas joined the Union.

Reading Check **Identifying** What was the role of Sam Houston in Texas history?

History ONLINE
Study Central™ To review this section, go to glencoe.com.

Section 2 Review

Vocabulary

1. Write a short paragraph in which you use all of the following vocabulary terms: Tejano, empresario, establish, decree, remove, annex.

Main Ideas

2. **Explaining** How did Stephen Austin try to resolve tensions with the Mexican government?

3. **Specifying** Why was the Battle of San Jacinto important?

Critical Thinking

4. **Contrasting** In a diagram like the one below, describe the Mexican government's expectations for the settlement of Texas. Describe how the actual settlement differed from these expectations and the result.

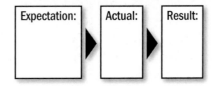

5. **Synthesizing** How did the Texan defeats at the Alamo and Goliad affect Texans?

6. **Persuasive Writing** Take the role of Stephen Austin. Write what you would say to President Santa Anna to persuade him to agree to Texans' demand for independence.

7. **Answer the Essential Question**
Why did Texans fight for their independence from Mexico?

Section 3 ★ War With Mexico

Essential Question ◄
How did Mexican lands in the West become part of the United States?

Reading Guide

Content Vocabulary

rancho *(p. 374)* Californios *(p. 376)*

ranchero *(p. 374)* cede *(p. 377)*

Academic Vocabulary

resource *(p. 374)* commence *(p. 375)*

Key People and Events

Santa Fe Trail *(p. 373)*

John C. Frémont *(p. 374)*

Winfield Scott *(p. 377)*

Treaty of Guadalupe Hidalgo *(p. 377)*

Mexican Cession *(p. 377)*

Gadsden Purchase *(p. 377)*

Reading Strategy

Taking Notes As you read, describe the achievements of each individual in the chart below.

	Achievements
William Becknell	
John C. Frémont	
Winfield Scott	

NEW YORK STANDARDS
The American Journey

U5.III.8 To describe the relationships between people and environments and the connections between people and places

U6.I.1 To understand the series of events and resulting conditions that lead to the American Civil War

U6.I.2 To understand how different experiences, beliefs, values, traditions, and motives cause individuals and groups to interpret historic events and issues from different perspectives

American Diary

Spanish conquistadors brought the first cattle and horses to North America. As Mexicans settled in present-day California, many became cowhands. They herded cattle on California's large ranches. These Mexican cowhands were called vaqueros and were the first cowboys of the American West. People of other nationalities soon populated the region, but Spanish culture still influences California's people today.

Mexican cowboys roping cattle

372

Section 1: The North's Economy

Essential Question What innovations in industry, travel, and communications changed the lives of Americans in the 1800s?

Section 2: The North's People

Essential Question How did immigration have an impact on cities, industry, and culture in the North?

Section 3: Southern Cotton Kingdom

Essential Question How did the South's industry and economy differ from the industry and economy of the North?

Section 4: The South's People

Essential Question How did unique elements of culture develop among enslaved African Americans in the South?

FOLDABLES® Study Organizer

Organizing Information Make this Foldable to help summarize what you learn about similarities and differences between the North and the South.

Step 1 Mark the center of a sheet of notebook paper.

Step 2 Fold the sheet of notebook paper into thirds.

Step 3 Sketch a map of the United States on the front and label your Foldable as shown.

North (1820–1860)
South (1820–1860)

Reading and Writing After you finish taking notes in your Foldable, list the causes and effects of the differences that led to conflict between these regions.

California gold miner ▶

WILLIAM HENRY HARRISON 1841

JOHN TYLER 1841–1845

★ **1845** James Marshall discovers gold in California

JAMES POLK 1845–1849

ZACHARY TAYLOR 1849–1850

MILLARD FILLMORE 1850–1853

FRANKLIN PIERCE 1853–1857

JAMES BUCHANAN 1857–1861

1840

1850

1860

★ **1845** Great Irish Famine begins

★ **1848** Johannes Rebmann is first European to see Kilamanjaro

★ **1857** Sepoy Rebellion begins in India

★ **1859** Darwin's *On the Origin of Species* is published

Kilimanjaro in Tanzania ▶

The North's Economy

Essential Question ◀

What innovations in industry, travel, and communications changed the lives of Americans in the 1800s?

Reading Guide

Content Vocabulary

clipper ship (p. 390)

telegraph (p. 391)

Morse code (p. 392)

Academic Vocabulary

innovation (p. 389)   transform (p. 391)

Key People

Elias Howe (p. 389)

Robert Fulton (p. 390)

Peter Cooper (p. 390)

Samuel Morse (p. 391)

John Deere (p. 393)

Cyrus McCormick (p. 393)

Reading Strategy

Taking Notes As you read, use the diagram below to describe the three phases of the development of industrialization in the North.

Development of Industrialization
Phase 1
↓
Phase 2
↓
Phase 3

NEW YORK STANDARDS
The American Journey

U5.III.1 To understand the way of life of an agrarian society

U5.III.2 To understand the nature and effect of changes on society and individuals as the United States began to move from an agrarian to an industrial economy

U5.III.8 To describe the relationships between people and environments and the connections between people and places

American Diary

Railroad travel in the mid-1840s was uncomfortable. English novelist Charles Dickens described what it was like to travel on a train. "There is a great deal of jolting, a great deal of noise, a great deal of wall, not much window, a locomotive engine, a shriek, and a bell. The cars are like shabby omnibusses, but larger; holding thirty, forty, fifty people. . . . In the center of the carriage there is usually a stove, fed with charcoal . . . which is for the most part red-hot. It is insufferably close."

—from American Notes for General Circulation

The number of railroad routes increased dramatically from 1840 to 1860.

Technology and Industry

Main Idea Industry, travel, and communications greatly expanded during the 1800s.

History and You How often do you use e-mail or text messaging during any one day? Read to learn about the invention of the telegraph, which greatly improved communications in the 1800s.

. . . .

Early trains differed from and offered few of the comforts of modern-day trains. They were noisy and often dirty. As Charles Dickens noted, they also provided a jolty ride. Locomotives were part of the wave of industrialization during the 1800s. **Innovations**— new ideas or methods—in industry and technology began changing the way Americans worked, traveled, and communicated.

Industrialization

The industrialization of the North developed in three phases. In the first phase, manufacturers made products by dividing the tasks involved among the workers. For example, one worker would spin thread all day, and another would weave cloth. This was faster than having one person spin and then weave. During the second phase, manufacturers built factories to bring specialized workers together. Products could be made more quickly than before.

In the third phase, factory workers used machinery to perform some of their work. Many of the new machines ran on water-power or steam power. For example, power-driven looms took over the task of weaving. The worker's job changed from weaving to tending the machine. This change produced more fabric in less time.

Mass production of cotton textiles began in New England in the early 1800s. **Elias Howe** invented the sewing machine in 1846. Using this machine and machine-made fabrics, workers produced clothing on a large scale. Other types of industries developed during the same period. By 1860, the Northeast's factories produced at least two-thirds of the country's manufactured goods.

Improved Transportation

Transportation improvements contributed to the success of America's new industries. Between 1800 and 1850, construction crews built thousands of miles of roads and canals.

Primary Source / Railroad Expansion, 1860

Major Railroads, 1860

Total Length of Railroad Tracks

1840	3,000 miles (4,828 km)
1850	9,000 miles (14,484 km)
1860	30,000 miles (48,280 km)

Railroads

ATLANTIC OCEAN

0   200 kilometers
0   200 miles
Albers Equal-Area projection

Making Tracks Trains were important not only for transporting people across the country, but they also allowed goods to be shipped greater distances than ever before. Beginning in the early 1800s, industrialization and technology began to change the way Americans worked, traveled, and communicated.

Critical Thinking

Making Inferences What region might have an advantage for transporting goods and people more easily?

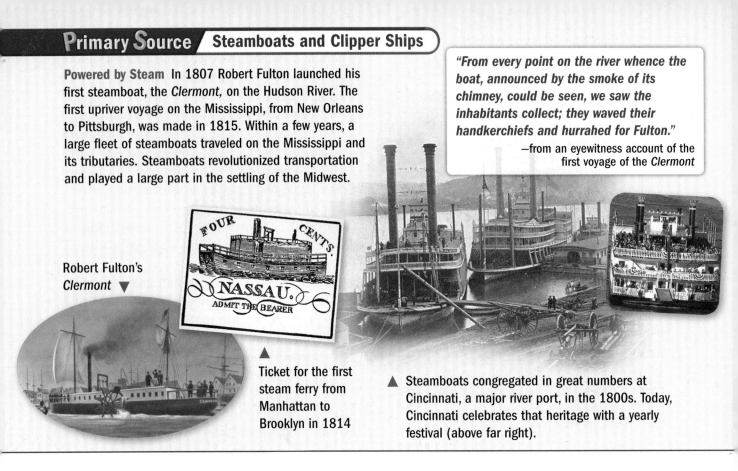

Powered by Steam In 1807 Robert Fulton launched his first steamboat, the *Clermont*, on the Hudson River. The first upriver voyage on the Mississippi, from New Orleans to Pittsburgh, was made in 1815. Within a few years, a large fleet of steamboats traveled on the Mississippi and its tributaries. Steamboats revolutionized transportation and played a large part in the settling of the Midwest.

"From every point on the river whence the boat, announced by the smoke of its chimney, could be seen, we saw the inhabitants collect; they waved their handkerchiefs and hurrahed for Fulton."
—from an eyewitness account of the first voyage of the *Clermont*

Robert Fulton's *Clermont* ▼

FOUR CENTS. NASSAU. ADMIT THE BEARER

▲ Ticket for the first steam ferry from Manhattan to Brooklyn in 1814

▲ Steamboats congregated in great numbers at Cincinnati, a major river port, in the 1800s. Today, Cincinnati celebrates that heritage with a yearly festival (above far right).

Canals opened new shipping routes by connecting many lakes and rivers. Upstream travel against the current was extremely difficult though. That changed in 1807, when inventor **Robert Fulton** demonstrated a reliable steamboat. Steamboats could carry goods and passengers more cheaply and quickly along inland waterways than flatboats or sail-powered vessels.

In the 1840s, builders began to widen and deepen canals to accommodate steamboats. By 1860 about 3,000 steamboats traveled the country's major rivers and canals, as well as the Great Lakes, spurring the growth of cities such as Cincinnati, Buffalo, and Chicago.

Sailing ships also were improved in the 1840s. The **clipper ships**—with sleek hulls and tall sails—were the pride of the open seas. They could sail 300 miles (483 km) per day, as fast as most steamships at that time. The ships got their name because they "clipped" time from long journeys. Before the clippers, the voyage from New York to Great Britain took about 21 to 28 days. A clipper ship could usually make that trip in half the time.

Locomotives

The development of railroads in the United States began with short stretches of tracks to connect mines with nearby rivers. Horses, rather than locomotives, pulled the early trains. The first steam-powered passenger locomotive, the *Rocket*, began operating in Britain in 1829.

Peter Cooper designed and built the first American steam locomotive in 1830. Called the *Tom Thumb*, it got off to a bad start. In a race against a horse-drawn train in Baltimore, the *Tom Thumb*'s engine failed. Engineers soon improved the engine, and within 10 years steam locomotives were pulling trains in the United States.

A Railway Network

In 1840 the United States had almost 3,000 miles (4,828 km) of railroad track. By 1860, it had almost 31,000 miles (49,890 km), mostly in the North and Midwest areas. One railway linked the cities of New York City and Buffalo. Another connected the Pennsylvania cities of Philadelphia and Pittsburgh.

Wind in the Sails Clipper ships were designed to carry small, but highly profitable, cargoes over long distances at high speeds. In 1851 one of those ships, the *Flying Cloud*, made the passage from New York to San Francisco in 89 days—a record never beaten by another sailing ship. The age of the clipper ship ended in the late 1800s due to decreased shipping costs on steamships. After that, only ships that could carry large cargoes could make a profit.

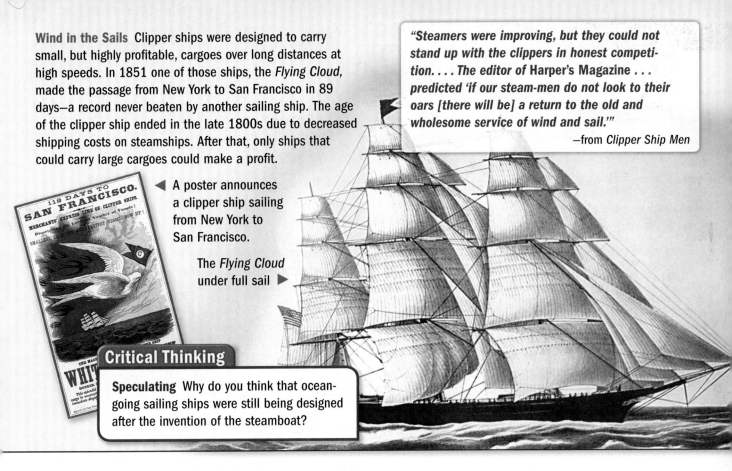

"Steamers were improving, but they could not stand up with the clippers in honest competition. . . . The editor of *Harper's Magazine* . . . predicted 'if our steam-men do not look to their oars [there will be] a return to the old and wholesome service of wind and sail.'"
—from *Clipper Ship Men*

◀ A poster announces a clipper ship sailing from New York to San Francisco.

The *Flying Cloud* under full sail ▶

Critical Thinking

Speculating Why do you think that ocean-going sailing ships were still being designed after the invention of the steamboat?

Yet another linked Baltimore and Wheeling, Virginia (now West Virginia). Railway builders connected these eastern lines to lines being built farther west in Ohio, Indiana, and Illinois. By 1860, a network of railroad track united the Midwest and the East.

Moving Goods and People

Along with canals, the railways **transformed,** or changed, trade in the nation's interior. The changes began with the opening of the Erie Canal in 1825 and the first railroads of the 1830s. Before this time, agricultural goods were carried down the Mississippi River to New Orleans. From there they were shipped to the East Coast or to other countries.

The development of the east-west canal and the rail network allowed grain, livestock, and dairy products to move directly from the Midwest to the East. Goods could now be moved faster and more cheaply. As a result, manufacturers in the East could offer them at lower prices.

The railroads also played an important role in the settlement and industrialization of the

Midwest. Fast, affordable train travel brought people into Ohio, Indiana, and Illinois. The populations of these states grew. As more people moved into the area, new towns and industries developed.

Faster Communication

The growth of industry and the new pace of travel created a need for faster methods of communication over the vast distances. The **telegraph**—an apparatus that used electric signals to transmit messages—filled that need.

Samuel Morse, an American inventor, was seeking support for a system of telegraph lines. On May 24, 1844, Morse got the chance to demonstrate that he could send messages instantly along wires. As a crowd in the U.S. capital watched, Morse tapped in the words "What hath God wrought!" A few moments later, the telegraph operator in Baltimore sent the same message back in reply. The telegraph worked! Soon telegraph messages were flashing back and forth between Washington, D.C., and Baltimore.

People IN HISTORY

John Deere
Inventor of the Steel-Tipped Plow

Because the heavy Midwestern soil stuck to cast-iron plows, farmers had to stop every few feet to clean the plow blades. Blacksmith John Deere set out to create a polished steel plow that would clean itself. The plows became a successful new business. Within 10 years he was selling 1,000 plows per year. Deere constantly improved his design. He was quoted as saying, *"I will never put my name on a product that does not have in it the best that is in me."*

Samuel Morse
Inventor of the Telegraph

Samuel Morse had trouble convincing Congress to build a telegraph line. When he finally did, however, Americans were thrilled with the telegraph's speed. In a letter to his brother, Sidney, Morse described the scene that day: *"The enthusiasm of the crowd . . . was excited to the highest pitch. . . . They gave the Telegraph three cheers, and I was called to make my appearance at the window where three cheers were given to me by some hundreds present."*

CRITICAL Thinking

1. **Analyzing** What did Samuel Morse and John Deere have in common?
2. **Identifying** What showed the popularity of the telegraph? Of the steel-tipped plow?

Morse transmitted his message in **Morse code.** This code, which Morse developed and which bears his name, is a series of dots and dashes representing the letters of the alphabet. A skilled Morse code operator could rapidly tap out words in the dot-and-dash alphabet.

Americans adopted the telegraph eagerly. A British visitor marveled at the speed with which Americans formed telegraph companies and erected telegraph lines. Americans, he wrote, were driven to "annihilate [wipe out] distance" in their vast country. To speed the transmission of news using the telegraph, the Associated Press was formed in 1848. By 1852, there were about 23,000 miles (37,015 km) of telegraph lines in the United States.

Reading Check **Explaining** How did canals and railways transform trade in the interior of the United States?

Agriculture

Main Idea Revolutionary inventions in the 1830s changed farming methods, and agriculture became more profitable.

History and You Have you or your family ever bought produce from a farmers market? Read to learn how agriculture boomed during the 1800s.

The railroads gave farmers access to new markets far from their homes in which to sell their products. At the same time, advances in agricultural technology allowed farmers to greatly increase the size of the harvests they produced.

In the early 1800s, few farmers had ventured into the treeless Great Plains west of Missouri, Iowa, and Minnesota. Even areas of mixed forest and prairie west of Ohio and Kentucky seemed too difficult for farming.

Settlers worried that their wooden plows could not break the prairie's matted sod. Further, they worried that the soil would not be fertile enough to support fields of crops.

Revolution in Agriculture

Three revolutionary inventions of the 1830s changed farming methods and encouraged settlers to cultivate larger areas of the Midwest. One invention was the steel-tipped plow that **John Deere** invented in 1837. Far sturdier than the wooden plow, Deere's plow easily cut through the hard-packed prairie sod. Equally important were the mechanical reaper, which sped up the harvesting of wheat, and the thresher, which quickly separated the grain from the stalk.

McCormick's Reaper

Born on a Virginia farm, **Cyrus McCormick** became interested in machines that would ease the burden of farmwork. McCormick designed and constructed the mechanical reaper. He made a fortune manufacturing and selling it.

For hundreds of years, farmers harvested grain with handheld sickles, or cutting tools. McCormick's reaper could harvest grain much faster than a person using a sickle.

History ONLINE
Student Web Activity Visit glencoe.com and complete the Chapter 13 Web Activity about agriculture in the mid-1800s.

Because farmers could harvest wheat so quickly, they began planting more of it. Growing wheat became profitable. McCormick's reaper ensured that raising wheat would remain the main economic activity on the Midwestern prairies.

New machines and the accessibility to railroads allowed farmers to devote more acres to cash crops—crops raised strictly for sale. Midwestern farmers began growing wheat as a cash crop and shipping it east by train and canal barge. Farmers in the Northeast and Middle Atlantic states increased their production of fruits and vegetables.

Despite improvements in agriculture, the North turned away from farming and toward industry. It was difficult to make a living farming the rocky soil of New England. Industry, however, flourished in the area. The number of people working in factories continued to rise.

Reading Check **Identifying** What innovation sped up the harvesting of wheat?

Section 1 Review

History ONLINE
Study Central™ To review this section, go to glencoe.com.

Vocabulary

1. Write a paragraph in which you explain why each of these terms appears in a chapter about American life in the first half of the nineteenth century: innovation, clipper ship, transform, telegraph, Morse code.

Main Ideas

2. **Summarizing** How were messages sent via telegraph? Why was this invention important?

3. **Identifying** List innovations in farming methods in the 1830s.

Critical Thinking

4. **Making Connections** Use a diagram like the one below to show factors that encouraged the settlement of the Midwest.

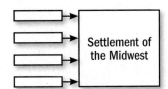

5. **Expository Writing** Write a paragraph discussing why industrial growth and the new pace of travel created a desire for faster communication.

Answer the
6. **Essential Question**
What innovations in industry, travel, and communications changed the lives of Americans in the 1800s?

Section 2

The North's People

Essential Question ◀

How did immigration have an impact on cities, industry, and culture in the North?

Reading Guide

Content Vocabulary

trade union (p. 396)

discrimination (p. 396)

strike (p. 396)

famine (p. 398)

prejudice (p. 396)

nativist (p. 399)

Academic Vocabulary

community (p. 396)

license (p. 397)

Key People and Events

Henry Boyd (p. 396)

Samuel Cornish (p. 396)

John B. Russwurm (p. 396)

Macon B. Allen (p. 397)

Sarah G. Bagley (p. 397)

Know-Nothing Party (p. 399)

Reading Strategy

Taking Notes As you read, use a diagram like the one below to list two reasons for the growth of cities.

NEW YORK STANDARDS
The American Journey

U5.III.2 To understand the nature and effect of changes on society and individuals as the United States began to move from an agrarian to an industrial economy

U5.III.3 To describe historic events through the eyes and experiences of those who were there

U5.III.8 To describe the relationships between people and environments and the connections between people and places

American Diary

"Over there [Germany], alas, common sense and free speech lie in shackles. . . . I invite you to come over here, should you want to obtain a clear notion of genuine public life, freedom of people and sense of being a nation. . . . I have never regretted that I came here, and never! never! again shall I bow my head under the yoke of despotism and folly."

—*August Blümner, a German immigrant quoted in* News from the Land of Freedom

Immigrants arriving in New York Harbor

Northern Factories

Main Idea Many workers in the mid-1800s saw the need for reforms in working conditions.

History and You Do you babysit or mow lawns to earn money? Is the pay fair? Read to learn why workers in the mid-1800s wanted to earn more pay and improve their working conditions.

. . . .

For many immigrants like August Blümner, America meant freedom and liberty. Immigrants often settled in cities and found work in the many mills and factories there. Working conditions were harsh, however, and reforms were needed.

Between 1820 and 1860, America's manufacturing increasingly shifted to mills and factories. As numerous machines took over more production tasks, these tasks were brought under one roof—creating the factory system. In addition to textiles and clothing, factories produced items such as shoes, watches, guns, sewing machines, and agricultural machinery.

Working Conditions

As the factory system developed, working conditions worsened. Employees worked long hours, averaging 11.4 hours per day by 1840. Factory work involved many dangerous conditions, and longer workdays caused on-the-job accidents.

For example, long leather belts connected the machines to the factory's water-powered driveshaft. These belts had no protective shields. Workers, especially children, often suffered injuries from the rapidly spinning belts. Many workers lost their fingers or broke their bones.

Employees often labored under unpleasant conditions. Factories were miserably hot and stifling in the summer. The machines gave off heat, and air-conditioning had not yet been invented. Most factories had no heating in the winter, and workers were cold.

Factory owners were often more concerned about profits than about employees' comfort and safety. No laws existed to regulate working conditions or to protect workers.

By the Numbers / Immigration in the Mid-1800s

Sources of Immigration Newcomers came to America from many different countries in the mid-1800s, but the overwhelming majority came from Ireland and Germany.

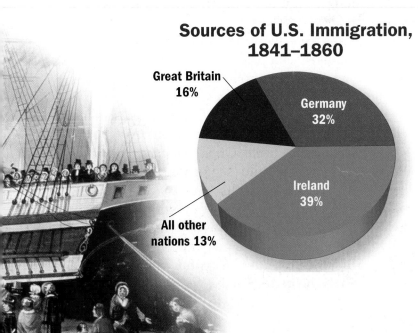

Sources of U.S. Immigration, 1841–1860

- Great Britain 16%
- Germany 32%
- Ireland 39%
- All other nations 13%

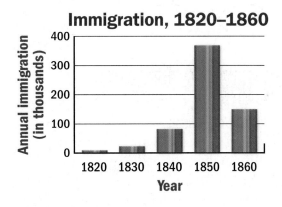

Immigration, 1820–1860

Annual immigration (in thousands) by Year: 1820, 1830, 1840, 1850, 1860

Critical Thinking

Predicting Why might people leave their homeland for another country?

Lowell Girls In Lowell, Massachusetts, the textile mills were staffed mainly by young female workers known as "Lowell girls." They toiled long hours in a hot, dangerous working environment for low wages. While they sought better working conditions, the girls had opportunities to attend social gatherings and educational programs.

"Pleasures there are, even in factory life; and we have many. . . . Where can you find a more pleasant place for contemplation?"
—Sarah G. Bagley, "Pleasures of Factory Life"

Power loom of the type used at the Lowell factories ▶

◀ Cover of the *Lowell Offering*, a magazine published by the women at the Lowell mills

Critical Thinking

Analyzing Refer to the quotation and the pictures, and describe what it was like to work in the Lowell mills.

Workers' Attempts to Organize

By the 1830s, workers began organizing to improve working conditions. Fearing the growth of the factory system, skilled workers formed **trade unions**—organizations of workers with the same trade, or skill. Steadily worsening working conditions also led unskilled workers to organize.

In the mid-1830s, skilled workers in New York City staged a series of **strikes.** They refused to work in order to put pressure on employers. Workers wanted to receive higher wages and to limit their workday to 10 hours. Groups of skilled workers formed the General Trades Union of New York.

In the early 1800s, going on strike was illegal. Striking workers could be punished for breaking the law, or they could be fired from their jobs. In 1842 a Massachusetts court ruled that workers did have the right to strike. It would be many years, however, before workers received other legal rights.

African American Workers

Slavery largely disappeared from the North by the 1830s. However, racial **prejudice**—an unfair opinion not based on facts—and **discrimination**—unfair treatment of a group—remained. For example, New York no longer required white men to own property in order to vote. However, few African Americans were allowed to vote. Rhode Island and Pennsylvania passed laws to keep free African Americans from voting.

Most **communities** would not allow free African Americans to attend public schools. Many communities barred them from public facilities as well. Often African Americans were forced into segregated, or separate, schools and hospitals.

A few African Americans rose in the business world. **Henry Boyd** owned a furniture manufacturing company in Cincinnati, Ohio. In 1827 **Samuel Cornish** and **John B. Russwurm** founded *Freedom's Journal*, the first African American newspaper, in New York City. In 1845 **Macon B. Allen** became the first African American **licensed,** or given official authority, to practice law in the United States. Most African Americans, however, were extremely poor.

Women Workers

Employers also discriminated against women, paying them less than male workers. Men excluded women from unions and wanted them kept out of the workplace.

Some female workers tried to organize in the 1830s and 1840s. **Sarah G. Bagley,** a weaver from Massachusetts, founded the Lowell Female Labor Reform Organization. Her group petitioned for a 10-hour workday in 1845. Because most of the petitioners were women, the legislature did not consider the petition. Women like Sarah Bagley, however, paved the way for later movements to correct the injustices against female workers.

✔ **Reading Check** **Describing** How did conditions for workers change as the factory system developed?

The Rise of Cities

Main Idea European immigrants often faced hardships and discrimination when they settled in Northern cities.

History and You Do you have Irish or German ancestors or know someone who does? Read to learn why many Irish and Germans came to the United States.

. . . .

The growth of factories and immigration—the movement of people into a country—went hand in hand with the growth of Northern cities. Both natural-born citizens and immigrants flocked to the cities, where most of the factories were located. American manufacturers welcomed immigrants, many of whom were willing to work for low pay.

Increase in Urban Population

Between 1820 and 1840, some Midwestern towns that had been small villages located along rivers developed into major cities.

Primary Source / Nativism

Anti-immigrant Sentiment Nativists feared the impact new immigrants would have on American culture. Many of the new immigrants were Catholic, while nativists were mainly Protestant. Nativists from the American Party (also called the Know-Nothing Party) tried to block immigration and limit the political rights of immigrants.

◀ American Party emblem, 1854

"Americans must rule America; *and to this end native-born citizens should be selected for all State, Federal and municipal offices of government employment, in preference to all others.*"
—the American Party platform, from the American National Convention, 1856

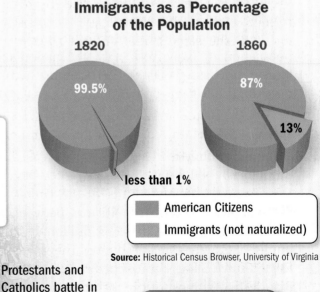

▶ Protestants and Catholics battle in the streets of Philadelphia in 1844 over the issue of Catholicism in the schools.

By the Numbers

Immigrants as a Percentage of the Population

1820 — 99.5%, less than 1%

1860 — 87%, 13%

■ American Citizens
■ Immigrants (not naturalized)

Source: Historical Census Browser, University of Virginia

Critical Thinking

Making Connections How was the issue of Catholicism in schools related to nativism?

Many Irish immigrants journeyed to the United States in the mid-1800s. Castle Garden, the building in the upper left, was the processing facility for immigrants at that time.

1. **Interpreting** According to this cartoon, how do the British feel about the migration? How do you know?

2. **Analyzing** What reason does the cartoon suggest for why the immigrants are leaving? How do you know?

   A. Uncle Sam (United States)
   B. Irish immigrants
   C. John Bull (Britain)
   D. British lion

St. Louis, Pittsburgh, Cincinnati, and Louisville profited from their waterfront locations. They became growing centers of trade that linked the farmers of the Midwest with the cities of the Northeast. After 1830, the Great Lakes became a center for shipping, and new urban centers such as Buffalo, Detroit, Milwaukee, and Chicago arose.

The larger cities became even larger. The population of New York City, the nation's largest city, passed 800,000. Philadelphia had more than 500,000 people in 1860.

Immigration

Immigration to the United States increased dramatically between 1840 and 1860. The largest group of immigrants to the United States at that time were from Ireland. Between 1840 and 1860, more than 1.5 million Irish immigrants arrived in the country. They came to the United States because of a potato blight that destroyed most of the Irish potato crops in the 1840s. A **famine,** an extreme shortage of food, struck Ireland. More than a million people died.

Mostly farmers, the Irish immigrants were too poor to buy land. For this reason many settled in the Northeast and took low-paying factory jobs in the cities. Many of the Irish men also worked on the railroads. Accounting for nearly half of the immigrants, Irish women became servants and factory workers in the Northern cities.

The second-largest group of immigrants in the United States between 1820 and 1860 came from Germany. Some sought work and opportunity. Others came because the German democratic revolution had failed. Many arrived with enough money to buy farms or open their own business. They prospered and founded their own communities and self-help organizations. Some German immigrants settled in New York and Pennsylvania, but many moved to the Midwest and the western territories.

The Impact of Immigration

The European immigrants who came to the United States between the years of 1820 and 1860 changed the character of the country.

These people brought their languages, customs, religions, and traditions with them. Some of their ways of life filtered into American culture.

Before the early 1800s, the country had relatively few Catholics. Most of them lived around Baltimore, New Orleans, and St. Augustine. Most Irish immigrants and about one-half of the German immigrants were Roman Catholics. Many Catholic immigrants settled in cities of the Northeast. The Church provided spiritual guidance and served as a center of community life for the newcomers.

The German immigrants brought their language as well as their religion. When they settled, they founded their own publications and established musical societies.

Immigrants Face Prejudice

In the 1830s and 1840s, anti-immigrant feelings rose. Some Americans feared that immigrants were changing the character of the United States too much.

People opposed to immigration were known as **nativists.** They believed that immigration threatened the future of "native"—American-born—citizens. Some nativists accused immigrants of taking jobs from "real" Americans and were angry that immigrants would work for lower wages. Others accused immigrants of bringing crime and disease to American cities. Immigrants who lived in city slums were likely targets of this prejudice.

The Know-Nothing Party

Nativists formed secret anti-Catholic societies. In the 1850s, they formed a new political party: the American Party. Because members of nativist groups often answered questions about their organization with the statement "I now nothing," their party came to be known as the **Know-Nothing Party.**

The Know-Nothings called for stricter citizenship laws. They wanted to extend the immigrants' waiting period for citizenship from 5 to 21 years and to ban foreign-born citizens from holding office.

In the mid-1850s, the Know-Nothing movement split into a Northern branch and a Southern branch over the question of slavery. At this time the slavery issue was also dividing the Northern and Southern states of the nation.

Reading Check **Identifying** Which two nations did most immigrants come from in the mid-1800s?

Section 2 Review

History ONLINE
Study Central™ To review this section, go to glencoe.com.

Vocabulary

1. Use each of these terms in a sentence that will help explain its meaning: trade union, strike, prejudice, discrimination, community, license, famine, nativist.

Main Ideas

2. **Listing** List some of the early attempts at work reforms in the North.

3. **Discussing** Why did some Americans object to immigration?

Critical Thinking

4. **Classifying** Create a diagram like the one below to identify the two major groups of immigrants to the United States in the first half of the 1800s and show where they settled.

Group	Area Settled

5. **Creative Writing** Imagine that you are an African American child living in the North in the mid-1800s. Write a poem in which you describe how you feel about your treatment.

6. **Answer the Essential Question** How did immigration have an impact on cities, industry, and culture in the North?

Southern Cotton Kingdom

Essential Question

How did the South's industry and economy differ from the industry and economy of the North?

Reading Guide

Content Vocabulary

cotton gin (p. 401)   capital (p. 403)

Academic Vocabulary

consequence (p. 402) process (p. 402)

Key People and Events

Eli Whitney (p. 401)

William Gregg (p. 403)

Joseph Reid Anderson (p. 403)

Reading Strategy

Taking Notes As you read, use a diagram like the one below to show reasons cotton production grew but industrial growth was slower in the South.

Boom in Cotton Production

Slow Industrial Growth

NEW YORK STANDARDS
The American Journey

U5.III.1 To understand the way of life of an agrarian society

U5.III.5 To define basic economic concepts such as scarcity, supply and demand, markets, resources, and economic systems

U5.III.7 To develop conclusions about economic issues and problems by creating broad statements that summarize findings and solutions

U5.III.8 To describe the relationships between people and environments and the connections between people and places

American Diary

"I have just returned from Philadelphia. My business there was to lodge a Model of my machine and receive a Patent for it. I accomplished everything agreeable to my wishes. I had the satisfaction to hear it declared by a number of the first men in America that my machine is the most perfect & the most valuable invention that has ever appeared in this Country. I have received my Patent."

—Eli Whitney, letter to his father, March 30, 1794

Cotton gin being used on Southern plantation

Visual Summary

Comparing North and South

The North and the South developed differently during the first half of the 1800s. The North built an industrial economy, while the South pursued an agricultural economy based on slavery. Those economies influenced the labor force and the development of transportation in the regions.

Plantation workers using a cotton gin ▶

	North	South
Economy	• Industrial • New technology fuels growth of industry • Industry develops rapidly Power loom ▶	• Agricultural • Revolutionary cotton gin makes cotton crop highly profitable • Industry develops slowly
People	• Immigrants, including many from Ireland, work factory jobs • Slavery has mostly disappeared by 1830s, but racial prejudice and discrimination remain ◀ Mill workers	• The South had more small farms than large plantations • Most small farmers work land themselves • Slavery on large cotton plantations grows due to increased demand for labor • By 1860 about 4 million African Americans lived under slavery
Transportation	• Roads, canals, and railroads are built for transportation and shipping	• Natural waterways for shipping; fewer railroads are built than in the North

◀ Steamboats in Cincinnati

STUDY TO GO Study anywhere, anytime! Download quizzes and flash cards to your PDA from glencoe.com.

GRADE 8 INTERMEDIATE TEST PRACTICE

TEST-TAKING TIP

Make sure the number of answer spaces on the answer sheet matches the number of questions on the test you are taking.

Reviewing Main Ideas

Directions: Choose the best answer for each of the following questions.

1 What happened in the first phase of industrialization in the North?

(1) Factory workers used machinery to perform some of their work.

(2) Manufacturers made products by dividing the tasks involved among the workers.

(3) Waterpower and steam power were used to produce more products in less time.

(4) Manufacturers built factories to bring specialized workers together.

2 The American Party was sometimes called the Know-Nothing Party because

(1) its opponents believed party members knew nothing about the important issues.

(2) party members did not support education.

(3) party members responded to questions about the group by saying, "I know nothing."

(4) party members were mainly Catholics who knew nothing about Protestantism.

3 What was the main reason that the Southern economy remained largely agricultural?

(1) Southerners lacked the capital to start industries.

(2) Cotton sales were very profitable.

(3) Southerners refused to work in factories.

(4) Costs to ship goods to markets were too high.

4 The largest group of whites in the South were

(1) yeomen. **(3)** the rural poor.

(2) tenant farmers. **(4)** plantation owners.

Short-Answer Question

Directions: Base your answer to question 5 on the following table and on your knowledge of social studies.

Occupational Distribution of American Workers

	1820	1860
Agriculture	79%	53%
Mining	0.4%	1.6%
Construction	—	4.7%
Manufacturing	3%	14%
Trade	—	8%
Transport	1.6%	6.4%
Service	4.1%	6.4%

5 Explain how the technological innovations of the early 1800s affected the change in the percentage of Americans working in agriculture and manufacturing.

Review the Essential Questions

6 Essay How did industrialization and immigration affect different parts of the United States in the first half of the 1800s?

To help you write your essay, review your answers to the Essential Questions in the section reviews and the chapter Foldables Study Organizer. Your essay should include:

- innovations in technology, communications, and transportation in the 1800s;
- the development of factories and cities in various parts of the United States;
- influences of immigration and patterns of settlement;
- reasons for and effects of the growing importance of cotton in the Southern economy; and
- the spread of slavery in the South.

GO ON

Document-Based Questions

Directions: Analyze the documents and answer the short-answer questions that follow.

Document 1

A Southern newspaper publisher wrote the following in 1856.

> Every Roman Catholic in the known world is under the absolute control of the Catholic Priesthood. . . . And it is . . . this power of the Priesthood to control the Catholic community, and cause a vast multitude of ignorant foreigners to vote as a unit . . .

Source: William G. Brownlow, *Americanism Contrasted*

7 Based on the document, what did the writer believe about Catholic immigrants to the U.S.?

Document 2

This map shows the 15 most populous American cities in 1840.

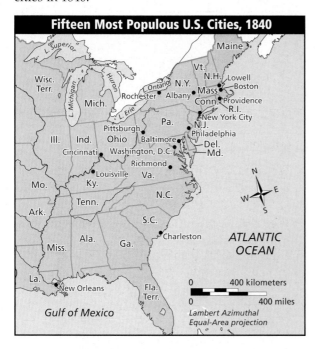

Fifteen Most Populous U.S. Cities, 1840

8 Use the map and your knowledge of geography and economics to explain the distribution of major U.S. cities in the mid-1800s.

Document 3

The following is an excerpt from a work contract from around 1830.

> We . . . agree to work for such wages per week, and prices by the job, as the Company may see fit to pay. . . . We also agree not to be engaged in any [labor union], whereby the work may be [delayed], or the company's interest in any work [harmed].

Source: Cocheco Manufacturing Company

9 Based on the excerpt, what can you conclude about the relationship between employees and employers in factories in the early 1800s?

Document 4

In this passage, Jacob Stroyer describes the aftermath of a beating he received as an enslaved boy.

> I went to mother with my complaint and she came out to the man who had whipped me. . . . Then he took a whip and started for her. . . . I ran back and forth between mother and him until he stopped beating her. [Afterward], he took me back to the stable yard and gave me a severe flogging.

Source: Jacob Stroyer, *My Life in the South*

10 According to the document, how did Jacob's mother react to his beating? What was the final outcome?

11 Expository Writing Using the information from the four documents and your knowledge of social studies, write an essay in which you:

- take the role of an immigrant to America in 1840 and decide whether to settle in the North or the South; and

- describe the conditions in both sections of the country that led to your decision.

Need Extra Help?											
If You Missed Questions. . .	1	2	3	4	5	6	7	8	9	10	11
Go to Page. . .	389	399	401–403	407	389–393	386–412	399	397–399	395–397	409–411	386–412

Chapter 14

The Age of Reform 1820–1860

During the 1800s, most American students attended one-room schools.

PRESIDENTS

JAMES MONROE 1817–1825

JOHN Q. ADAMS 1825–1829

ANDREW JACKSON 1829–1837

MARTIN VAN BUREN 1837–1841

U.S. Events

World Events

1820

1830

★ **1821** Sequoya develops Cherokee alphabet

★ **1827** New York bans slavery

1830 *Book of Mormon* published

★ **1821** Mexico becomes independent nation

★ **1837** Victoria becomes queen of England

Section 1: Social Reform

Essential Question How did religion influence the social reforms in the United States during the early and mid-1800s?

Section 2: The Abolitionists

Essential Question How did abolitionists influence the antislavery movement?

Section 3: The Women's Movement

Essential Question What were the effects of the women's rights movement of the middle to late 1800s?

Elizabeth Cady Stanton at the Seneca Falls Convention ▶

FOLDABLES Study Organizer

Organizing Information

Make this Foldable to organize what you learn about the reform movements of the 1800s.

Step 1 Fold a sheet of paper in half lengthwise.

Step 2 Fold the paper into three equal sections.

Step 3 Cut the folds on the top flap.

Step 4 Label the tabs as shown.

Reform and Society | Reform and Slavery | Reform and Women

Reading and Writing As you read the chapter, take notes in your Foldable about how reformers addressed problems in society and issues facing enslaved people and women.

WILLIAM HENRY HARRISON 1841

JOHN TYLER 1841–1845

JAMES POLK 1845–1849

★ **1848** Seneca Falls Convention held

ZACHARY TAYLOR 1849–1850

MILLARD FILLMORE 1850–1853

FRANKLIN PIERCE 1853–1857

JAMES BUCHANAN 1857–1861

1840   1850   1860

★ **1843** Maori revolt against British in New Zealand

★ **1847** Liberia claims independence

★ **1850** Taiping Rebellion begins in China

★ **1853** Crimean War begins

★ **1859** Belgian inventor Lenoir builds first practical internal-combustion engine

Section 1

Social Reform

Essential Question

How did religion influence the social reforms in the United States during the early and mid-1800s?

Reading Guide

Content Vocabulary

revival *(p. 419)*

normal school *(p. 420)*

utopia *(p. 419)*

transcendentalist *(p. 421)*

temperance *(p. 419)*

civil disobedience *(p. 421)*

Academic Vocabulary

lecture *(p. 419)*

author *(p. 421)*

Key People and Events

Second Great Awakening *(p. 419)*

temperance movement *(p. 419)*

Reading Strategy

Taking Notes As you read, use a diagram like the one below to identify the reformers' contributions.

Reformer		Contribution
Thomas Gallaudet	→	
Dorothea Dix	→	

NEW YORK STANDARDS
The American Journey

U5.III.2 To understand the nature and effect of changes on society and individuals as the United States began to move from an agrarian to an industrial economy

U5.III.4 To explore the meaning of American culture by identifying the key ideas, beliefs, patterns of behavior, and traditions that help define it and unite all Americans

U6.I.1 To understand the series of events and resulting conditions that led to the American Civil War

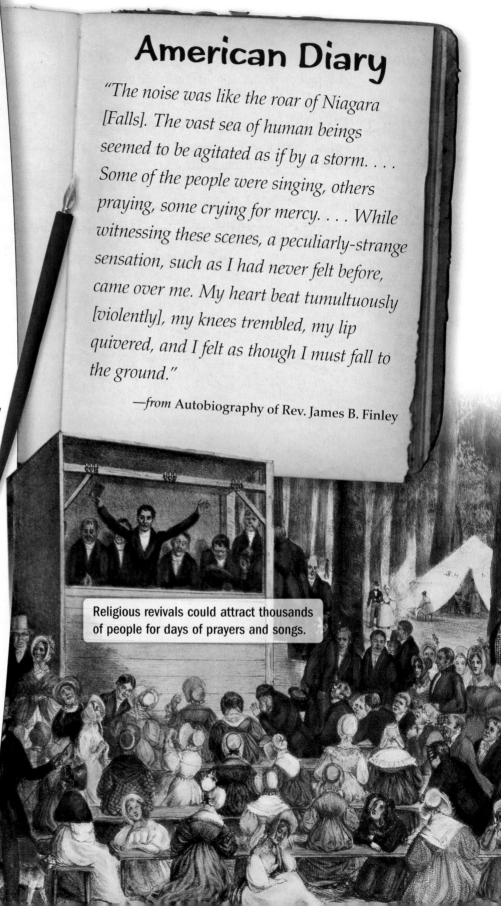

American Diary

"The noise was like the roar of Niagara [Falls]. The vast sea of human beings seemed to be agitated as if by a storm. . . . Some of the people were singing, others praying, some crying for mercy. . . . While witnessing these scenes, a peculiarly-strange sensation, such as I had never felt before, came over me. My heart beat tumultuously [violently], my knees trembled, my lip quivered, and I felt as though I must fall to the ground."

—from Autobiography of Rev. James B. Finley

Religious revivals could attract thousands of people for days of prayers and songs.

Religion and Reform

Main Idea The Second Great Awakening influenced social and educational reforms.

History and You Do you volunteer to help people, such as the elderly, with their daily chores? You are probably familiar with individuals or organizations who help people in need. Read about how reformers felt a responsibility to help others.

Religious camp meetings, called **revivals,** were quite common in the early 1800s. People would travel great distances to hear preachers speak and to pray, sing, weep, and shout. This was the time when a wave of religious fervor—known as the **Second Great Awakening**—stirred the nation. The first Great Awakening had spread through the colonies in the mid-1700s.

There was a new spirit of reform throughout America in the early 1800s. This spirit brought changes to American religion, education, and literature. Some reformers sought to improve society by forming **utopias.** These communities were based on a vision of the perfect society. However, most were founded on impractical ideas and only a few groups, like the Mormons, were able to establish stable, lasting communities.

The Religious Influence

Attending revivals often made men and women eager to reform both their own lives and the world. Some people became involved in missionary work and social reform movements. Among those movements was the push to ban alcohol.

Lyman Beecher, a Connecticut minister, crusaded against the use of alcohol. He wanted to protect society from "rum-selling, tippling folk, infidels [nonbelievers], and ruffscruff." Beecher and other reformers called for **temperance,** drinking little or no alcohol. They used **lectures,** pamphlets, and revival-style rallies to warn people of the dangers of liquor.

The **temperance movement** led to some victories when Maine and other states passed laws banning the manufacture and sale of alcoholic beverages. Most of these laws, however, were later repealed, or canceled.

Primary Source / Responsibility for Others

Helping Others Reformer Dorothea Dix encouraged others to help the less fortunate. She said, "Become the [protectors] of your race, the just guardians of the solemn rights you hold in trust. Raise up the fallen, [aid] the desolate, restore the outcast, defend the helpless, and for your eternal and great reward receive the [blessing]."

—from *Memorial to the Massachusetts Legislature*

Dorothea Dix ▶

Critical Thinking

Comparing Do you know any people today who share beliefs similar to Second Great Awakening reformers? What are their beliefs?

Primary Sources
INTERPRETING
POLITICAL CARTOONS

This cartoon, by Nathaniel Currier, is titled "The Drunkard's Progress." It was created in 1846, during the temperance movement.

1. **Summarizing** How would you describe the "progress" from step 1 through step 9?
2. **Making Inferences** Who do the people under the arch represent? Why are they shown in the cartoon?

Reforming Education

Reformers also wanted to improve education. In the mid-1850s, most schools were poorly funded, and many teachers lacked training. Some people opposed compulsory, or required, education.

In addition, restrictions were placed on who could attend school. Girls were often excluded because parents thought education was wasted on future wives and mothers. Many African Americans were also denied the right to attend school.

Massachusetts lawyer Horace Mann was a leader of educational reform. Partly because of his efforts, in 1839 Massachusetts founded the nation's first state-supported **normal school** where high-school graduates were trained to become teachers. Other states soon adopted Mann's reforms.

Many new colleges and universities were created during the age of reform. Most admitted only men, but gradually, higher education became available to groups that had been denied the opportunity. Oberlin College of Ohio, for example, founded in 1833, admitted both women and African Americans.

People With Special Needs

Some reformers focused on the problem of teaching people with disabilities. Thomas Gallaudet (GA•luh•DEHT) developed a method to educate people who were hearing impaired. He opened the Hartford School for the Deaf in Connecticut in 1817. At about the same time, Samuel Gridley Howe advanced the cause of people who were visually impaired. He developed books with large raised letters that people with sight impairments could "read" with their fingers. Howe headed the Perkins Institute, a school for the blind, in Boston.

Schoolteacher Dorothea Dix began visiting prisons in 1841. She found some prisoners chained to the walls with little or no clothing, often in unheated cells. Dix also learned that some of the inmates were guilty of no crime. They were people who were mentally ill. Dix made it her life's work to educate the public about the poor conditions for prisoners and the mentally ill.

Reading Check **Identifying** How did Samuel Howe help the visually impaired?

Cultural Trends

Main Idea A distinct type of American literature emerged in the 1820s.

History and You Have you read works by Thoreau, Emerson, or Dickinson? Read to learn how these writers changed American literature.

· ·

The changes in American society also influenced art and literature. Beginning in the 1820s, American artists developed their own style and explored American themes.

The American spirit of reform influenced the **transcendentalists.** These thinkers and writers stressed the relationship between humans and nature and the importance of the individual conscience. Margaret Fuller, Ralph Waldo Emerson, and Henry David Thoreau were leading transcendentalists.

Through her writings, Fuller supported women's rights. In his works, Emerson urged people to listen to the inner voice of conscience and to overcome prejudice. Thoreau practiced **civil disobedience** by refusing to obey laws he considered unjust. In 1846 Thoreau went to jail rather than pay a tax to support the Mexican War.

Numerous poets also created great works during this period. Henry Wadsworth Longfellow wrote narrative, or story, poems such as the *Song of Hiawatha*. Poet Walt Whitman captured the new American spirit and confidence in his *Leaves of Grass*. Emily Dickinson wrote simple, deeply personal poems. In a poem called "Hope," written in 1861, she compares hope to a bird:

PRIMARY SOURCE

"'Hope' is the thing with feathers—
That perches in the soul—
And sings the tune without the words—
And never stops—at all—"

—from *Emily Dickinson: Selected Poems*

During this time, women were the **authors** of the most popular fiction. Harriet Beecher Stowe wrote the most successful best-seller of the mid-1800s, *Uncle Tom's Cabin.* Stowe's novel explores the injustice of slavery, an issue that took on new urgency during the age of reform.

Reading Check **Identifying Cause and Effect** How did the spirit of reform influence American authors?

Section 1 Review

History ONLINE
Study Central™ To review this section, go to glencoe.com.

Vocabulary

1. Use the following key terms to write a paragraph about social reform: revival, utopia, temperance, lecture, normal school, transcendentalist, civil disobedience, author.

Main Ideas

2. Identifying What problems spurred reform in the area of education?

3. Explaining What themes did the transcendentalists focus on in their writings?

Critical Thinking

4. Synthesizing In what ways did the writers of the mid-1800s demonstrate the American spirit of the times?

5. Analyzing What reforms resulted from the Second Great Awakening? Use a diagram like the one below to organize your answer.

6. Persuasive Writing Create a brochure about the newly established Oberlin College to send to potential students. Explain why the college differs from others, and describe the advantages of this college experience.

Answer the
7. Essential Question
How did religion influence the social reforms in the United States during the early and mid-1800s?

The Age of Reform **Chapter 14** 421

TIME NOTEBOOK

What were people's lives like in the past?

These two pages will give you some clues to everyday life in the United States as you step back in time with TIME Notebook.

PHOTO RESEARCHERS

Profile

"My best friends solemnly regard me as a madman." That's what the artist **JOHN JAMES AUDUBON** *writes about himself in his journal. And he does seem to be a bit peculiar. After all, he put a band around a bird's foot so he could tell if it returned from the South in the spring. No one's ever done that before. Audubon is growing more famous thanks to his drawings. His love of the wild and his skill as an artist have awakened a new sense of appreciation for animal life in the United States. Here is what he wrote while on a trip to New Orleans in 1821.*

"I took a walk with my gun this afternoon to see . . . millions of Golden Plovers [medium-sized shorebirds] coming from the northeast and going nearly south—the destruction . . . was really astonishing—the Sportsmen here are more numerous and at the same time more expert at shooting on the wing than anywhere in the United States. . . . 400 Gunners were out. Supposing that each man killed 40 dozen that day, 192,000 plovers must have been destroyed."

PLUVIALIS DOMINICA, **AMERICAN GOLDEN PLOVER, DRAWN BY AUDUBON**

THE NATURAL HISTORY MUSEUM / ALAMY

VERBATIM

WHAT PEOPLE ARE SAYING

❝ What hath God wrought? ❞
> **SAMUEL MORSE,**
> *in the first official message sent over his telegraph in 1844*

❝ O, Susanna,
Now don't you cry for me,
For I come from Alabama
With my banjo on my knee. ❞
> **STEPHEN FOSTER,**
> *author of this campfire tune in 1848*

❝ . . . Some very good houses, broad streets, and marble-fronted shops . . . though it is never likely to vie, in point of elegance or beauty, with Cincinnati. ❞
> **CHARLES DICKENS,**
> *British author, on his visit to St. Louis in 1842*

❝ The tide of emigration seems as usual to be flowing to the west. . . . Counties which three or four years ago were but a trackless wilderness, contain now five, six, and seven hundred voters. ❞
> *INDIANAPOLIS JOURNAL, 1829*

❝ In 1840 I was called from my farm to undertake the administration of public affairs and I foresaw that I was called to a bed of thorns. I now leave that bed which has afforded me little rest . . . ❞
> **U.S. PRESIDENT JOHN TYLER,**
> *on why he won't run for reelection in 1844*

Wright & Ditson REGULATION. LEAGUE BALL

SPORTS

Baseball for Beginners

Want to take up the new game of baseball? Keep your eye on the ball— because the rules keep changing!

1845
• bases are set 90 feet (27 m) apart in a diamond shape
• only nine men play on each side
• pitches are thrown underhand
• a ball caught on the first bounce is an "out"
1846
• at first base, a fielder can tag the bag before the runner reaches it and so make an out
1847
• players may no longer throw the ball at a runner to put him out

◀ Selling enslaved people at auction

▲ Defenders of slavery described plantations as ideal settings where enslaved persons were well treated.

▲ Poster announcing the raffle of a horse and an enslaved female

RAFFLE
DARK BAY HORSE, "STAR."
MULATTO GIRL, "SARAH,"
Will be Raffled for
CHANCES AT ONE DOLLAR EACH.
JOSEPH JENNINGS.

"In all social systems there must be a class to do the menial duties, to perform the drudgery of life. That is, a class requiring but a low order of intellect and but little skill. . . . Such a class you must have, or you would not have that other class which leads progress, civilization, and refinement. . . . Fortunately for the South, she found a race adapted to that purpose."
—Senator James Henry Hammond in a speech to Congress, 1858

Critical Thinking

Analyzing Primary Sources What pro-slavery arguments are discussed in the quotations from Weld and Hammond?

PRIMARY SOURCE

"What, to the American slave, is your 4th of July? I answer; a day that reveals to him, more than all other days in the year, the gross injustice and cruelty to which he is the constant victim. To him, your celebration is a sham . . . your national greatness, swelling vanity; your sounds of rejoicing are empty and heartless; . . . your shouts of liberty and equality, hollow mockery."
—from *Frederick Douglass: Selected Speeches and Writings*

Douglass was editor of the antislavery newspaper *North Star* and won admiration as a powerful and influential speaker and writer. He even traveled abroad. Douglass spoke to huge antislavery audiences in London and the West Indies.

Douglass returned to the United States because he believed abolitionists must fight slavery at its source. He insisted that African Americans receive not just their freedom but full equality with whites as well. In 1847 friends helped Douglass buy his freedom from the slaveholder from whom he had fled in Maryland.

Sojourner Truth

"I was born a slave in Ulster County, New York," Isabella Baumfree began when she told her story to audiences. Called "Belle," she lived in the cellar of a slaveholder's house. She escaped in 1826 and gained official freedom in 1827 when New York banned slavery. Quaker friends then helped her find her son who had been sold as a slave. She eventually settled in New York City with her two youngest children. In 1843 Belle chose a new name:

PRIMARY SOURCE

"The Lord [named] me Sojourner . . . Truth, because I was to declare the truth to the people."
—from *Sojourner Truth: Slave, Prophet, Legend*

Sojourner Truth worked with a number of other abolitionists, including William Lloyd Garrison and Frederick Douglass, to bring about the end of slavery. She traveled throughout the North and spoke about her experiences as an enslaved person. Sojourner Truth was also an active supporter of the women's rights movement.

Primary Source | Reactions Against Abolitionism

Anti-Abolitionists Opposition to abolitionism was almost as strong in the North as it was in the South. Southerners viewed abolitionism as an attack on their way of life. Many Northerners feared the effect abolition might have upon them. In both areas, anti-abolitionists violently responded to literature that supported abolitionism.

In 1837 in Alton, Illinois, a mob killed abolition- ist newspaper editor Elijah Lovejoy, destroyed his press (right), and burned his house (below).

▲ Southerners burn antislavery documents in Charleston, South Carolina, in 1830.

"And men, like the abolitionist . . . [who goes] about meddling with other Peoples' affairs . . . [should] pay attention to his own affairs, & let his neighbor alone. . . . If these matters are going to be [agitated it will] . . . lead to the separation of the Union."
—from a letter by E. W. Taylor (a New Yorker who moved to South Carolina)

Critical Thinking

Analyzing Why did anti-abolitionists destroy pro-abolition literature?

The Underground Railroad

Some abolitionists risked prison—even death—by helping African Americans escape from slavery. The network of escape **routes**— lines of travel—from the South to the North was called the **Underground Railroad.**

Passengers on this "railroad" traveled through the night, often on foot, and went north. The North Star was their guide. Dur- ing the day passengers rested at "stations"— barns, basements, and attics—until the next night's journey. The railroad's "conductors" were whites and African Americans who helped guide the runaways to freedom in the Northern states or Canada. Harriet Tubman became the most famous conductor on the Underground Railroad.

The Underground Railroad helped only a tiny fraction of the enslaved population. Still, the Railroad gave hope to people who suf- fered in slavery. It also gave abolitionists a way to help some enslaved people.

Reading Check **Explaining** What were "stations" on the Underground Railroad?

Clashes Over Abolitionism

Main Idea Many Southerners and Northerners opposed abolition.

History and You Can you think of a time when you feared change, even if it was for the better? Read to learn why many people opposed abolition.

The antislavery movement triggered a strong reaction against abolitionism. Many Southerners opposed the idea of ending slav- ery. They held that abolitionism threatened the South's way of life, which depended on enslaved labor.

Not all Northerners were abolitionists. The abolitionists in the North made up only a small fraction of the population. Many Northerners saw the antislavery movement as a threat to the nation's social order. They believed that once freed, the African Ameri- cans could never blend into American soci- ety. Other Northerners feared that the abolitionists could begin a war between the North and South.

Many Northerners also had economic fears. They did not want to lose their jobs to the emancipated workers who might travel to the North and work for cheaper wages.

Opposition to abolitionism sometimes erupted into violence against the abolitionists themselves. Philadelphia's antislavery headquarters was burned, which set off a bloody race riot. A Boston mob attacked and threatened to hang abolitionist William Lloyd Garrison. Authorities saved his life by putting him in jail.

Elijah Lovejoy in Illinois was not so lucky. Angry whites invaded his antislavery newspaper offices and wrecked his presses three times. Each time Lovejoy installed new presses and resumed publication. The fourth time the mob set fire to the building. When Lovejoy came out of the blazing building, he was shot and killed.

The South Reacts

Southerners fought abolitionism with arguments in defense of slavery. They claimed that slavery was essential to the Southern economy and had allowed Southern whites to reach a high level of culture.

Southerners also argued that they treated enslaved people well. They claimed that Northern workers were worse off than enslaved workers because they worked in factories for long hours at low wages. These jobs were repetitious and often dangerous. Also, Northern workers had to pay for their own goods and services from their small earnings, whereas the system of slavery provided food, clothing, and **medical** care to its workers.

Other defenses of slavery were based on racism. Many whites believed that African Americans were better off under white care than on their own.

The conflict between pro-slavery and antislavery groups continued to mount. At the same time, a new women's rights movement was growing.

Reading Check **Explaining** How did many Southerners defend the instituion of slavery?

Section 2 Review

History ONLINE
Study Central™ To review this section, go to glencoe.com.

Vocabulary

1. Write complete sentences that define the following terms: abolitionist, route, Underground Railroad, medical.

Main Ideas

2. Specifying What effect did the American Colonization Society have on slavery? How did enslaved African Americans view that group and its efforts?

3. Discussing Discuss the role of African Americans in the abolitionist movement.

4. Comparing and Contrasting How did Northerners and Southerners view abolitionism differently?

Critical Thinking

5. Outlining Use a format like the one below to make an outline of this section. Write each main heading on a line with a Roman numeral, and then list important facts below it. The number of key facts may vary from this sample.

I. First main heading
   A. Key fact #1
   B. Key fact #2
II. Second main heading
   A. Key fact #1
   B. Key fact #2
III. Third main heading
   A. Key fact #1
   B. Key fact #2

6. Creative Writing Write a conversation that might have taken place between a Southern plantation owner and a Massachusetts abolitionist about the abolition of slavery. Have each character explain his or her point of view.

Answer the
7. Essential Question
How did abolitionists influence the antislavery movement?

The Underground Railroad

The Underground Railroad was a loosely organized system of secret routes for helping enslaved people escape to Canada or to areas of safety in free states. However, the popular notion of lantern-wielding "conductors" guiding families of enslaved people through forests in the South is largely inaccurate. In fact, few Southerners were willing to assist an enslaved person escape. For the most part, fugitives were on their own until they reached border states. There they could find assistance from loosely-connected groups of abolitionists. This network was the true Underground Railroad.

How Did Geography Affect the Underground Railroad?

Few abolitionists escorted runaways from the Deep South into free territory. Most runaways—typically single young men—probably lived in the upper South, close to free territories. Anti-slavery Northerners—mostly free African Americans—in border towns such as Ripley, Ohio, and Wilmington, Delaware, hid escapees from police and professional slave catchers and helped them move farther north.

The Underground Railroad, Charles T. Webber, 1893
The painting portrays a group of enslaved African Americans arriving at a safe house "station" on the Underground Railroad. Three abolitionists, Levi Coffin and his wife, Catharine, as well as Hannah Haddock, are also pictured. The scene most likely takes place at the Coffin farm in Cincinnati, Ohio.

This "hidey hole" built in a safe house in Fountain City, Indiana, was used to conceal fugitives from the police and professional slave catchers. The beds could be moved in front of the hole to conceal it. ▼

A MAN KIDNAPPED!

A PUBLIC MEETING AT

FANEUIL HALL!

WILL BE HELD

THIS FRIDAY EVEN'G,

May 26th, at 7 o'clock.

To secure justice for A MAN CLAIMED AS A SLAVE by a

VIRGINIA KIDNAPPER!

And NOW IMPRISONED IN BOSTON COURT HOUSE, in defiance of the Laws of Massachusetts, Shall he be plunged into the Hell of Virginia Slavery by a Massachusetts Judge of Probate!

BOSTON, May 26th, 1854.

◄ This poster refers to Anthony Burns, a runaway enslaved man. Burns's arrest and trial under the Fugitive Slave Act of 1850 sparked protests by abolitionists in Boston and other Northern cities.

Escape Routes Escapees used two main corridors to flee into the North. Enslaved people from inland Southern states generally made their way toward Ohio, Illinois, Indiana, and Michigan. Runaways from Southern states along the Atlantic coast tended to follow the coastline into Pennsylvania, New Jersey, and New York. Many of these runaways eventually headed into Canada. ▼

Routes to Freedom

Legend:
- Slaveholding regions
- Non-slaveholding regions
- Underground Railroad route
- 1860 boundary

Ellen Craft (1826–1891) was the daughter of an African American enslaved woman and her slaveholder. Passing as white, Ellen escaped from slavery in Georgia in 1848 by dressing as a Southern male slaveholder (pictured below left). Her darker-skinned husband, **William Craft** (pictured right), accompanied her by pretending to be her valet.

Analyzing Geography

1. **Place** From which state do you think more African Americans successfully escaped slavery to freedom: Kentucky or Alabama? Explain your answer.

2. **Regions** On the map, locate the cities of Toledo, Cleveland, and Buffalo. Why do you think these cities became important points along the Underground Railroad?

The Women's Movement

Essential Question ◄

What were the effects of the women's rights movement of the middle to late 1800s?

Reading Guide

Content Vocabulary

suffrage (p. 435)   coeducation (p. 437)

Academic Vocabulary

capable (p. 437)   ministry (p. 438)

Key People and Events

Lucretia Mott (p. 435)

Elizabeth Cady Stanton (p. 435)

Susan B. Anthony (p. 437)

Catherine Beecher (p. 437)

Emma Hart Willard (p. 437)

Mary Lyon (p. 438)

Elizabeth Blackwell (p. 438)

Reading Strategy

Taking Notes As you read, use a diagram like the one below to identify the contributions these individuals made to women's rights.

Individual	Contribution
Lucretia Mott →	
Elizabeth Cady Stanton →	
Susan B. Anthony →	

NEW YORK STANDARDS
The American Journey

U5.III.2 To understand the nature and effect of changes on society and individuals as the United States began to move from an agrarian to an industrial economy

U5.III.3 To describe historic events through the eyes and experiences of those who were there

U5.III.4 To explore the meaning of American culture by identifying the key ideas, beliefs, patterns of behavior, and traditions that help define it and unite all Americans

American Diary

When Lucy Stone attended college, she faced many challenges. Her daughter, Alice Stone Blackwell, recalled, "At the low wages then paid to women, it took Lucy nine years to save up money enough to enter college." Stone attended Oberlin College in Ohio, which was the first college in the United States to admit women. Stone graduated from Oberlin in 1847 and became a strong supporter of women's rights.

—from Lucy Stone: Pioneer of Woman's Rights

Mount Holyoke Female Seminary in South Hadley, Massachusetts, was the first women's college in the United States.

Women and Reform

Main Idea Women organized to win equal rights.

History and You Can you imagine a time when women were not allowed to vote and had limited access to education and jobs? Read to learn how women worked to change their status in America.

Many women abolitionists also worked for women's rights. Like many of the women reformers, **Lucretia Mott** was a Quaker. Quaker women enjoyed a certain amount of equality in their own communities. Mott helped fugitive enslaved workers and organized the Philadelphia Female Anti-Slavery Society. At the world antislavery convention in London, she met **Elizabeth Cady Stanton.** There, they joined forces to work for women's rights.

The Seneca Falls Convention

In July 1848, Stanton, Mott, and other women organized the first women's rights convention in Seneca Falls, New York. About 200 women and 40 men attended.

The convention issued a Declaration of Sentiments and Resolutions. The declaration called for an end to laws that discriminated against women. It also demanded that women be allowed to enter the all-male world of trades, professions, and businesses. The most controversial issue at the Seneca Falls Convention, however, was about **suffrage,** or the right to vote.

Elizabeth Stanton insisted that the declaration include a demand for woman suffrage. The delegates, however, thought the idea of women voting was too radical. Lucretia Mott told her friend, "Lizzie, thee will make us ridiculous." Standing with Stanton, the abolitionist Frederick Douglass argued powerfully for women's right to vote. After a heated debate, the convention voted to include the demand for woman suffrage in the United States.

Growth of the Women's Movement

The Seneca Falls Convention paved the way for the growth of the women's rights movement. During the 1800s women held several national conventions, including the first national women's rights convention, in Worcester, Massachusetts. A number of reformers, both male and female, joined the growing movement.

Time Line / **Women's Rights**

Struggling for Equality Women who fought to end slavery also began to argue for their own rights and an equal place in society.

★ **1833** Oberlin College admits women and African Americans

★ **1844** Female textile workers in Massachusetts form labor association

★ **1837** Mary Lyon establishes Mount Holyoke Female Seminary

★ **1848** First women's rights convention held in Seneca Falls, New York

◄ Mary Lyon

Critical Thinking

Speculating Why do you think the Declaration of Independence is often referred to by people struggling to gain rights?

Primary Source

The Seneca Falls Declaration

The first women's rights convention adopted resolutions proclaiming women's equality and calling for women's right to vote, to speak publicly, and to run for office. Before the meeting, the women published a "Declaration of Sentiments" in the local newspaper to state their goals.

▲ Elizabeth Cady Stanton

When, in the course of human events, it becomes necessary for one portion of the family of man to assume among the people of the earth a position different from that which they have **hitherto** occupied, but one to which the laws of nature and of nature's God entitle them, a decent respect to the opinions of mankind requires that they should declare the causes that impel them to such a course.

We hold these truths to be self-evident: that all men and women are created equal; that they are **endowed** by their Creator with certain **inalienable** rights; that among these are life, liberty, and the pursuit of happiness. . . .

The history of mankind is a history of repeated injuries and **usurpations** on the part of man toward woman, having in direct object the establishment of an absolute tyranny over her. To prove this, let facts be submitted to a candid world. . . .

Now, in view of this entire **disfranchisement** of one-half the people of this country, their social and religious **degradation**—in view of the unjust laws above mentioned, and because women do feel themselves aggrieved, oppressed, and fraudulently deprived of their most sacred rights, we insist that they have immediate admission to all the rights and privileges which belong to them as citizens of the United States.

This document reflects the ideas in the Declaration of Independence. Like the patriots of 1776, women are announcing the need for revolutionary change.

Here two important words—*and women*—are added to Thomas Jefferson's famous phrase.

During this time, husbands were legal masters of their wives.

A list of specific grievances follows this paragraph.

In addition to the right to vote, most educational and employment opportunities at this time were unavailable to women.

In 1920—more than 70 years after Seneca Falls—American women finally gained the right to vote.

VOCABULARY

hitherto (HIH·thuhr·TOO): before

endowed (ihn·DAU·ehd): provided

inalienable (ih·NAYL·yuh·nuh·buhl): impossible to surrender

usurpations (YOO·suhr·PAY·shuhnz): wrongful seizures of power

disfranchisement (DIHS·FRAN·CHYZ·muhnt): deprivation of rights, especially the right to vote

degradation (DEH·gruh·DAY·shuhn): lowering in status

Critical Thinking

1. **Drawing Conclusions** Why did the authors of this document use the Declaration of Independence as a model?
2. **Speculating** How do you think the authors would have responded to critics who ridiculed them as being too bold?
3. **Making Inferences** How did this document, along with the women's convention, help women acquire more rights?

History ONLINE

For additional test practice, use **Self-Check Quizzes**—Chapter 14 at glencoe.com.

Document-Based Questions

Directions: Analyze the documents and answer the short-answer questions that follow.

Document 1

This excerpt is from an 1848 report that Horace Mann wrote to the Massachusetts Board of Education.

> According to the European theory, men are divided into classes,—some to toil and earn, others to seize and enjoy. According to the Massachusetts theory, all are to have an equal chance for earning, and equal security in the enjoyment of what they earn. . . . Education, then, beyond all other devices of human origin, is the great equalizer of the conditions of men.

Source: Horace Mann, "Report No. 12 of the Massachusetts School Board"

6 What did Mann consider the difference to be between European and Massachusetts theories of society?

Document 2

The following is taken from Ralph Waldo Emerson's essay "Self-Reliance."

> And so the reliance on Property, including the reliance on governments which protect it, is the want of self-reliance. Men have looked away from themselves and at things so long, that they have come to esteem . . . the religious, learned, and civil institutions as guards of property. . . . They measure their esteem of each other, by what each has, not by what each is.

Source: Ralph Waldo Emerson, *Essays: First Series*

7 Based on the document, what does Emerson see as one of the basic problems within American society?

Document 3

The following is one of a series of cards issued in 1863 by H. T. Helmbold, a drug and chemical company, to promote its products.

THE PARTING "Buy us too."

Source: Library of Congress, LC-USZC4-2525

8 Based on the image, do you believe Helmbold issued the cards to rally support for or against the abolition of slavery? Explain.

Document 4

The following is an excerpt from an 1853 essay that appeared in *Harper's New Monthly Magazine*.

> There is danger that laws giving the right of separate property, and of course the management of separate property, to the wife, may in time vitally affect that oneness which is so essential to the marriage idea.

Source: Henry Raymond, "Woman's Rights"

9 Why does the writer suggest that women should not receive marriage property rights?

10 **Creative Writing** Using the information from the four documents and your knowledge of social studies, write an essay in which you:

- assume the role of a mid-1800s reformer and explain your goals for American society; and
- describe the challenges you face and how you will address them.

Need Extra Help?										
If you missed questions. . .	1	2	3	4	5	6	7	8	9	10
Go to page. . .	421	431	435	419	418–438	420	421	424–431	438	418–438

Unit 5

Civil War and Reconstruction
1840–1896

Chapter 15
. . . .
Toward Civil War
1840–1861

Chapter 16
. . . .
The Civil War
1861–1865

Chapter 17
. . . .
**Reconstruction
and the New South**
1865–1896

Spent cannon round from
the attack on Fort Sumter,
April 1861

442

"It is well that war is so terrible; we would grow too fond of it."
—Robert E. Lee

Union soldiers with a cannon, June 1862

443

Unit 5

Reading History

Identifying Cause and Effect

Learn It! A *cause* is an action or event that makes something happen. What happens as a result is the *effect*.

Cause
The slavery issue splits the Democratic Party.

Effect
Northern Democrats nominate Stephen Douglas.

Effect
Southern Democrats nominate John C. Breckinridge.

—from Chapter 15, p. 463

The issue of slavery split the Democratic Party. The northern Democrats nominated Stephen Douglas. They supported popular sovereignty. Southern Democrats vowed to uphold slavery. Their candidate was John C. Breckinridge.

Practice It! Read the paragraph and write down the cause and effect(s) on another sheet of paper.

—from Chapter 17, p. 531

In the 1870s, Reconstruction governments created public schools for both races. Within a few years, about 50 percent of white children and 40 percent of African American children in the South were enrolled.

Cause

Effect

Effect

The Fugitive Slave Act

Main Idea The Fugitive Slave Act required all citizens to help catch runaways, yet many Northerners refused to cooperate.

History and You Have you ever tried to protect someone from a bully? Read how Northerners tried to thwart the efforts of slave hunters.

. . . .

As part of the Compromise of 1850, Senator Henry Clay of Kentucky convinced Congress to pass the **Fugitive Slave Act** as an attempt to pacify slaveholders. The Fugitive Slave Act of 1850 required all citizens to help catch runaways. Anyone who aided a fugitive could be fined or imprisoned. People in the South believed the law would force Northerners to recognize the rights of Southerners. Instead, enforcement of the law convinced more people in the North of the evils of slavery.

After the passage of the Fugitive Slave Act, slaveholders stepped up their efforts to catch runaway enslaved people. They even tried to capture runaways who had lived in freedom in the North for years. Sometimes they seized African Americans who were not trying to escape and forced them into slavery.

History ONLINE
Student Web Activity Visit glencoe.com and complete the Chapter 15 Web Activity about the Underground Railroad.

In spite of the penalties, some Northerners refused to cooperate with the law. They justified their opposition on moral grounds. In his 1849 essay "Civil Disobedience," Henry David Thoreau wrote that if the law "requires you to be the agent [cause] of injustice to another, then I say, break the law."

The Underground Railroad, a **network,** or interconnected system, of free African Americans and whites, helped runaways make their way to freedom. Antislavery groups tried to rescue African Americans who were being pursued or to free those who were captured. In Boston, members of one such group followed federal agents shouting, "Slave hunters—there go the slave hunters." People contributed funds to buy the freedom of African Americans. Northern juries refused to convict those accused of violating the Fugitive Slave Act.

✔ **Reading Check** **Explaining** What was the purpose of the Underground Railroad?

Primary Source / **Reward Poster**

A poster advertises a substantial reward for a runaway enslaved man.

Critical Thinking

Making Inferences Under the Fugitive Slave Act of 1850, any citizen might be required to help capture a runaway slave. Why do you think some people condemned this law?

Slavery and Sectionalism NATIONAL GEOGRAPHIC

The Compromise of 1850

Kansas-Nebraska Act, 1854

Free states
Slave states
Indian Territory
Territory open to slaveholding
Territory closed to slaveholding

◀ Stephen Douglas sponsored the controversial Kansas-Nebraska Act.

Map Skills

Regions What territories were non-slaveholding in 1854?

Maps In Motion See StudentWorks™ Plus or glencoe.com.

The Kansas-Nebraska Act

Main Idea The Kansas-Nebraska Act resulted from another dispute over slavery in Congress.

History and You Do you recall how the Missouri Compromise limited slavery in the territories? Read how this agreement fell apart in the 1850s.

Franklin Pierce, a New Hampshire Democrat, became president in 1853. Pierce intended to enforce the Fugitive Slave Act.

In 1854 Stephen A. Douglas, the Illinois senator who forged the Compromise of 1850, introduced a bill in Congress. He proposed organizing the region west of Missouri and Iowa as the territories of Kansas and Nebraska. Douglas hoped his plan to expand the nation would be acceptable to both the North and the South.

Because of their location, Kansas and Nebraska seemed likely to become free states. Both lay north of 36°30′N latitude, the line set in the Missouri Compromise as the limit of slavery. Douglas knew Southerners would object to admitting Kansas and Nebraska as free states because it would give free states more votes in the Senate. As a result, Douglas proposed abandoning the Missouri Compromise and letting the settlers in each territory vote on whether to allow slavery. He called this **popular sovereignty**—allowing the people to decide.

Passage of the Act

Many Northerners protested. Douglas's plan to repeal the Missouri Compromise would allow slavery into areas that had been free for more than 30 years. Southerners in Congress, however, supported the bill. They expected Kansas to be settled mostly by slaveholders from Missouri who would vote to keep slavery legal. With some support from Northern Democrats and the backing of President Pierce, Congress passed the **Kansas-Nebraska Act** in 1854.

Conflict in Kansas

Right after the law passed, pro-slavery and antislavery groups rushed into Kansas. When elections took place, a pro-slavery legislature was elected.

Although only about 1,500 voters lived in Kansas at the time, more than 6,000 people cast ballots. Thousands of pro-slavery supporters from Missouri crossed the border just to vote in the election. These Missourians traveled in armed groups and became known as **border ruffians.**

Soon, the new Kansas legislature passed laws supporting slavery. One law even restricted political office to pro-slavery candidates.

The antislavery people refused to accept these laws. Instead they armed themselves, held their own elections, and adopted a constitution that banned slavery. By January 1856, rival governments existed in Kansas—one for and one against slavery.

"Bleeding Kansas"

With both sides arming themselves, an outbreak of violence became **inevitable,** or unavoidable. In May 1856, 800 slavery supporters attacked the town of Lawrence, a stronghold of antislavery settlers. The attackers burned the Free State Hotel and destroyed two newspaper offices and many homes. Soon after, antislavery forces retaliated.

John Brown, a fervent abolitionist, believed God chose him to end slavery. The attack on Lawrence enraged Brown. He vowed to "strike terror in the hearts of the pro-slavery people." One night Brown led a group along Pottawatomie Creek, where they seized and killed five supporters of slavery.

Armed bands soon roamed the territory. Newspapers referred to "Bleeding Kansas" and "the Civil War in Kansas." A **civil war** is a conflict between citizens of the same country. In October 1856 the territorial governor sent federal troops to stop the bloodshed.

Violence also broke out in Congress. Senator Charles Sumner of Massachusetts lashed out against pro-slavery forces in Kansas. He also criticized pro-slavery senators, such as Andrew P. Butler of South Carolina. Two days later, Butler's cousin, Representative Preston Brooks, walked into the Senate chamber and hit Sumner with a cane. Sumner fell to the floor, unconscious and bleeding. This incident and the Kansas feud revealed the rising hostility between North and South.

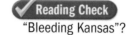 **Reading Check** **Explaining** What events led to "Bleeding Kansas"?

Section 2 Review

History ONLINE
Study Central™ To review this section, go to glencoe.com.

Vocabulary

1. Use each of these terms in a sentence that will help explain its meaning: network, popular sovereignty, border ruffians, inevitable, civil war.

Main Ideas

2. Listing What were some ways that Northerners defied the Fugitive Slave Act?

3. Explaining How would the issue of slavery in Kansas and Nebraska be decided under the Kansas-Nebraska Act?

Critical Thinking

4. Contrasting How did Southerners expect Northerners to react to the Fugitive Slave Act? How did Northerners actually react?

5. Sequencing Use a diagram like the one below to list the steps leading to bloodshed in Kansas.

6. Persuasive Writing Decide whether you would have been for or against the Kansas-Nebraska Act and the concept of popular sovereignty. Then write a newspaper editorial arguing your position.

Answer the
7. Essential Question
How did popular sovereignty lead to violence in Kansas?

Challenges to Slavery

Essential Question

What was the significance of the *Dred Scott* decision?

Reading Guide

Content Vocabulary
arsenal (p. 461) martyr (p. 461)

Academic Vocabulary
rigid (p. 458) topic (p. 460)

Key People and Events
Republican Party (p. 457)
John C. Frémont (p. 457)
James Buchanan (p. 457)
Dred Scott (p. 458)
Abraham Lincoln (p. 460)

Reading Strategy
Taking Notes As you read, use a diagram like the one below to note each party's candidate and platform in the 1856 presidential election. Also record the election result.

Republican:	— Platform:
Democrat:	— Platform:
American Party:	— Platform:

Election Result:

NEW YORK STANDARDS
The American Journey

U6.I.1 To understand the series of events and resulting conditions that led to the American Civil War

U6.I.2 To understand how different experiences, beliefs, values, traditions, and motives cause individuals and groups to interpret historic events and issues from different perspectives

U6.I.3 To participate in a negotiating and compromising role-playing activity that mirrors the attempts at political compromise in the 1850's

American Diary

A few years after the attacks in Kansas, John Brown led a raid in Harpers Ferry, Virginia. Many people considered Brown and his followers to be ruthless murderers. The Fredericksburg Herald declared that, "shooting is a mercy they should be denied." Others viewed Brown as a freedom fighter. When Brown was executed in 1859, writer Henry David Thoreau wrote, "He is not Old Brown any longer, [but] an angel of light."

—quoted in "John Brown at Harpers Ferry" and from Thoreau's "A Plea for Capt. John Brown"

John Brown leaving Charleston jail on his way to his execution

A New Political Party

Main Idea Opponents of slavery from different political parties came together to form the new Republican Party.

History and You Which of today's political issues is most important to your family? Read to learn how the parties stood on key issues of the 1854 and 1856 elections.

. . . .

Even before Brown's raid, other events drove the North and South further apart. After the Kansas-Nebraska Act, the Democratic Party began to divide along sectional lines, with Northern Democrats leaving the party. Differing views over the slavery issue destroyed the Whig Party.

The Election of 1854

In 1854 additional antislavery Whigs and Democrats joined forces with Free-Soilers to form the **Republican Party.** The Republicans challenged the pro-slavery Whigs and Democrats, choosing candidates to run in the state and congressional elections of 1854. Their main message was that the government should ban slavery from new territories. The Republican Party quickly showed its strength in the North. In the election, the Republicans won control of the House of Representatives and of several state governments. In the South, the Republican Party had almost no support.

Almost three-fourths of the Democratic candidates from free states lost in 1854. The Democrats were increasingly becoming a Southern party.

The Election of 1856

Democrats and Republicans met again in the presidential election of 1856. The Whig Party, disintegrating over the slavery issue, did not offer a candidate of its own.

The Republicans chose **John C. Frémont** of California as their candidate for president. Frémont gained fame as an explorer in the West. The party platform called for free territories, and its campaign slogan became "Free soil, Free speech, and Frémont."

The Democratic Party nominated **James Buchanan** of Pennsylvania, an experienced diplomat and former member of Congress. Buchanan wanted to appease the South in order to save the Union. As a result, the party endorsed the idea of popular sovereignty.

Primary Source / Hero or Villain?

Views of John Brown Some Northerners regarded John Brown as a hero. In a letter to Brown, a free African American in Indiana wrote: "I thank you that you have been brave enough to reach out your hands to the crushed and blighted of my race." A Southern newspaper, however, wrote: "The miserable old traitor and murderer belongs to the gallows, and the gallows will have its own."

Critical Thinking

Evaluating In what ways might a Northerner and a Southerner view John Brown's actions differently?

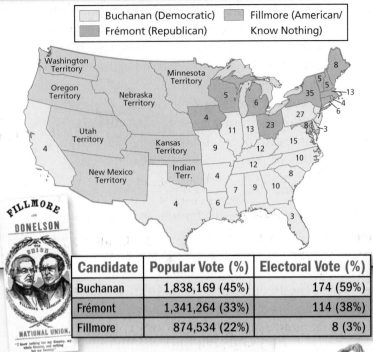

Buchanan (Democratic)
Frémont (Republican)
Fillmore (American/Know Nothing)

Candidate	Popular Vote (%)	Electoral Vote (%)
Buchanan	1,838,169 (45%)	174 (59%)
Frémont	1,341,264 (33%)	114 (38%)
Fillmore	874,534 (22%)	8 (3%)

▲ Third-party candidate Fillmore appealed to voters concerned about immigration and Catholicism.

Democrats stressed that Buchanan was the candidate of conciliation and stability and believed that a Frémont victory would lead to civil war. ▶

JAMES BUCHANAN, DEMOCRATIC CANDIDATE FOR PRESIDENT OF THE UNITED STATES.

Northern States for Buchanan The presidential election of 1856 was decided in the swing states of Pennsylvania, Illinois, and Indiana. Democratic candidate James Buchanan won all three. Only 1,200 of Republican John Frémont's 1.34 million popular votes came from slaveholding states.

The Republican ticket of John C. Frémont and William L. Dayton opposed slavery's expansion into the territories. ▶

Map Skills

Regions In which region was Frémont most successful? Which states in that area did he not win?

Maps In Motion See StudentWorks™ Plus or glencoe.com.

The American Party, or Know Nothings, grew quickly between 1853 and 1856 by attacking immigrants. The Know Nothings nominated former president Millard Fillmore. Most of the Northern delegates, however, walked out of the convention when the party refused to call for the repeal of the Kansas-Nebraska Act.

The presidential vote divided along **rigid**—firm and inflexible—sectional lines. Buchanan won the election. He took all Southern states except Maryland and received 174 electoral votes compared to 114 for Frémont and 8 for Fillmore. Frémont did not receive a single electoral vote south of the Mason-Dixon line, but he carried 11 of the 16 free states.

✔ **Reading Check** **Identifying** Which political party was emerging as the party of the South in the 1854 and 1856 elections?

The *Dred Scott* Case

Main Idea The Supreme Court's decision in the *Dred Scott* case dealt a severe blow to antislavery forces and further divided the country.

History and You How would you feel if the Supreme Court decided that you were "property"? Read to find out how the decision in the *Dred Scott* case shocked the nation.

Dred Scott was an enslaved African American bought by an army doctor in Missouri, a slave state. In the 1830s, the doctor moved his household to Illinois, a free state, and then to the Wisconsin Territory, where slavery was banned by the Northwest Ordinance of 1787. Later the family returned to Missouri, where the doctor died. In 1846, with the help of antislavery lawyers, Scott sued for his freedom.

Scott claimed he should be free because he once lived in areas of the North where slavery was prohibited.

Eleven years later, as anger grew over the slavery issue, the case reached the Supreme Court. The case attracted enormous attention across the country. While the immediate issue was Dred Scott's status, the Court also had the opportunity to rule on the question of slavery in the territories.

The Court's Decision

The Court's decision electrified the nation. Chief Justice Roger B. Taney (TAW•nee) said that Dred Scott was still an enslaved person. As such, Scott was not a citizen and had no right to bring a lawsuit. Taney continued on, addressing broader issues.

Taney wrote that Scott's residence on free soil did not make him free. An enslaved person was property, and the Fifth Amendment prohibits Congress from taking away property without "due process of law."

Finally, Taney wrote that Congress had no power to prohibit slavery in any territory. The Missouri Compromise—which banned slavery north of 36°30'N latitude—was unconstitutional. For that matter, so was popular sovereignty. Not even the voters in a territory could prohibit slavery because that would amount to taking away a person's property. In effect, the decision meant that the Constitution protected slavery.

Reaction to the Decision

Rather than settling the issue, the decision divided the country even more. The Court upheld what many in the South had always maintained: Nothing could legally stop the spread of slavery. The Republicans' main issue—limiting the spread of slavery—was ruled unconstitutional.

Republicans and other antislavery groups were outraged. They called the *Dred Scott* decision "a wicked and false judgment" and "the greatest crime" ever committed in the nation's courts.

Reading Check Applying Based on the *Dred Scott* decision, could voters ban slavery? Explain.

Primary Source / **The *Dred Scott* Decision**

A Controversial Ruling In his ruling in the *Dred Scott* case, Chief Justice Roger B. Taney declared the Missouri Compromise unconstitutional because it deprived slaveholders of their property without due process or compensation. Southerners praised the decision, which opened all U.S. territory to slavery.

Supreme Court Chief Justice Roger B. Taney ▶

◀ Newspaper announcing the *Dred Scott* decision

"They [African Americans] had for more than a century before been regarded as beings of an inferior order and altogether unfit to associate with the white race . . . and so far inferior that they had no rights which the white man was bound to respect. . . . No one . . . should induce the Court to give to the words of the Constitution a more liberal construction in their favor than they were intended to bear when the instrument was framed and adopted."
—Roger Taney, *Dred Scott* v. *Sandford* decision, March 1857

▲ The Old Courthouse in St. Louis where the *Dred Scott* case was heard

Critical Thinking

Assessing How do you think the *Dred Scott* decision affected sectional tensions in the country?

A Raid to Fight Slavery John Brown gained notoriety fighting against pro-slavery forces in Kansas in the mid-1850s. Financed by wealthy abolitionists, Brown led a raid in 1859 to capture the federal arsenal at Harpers Ferry, Virginia. Brown hoped to use the weapons at the arsenal to spark an uprising by enslaved people in Virginia.

John Brown and his men barricaded themselves in this brick engine house to fight off attacks from federal troops. ▼

"Now if . . . I should forfeit my life for the furtherance of the ends of justice and MINGLE MY BLOOD . . . with the blood of millions in this slave country whose rights are disregarded by wicked, cruel, and unjust enactments—I submit; so LET IT BE DONE."
—John Brown's statement to the Virginia Court

▲ Federal troops commanded by Colonel Robert E. Lee crushed Brown's raid. More than half of Brown's force, including two of his sons, died in the fighting. Brown and his surviving men were captured and Brown was later hanged.

Critical Thinking

Drawing Conclusions Was the raid on Harpers Ferry a success for abolitionists? Why or why not?

Lincoln and Douglas

Main Idea The Lincoln-Douglas debates placed the little-known Lincoln into the national spotlight.

History and You Do you like to root for the underdog? Read how Abraham Lincoln skillfully debated against the powerful Stephen Douglas.

In the congressional election of 1858, the Senate race in Illinois was the center of national attention. The contest pitted the current senator, Democrat Stephen A. Douglas, against Republican challenger **Abraham Lincoln.** People considered Douglas a likely candidate for president in 1860. Lincoln was nearly an unknown.

Douglas, a successful lawyer, joined the Democratic Party and won election to the House in 1842 and to the Senate in 1846. Short, stocky, and powerful, Douglas was called "the Little Giant." He disliked slavery but thought that the controversy over it would interfere with the nation's growth. He believed the issue could be resolved through popular sovereignty.

Born in the poor backcountry of Kentucky, Abraham Lincoln moved to Indiana as a child, and later to Illinois. Like Douglas, Lincoln was intelligent, ambitious, and a successful lawyer. He had little formal education—but excellent political skills. He had served in the Illinois legislature and in the U.S. House of Representatives. Lincoln saw slavery as morally wrong but admitted there was no easy way to end slavery where it existed. He was certain, though, that slavery should not be allowed to spread.

The Lincoln-Douglas Debates

Not as well-known as Douglas, Lincoln challenged the senator to a series of debates. Douglas reluctantly agreed. The two met seven times in August, September, and October of 1858 in cities and villages throughout Illinois. Thousands came to these debates. The main **topic,** or subject of discussion, was slavery.

During the debate at Freeport, Lincoln pressed Douglas about his views on popular sovereignty. Could the people of a territory legally exclude slavery before becoming a state? Douglas replied that the people could exclude slavery by refusing to pass laws protecting slaveholders' rights. Douglas's response, which satisfied antislavery followers but lost him support in the South, became known as the Freeport Doctrine.

Douglas claimed that Lincoln wanted African Americans to be fully equal to whites. Lincoln denied this. Still, Lincoln said, "in the right to eat the bread . . . which his own hand earns, [an African American] is my equal and the equal of [Senator] Douglas, and the equal of every living man." The real issue, Lincoln said, is "between the men who think slavery a wrong and those who do not think it wrong. The Republican Party think it wrong."

Following the debates, Douglas won a narrow victory in the election. Lincoln lost the election but did not come away empty-handed. He gained a national reputation as a man of clear thinking who could argue with force and persuasion.

The Raid on Harpers Ferry

After the 1858 election, Southerners felt threatened by Republicans. In late 1859, an act of violence added to their fears. On October 16 the abolitionist John Brown led a group on a raid on Harpers Ferry, Virginia. His target was an **arsenal,** a storage site for weapons. Brown hoped to arm enslaved African Americans and start a revolt against slaveholders. Abolitionists had paid for the raid.

Brown's raid was defeated by local citizens and federal troops. Convicted of treason and murder, Brown was sentenced to hang. His execution shook the North. Some antislavery Northerners denounced Brown's use of violence. Others saw Brown as a **martyr**—a person who dies for a great cause.

John Brown's death rallied abolitionists. When Southerners learned of Brown's abolitionist ties, their fears of a great Northern conspiracy against them seemed to be confirmed. The nation was on the brink of disaster.

Reading Check **Identifying** Why did John Brown raid the arsenal at Harpers Ferry?

Section 3 Review

History ONLINE
Study Central™ To review this section, go to glencoe.com.

Vocabulary

1. Define each of the following terms, and use each in a sentence: rigid, topic, arsenal, martyr.

Main Ideas

2. **Specifying** What issue led to the formation of the Republican Party, and what stand did the new party take on that issue?

3. **Explaining** What reasons did Taney give for Dred Scott's status as an enslaved person?

4. **Identifying** How did the Lincoln-Douglas debates benefit Lincoln?

Critical Thinking

5. **Identifying Points of View** Use a diagram like the one below to compare the views of Lincoln and Douglas on the issue of slavery.

6. **Making Inferences** Why do you think the raid on Harpers Ferry by a mere 18 men seemed so threatening to Southerners?

7. **Persuasive Writing** Write a rebuttal, or response, to Roger B. Taney on the *Dred Scott* decision. Address the points he made in his remarks on the Court's decision.

8. **Answer the Essential Question**
What was the significance of the *Dred Scott* decision?

Section 4 ★ Secession and War

Essential Question ◄

What role did the theory of states' rights play in the outbreak of the Civil War?

Reading Guide

Content Vocabulary
secession (p. 463)   states' rights (p. 464)

Academic Vocabulary
reject (p. 464)   justify (p. 464)

Key People and Events
John Crittenden (p. 463)
Confederate States of America (p. 464)
Jefferson Davis (p. 464)
Fort Sumter (p. 466)

Reading Strategy
Taking Notes As you read, list the major events on a time line like the one below.

| Nov. 1860 | Feb. 1861 | April 1861 |
| Dec. 1860 | March 1861 |

NEW YORK STANDARDS
The American Journey

U5.III.9 To use a number of research skills (e.g., computer databases, periodicals, census reports, maps, standard reference works, interviews, surveys) to locate and gather geographic information about issues and problems

U6.I.1 To understand the series of events and resulting conditions that led to the American Civil War

U6.I.2 To understand how different experiences, beliefs, values, traditions, and motives cause individuals and groups to interpret historic events and issues from different perspectives

U6.II.1 To understand the development and progress of the Civil War

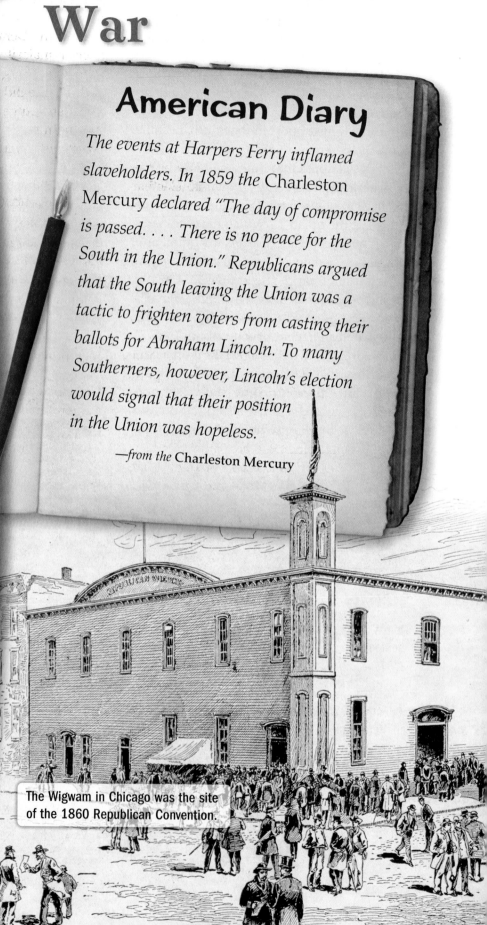

American Diary

The events at Harpers Ferry inflamed slaveholders. In 1859 the Charleston Mercury declared "The day of compromise is passed. . . . There is no peace for the South in the Union." Republicans argued that the South leaving the Union was a tactic to frighten voters from casting their ballots for Abraham Lincoln. To many Southerners, however, Lincoln's election would signal that their position in the Union was hopeless.

—from the Charleston Mercury

The Wigwam in Chicago was the site of the 1860 Republican Convention.

1848–1854

1848 The Free-Soil Party forms to oppose slavery in territories.

Van Buren-Adams poster, 1848 ▶

1850

- The Compromise of 1850 temporarily eases debate on slavery in Congress.
- The Fugitive Slave Act stirs up antislavery feelings in North.

1854

- The Kansas-Nebraska Act declares popular sovereignty in territories.
- Missouri voters help elect pro-slavery legislature in Kansas.
- The Republican Party forms as antislavery party.

1855–1859

1856

Jan. Kansas antislavery forces set up a rival government.

May Slavery supporters unleash violence in Kansas.

Oct. Federal troops are sent to end violence in "Bleeding Kansas."

1857 The *Dred Scott* decision rules that slavery is protected by the Constitution.

1858 Lincoln-Douglas debates focus on slavery and give Lincoln national recognition.

1859

Oct. John Brown raids Harpers Ferry arsenal uniting abolitionists.

1860–1861

1860

Nov. Lincoln is elected president.

Dec. South Carolina secedes; other Southern states follow.

1861

Feb. Southern states form Confederate States of America.

March Lincoln speaks of preserving the Union and preventing war in his Inaugural Address.

April The Confederate attack on Fort Sumter begins the Civil War.

▲ Confederate attack on Fort Sumter

◀ Fighting at Harpers Ferry

Study anywhere, anytime! Download quizzes and flash cards to your PDA from glencoe.com.

YOU DECIDE

Did the South Have the Right to Secede?

Building Background

When Abraham Lincoln was inaugurated to his first term as president, on March 4, 1861, the unfinished Capitol dome seemed to reflect the uncertain future of the United States. Seven Southern states had already voted to secede from the Union and form the Confederate States of America.

The Confederate president, Jefferson Davis, had been inaugurated earlier, on February 18. Each man's inauguration address presented a different view on the basic question of whether a state had the right to secede from the Union.

NO

ABRAHAM LINCOLN

One section of our country believes slavery is right and ought to be extended, while the other believes it is wrong and ought not to be extended. This is the only substantial dispute. . . .

The [President] derives all his authority from the people, and they have referred none upon him to fix terms for the separation of the States. The people themselves can do this if also they choose, but the Executive as such has nothing to do with it. His duty is to administer[1] the present Government as it came to his hands and to transmit it unimpaired[2] by him to his successor. . . .

We are not enemies, but friends. We must not be enemies. Though passion may have strained it must not break our bonds of affection. The mystic chords of memory, stretching from every battlefield and patriot grave to every living heart and hearthstone all over this broad land, will yet swell the chorus of the Union, when again touched, as surely they will be, by the better angels of our nature.

Abraham Lincoln's first inauguration, March 4, 1861

---

[1] **administer** manage

[2] **unimpaired** unharmed

468

YES

JEFFERSON DAVIS

An agricultural people, whose chief interest is the export of a commodity required in every manufacturing country, our true policy is peace, and the freest trade which our necessities will permit. . . . There can be but little rivalry between ours and any manufacturing or navigating community, such as the Northeastern States of the American Union. It must follow, therefore, that a mutual interest would invite good will and kind offices. If, however, passion or the lust of dominion[3] should cloud the judgment or inflame the ambition of those States, we must prepare to meet the emergency and to maintain, by the final arbitrament[4] of the sword, the position which we have assumed among the nations of the earth. We have entered upon the career of independence, and it must be inflexibly pursued. . . . As a necessity, not a choice, we have resorted to the remedy of separation; and henceforth our energies must be directed to the conduct of our own affairs, and the perpetuity[5] of the Confederacy which we have formed.

---

[3] **dominion** territory

[4] **arbitrament** power to decide

[5] **perpetuity** lasting life

DBQ Document-Based Questions

1. **Identifying** What are Abraham Lincoln's and Jefferson Davis's basic arguments against or in favor of secession?

2. **Making Inferences** What issue seems most important to Lincoln? To Davis?

3. **Analyzing** Did either president refer to the economies of the different regions? If so, how were they described?

4. **Evaluating** In your opinion, which of the two addresses makes the more powerful appeal to emotions? Explain your answer in a short essay.

Jefferson Davis's inauguration in Montgomery, Alabama, February 18, 1861

GRADE 8 INTERMEDIATE TEST PRACTICE

TEST-TAKING TIP

Read all the choices before selecting your answer. You may overlook the correct answer if you are hasty!

Reviewing Main Ideas

Directions: Choose the best answer for each of the following questions.

1 Which of the following was a proposal to ban slavery in any lands acquired from Mexico?

(1) Compromise of 1850

(2) Wilmot Proviso

(3) Missouri Compromise

(4) Freeport Doctrine

2 What resulted from the Fugitive Slave Act?

(1) Passage of the law quieted widespread violence in Kansas and Nebraska.

(2) Most Northerners believed Southern slaveholders' rights should be upheld.

(3) Abolitionists were jailed in the North.

(4) The law angered the North, convincing many of the evils of slavery.

3 The Supreme Court's decision in the *Dred Scott* case stated that

(1) enslaved persons could bring lawsuits.

(2) Congress had no power to prohibit slavery in any territory.

(3) the slave trade should be abolished.

(4) the Missouri Compromise was constitutional.

4 Which was included in the Republican Party platform of the election of 1860?

(1) The question of slavery should be decided by popular sovereignty.

(2) In a free society, the minority has the right to break up the government.

(3) Slavery should be left where it existed but be excluded from the territories.

(4) Slavery should be protected in all territories south of 36°30'N latitude.

Short-Answer Question

Directions: Base your answer to question 5 on the political cartoon below and on your knowledge of social studies.

SOUTHERN CHIVALRY — ARGUMENT versus CLUB'S.

Source: Bettmann/CORBIS

5 This cartoon shows the attack on Massachusetts Senator Charles Sumner in the Senate chamber. What emotions might the event in this cartoon have stirred up in the North and in the South?

Review the Essential Questions

6 Essay Describe the various attempts to find a compromise between the demands of the North and the South.

To help you write your essay, review your answers to the Essential Questions in the section reviews and the chapter Foldables Study Organizer. Your essay should include:

- the compromises Congress made regarding sectionalism and slavery; and
- reactions by antislavery and pro-slavery forces.

GO ON

Document-Based Questions

Directions: Analyze the documents and answer the short-answer questions that follow.

Document 1

In this passage, Erastus D. Ladd describes voters from Missouri crossing the border to vote in an 1855 election in Kansas.

> They claimed to have a legal right to vote in the Territory [Kansas], and that they were residents by virtue of their being then in the Territory. They said they were free to confess that they came from Missouri; that they lived in Missouri, and voted as Missourians.

Source: Albert Bushnell Hart, *Source-Book of American History*

7 Were the actions of these voters legal? How did the voters from Missouri justify voting in Kansas?

Document 2

This is an excerpt from a speech by Georgia congressperson Robert Toombs in 1849.

> I do not . . . hesitate to avow [admit] before this House and the country, and in the presence of the living God, that if by your legislation you seek to drive us from the territories of California and New Mexico, purchased by the common blood and treasure of the whole people, and to abolish slavery in this District, thereby attempting to fix a national degradation [shame] upon half the States of this Confederacy, I am for disunion.

Source: Representative Robert Toombs of Georgia

8 Based on the excerpt, do you think Toombs favored or opposed the legalization of slavery in California and New Mexico? On what did Toombs base his views?

Document 3

In this passage from 1851, Richard Henry Dana, Jr., speaks of the Fugitive Slave Act of 1850.

> If the law were constitutional, which I firmly believe it is not, it would be the duty of a citizen not to resist it by force, unless he was prepared for revolution and civil war; but we rejoice in the escape of a victim of an unjust law as we would in the escape of an ill-treated captive deer or bird.

Source: Charles Francis Adams, *Richard Henry Dana*

9 Suppose Dana was a member of a jury during a trial of someone accused of breaking the Fugitive Slave Act. Based on the passage, do you think he would find the accused guilty or not guilty? Why?

Document 4

This is a campaign ribbon from the 1856 presidential election.

Source: David J. & Janice L. Frent Collection/CORBIS

10 Does this ribbon support or oppose John C. Frémont for president? Explain.

11 **Expository Writing** Using the information from the four documents and your knowledge of social studies, write an essay in which you:

- identify ways Northerners and Southerners appealed to emotion *and* to legal arguments to justify their positions; and

- explain which type of argument you find most persuasive, and why.

Need Extra Help?											
If you missed questions. . .	1	2	3	4	5	6	7	8	9	10	11
Go to page. . .	450	453	458–459	463	455	448–466	454–455	451	453	457–458	448–466

Chapter 16

The Civil War
1861–1865

Civil War: First at Vicksburg, 1863 by H. Charles McBarron, Jr.

PRESIDENTS

ABRAHAM LINCOLN

U.S. Events

World Events

1861
★ 1861
Conflict at Fort Sumter,
South Carolina, begins
Civil War

★ 1861
Robert E. Lee
named commander
of Confederate armies

1862

★ 1861
• Russia emancipates serfs
• First ironclad warship
  completed in England

★ 1862
International Red Cross
established; American
Red Cross organized 10
years later

Section 1: The Two Sides

Essential Question What were the strengths and weaknesses of the North and the South?

Section 2: Early Stages of the War

Essential Question Why did neither the Union nor the Confederacy gain a strong advantage during the early years of the war?

Section 3: Life During the War

Essential Question What social, political, and economic changes resulted from the war?

Section 4: The Strain of War

Essential Question How did the events at Gettysburg and Vicksburg change the course of the war?

Section 5: The War's Final Stages

Essential Question What events led to the end of the war?

History ONLINE
Chapter Overview Visit glencoe.com and click on **Chapter 16—Chapter Overviews** to preview chapter information.

FOLDABLES®
Study Organizer

Organizing Information
Make this Foldable to help organize what you learn about the Civil War.

Step 1 Fold a sheet of paper in half from side to side.

Fold it so the left edge lies about $\frac{1}{2}$ inch from the right edge.

Step 2 Turn the paper and fold it into thirds.

This will make three tabs.

Step 3 Unfold and cut the top layer only along both folds.

Step 4 Label your Foldable as shown.

Before the War | During the War | After the War
The Civil War

Reading and Writing As you read the chapter, list events that occurred before, during, and after the Civil War under the appropriate tabs of your Foldable.

★ **1863**
- Emancipation Proclamation issued
- Grant named commander of Union armies

★ **1864** Sherman's March to the Sea begins

ANDREW JOHNSON

★ **1865** Civil War ends

1863

1864

1865

★ **1863** London subway opens

★ **1864** First Geneva Convention establishes rules for treatment of prisoners of war

★ **1865** French writer Jules Verne publishes a novel about a trip to the moon

Section 1 The Two Sides

Essential Question ◄

What were the strengths and weaknesses of the North and the South?

Reading Guide

Content Vocabulary

border state (p. 475)   export (p. 477)
blockade (p. 477)

Academic Vocabulary

contrast (p. 476)   challenge (p. 479)

Key People and Events

Abraham Lincoln (p. 475)
Anaconda Plan (p. 477)

Reading Strategy

Taking Notes As you read, take notes on the differences and similarities between the two sides.

North   South

NEW YORK STANDARDS
The American Journey

U6.II.1 To understand the development and progress of the Civil War

U6.II.4 To describe the relationships between people and environments and the connections between people and places

U6.II.5 To identify and collect economic information related to the Civil War from standard reference works, newspapers, periodicals, computer databases, textbooks and other primary and secondary sources

American Diary

At the Battle of Malvern Hill in 1862, a Union sergeant named Driscoll shot a young Confederate soldier. Hurrying forward, Driscoll turned the soldier's face up to see if the young man was dead. But when he looked at the dying soldier's face, he received a terrible shock. Looking up, the boy murmured, "Father," and then closed his eyes forever. The soldier was his son, who had gone south before the war.

Goals and Strategies

Main Idea The North and the South had many different strengths, strategies, and purposes in the Civil War.

History and You Is it better for an army to have plenty of soldiers or a powerful will to fight? Why? Read to learn how these characteristics affected the Civil War.

Like the Driscolls, many families were divided by the war. Neither side imagined, however, that the war would cost such a terrible price in human life. During the four years of fighting, hundreds of thousands of Americans had lost their lives. Many thousands more were wounded in battle.

The Border States

For most states, choosing sides in the Civil War was easy. The **border states** of Delaware, Maryland, Kentucky, and Missouri, however, were bitterly divided. Slavery was legal in all four states, though none had many enslaved people. All four had ties to the North and the South.

These states were vital to the Union because of their strategic locations. Missouri could control parts of the Mississippi River and major routes to the West. Kentucky controlled the Ohio River. Delaware was close to Philadelphia.

Maryland, perhaps the most important of the border states, was close to Richmond, the Confederate capital. Most significantly, Washington, D.C., lay within the state. If Maryland seceded, the North's government would be surrounded.

President **Abraham Lincoln** worked tirelessly to keep the four border states in the Union. In the end, he was successful.

Still, many border state residents supported the Confederacy. The president had his hands full trying to restrain these opponents of the war. In September 1861, Lincoln wrote:

PRIMARY SOURCE

"I think to lose Kentucky is nearly the same as to lose the whole game. . . . We would as well consent to separation at once, including the surrender of this capitol."

—from *Abraham Lincoln: His Speeches and Writings*

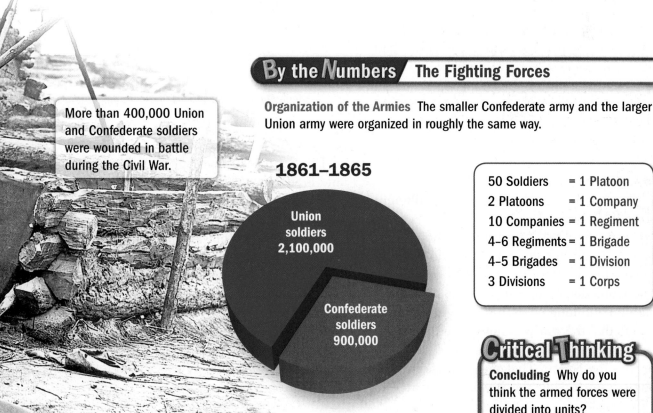

More than 400,000 Union and Confederate soldiers were wounded in battle during the Civil War.

By the Numbers / The Fighting Forces

Organization of the Armies The smaller Confederate army and the larger Union army were organized in roughly the same way.

1861–1865

Union soldiers 2,100,000

Confederate soldiers 900,000

50 Soldiers	= 1 Platoon
2 Platoons	= 1 Company
10 Companies	= 1 Regiment
4–6 Regiments	= 1 Brigade
4–5 Brigades	= 1 Division
3 Divisions	= 1 Corps

Critical Thinking

Concluding Why do you think the armed forces were divided into units?

Resources in the North and South

Union   Confederacy

Source: U.S. Census Bureau, *Historical Statistics of the United States*

Graph Skills

Comparing In what areas did the North have the greatest advantage over the South?

Graphs In Motion See StudentWorks™ Plus or glencoe.com.

Comparing North and South

When the war began, both sides had advantages and disadvantages. How they would use those strengths and weaknesses would determine the war's outcome.

The North had a larger population and better resources than the South. The South had other advantages, such as excellent military leaders and a strong fighting spirit. Also, because most of the war was fought in the South, the Confederacy knew the land and had the will to defend it.

War Aims

The North and the South had different aims in fighting the Civil War. The South's goal was to establish itself as an independent nation. To do this, the South did not have to invade the North or destroy the Union army. The Confederacy needed only to fight hard enough and long enough to convince Northerners that the war was not worth its cost.

In **contrast,** the Northern goal was to restore the Union. That meant invading the South and forcing the breakaway states to give up their quest for sovereignty. Although slavery helped drive a wedge between Northerners and Southerners, President Lincoln's original aim was not to defeat slavery. He wrote in 1862:

PRIMARY SOURCE

"If I could save the Union without freeing *any* slave I would do it."
—from *Abraham Lincoln: His Speeches and Writings*

Confederate Strategies

The South expected support from Britain and France, whose supply of Southern cotton was being disrupted by the war. Southerners reasoned that these nations might pressure the North to end the war.

The South's basic strategy, however, was to conduct a defensive war. This meant that the South would hold on to as much territory as possible. Southerners felt that if they showed determination to be independent, Northerners would tire of the war. The only exception to this defensive strategy was a plan to attack Washington, D.C.

Union Strategies

The North's war plan came from General Winfield Scott, hero of the war with Mexico. Knowing that the North would have to subdue the South completely, he proposed three main strategies for winning the war.

First, the Union should **blockade,** or close, Southern ports. This strategy would prevent supplies from reaching the Confederacy. It also would keep the South from **exporting** its cotton crop—or selling it to other countries.

Second, the North intended to gain control of the entire Mississippi River, which would split the Confederacy in two and cut Southern supply lines. Scott's plan was called the **Anaconda Plan,** after the snake that squeezes its prey to death.

Third, the North planned to capture Richmond, Virginia, the Confederate capital.

Reading Check **Explaining** Why was it to the South's advantage to fight a defensive war?

Americans Against Americans

Main Idea Soldiers in the Civil War came from every region, and each side expected an early victory.

History and You What motivates men and women to join the armed forces today? Read to find out about the backgrounds of the Civil War soldiers.

The Civil War was more than a war between the states. It pitted brother against brother and neighbor against neighbor. Kentucky senator John Crittenden had two sons who became generals. One fought for the Confederacy, the other for the Union. Even President Lincoln's wife, Mary Todd Lincoln, had relatives in the Confederate army.

Many left their homes and families to enlist in the Union or Confederate armies. Soldiers on both sides had many reasons for signing up. Some were motivated by patriotism and loyalty to their causes.

Economics & History

Enlisted men in both the Union and Confederate armies were paid monthly. Compare the pay rates to those in later wars.

Army Salaries (monthly)

Rank	Civil War	World War II 1942	Vietnam War 1965	Iraq War 2007
Private	*$13	$50	$85	$1,203 – 1,543.20
Corporal	$14	$66	$210	$1,699.50
Sergeant	$17	$78	$261	$1,854 – 2,339.10
Sergeant Major	$21	$138	$486	$4,110

*Until 1864, African Americans in the Civil War were paid only $7.00 per month.

Source: *Bureau of Economic Analysis*; Princeton Review; www.militaryfactory.com

$7.20	Overcoat	$1.14	Pair of Shoes
$6.71	Dress Coat	$1.35	Hat
$2.95	Blanket	$0.88	Undershirt
$2.63	Blouse	$0.55	Underwear
$3.03	Trousers	$0.26	Socks

Soldiers had to replace any of the clothing they lost out of their own pay.

Union soldier's cap ▲

$100 BOUNTY
$13 PAY PER MONTH
$6 STATE PAY for MARRIED MEN
$4 STATE PAY for SINGLE MEN
$3.50 PER MONTH FOR CLOTHES & RATIONS FOUND.
THE
N GUARDS!
LEGION, Colonel William Bryan, now encamped at Beverly. A few more
YOUNG MEN WANTED
FILL THIS COMPANY.
N AND PROCEED TO CAMP AT ONCE
TING STATION,
AN'S, SECOND ST.
Market and Plum Sts.
, N. JERSEY.
APT. R. GRAHAM CLARKE.

To get more men to enlist, Union recruiters put up posters offering a sign-up bonus or bounty.

Critical Thinking

Calculating What was a private's weekly salary in the Civil War?

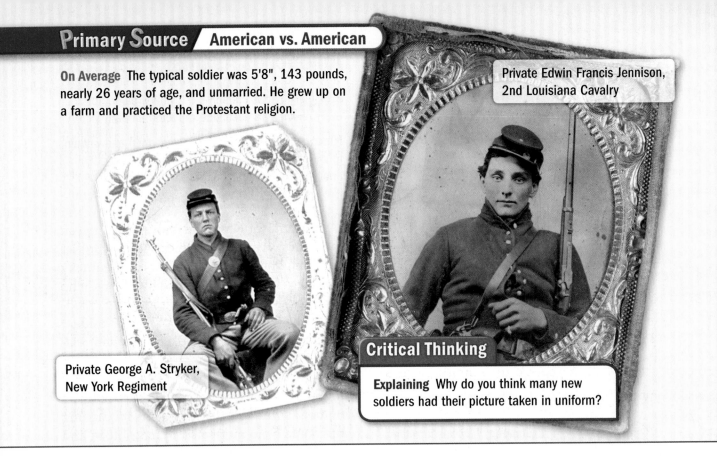

On Average The typical soldier was 5'8", 143 pounds, nearly 26 years of age, and unmarried. He grew up on a farm and practiced the Protestant religion.

Private Edwin Francis Jennison, 2nd Louisiana Cavalry

Private George A. Stryker, New York Regiment

Critical Thinking

Explaining Why do you think many new soldiers had their picture taken in uniform?

Others thought they would be called cowards if they did not serve. Still others yearned for excitement. The sister of William Stone of Louisiana wrote that her brother was:

PRIMARY SOURCE

"wild to be off to Virginia [to join the Confederate army]. He so fears that the fighting will be over before he can get there."

—from *Brokenburn: The Journal of Kate Stone*

The quest for excitement was especially strong among younger soldiers. Many recruits on both sides were hardly adults. Tens of thousands of soldiers were under 18, and some were younger than 14. To get into the army, many teenagers ran away from home or lied about their ages.

Although teenage boys were accepted into military service, one group of men was not permitted to fight during the early days of the war. Unwilling to provide enslaved people with weapons, the Confederacy barred African Americans from the army. The Union also refused to let freed people enlist. Northern leaders worried that white troops would not accept African American soldiers. Later in the war, though, this policy was changed.

False Hopes

When the war began, each side expected an easy victory. Northerners could not imagine the Confederates holding out for long against the Union's greater resources. They boasted that the war would end in a quick and glorious triumph for the Union.

Confederates found it impossible to believe that the North could ever subdue the fighting spirit of the South. Both sides were wrong. In the end, the war lasted far longer than most Americans could have guessed.

Who Were the Soldiers?

Soldiers came from every region and all walks of life. Most, though, came from farms. Almost half of the North's troops and more than 60 percent of the South's had owned or worked on farms. Lincoln's early terms of enlistment asked governors to supply soldiers for 90 days. When the conflict did not end quickly, soldiers' terms became longer.

By the summer of 1861, the Confederate army had about 112,000 soldiers, who were sometimes called Rebels. The Union had about 187,000 soldiers, or Yankees, as they were also known. By the end of the war, about 900,000 men fought for the Confederacy and about 2.1 million men for the Union. The Union army included just under 200,000 African Americans and about 10,000 Latino soldiers.

The Life of a Soldier

In both the North and the South, civilians and soldiers suffered terrible hardships and faced new **challenges.** In letters to their families and friends at home, soldiers described what they saw and how they felt. Many wrote about their boredom, discomfort, sickness, fear, and horror.

Most of the time the soldiers lived in camps. Camp life had its pleasant moments of songs, stories, letters from home, and baseball games. Often, however, a soldier's life was dull—a seemingly unchanging routine of drills, bad food, marches, and rain.

During lulls between battles, Confederate and Union soldiers sometimes forgot they were enemies. A private described his wartime experiences:

PRIMARY SOURCE

"A part of Co K and some of the enemy came together and stacked arms and talked for a long time. Our men cooked coffee and treated them and [afterward] . . . each one took up his position again and they began to fire at each other again, but not as hard as before."

—from *The Life of Billy Yank*

The Reality of War

In spite of fleeting moments of calm, the reality of war was never far away. Both sides suffered terrible losses. The new rifles used during the Civil War fired with greater accuracy than the muskets of earlier wars.

Medical facilities were overwhelmed by the thousands of casualties. After the Battle of Shiloh, the wounded lay in the rain for more than 24 hours waiting for treatment. A Union soldier recalled, "Many had died there, and others were in the last agonies as we passed. Their groans and cries were heart-rending."

Faced with such horrors, many men deserted. About one of every 11 Union soldiers and one of every 8 Confederates ran away because of fear, hunger, or sickness.

✔ **Reading Check** **Explaining** Why did both sides think the war would end quickly?

Section 1 Review

History ONLINE
Study Central™ To review this section, go to glencoe.com.

Vocabulary

1. Write a short paragraph in which you use all the following vocabulary terms: border state, contrast, blockade, export, challenge.

Main Ideas

2. **Explaining** Why were the border states important to both the North and South?

3. **Evaluating** What was the purpose of the Anaconda Plan?

Critical Thinking

4. **Predicting** What do you think would be the South's greatest advantage in the war?

5. **Comparing** Create a diagram to compare Northern and Southern aims and strategies.

	North	South
Aims		
Strategies		

6. **Descriptive Writing** You are a Southerner or Northerner in 1861. Write a journal entry that explains your reasons for joining the Confederate or Union army.

Answer the
7. **Essential Question**
What were the strengths and weaknesses of the North and the South?

Section 2

Early Stages of the War

Essential Question ◄

Why did neither the Union nor the Confederacy gain a strong advantage during the early years of the war?

Reading Guide

Content Vocabulary

tributary *(p. 482)* casualty *(p. 483)*
ironclad *(p. 483)*

Academic Vocabulary

abandon *(p. 481)* impact *(p. 487)*

Key People and Events

Stonewall Jackson *(p. 481)*

Ulysses S. Grant *(p. 482)*

Battle of Shiloh *(p. 483)*

Robert E. Lee *(p. 485)*

Battle of Antietam *(p. 486)*

Frederick Douglass *(p. 487)*

Emancipation Proclamation *(p. 487)*

Reading Strategy

Taking Notes As you read, place the early Civil War battles described in the text on a time line and take notes on what happened during each one.

NEW YORK STANDARDS
The American Journey

U6.II.1 To understand the development and progress of the Civil War

U6.II.2 To investigate key turning points in the Civil War in New York State and United States history and explain why these events or developments are significant

U6.II.3 To map information about people, places, and environments

American Diary

Captain Van Brunt, of the U.S. Navy, described the historic first battle between metal-plated ships in 1862: "[The Monitor] laid herself right alongside of the Merrimack, and the contrast was that of a pigmy to a giant. Gun after gun was fired by the Monitor, which was returned with whole broadsides from the rebels with no more effect, apparently, than so many pebblestones thrown by a child."

—*quoted in* Official Records of the Union and Confederate Navies in the War of the Rebellion, *1898*

War on Land and Sea

Main Idea The Confederates decisively won the First Battle of Bull Run.

History and You Would you eat a picnic lunch while a battle was raging all around you? Read to learn what happened in 1861 when many people did exactly that.

. . . .

The Civil War was fought on sea as well as on land. While the Union and Confederacy mobilized their armies, the Union navy began operations against the South. In April 1861, President Lincoln proclaimed a blockade of all Confederate ports.

Southerners hoped to break the Union blockade with a secret weapon—the *Merrimack*, an **abandoned** Union warship. The Confederates rebuilt and covered the wooden ship in iron. The armored vessel, renamed the *Virginia*, could withstand Union cannon fire.

First Battle of Bull Run

Pressure mounted in the summer of 1861, leading to the first major battle of the Civil War. On July 21, about 30,000 inexperienced Union troops commanded by General Irvin McDowell attacked a smaller, equally inexperienced Confederate force led by General P. G. T. Beauregard. The fighting took place in northern Virginia, about 5 miles (8 km) from the town of Manassas Junction near a small river called Bull Run. Hundreds of Washington, D.C., residents went to the battle site to picnic and watch.

The Yankees drove the Confederates back at first. Then the Rebels rallied, inspired by reinforcements under General Thomas Jackson. Jackson was seen holding out heroically, "like a stone wall," and became known thereafter as **"Stonewall" Jackson.** The Confederates unleashed a savage counterattack that forced Union lines to break. The Union retreat turned into a mad stampede when retreating Union troops collided with the civilians, fleeing in panic back to Washington, D.C.

The outcome shocked Northerners. They began to understand that the war could be a long, difficult, and costly struggle. President Lincoln appointed a new general, George B. McClellan, to head and organize the Union army of the East—called the Army of the Potomac—and to train the troops.

Primary Source / Naval Warfare

The Ironclads The *Monitor* was small for a warship—about 172 feet (52 m) long—and constructed almost entirely of iron. A revolving armored tower called a turret housed the guns.

The Union's *Monitor* (below) battled the ironclad *Merrimack* (left), called the *Virginia* by the Confederates, on March 9, 1862.

iron turret rotates on a pivot

11-inch (28-cm) cannon housed inside rotating turret

layered armor plating

Critical Thinking

Making Inferences What advantages would an iron warship have over a wooden ship? Explain.

The loss at Bull Run discouraged Union supporters. Although dismayed by the results, President Lincoln was also determined. Within days he issued a call for more volunteers for the army. He signed two bills requesting a total of 1 million soldiers to serve for three years. Victories in the West raised Northern spirits and also increased enlistment.

The War in the West

In the West, the major Union goal was to control the Mississippi River and its **tributaries,** the smaller rivers that flow into a larger river. With control of the river, Union ships on the Mississippi could prevent the states of Louisiana, Arkansas, and Texas from supplying the rest of the Confederacy. Control would also let Union gunboats and troops move into the heart of the South.

The battle for the rivers began in February 1862 when Union forces captured Fort Henry on the Tennessee River. The assault was led by naval commander Andrew Foote and army general **Ulysses S. Grant.** Soon afterward, Grant and Foote moved against Fort Donelson on the Cumberland River. The Confederates in Fort Donelson realized that they had no chance of winning the battle, so they asked Grant what terms, or incentives, he would give them to give up the fort. Grant said:

PRIMARY SOURCE

"No terms except an unconditional and immediate surrender can be accepted."
—General Grant to General Buckner, February 1862

"Unconditional Surrender" Grant became the North's new hero.

War of the Ironclads

As conflict was raging on the rivers of the West, ships of the Union and Confederate navies were fighting in the Atlantic Ocean.

War in the West, 1862–1863   NATIONAL GEOGRAPHIC

Union states
Confederate states
Union victory
Confederate victory

Shiloh April 7, 1862
At dawn, Union forces launched a counterattack **A** against Confederate forces **B**. By mid-afternoon, the Confederate forces were driven back **C**. Confederate General Beauregard ordered a retreat, forming a rear guard. The remaining Confederate forces moved south toward Corinth **D**.

On March 8, 1862, the *Merrimack,* renamed the *Virginia,* attacked a group of Union ships off the coast of Virginia. The North's wooden warships could not damage the Confederate ship—shells simply bounced off its iron sides. Some Northern leaders feared the South would use the **ironclad** warship to destroy the Union navy, steam up the Potomac River, and bombard Washington, D.C.

The North, though, had an ironclad ship of its own, the *Monitor,* and this ship rushed toward Virginia. On March 9, the two ironclads met in battle. Neither ship could sink the other. Although the battle was indecisive, it was also historic because it was the first ever between metal-covered ships.

The Battle of Shiloh

Meanwhile, in the West, General Grant and about 40,000 troops headed south along the Tennessee River toward Corinth, Mississippi, an important railroad junction. In early April 1862, the Union army camped at Pittsburg Landing, 20 miles (32 km) from Corinth. Nearby was a church named Shiloh. Additional Union forces came from Nashville to join Grant.

Confederate leaders decided to strike first, before the reinforcements arrived. Early in the morning of April 6, Confederate forces led by Albert Sidney Johnston and P. G. T. Beauregard launched a surprise attack on the Union troops. The **Battle of Shiloh** lasted two days, with some of the most bitter, bloody fighting of the war. Even though Shiloh was a narrow victory for the Union forces, the losses were enormous. Together the two armies suffered more than 23,000 **casualties**—people killed or wounded.

After Shiloh, Union forces gained control of Corinth on May 30. Memphis, Tennessee, fell to Union armies on June 6. The North seemed well on its way to controlling the Mississippi River.

The Battle of Shiloh

More than 23,000 troops were killed or wounded in the Battle of Shiloh. This was the highest number of casualties of any Civil War battle to date. The Union victory was an important step toward the goal of controlling the Mississippi River.

Critical Thinking

Analyzing Did either Beauregard or Sherman accept the fact that his side might lose the Battle of Shiloh? Do you think their statements reflect what most military leaders would say in this situation? Explain.

Day One

A surprise attack by the Confederate army gave it an early advantage. Union general William T. Sherman remarked to General Grant, *"Well, Grant, we've had the devil's own day of it, haven't we?"*

"Yes," Grant replied, *"Lick 'em tomorrow, though."*

◀ William T. Sherman

Day Two

With Union reinforcements, the battle changed direction, resulting in a Union victory. Confederate general P. G. T. Beauregard lamented, *"I thought I had General Grant just where I wanted him and could finish him up in the morning."*

P. G. T. Beauregard ▶

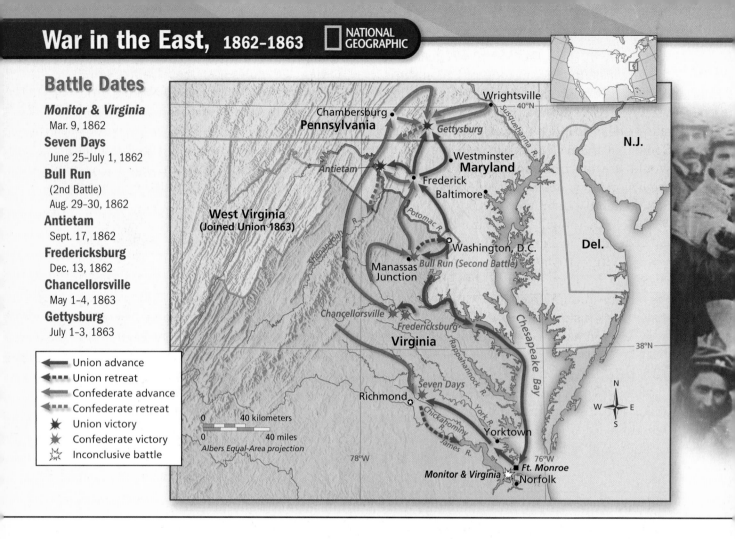

War in the East, 1862-1863

NATIONAL GEOGRAPHIC

Battle Dates

Monitor & Virginia
Mar. 9, 1862

Seven Days
June 25-July 1, 1862

Bull Run
(2nd Battle)
Aug. 29-30, 1862

Antietam
Sept. 17, 1862

Fredericksburg
Dec. 13, 1862

Chancellorsville
May 1-4, 1863

Gettysburg
July 1-3, 1863

Union advance
Union retreat
Confederate advance
Confederate retreat
Union victory
Confederate victory
Inconclusive battle

0   40 kilometers
0   40 miles
Albers Equal-Area projection

New Orleans Falls

A few weeks after Shiloh, the North won another important victory. On April 25, 1862, Union naval forces under David Farragut captured New Orleans, Louisiana, the largest city in the South. Farragut, who was of Spanish descent, grew up in the South but remained loyal to the Union. His capture of New Orleans, near the mouth of the Mississippi River, meant that the Confederacy could no longer use the river to carry its goods to sea. Together with Grant's victories to the north, the capture of New Orleans gave the Union control of most of the Mississippi River. Only the city of Vicksburg, Mississippi, blocked Union control of the river and the success of the Union's western strategy.

Reading Check Comparing and Contrasting
How was the Battle of Shiloh like the First Battle of Bull Run? How were the two battles different?

War in the East

Main Idea The South won several important victories in the East during 1862, but the Union responded with a vital triumph of its own.

History and You What is the most valuable thing you have lost? Read to learn what happened when a Confederate officer lost some important papers.
· ·

While Union and Confederate forces were struggling for control of Tennessee and the Mississippi River, another major campaign was being waged in the East to capture Richmond, Virginia. Richmond, the capital of the Confederacy, was close to the northern Confederate border and vulnerable to attack. Yet it was a matter of pride to defend it at all costs. Repelling one Union advance after another, Confederate armies prevented the fall of Richmond until the end of the war.

By the Numbers

The Battle of Antietam was the bloodiest one-day battle in the war and in American history. Several battles in the East were costly in terms of total casualties (killed, wounded, missing, and captured).

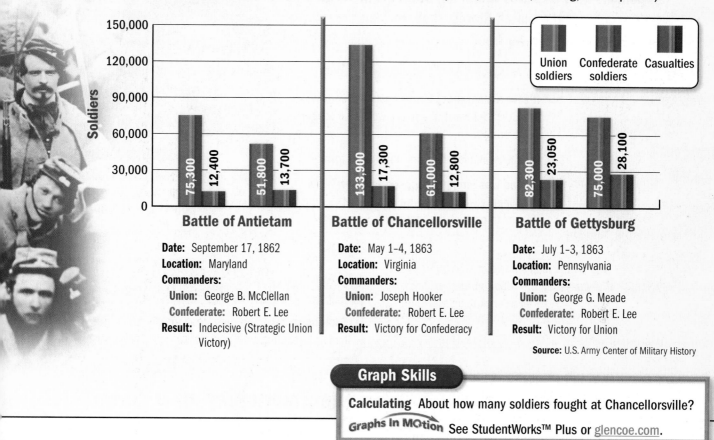

Battle of Antietam
- **Date:** September 17, 1862
- **Location:** Maryland
- **Commanders:**
  - **Union:** George B. McClellan
  - **Confederate:** Robert E. Lee
- **Result:** Indecisive (Strategic Union Victory)

Battle of Chancellorsville
- **Date:** May 1–4, 1863
- **Location:** Virginia
- **Commanders:**
  - **Union:** Joseph Hooker
  - **Confederate:** Robert E. Lee
- **Result:** Victory for Confederacy

Battle of Gettysburg
- **Date:** July 1–3, 1863
- **Location:** Pennsylvania
- **Commanders:**
  - **Union:** George G. Meade
  - **Confederate:** Robert E. Lee
- **Result:** Victory for Union

Source: U.S. Army Center of Military History

Graph Skills

Calculating About how many soldiers fought at Chancellorsville?

Graphs In MOtion See StudentWorks™ Plus or glencoe.com.

Victories for the Confederacy

Southern victories in the East were largely the result of the leadership of General **Robert E. Lee** and Stonewall Jackson. Through knowledge of the terrain, speed of movement, and the ability to inspire their troops, Confederate forces managed to defeat Union forces sometimes twice as large as their own.

In 1862 Confederate forces turned back General George B. McClellan at the Seven Days' Battle, General John Pope at the Second Battle of Bull Run, and General Ambrose Burnside at Fredericksburg. In May 1863, at Chancellorsville, Virginia, Lee's army defeated a Union army twice its size. "My God, my God," Lincoln said when he learned of the defeat, "What will the country say!"

Victories in the East did not include victories outside the Confederacy. Lee's two attempts to invade the North failed. In September 1862, Lee's army was turned back at the Battle of Antietam. Less than a year later, Confederate forces would face the same fate at Gettysburg. You will read about the Battle of Gettysburg in Section 4.

Invasion of the North

Washington, D.C., presented a tempting target for the Confederates, but the city was too well guarded for Lee to consider an attack. On the urging of Confederate president Jefferson Davis, Lee moved his troops instead into western Maryland—Union territory. His goal now was to sweep into Pennsylvania and carry the war into the Northern states. Lee knew that McClellan was pursuing him with a sizable force, so he concentrated on moving forward. Lee's forces crossed into Maryland and began an invasion of the North.

Lincoln declared in the Emancipation Proclamation that:

"all persons held as slaves within any state . . . in rebellion against the United States, shall be then, thenceforward and forever free."

Results of the Proclamation

✔ It sent a clear message to enslaved people and the Confederacy that slavery would no longer be tolerated.

✔ African American military units were formed.

✔ Europe was strongly opposed to slavery. No European government would defend the South in its war to protect the institution of slavery.

"If my name ever goes into history, it will be for this act."
—Abraham Lincoln, 1863

"The white man's happiness cannot be purchased by the black man's misery."
—Frederick Douglass, 1849

Critical Thinking

Explaining What political reasons did Lincoln have for issuing the Emancipation Proclamation?

The Battle of Antietam

Once in Maryland, Lee split his army in four parts and instructed them to move in different directions. He hoped to confuse McClellan about the size and destination of his army. A Confederate officer, however, lost his copy of Lee's orders describing this plan. The paper was found by two Union soldiers, who brought it to McClellan.

McClellan did not attack immediately. Lee reassembled his troops, and on September 17, 1862, the two sides met in the **Battle of Antietam** near Sharpsburg, Maryland.

About 6,000 soldiers were killed. About 17,000 more were badly wounded. It was the deadliest single day of fighting during the war. Antietam was an important victory for the Union. Because of the great losses, Lee chose to retreat to Virginia after the fighting. At least for the time being, his strategy of invading the North had failed. The Union could breathe a little more easily.

Reading Check **Summarizing** What was the outcome of the Battle of Antietam?

The Emancipation Proclamation

Main Idea Lincoln's Emancipation Proclamation had an enormous effect in America and abroad.

History and You How do you make difficult decisions? Read to learn about the debate over the war's purpose and how Lincoln eventually settled on a course of action.

At first, Abraham Lincoln cast the Civil War as a battle for the Union rather than as a fight against slavery. As the conflict progressed, however, Lincoln changed the way he thought about slavery and its role in the war.

The Debate

Lincoln hated slavery, yet he was reluctant to make the Civil War a battle to end it. He feared that many Union supporters would strongly oppose such a decision. At the beginning of the war, Lincoln hesitated to move against slavery because of the border states.

Even many Northerners who disapproved of slavery were not eager to risk their lives to end it. Other Americans held a different opinion, however.

From the start of the war, abolitionists, including orator **Frederick Douglass** and newspaper editor Horace Greeley, urged Lincoln to make the war a fight to end slavery. These Northerners made several arguments to support their position. First, they argued, slavery was a moral wrong that needed to be abolished. Second, they pointed out that slavery was the root of the divisions between North and South. Therefore, the nation could never be fully restored if slavery continued.

Finally, Douglass and others brought up the issue of foreign policy. Britain and France each sympathized with the South for economic reasons. Southern leaders were trying to persuade Britain and France to recognize the Confederacy's independence.

Public opinion in England and France was strongly antislavery. By casting the war as a fight for freedom, Douglass pointed out, Lincoln would make Britain and France less willing to support the South. That, in turn, would help the Union cause.

Lincoln Decides

Lincoln knew that the Constitution did not give him the power to end slavery. The Constitution did, however, give him the power to take property from an enemy in wartime—and, by law, enslaved people were property. On September 22, 1862, soon after the North's victory at Antietam, Lincoln announced that he would issue the **Emancipation Proclamation**—a decree freeing all enslaved people in rebel territory on January 1, 1863.

Effects of the Proclamation

The Emancipation Proclamation did not actually free a single enslaved person. The proclamation applied only to enslaved people in areas held by the Confederacy. There Lincoln had no power to enforce the new policy.

The proclamation had an important **impact** in America, however. By issuing the Emancipation Proclamation, the government declared slavery to be wrong. If the Union won the war, slavery would be banned forever.

✓ **Reading Check** **Summarizing** Why did abolitionists believe that Lincoln should make the end of slavery a goal of the war?

Section 2 Review

History ONLINE
Study Central™ To review this section, go to glencoe.com.

Vocabulary

1. Use each of these terms in a sentence that will help explain its meaning: abandon, tributary, ironclad, casualty, impact.

Main Ideas

2. **Analyzing** What factors helped the Confederates win the First Battle of Bull Run?

3. **Summarizing** What was the final outcome of the Battle of Shiloh?

4. **Explaining** What did the Emancipation Proclamation state?

Critical Thinking

5. **Analyzing** Why was controlling the Mississippi River vital to the North and the South? Explain your answer in a diagram like the one shown here.

○—(Control of the Mississippi)—○

6. **Evaluating** Which of Frederick Douglass's arguments for making the abolition of slavery an aim of the war do you find most convincing? Why?

7. **Expository Writing** You read about General Lee's lost battle orders. Write a short paragraph explaining the role of chance and error in this discovery, as well as General McClellan's use of the information.

Answer the
8. **Essential Question**
Why did neither the Union nor the Confederacy gain a strong advantage during the early years of the war?

America's LITERATURE

Meet the Author

Stephen Crane (1871–1900) had never seen a battlefield when he wrote *The Red Badge of Courage,* which he based on accounts of the Confederate victory at Chancellorsville. Even so, he described the experience of war so realistically that even combat veterans admired his work.

Building Background

The American novelist Stephen Crane, who created the most famous depiction of Civil War combat in his 1895 novel *The Red Badge of Courage,* did not describe warfare in traditional, heroic terms. Instead, he tried to present an objective, almost scientific examination of the effect of battle on individuals. As you read this excerpt from *The Red Badge of Courage,* be aware of how Crane creates an effect of realism.

Vocabulary

careering speeding

exasperation extreme irritation

impotency powerlessness

imprecations curses

pummeling beating

exultant very joyful

THE RED BADGE OF COURAGE

Stephen Crane

He was at a task. He was like a carpenter who has made many boxes, making still another box, only there was furious haste in his movements. He, in his thought, was **careering** off in other places, even as the carpenter who as he works whistles and thinks of his friend or his enemy, his home or a saloon. And these jolted dreams were never perfect to him afterward, but remained a mass of blurred shapes.

Presently he began to feel the effects of the war atmosphere—a blistering sweat, a sensation that his eyeballs were about to crack like hot stones. A burning roar filled his ears.

Following this came a red rage. He developed the acute **exasperation** of a pestered animal, a well-meaning cow worried by dogs. He had a mad feeling against his rifle, which could only be used against one life at a time. He wished to rush forward and strangle with his fingers. He craved a power that would enable him to make a world-sweeping gesture and brush all back. His **impotency** appeared to him, and made his rage into that of a driven beast.

A burning roar filled his ears.

Buried in the smoke of many rifles his anger was directed not so much against the men whom he knew were rushing toward him as against the swirling battle phantoms which were choking him, stuffing their smoke robes down his parched throat. He fought frantically for respite for his senses, for air, as a babe being smothered attacks the deadly blankets.

There was a blare of heated rage mingled with a certain expression of intentness on all faces. Many of the men were making low-toned noises with their mouths, and these subdued cheers, snarls, **imprecations,** prayers, made a wild, barbaric song that went as an undercurrent of sound, strange and chantlike with the resounding chords of the war march. The man at the youth's elbow was babbling. In it there was something soft and tender like the monologue of a babe. . . .

The lieutenant of the youth's company had encountered a soldier who had fled screaming at the first volley of his comrades. Behind the lines these two were acting a little isolated scene. The man was blubbering and staring with sheeplike eyes at the lieutenant, who had seized him by the collar and was **pummeling** him. He drove him back into the ranks with many blows. The soldier went mechanically, dully, with his animal-like eyes upon the officer. Perhaps there was to him a divinity expressed in the voice of the other— stern, hard, with no reflection of fear in it. He tried to reload his gun, but his shaking hands prevented. The lieutenant was obliged to assist him.

The men dropped here and there like bundles. The captain of the youth's company had been killed in an early part of the action. His body lay stretched out in the position of a tired man resting, but upon his face there was an astonished and sorrowful look, as if he thought some friend had done him an ill turn. . . .

At last an **exultant** yell went along the quivering line. The firing dwindled from an uproar to a last vindictive popping. As the smoke slowly eddied away, the youth saw that the charge had been repulsed. The enemy were scattered into reluctant groups. He saw a man climb to the top of the fence, straddle the rail, and fire a parting shot. The waves had receded, leaving bits of dark *débris* upon the ground.

Analyzing Literature

1. **Respond** What surprised you most about Stephen Crane's description of combat?

2. **Recall and Interpret**
   (a) What is the "dark *débris*" left on the battlefield?
   (b) What is the effect of using this phrase?

3. **Evaluate and Connect**
   (a) In your opinion, which details in this passage contribute most powerfully to the effect of realism Crane was striving to create?
   (b) What conclusions can you draw from Crane's depiction of battle?

Section 3 — Life During the War

Essential Question ◄
What social, political, and economic changes resulted from the war?

Reading Guide

Content Vocabulary
habeas corpus *(p. 495)*
draft *(p. 496)*
bounty *(p. 496)*
greenback *(p. 497)*
inflation *(p. 497)*

Academic Vocabulary
distribute *(p. 493)*   substitute *(p. 496)*

Key People and Events
Mary Edwards Walker *(p. 492)*
Dorothea Dix *(p. 492)*
Clara Barton *(p. 492)*
Sally Tompkins *(p. 492)*
bread riots *(p. 494)*

Reading Strategy
Taking Notes As you read the section, complete a diagram like the one below by describing three ways that women in the North and the South contributed to the war effort.

Contributions

NEW YORK STANDARDS
The American Journey

U6.II.1 To understand the development and progress of the Civil War

U6.II.4 To describe the relationships between people and environments and the connections between people and places

U6.II.5 To identify and collect economic information related to the Civil War from standard reference works, newspapers, periodicals, computer databases, textbooks and other primary and secondary sources

American Diary

Drummer boy Delavan Miller, who served in a New York Regiment, recalls: "The day after a battle is always a sad one in a regiment. Men search for missing comrades and some are found cold in death who were full of life the day before. No jests are spoken. The terribleness of war has been forcibly impressed on all participants."

—from Drum Taps in Dixie

Men with the 36th Pennsylvania Infantry Regiment drill at their winter quarters near Langley, Virginia.

A Different Way of Life

Main Idea The Civil War affected civilians as well as soldiers.

History and You How does war change the everyday life of citizens? Read on to find out how Americans tried to adjust to wartime conditions.

Thirteen-year-old Delavan Miller served as a drummer for a New York regiment. He recalls that:

PRIMARY SOURCE

"The great majority of the men really felt that the war would be ended before we had a chance to take a hand in. I may say that the drummer boys, full of young red blood, were as eager for [battle] as the older men, but most of us had got enough of war before we reached Appomattox."

—from *Drum Taps in Dixie*

Life at Home

When the Civil War began, Miller, like many other teenagers, left everything that was familiar to him to serve in the military. This meant leaving family, friends, and school.

Almost everyone who stayed home was touched in some way by the war. Only about one-half of the 12 million school-age children attended school. Many of those who did not worked to help support their families. Schools closed during the war in some areas, especially those near the scenes of battles and skirmishes. Many schools and churches served as hospitals for the wounded.

Shortages in the South

Although the war affected everyone, life in the South changed most dramatically. Both armies spent most of their time on Southern soil, and the South therefore suffered the greatest destruction. Southerners who lived in the paths of marching armies lost crops and homes. Thousands became refugees, and even those who lived outside the war zones suffered. As one observer noted, the South depended on the outside world "for everything from a hairpin to a toothpick, and from a cradle to a coffin." As the war dragged on, shortages of food, supplies, and even household items became commonplace.

Reading Check **Explaining** What problems did the Southern people face during the war?

If You Were There — Drummer Boys in the Civil War

Duties and Tasks At 13, you join the army and train as a drummer. Your day begins at 5 A.M. Your drums call the soldiers to meals, roll call, drills, bed, and lights out. You also do chores for officers and surgeons. Your meals, when you can eat, are usually plain biscuits called hardtack and barely cooked bacon.

◄ "Drummer" Jackson served with an African American regiment.

Critical Thinking

Making Inferences What is your daily routine like? How do you think you would have handled the life of a drummer?

New Roles for Women

Main Idea Many Northern and Southern women took on new responsibilities during the war.

History and You Think of ways that your family would be affected by a war in your backyard. Read to learn the many ways families were affected by the Civil War.

. . . .

Against the advice of family and friends, Kate Cumming, a young woman from Mobile, Alabama, left home to begin a career as a nurse with the Confederate Army of the Mississippi. Cumming was one of the many women whose lives changed greatly because of the Civil War.

In both the North and the South, women kept the farms and factories going. They ran offices, taught school, and kept government records. Women suffered the stress of having husbands away at war and the pain of losing family members. They scrimped and saved to make do without many things they were used to, and they prayed to keep their families together.

Treating the Sick and Wounded

In the Civil War, for the first time, thousands of women served as nurses. At first many doctors did not want women nurses, saying that women were too delicate for the grisly work required on the battlefields. Men thought of nursing as work for males and believed it was improper for women to tend the bodies of unknown men.

Strong-minded women disregarded these objections. **Mary Edwards Walker** became the first woman army surgeon and later received the Congressional Medal of Honor. **Dorothea Dix** convinced officials to let women work as nurses and recruited large numbers of women to serve. Another Northerner, **Clara Barton,** became famous for her work with wounded soldiers. In the South, **Sally Tompkins** established a hospital for soldiers in Richmond, Virginia.

Kate Cumming, who nursed the wounded in Corinth after the Battle of Shiloh, wrote, "Nothing that I had ever heard or read had given me the faintest idea of the horrors witnessed here."

Primary Source / Women in the War

New Roles Women filled many roles during the Civil War. Many offered their services as nurses. A few were spies, and as many as 400 disguised themselves as men to serve as Union or Confederate soldiers. They cut their hair, donned men's clothing, and changed their names to fight alongside men in battle. Many were following brothers or husbands to war, but some wanted to fight because they believed in the cause.

"Francis Clailin" ▶

Frances Louisa Clayton changed her name to Francis Clailin and enlisted as a Union soldier to be with her husband. Like the woman described below, Clayton's identity was revealed in a hospital.

"Maybe she would have remained undiscovered for a long time if she hadn't fainted. She was given a warm bath which gave the secret away."

Nurse in field hospital ▼

Frances Clayton ▶

Spies

Some women were spies. Rose O'Neal Greenhow entertained Union leaders in Washington, D.C. She gathered information about Union plans that she passed to the South. Greenhow eventually was caught, convicted of treason, and exiled. Belle Boyd, of Front Royal, Virginia, informed Confederate generals of Union army movements in the Shenandoah Valley.

Some women disguised themselves as men and became soldiers. Loretta Janeta Velázquez fought for the South at the First Battle of Bull Run and at the Battle of Shiloh. Later she became a Confederate spy.

Harriet Tubman, an important "conductor" on the Underground Railroad, also served as a spy and scout for the Union. In 1863 Tubman led a mission that freed hundreds of enslaved people and disrupted southern supply lines.

Reading Check **Making Inferences** How do you think women felt about how the war changed their lives?

Elizabeth Van Lew lived in Richmond and secretly sent information about Confederate activities to President Lincoln.

"For my loyalty to my country I have two beautiful names— here I am called 'Traitor,' farther North a 'Spy.'"

Elizabeth Van Lew ▲

Critical Thinking

Analyzing Did the Civil War change the traditional roles of women? How?

Prison Camps and Field Hospitals

Main Idea When Americans went to war, most were not prepared for the horrors of battle.

History and You What goes through the mind of a doctor or nurse in the middle of battle? Read to learn about battlefield medicine.

After the terror on the battlefield, many men suffered the agony of their wounds. Still others faced the humiliation and suffering of being taken prisoner.

In the Hands of the Enemy

Throughout the war, each side treated its enemy soldiers with a mixture of sympathy and hostility. At first, the two sides exchanged prisoners. However, when each realized that the men simply returned to fight again, they set up prison camps. Prisoners were generally allowed to keep their blanket and a cup or canteen when they were captured. These few provisions were all they had during their imprisonment. Food shortages also added to the suffering. Volunteers **distributed,** or gave out, bread and soup among the wounded, but in the prisons there was little or nothing to eat.

Andersonville prison, in Georgia, was opened in early 1864. It was built to hold 10,000 prisoners, but by August, 33,000 were crammed into it. The men slept in shallow holes dug in the ground and daily received a teaspoon of salt, three tablespoons of beans, and eight ounces of cornmeal. They drank and cooked with water from a stream that also served as a sewer. Almost 13,000 Union prisoners died there, mostly from disease.

The Union prison in Elmira, New York, was no better. Captured soldiers from the sunny South suffered through the winter months without blankets and warm clothes. The hospital was in a flooded basement, and a pond within the compound served as both toilet and garbage dump. Almost one quarter of all prisoners at Elmira died.

Field Hospitals

Surgeons traveled with the troops and set up hospitals near battlefields. There, with bullets and cannonballs flying past their heads, they bandaged wounds and amputated limbs. A nurse recalls:

PRIMARY SOURCE

"We have to walk, and when we give the men anything kneel, in blood and water; but we think nothing of it."
—from Kate: The Journal of a Confederate Nurse

The war produced many casualties, and doctors struggled to tend to the wounded. Disease was a constant threat, and some regiments lost half their men to illness before ever going into battle. Crowded together in army camps and drinking from unsanitary water supplies, many soldiers became sick. Smallpox, when it erupted, could be deadly, as could a number of other diseases, including dysentery, typhoid, and pneumonia.

Reading Check Comparing and Contrasting How were the prison camps at Andersonville and Elmira alike, and how were they different?

Political and Economic Change

Main Idea The Civil War led to political change and strained the economies of the North and the South.

History and You Can you think of a time when you disagreed with or opposed something? Did you take action? Read to learn why and how people opposed the Civil War, and how Presidents Lincoln and Davis responded.

Throughout the Civil War, numerous smaller "civil wars" raged in the North and the South.

In the South

Many Southerners opposed the war in the first place. After two years, the war had taken huge amounts of food, materials, and money, and shortages were widespread.

Bread riots erupted throughout the South as hungry people took to the streets. In Richmond, a mob, mostly made of women and

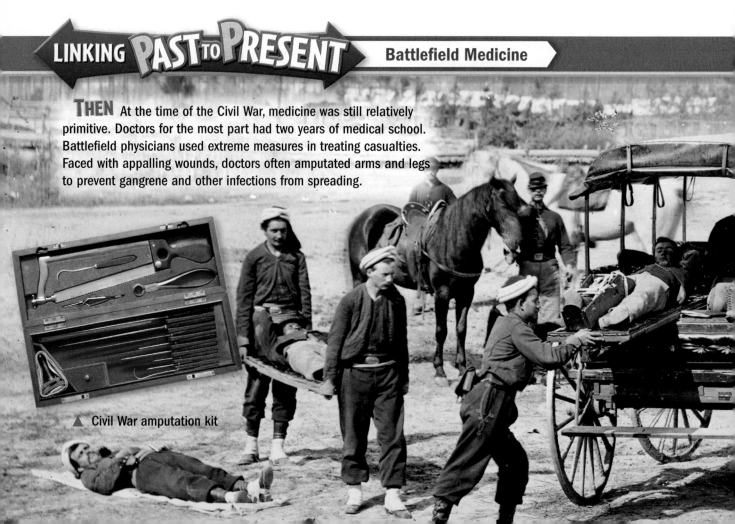

LINKING PAST TO PRESENT — Battlefield Medicine

THEN At the time of the Civil War, medicine was still relatively primitive. Doctors for the most part had two years of medical school. Battlefield physicians used extreme measures in treating casualties. Faced with appalling wounds, doctors often amputated arms and legs to prevent gangrene and other infections from spreading.

▲ Civil War amputation kit

African Americans in the War

Main Idea African Americans showed courage and skill as soldiers in the Union army.

History and You What does it mean to act bravely? Read to learn about the 54th Massachusetts regiment and the battle for Fort Wagner.

At first, both the North and the South barred African Americans from serving in their armies. As time passed, the North relaxed its rules.

In the South

African Americans made up more than 30 percent of the Southern population, but Confederate leaders never seriously considered allowing them to enlist. Confederate leaders feared that African American soldiers, once armed, would attack their fellow troops or even begin a general revolt. The Confederates felt that the advantage of having more soldiers in their army did not justify this risk.

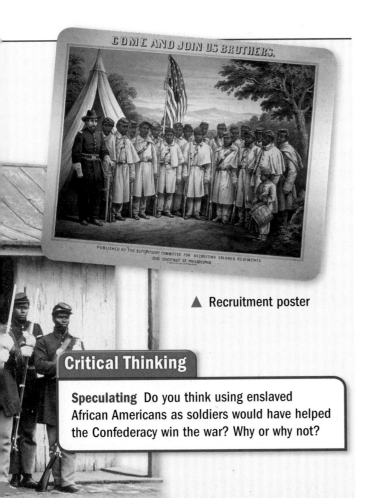

▲ Recruitment poster

Critical Thinking

Speculating Do you think using enslaved African Americans as soldiers would have helped the Confederacy win the war? Why or why not?

History ONLINE
Student Web Activity Visit glencoe.com and complete the Chapter 16 Web Activity about African Americans in the war.

In the North

President Lincoln at first resisted appeals to enlist African Americans in the Union army. He feared that such a policy would be resented in the border states. By 1862, though, it was evident that the North needed more soldiers, and many Union African Americans were eager to fight. As a result, Congress decided to allow the formation of all-African American regiments.

These new soldiers were in a tough position. Many white regiments from the North doubted their fighting ability. Others resented their presence. Many Southern troops hated the African American soldiers and often focused their fiercest gunfire on African American Northern regiments.

Still, African Americans joined. By the end of the war, they comprised about 10 percent of the Union army. Some were freed people from the North; others were runaway enslaved African Americans from the South. These men fought hard and effectively, too. As one white Union officer wrote about an all-African American Kansas regiment:

PRIMARY SOURCE

"They make better soldiers in every respect than any troops I have ever had under my command."
—Union general James G. Blunt

The 54th Massachusetts

The best-known African American regiment was the **54th Massachusetts.** In 1863 this regiment took part in an assault on Fort Wagner in South Carolina. The 54th served in the front lines of this battle. Confederate gunfire battered the men, causing nearly 300 casualties in this regiment alone. **Nevertheless,** the soldiers bravely fought on. Though the Union could not capture the fort, the 54th became famous for the courage and sacrifice of its members.

✓ **Reading Check** Comparing and Contrasting How were Union and Confederate policies regarding African American soldiers alike and different?

YOU DECIDE

Should Lee Have Invaded the North?

The war was fought in Southern territory for the most part. Lee's first invasion was turned back at Antietam. In 1863 he tried again.

The Alternatives

Play it safe

Should the South continue its defensive strategy?

Be bold

Should Lee launch a second invasion of the North?

Considering the Consequences

If the invasion fails

- The Confederacy makes no further attempt to invade the North.
- The tide of war turns in favor of the North.

If the invasion succeeds

- The Confederacy likely gains support from Europe.
- Union antiwar feeling grows.

The Decision

Could Lee's forces conquer the army of the Potomac on its own soil? Confident after the brilliant victory at Chancellorsville, Lee decided to invade the North.

The Results

- Lee's army in northern Virginia is defeated.
- The Confederacy makes no further attempt to invade the North.
- The tide of war turns in favor of the North.

DBQ Document-Based Questions

1. **Analyzing** In your opinion, did Lee have valid reasons for invading the North?

2. **Explaining** What do you think was the best reason for not invading the North?

The Tide of War Turns

Main Idea The Battle of Gettysburg marked a turn in the war as the Union forces defeated the Confederates.

History and You Have you ever made a decision that seemed right at the time but turned out to be disastrous? Read to learn what happened when General Lee decided to invade the North.

In spring of 1863, the South had the upper hand, but that was soon to change. The Confederate victory at Chancellorsville ruined Union plans for attacking Richmond. Robert E. Lee, emboldened by his victories, decided to take the war into the North. A win there might impress France and Britain.

The South's strategy recalled that of the colonies in the Revolutionary War—though far outnumbered, they were aided by France and had won. Now, France and Britain missed the goods—especially cotton—they were accustomed to buying from Southern planters. If the Confederates appeared to be winning, those nations might help.

The Battle of Gettysburg

In July 1863, a small town in southern Pennsylvania became the site of one of the most decisive battles in the Civil War. Gettysburg was not a capital, a strategic port, or the location of an important fort. That such serious fighting took place there was almost an accident.

The Confederates entered the town for much-needed supplies. General Lee hoped to avoid fighting troops in an unfamiliar area. However, the two sides **encountered** one another. When Lee's armies crawled out of Gettysburg four grueling days later, it was after sustaining 25,000 casualties. The Union—the victor—suffered the loss of 23,000.

The battle started at 5:30 A.M. on July 1. Outnumbered, Union troops retreated to a section of high ground called Cemetery Ridge. Reinforcements for both sides arrived, and on the second day of fighting, Southern generals tried to dislodge Union forces from hills named Round Top and Little Round Top. However, after furious fighting, Union forces under the command of General George Meade held their positions.

That night, Meade made the decision not to retreat. The next day, Lee also made an important decision. He ordered an attack designed to "create a panic and virtually destroy the [Union] army."

The Confederates started by firing nearly 140 cannons at the Union lines. Then, under the leadership of General George Pickett, thousands of Confederate troops attacked the Union's center position at Cemetery Ridge. Putting themselves directly in the way of musket and artillery fire, they advanced across open land.

At first, it seemed that **Pickett's Charge** might work—the Confederates broke the first line of Union defense. In the end, however, three-quarters of those who started the attack lay dead or wounded on the ground. Lee later wrote:

PRIMARY SOURCE

"The army did all it could. I fear I required of it impossibilities."

—from *Memoirs of Robert E. Lee*

Gettysburg put an end to one goal of Confederate foreign policy: gaining help from Britain and France. The South hoped to receive from the British two ironclads that would be used to sweep Union shipping from the Atlantic. However, in October 1863, the British government decided not to release the ships.

The Vicksburg Siege

On July 4, the day that Lee retreated from Gettysburg, the Confederacy suffered another major military blow. The important river city of Vicksburg, Mississippi, fell under the control of Union troops led by Ulysses S. Grant.

The Battle of Gettysburg, Day 3 — NATIONAL GEOGRAPHIC

Pickett's Charge came at the height of the three-day battle. More than 12,000 Confederate troops marched across an open field to attack the Union's center position. The effort ended in disaster.

▲ Today, the Gettysburg battlefield's 1,400 monuments commemorate "the great deeds of valor."

Map legend:
- Confederate troops
- Union troops
- Confederate troop movements

"The sacrifice of life on that blood soaked field . . . was too awful for the heralding of victory, even for our victorious foe."

—George E. Pickett, in a letter to his fiancée

Critical Thinking

Concluding Why did Pickett think that the North did not want to celebrate the victory?

Primary Source

The Gettysburg Address

On November 19, 1863, President Abraham Lincoln gave a short speech at the dedication of a national cemetery on the battlefield of Gettysburg. His simple yet eloquent words expressed his hopes for a nation divided by civil war.

▲ Monument at Gettysburg

Four **score** and seven years ago our fathers brought forth on this continent a new nation, conceived in liberty, and dedicated to the **proposition** that all men are created equal.

> Lincoln is referring to the nation declaring its independence in 1776—87 years before.

Now we are engaged in a great civil war, testing whether that nation, or any nation so conceived and so dedicated, can long **endure.** We are met on a great battlefield of that war. We have come to dedicate a portion of that field as a final resting place for those who here gave their lives that that nation might live. It is altogether fitting and proper that we should do this.

> Union soldiers were fighting to keep the nation (North and South) together.

But, in a larger sense, we can not dedicate—we can not **consecrate**—we can not **hallow**—this ground. The brave men, living and dead, who struggled here, have consecrated it far above our poor power to add or detract. The world will little note nor long remember what we say here, but it can never forget what they did here. It is for us, the living, rather, to be dedicated here to the unfinished work which they who fought here have thus far so nobly advanced. It is rather for us to be here dedicated to the great task remaining before us—that from these honored dead we take increased devotion to that cause for which they gave the last full measure of devotion; that we here highly **resolve** that these dead shall not have died in vain; that this nation, under God, shall have a new birth of freedom; and that government of the people, by the people, for the people, shall not perish from the earth.

> The soldiers who died made the supreme sacrifice. Lincoln believes it is up to those who are still living to carry on their unfinished work.

> The U.S. government was created to serve the people. People are the source of the government's power.

VOCABULARY

score: twenty
proposition (PRAH·puh·ZI·shun): an idea or a belief
endure: to continue or last
consecrate (KAHN·suh·KRAT): to dedicate to a sacred purpose
hallow (HA·LOH): to respect greatly
resolve: to make a firm decision

Critical Thinking

1. **Making Inferences** How is the Civil War going to "test" whether or not the United States can endure?

2. **Interpreting** Why do you think Lincoln thought it was so important to honor those who fought and died at Gettysburg?

3. **Finding the Main Idea** According to Lincoln, why was the war being fought?

Grant first launched his attack in April, surrounding the 30,000 Confederate troops holding Vicksburg. In May, Grant began a **siege** against the town, blockading it to prevent food and supplies from entering. Union gunships on the river supported Grant's 77,000 troops by firing thousands of mortar shells into the city.

During the 47-day siege, both sides suffered heavy casualties. More than 9,000 Confederate and 10,000 Union troops died, many of disease or starvation. Remarkably, fewer than 20 civilians were killed in the siege.

The bad news did not end there for the South, though. A few days later, it lost Port Hudson in Louisiana, its last stronghold on the vital Mississippi River. The Union strategy to split the South in two had succeeded. Arkansas, Louisiana, and Texas were now cut off. In a single month, July 1863, the Civil War reached a major turning point.

Lincoln's Gettysburg Address

On November 19, 1863, Soldiers' National Cemetery was dedicated at Gettysburg. At the ceremony, former governor of Massachusetts Edward Everett delivered a two-hour speech. After him, President Abraham Lincoln spoke for about two minutes. In 272 words, Lincoln was able to honor the soldiers and the cause for which they had fought and died, as well as state his vision for the country.

PRIMARY SOURCE

"These dead shall not have died in vain. . . . Government of the people, by the people, for the people shall not perish from the earth."

—from the Gettysburg Address

Reactions to Lincoln's **Gettysburg Address** in the press were mixed. Everett, along with the *New York Times, Chicago Tribune,* and *Springfield* (Mass.) *Republican,* thought the speech was a success. The *Republican* wrote, "His little speech is a perfect gem; deep in feeling, compact in thought and expression, and tasteful . . . in every word and comma."

Reading Check **Explaining** How do the events of this section demonstrate that the "tide" of war turned?

Section 4 Review

History ONLINE
Study Central™ To review this section, go to glencoe.com.

Vocabulary

1. Define each of these terms in a sentence that will help explain its meaning: entrench, nevertheless, encounter, siege.

Main Ideas

2. Explaining Why was the battle of Chancellorsville important?

3. Contrasting How were African American soldiers treated differently than white soldiers?

4. Explaining In the Gettysburg Address, what did Lincoln say was the duty of "the living" to accomplish?

Critical Thinking

5. Making Inferences Why do you think many leaders called for African Americans to be allowed to fight in the Civil War?

6. Organizing Using a graphic organizer similar to the one below, list the results of the Battle of Gettysburg.

7. Expository Writing Refer to Lincoln's Gettysburg Address in this section. Write an essay discussing Lincoln's ideas on freedom and the importance of saving the Union.

Answer the
8. Essential Question
How did the events at Gettysburg and Vicksburg change the course of the war?

The Civil War **Chapter 16** **505**

Section 5 ★ The War's Final Stages

Essential Question ◄
What events led to the end of the war?

Reading Guide

Content Vocabulary
total war (p. 507)   resistance (p. 509)

Academic Vocabulary
series (p. 507)   interpret (p. 509)

Key People and Events
David Farragut (p. 509)
March to the Sea (p. 510)
Appomattox Court House (p. 512)

Reading Strategy
Taking Notes As you read, take notes on the significance of battles late in the war.

Battle	Importance

NEW YORK STANDARDS
The American Journey

U6.II.1 To understand the development and progress of the Civil War

U6.II.2 To investigate key turning points in the Civil War in New York State and United States history and explain why these events or developments are significant

U6.II.3 To map information about people, places, and environments

American Diary

After Union forces took control of Atlanta on September 2, 1864, General William Sherman ordered the city burned and the citizens to leave. When the mayor of Atlanta pleaded with Sherman to change his mind, Sherman refused. He responded: "War is cruelty, and you cannot refine it. . . . You might as well appeal against the thunderstorm as against these terrible hardships of war."

—*from* Memoirs of General William T. Sherman

Atlanta and many other Southern cities, including Richmond as shown here, suffered large-scale destruction as the war continued.

506

Total War Strikes the South

Main Idea After a long, bloody summer, Union forces captured major Southern strongholds, and as a result, Lincoln won reelection.

History and You Have you ever had a goal that was difficult to reach? Did you have a strategy to reach your goal? Read to learn how Grant and the Union forces executed their plan.

. . . .

General William Sherman's destruction of Atlanta and other areas of the South was part of a deliberate strategy to bring the horrors of war—terror, starvation, violence, and homelessness—to the Southern people. This systematic destruction of an entire land—not just its army—is called **total war.**

Union Strategy

By 1864, Union forces surrounded the South. Union ships blocked the Confederate coast, strangling its export economy and cutting off supplies. The Union controlled the Mississippi River, and the western Confederate states were cut off. A bold plan of attack was needed. General Grant would be the one to draw up such a plan.

Grant in Charge

Ulysses S. Grant was only an average student and a failure as a farmer and businessperson. At soldiering, however, he was brilliant. He chalked up victories at Shiloh and Vicksburg and at another important battle in Chattanooga, Tennessee. In March 1864, President Lincoln put General Grant in charge of all the Union armies.

Grant then devised his plan. He would deliver killing blows from all sides. His armies would move on to Richmond, the Confederate capital. At the same time, William Tecumseh Sherman would lead his troops in attacks across the Deep South.

Grant soon put his strategy into effect. In May and June of 1864, Grant's army of 115,000 men smashed into Lee's 64,000 troops in a **series** of three battles near Richmond, Virginia—the battles of the Wilderness, Spotsylvania Courthouse, and Cold Harbor. Each time Confederate lines held, but each time Grant quickly resumed the attack.

"Whatever happens, there will be no turning back," Grant promised Lincoln. He was determined to march southward, attacking Lee's forces relentlessly until the Confederacy surrendered.

By the Numbers / Costs of the War

The South in Ruins By the end of the war, many Southern roads, railroads, farms, and industrial plants were in ruins.

Millions of Dollars

Union | Confederacy

Physical Destruction: $2,302,000 | $0
Government Expenditures: $1,032,000 | $1,487,000

Source: *EH.Net Encyclopedia*

Critical Thinking

Interpreting Were most battles fought on Union or Confederate soil? How can you tell?

The Wilderness Campaign

In the northeast corner of the Confederacy, about halfway between Washington, D.C., and Richmond, Virginia, lay an area of dense woods called the Wilderness. Here, on May 5, 1864, the six bloodiest weeks of the war began. For two days, the forces of Grant and Lee struggled among a tangle of trees through which they could scarcely see. Said a Union private, "It was a blind and bloody hunt to the death."

Lee had only about 60,000 men to Grant's more than 100,000. Both sides suffered huge casualties. Grant, who lost 17,000 men, cried in his tent at the end of the second day. Meanwhile, brushfires raged through the forest, burning alive 200 wounded men. On the morning of the third day, with no clear winner, Grant moved his forces south toward Richmond.

The next battles were fought at nearby Spotsylvania Courthouse and at Cold Harbor. On June 2, the night before this third battle began, a Union general observed that men were "writing their names and home addresses on slips of paper and pinning them to the backs of their coats" to help people identify their bodies. The war seemed hopeless. Grant, however, was determined. He explained to the White House:

PRIMARY SOURCE

"I propose to fight it out on this line, if it takes all summer."

—Dispatch to Washington, May 11, 1864

Grant's critics in the North called him a "butcher" because of the huge loss of life among his own troops—50,000 in 30 days. Lincoln, however, said, "I can't spare this man. He fights."

People IN HISTORY

Robert E. Lee

General, commander in chief of the Confederate armies

Lee, a brilliant scholar and a daring soldier, was willing to take risks. However, when his orders caused enormous loss of lives, he was filled with sadness. When he finally surrendered, he told his troops he had *"unceasing admiration of your constancy and devotion to your country."*

Abraham Lincoln

Sixteenth president of the United States

Lincoln would not give up. He lost seven elections on the way to winning the presidency. His perseverance helped him stand against all opposition to the war. He believed, *"A house divided against itself cannot stand."* He would see the war through until the country was reunited.

The Petersburg Siege

Continuing his movement south, Grant went on to Petersburg, a railroad center that was vital to the Confederate movement of troops and supplies. If Grant could take Petersburg, then Richmond would be cut off from the rest of the Confederacy. Grant laid siege. The Confederates defended the city, but they could not win. Trains brought food and reinforcements to the Union troops. The Confederates could get neither. For nine long months, however, they held out.

Sherman in Georgia

Meanwhile, William Tecumseh Sherman took off for Georgia. In early July, his troops circled Atlanta. There they faced the brilliant Confederate general, John Hood, whose forces put up major resistance. Sherman laid siege. Finally, on September 1, Hood abandoned the city. The mood in the South was desperate. Mary Chesnut, a Georgian who kept a diary throughout the war, wrote, "There is no hope, but we will try to have no fear."

Farragut at Mobile Bay

The highest-ranking officer in the Union navy was **David Farragut,** the son of a Latino military man. Young David Farragut joined the navy when he was only 12 years old. Now, in August 1864, he was leading a fleet of 18 ships through a narrow channel into Mobile Bay in Alabama. The Confederates had two forts on either side of the channel, and they had mined the waters with torpedoes. Guns were firing from both forts. What was Farragut to do? He gave his famous order, "Damn the torpedoes, full speed ahead!"

Farragut, who was suffering from dizziness, had himself tied to the ship's rigging so he could stay in the battle. His invasion was a success, and the last Southern port east of the Mississippi was blocked.

The Election of 1864

Through most of 1864, opposition to the war in the North grew stronger. A presidential election was coming up in November, and it looked unlikely that Lincoln would win reelection. His loss could mean an end to the war and recognition of the Confederate government as an independent country. Southerners clung to this hope.

After Atlanta fell and Mobile Bay was blocked, Northerners began to believe again that they could win. Lincoln won a second term handsomely—with 55 percent of the popular vote, 212 to 21 electoral votes.

Lincoln interpreted, or explained, his reelection as a clear sign from the voters to end slavery permanently by amending the Constitution. On January 31, 1865, Congress passed the Thirteenth Amendment, which banned slavery in the United States.

Reading Check Summarizing What was the Union strategy in 1864, and what were the results?

Ulysses S. Grant

General of the United States Army and eighteenth president of the United States

Grant was a fearless soldier and an expert horseman at a time when soldiers rode horses in battle. Grant's strategy seemed ruthless at times, but he said, *"I have never advocated [war] except as a means of peace."*

CRITICAL Thinking

1. **Synthesizing** What characteristics do you think these three men shared?

2. **Describing** Select a quote from one of the men described. What does the quote reveal about that person?

The Final Battles, 1864–1865 NATIONAL GEOGRAPHIC

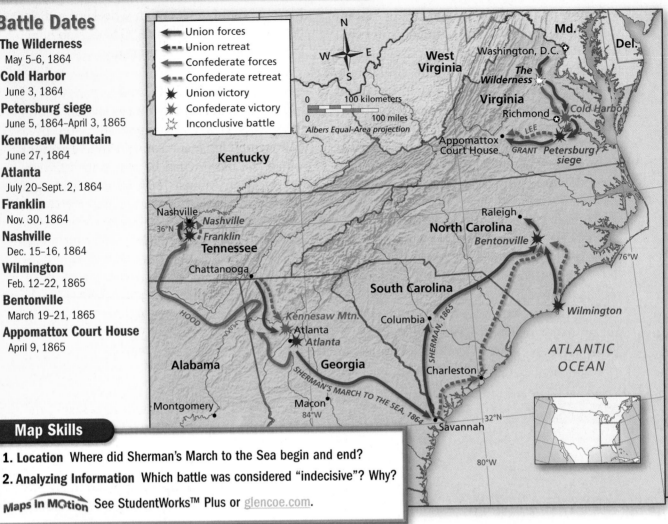

Battle Dates

The Wilderness
May 5–6, 1864

Cold Harbor
June 3, 1864

Petersburg siege
June 5, 1864–April 3, 1865

Kennesaw Mountain
June 27, 1864

Atlanta
July 20–Sept. 2, 1864

Franklin
Nov. 30, 1864

Nashville
Dec. 15–16, 1864

Wilmington
Feb. 12–22, 1865

Bentonville
March 19–21, 1865

Appomattox Court House
April 9, 1865

Map Skills

1. **Location** Where did Sherman's March to the Sea begin and end?
2. **Analyzing Information** Which battle was considered "indecisive"? Why?

Maps In Motion See StudentWorks™ Plus or glencoe.com.

The War's End

Main Idea After four years of fighting against unfavorable odds, the South finally surrendered.

History and You How would you treat an enemy who said, "I give up"?

From the beginning of the war, the Union army wanted to capture the Confederate capital. When Grant finally drove Lee's army out of Petersburg, Virginia, Jefferson Davis knew that Richmond was doomed.

Sherman's March to the Sea

The last months of the war saw the Union determined to break the will of the South. Sherman and his men became destroyers.

Before Sherman's army left Atlanta in November, it burned much of this beautiful city. From Atlanta, Sherman's troops burned cities and farmlands as they marched across Georgia to the Atlantic coast. This trail of destruction is known as Sherman's **March to the Sea.**

Sherman continued his path of destruction through the Carolinas to join Grant's forces near Richmond. Union troops took what food they needed, tore up railroad lines and fields, and killed livestock in an effort to destroy anything that was useful to the South.

White Southerners deplored Sherman's march, but thousands of African Americans left their plantations to follow the protection of his army. For them, this was a march to freedom.

The Union Advances

1861

Early Stages Confederate troops won most of the battles in the first year of the Civil War.

1863

Union Gains Union control of the Mississippi River cut off Texas and Arkansas, the South's leading food producers, from the Confederacy.

1865

Final Stages By 1865, the Union controlled large parts of the Confederacy.

By the Numbers

Lives Lost More lives were lost in the Civil War than in any other major American conflict. Deadly weapons, poor medical practices, infection, and disease all contributed.

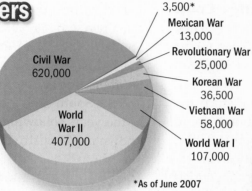

Civil War 620,000
World War II 407,000
Iraqi War 3,500*
Mexican War 13,000
Revolutionary War 25,000
Korean War 36,500
Vietnam War 58,000
World War I 107,000

*As of June 2007

Sources: *United States Civil War Center, For the Common Defense*

Unknown Soldiers A gravestone in Gettysburg Cemetery commemorates the loss of 425 Civil War soldiers who were never identified.

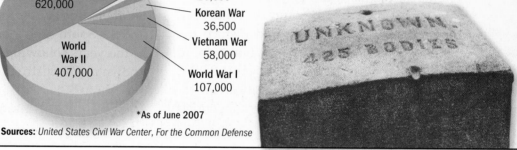

The Fall of Richmond

Meanwhile, Grant continued the siege of Petersburg. Lee and his troops defended the town, but sickness, casualties, and desertion weakened them. Finally, on April 2, 1865, the Confederate lines broke and Lee withdrew.

Word of Lee's retreat came to the Confederate president. As the Union army marched toward Richmond, Davis and his cabinet gathered documents, gave orders that bridges and weapons useful to the enemy be set on fire, and fled the city. An observer wrote:

PRIMARY SOURCE

"The trains came and went, wagons, vehicles, and horsemen rumbled and dashed to and fro.... As night came on ... rioting and robbing took place."
—from *Battles and Leaders of the Civil War*

The armory, with its stores of ammunition, exploded. Boom after boom rang through the city, and fires raged out of control.

Two days later, President Lincoln and his son Tad arrived to tour the fallen capital. Said Lincoln, "Thank God I have lived to see this. It seems to me that I have been dreaming a horrid nightmare for four years, and now the nightmare is over."

Joyful African Americans followed Lincoln everywhere, singing, laughing, and reaching out to touch him. When one man knelt down to thank him, Lincoln replied, "Don't kneel to me. You must kneel to God only, and thank Him for your freedom."

At the Confederate president's house, Lincoln sat in a chair in Davis's office and "looked far off with a dreamy expression."

At Libby Prison, where the Union held Confederate prisoners of war, Lincoln was asked what to do with the prisoners and replied, "If I were in your place, I'd let 'em up easy, let 'em up easy."

Surrender at Appomattox

The formal end of the war came a few days later, on April 9, 1865. Two days earlier, Grant asked Lee to surrender, writing, "The result of last week must convince you of the hopelessness of further resistance."

Yet Lee believed he must fight on. However, when the Union captured the train carrying food to his troops and Lee was completely surrounded, he knew it was over.

In the little town of **Appomattox Court House,** Virginia, Grant met with Lee. They shook hands and talked a little. Then Grant offered his terms. Lee's soldiers could keep their small firearms, the officers could keep their horses, and no one would disturb the soldiers as they made their way home. In an act of generosity, Grant also gave 25,000 rations to feed Lee's troops. Dignity and compassion were the order of the day that ended America's deadliest war.

The Toll of War

More lives were lost in the Civil War than in any other conflict in American history. More than 600,000 soldiers died. The war cost billions of dollars. In the South, cities and farmlands were destroyed, and it would take years and a massive national effort to rebuild.

The war had other consequences as well. The North's victory saved the Union. The federal government was strengthened and was now clearly more powerful than the states. Finally, the war freed millions of African Americans. The end of slavery, however, did not solve the problems that the newly freed African Americans were to face.

Following the war, many questions remained. No one yet knew how to bring the Southern states back into the Union, nor what the status of African Americans would be in Southern society. Americans from the North and the South tried to answer these questions in the years following the Civil War—an era known as Reconstruction.

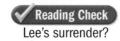 **Reading Check** **Evaluating** What events led to Lee's surrender?

Section 5 Review

History ONLINE
Study Central™ To review this section, go to glencoe.com.

Vocabulary

1. Define each of the following terms, and use them in a paragraph about the last year of the Civil War: total war, series resistance, interpret.

Main Ideas

2. **Explaining** How did events on the battlefield affect Lincoln's reelection?

3. **Describing** Why did Sherman burn and destroy the South's land?

4. **Explaining** What were Grant's terms of surrender at Appomattox Court House?

Critical Thinking

5. **Analyzing** Complete a graphic organizer similar to the one below to explain the effects of the Civil War on the nation.

6. **Descriptive Writing** Take on the role of a reporter living in Georgia during Sherman's March to the Sea. Write a brief article describing the Union's actions and their effects on the people living there.

7. **Answer the Essential Question** What events led to the end of the war?

1861

Feb. Southern states form the Confederacy

Apr. Union surrenders Fort Sumter

June Four border states stay in the Union

July First major battle fought at Bull Run in Virginia

1862

Mar. The *Monitor* and the *Virginia* fight the first battle between ironclad ships

Virginia

Apr. Farragut's naval forces capture New Orleans

Sept. Antietam is the first major battle on Northern soil

1863

Jan. Lincoln issues Emancipation Proclamation

July Lee's invasion of the North turned back at Gettysburg

July Fall of Vicksburg results in Union control of the Mississippi River

1864

Mar. General Ulysses Grant assumes command of all Union armies

Nov. Lincoln reelected to second term

1865

Feb. Sherman's forces march through the Carolinas

Apr. 2 Lee evacuates Richmond; Union forces capture capital

Apr. 9 Surrender at Appomattox Court House

Apr. 14 Lincoln is assassinated

▲ A Union soldier with his family in a Washington, D.C., camp in 1862

STUDY TO GO Study anywhere, anytime! Download quizzes and flash cards to your PDA from glencoe.com.

GRADE 8 INTERMEDIATE TEST PRACTICE

TEST-TAKING TIP

Answer the questions you know first and go back to those for which you need more time.

Reviewing Main Ideas

Directions: Choose the best answer for each of the following questions.

1 What was one advantage the Southern states had during the Civil War?

(1) They received military support from Britain and France.

(2) Many battles occurred on lands with which Southerners were more familiar.

(3) The largest weapons factories were located in the South.

(4) Most people in the country agreed with the position of the Southern states.

2 By gaining control of the Mississippi and Tennessee Rivers, what was the Union able to do?

(1) capture Fort Sumter

(2) force the Confederacy to surrender

(3) split the Confederacy

(4) defeat the Confederate forces at Gettysburg

3 During the war, the economy of the South

(1) was severely strained from the blockade instituted by the North and the destruction of Southern land and property.

(2) remained unchanged because most of the battles took place on Northern soil.

(3) was strengthened due to inflation.

(4) was strengthened because bounties were paid to army recruits.

4 Which Union general proved to be most effective?

(1) General McClellan   **(3)** General Burnside

(2) General Grant   **(4)** General Hooker

Short-Answer Question

Directions: Base your answer to question 5 on the excerpt below and on your knowledge of social studies.

> With malice toward none, with charity for all, with firmness in the right as God gives us to see the right, let us strive on to finish the work we are in, to bind up the nation's wounds, to care for him who shall have borne the battle and for his widow and his orphan—to do all which may achieve and cherish a just and lasting peace among ourselves and with all nations.
>
> —from Abraham Lincoln's second Inaugural Address

5 In his address, Lincoln did not focus on the Union victory in the Civil War. State *two* reasons why this is so.

Review the Essential Questions

6 Essay How did the Civil War affect the North and the South?

To help you write your essay, review your answers to the Essential Questions in the section reviews and the chapter Foldables Study Organizer. Your essay should include:

- the strengths and weaknesses of the two sides;
- the results of early battles;
- social, political, and economic changes;
- how Vicksburg and Gettysburg changed the course of the war; and
- the aftermath of war.

GO ON

History ONLINE

For additional test practice, use **Self-Check Quizzes**–Chapter 16 at glencoe.com.

Document-Based Questions

Directions: Analyze the documents and answer the short-answer questions that follow.

Document 1

In July 1861 Confederate diplomat John Slidell describes one advantage the South holds.

> We shall have the enormous advantage of fighting on our own territory and for our very existence.

Source: James M. McPherson, *Ordeal By Fire*

7 Why would fighting on familiar territory be an advantage?

Document 2

A Union cavalry man taken prisoner describes the conditions of the Andersonville prison.

> July 6. Boiling hot, camp reeking with filth, and no sanitary privileges; men dying off over 140 per day . . . .Disease is here and mowing down good and true men. . . .Bread today and it is so coarse as to do more hurt than good to a majority of the prisoners.

Source: *Eyewitness to America*

8 What was life like for prisoners during the Civil War?

Document 3

The diaries of Mary Chesnut of South Carolina describe life in the South during the Civil War.

> Since we left Chester nothing but solitude, nothing but tall blackened chimneys, to show that any man has trod here before. This is Sherman's track.

Source: Mary Boykin Chesnut, *A Diary From Dixie*

9 What does this excerpt reveal about Sherman's strategy in fighting the South?

Document 4

This political cartoon appeared in an August 1862 edition of *Punch,* a British magazine.

Source: Corbis

10 Based on this cartoon, identify two challenges the Union faced in fighting the war.

Document 5

Frederick Douglass led the movement to allow African American men to enlist.

> Once let the black man get upon his person the brass letters U.S. . . . and a musket on his shoulder and bullets in his pocket, and there is no power on earth which can deny that he has earned the right to citizenship [in the United States].

Source: James M. McPherson, *Battle Cry of Freedom*

11 Based on this document, identify **one** reason Douglass wanted African American men to fight in the war.

12 **Expository Writing** Using the information from the five documents and your knowledge of social studies, write an essay in which you:

- discuss the main goals for the Union and the Confederacy in fighting the Civil War; and

- discuss the effects of the war on soldiers and civilians.

Need Extra Help?												
If you missed questions. . .	1	2	3	4	5	6	7	8	9	10	11	12
Go to page. . .	476	482–483	494–497	500	506–512	472–512	475–476	493	506–510	498–505	501	472–512

Reconstruction and the New South 1865–1896

A teacher and her students in front of the Freedmen's School in North Carolina

  ABRAHAM LINCOLN 1861–1865 **ANDREW JOHNSON 1865–1869**

1867
- Alaska purchased
- First Reconstruction Act passed

★ **1870** Fifteenth Amendment ratified

 ULYSSES S. GRANT 1869–1877

1877 ★ Reconstruction ends

PRESIDENTS

U.S. Events

World Events

1860

1870

★ **1866** First transatlantic cable connects North America to Europe

★ **1868** Meiji era begins in Japan

★ **1871** Bismarck unifies Germany

★ **1874** First major exhibit of impressionist art in Paris

Section 1: Reconstruction Plans

Essential Question How did plans to unify the nation differ after the Civil War?

Section 2: Radicals in Control

Essential Question What were the results of Radical Reconstruction?

Section 3: The South During Reconstruction

Essential Question In what ways did government in the Southern states change during Reconstruction?

Section 4: Change in the South

Essential Question How did the South change politically, economically, and socially when Reconstruction ended?

FOLDABLES
Study Organizer

Organizing Information Make this Foldable to help you summarize what you learn about Reconstruction and the New South.

Step 1 Fold an 11" x 17" piece of paper lengthwise to create a shutterfold.

Step 2 Fold a 3-inch tab along the bottom, and glue or staple the seams to create four pockets.

Step 3 Label the Foldable as shown.

Reading and Writing As you read the chapter, take notes on notecards about key events and issues covered in each section. Use your Foldable to store the cards, and then answer the Essential Questions for each section.

Jane Addams, founder of Hull House ▶

RUTHERFORD B. HAYES 1877–1881

JAMES GARFIELD 1881

CHESTER ARTHUR 1881–1885

GROVER CLEVELAND 1885–1889

★ **1890** Hull House opens in Chicago

BENJAMIN HARRISON 1889–1893

GROVER CLEVELAND 1893–1897

1880 — **1890** — **1900**

★ **1882** Beginning of British occupation of Egypt

★ **1886** First May Day celebration held in Paris

★ **1891** Famine spreads throughout Russia

★ **1896** Ethiopia defeats invading Italians

Section 1 Reconstruction Plans

Essential Question ◄
How did plans to unify the nation differ after the Civil War?

Reading Guide

Content Vocabulary
Reconstruction (p. 519)   amnesty (p. 519)

Academic Vocabulary
radical (p. 520)   adjust (p. 520)

Key People and Events
Ten Percent Plan (p. 519)
Radical Republicans (p. 520)
Thaddeus Stevens (p. 520)
Wade-Davis Bill (p. 520)
Freedmen's Bureau (p. 520)
John Wilkes Booth (p. 521)
Andrew Johnson (p. 521)

Reading Strategy
Taking Notes As you read, use a diagram like the one below to describe each Reconstruction plan.

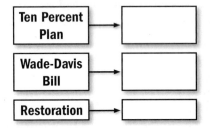

Ten Percent Plan → [ ]

Wade-Davis Bill → [ ]

Restoration → [ ]

NEW YORK STANDARDS
The American Journey

U6.III.1 To understand how the Civil War affected the development of the postwar United States and influenced other countries

U6.III.2 To describe how ordinary people and famous historic figures in the local community, the State, and the United States have advanced fundamental democratic values, beliefs, and traditions expressed in the Declaration of Independence, the New York State and United States constitutions, the Bill of Rights, and other important historic documents

U6.III.4 To value the principles, ideals, and core values of the American democratic system based upon the premises of human dignity, liberty, justice, and equality

American Diary

Major Henry Rathbone tried to seize John Wilkes Booth after Booth shot President Lincoln at Ford's Theater. As Booth leaped over the railing of the presidential box onto the stage, Rathbone cried, "Stop that man." Rathbone later stated: "I then turned to the President. . . . I saw that he was unconscious, and, supposing him mortally wounded, rushed to the door for the purpose of calling medical aid."

—*from* The Assassination of President Lincoln and the Trial of the Conspirators

The funeral train that carried Lincoln's body traveled more than 1,700 miles (2,736 km) and stopped in 10 major cities before arriving in Springfield, Illinois.

The amendment also barred former Confederate leaders from holding national or state office unless pardoned by Congress. The Fourteenth Amendment also excluded Native Americans from citizenship.

Congress declared that Southern states had to ratify the amendment to rejoin the Union. Of the 11 Southern states, only Tennessee ratified it. The refusal of the other Southern states to ratify delayed the amendment's adoption until 1868.

Republican Victory

In the congressional elections of 1866, President Johnson campaigned vigorously against the Radical Republicans. Many Northerners objected to the nasty tone of Johnson's campaign and feared clashes between whites and African Americans. The Republicans won a solid victory, giving Congress the signal to take Reconstruction into its own hands.

Reading Check **Explaining** Why did Johnson consider the civil rights bill unconstitutional?

Radical Reconstruction

Main Idea Radical Republicans were able to put their version of Reconstruction into action.

History and You If you were a member of Congress at this time, what changes would you like to see in a Reconstruction plan? Read to find out how the Radical Republicans shaped Reconstruction.

President Johnson could do little to stop Republicans because they could easily override his vetoes in Congress. Thus began a period known as Radical Reconstruction.

Reconstruction Acts of 1867

The **First Reconstruction Act** passed in 1867 called for the creation of new governments in the 10 Southern states that had not ratified the Fourteenth Amendment. Tennessee, which ratified, kept its government and rejoined the Union.

History ONLINE
Student Web Activity Visit glencoe.com and complete the Chapter 17 Web Activity about Reconstruction.

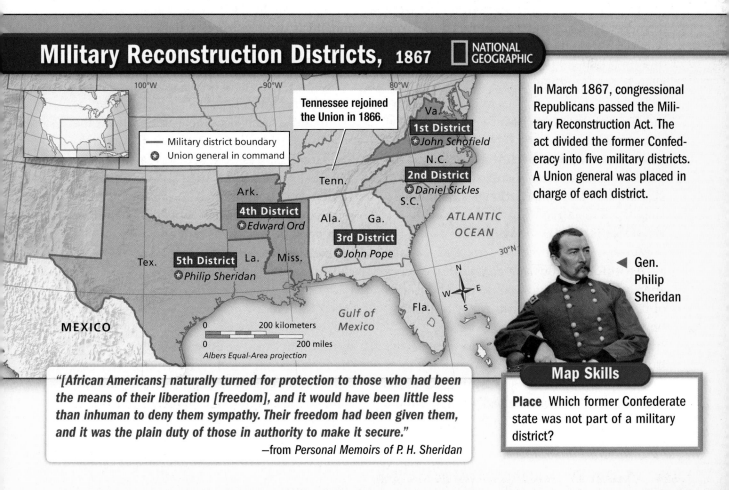

Military Reconstruction Districts, 1867 NATIONAL GEOGRAPHIC

Tennessee rejoined the Union in 1866.

— Military district boundary
● Union general in command

1st District ● John Schofield
2nd District ● Daniel Sickles
3rd District ● John Pope
4th District ● Edward Ord
5th District ● Philip Sheridan

In March 1867, congressional Republicans passed the Military Reconstruction Act. The act divided the former Confederacy into five military districts. A Union general was placed in charge of each district.

◄ Gen. Philip Sheridan

Map Skills

Place Which former Confederate state was not part of a military district?

"[African Americans] naturally turned for protection to those who had been the means of their liberation [freedom], and it would have been little less than inhuman to deny them sympathy. Their freedom had been given them, and it was the plain duty of those in authority to make it secure."
—from *Personal Memoirs of P. H. Sheridan*

Chance & Error in History

What If Lincoln Had Survived?

Abraham Lincoln wanted the South to be treated compassionately when the war ended. The Radicals expected that the new president, Andrew Johnson, would adopt a firm policy toward the South.

Second Inaugural Address, March 1865

"With malice toward none, with charity for all, with firmness in the right as God gives us to see the right, let us strive on to finish the work we are in, to bind up the nation's wounds, to care for him who shall have borne the battle and for his widow and his orphan."

—Abraham Lincoln

◀ Lincoln's funeral procession, Columbus, Ohio

Critical Thinking

1. **Contrasting** Describe the leadership qualities of Abraham Lincoln and Andrew Johnson.
2. **Speculating** How do you think Reconstruction might have been different if Lincoln had not been assassinated? Explain.

◀ President Johnson and the Radicals had little in common, and Johnson had little popular support. Many people thought Johnson was self-righteous, hot-tempered, stubborn, and crude.

The act divided the 10 Southern states into 5 military districts, each run by a military commander until new governments were formed. The act also guaranteed African American men the right to vote in state elections and banned former Confederate leaders from holding political office.

To rejoin the Union, the states had to ratify the Fourteenth Amendment and submit new state constitutions to Congress for approval. A **Second Reconstruction Act** required the military commanders to register voters and prepare for state constitutional conventions.

Readmission of States

Many white Southerners refused to take part in the elections for constitutional conventions and state governments. Thousands of newly registered African American voters, however, voted.

In the elections, Republicans gained control of Southern state governments. By 1868, seven Southern states—Alabama, Arkansas, Florida, Georgia, Louisiana, North Carolina,

and South Carolina—had established new governments and met the requirements for readmission. By 1870, Mississippi, Virginia, and Texas were restored to the Union.

Impeaching the President

Strongly opposed to Radical Reconstruction, President Johnson had the power as commander in chief of the army to direct the actions of the military governors. For this reason, Congress passed a series of laws to limit the president's power, such as the **Tenure of Office Act.** It prohibited the president from removing government officials, including members of his own cabinet, without the Senate's approval.

The conflict between Johnson and the Radicals grew more intense. In August 1867—when Congress was not in session—Johnson **suspended** (removed from office temporarily) Secretary of War **Edwin Stanton** without the Senate's approval. When the Senate met again and refused to approve the suspension, Johnson removed Stanton from office.

Rutherford B. Hayes ▶

Disputed Election of 1876 NATIONAL GEOGRAPHIC

One of Oregon's three electoral votes was in doubt.

Disputed electoral vote

Northern troops still occupied three states.

People living in territories could not vote in national elections.

Critical Thinking

Comparing Which laws are most similar to each other?

Candidate	Electoral Vote	Popular Vote	Political Party
Hayes	185	4,036,572	Republican
Tilden	184	4,284,020	Democrat

The new government would give more aid to the South. Republicans agreed to withdraw all remaining troops from Southern states. Without soldiers to support them, the remaining Republican governments in South Carolina and Louisiana quickly collapsed. The Democrats, in turn, promised to maintain African American rights.

A New Policy

In his Inaugural Address, Hayes declared that what the South needed most was the restoration of "wise, honest, and peaceful local self-government." During a goodwill trip to the South, Hayes announced his intention of letting Southerners handle racial issues. Hayes's message was clear. The federal government would no longer attempt to reshape Southern society. Reconstruction had come to an end.

✓ **Reading Check** **Summarizing** How did the Compromise of 1877 affect Reconstruction?

Change in the South

Main Idea After Reconstruction, the South experienced a political shift and industrial growth.

History and You Do you recall that lack of industry put the South at a disadvantage during the Civil War? Read to learn how Southerners vowed to create a strong industrial "New South."

. . . .

Many Southern whites hated Republicans for their role in the Civil War and in Reconstruction. When Reconstruction ended, power in the South shifted to the Democrats.

Democrats in Control

In some regions, the ruling Democrats were the large landowners and other groups that held power before the Civil War. In many areas, however, new leaders took charge. Among their ranks were merchants, bankers, and other business leaders who supported economic development.

Change in Politics

These Democrats called themselves "Redeemers" because they had "redeemed," or saved, the South from Republican rule. The Redeemers adopted conservative policies, such as lower taxes and reduced government spending. They drastically cut, or even eliminated, many social services started during Reconstruction, including public education. Their one-party rule and conservative policies dominated Southern politics well into the 1900s.

Rise of the "New South"

By the 1880s, forward-looking Southerners were convinced that their region must develop a strong industrial economy. They argued that the South lost the Civil War because its industry did not match the North's. Henry Grady, editor of the *Atlanta Constitution*, headed a group that urged Southerners to "out-Yankee the Yankees" and build a "New South." This "New South" would have industries based on the region's abundant coal, iron, tobacco, cotton, and lumber. Southerners would create this new economy by embracing a spirit of hard work and regional pride.

Industry in the South made dramatic gains in the 1880s. Textile mills sprang up across the South. The American Tobacco Company, developed largely by James Duke of North Carolina, eventually controlled almost all tobacco manufacturing in the nation. By 1890, Southern mills produced nearly 20 percent of the nation's iron and steel. Much of the industry was in Alabama near deposits of iron ore.

Southern industry grew as a result of a cheap and reliable workforce. Most factory workers put in long hours for low wages. A railroad-building boom also aided industrial development. By 1870, the Southern railroad system, which had been destroyed during the war, was largely rebuilt. The miles of rail track more than doubled between 1880 and 1890. Still, the South did not develop an industrial economy as strong as the North's. Agriculture remained the South's main economic activity.

Primary Source / Sharecropping

Denied Land During the Civil War, formerly enslaved African Americans hoped to acquire abandoned or confiscated Confederate lands. The government under President Johnson, however, returned Southern plantations to their former slaveholders.

Formerly enslaved African Americans often ended up working as sharecroppers on land that belonged to their former owners. ▼

Southern laws forced sharecroppers to work the land until they paid off their debts. A system emerged in the South that closely resembled slavery. ▼

Typical sharecropper contract ▶

To secure payment of said rent and supply bill, the said Dawson [the sharecropper] grants unto said Solid South [the landowner] a special privilege and right of pledge on all the products raised on said land, and on all his stock, farming implements, and personal property, and hereby waives in favor of said Solid South the benefit of any and all homestead laws and exemption laws now in force, or which may be in force, in Louisiana, and agrees that all his property shall be seized and sold to pay said rent and supply bill in default of payment thereof as herein agreed. Any violation of this contract shall render the lease void.

Rural Economy

Supporters of the New South hoped to change Southern agriculture as well as industry. Their goal was small, profitable farms raising a variety of crops rather than large plantations devoted to cotton. A different economy emerged, however. Some plantations were broken up, but many large landowners held on to their land. When estates were divided, much of the land went to sharecropping and tenant farming, neither of which was profitable.

Debt also caused problems. Poor farmers used credit to buy supplies. Merchants who sold on credit charged high prices, and farmers' debts rose. To repay debts, farmers grew **cash crops**—crops that could be sold for money. As in the past, the main cash crop was cotton. Too much cotton forced prices down, however. Farmers then had to grow even more cotton to try to recover their losses. Sharecropping and reliance on one cash crop kept Southern agriculture from advancing.

Reading Check **Describing** Why did industry in the South grow during this period?

Agricultural Production in the South, 1850–1890

Increased ▶ production lowered cotton prices and left much of the rural South in poverty after the Civil War.

Source: *Historical Statistics of the South*

Critical Thinking

Comparing and Contrasting How was the South after the Civil War similar to and different from the South before the Civil War?

Graphs In Motion See StudentWorks™ Plus or glencoe.com.

A Divided Society

Main Idea As Reconstruction ended, true freedom for African Americans became a distant dream.

History and You How would you feel if you had to pass a test on a subject you never studied in order to graduate? Read to learn about a test African Americans in the South had to pass in order to vote.

As Reconstruction ended, African Americans' dreams for justice faded. In the last 20 years of the 1800s, racism became firmly set in the culture. Individuals took steps to keep African Americans separated from whites and to deny them basic rights.

Voting Restrictions

The Fifteenth Amendment prohibited any state from denying an individual the right to vote because of race. Southern leaders, however, found ways to get around the amendment and prevent African Americans from voting.

Many Southern states required a **poll tax,** a fee people had to pay to vote. Because many African Americans could not afford the tax, they could not vote. The tax also kept many poor whites from voting.

Another approach was to make prospective voters take a **literacy test** in which they had to read and explain difficult parts of state constitutions or the federal Constitution. Because most African Americans had little education, literacy tests prevented many from voting.

Literacy tests could also keep some whites from voting. For this reason some states passed **grandfather clauses.** These laws allowed people who did not pass the literacy test to vote if their fathers or grandfathers voted before Reconstruction. Because African Americans could not vote until 1867, they were excluded. By the end of the 1800s, such laws and the constant threat of violence caused African American voting to decline drastically.

Jim Crow Laws

By the 1890s, **segregation,** or the separation of the races, had become a common feature of the South. Southern states passed so-called **Jim Crow laws** that required African Americans and whites to be separated in almost every public place.

In 1896 the Supreme Court upheld segregation laws in *Plessy v. Ferguson.* The case involved a Louisiana law requiring separate sections on trains for African Americans. The Court ruled that segregation was legal as long as African Americans had access to public places equal to those of whites.

One problem, however, was that the facilities were separate but in no way equal. Southern states spent much more money on schools and other facilities for whites than on those for African Americans. This "separate but equal" doctrine gave legal support to Southern segregation for more than 50 years. White violence against African Americans also rose. One form of violence was **lynching,** in which an angry mob killed a person by hanging. African Americans were lynched because they were suspected of crimes—or because they did not behave as whites thought they should behave.

Reconstruction's Impact

Reconstruction was both a success and a failure. It helped the South rebuild its economy. Yet much of the South remained agricultural and poor. African Americans gained greater equality, created their own institutions, and shared in government with whites. Their advances, however, did not last. In the words of African American writer and civil rights leader W.E.B. Du Bois, "The slave went free; stood a brief moment in the sun; then moved back again toward slavery."

Reading Check **Describing** How was segregation applied?

Section 4 Review

History ONLINE
Study Central™ To review this section, go to glencoe.com.

Vocabulary

1. Use each of these terms in a sentence that will help explain its meaning: outcome, commission, cash crop, poll tax, literacy test, grandfather clause, segregation, lynching.

Main Ideas

2. Explaining How did the Amnesty Act help Democrats regain control of Southern state governments?

3. Describing How did forward-thinking Southerners want to change the South's economy?

4. Explaining Why did African American voting in the South decline drastically by the late 1800s?

Critical Thinking

5. Determining Cause and Effect Use a diagram like the one below to describe the two issues that split the Republican Party for the 1872 election. Then name the group these dissatisfied Republicans came together to form.

Issues That Divided Republicans

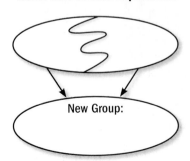

New Group:

6. Analyzing Did agriculture in the New South achieve the shift envisioned by its supporters? Why or why not?

7. Descriptive Writing You are an African American in 1899. When you took a seat on a train, the white conductor told you to move to a separate section. Write a letter to W.E.B. Du Bois, describing the incident and your feelings about it.

Answer the
8. Essential Question

How did the South change politically, economically, and socially when Reconstruction ended?

Visual Summary

◀ Freedmen's school

Reconstruction Plans

- The South is rebuilt and readmitted to the Union during Reconstruction.
- Lincoln's Ten Percent Plan is designed to heal the Union quickly.
- The Radical Republicans' Wade-Davis Bill has strict requirements for states to be readmitted.
- The Freedmen's Bureau helps African Americans adjust to freedom.
- Abraham Lincoln is assassinated in April 1865.
- President Johnson's "Restoration" plan calls for states to ratify the amendment to abolish slavery.

Lincoln's funeral ▼

Radical Reconstruction

- Radical Republicans believe Johnson's plan is too easy on the South.
- Southern states pass black codes to control freed African Americans, but Congress passes the Civil Rights Act of 1866 to protect their freedoms.
- The Fourteenth Amendment gives African Americans citizenship and equal protection of the laws.
- Radical Republicans win Congress and enact their own Reconstruction plans.
- Congress impeaches Johnson but fails to convict him.
- The Fifteenth Amendment gives African American men the right to vote.

Andrew Johnson ▲

Reconstruction in the South

- African Americans vote and take part in Southern politics.
- Some whites resist the expansion of African Americans' rights and form the Ku Klux Klan.
- Sharecropping limits economic opportunities for African Americans.

Reconstruction Ends

- Republicans lose power as a result of political corruption and economic crisis.
- Democrats regain control of Southern state governments.
- Southern Democrats encourage economic growth but limit the rights of African Americans.

STUDY TO GO Study anywhere, anytime! Download quizzes and flash cards to your PDA from glencoe.com.

Southern Industry After the Civil War

Before the Civil War, the backbone of the Southern economy was agriculture. After Reconstruction, industry in the South made dramatic gains.

How Did Geography Affect Southern Industry?

Many Southern industries after the Civil War centered around regional agricultural products such as tobacco and cotton. In the 1880s textile mills sprang up throughout the South. Additionally, Southern forests provided lumber for new homes, factories, railroad ties, and above all, furniture.

Other Southern industries centered on the region's rich reserves of coal and iron. By 1900, the South led the world in coal production; this same period saw a large growth in iron and steel mills.

▲ While the economy of the Old South focused on cotton and tobacco production, distinct industrial regions began to develop after the Civil War.

Manufacturing in the Southern States, 1860–1900*

State	1860	1880	1900
Alabama	1,459	2,070	5,602
Arkansas	518	1,202	4,794
Florida	185	426	2,056
Georgia	1,890	3,593	7,504
Louisiana	1,744	1,553	4,350
Mississippi	976	1,479	4,772
North Carolina	3,689	3,802	7,226
South Carolina	1,230	2,078	3,762
Tennessee	2,572	4,326	8,016
Texas	983	2,996	12,289
TOTAL	15,246	23,525	60,371

*Number of Manufacturing Establishments

Thomas Nast's illustration for an 1882 cover of *Harper's Weekly* compares the Old South's "King Cotton" of 1861 to the New South's "Queen of Industry." ▶

What they were saying . . .

Atlanta *Constitution* editor Henry Grady was one of the leaders calling for a "New South," a South that is industrialized and part of a modern national economy.

"We are going to take a noble revenge . . . by invading every inch of your territory [the North] with iron, as you invaded ours twenty-nine years ago."

◀ After the Civil War, Southerners built a number of iron and steel mills. Many mills were located near the iron ore deposits around Birmingham, Alabama. Founded in 1871, Birmingham became a prime industrial center of the New South. Between 1880 and 1900, the area in and around Birmingham was second only to Pittsburgh, Pennsylvania, in the number of new furnaces for making iron.

Although tobacco was grown in the South before the Civil War, it was rarely processed there. By 1900, tobacco processing had become a major Southern industry. ▶

◀ One of the first industries to gain strength in the "New South" was the textile industry. Textile mills produced cotton cloth.

▲ The lumber industry thrived in many parts of the South.

Analyzing Geography

1. **Location** In which parts of the "New South" did coal mining predominate? Textile manufacturing? Tobacco?

2. **Human-Environment Interaction** In what ways did Southern agriculture influence the types of industries that arose in the New South?

GRADE 8 INTERMEDIATE TEST PRACTICE

TEST-TAKING TIP

Be sure to pay attention to specific words in a question. Words can act as clues to help you identify the correct answer.

Reviewing Main Ideas

Directions: Choose the best answer for each of the following questions.

1 Which of the following was a provision of the 1864 Wade-Davis bill?

(1) African American males in a state had to swear loyalty to the Union.

(2) Ex-Confederates could not hold public office.

(3) Confederate states could be readmitted to the Union even if they kept slavery.

(4) Half of all delegates to a constitutional convention had to be formerly enslaved people.

2 What was Andrew Johnson's reaction to the Civil Rights Act of 1866?

(1) He supported the law even though he believed it did not protect African Americans.

(2) He said it was unconstitutional because it was passed by a Congress that did not include representatives from all the states.

(3) He persuaded Congress to pass the bill.

(4) He vetoed it because it gave states too much power.

3 Southern whites who supported the Republicans were called

(1) scalawags. **(3)** carpetbaggers.

(2) sharecroppers. **(4)** freed men and women.

4 During the Grant administration,

(1) Radical Republicans became more powerful.

(2) corruption charges weakened Democrats.

(3) many Northerners began to think the South should solve its own problems.

(4) most white Southerners supported Republicans.

Short-Answer Question

Directions: Base your answer to question 5 on the excerpt below and on your knowledge of social studies.

> I have confidence . . . in the endurance, capacity, and destiny of my people [African Americans]. We will . . . seek our places, sometimes in the field of letters, arts, sciences, and the professions. More frequently mechanical pursuits will attract and elicit our efforts; more still of my people will find employment . . . as the cultivators of the soil. The bulk of this people—by surroundings, habits, adaptation, and choice—will continue to find their homes in the South. . . . Whatever our ultimate position in the . . . Republic . . . we will not forget our instincts for freedom nor our love of country.
>
> —Senator Blanche K. Bruce, from a speech in 1876

5 According to the document, how did Bruce expect most African Americans to earn a living? How did he view their futures?

Review the Essential Questions

6 **Essay** What do you think was Reconstruction's greatest success? What was its greatest failure? Explain your answers.

To help you write your essay, review your answers to the Essential Questions in the section reviews and the chapter Foldables Study Organizer. Your essay should include:

- the various plans for Reconstruction;
- the actions of the Radical Republicans and their conflicts with Johnson;
- the changes in the South and white Southern responses; and
- reasons why Reconstruction ended.

GO ON ➡

History ONLINE

For additional test practice, use **Self-Check Quizzes**—Chapter 17 at glencoe.com.

Document-Based Questions

Directions: Analyze the documents and answer the short-answer questions that follow.

Document 1

New England journalist Sidney Andrews recorded these remarks in 1865 from a man in Charleston, South Carolina.

> You Northern people are making a great mistake in your treatment of the South. We are thoroughly whipped; we give up slavery forever; and now we want you to quit [criticizing] us. Let us back into the Union, and then come down here and help us build up the country.

Source: Sidney Andrews, *The South Since the War*

7 Based on the excerpt, do you think the person Andrews spoke to would most likely support Lincoln's Ten Percent Plan or the Wade-Davis Bill? Explain.

Document 2

President Andrew Johnson made these remarks in his veto of the First Reconstruction Act of 1867.

> The power . . . given to the commanding officer . . . of each district is that of an absolute monarch. His mere will is to take the place of all law. . . .
> It reduces the whole population of the ten States . . . to the most abject and degrading slavery.

Source: Andrew Johnson, "From Revolution to Reconstruction"

8 According to the document, why did Johnson veto the First Reconstruction Act?

Document 3

The illustration at the top right is from the December 28, 1868, *Harper's Weekly* magazine. It shows two members of the Ku Klux Klan.

Source: Corbis

9 Why did Klan members wear disguises?

Document 4

The following are examples of Jim Crow laws passed throughout the South.

> No person or corporation shall require any white female nurse to nurse in wards or rooms in hospitals, either public or private, in which negro men are placed. *Alabama*
>
> The schools for white children and the schools for negro children shall be conducted separately. *Florida*
>
> Books shall not be interchangeable between the white and colored schools, but shall continue to be used by the race first using them. *North Carolina*

Source: Martin Luther King, Jr., National Historic Site

10 How were African American freedoms limited?

11 **Expository Writing** Using the information from the four documents and your knowledge of social studies, write an essay in which you:

- describe the political issues related to Reconstruction, including the effect of Lincoln's death on the process; and

- describe how Reconstruction affected the various groups in the South.

Need Extra Help?											
If you missed questions. . .	1	2	3	4	5	6	7	8	9	10	11
Go to page. . .	520	524	529	535	530	518–540	519–520	525	530	539–540	518–540

Unit 6

Reshaping the Nation
1858–1914

The gramophone was an early player of musical recordings.

"Once I moved about like the wind. Now I surrender to you and that is all."
—Geronimo

Grand Opening of the Brooklyn Bridge, May 24, 1883

547

Comparing and Contrasting

Learn It! When you *compare* people, things, or ideas, you look for similarities among them. When you *contrast*, you look for differences.

Central Pacific
Hired Chinese laborers

Similarities
Both companies were working to build the transcontinental railroad. Workers labored for low wages in harsh conditions.

Union Pacific
Hired Irish and African American workers

—*from Chapter 18, p. 556*

Two companies accepted the challenge to build the [transcontinental] railroad. . . .The Central Pacific hired about 10,000 Chinese laborers to work on its tracks. The first Chinese were hired in 1865 at about $28 per month. The Union Pacific relied on Irish and African American workers. All workers toiled for low wages in harsh conditions.

Practice It! Read the paragraph. Then on another sheet of paper, draw a Venn diagram and compare and contrast forms of public transportation in the late 1800s.

—*from Chapter 20, p. 625*

As cities grew, people needed new means of transportation. Streetcars, which horses pulled on tracks, provided public transportation at the time. In 1873 San Francisco began construction of cable-car lines. A large underground cable powered by a motor at one end of the rail line moved passengers along.

Streetcars

Similarities

Cable-cars

Academic Vocabulary Preview

Listed below are the academic vocabulary words and their definitions that you will come across as you study Unit 6. The activities in the Practice It! column will help you study the words and definitions.

Academic Vocabulary	Definition	Practice It!
Chapter 18 Opening the West		
sum (SUHM) *p. 553*	amount; total	**Identify** *the term from Chapter 18 that best completes each sentence.*
extract (ehk · STRAKT) *p. 553*	to remove, usually by force	**1.** Mining companies use machinery to _____ ore from the land.
locate (LOH · kayt) *p. 561*	to establish; settle	**2.** At one time, the United States had a gold-based _____, instead of metal coins and paper notes.
factor (FAK · tuhr) *p. 563*	contributing circumstance	
ensure (ihn · SHUR) *p. 567*	make certain	
widespread (WYD · SPREHD) *p. 569*	far-reaching	**3.** Some prospectors made large _____(s) of money during the California Gold Rush.
create (kree · AYT) *p. 575*	to form; to make	
currency (KUHR · uhnt · see) *p. 577*	metal coins and paper notes used as money	
Chapter 19 The Industrial Age		
labor (LAY · buhr) *p. 585*	to work	**Identify** *the term from Chapter 19 that best matches the underlined word or phrase.*
individual (IHN · duh · VIHJ · wuhl) *p. 585*	person	**4.** The telegraph was used to <u>send</u> messages in Morse code.
transmit (trants · MIHT) *p. 589*	send from one place to another	
mechanism (MEH · kuh · NIH · zuhm) *p. 592*	mechanical device	**5.** In the early 1900s, labor unions helped create safer <u>working conditions</u> in urban factories.
partner (PAHRT · nuhr) *p. 597*	associate who agrees to operate a business with another	**6.** African American inventors developed much-needed <u>mechanical devices</u> for consumers and industry.
trend (TREHND) *p. 599*	general direction or movement	
identify (eye · DEHN · tuh · FY) *p. 604*	recognize	
environment (ihn · VY · ruhn · muhnt) *p. 605*	the conditions of a location	
Chapter 20 An Urban Society		
attitude (A · tuh · TOOD) *p. 617*	way of thinking and acting	**Choose** *the word that best matches the meaning of each vocabulary term listed below.*
affect (uh · FEHKT) *p. 617*	to have an impact on	

major (MAY · juhr) *p. 621*	greater in size, extent, or importance	**7. major** **9. minor**
		  a. greater a. equal
		  b. lower b. lesser
		  c. wiser c. greater

minor (MY · nuhr) *p. 623*	lesser in size, extent, or importance	

philosophy (fuh · LAH · suh · fee) *p. 627*	a set of ideas and beliefs	**8. philosophy** **10. isolate**
		  a. education a. gather
		  b. beliefs b. control
		  c. government c. separate

isolate (EYE · suh · LAYT) *p. 628*	cut off; separate	

Opening the West 1858–1896

Railroad companies hired buffalo hunters to provide their workers with fresh meat.

▲ Ruins after Chicago Fire

★ **1871** Great Chicago Fire destroys most of city

PRESIDENTS

 JAMES BUCHANAN 1857–1861

 ABRAHAM LINCOLN 1861–1865

 ANDREW JOHNSON 1865–1869

 ULYSSES S. GRANT 1869–1877

 RUTHERFORD B. HAYES 1877–1881

 JAMES GARFIELD 1881

U.S. Events

World Events

1860

★ **1861** Italians establish a united kingdom

★ **1869** Suez Canal opens

1870

1871 ★ Stanley and Livingstone meet in Africa

1880

★ **1878** Russo-Turkish War ends

History ONLINE
Chapter Overview Visit glencoe.com and click on **Chapter 18—Chapter Overviews** to preview chapter information.

Section 1: The Mining Booms

Essential Question What were the causes and effects of mining booms in the West?

Section 2: Ranchers and Farmers

Essential Question How did cattle ranchers and farmers adapt to life in the West?

Section 3: Native American Struggles

Essential Question How did westward expansion affect Native Americans?

Section 4: Farmers in Protest

Essential Question Why did economic reform movements develop in the late 1800s?

Apache leader Geronimo ▶

FOLDABLES Study Organizer

Organizing Information

Make this Foldable to help organize what you learn about the opening of the West in the late 1800s.

Step 1 Fold an 11" x 17" piece of paper lengthwise to create 4 equal sections.

Step 2 Label your Foldable as shown.

| The Mining Booms | Ranchers & Farmers | Native American Struggles | Farmers in Protest |

Reading and Writing As you read the chapter, use the Foldable to take notes on each section. Be sure to write down important people, dates, and events.

CHESTER ARTHUR 1881–1885

★ **1882** Congress limits immigration with Chinese Exclusion Act

GROVER CLEVELAND 1885–1889

★ **1886**
• Geronimo surrenders to U.S. military
• U.S. accepts Statue of Liberty from France

BENJAMIN HARRISON 1889–1893

★ **1892**
• Populist Party forms
• Sierra Club organizes in San Francisco

GROVER CLEVELAND 1893–1897

1890   **1900**

★ **1882** Triple Alliance forms among Germany, Austria, Italy

★ **1885** European powers divide Africa

★ **1891** Construction of Trans-Siberian railroad begins

★ **1896** First modern Olympics held in Athens

Section 1 ★ The Mining Booms

Essential Question ◄
What were the causes and effects of mining booms in the West?

Reading Guide

Content Vocabulary
vigilante (p. 553)
subsidy (p. 555)
transcontinental (p. 555)
time zone (p. 557)

Academic Vocabulary
sum (p. 553)   extract (p. 553)

Key People and Events
Comstock Lode (p. 553)
Leland Stanford (p. 556)

Reading Strategy
Taking Notes As you read, identify the effects of the mining booms.

NEW YORK STANDARDS
The American Journey

U7.I.1 To understand how industrialization led to significant changes in the economic patterns for producing, distributing, and consuming goods and services

U7.I.2 To explain how societies and nations attempt to satisfy their basic needs and wants by utilizing scarce capital, natural, and human resources

U7.II.1 To understand how industrialization altered the traditional social pattern of American society and created a need for reform

American Diary

In 1859 a Kansas newspaper article tried to inspire people to travel to Pikes Peak in Colorado where gold had been discovered: "Hurra for Pike's Peak! Hurra for Pike's Peak! / There's gold in the Mount'n, there's gold in the vale, / There's plenty for all who are willing to seek / Believe me; believe me—'tis no idle tale. / Come, hurra for Pike's Peak!" Stories about the discoveries of gold and silver lured thousands of fortune seekers west.

—from "A Call to the Mines"

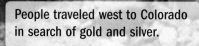

People traveled west to Colorado in search of gold and silver.

Gold, Silver, and Boomtowns

Main Idea Miners found gold in the West, leading to the creation of new states.

History and You What opportunities today might tempt your family to move to a new state? Read to learn how the discovery of gold encouraged people to move West.

By the mid-1850s, the California Gold Rush had ended. Disappointed miners, still hoping to strike it rich, began prospecting in other parts of the West.

In 1858 gold was found at Pikes Peak in the Colorado Rockies. Newspapers claimed that miners were making $20 a day panning for gold—a large **sum,** or amount of money, at a time when servants earned less than a dollar a day. By the spring of 1859, about 50,000 prospectors had flocked to the goldfields of Colorado.

Prospectors skimmed gold dust from streams or scratched gold particles from the land. Most of the gold, however, was deep in underground lodes, which are rich streaks of ore running between rock layers. Mining this ore and then **extracting,** or removing, the gold particles required machinery, workers, and an organized business. Companies stood a better chance of getting rich from mining for gold than did individuals.

Boom and Bust

In 1859 several prospectors found one of the world's richest deposits of silver-bearing ore near Nevada's Carson River. The discovery was called the **Comstock Lode** after Henry Comstock, who owned a share of the claim. Thousands of mines opened near the site, but only a few were profitable.

Gold strikes created boomtowns—towns that developed almost overnight around mining sites. The Comstock boomtown was Virginia City, Nevada. Boomtowns were lively, and often lawless, places. Money came quickly—and was often lost just as quickly through spending and gambling. Violence was also part of life in boomtowns, where many people carried guns and a lot of cash. Few boomtowns had police or prisons, so ordinary people known as **vigilantes** sometimes acted to punish criminals.

Men mostly lived in boomtowns, but some women opened businesses or worked as laundresses, cooks, or entertainers. Women often founded schools and churches.

By the Numbers / Life of a Mining Boomtown

A Boomtown's Population Virginia City, Nevada, became one of the largest cities in the West after gold was discovered in the region. Once all of the gold was extracted from the ground, however, Virginia City's population declined.

Population of Virginia City, Nevada

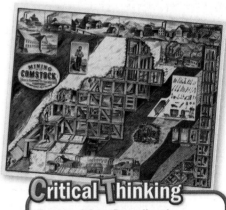

*Estimate according to various Nevada historical sources
Source: Nevada State Library and Archives, 2007.

Critical Thinking

Summarizing Describe the changes in population in Virginia City, Nevada, from 1860 to 1920.

Mining and the West, 1848–1890

NATIONAL GEOGRAPHIC

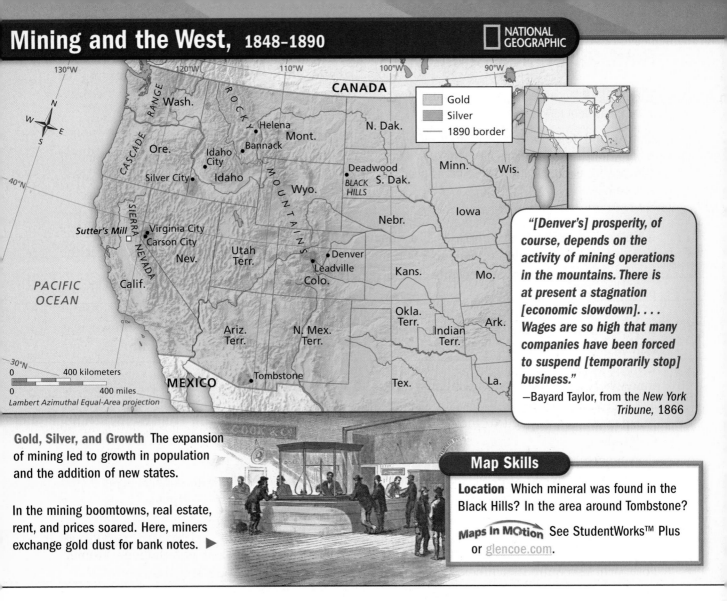

"[Denver's] prosperity, of course, depends on the activity of mining operations in the mountains. There is at present a stagnation [economic slowdown]. . . . Wages are so high that many companies have been forced to suspend [temporarily stop] business."

—Bayard Taylor, from the *New York Tribune*, 1866

Gold, Silver, and Growth The expansion of mining led to growth in population and the addition of new states.

In the mining boomtowns, real estate, rent, and prices soared. Here, miners exchange gold dust for bank notes. ▶

Map Skills

Location Which mineral was found in the Black Hills? In the area around Tombstone?

Maps In Motion See StudentWorks™ Plus or glencoe.com.

Despite the promise of prosperity, many mining "booms" were followed by "busts." When the ore was gone, people left, and the boomtowns became ghost towns.

The United States Expands West

As the gold and silver disappeared, the mining of other metals, including copper, lead, and zinc, increased. As these mining areas developed and became more populated, they eventually became states. Colorado joined the United States in 1876. North Dakota, South Dakota, Washington, and Montana became states in 1889. Wyoming and Idaho were admitted to the Union in 1890.

Reading Check **Explaining** Why did many boomtowns turn into ghost towns?

Railroads Connect East and West

Main Idea Railroads transported gold and silver to market and brought supplies to the miners.

History and You What type of transportation would you take if you had to travel from the East Coast to the West Coast? Read to learn how people and goods were transported in the mid-1800s.

The western mines operated far from the industrial centers of the East and Midwest. For this reason, transportation played a vital role in the survival of mining communities. Gold and silver had little value unless they could reach factories, ports, and markets.

At the same time, people living in the boom-towns needed shipments of food and other supplies.

Wagons and stagecoaches could not move people and goods fast enough to meet these demands, but railroads did. The nation's railroad network expanded rapidly between 1865 and 1890. During that time, the length of track in the United States soared from about 35,000 miles (56,327 km) to more than 150,000 miles (241,402 km).

Government and the Railroads

Railroad construction was often supported by large government **subsidies**—financial aid and land grants from the government. Railroad executives made the argument that their companies should receive free public land on which to lay track because a rail network connecting East and West would bring important benefits to the entire nation.

The national government and states agreed. In all, the federal government granted more than 130 million acres (52,609,180 ha) of land to the railroad companies. Much of the land was purchased or obtained by treaties from Native Americans. The government grants included the land for the tracks plus strips of land along the railway, 20 to 80 miles (32 to 129 km) wide. Railroad companies sold those strips of land to raise additional money.

States and local communities also helped the railroads. Towns offered cash subsidies to make sure that the railroads were constructed near their communities. For example, Los Angeles gave the Southern Pacific Railroad money and paid for a passenger terminal to ensure that the railroad would be built near the town.

Spanning the Continent

The search for a route for a **transcontinental** rail line—one that would span the continent and connect the Atlantic and Pacific coasts—began in the 1850s. Southerners wanted the route to run through the South, and Northerners wanted it to pass through the North. During the Civil War, the Union government chose a northerly route. The government offered land grants to railroad companies willing to build the transcontinental line.

The challenge was enormous—laying track for more than 1,700 miles (2,736 km) across hot plains and through rugged mountains.

The Steam Locomotive

The railroads that were so important to the growth of the West were dependent upon the technology of the steam locomotive.

1 The **firebox** burns coal, wood, or sometimes oil.

2 Water in the **boiler**, heated by gases from the firebox, creates steam.

3 The smoke box draws hot gases from the firebox and keeps an even fire burning.

4 In the **steam header tank**, the heated steam expands and creates great pressure.

5 Hot steam is piped to the **pistons**. The pistons power the **drive rods**, which in turn push the **drive wheels**.

Critical Thinking

Making Inferences What advantages did steam locomotives have over other forms of transportation available in the mid-1800s?

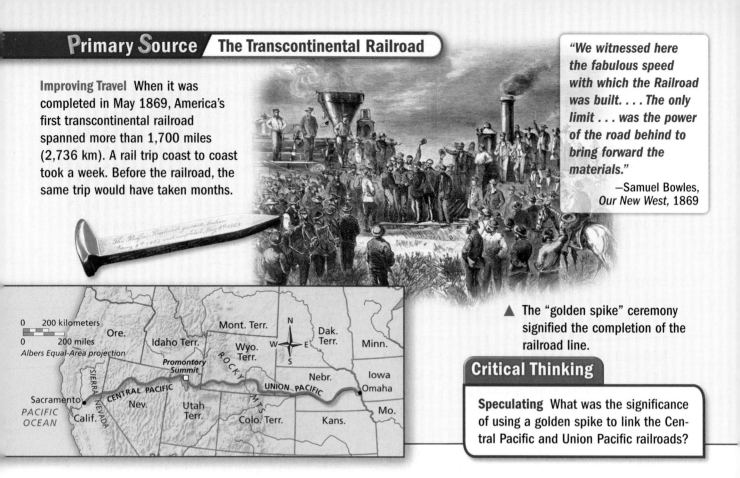

Primary Source / The Transcontinental Railroad

Improving Travel When it was completed in May 1869, America's first transcontinental railroad spanned more than 1,700 miles (2,736 km). A rail trip coast to coast took a week. Before the railroad, the same trip would have taken months.

"We witnessed here the fabulous speed with which the Railroad was built. . . . The only limit . . . was the power of the road behind to bring forward the materials."
—Samuel Bowles, Our New West, 1869

▲ The "golden spike" ceremony signified the completion of the railroad line.

Critical Thinking

Speculating What was the significance of using a golden spike to link the Central Pacific and Union Pacific railroads?

Two companies accepted the challenge to build the railroad. The Union Pacific Company began laying track westward from Omaha, Nebraska, while the Central Pacific Company worked eastward from the city of Sacramento, California.

The two companies competed furiously. Each wanted to cover a greater distance than the other in order to receive more of the government subsidies.

The Central Pacific hired about 10,000 Chinese laborers to work on its tracks. The first Chinese were hired in 1865 at about $28 per month. The Union Pacific relied on Irish and African American workers. All workers toiled for low wages in harsh conditions. In the choking heat of summer and the icy winds of winter, the workers cleared forests, blasted tunnels through mountains, and laid hundreds of miles of track across the vast center of the country. In the end, the Central Pacific workers, who covered a much harsher terrain, laid 742 miles (1,194 km) of track. The Union Pacific workers laid 1,038 miles (1,670 km) of track.

The Transcontinental Railway

On May 10, 1869, construction was completed. A Chinese crew was chosen to lay the final 10 miles (16 km) of track, which was completed in only 12 hours. The two sets of track met at Promontory Summit in Utah Territory. **Leland Stanford,** governor of California, drove a final golden spike into a tie to join the two railroads. Almost as the event occurred, telegraph lines flashed the news across the country: "The last rail is laid. . . . [T]he last spike driven. . . . The Pacific Railroad is completed."

Effects of the Railroads

By 1883, two more transcontinental lines and dozens of shorter lines connected cities in the West with the rest of the nation. The economic consequences were enormous. The railroads brought thousands of workers west. Trains carried metals and produce east and manufactured goods west. As more tracks were laid, more steel was needed, and the demand boosted the nation's steel industry.

Document-Based Questions

Directions: Analyze the documents and answer the short-answer questions that follow.

Document 1

This is an excerpt from Grenville M. Dodge's 1869 report on the transcontinental railway.

Telegraphic wires were so connected that each blow of the descending [sledgehammer] could be reported instantly to all parts of the United States. . . . And with the last blow of the sledge a cannon was fired at Fort Point [in San Francisco].

Source: Ed. David Colbert, *Eyewitness to America*

7 Based on the excerpt, was the completion of the railroad considered an important national event? How do you know?

Document 2

J. Ross Browne recorded these impressions of Virginia City, Nevada, in 1865.

The business part of the town has been built up with astonishing rapidity. In the spring of 1860 there was nothing of it save a few frame shanties and canvas tents, and one or two rough stone cabins. It now presents some of the distinguishing features of a metropolitan city.

Source: *The Mammoth Book of Eyewitness America*

8 According to Browne, how had Virginia City changed?

9 What might be distinguishing features of a metropolitan city in 1865?

Document 3

This 1891 cartoon is about the Populist Party.

A PARTY OF PATCHES.

Source: The Granger Collection, New York

10 The title of the cartoon is "A Party of Patches." What does this say about the organization of the party?

11 **Expository Writing** Using the information from the three documents and your knowledge of social studies, write an essay in which you:

- explain why railroads are the key to understanding the development of the American West; and

- discuss at least one problem or conflict directly related to the spread of railroads in the West.

Need Extra Help?											
If you missed questions. . .	1	2	3	4	5	6	7	8	9	10	11
Go to page. . .	553	564	570	577	568–571	552–578	554–557	557	557	577–578	552–578

The Industrial Age 1865–1914

Working at a factory in Dayton, Ohio, 1902

A. Johnson
1865–1869

1869 ★
First trans-continental railroad completed

U. S. Grant
1869–1877

★ **1870**
Rockefeller organizes Standard Oil Company

1876 ★
Bell patents the telephone

R. B. Hayes
1877–1881

★ **1879**
Edison invents electric light

J. Garfield
1881

PRESIDENTS

U.S. Events

World Events

1860

1870

1880

1867 ★
Diamonds discovered in Cape Colony, a province in South Africa

★ **1880**
Unions win the right to strike in Great Britain

Section 1: Railroads Lead the Way

Essential Question How did railroad expansion affect the United States economy?

Section 2: Inventions

Essential Question How did the inventions of the late 1800s revolutionize society?

Section 3: An Age of Big Business

Essential Question How did Americans build fortunes in the oil and steel industries?

Section 4: Industrial Workers

Essential Question Why did workers form labor unions in the middle to late 1800s?

FOLDABLES Study Organizer

Organizing Information Make this Foldable to help organize what you learn about the growth of industry in the late 1800s.

Step 1 Fold four sheets of paper in half from top to bottom.

Step 2 On each folded paper, make a cut 1 inch from the side on the top flap.

Step 3 Place the folded papers one on top of the other, and staple the sections together. Label the pages with headings appropriate for the sections.

Railroad Industry

Main ideas, dates, events, diagrams, etc.

Reading and Writing As you read, note dates, events, and visuals from the chapter to help you summarize its main ideas.

Model T touring car, 1908 ▶

 C. Arthur 1881–1885

 G. Cleveland 1885–1889

 B. Harrison 1889–1893

★ **1890** Sherman Antitrust Act passes

★ **1892** Iron- and steel- workers strike in the U.S.

 G. Cleveland 1893–1897

 W. McKinley 1897–1901

 T. Roosevelt 1901–1909

★ **1903** First pow- ered flight by Wright brothers

★ **1908** Ford introduces Model T

1890

1900

1893 ★ Karl Benz builds four- wheel car

1895 ★ Marconi sends first radio signals

★ **1895** Lumière brothers introduce motion pictures

 ◀ French inventor Louis Lumière

Section 1 ★ Railroads Lead the Way

Essential Question ◄

How did railroad expansion affect the United States economy?

Reading Guide

Content Vocabulary

consolidation (p. 585)

railroad baron (p. 585)

standard gauge (p. 586)

rebate (p. 587)

pool (p. 587)

Academic Vocabulary

labor (p. 585) individual (p. 585)

Key People and Events

George Westinghouse (p. 587)

Eli H. Janney (p. 587)

Gustavus Swift (p. 587)

George M. Pullman (p. 587)

Reading Strategy

Taking Notes As you read, use a diagram like the one below to record the effects of railroad expansion in the United States.

NEW YORK STANDARDS
The American Journey

U7.I.1 To understand how industrialization led to significant changes in the economic patterns for producing, distributing, and consuming goods and services

U7.I.3 To define basic economic concepts such as scarcity, supply and demand, markets, resources, and economic growth

U7.I.5 To understand how people in the United States and throughout the world are both producers and consumers of goods and services

American Diary

In 1869 writer Samuel Bowles described his journey west: "Marked, indeed, was the contrast between the stage [stagecoach] ride . . . and the Railroad ride . . . across the Plains. The then long-drawn, tedious [boring] endurance of six days and nights, running the gauntlet of hostile Indians, was now accomplished in a single twenty-four hours, safe in a swiftly-moving train, and in a car that was an elegant drawing-room by day and a luxurious bedroom at night."

—from Our New West

Railroad Expansion

Main Idea The railroad system expanded rapidly in the late 1800s, building large fortunes for some wealthy businesspeople.

History and You In what industries do people make large amounts of money today? Read to learn about the profits generated by railroad expansion.

....

During the Civil War, trains carried troops and supplies to the front. After the war, the railroad system grew rapidly and drove economic growth in the United States. In 1860 the United States had about 30,000 miles (48,280 km) of railroad track. By 1900, the nation had nearly 193,000 miles (310,603 km) of track. Work songs such as "John Henry" and "I've Been Working on the Railroad" were popular among those who **labored,** or worked, to build these miles of track.

Railroad expansion was accompanied by **consolidation**—the practice of combining separate companies—in the industry. Large railroad companies bought smaller companies or drove them out of business. Consolidation made the large companies more efficient. These companies established standard prices and made industrial processes more uniform.

Railroad Barons

After consolidation, a few powerful **individuals,** or persons, known as **railroad barons** controlled the nation's rail traffic. New Yorker Cornelius Vanderbilt, one of the first railroad barons, made a fortune by consolidating several companies. His railroad empire stretched from New York City to the Great Lakes. Another railroad baron, James J. Hill, built the Great Northern line between Minnesota and Washington State. Other barons, including Collis P. Huntington and Leland Stanford, founded the Central Pacific, which connected California and Utah. The railroad barons were aggressive and competitive. They lived in an age when there were few laws that regulated business.

Reading Check **Analyzing** What are the advantages and disadvantages of consolidation?

By the Numbers / Railroad Tracks

Connecting the Country Railroads expanded rapidly in the years following the Civil War. By the late 1800s, all major U.S. cities from the West Coast to the East Coast were connected by rail.

U.S. Railroad Track Miles

Miles of track:
- 1860: 30,635
- 1870: 52,922
- 1880: 92,147
- 1890: 163,597
- 1900: 193,346

Source: Association of American Railroads; *Historical Statistics of the United States: Colonial Times to 1970*

The Union Pacific Railroad depot at La Grande, Oregon, c. 1870

Critical Thinking
Calculating Which decade saw the largest increase in track miles?

The Growth of Railroads National Geographic

Time Zones Before railroads, each community established its own time. In order to create sensible schedules, the railroad companies divided the country into four time zones. Each zone was one hour apart from the zone on either side of it.

Railroads in 1890

Legend:
- Pacific Time Zone
- Mountain Time Zone
- Central Time Zone
- Eastern Time Zone
- Railroads built by 1870
- Railroads built by 1890

*Time zones and borders shown as of 1890

▲ This advertisement shows the "Hotel" car introduced by George Pullman in 1867. It had both sleeping and dining facilities and greatly improved the experience of rail travel.

Map Skills

Regions Which time zone regions had the greatest lengths of railroad tracks? Why was that so?

Maps In Motion See StudentWorks™ Plus or glencoe.com.

Railroads Stimulate the Economy

Main Idea Railroads brought major changes to American industry and American life in general.

History and You Think about how the expansion of one industry leads to the growth of others. Read to learn how railroads influenced other industries.

. . . .

Railroads carried raw materials such as iron ore, coal, and timber to factories. They also carried manufactured goods from factories to markets and transported produce from farming areas to the cities.

At first the demand for iron tracks and locomotives helped the iron mining and processing industries grow. Around 1880, railroad companies began using tracks of steel—a strong metal made by adding carbon and other elements to refined iron. The use of steel in railroad tracks stimulated America's steel industry. Railroads also had an effect on the lumber industry, which supplied wood for railway ties, and the coal industry, which provided fuel. In addition, railroad companies provided work for thousands of people.

Improving the Railroads

Increased use made it necessary for railroads to expand and unify their systems. While railroads were being built across the country, different lines used rails of different gauges, or widths. As a result, trains of one line could not use another line's tracks. The gaps in service made travel extremely slow.

As the railroad companies consolidated, companies adopted a **standard gauge** of 4 feet, 8.5 inches (1 m, 41.6 cm) as the width of the railroad track. A standard gauge allowed faster shipment of goods at a reduced cost. It was no longer necessary to load and unload goods from one train to another.

Railroad Technology

Railway transportation also improved with the introduction of new technology. Four developments were particularly important. Inventor **George Westinghouse** devised air brakes that improved the system for stopping trains, making train travel safer. Janney car couplers, named after inventor **Eli H. Janney,** made it easier for railroad workers to link cars. Refrigerated cars, developed by **Gustavus Swift,** enabled the railroads to ship meat and other perishable goods over long distances. Finally, **George M. Pullman** developed the Pullman sleeping car—a luxury railway car with seats that converted into beds for overnight journeys.

Competing for Customers

Railroad companies competed fiercely with one another to keep old customers and to win new ones. Large railroads offered secret discounts called **rebates** to their biggest customers. Smaller railroads that could not match these rebates were often forced out of business. Giving discounts to big customers, however, raised freight rates for farmers and other customers who shipped small amounts of goods.

The railroad barons also made secret agreements among themselves, known as **pools.** They divided business among their companies and set rates. With no other competition in its region, a railroad could charge higher rates and earn greater profits. There were some laws to regulate the railroads, but they did little to stop the barons.

Railroads Change America

The growing railroad network helped American industry expand into the West. For example, the manufacturing center for agricultural equipment moved from central New York State to Illinois and Wisconsin. Trains also redistributed the American population. They transported homesteaders into the Great Plains and the West and people from rural areas to the cities.

Reading Check **Describing** What were some of the new technologies that improved railroad travel?

Section 1 Review

History ONLINE
Study Central™ To review this section, go to glencoe.com.

Vocabulary

1. Use each of these terms in a sentence that will help explain its meaning: labor, consolidation, individual, railroad baron, standard gauge, rebate, pool.

Main Ideas

2. Explaining How did railroad barons build their fortunes?

3. Evaluating Do you think Congress should have allowed railroad barons to make agreements about business and rates? Explain your answer.

Critical Thinking

4. Classifying What are some industries that benefited from the expansion of the railroad system?

5. Making Inferences Do you think owners of small farms supported the rebates given by railroad companies?

6. Expository Writing Write a paragraph explaining how the adoption of standard-gauge track affected the railroads.

Answer the
7. Essential Question
How did railroad expansion affect the United States economy?

The Industrial Age **Chapter 19** **587**

Section 2 · Inventions

Essential Question

How did the inventions of the late 1800s revolutionize society?

Reading Guide

Content Vocabulary

Model T (p. 593)

mass production (p. 593)

assembly line (p. 593)

Academic Vocabulary

transmit (p. 589) mechanism (p. 592)

Key People and Events

Cyrus Field (p. 589)

Alexander Graham Bell (p. 590)

George Eastman (p. 590)

John Thurman (p. 590)

Lewis Howard Latimer (p. 592)

Granville Woods (p. 592)

Elijah McCoy (p. 592)

Jan E. Matzeliger (p. 592)

Henry Ford (p. 592)

Reading Strategy

Taking Notes As you read, use a chart like the one below to identify the effects of major inventions.

	Effects
Telegraph	
Telephone	
Electric lightbulb	

NEW YORK STANDARDS
The American Journey

U7.I.1 To understand how industrialization led to significant changes in the economic patterns for producing, distributing, and consuming goods and services

U7.I.3 To define basic economic concepts such as scarcity, supply and demand, markets, resources, and economic growth

U7.II.2 To investigate key turning points in New York State and United States history and explain why these events or developments are significant

American Diary

The Cleveland Plain Dealer described the lighting of a park in 1879: "Thousands of people gathered . . . and as the light shot around and through the Park a shout was raised. . . . Soon afterward a section of artillery on the lake shore began firing a salute in honor of the occasion. The Telegraph Supply Company's establishment . . . was thrown open to as many people as could be accommodated . . . [to] inspect the machinery which sends light over the wire."

—from Men and Volts

Electricity lights up Luna Park on Coney Island in New York, 1890.

588

Communications

Main Idea New inventions revolutionized communications, making faraway places seem closer.

History and You Do you talk on a cell phone or e-mail people in other states or countries? Read to learn how long-distance communication changed in the late 1800s.

. . . .

By 1910, Americans in cities drove cars through streets lit with electric lights. They went to department stores where they bought everything from kitchen sinks to shoes. Americans also could do their shopping by mail—or pick up the telephone and order groceries from the local store. The automobile, the electric light, and the telephone were invented after 1870. Within a generation, they became part of everyday life for millions of people. These new inventions helped people communicate more quickly over long distances. Improvements in communication helped unify the country and promoted economic growth.

The Telegraph

Samuel Morse had introduced the telegraph in 1844. By 1860 the United States had thousands of miles of telegraph lines, managed mostly by the Western Union Telegraph Company. At telegraph offices, trained operators **transmitted**, or sent, messages in Morse code.

Telegrams offered almost instant communication and served many purposes. Shopkeepers relied on telegrams to order goods, and reporters used them to transmit stories to their newspapers. Americans also used telegrams to send personal messages.

The telegraph soon linked the United States and Europe. In the 1860s, news from Europe was relayed to the United States by ship and took several weeks. **Cyrus Field** wanted to speed up the process. In 1866, after several unsuccessful attempts, Field managed to lay a telegraph cable across the Atlantic Ocean. The new transatlantic telegraph transmitted messages in a matter of seconds, bringing the United States and Europe closer together.

Primary Source / **Lewis Latimer**

Improving Technology Lewis Latimer was a draftsman and an inventor who received numerous patents for his inventions. In 1876 he was hired to draft the patent drawings for Alexander Graham Bell's telephone. Later, he improved on Edison's version of the lightbulb, creating one that lasted much longer. Latimer directed the installation of electric streetlights in New York City, Philadelphia, Montreal, and London.

Critical Thinking

Making Connections What types of technology today make your life easier?

Primary Source | The Wright Brothers

Taking Flight Inventors experimented with engine-powered aircraft in the 1800s, but attempts were not successful until 1903. Orville and Wilbur Wright made the world's first flight in an engine-powered glider at Kill Devil Hill, near Kitty Hawk, North Carolina.

◄ Orville and his brother Wilbur operated a bicycle shop in Dayton, Ohio, in the 1890s. Both expert mechanics, they became interested in the concept of human flight.

▲ On December 17, 1903, the Wright brothers fitted their glider with a gasoline engine. They made four flights at Kitty Hawk, the longest covering 852 feet (260 m) and lasting 59 seconds.

◄ The Wright brothers designed and tested gliders. From these experiments, they learned how to control an aircraft.

The Telephone Rings In

Alexander Graham Bell invented a device that revolutionized communications even more. Born and educated in Scotland, Bell moved to the United States, where he studied methods for teaching hearing-impaired people to speak. He also experimented with sending voices through electrical wires.

By 1876 Bell developed a device that transmitted speech—the telephone. While preparing to test the device, he accidentally spilled battery acid on his clothes. Panicked, Bell called out to his assistant in another room: "Mr. Watson, come here. I want you!" Watson heard Bell's voice coming through the telephone. The invention was a success.

Bell formed the Bell Telephone Company in 1877. By the 1890s, he had sold hundreds of thousands of phones. Businesses were the first customers to use telephones. Before long, though, telephones were common in homes.

Reading Check **Comparing** Describe the difference between a telegraph and a telephone.

The Genius of Invention

Main Idea Revolutionary new inventions changed business and everyday life in the 1800s.

History and You Have you ever had an idea for an invention that would make life easier? Read about inventions that improved people's lives.

The late 1800s saw a burst of inventiveness in the United States. Between 1860 and 1890, the United States government granted more than 400,000 patents for new inventions.

Many of the inventions were designed to help businesses operate more efficiently. Among these were Christopher Sholes's typewriter (1868) and William Burroughs's adding machine (1888).

Other inventions affected everyday life. In 1888 **George Eastman** invented a small box camera—the Kodak—that made it easier and less costly to take photographs. **John Thurman** developed a vacuum cleaner in 1899 that simplified housework.

590 **Chapter 19** *The Industrial Age*

In 1908 Wilbur created a sensation in France by controlling his aircraft in different types of wind. He also set new distance and altitude records. ▶

"The airplane became the promise of the future, and pilots were the popular heroes. . . . Even the routine flights of today retain a touch of magic, reminiscent of the Wright brothers' real intent, which was not speed, money, or military might but simply to break the bonds of Earth and see the world in a new way."

—Astronaut Edwin "Buzz" Aldrin, May 1998

◀ As shown by this aerial bomb test in 1911, the Wrights' invention soon attracted the attention of the U.S. military as well as militaries around the world.

Critical Thinking

Analyzing Primary Sources According to Buzz Aldrin, what was the Wright brothers' greatest accomplishment?

The Wizard of Menlo Park

Thomas Edison was called "dull" by his teachers. Because of his poor hearing, he had trouble in school and often did not attend. His mother finally removed him from school and taught him at home. Edison loved anything related to science, and his mother allowed him to set up a chemistry lab in the family's basement.

When he was 12, Edison got a job working for the railroad, where he set up a new lab in an empty freight car. One day, Edison saved the life of a child who had fallen onto the tracks of an oncoming train. The child's father took an interest in Edison and taught him to use the telegraph. Edison's first invention was a gadget that sent automatic telegraph signals—which he invented so he could sleep on the job.

While still in his 20s, Edison decided to go into the "invention business." In 1876 he set up a workshop in Menlo Park, New Jersey. Out of this famous laboratory came the phonograph, the motion picture projector, the telephone transmitter, and the storage battery. Edison's most important invention by far, though, was the electric lightbulb.

Edison developed the first workable lightbulb in 1879. He then designed power plants that could produce electric power and distribute it to lightbulbs. For Christmas in 1880, Edison used 40 bulbs to light up Menlo Park. Visitors flocked to see the "light of the future." Then, in 1882, Edison built the first central electric power plant in New York City—illuminating 85 buildings!

Inventor George Westinghouse took Thomas Edison's work with electricity even further. In 1885 Westinghouse developed and built transformers that could send electric power more cheaply over longer distances. As a result of Westinghouse's work, factories, trolleys, streetlights, and lamps throughout the United States could be powered by electricity. Westinghouse also created a method for transporting natural gas and invented many safety devices.

Lightbulbs and Vacuum Cleaners The late 1800s could be called the age of invention. The inventions helped change the everyday lives of Americans.

▼ Alexander Graham Bell's first phone

In 1888 George Eastman marketed the Kodak camera. After taking 100 pictures, a user could send it back to the company. The developed photos and a reloaded camera were returned to the customer by mail. ▲

★ **1876** Telephone

★ **1879** Lightbulb

★ **1888** Kodak camera

★ **1868** Typewriter

★ **1877** Phonograph

★ **1888** Adding machine

★ **1899** Motorized vacuum cleaner

▼ Alexander Graham Bell patented the telephone in 1876. There were two million in use by 1900.

◄ Thomas Edison's invention of the phonograph in 1877 attracted worldwide attention.

Critical Thinking

Evaluating Which invention do you think affected people's lives the most? Why?

African American Inventors

A number of African Americans contributed to the era of invention. Engineer **Lewis Howard Latimer** developed an improved wire for the lightbulb and joined Thomas Edison's company. **Granville Woods,** an electrical and mechanical engineer from Ohio, patented dozens of inventions. Among them were an electric incubator and railroad improvements such as an electromagnetic brake and an automatic circuit breaker. **Elijah McCoy** invented a mechanism, or mechanical device, for oiling machinery.

Jan E. Matzeliger, another African American inventor, developed a shoe-making machine that performed many steps previously done by hand. His device, which revolutionized the shoe industry, was used in in the United States and overseas.

✓ **Reading Check** **Evaluating** Which of Edison's inventions do you think is the most valuable to our world today? Explain your reasoning.

A Changing Society

Main Idea Henry Ford's automobile and assembly line changed industry and society forever.

History and You How might your life be different if the automobile had never been invented? Read to learn about the invention of the automobile.

In the 1900s, improvements ushered in a new era of transportation. After much experimentation, the automobile became a practical machine for traveling from place to place.

Henry Ford's Automobiles

Henry Ford had a vision. He wanted to build an inexpensive car that would last a lifetime. While working as an engineer in Detroit, Michigan, in the 1890s, Ford experimented with an automobile engine that was powered by gasoline. In 1903 he established his own auto-making company in Detroit and began designing cars.

In 1906 Ford had an idea for a new type of car. He told Charles Sorenson, later Ford's general superintendent, "We're going to get a car now that we can make in great volume and get the prices way down." For the next year, Ford and Sorenson worked on the **Model T,** building the car and testing it on rough roads. In 1908 Ford introduced the Model T to the public. Sorenson described the sturdy black vehicle as "a car which anyone could afford to buy, which anyone could drive anywhere, and which almost anyone could keep in repair." These qualities made the Model T immensely popular. During the next 18 years, Ford's company sold 15 million Model Ts.

Henry Ford also pioneered a new, less expensive way to manufacture cars—the **assembly line.** On the assembly line, each worker performed an assigned production task again and again. The assembly line revolutionized other industries as well. It enabled manufacturers to produce large quantities of goods more quickly. This **mass production** of goods decreased manufacturing costs, so products could be sold more cheaply.

Selling Goods

Merchants looked for more efficient ways to sell their goods. One method was through the mail. Before 1863 people picked up their mail at post offices. After 1863 mail was delivered directly to people's homes.

Merchants could now send goods cross country nearly as easily as across town. Some firms developed mail order businesses—receiving and shipping orders by mail. Companies such as Montgomery Ward and Sears Roebuck published catalogs that offered a wide range of goods from shoes to farm equipment.

Chain stores—stores with identical branches in many places—grew rapidly. F. W. Woolworth's chain of "five-and-ten-cent stores" specialized in the sale of everyday household and personal items at bargain prices. By 1911, more than 1,000 Woolworths were in operation. The Woolworth Building, erected in New York City in 1913, stood 792 feet (241 m) tall—the tallest building in the world at that time.

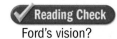 **Reading Check** **Identifying** What was Henry Ford's vision?

Section 2 Review

History ONLINE
Study Central™ To review this section, go to glencoe.com.

Vocabulary

1. Use each of these terms in a sentence that will help explain its meaning: transmit, mechanism, Model T, assembly line, mass production.

Main Ideas

2. Assessing What was the significance of the transatlantic telegraph cable?

3. Explaining How did George Westinghouse build upon Thomas Edison's inventions?

4. Analyzing What effect did the assembly line have on the manufacturing industry?

Critical Thinking

5. Evaluating In your opinion, what were the five most important inventions of this time? List them in order in a chart, and provide your reasons.

Top 5 Inventions	Reasons

6. Concluding How did companies change the way goods were sold to the public in the late 1800s?

7. Expository Writing Some people believe that the Internet has been the most revolutionary invention in communications since the telegraph. Write a paragraph in which you compare the two inventions and explain whether you support this view.

8. Answer the Essential Question
How did the inventions of the late 1800s revolutionize society?

Section 3

An Age of Big Business

Essential Question ◄

How did Americans build fortunes in the oil and steel industries?

Reading Guide

Content Vocabulary

corporation (p. 596)   trust (p. 597)

stock (p. 596)   monopoly (p. 597)

shareholders (p. 596)   merger (p. 599)

dividend (p. 596)

Academic Vocabulary

partner (p. 597)   trend (p. 599)

Key People and Events

John D. Rockefeller (p. 597)

Andrew Carnegie (p. 598)

Sherman Antitrust Act (p. 599)

Reading Strategy

Taking Notes As you read, create a diagram like the one below to organize information about the oil and steel industries.

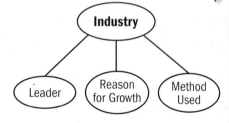

Industry → Leader, Reason for Growth, Method Used

NEW YORK STANDARDS
The American Journey

U7.I.1 To understand how industrialization led to significant changes in the economic patterns for producing, distributing, and consuming goods and services

U7.I.2 To explain how societies and nations attempt to satisfy their basic needs and wants by utilizing scarce capital, natural, and human resources

U7.I.3 To define basic economic concepts such as scarcity, supply and demand, markets, resources, and economic growth

American Diary

A man once told author Ida M. Tarbell that, "The only time I ever saw John Rockefeller enthusiastic was when a report came in from the creek that his buyer had secured a cargo of oil at a figure much below the market price. He bounded from his chair with a shout of joy, danced up and down, hugged me, threw up his hat, acted so like a madman that I have never forgotten it."

—*from* The History of the Standard Oil Company

Oil wells in Los Angeles, California, area during the late 1800s

Foundations for Growth

Main Idea New technology and abundant natural resources led to economic growth.

History and You If you wanted to start your own small business, what resources would you need? Read about the resources that were available for the oil and steel industries.

. . . .

In western Pennsylvania, a sticky black substance—petroleum—seeped from the ground. For a while, promoters sold the oil as medicine. Then, in the 1850s, researchers found they could burn petroleum to produce heat and smoke-free light. It could also be used to lubricate machinery. Suddenly, oil became valuable.

Edwin L. Drake believed that he could find petroleum by digging a well. Many people thought Drake was wrong. At that time, few people knew that pools of oil did indeed exist underground. They did not imagine that oil wells could lead to great fortune.

In 1859 Drake drilled a well in Titusville, Pennsylvania, and struck oil. This led to the creation of a multimillion-dollar petroleum industry.

Factors of Production

During the late 1800s, new technology, transportation, and business methods allowed the country to tap its rich supply of natural resources and increase production.

The change from an agricultural economy to an industrial one was possible because the United States had the resources needed for a growing economy. Among these resources were what economists call the factors of production: land, labor, and capital.

The first factor of production, land, refers not just to the land itself but all natural resources. The United States held a variety of natural resources that were useful for industrial production.

The second factor of production is labor. Large numbers of workers were needed to turn raw materials into goods. This need was met by rapid population growth. Between 1860 and 1900, the population of the country more than doubled.

The third factor of production is capital, which are the manufactured goods used to make other goods and services. The machines, buildings, and tools used to assemble automobiles, for example, are capital goods.

Primary Source / Big Business

Monopolies Big corporations were often portrayed as "monopoly monsters" that were too powerful to be controlled.

The United States is swallowed by the Giant of Monopoly, ca. 1890. ▶

Critical Thinking

Evaluating Why might laws be passed to control monopolies?

The term *capital* also means "money for investment." One source of money is the sale of stock by corporations. Another is corporate savings, or businesses investing some of their earnings in better equipment.

Raising Capital

With the economy growing after the Civil War, many railroads and other businesses looked for ways to expand. To do so, they had to raise capital. They needed capital to buy raw materials and equipment, to pay workers, and to cover shipping and advertising costs.

One way a company could raise capital was by becoming a **corporation.** A corporation is a company that sells shares, or **stock,** of its business to the public. People who invest in the corporation by buying stock are its **shareholders,** or partial owners.

During periods of strong economic growth, shareholders earn **dividends**—cash payments from the corporation's profits—on the stock they own. If the company fails, however, the shareholders lose their investment. In the late 1800s, hundreds of thousands of people bought and sold stocks in special markets known as stock exchanges.

The growth of corporations helped fuel America's industrial expansion in the years following the Civil War. Railroads were the first businesses to form corporations, followed by manufacturing firms and other businesses. Banks also played a major role in this period of economic growth. They made profits by lending money to new businesses.

Reading Check **Explaining** Why is capital important for economic growth?

Primary Source / **Factors of Production**

"I am a woman who came from the cotton fields of the South. I was promoted from there to the wash-tub. Then I was promoted to the cook kitchen, and from there I promoted myself into the business of manufacturing hair goods and preparations. . . . I have built my own factory on my own ground."
—Madam C. J. Walker, quoted in *On Her Own Ground*

Land
Natural resources

Labor
Human skills and effort

Capital
Buildings, tools, equipment

▲ Madam C. J. Walker, American entrepreneur

Entrepreneurs People bring together the factors of production to create products and services. They accept the risk of running a business to earn a profit.

Products and Services

Critical Thinking

1. **Categorizing** You use a calculator to complete your math homework. Which factor of production is your calculator?

2. **Theorizing** What qualities should a person have to become a successful entrepreneur?

This 1800s cartoon represents John D. Rockefeller's near-total control of the oil industry.

1. **Identifying** What type of character does Rockefeller represent in this cartoon?

2. **Analyzing** Why is Rockefeller shown holding the world in his hand?

A. John D. Rockefeller
B. oil lamp
C. world

The Oil Business

Main Idea John D. Rockefeller's Standard Oil Company controlled the booming oil industry.

History and You Recall how the railroad barons became powerful. Read how similar events occurred in the oil industry.

The oil industry grew rapidly in the late 1800s. As word of Edwin Drake's success spread, prospectors and investors hurried to western Pennsylvania. "Oil rush" towns with names such as Oil City and Petroleum Center sprang up overnight. The oil boom expanded as prospectors struck oil in Ohio and West Virginia.

Great fortunes were made from oil. Born in Richford, New York, in 1839, **John D. Rockefeller** was the most famous figure of the oil industry. When Rockefeller was 26 years old, he and four **partners,** or associates who agree to operate a business together, built an oil refinery—a plant to process oil—in Cleveland, Ohio.

In 1870 Rockefeller organized the Standard Oil Company of Ohio and set out to dominate the oil industry. One method he used was horizontal integration—combining competing companies into one corporation. Standard Oil grew powerful and wealthy.

The Standard Oil Trust

Rockefeller lowered his prices to drive his competitors out of business, pressured customers not to deal with rival companies, and persuaded the railroads to give him special rates. In 1882 he formed a **trust,** a group of companies managed by the same board of directors. Rockefeller did this by acquiring stock in many different oil companies. The shareholders of these companies traded their stock for Standard Oil stock, which paid higher dividends. As a result, Standard Oil became part owner of the other companies. Rockefeller had created a **monopoly**—total control of an industry by a single producer.

Reading Check **Describing** How did Standard Oil become a monopoly?

Economics & History

During the late 1800s, vertical and horizontal integration helped businesses grow into monopolies.

Vertical Integration
Purchase of companies at all levels of production

Ace Meat Industries
- Delivery wagons
- Meat packing plants
- Cooled warehouse
- Refrigerated railroad cars
- Slaughterhouse
- Cattle

Horizontal Integration
Purchase of competing companies in same industry

U.S. Oil Company

Independent Oil Refineries

Diagram Skills

Contrasting What is the difference between vertical integration and horizontal integration?

The Steel Business

Main Idea New processes for making steel created an important industry.

History and You Have you heard of Carnegie Hall in New York City? Read to learn about the influential man for whom this cultural landmark is named.

Steel also became a huge business in the late 1800s. A strong and long-lasting form of iron treated with carbon, steel was the ideal material for railroad tracks, bridges, and many other products.

Steel Industry Growth

Two new methods of making steel—the Bessemer process, developed by English inventor Henry Bessemer, and the open-hearth process—changed the industry. With these new methods, mills could produce steel at affordable prices and in large quantities. In the 1870s, large steel mills were built near sources of iron ore in western Pennsylvania and eastern Ohio. Pittsburgh, Pennsylvania, became the steel capital of the United States. Cleveland, Chicago, Detroit, and Birmingham, Alabama, also became important hubs for steel production.

Andrew Carnegie

The leading figure in the early years of the American steel industry was **Andrew Carnegie,** the son of a Scottish immigrant. Starting as a messenger and telegraph operator, Carnegie worked his way up to become manager of the Pennsylvania Railroad. In 1865 he invested in the growing iron industry. Carnegie soon realized that there was an enormous market for steel. After learning about the Bessemer process, he built a steel plant near Pittsburgh.

Working Conditions

Main Idea Factory workers toiled under terrible conditions.

History and You When you are working on a project, do you take breaks? Why are breaks necessary? Read to learn what life was like for factory workers.

The industrial growth of the late 1800s created new jobs. Yet factory workers paid a price for economic progress. As mass production increased, factories became larger and less personal.

Industrial laborers worked for 10 or 12 hours a day, six days a week. They could be fired at any time for any reason. Many lost their jobs during business downturns or were replaced by immigrants who were willing to work for lower pay.

People worked in unsafe and unhealthy factory conditions, and accidents were common in factories and mines. Steelworkers suf-fered burns. Coal miners died in cave-ins and from the effects of gas and coal dust. Garment workers toiled in crowded and dangerous urban factories called **sweatshops.**

Women and Children

By 1900 more than one million women had joined the industrial workforce. Because there were no laws that regulated workers' salaries, women, in general, earned about half of what men did for the same work.

Hundreds of thousands of children under 16 years of age also worked in factories. Many states passed child-labor laws that said children working in factories had to be at least 12 years old and should not work more than 10 hours a day. Employers, however, widely ignored child-labor laws.

Reading Check **Calculating** How many hours a week did industrial laborers typically work?

History ONLINE
Student Web Activity Visit glencoe.com and complete the Chapter 19 Web Activity about industrial workers.

By the Numbers / Cost of Living

Working for a Living For industrial workers in the early 1900s, life was difficult. Most family members, including children, worked for long hours and low pay. Employers often hired and paid on a weekly or daily basis. A worker did not get paid if he or she was unable to work because of illness or if an employer closed the factory because business was slow.

Average Hourly Wages*
Bricklayers: 50¢
Plasterers: 50¢
Newspaper compositors: 36¢
Machine woodworkers: 25¢
Construction workers: 17¢
Metalworkers: 16¢

(*in Chicago, 1903)

Average Expenses*
Rent: $4–10 per month
Butter: 22¢ per pound
Milk: 6¢ per quart
Bread: 5¢ per loaf
Rib roast: 13¢ per pound
Postage: 2¢ per ounce

(*in Chicago, 1903)

Critical Thinking

Speculating What do you think is the biggest expense today for workers?

Workers repair train wheels in 1904.

Growth of Labor Unions

Main Idea Workers organized unions in order to acquire better wages, benefits, and working conditions.

History and You Have you ever been a part of a group that was working for a common goal? Did the group achieve its goal? Why or why not? Read to learn about labor unions and their goals.

. . . .

Dissatisfied workers organized into groups—labor unions—to demand better pay and working conditions from their employers. Earlier in the 1800s, skilled workers had formed unions to represent workers in certain crafts or trades, such as carpentry. These **trade unions** had little influence because each represented only one trade and were too small to be effective. By the mid-1800s, as working conditions worsened, labor leaders looked to expand their unions.

In 1869 garment cutters in Philadelphia founded a trade union known as the Noble and Holy Order of the **Knights of Labor.** Employers fired workers who joined labor organizations, so the Knights met secretly and used special handshakes to **identify,** or recognize, one another.

Under the leadership of **Terence V. Powderly,** the Knights of Labor became a national labor organization in the 1880s. Unlike most unions, the Knights recruited people who were traditionally kept out of trade unions, including women, African Americans, immigrants, and unskilled laborers.

The Knights of Labor grew to more than 700,000 members by 1886. A wave of strikes, however, turned public opinion against the union, and it lost power in the 1890s.

In 1881 a group of national trade unions formed the **American Federation of Labor** (AFL). The AFL represented skilled workers in various crafts.

The Labor Movement, 1877–1914 — NATIONAL GEOGRAPHIC

Unions Struggle After the Civil War, labor leaders sought to organize large national unions. In the late 1800s, however, government opposition, internal divisions, and public disapproval limited the movement's progress.

◀ Unions gained strength in the late 1800s and worked more actively for workers' rights.

▼ Labor unrest during the Pullman Strike, 1894

1 1877 Great Railway Strike
Workers protest pay cuts

2 1886 Haymarket Affair
Labor rally ends in violence

3 1892 New Orleans
Workers from 42 unions demand shorter hours and better pay

4 1892 Homestead Strike
Steelworkers protest wage cut

5 1892 Silver Mine Unrest
State jails hundreds of striking workers

6 1894 Pullman Strike
Federal troops end riots

7 1902 Anthracite Coal Strike
Miners strike to win union recognition

8 1914 Ludlow Massacre
State militia burns striking miners' tent colony

Critical Thinking

Identifying Which strikes involved miners?

People IN HISTORY

Samuel Gompers

Leader of the American Federation of Labor

Samuel Gompers did not think that unions should always support the same political party. Rather, Gompers argued that unions should support any political party that worked for the unions' goals. He also believed the best way to achieve labor's goals was through collective bargaining. Gompers stressed that *"the individual workman is as weak against the combination of wealth as would be a straw in a cyclone."* Workers could only *"stand on an equal footing with the employers"* when they were organized into labor unions.

Mary Harris Jones

Labor organizer

Mary Harris Jones, also known as "Mother Jones," traveled across the country organizing workers for the United Mine Workers union. She also supported strikes and tried to sway public opinion in favor of unions. Denounced in the United States Senate, Jones believed that *"there are no limits to which powers of privilege will not go to keep the workers in slavery."*

CRITICAL Thinking

1. **Identifying** According to Gompers, how could labor unions help workers?
2. **Synthesizing** How did Gompers and Jones view employers?

The AFL was led by **Samuel Gompers,** the tough and practical-minded president of the Cigar Makers' Union. The organization pressed for higher wages, shorter hours, better working conditions, and the right to **collective bargaining**—when unions represent workers in labor discussions with management.

Although violent strikes turned public feeling against workers and unions in the late 1880s, the AFL survived and grew. By 1904, the AFL claimed more than 1.6 million members.

Women and the Unions

Many unions would not admit women workers, so some women formed their own unions. Mary Harris Jones, also known as Mother Jones, spent 50 years fighting for workers' rights.

In 1911 a fire broke out at the Triangle Shirtwaist Company factory, a sweatshop in New York City. The workers, mostly young immigrant women, could not escape because the company locked the doors to prevent employees from leaving early. Nearly 150 workers died. The disaster led the International Ladies' Garment Workers Union (ILGWU) to push for a safer working **environment.**

The Unions Act

Economic depressions in the 1870s and the 1890s forced companies to lower wages and, in some cases, fire workers. Unions responded with large strikes that sometimes sparked violence.

After a financial panic in 1873, an economic depression hit the nation. To cut costs, companies forced their workers to take pay cuts.

In July 1877, angry strikers burned rail yards, ripped up track, and destroyed railroad property. The companies hired **strikebreakers** to replace the striking workers, and federal troops restored order.

Antilabor feeling grew stronger after a bloody clash between police and strikers in Chicago's Haymarket Square in May 1886. Striking workers from the McCormick Harvester Company gathered to protest the killings of four strikers the previous day. When police ordered the crowd to break up, an unidentified person threw a bomb that killed a police officer. Several more were killed in a riot that followed. Following the Haymarket Riot, many Americans associated the labor movement with terrorism and disorder.

In 1892 workers went on strike at Andrew Carnegie's steel plant in Homestead, Pennsylvania. In the attempt to weaken the steelworkers' union, plant managers had cut workers' wages. When the union called a strike, Homestead managers hired nonunion workers and brought in 300 armed guards to protect them. A fierce battle left at least 10 people dead.

Pennsylvania's governor sent the state's militia to Homestead to restore order. The plant reopened with nonunion workers, protected by the troops. After the failure of the Homestead Strike, the number of members in the steelworkers' union dwindled.

The employees of George Pullman's railway-car plant near Chicago went on strike in May 1894, when the company cut their wages. Pullman responded by closing the plant. One month later, workers in the American Railway Union supported the strikers by refusing to handle Pullman cars. As a result, rail traffic was paralyzed.

Pullman and the railroad owners fought back with the help of the government. They persuaded U.S. Attorney General Richard Olney to obtain an **injunction,** or court order, to stop the union from "obstructing the railways and holding up the mails." Yet the union and its leader, **Eugene V. Debs,** still refused to end the strike. Debs was sent to jail.

President Grover Cleveland sent federal troops to Chicago, and soon the strike was over. The failure of the Pullman Strike dealt another blow to the union movement. Despite these setbacks, however, workers continued to organize to campaign for better wages and working conditions.

Reading Check **Explaining** Why were there growing antilabor feelings during the late 1800s?

History ONLINE
Study Central™ To review this section, go to glencoe.com.

Section 4 Review

Vocabulary

1. Use each of these terms in a sentence that will help explain its meaning: sweatshop, trade union, identify, collective bargaining, environment, strikebreaker, injunction.

Main Ideas

2. **Describing** How were women and children treated as members of the industrial workforce?

3. **Making Inferences** Why did employers fire workers who joined labor organizations?

Critical Thinking

4. **Comparing** Compare the Pullman Strike and the Homestead Strike. Create a Venn diagram like the one below to identify their similarities.

5. **Evaluating** Were the early labor unions successful? Explain.

6. **Persuasive Writing** As a member of Congress, write a speech supporting federal child-labor laws.

Answer the
7. **Essential Question**
Why did workers form labor unions in the middle to late 1800s?

Visual Summary

Main Idea	Supporting Details
Expansion of Railroads	• From 1860 to 1900, more than 163,000 miles (262,323 km) of new railroad track is laid in the United States. • The width of railroad track becomes standard, simplifying transport by train. • Improvements are introduced such as air brakes, linking systems, refrigerated cars, and sleeping cars.
New Inventions	• Transatlantic telegraph • Telephone • Camera • Vacuum cleaner • Electric lightbulb • Model-T car
Growth of Big Business	• U.S. has plentiful resources, including those making up the factors of production—land, labor, and capital. • A few giant corporations, especially in oil and steel, hold substantial economic power. • Trusts and monopolies make corporations efficient but create less competiton, hurting consumers.
Philanthropy	• Carnegie builds Carnegie Hall, one of the world's most famous music halls, and more than 2,000 libraries nationwide. • Rockefeller establishes the University of Chicago and New York's Rockefeller Institute for Medical Research.
Workers' Rights	• Factory workers, miners, and other laborers work long hours, often under dangerous conditions. • Trade unions, such as the AFL, expand in order to represent more workers. • Workers strike in several industries, sometimes sparking violence.

◀ Pullman Strike, 1894

STUDY TO GO Study anywhere, anytime! Download quizzes and flash cards to your PDA from glencoe.com.

GRADE 8 INTERMEDIATE TEST PRACTICE

TEST-TAKING TIP

Answer the questions you know first. Then go back to answer those for which you need more time.

Reviewing Main Ideas

Directions: Choose the best answer for each of the following questions.

1 Large railroads of the 1800s offered their biggest customers secret discounts called

- **(1)** tariffs.
- **(2)** tolls.
- **(3)** rebates.
- **(4)** pools.

2 Which of the following was invented by George Eastman?

- **(1)** lightbulb
- **(2)** typewriter
- **(3)** phonograph
- **(4)** Kodak camera

3 Which factor of production refers to buildings, machinery, and tools?

- **(1)** land
- **(2)** dividends
- **(3)** labor
- **(4)** capital

4 The 1892 Homestead Strike erupted after

- **(1)** railway workers paralyzed rail traffic in protest over job cuts.
- **(2)** managers at Andrew Carnegie's steel plant cut workers' wages to weaken the union.
- **(3)** workers from the McCormick Harvester Company demanded a 40-hour workweek.
- **(4)** a fire killed workers at a garment factory, leading to calls for safer working conditions.

Short-Answer Question

Directions: Base your answer to question 5 on the excerpt below and on your knowledge of social studies.

> We want eight hours [work day] and nothing less. We have been accused of being selfish, and it has been said that we will want more; that last year we got an advance of ten cents and now we want more. We do want more. You will find that a man generally wants more. . . . You ask a workingman, who is getting two dollars a day, and he will say that he wants ten cents more. . . . The man who receives five thousand dollars a year wants six thousand dollars a year, and the man who owns eight or nine hundred thousand dollars will want a hundred thousand dollars more to make it a million.
>
> —Samuel Gompers, labor union leader

5 Restate the main idea of this excerpt in your own words.

Review the Essential Questions

6 Essay Explain why the late 1800s and early 1900s became known as the Age of Big Business.

To help you write your essay, review your answers to the Essential Questions in the section reviews and the chapter Foldables Study Organizer. Your essay should include:

- the effect of railroad expansion;
- the abundance of inventions in the late 1800s and their impact;
- factors of production and the business practices of industrial leaders; and
- government responses to labor unions.

History ONLINE

For additional test practice, use **Self-Check Quizzes**—Chapter 19 at glencoe.com.

Document-Based Questions

Directions: Analyze the documents and answer the short-answer questions that follow.

Document 1

The following words are from the workers' song "Drill, Ye Tarriers, Drill." "Tarrier" was the name given to Irish drillers who dug tunnels for the railroads.

> The new foreman is Dan McCann, / I'll tell you sure he's a blame mean man, / Last week a premature blast went off, / And a mile in the air went big Jim Goff.
>
> [Chorus:] Then drill, ye tarriers, drill, / Drill, ye tarriers, drill, / Oh it's work all day without sugar in your tay / When ye work beyant [beyond] on the railway, / And drill, ye tarriers, drill.
>
> When pay day next it came around, / Poor Jim's pay a dollar short he found, / "What for?" says he, then came this reply, / "You were docked for the time you were up in the sky."

Source: Norm Cohen, *Long Steel Rail: The Railroad in American Folksong*

7 How does the song reflect the challenges that railroad workers faced?

Document 2

Tall skyscrapers were built in the late 1800s. In 1879 Benjamin Oppenheimer submitted the drawing to the right with his patent application.

8 What do you think is the purpose of Oppenheimer's invention?

Source: A. E. Brown and H. A. Jeffcott, Jr., *World's Wackiest Inventions*

Document 3

John D. Rockefeller stated the following:

> God gave me my money. . . . Having been endowed with the gift I possess, I believe it is my duty to make money and still more money and to use the money I make for the good of my fellow man according to the dictates of my conscience.

Source: Suzy Platt, *Respectfully Quoted*

9 How did Rockefeller explain his own wealth? How do you think he might explain why some people are not wealthy?

Document 4

The following article, "Christianity and Wealth," is by Congregationalist minister Washington Gladden.

> During the past fourteen years the wealth of this nation has increased much faster than the population, but the people who work for wages are little if any better off than they were fourteen years ago. . . .
>
> But this is not saying that . . . the state [should] . . . take the property of the rich and distribute it among the poor. . . . There are, however, one or two things that [are] . . . the immediate duty of the state. Certain outrageous monopolies exist that the state is bound to crush. . . . Another gigantic public evil that the state must exterminate is that of gambling in stocks and produce.

Source: Washington Gladden, *Century Illustrated*

10 What problems does Gladden describe in the excerpt? What solution does he propose?

11 Expository Writing Using the information from the four documents and your knowledge of social studies, write an essay in which you:
- explain why this time period might be referred to as the beginning of modern America; and
- name at least one way American society today resembles the Industrial Age and one way it is different.

Need Extra Help?											
If you missed questions...	1	2	3	4	5	6	7	8	9	10	11
Go to page...	587	590	595	606	605	584–606	603	590	597	603	584–606

Chapter 20

An Urban Society 1865-1914

The Brooklyn Bridge with a view of the surrounding area, 1898

ANDREW JOHNSON 1865–1869

ULYSSES S. GRANT 1869–1877

RUTHERFORD B. HAYES 1877–1881

JAMES GARFIELD 1881

CHESTER ARTHUR 1881–1885

GROVER CLEVELAND 1885–1889

BENJAMIN HARRISON 1889–1893

PRESIDENTS

U.S. Events

World Events

1865

1875

1885

★ **1866**
Transatlantic telegraph line successfully completed

1882 ★
Robert Louis Stevenson's *Treasure Island* published

1889 ★
Eiffel Tower erected

Section 1: The New Immigrants

Essential Question What were some characteristics of the new wave of immigrants that arrived after 1865?

Section 2: Moving to the City

Essential Question How did cities change during the late 1800s?

Section 3: A Changing Culture

Essential Question In what ways did American culture change in the late 1800s?

FOLDABLES
Study Organizer

Organizing Information

Make this Foldable to help organize what you learn about changes to the culture of the United States.

Step 1 Place two sheets of paper on top of one another about one inch apart.

Step 2 Fold the papers to form four equal tabs.

Step 3 Staple the sheets, and label each tab as shown.

Reading and Writing As you read the chapter, write down key events and ideas that relate to the Essential Questions.

An Urban Society 1865-1914

Section 1: The New Immigrants
Essential Question:
Section 2: Moving to the City
Essential Question:
Section 3: A Changing Culture
Essential Question:

◀ Ford factory, Detroit, Michigan

★ **1892** Ellis Island admits immigrants

GROVER CLEVELAND 1893–1897

WILLIAM McKINLEY 1897–1901

THEODORE ROOSEVELT 1901–1909

1906 ★ San Francisco rocked by earthquake

WILLIAM HOWARD TAFT 1909–1913

★ **1913** Ford develops first moving assembly line

1895

1905

1915

1895 ★ First complete performance of *Swan Lake*

1900 ★ First trial flight of Zeppelin

★ **1907** Cubism arises in art

Section 1 — The New Immigrants

Essential Question ◄

What were some characteristics of the new wave of immigrants that arrived after 1865?

Reading Guide

Content Vocabulary

emigrate (p. 613)

sweatshop (p. 615)

ethnic group (p. 614)

assimilate (p. 616)

steerage (p. 614)

Academic Vocabulary

attitude (p. 617)   affect (p. 617)

Key People and Events

Emma Lazarus (p. 614)

Chinese Exclusion Act (p. 617)

Immigration Act of 1917 (p. 617)

Reading Strategy

Taking Notes As you read, place the immigration laws on a time line like the one below, and take notes on the purpose of each law.

1882	1892	1902	1907	1917

NEW YORK STANDARDS
The American Journey

U7.II.1 To understand how industrialization altered the traditional social pattern of American society and created a need for reform

U7.II.2 To investigate key turning points in New York State and United States history and explain why these events or developments are significant

U7.II.6 To understand how scarcity requires people and nations to make choices that involve costs and future considerations

American Diary

At the end of a long ocean voyage, immigrants waited for entry into the United States. "The steerage passengers have before them more rigid examinations . . . so in spite of . . . the glad greetings shouted to and fro, they sink again into awe-struck and confused silence. When the last . . . passenger has disappeared from the dock, the immigrants with their baggage are loaded into barges and taken to Ellis Island for their final examination."

—from On the Trail of the Immigrant *by Edward A. Steiner*

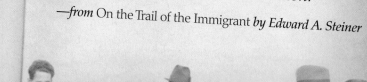

Newly arrived immigrants at Ellis Island

A Flood of Immigrants

Main Idea New immigrants began to arrive in the late 1800s, seeking opportunities in the United States.

History and You Have you seen pictures of or visited the Statue of Liberty? Read to learn the statue's significance to millions of immigrants.

$\bullet$

Before 1865, most immigrants to the United States—except for enslaved Africans—came from northern and western Europe. After the Civil War, immigrants from other countries began making the journey to the United States.

New Immigration

In the mid-1880s, the pattern of immigration started to change. Large groups of "new" immigrants arrived from eastern and southern Europe. Greeks, Russians, Hungarians, Italians, Turks, and Poles were among the newcomers. At the same time, the number of "old" immigrants from northern and western Europe started to decrease. By 1907, 80 percent of immigrants came from southern and eastern Europe.

Many of these newcomers were Catholics or Jews. Few spoke English. Because of this, they did not blend into American society as easily as the "old" immigrants had. Often, they clustered together in neighborhoods made up of people of the same nationality.

After 1900, immigration from Mexico also increased. In addition, many people came to the United States from China and Japan. They, too, brought unfamiliar languages and religious beliefs and had difficulty blending into American society.

Leaving Troubles Behind

Why did so many people leave their homelands for the United States in the late 1800s and early 1900s? They were "pushed" away by difficult conditions at home. At the same time, many were "pulled" to the United States by new opportunities.

Many people **emigrated,** or left their homelands, because of economic troubles. In Italy and Hungary, overcrowding and poverty made jobs scarce. Farmers in Croatia and Serbia could not own enough land to support their families. Sweden suffered major crop failures. New machines such as looms put many craft workers out of work.

Primary Source / **Responding to New Immigrants**

Differing Opinions People had different opinions about immigration. Although some believed the United States should welcome immigrants with open arms, others saw the flood of people entering the country as a problem. These views were reflected in political cartoons of the day.

◀ This magazine cover demonstrates one reaction to making Ellis Island a new processing station for immigrants. The cartoon on the cover shows the Statue of Liberty frowning as immigrants are dumped at her feet.

Critical Thinking

Comparing and Contrasting What symbols does the artist use to represent the United States? What message is the artist trying to convey about new immigrants?

Seeking Fairness

Persecution also drove people from their homelands. Some countries passed laws or set policies against certain **ethnic groups**—minorities that spoke different languages or followed different customs from those of most people in a country. Members of these ethnic groups often emigrated to escape discrimination or unfair laws. Many Jews fled persecution in Russia in the 1880s and came to the United States.

Seeking Opportunity

Immigrants saw the United States as a place of jobs, plentiful land, and opportunities for a better life. Although some immigrants returned to their homelands after a few years, most came to America to stay.

Immigrants often had a difficult journey to America. Many had to first travel to a seaport to board a ship. Often they traveled for hundreds of miles and through foreign countries to get to port cities.

Then came the long ocean voyage to the United States—12 days across the Atlantic or several weeks across the Pacific. Immigrants usually could afford only the cheapest tickets and traveled in **steerage**—cramped quarters on the lower decks of the ships.

Entering America

Most immigrants landed at New York City. After 1886, the magnificent sight of the Statue of Liberty greeted immigrants as they sailed into New York Harbor. The statue, a gift from the people of France, seemed to promise hope for a better life in the new country. On its base, the stirring words of **Emma Lazarus,** an American poet, welcomed the many immigrants arriving in the country from Europe: "Give me your tired, your poor, Your huddled masses yearning to breathe free, The wretched refuse of your teeming shore. Send these, the homeless, tempest-tossed to me, I lift my lamp beside the golden door!"

Primary Source / Statue of Liberty

The statue, shown here under construction in Paris, was a gift of friendship from the people of France. The statue's full name is "Liberty Enlightening the World." ▼

The torch is a symbol of liberty. The crown's rays stand for the seven seas and seven continents of the world. ▶

Lady Liberty holds a tablet that represents the book of law. In Roman numerals it reads "July 4, 1776." ▼

Statue Facts	
Overall height, base to tip of torch	305 feet, 6 inches
Height from her heel to top of her head	111 feet, 6 inches
Height of face	8 feet
Width of waistline	35 feet
Total weight	225 tons
Number of steps from base to head	154

Source: Ellis Island Foundation.

◀ At her feet lies a broken chain, meaning freedom from tyranny.

Before the new arrivals could actually pass through the "golden door" to America, however, they had to register at government reception centers. In the East, immigrants were processed at Castle Garden, a former fort on Manhattan Island. After 1892, they went through Ellis Island in New York Harbor. Most Asian immigrants arrived in the United States on the West Coast in California and went through the processing center on Angel Island in San Francisco Bay.

Examiners at the centers recorded the immigrants' names—sometimes shortening or simplifying a name they found too difficult to write. The examiners asked the immigrants where they came from, their occupation, and whether they had relatives in the United States. New immigrants also were given health examinations. Immigrants with contagious illnesses could be refused permission to enter the United States.

Reading Check Explaining Why was the voyage to America often difficult?

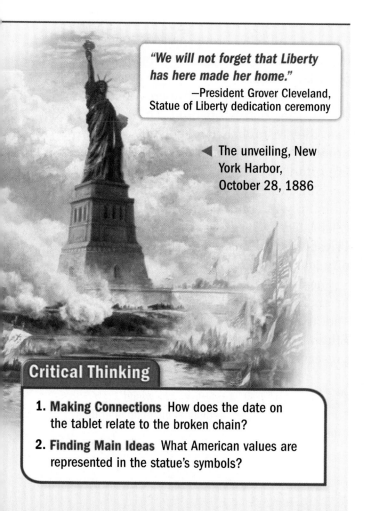

"We will not forget that Liberty has here made her home."
—President Grover Cleveland, Statue of Liberty dedication ceremony

◀ The unveiling, New York Harbor, October 28, 1886

Critical Thinking

1. **Making Connections** How does the date on the tablet relate to the broken chain?

2. **Finding Main Ideas** What American values are represented in the statue's symbols?

The Immigrant Experience

Main Idea Immigrants adjusted to life in America, finding work, forming communities, and adapting to a new culture.

History and You Are you familiar with parts of cities that are known as Little Italy or Chinatown? Read to learn how these neighborhoods might have formed.

After passing through the reception centers, most immigrants gained entry to the United States. Where would they go? How would they live? Some had relatives or friends to stay with and to help them find jobs. Others knew no one and would have to strike out on their own.

Finding Work

An immigrant's greatest challenge was finding work. Sometimes organizations in his or her homeland recruited workers for jobs in the United States. These organizations supplied American employers with unskilled workers who worked unloading cargo or digging ditches.

Some of America's fastest-growing industries hired immigrant workers. In the steel mills of Pittsburgh, for example, most of the laborers in the early 1900s were immigrant men. They might work 12 hours per day, seven days per week.

Many immigrants, including women and children, worked in **sweatshops** in the garment industry. These were dark, crowded shops where workers made clothing. The work was repetitious and hazardous, the pay low, and the hours long.

Pauline Newman, who later became an official in the International Ladies' Garment Workers Union, worked in a New York sweatshop as a child. She recalled: "We started work at 7:30 [in the morning] and during the busy season we worked until nine o' clock in the evening. They didn't pay any overtime and didn't give you anything for supper money. At times they would give you . . . a little apple pie . . . for your supper."

Primary Sources
INTERPRETING POLITICAL CARTOONS

This cartoon comments on successful Americans who wanted to limit immigration.

LOOKING BACKWARD THEY WOULD CLOSE TO THE NEWCOMER THE BRIDGE THAT CARRIED THEM AND THEIR FATHERS OVER.

1. **Interpreting** How are the successful Americans treating the new immigrant?

2. **Analyzing** If the Americans looked backward, as the title suggests, what would they see? What is the cartoonist saying?

A. New, poor immigrant   B. Successful Americans
C. Immigrant forefathers of the Americans

Adjusting to America

In their new homes, immigrants tried to preserve their own cultures. At the same time, most wanted to **assimilate,** or become part of the American culture. These two desires sometimes came into conflict.

Many immigrant parents continued to speak their native languages. Their children spoke English at school and with friends, but they spoke their native language at home. The grandchildren of many immigrants spoke only English.

Furthermore, in the United States, women generally had more freedom than women in European and Asian countries. New lifestyles conflicted with traditional ways and sometimes caused family friction.

Building Communities

Most of the new immigrants were from rural areas. Because they lacked the money to buy farmland in America, however, they often settled in industrial cities. With little or no education, they usually worked as unskilled laborers.

People of the same ethnic group tended to form separate communities. As a result, neighborhoods of Jewish, Italian, Polish, Chinese, and other groups quickly developed in New York, Chicago, San Francisco, and other large cities.

Immigrants sought to re-create some of the life they had left behind. The communities they established revolved around a number of traditional institutions. Most important were the houses of worship—the churches and the synagogues—where worship was conducted and holidays were celebrated as they were in their homelands. Priests and rabbis often acted as community leaders.

The immigrants published newspapers in their native languages, opened stores and theaters, and organized social clubs. Ethnic communities helped the immigrants preserve their cultural heritage.

Reading Check **Analyzing** Why would immigrants re-create traditional institutions in their new land?

The Nativist Movement

Main Idea Some people opposed immigration, while others appreciated the positive contributions made by immigrants.

History and You Did any of your relatives immigrate to the United States from another country? If so, when? Read to find out how immigrants were regarded by American society.

. . . .

Assimilation also was slowed by the **attitudes**—ways of thinking and acting—of many native-born Americans, who resented the new wave of immigrants. They feared that the new immigrants would take away their jobs or drive down everyone's wages by accepting lower pay. These Americans also argued that the new immigrants—with their foreign languages, unfamiliar religions, and distinctive customs—would not fit into American society.

People found it easy to blame immigrants for increasing crime, unemployment, and other problems. The nativist movement, which had opposed immigration since the 1830s, gained strength during the late 1800s. Calls for restrictions on immigration mounted.

Lawmakers responded quickly to the tide of anti-immigrant feeling. In 1882 Congress passed the **Chinese Exclusion Act,** which prohibited Chinese workers from entering the United States for 10 years. Congress extended this law in 1892 and again in 1902. Similarly, in 1907 the federal government and Japan came to a "gentleman's agreement" that aimed to limit the number of Japanese immigrants.

Other legislation **affected,** or had an impact on, immigrants from all nations. In 1897 Congress passed a bill that required immigrants to be able to read and write in some language. Although the president vetoed the bill, Congress later passed the **Immigration Act of 1917,** which included a similar literacy requirement.

On the other hand, some Americans supported immigration. These people recognized that immigrants supplied the country's industries with workers. We now appreciate that immigrants also enriched the country with the culture of their homelands.

Reading Check **Explaining** Why did some Americans blame immigrants for the nation's problems?

Section 1 Review

History ONLINE
Study Central™ To review this section, go to glencoe.com.

Vocabulary

1. Use each of these terms in a sentence that will help explain its meaning: emigrate, ethnic group, steerage, sweatshop, assimilate, attitude, affect.

Main Ideas

2. Contrasting How did immigration change after 1865?

3. Describing What were the working conditions in sweatshops?

4. Evaluating What is your opinion of the nativist movement?

Critical Thinking

5. Determining Cause and Effect What was the effect of each of the following immigration laws?

Chinese Exclusion Act	
"Gentleman's Agreement"	
Immigration Act of 1917	

6. Speculating What was an immigrant's greatest challenge upon arriving in the United States?

7. Expository Writing Write a paragraph explaining what happened at government reception centers for immigrants.

8. **Answer the Essential Question** What were some characteristics of the new wave of immigrants that arrived after 1865?

TIME NOTEBOOK

What were people's lives like in the past?

These two pages will give you some clues to everyday life in the United States as you step back in time with TIME Notebook.

AMERICA'S FIRST AUTO RACE
Built for Speed

BETTMANN / CORBIS

In 1893 two brothers, **CHARLES** and **FRANK DURYEA**, built the first American automobile in Springfield, Massachusetts. It could travel up to 7.5 miles per hour (mph). In 1895 the two bicycle mechanics held the first automobile race. The course was 54 miles (87 km), going from Chicago to Evanston, Illinois, and back again. Six cars started the race that snowy morning—the Duryea's second automobile, two electric cars, and three gas-powered Benzes from Germany. Here is how Frank Duryea describes the race:

The machine made good going of the soft unpacked snow in Jackson Park. . . . While still in the lead, the left front wheel struck a bad rut at such an angle that the steering arm was broken off. . . . We, fortunately, located a blacksmith shop where we forged down, threaded, and replaced the arm. . . . The Macy Benz passed us and held the lead as far as Evanston, where we regained it. Having made the turn at Evanston, elated at being in the lead again, we started on the home trip.

". . . One of the two cylinders ceased firing. . . . This repair was completed in fifty-five minutes and we got going, feeling that the Macy Benz must surely be ahead of us, but learned later that the Macy did not get that far. After a stop for gasoline . . . we continued on to the finish. . . . The motor had at all times shown ample power, and at no time were we compelled to get out and push."

Averaging 7.3 mph, Frank Duryea's car was the first to finish the race in just over 10 hours. He won the $2,000 prize.

VERBATIM
WHAT PEOPLE ARE SAYING

Assassination can be no more guarded against than death by lightning; and it is best not to worry about either.
> **PRESIDENT JAMES GARFIELD,**
> *Second United States president to be assassinated; he died from a gunshot wound in 1881*

The greatest bane [curse] of modern civilization.
> **DR. JOHN HARVEY KELLOGG,**
> *describing modern cooking in 1894. He had just invented a new "toasted corn flake" for the breakfast table*

I pledge allegiance to the flag of the United States of America . . .
> **YOUTH'S COMPANION,**
> *the first magazine to publish the Pledge of Allegiance in 1892*

We sat and looked as the lamp continued to burn, and the longer it burned, the more fascinated we were. None of us could go to bed. There was no sleep for any of us for 40 hours.
> **THOMAS EDISON,**
> *on inventing the lightbulb, which he patented in 1883*

I asked a man in prison once how he happened to be there and he said he had stolen a pair of shoes. I told him if he had stolen a railroad, he would be a United States senator.
> **"MOTHER" MARY JONES,**
> *labor activist*

CORBIS

The Eighth Wonder of the World

Fourteen years after construction began, the **BROOKLYN BRIDGE** —the largest suspension bridge in the world—opens in 1883. Schools and shops in Brooklyn are closed so everyone can celebrate.

With a span half again as long as that of any previous bridge, it hangs from steel cables. Its designer and builder, John Roebling, was killed on the job. His son, Washington, continued directing the work until he was injured. Then Washington's wife, Emily, completed the job, making her possibly the first woman field engineer.

618

The Well-Dressed Cowhand

These are prices from the Montgomery Ward catalogs of the 1880s.

Stetson hat $10.00
Cotton shirt (no collar) $1.25
Chaps and pants $8.00
Leather boots $20.00
Spurs $0.70
Colt pistol $12.20
Holster, cartridge belt $2.00
Saddle $40.00
Horse (usually
provided by ranch) $35.00
Lariat (lasso) $7.75

BETTMANN / CORBIS

MILESTONES

EVENTS AND PEOPLE OF THE TIME

OFFERED. A "company of fifty lady sharpshooters" to President William McKinley in 1898 at the start of the Spanish-American War, by the famous sharpshooter and performer, Annie Oakley. She promised each would bring along her own rifle and ammunition—McKinley has yet to respond to the offer.

CALLED. Government officials by President Rutherford B. Hayes, who took office in 1877; he was the first president to use the new telephone in the White House.

DRAWN. The first comic strip, *The Yellow Kid*, by R. F. Outcault in 1896—it has provided the name for dishonest reporting: "yellow journalism."

DEDICATED. The new Statue of Liberty in New York Harbor by President Cleveland in 1886.

SHOWN. First moving picture in 1896; featured are two girls dancing with umbrellas and two men boxing.

OPENED. Hull House in Chicago by Jane Addams in 1889—providing meals, health care, and education for the poor, including many immigrants.

HULTON-DEUTSCH COLLECTION / CORBIS

ANNIE OAKLEY

NUMBERS

UNITED STATES AT THE TIME

5 The number of transcontinental railroads crisscrossing the country in 1900

10 The number of years Chinese people must wait after applying to immigrate to the United States, according to the Chinese Immigration Act passed by Congress in 1882

21 The age of Frances Folsom when she married President Cleveland in 1886, making her the youngest First Lady

27,000,000

The number of visitors to the Chicago Exposition—sometimes called the first world's fair—in 1893, where visitors rode G.W. Ferris's new 250-foot-high invention, the Ferris wheel

VISUAL ARTS LIBRARY (LONDON) / ALAMY

200 Approximate number of Sioux Indians, mostly women and children, killed at Wounded Knee, South Dakota, when they were attacked by the American 7th Cavalry

CRITICAL THINKING

Describing Name the inventions and structures mentioned in this Notebook. How did each change the lives of Americans?

Analyzing Primary Sources Based on Duryea's diary of the race, why was it considered a daring and unusual adventure to race, or even drive, a car in 1893?

Section 2 — Moving to the City

Essential Question ◄

How did cities change during the late 1800s?

Reading Guide

Content Vocabulary

tenement (p. 622)

slum (p. 622)

suburb (p. 622)

settlement house (p. 623)

Hull House (p. 623)

skyscraper (p. 624)

Academic Vocabulary

major (p. 621)

minor (p. 623)

Key People and Events

Gilded Age (p. 622)

Jane Addams (p. 623)

Louis Sullivan (p. 624)

Frederick Law Olmsted (p. 625)

Reading Strategy

Taking Notes As you read, describe three effects of the growth of cities.

Growth of Cities

NEW YORK STANDARDS
The American Journey

U7.II.1 To understand how industrialization altered the traditional social pattern of American society and created a need for reform

U7.II.5 To describe historic events through the eyes and experiences of those who were there

U7.III.1 To understand how industrialization led to a need for reevaluating and changing the traditional role of government in relation to the economy and social conditions

American Diary

Americans across the United States were leaving farms and towns and moving to cities. Henry Fletcher wrote, "Undeniably the city has superior attractions as a place of residence for the well-to-do; even the poorest classes, who live in filthy tenements and are completely shut out from the enjoyments of nature, seem to find in the noises, the crowds, the excitements, even in the sleepless anxieties of the daily struggle for life, a charm they are powerless to resist."

—from "The Drift of Population to Cities: Remedies"

Chicago, Illinois, grew from 109,000 residents in 1860 to nearly 1.7 million in 1900.

620

Growth of Cities

Main Idea Immigrants and others flooded to American cities, where extremes of poverty and wealth existed.

History and You What is the largest city in your state? Read to learn how many American cities grew rapidly during the late 1800s.

- -

American cities grew rapidly after the Civil War. In 1870 one American in four lived in cities with 2,500 or more people. By 1910, nearly half of the American population were city dwellers. The United States was changing from a rural to an urban nation.

Immigrants played an enormous part in the growth of cities. In **major,** or larger, urban centers such as New York, Detroit, and Chicago, immigrants and their children made up 80 percent or more of the population in 1890. Native-born Americans also contributed to the urban growth, moving in huge numbers from farming areas to cities, looking for jobs.

The industrialization of America had changed work on farms. New farm machinery made it possible to produce crops using fewer farmworkers. In addition, women in rural areas no longer had to make clothing and household goods. These items, made by machine, could now be bought in stores or from catalogs. Freed from such chores, many women left farms to look for jobs in the cities.

African Americans also migrated to cities in large numbers. After the Civil War, many African Americans began moving to Southern cities in search of jobs. Beginning in 1914, a large number of African Americans moved to Northern cities, where they hoped to find less discrimination.

Transportation and Resources

America's expanding railroad network fed the growth of cities. Railroads helped people move, and they also transported the raw materials for industry. Trains carried cattle to Chicago and Kansas City, making these cities large meatpacking centers.

Some cities flourished because of nearby resources. Pittsburgh developed rapidly as a center for iron and steel manufacturing because both iron ore and coal—to fuel the industry's huge furnaces—were found in the area. Seaports such as New York and San Francisco developed as American trade with the rest of the world increased.

By the Numbers / Urban and Rural Population Growth

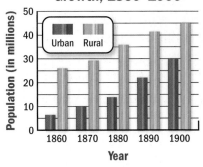

Urban and Rural Population Growth, 1860–1900

Source: *Historical Statistics of the United States.*

Critical Thinking

Analyzing Which year saw the least difference between urban and rural populations?

Primary Source — Life in the Tenements

Crowded Conditions Immigrant families usually lived in tenements in Irish, German, Jewish, or other ethnic neighborhoods. A typical tenement apartment consisted of three rooms, most without windows. Such an apartment might house a family of seven or more.

"To-day three-fourths of its [New York's] people live in the tenements, and the . . . drift of the population to the cities is sending ever-increasing multitudes to crowd them. The fifteen thousand tenant houses that were the despair of the sanitarian [public health specialist] in the past generation have swelled into thirty-seven thousand, and more than twelve hundred thousand persons call them home."
—Jacob Riis, *How the Other Half Lives*, 1890

Many immigrant families did piecework in their tenement apartments, making clothing for the garment industry.

Jacob Riis, a newspaper reporter and reformer, documented the living conditions in New York tenements.

◀ A crowded tenement building in New York City

Critical Thinking

Speculating Why do you think that so many immigrants ended up living in tenements in ethnic neighborhoods?

Tenement Living

In the biggest, most crowded cities, the poorest residents—including most immigrants—lived in **tenements.** Originally a tenement was simply a building in which several families rented rooms. By the late 1800s, however, a tenement had come to mean an apartment building in the **slums**—poor, run-down urban neighborhoods.

Several people lived in each room. Usually several families had to share a cold-water tap and a toilet. A government inspector wrote of the "filthy and rotten tenements" of the Chicago slums in 1896, where children filled "every nook, eating and sleeping in every windowsill, pouring in and out of every door."

The Middle Class

The cities also had a growing middle class, which included the families of doctors, lawyers, and ministers, as well as managers, salaried office clerks, and others. The middle class enjoyed a comfortable life. Many families moved to the **suburbs,** residential areas that sprang up outside city centers. There they lived in houses with hot water, indoor toilets, and—by 1900—electricity. Middle-class families might have servants and the leisure time to enjoy music, art, and literature.

The Very Rich

At the top of the economic and social ladder were the very rich. They built enormous mansions in the cities and huge estates in the country. In these mansions, the rich lived lives of extreme luxury. Because of their extravagant wealth—and the terrible poverty that lay beneath it—this time period became known as the **Gilded Age.** The word *gilded* refers to something covered with a thin layer of gold.

 Reading Check **Describing** Why was tenement living difficult?

Cities in Crisis

Main Idea Growing cities suffered from health and sanitation problems, poverty, fire, and crime.

History and You How do cities handle health and sanitation today? Read to learn about the problems of city life in the 1800s.

The rapid growth of cities produced serious problems. Garbage and horse manure accumulated in city streets, and the sewers could not handle the flow of human waste. Fires were another ever-present threat.

Health problems were widespread in the cities, because the filth was a breeding ground for quickly spreading diseases. In one Chicago neighborhood in 1900, babies often died of whooping cough, diphtheria, or measles before reaching their first birthday. One section of New York City was called the "lung block" because so many of its residents were suffering from tuberculosis. In an effort to control the spread of disease, New York City began to screen schoolchildren for contagious diseases, provide visiting nurses to mothers with young children, and establish public health clinics.

Yet disease was not the only threat to city life. Poverty in the cities led to crime as well. Orphaned and homeless children sometimes resorted to committing **minor,** or less serious, crimes in order to survive. Gangs roamed the poor neighborhoods.

The problems of the cities did not go unnoticed. Many dedicated people worked to improve urban life and help the poor. Some of this help came from religious groups that ran orphanages, prisons, hospitals, and recreation centers. The poor also received assistance from establishments called **settlement houses.** One of the most famous settlement houses was Chicago's **Hull House,** founded by **Jane Addams** in 1889.

Reading Check **Explaining** Why did disease spread so rapidly in large cities?

Primary Source / Settlement Houses

An Approach to Social Reform During the late 1800s, reformers such as Jane Addams established settlement houses in poor neighborhoods. The women who ran settlement houses provided everything from medical care, recreation programs, and English classes to hot lunches for factory workers.

Hull House, begun in Chicago by Jane Addams and Ellen Gates Starr in 1889, was surrounded by tenements and factories. ▶

"The Settlement, then, is an experimental effort to aid in the solution of the social and industrial problems which are engendered by the modern conditions of life in a great city. . . . It is an attempt to relieve, at the same time, the over-accumulation at one end of society and the destitution at the other."
—Jane Addams, *Philanthropy and Social Progress*

▼ The crowded areas of Chicago near Hull House had poor sanitation, and most residents lived in poverty.

Children at Hull House ▼

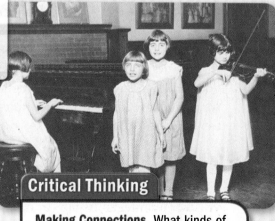

Critical Thinking

Making Connections What kinds of organizations offer help to people today?

The Great Bridge To accommodate the growing population of New York City, the Brooklyn Bridge was built over the East River to connect Manhattan and Brooklyn. Its long, high span was designed to allow for the passage of ships beneath. The bridge took 14 years to build. When completed in 1883, it was the longest suspension bridge in the world.

Workers finish a cable on the Brooklyn Bridge during construction. ▶

◀ The Brooklyn Bridge was the first suspension bridge to use woven steel cable wire, a technology developed by John Roebling, chief engineer. Four suspension cables support the bridge, and each cable contains 5,434 wires.

"The contemplated work [the bridge] . . . will not only be the greatest bridge in existence, but it will be the greatest engineering work of this continent, and of the age. . . . [It will be] a great work of art, and . . . a successful specimen of advanced bridge engineering."

—John A. Roebling, quoted in *The Great Bridge*

◀ The Brooklyn Bridge, view from the Brooklyn side toward Manhattan, 1883

Critical Thinking

Explaining Why was it important for the Brooklyn Bridge to be a suspension bridge? What innovation made this possible?

The Changing City

Main Idea New technology in transportation and architecture reshaped cities.

History and You What is the tallest building you have ever visited? Read to learn how skyscrapers forever changed American cities.

Urban growth led to new developments. In the late 1800s, the look and feel of American cities changed with the introduction of skyscrapers, new kinds of public transportation, new bridges, and public parks.

Building Up—Not Out

Because of the limited space in cities, imaginative architects began building upward rather than outward. In the 1860s, architects started to use iron frames to strengthen the building walls. Iron supports—together with the safety elevator that Elisha Otis invented in 1852—made taller buildings possible.

In 1884 William LeBaron Jenney constructed a 10-story office building in Chicago. Supported by an iron-and-steel frame, it was the world's first **skyscraper. Louis Sullivan** was one of the first to design skyscrapers. Soon architects were designing higher structures. New York's Woolworth Building, completed in 1913, soared an incredible 55 stories—792 feet (241 m) high. People called the building the Cathedral of Commerce.

New Designs

Some people looked to reshape the urban landscape. A group known as the "City Beautiful" movement believed city dwellers should be able to enjoy the beauties of nature.

Leisure and the Arts

Main Idea American culture moved away from European influence and became distinctively American.

History and You What are your favorite movies? Read to learn which famous inventor introduced the first "moving pictures."

. . . .

During this era, Americans enjoyed increasing amounts of leisure time. Unlike round-the-clock farmwork, professional and industrial jobs gave people hours and even days of free time. To fill their leisure time, Americans developed new forms of recreation, including sports, art, and music.

A Changing World of Sports

A favorite leisure-time activity for many people was watching and following sports. Baseball became the most popular **spectator sport** in America. By the early 1900s, the National and American Leagues were founded—each made up of teams from major cities. Their games drew large crowds of enthusiastic fans, and in 1903 the first World Series was held.

NOW Football has evolved into an exciting style of play. Rule changes and better protective gear have made the game safer. Each week millions watch high school, college, and pro teams in action.

Critical Thinking

Comparing What do you think is the biggest difference in football between the two eras?

Another popular spectator sport was football, which developed from the English game of rugby. The first college football game was played between Rutgers and Princeton in 1869. By the 1890s, college football games were drawing huge crowds.

Basketball, invented by Dr. James Naismith of Springfield, Massachusetts, also became popular. Naismith developed the game in the 1890s as an indoor winter sport for the students in his YMCA physical education classes. Considered the only major sport that is completely American in origin, basketball soon spread to other countries.

Americans not only watched but also participated in sports. The wealthy played tennis and golf, usually in exclusive private clubs. Bicycling grew in popularity after the "safety" bicycle was developed. Older bicycles had a large wheel in front and a small one in back, but the new ones had two air-filled rubber tires of the same size.

These improvements helped bicycle riding take the country by storm. One romantic song celebrated the bicycle: "It won't be a stylish marriage, I can't afford a carriage, But you'll look sweet upon the seat of a bicycle built for two."

Vaudeville and Movies

Not only did Americans watch sports, they also became eager fans of shows and movies. Large cities had many theaters. Plays performed ranged from serious dramas by Shakespeare to **vaudeville** shows, which were variety shows with dancing, singing, comedy, and magic acts.

Many people could afford the price of a ticket, and in the early 1900s, vaudeville offered the most popular shows in town. The circus was another popular attraction that brought large crowds. In 1910 the United States had about 80 traveling circuses that moved from town to town.

Prominent inventor Thomas Edison introduced "moving pictures" in the 1880s. The "movies" soon became enormously popular in the United States.

Theaters called nickelodeons got their name because they charged five cents to see short films. The nickelodeons marked the beginning of today's film industry.

American Artists and Musicians

For most of the 1800s, the work of American artists and musicians reflected a European influence. After the Civil War, Americans began to develop a distinctively American style.

Some American painters pursued realist themes in their works. Thomas Eakins of Philadelphia painted the human anatomy and surgical operations as well as rowers and other athletes. One of Eakins's students, Henry Tanner, depicted warm family scenes of Americans in the South. Frederic Remington portrayed the American West, focusing on subjects such as cowhands and Native Americans. Winslow Homer painted Southern farmers, Adirondack campers, and stormy sea scenes. James Whistler's *Arrangement in Grey and Black,* commonly known as "*Whistler's Mother,*" is one of the best-known American paintings. Mary Cassatt was influential in the Impressionist school of painting that arose during the late 1800s. Impressionists tried to capture the play of light, color, and patterns as they made immediate impressions on the senses.

Distinctively American kinds of music were also becoming popular. Bandleader John Philip Sousa composed many rousing marches, including "The Stars and Stripes Forever."

African American musicians in New Orleans in the late 1800s developed another entirely new kind of music—jazz. **Jazz** combined elements of work songs, gospel music, spirituals, and African rhythms. One of jazz's major characteristics was syncopation, a shifting of the usual musical accent. Related to jazz was **ragtime** music. One of the best ragtime composers was Scott Joplin. He wrote "Maple Leaf Rag" and many other well-known works.

The symphony orchestras of New York, Boston, and Philadelphia, all founded before 1900, were among the world's finest orchestras. Great singers and conductors from all over the world came to perform at New York's Metropolitan Opera House.

Reading Check **Describing** What elements make up jazz music?

Section 3 Review

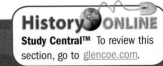
History ONLINE
Study Central™ To review this section, go to glencoe.com.

Vocabulary

1. Use each of these terms in a sentence that will help explain its meaning: philosophy, land-grant college, isolate, realism, regionalism, yellow journalism, spectator sport, vaudeville, jazz, ragtime.

Main Ideas

2. **Explaining** What was the goal of progressive education?

3. **Contrasting** How did realism and regionalism differ?

4. **Describing** What forms of entertainment were popular during this era?

Critical Thinking

5. **Making Connections** Identify the causes that sparked an increase in the number of publications in the late 1800s.

6. **Making Inferences** In what ways did schools have a negative effect on Native Americans?

7. **Creative Writing** Write a local newspaper article in the style of yellow journalism.

8. **Answer the Essential Question** In what ways did American culture change in the late 1800s?

City Life

- Industry and immigration lead to the growth of cities.
- In the poorest parts of crowded cities, people live in tenements and slums.
- Overcrowding leads to sanitation problems, disease, and crime.
- "The Gilded Age" refers to American riches overshadowing the poverty in many areas.

Immigration

- New groups of immigrants arrive in the U.S. from eastern and southern Europe.
- Reasons for immigration include: economic troubles, persecution in the native country, and better opportunities in the United States.
- New industries, such as steel and garment manufacturing, offer low-paying jobs for immigrant workers.
- Ethnic groups establish separate communities to re-create former lifestyles.
- Nativists fear immigration and call for restrictions.

Technology and Culture

- Architects address the lack of space in cities by building skyscrapers.
- Streetcars, trolleys, subways, and bridges all improve transportation in cities.
- The American educational system expands and offers new opportunities.
- Public libraries and new forms of literature and journalism add to culture in the cities.

Leisure Activities

- Middle-class Americans have newfound leisure time for sports, arts, and music.
- Sports, including baseball, football, and basketball, grow in popularity.
- Vaudeville shows, traveling circuses, and the first movies offer other new forms of entertainment.
- Distinctively American forms of music, including jazz and ragtime, become popular.

STUDY TO GO Study anywhere, anytime! Download quizzes and flash cards to your PDA from glencoe.com.

GRADE 8 INTERMEDIATE TEST PRACTICE

TEST-TAKING TIP

Consider carefully before changing your answer to a multiple-answer test question. Unless you misread the question, your first answer choice is often correct.

Reviewing Main Ideas

Directions: Choose the best answer for each of the following questions.

1 Most of the immigrants who arrived in the United States in the late 1800s

  (1) came from Latin America.

  (2) immediately blended into American society.

  (3) were from rural areas.

  (4) sought highly skilled technical jobs.

2 By the 1900s, where were middle-class Americans increasingly likely to live?

  (1) in rural areas

  (2) in the suburbs

  (3) in slums

  (4) in tenements

3 What was Frederick Law Olmsted's major contribution to American cities?

  (1) His safety elevator made taller buildings possible.

  (2) He founded settlement houses to help the urban poor.

  (3) He invented the electric trolley car, making city travel easier.

  (4) He led the "City Beautiful" movement, which promoted urban parks.

4 Supporters of "progressive education" emphasized which of the following?

  (1) character education

  (2) rote memorization of facts

  (3) the opening of libraries

  (4) land-grant schools for women

Short-Answer Question

Directions: Base your answer to question 5 on the table below and on your knowledge of social studies.

Family Characteristics of Major Immigrant Groups, 1909–1914

Group	Percentage Returning to Europe	Males per 100 Females	Percentage Under Age 14
Czechs	5	133	19
English	6	136	16
Finnish	7	181	8
Germans	7	132	18
Greeks	16	170	4
Hungarians	22	141	16
Italians	17	320	12
Poles	13	188	10
Slovaks	19	162	12

Source: "Immigrant America," Digital History

5 According to the table, which group was the most likely to return to Europe? Which group had the most uneven ratio between the sexes?

Review the Essential Questions

6 Essay Explain how immigration contributed to (a) the rise of the modern city; (b) the expansion of education; and (c) the development of a distinctly American culture by the early 1900s.

To help you write your essay, review your answers to the Essential Questions in the section reviews and the chapter Foldables Study Organizer. Your essay should include:

- characteristics and challenges of immigrants;
- changes and living conditions of cities;
- expansion of education and reading; and
- leisure activities and the arts.

GO ON ▶

Document-Based Questions

Directions: Analyze the documents and answer the short-answer questions that follow.

Document 1

> The immigrant of the former time came almost exclusively from western and northern Europe. . . . Immigrants from southern Italy, Hungary, Austria, and Russia . . . made up hardly more than one per cent of our immigration. To-day the proportion has risen to something like forty per cent. . . . These people . . . are beaten men from beaten races; representing the worst failures in the struggle for existence. . . . They have none of the ideas and [abilities] which fit men to take up readily and easily the problem of self-care and self-government.

Source: F. A. Walker, "Restriction of Immigration," 1907

7 Identify *two* reasons Walker opposed immigration from southern and eastern Europe.

Document 2

U.S. President Theodore Roosevelt stated the following.

> There is no room in this country for hyphenated Americanism. . . .
> . . . The one absolutely certain way of bringing the nation to ruin . . . would be to permit it to become a tangle of squabbling nationalities.

Source: address to Knights of Columbus, 1915

8 What did Roosevelt mean by "hyphenated Americanism"?

9 Based on the quote, did he favor or oppose the acceptance of immigrants into the American society? Explain your answer.

Document 3

This photo of three homeless boys sleeping in an alley appeared in Jacob Riis's *How the Other Half Lives: Studies Among the Tenements of New York*, 1890.

Source: Bettmann/CORBIS

10 Who was the "other half" referred to in the title of Riis's book? What did Riis hope to accomplish by publishing pictures such as this?

Document 4

In this passage, African American composer W. C. Handy—the "Father of the Blues"—explains what the blues are all about.

> My purpose was to capture in fixed form the highly distinctive music of my race. Everything I have written has its roots deep in the folk life of the South.

Source: "The Birth of the Blues," 1911

11 Based on the passage, what was the inspiration for Handy's music?

12 **Expository Writing** Using the information from the four documents and your knowledge of social studies, write an essay in which you:

- identify ways that American society by the early 1900s had become a true "melting pot" of assimilated cultures; and

- point out ways in which Americans remained separated in the early 1900s.

Need Extra Help?												
If you missed questions. . .	1	2	3	4	5	6	7	8	9	10	11	12
Go to page. . .	613	622	625	627	614	612–632	617	617	619	622–623	621	612–632

Unit 7

Reform and Empire
1865-1920

Chapter 21
The Progressive Era
1877-1920

Chapter 22
Rise to World Power
1865-1917

Chapter 23
World War I
1914-1919

Program cover for women's right to vote demonstration, Washington, D.C., 1913

636

"Give me your tired,
your poor,
your huddled masses
yearning to
breathe free . . ."
—Emma Lazarus

Members of the famous 369th Colored Infantry return from World War I.

Reading History

Paraphrasing

Learn It!

When you paraphrase, you use your own words to retell the information. You can improve your understanding of difficult passages by rewording, or paraphrasing, them.

Paraphrased Version

As the army asks for your solid and steady support, think about the courage and strength of our ancestors. Your support will help ensure that America's democratic values will not be destroyed.

—from Chapter 23, p. 722

General John J. Pershing

"Invoking the spirit of our forefathers, the army asks for your unflinching support, to the end that the high ideals for which America stands may endure upon the earth."

Practice It!

Read the quote below. On another sheet of paper, paraphrase the passage by completing the sentences with your own words.

—from Chapter 21, p. 662

W.E.B. Du Bois

"Freedom . . . we still seek,— the freedom of life and limb, the freedom to work and think, the freedom to love and aspire. Work, culture, liberty,—all these we need, not singly but together, . . . all striving toward that vaster ideal . . . the ideal of human brotherhood, gained through the unifying ideal of Race."

Paraphrased Version

We still need _____
_____.
By making sure each of us has all these freedoms, together we _____
_____.

Called **muckrakers,** these reporters "raked"—or exposed—the "muck"—dirt and corruption—underlying society.

One of the most effective muckrakers was Lincoln Steffens. Working for *McClure's Magazine,* Steffens exposed corrupt machine politics in New York and other cities. **Ida Tarbell,** also with *McClure's,* described the oil trust's unfair practices. Her articles increased public pressure for more government control over big business.

In his novel *The Jungle* (1906), **Upton Sinclair** described the horrors of the Chicago meatpacking industry. His vivid descriptions shocked people in America. In response, Congress passed the Meat Inspection Act and the Pure Food and Drug Act in 1906. Now food and medicine had to be **accurately** labeled, and harmful food could not be sold.

Progressives also backed many reforms designed to increase the people's direct control of government. Robert La Follette reformed Wisconsin's electoral system. He introduced the "Wisconsin idea," a direct primary election in which party candidates were chosen by voters instead of by party bosses and state conventions.

The Oregon System

Oregon also made important reforms. With the **initiative,** voters could place an issue on the ballot in a state election. Voters could accept or reject measures that the state legislature enacted with the **referendum.** The **recall** allowed voters to remove incompetent elected officials. These reforms, called the Oregon System, were adopted by other states.

The Seventeenth Amendment

Progressives also changed the way U.S. senators were elected. The Constitution gave state legislatures the responsibility of choosing senators. Party bosses and business interests, however, often controlled the process. Progressives wanted to give people the opportunity to vote for their senators directly. Support for this idea grew. In 1912 Congress passed the Seventeenth Amendment to the Constitution. This amendment set forth the direct election of senators. Ratified in 1913, the amendment gave the people a voice in choosing their representatives.

Reading Check **Summarizing** How did progressive reformers reinforce democratic ideas?

Section 1 Review

History ONLINE
Study Central™ To review this section, go to glencoe.com.

Vocabulary

1. Define each of the following terms in a sentence: oligopoly, behalf, muckraker, accurate, initiative, referendum, recall.

Main Ideas

2. Listing Identify some ways in which political machines were corrupt in the late 1800s.

3. Discussing Why did reformers want regulation of the railroads, and what was the government's response?

4. Identifying How did muckrakers bring about reform?

Critical Thinking

5. Determining Cause and Effect Use a diagram like the one below to show which problem reformers were trying to resolve with each legislation.

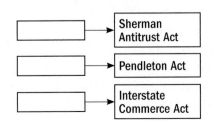

6. Persuasive Writing You are a muckraker. Choose something you think is unfair in your school or community and write a two- or three-paragraph article about it. Try to move your readers to improve the situation.

Answer the
7. Essential Question
How did the progressives fight corruption in business and in government?

America's LITERATURE

Meet the Author

Elizabeth Winthrop (1948–) was inspired to write *Counting on Grace* after seeing a photograph of a 12-year-old girl named Addie at work in a textile mill in Vermont. The photograph, taken by child labor photographer Lewis Hine in 1910, has been reprinted hundreds of times and has even appeared on a U.S. postage stamp.

Building Background

In *Counting on Grace*, the main character is a 12-year-old girl who leaves school to work at the thread mill in a Vermont town in 1910. Grace had been in the mill "lots of times" before to play and bring lunch to her family. Now she works to help support her family. Her mother, Mamère, her father, and her sister, Delia, also work in the mill. French Johnny, a French-Canadian second hand in the mill, is in charge of the spinning rooms where Grace and her family work. As you read Grace's description, think about the difficulties that the workers had to endure.

Vocabulary

bobbin a small round device on which thread or yarn is wound

mumblety-peg game in which players throw or flip a jackknife in various ways so that the knife sticks in the ground

dawdles wastes time

This photograph of mill worker Addie Card inspired Elizabeth Winthrop to write the novel *Counting on Grace.* ▶

COUNTING ON GRACE

Elizabeth Winthrop

I've been in the mill lots of times. Summers ever since I was nine, I've been cooking the hot meal for Mamère and Papa and Delia and taking in the dinner pails in the middle of the day. Delia let me push her **bobbin** dolly. I played **mumblety-peg** or roll the bobbin with Dougie and Bridget and Felix when he was a summer sweeper boy in the spinning room. And grease skating. That's the best. Thomas invented that game. Too bad he can't play it no more with his twisted foot.

With all the oil dripping off the machines, bare feet slide around easy. The boys draw a line at the end of one alley, between the frames where French Johnny can't see us, and we run and set our legs into a

By 1917, the National American Woman Suffrage Association had more than 2 million members. In a speech to the association in 1902, Catt said:

PRIMARY SOURCE

"The whole aim of the [women's] movement has been to destroy the idea that obedience is necessary to women . . . and to train men to such comprehension of equity [fairness] they would not exact [demand] it."
—quoted in *The American Reader*

Opposition to Woman Suffrage

Groups protested the idea of giving women the vote. Some women, as well as men, supported these groups. They claimed that woman suffrage would upset society's "natural" balance and lead to divorce and neglect of children. As the progressive movement gained momentum, however, many middle-class women concluded that they needed the vote to promote the reforms they favored. Many working-class women also wanted the vote to pass labor laws protecting women. The suffrage movement also gained strength when respected people such as Jane Addams spoke out in support of the vote for women.

As the movement grew, women began lobbying lawmakers, organizing marches, and delivering speeches on street corners. On March 3, 1913, the day before President Woodrow Wilson's inauguration, suffragists marched on Washington, D.C.

The suffragists won their early victories in the West. First as a territory and then as a state, Wyoming led the nation in giving women the vote. Between 1910 and 1913, five other states adopted woman suffrage. By 1919, women could vote in at least some elections in most of the 48 states.

Continuing the Fight

Meanwhile, suffragists continued their struggle to win the vote everywhere. Alice Paul, a Quaker social worker, founded the National Woman's Party in 1916. She sought greater economic and legal equality, as well as suffrage, for women.

In 1917 Alice Paul met with President Woodrow Wilson but failed to win his support for woman suffrage. In response, Paul led women protesters in front of the White House. They were arrested for blocking the sidewalk.

Voting Rights for Women, 1919 — NATIONAL GEOGRAPHIC

Legend:
- Equal suffrage, date effective
- Partial suffrage
- No statewide suffrage

Map Skills

Place What was the status of woman suffrage in your state by 1919?

Maps In MOtion See StudentWorks™ Plus or glencoe.com.

Campaigning Against Alcohol The Woman's Christian Temperance Union (WCTU), founded in 1874, became the largest and most powerful women's organization in the country. To promote temperance, the WCTU used education on the dangers of alcohol.

Frances Willard, president of the WCTU, believed in the motto "Do Everything." She thought all social problems were connected and activists should embrace many social reforms. ▶

The WCTU joined with the Anti-Saloon League to push through the Eighteenth Amendment in 1919. The amendment outlawed making and selling alcohol. ▼

◀ The WCTU was founded after the successful Women's Crusade of the winter of 1873–1874. During the Crusade, women demonstrated outside saloons, praying and singing hymns.

Critical Thinking

Drawing Conclusions Do you agree with Frances Willard that all social problems are connected? Explain.

After their arrest, the women started a much-publicized hunger strike. Alva Belmont, one of the protesters, proudly said that all the women did was stand there "quietly, peacefully, lawfully, and gloriously."

Women Vote Nationally

By 1917, the national tide was turning in favor of woman suffrage. New York and, a year later, South Dakota and Oklahoma, granted equal suffrage. As more states granted women the right to vote, Congress debated the issue.

In 1918 the House of Representatives passed a woman suffrage amendment. The next year, the Senate also passed the amendment. After three-fourths of the states had ratified it, the Nineteenth Amendment went into effect in 1920. The amendment came in time for women to vote in that year's presidential election. For the first time, American women could take part in the election of their leaders on a national level.

Reading Check **Explaining** Why were some groups against giving women the right to vote?

Women and Social Reform

Main Idea Women were active in many social reform efforts to improve the lives of others.

History and You Do you know anyone who has worked hard for a cause? Read to learn how women worked for reforms to help improve life for themselves and others.

. . . .

During the Progressive Era, women became involved in many reform movements in addition to woman suffrage.

Working for a Better Life

Many middle-class women worked to improve the lives of others. They helped working-class people, immigrants, and society as a whole. The women supported and staffed libraries, schools, and settlement houses. They also raised money for various charities.

Some women worked for other causes. They sponsored laws to regulate the labor of both women and children and to require the regular inspection of workplaces by the government.

Their pressure on Congress helped create the Children's Bureau in the Labor Department. Women also worked for reforms in the food and medicine industries. They pressured state legislatures to provide pensions for widows and for abandoned mothers with children.

Working women also were active in the reform movement. In 1903 the Women's Trade Union League (WTUL) was formed. The WTUL urged working women to form labor unions. It also supported laws to protect the rights of women factory workers. WTUL members raised money to help striking workers pay bail for women who were arrested for striking.

The Temperance Crusade

The crusade against alcohol was led by the Woman's Christian Temperance Union (WCTU), founded in 1874, and the Anti-Saloon League, set up 20 years later. They called for temperance, urging individuals to stop drinking. They also supported **prohibition**—laws that would ban making or selling alcohol.

In 1879 **Frances Willard** became head of the WCTU. Willard educated the public about the dangers of alcohol abuse. The WCTU's goal was prohibition, but it also supported other causes, including prison reform, woman suffrage, improved working conditions, and world peace. Through state WCTU chapters, women combined their role as guardians of the home with social activism.

Carry Nation was a colorful crusader for temperance in the early 1900s. During her protests, she would enter saloons and destroy the bottles and kegs of alcohol there with an ax.

Progressive reformers also wanted to ban alcohol for social reasons. Other Americans opposed alcohol for moral reasons. In response, Congress in 1917 passed a constitutional amendment declaring it illegal to make, transport, or sell alcohol in the United States. The Eighteenth Amendment, known as the Prohibition Law, was ratified in 1919.

Reading Check **Describing** What was the goal of the temperance movement?

Section 2 Review

History ONLINE
Study Central™ To review this section, go to glencoe.com.

Vocabulary

1. Use complete sentences to define the following terms: professional, intelligence, suffragist, prohibition.

Main Ideas

2. **Summarizing** In what ways did middle-class women's roles change near the end of the 1800s?

3. **Explaining** Why was 1920 a good year for the passage of the Nineteenth Amendment?

4. **Identifying** In what ways did reformers try to improve the lives of working women?

Critical Thinking

5. **Drawing Conclusions** Why was gaining the right to vote important to women?

6. **Creative Writing** Write a dialogue between a man and a woman before 1920 in which they discuss whether women should be allowed to vote for the president.

7. **Sequencing** Complete a time line like the one below to show important steps in woman suffrage.

1890   1896   1916 1920

Answer the
8. **Essential Question**
How did reforms affect the lives of women and other groups in the late 1800s?

Essential Question

Why were Theodore Roosevelt and William Howard Taft known as progressive presidents?

Reading Guide

Content Vocabulary

trustbuster (p. 657)   Square Deal (p. 658)

arbitration (p. 658)   conservation (p. 659)

Academic Vocabulary

inspect (p. 658)   primary (p. 660)

Key People and Events

Federal Reserve Act (p. 661)

Clayton Antitrust Act (p. 661)

Reading Strategy

Taking Notes As you read, use a diagram like the one below to identify how the beliefs of Theodore Roosevelt were similar to but different from William Howard Taft's.

Roosevelt   Taft

NEW YORK STANDARDS
The American Journey

U7.III.2 To investigate key turning points in New York State and United States history and explain why these events or developments are significant

U7.III.3 To gather and organize information about the important achievements and contributions of individuals and groups living in New York State and the United States

U7.III.4 To classify major developments into categories such as social, political, economic, geographic, technological, scientific, cultural, or religious

American Diary

Progressive reformers wanted to protect America's wilderness and environment. President Theodore Roosevelt was an enthusiastic supporter of their cause. Describing his travels in California in 1903, he wrote: "The first night was clear and we lay down in the darkening aisles of the great sequoia grove. The majestic trunks, beautiful in symmetry [proportion], rose round us like the pillars of a mightier cathedral than ever was conceived."

—*quoted in* Roosevelt the Explorer

Theodore Roosevelt riding at a western ranch

Theodore Roosevelt

Main Idea Theodore Roosevelt believed that businesses must be regulated.

History and You Are there powerful businesses in your community? Read to learn how big business was regulated when Theodore Roosevelt was president.

. . . .

Theodore Roosevelt won the Republican vice presidential nomination in 1900. Mark Hanna, the Republican leader, called Roosevelt "that cowboy" and warned that only one life would stand between Roosevelt and the White House. When the Republicans won, Hanna told President McKinley, "Now it is up to you to live." Less than one year later, McKinley was assassinated. Suddenly 42-year-old Theodore Roosevelt became president. He was the youngest president in the nation's history. When Roosevelt moved into the White House in 1901, he brought progressive ideas with him.

The "Trustbuster"

President McKinley favored big business. President Roosevelt, in contrast, supported the regulation of business and other progressive reforms. During his term, Roosevelt tackled certain trusts that violated the Sherman Antitrust Act.

His first target was the Northern Securities Company. This railroad monopoly fought the accusations of illegal activity all the way to the Supreme Court. In 1904 the Supreme Court decided that Northern Securities had illegally limited trade. The Court ordered that the trust be taken apart.

During the rest of Roosevelt's term, he obtained indictments, or legal charges, against trusts in the beef, oil, and tobacco industries. Although called a **trustbuster,** Roosevelt did not want to break up all trusts. He thought trusts should be regulated, not destroyed. He grouped trusts into "good" and "bad" ones. Good trusts, he believed, were concerned with public welfare, but bad trusts were not.

Labor Crisis

In 1902 Roosevelt faced a major labor crisis. More than 100,000 Pennsylvania coal miners, members of the United Mine Workers, went on strike. They demanded better pay, an eight-hour workday, and recognition of the union's right to represent its members in discussions with mine owners.

By the Numbers / Protecting America's Wilds

Theodore Roosevelt is said ▶ to have remarked that "birds in the trees and on the beaches were much more beautiful than on women's hats."
—from Theodore Roosevelt: *The Naturalist*

Setting Aside American Lands While he was president, Roosevelt used his authority to create a number of parks, preserves, and monuments to protect birds, wildlife, and millions of acres of American land.

Lands Protected Under Theodore Roosevelt	
4	Federal Game Preserves
5	National Parks
18	National Monuments
51	Federal Bird Preserves
150	National Forests

Critical Thinking

Speculating What might happen if the federal government did not protect natural resources and wildlife?

The mine owners refused to negotiate with the workers. The coal strike dragged on for months. As winter approached, coal supplies dwindled. Public feeling began to turn against the owners. As public pressure mounted, Roosevelt invited representatives of the owners and miners to a meeting at the White House. He was angry when the owners refused to negotiate. Roosevelt threatened to send federal troops to work in the mines and produce the coal. The owners finally agreed to arbitration—settling the dispute by agreeing to accept the decision of a neutral outsider. Mine workers won a pay increase and a reduction in hours, but they did not gain recognition for their union.

Roosevelt's action marked a departure from normal patterns of labor relations at the time. Earlier presidents used troops against strikers. In contrast, Roosevelt used the government's power to force the company owners to negotiate. In other labor actions, however, Roosevelt supported employers in disputes with workers.

Square Deal

Roosevelt ran for president in 1904. He promised the people a Square Deal—fair and equal treatment for all. He easily won the election with more than 57 percent of the popular vote.

Roosevelt's Square Deal called for the government regulation of business. This attitude toward business differed from the presidency of Thomas Jefferson. That approach was called laissez-faire (LEH•say FEHR). This French term generally means "let people do as they choose." In economics, it refers to an economic policy in which there is little government involvement in the affairs of businesses.

Roosevelt introduced a new era of government regulation. He supported the Meat Inspection Act and the Pure Food and Drug Act. These acts gave the Department of Agriculture and the Food and Drug Administration the power to visit businesses and inspect, or carefully examine, the products that were produced there.

LINKING PAST TO PRESENT — Conserving Wild Places

THEN By the mid-1800s, Americans began to view wild places as more than obstacles to overcome or resources to use. The nation began setting aside areas of natural beauty for future generations. President Theodore Roosevelt greatly expanded the system of national parks and forests.

"There are no words that can tell the hidden spirit of the wilderness, that can reveal its mystery . . . and its charm."
—Theodore Roosevelt

◄ Visitors enjoying Yosemite National Park, 1920

The conservation movement began partly as a response to uncontrolled logging. Roosevelt understood, though, that the nation also needed to use its resources: "Conservation means development as much as it does protection." ▼

Conserving the Wilderness

Roosevelt had a lifelong enthusiasm for the great outdoors and the wilderness. He strongly believed in the need for **conservation,** the protection and preservation of the country's natural resources.

As president, Roosevelt took steps to conserve the country's forests, mineral deposits, and water resources. In 1905 he proposed the U.S. Forest Service. He pressured Congress to set aside millions of acres of national forests to create the nation's first wildlife sanctuaries. Roosevelt also formed the National Conservation Commission, which produced the first survey of the country's natural resources.

Roosevelt has been called America's first environmental president. He made conservation an important public issue. Roosevelt, however, also saw the need for economic growth and development. He tried to balance business interests with conservation.

Reading Check **Describing** What was Roosevelt's approach to labor relations?

William Howard Taft

Main Idea Conflict between Roosevelt and Taft led to Woodrow Wilson's election as president.

History and You Has a friend ever disappointed you by an action he or she has taken? Read to learn about the conflict between Theodore Roosevelt and William Howard Taft.

No president had ever served more than two terms. In keeping with that tradition, Roosevelt decided not to run for reelection in 1908. Instead he chose William Howard Taft to run for president. Taft easily defeated Democrat William Jennings Bryan.

Taft lacked Roosevelt's flair. Still, he carried out—and went beyond—many of Roosevelt's policies. The Taft administration won more antitrust cases in four years than Roosevelt won in seven. Taft also favored safety standards for mines and railroads.

Taft supported the Sixteenth Amendment. It allowed Congress to tax citizens' incomes to collect money for the federal government.

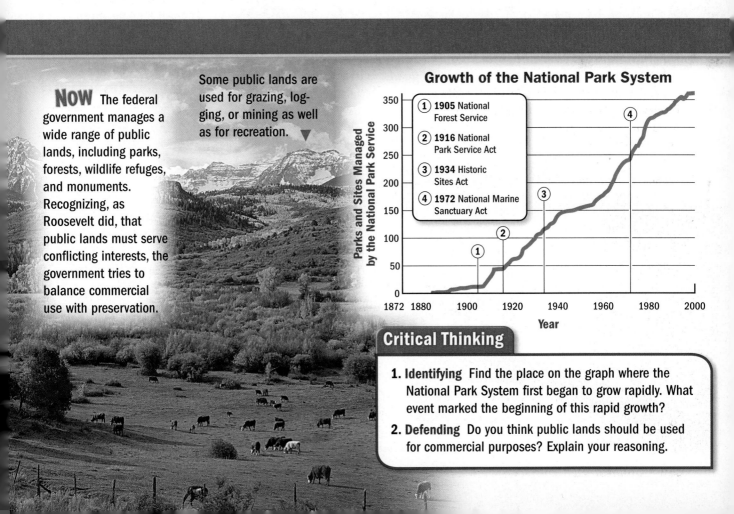

NOW The federal government manages a wide range of public lands, including parks, forests, wildlife refuges, and monuments. Recognizing, as Roosevelt did, that public lands must serve conflicting interests, the government tries to balance commercial use with preservation.

Some public lands are used for grazing, logging, or mining as well as for recreation. ▼

Growth of the National Park System

Parks and Sites Managed by the National Park Service

1. **1905** National Forest Service
2. **1916** National Park Service Act
3. **1934** Historic Sites Act
4. **1972** National Marine Sanctuary Act

Critical Thinking

1. **Identifying** Find the place on the graph where the National Park System first began to grow rapidly. What event marked the beginning of this rapid growth?

2. **Defending** Do you think public lands should be used for commercial purposes? Explain your reasoning.

Progressives believed income taxes to be fairer and hoped the taxes would allow the government to lower tariffs and relieve the hardship of the poor. The Sixteenth Amendment, added to the Constitution in 1913, did not state how income would be taxed. Congress passed further laws so that higher incomes were taxed at a higher rate than lower incomes.

Taft made progressive reforms. Yet he disappointed many progressives such as Theodore Roosevelt. The two important areas where progressives believed Taft was weak were tariffs and conservation. Taft failed to fight for a lower tariff, and he altered a number of conservation policies so that they favored businesses.

Roosevelt Challenges Taft

By 1912, Roosevelt had become disappointed in Taft. Claiming that Taft "completely twisted around" his own policies, Roosevelt decided to challenge Taft for the Republican presidential nomination.

The showdown between Roosevelt and Taft came at the Republican national convention in Chicago in June. Roosevelt had won every **primary**—an election in which a political party chooses its candidates—and had many supporters. Taft, however, had the backing of party leaders. Taft also had the support of business interests that controlled the party machinery. Taft was nominated on the first ballot.

Roosevelt charged the Republican Party leaders with stealing the nomination from him. He led his supporters out of the convention hall. They formed a new party, the Progressive Party. In August the Progressives held their own convention in Chicago and nominated Roosevelt for president.

A reporter asked Roosevelt about his health. The candidate thumped himself on the chest and declared, "I feel as strong as a bull moose!" From then on, the Progressive Party was known as the Bull Moose Party.

Economics & History

Before the Civil War, the federal government received most of its funds from tariffs, or taxes on imported goods. During the Civil War, the government placed a tax on people's incomes. This type of tax, however, remained controversial for many years.

Federal Income Taxes		
	Earnings	**Tax Rate**
1864	$600–$5,000	5%
	over $10,000	10%
1894	**Earnings**	**Tax Rate**
	all	2%

★ **1862** First federal income tax passed
★ **1872** Federal income tax repealed
★ **1894** Everyone required to pay 2% of income
★ **1895** Income tax ruled unconstitutional
★ **1913** Income tax made permanent

Income taxes today are progressive—rates are based on ability to pay. People who earn more pay a larger percentage of their income in taxes than do people who earn less.

Sources of Funds for the Federal Government Today

Today, income taxes from individuals and businesses are the main source of funds for the federal government.

- Retirement and unemployment taxes 36%
- Borrowing 1%
- Other taxes 7%
- Individual income taxes 43%
- Business income taxes 13%

Source: Internal Revenue Service

Critical Thinking

Calculating Suppose you earned $1,000 in 1894. How much income tax would you pay? Your friend earned $2,000. How much tax would he or she pay?

Rebirth of the Ku Klux Klan The Ku Klux Klan (KKK) underwent a resurgence in the early 1900s following the release of D.W. Griffith's 1915 movie *The Birth of a Nation*, which presented a romantic vision of the KKK. Following a brief growth spurt, in which membership climbed into the millions, the Klan began to decline in 1924 after a series of scandals involving the group's leadership. Membership shrank and politicians who supported the Klan were voted out of office. The Klan declared bankruptcy and disbanded again in 1944.

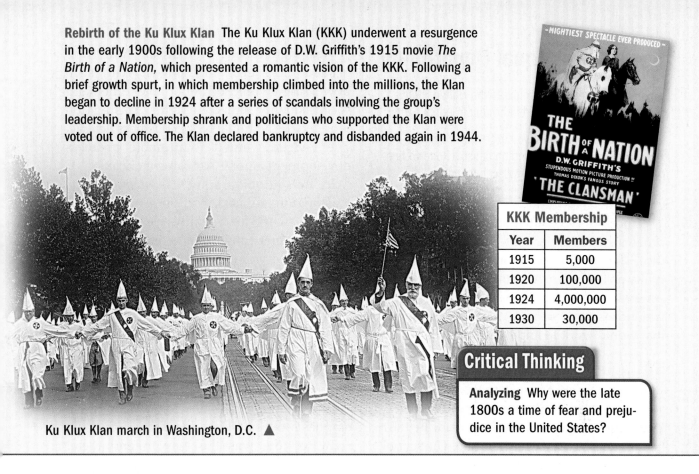

Ku Klux Klan march in Washington, D.C. ▲

KKK Membership

Year	Members
1915	5,000
1920	100,000
1924	4,000,000
1930	30,000

Critical Thinking

Analyzing Why were the late 1800s a time of fear and prejudice in the United States?

Calling for "100 percent Americanism," the number of Klan supporters continued to grow and even spread beyond the South. Many Klan members were from Northern as well as Southern cities and towns.

Racial Violence

Many people lost their jobs during the economic depressions of 1893 and 1907. Frustrated and desperate, they sometimes unleashed their anger against African Americans and other minorities. More than 2,600 African Americans were lynched between 1886 and 1916, mostly in the South. Lynching also was used to terrorize Chinese immigrants in the West.

Progressivism and Prejudice

In the late 1800s and the early 1900s, many Americans held **biased,** or prejudiced, views. They believed that white, male, native-born Americans had the right to make decisions for all of society.

Most of the progressive reformers came from the middle and upper classes. They saw themselves as moral leaders who worked to improve the lives of less fortunate people in their communities and throughout the nation. The reforms they supported, though, often discriminated against one group as they tried to help another group.

Trade unions often did not allow African Americans, women, or immigrants to join. The unions argued that skilled laborers could obtain better working conditions if they did not demand improved conditions for all workers.

Sometimes progressive reforms were really efforts to control a particular group. The temperance movement, for example, was partly an attempt to control the behavior of Irish Catholic immigrants. Civil service reforms required job applicants to be educated. This change reduced the political influence that immigrants, who were largely uneducated, began to achieve in some cities. In spite of their mixed results, though, progressive reforms did improve conditions for many Americans.

Reading Check **Identifying** Which Supreme Court decision legalized segregation?

Struggle for Equal Opportunity

Main Idea Minority groups in the United States sought to end discrimination and obtain equal rights.

History and You Have you ever been part of a group that worked for a common cause? Read to find out how some groups fought discrimination.

Minorities were often banned from joining progressive organizations because of prejudice. They had to battle for justice and opportunity on their own. African Americans, Native Americans, Mexican Americans, and Jewish Americans took steps to form organizations that would work to improve their lives.

Struggle for Equality

African Americans rose to the challenge of achieving equality. Born enslaved, **Booker T. Washington** taught himself to read. In 1881 he founded the Tuskegee Institute. The school taught African Americans farming and industrial skills.

Washington believed African Americans needed more economic power. With such power, they would be better able to demand social equality and civil rights. Washington founded the National Negro Business League. The League wanted to promote business development among African Americans.

In his autobiography, *Up from Slavery,* Washington advised African Americans to patiently work for equality. He argued that African Americans needed education and skills. These would help African Americans become more valuable members of their community and lead to equality.

W.E.B. Du Bois also worked for civil rights. He was the first African American to receive a doctoral degree from Harvard University. As an educator, Du Bois took a different approach than did Booker T. Washington. Du Bois rejected Washington's emphasis on job skills and argued that the right to vote was the way to end racial inequality, stop lynching, and gain better schools. "The power of the ballot we need in

People IN HISTORY

Booker T. Washington

African American educator and leader

Washington urged African Americans to work hard for economic security before looking for ways to end discrimination and segregation. In one speech, he said that the opportunity to *"earn a dollar in a factory"* was worth much more than the opportunity to *"spend a dollar in an opera house."*

W.E.B. Du Bois

Sociologist and advocate of civil rights for African Americans

Du Bois believed that African Americans should protest their unequal treatment in American society. An African American, he wrote, *"simply wishes to . . . be both a Negro and an American, without being cursed and spit upon by his fellows, without having the doors of Opportunity closed roughly in his face."*

CRITICAL Thinking

1. **Making Inferences** What did Washington mean when he said the opportunity to earn a dollar was worth more than the opportunity to spend one in an opera house?

2. **Synthesizing** Which leader would be more likely to protest having separate schools for African Americans and whites? Explain your answer.

sheer self-defense," he said, "else what shall save us from a second slavery?" Du Bois helped start the Niagara Movement in 1905. This movement demanded equal economic and educational opportunity for African Americans and insisted on an end to legalized segregation and discrimination.

Although it never gained great support, the Niagara Movement led to the creation of the National Association for the Advancement of Colored People in 1910. This organization was greatly influential in the fight for African American civil rights throughout the twentieth century.

Some African Americans thought that they would be better off in separate societies. These societies could be located either in the United States or in Africa. To achieve this goal, groups were founded to establish African American towns. A back-to-Africa movement began, but its ideas were not popular. The goals of these movements gained few supporters among African Americans.

African American Women Take Action

African American women also formed groups to end discrimination. The National Association of Colored Women fought lynchings and other forms of racial violence. Ida B. Wells was editor of an African American newspaper in Memphis, Tennessee. She was forced to leave town after publishing the names of people involved in a lynching. Wells started a national crusade against the terrible practice of lynching.

In 1895 Wells published a book, *A Red Record*. She showed that lynching was used mainly against African Americans who became prosperous or who had competed with white businesses. "Can you remain silent and inactive when such things are done in your own community and country?" she asked. Although Congress rejected an anti-lynching bill, the number of lynchings declined significantly due in great part to the efforts of Wells and other activists.

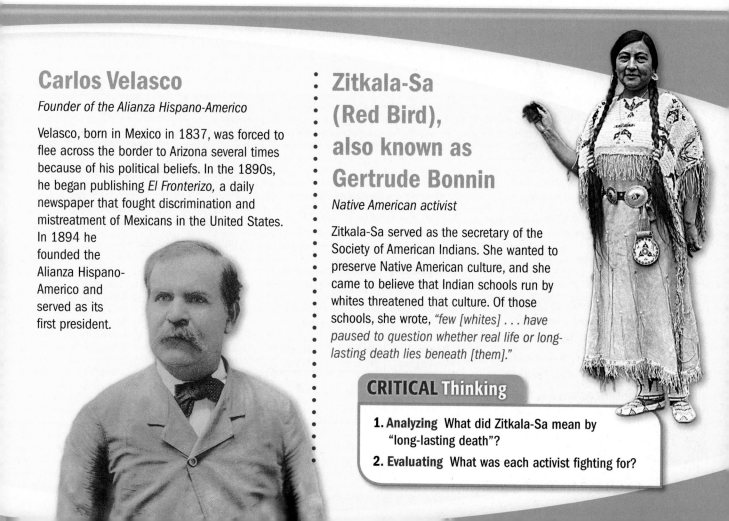

Carlos Velasco

Founder of the Alianza Hispano-Americo

Velasco, born in Mexico in 1837, was forced to flee across the border to Arizona several times because of his political beliefs. In the 1890s, he began publishing *El Fronterizo*, a daily newspaper that fought discrimination and mistreatment of Mexicans in the United States. In 1894 he founded the Alianza Hispano-Americo and served as its first president.

Zitkala-Sa (Red Bird), also known as Gertrude Bonnin

Native American activist

Zitkala-Sa served as the secretary of the Society of American Indians. She wanted to preserve Native American culture, and she came to believe that Indian schools run by whites threatened that culture. Of those schools, she wrote, *"few [whites] . . . have paused to question whether real life or long-lasting death lies beneath [them]."*

CRITICAL Thinking

1. **Analyzing** What did Zitkala-Sa mean by "long-lasting death"?
2. **Evaluating** What was each activist fighting for?

History ONLINE
Student Web Activity Visit glencoe.com and complete the Chapter 21 Web Activity about the Progressive Era.

African American Successes

African Americans achieved success in many professions. George Washington Carver, a chemist at Tuskegee Institute, helped improve the South's economy through his research on plant products. Maggie Lena founded the St. Luke Penny Savings Bank in Richmond. She served as America's first woman bank president.

Other Groups

The federal government's efforts to blend Native Americans into white society threatened their traditional cultures. In 1911 Native American leaders formed the Society of American Indians to improve living conditions for Native Americans and to teach white America about native cultures. One society founder, Dr. Carlos Montezuma, revealed government abuses of Native American rights. Montezuma believed that Native Americans should leave the reservations and make their own way in white society.

In the early 1900s, the Mexican American population quickly grew. Many crossed the border to escape conflict and economic woes in Mexico. Like other groups, Mexican Americans faced discrimination and violence.

Mexican Americans often relied on their own efforts. Their *mutualistas*—self-defense groups—provided insurance and legal help. One of the first *mutualistas* was the *Alianza Hispano-Americo* (Hispanic American Alliance). Another, the *Orden Hijos de America* (Order of Sons of America), promoted Mexican American rights. In labor camps and Mexican neighborhoods called **barrios,** *mutualistas* handled issues such as overcrowding and poor public services.

Jewish Americans also faced prejudice during this period. A number of organizations, including the American Jewish Committee and the Anti-Defamation League, formed to fight anti-Semitism and other types of bigotry. Many of these groups continue their work today, addressing injustices both in America and around the world.

Reading Check **Identifying** What was the purpose of the Niagara Movement?

Section 4 Review

History ONLINE
Study Central™ To review this section, go to glencoe.com.

Vocabulary

1. Define the following terms in complete sentences: discrimination, deny, bias, *mutualista*, barrio.

Main Ideas

2. **Discussing** Why did many Americans and recent immigrants face discrimination in the Progressive Era?

3. **Summarizing** How did Mexican Americans organize to fight discrimination and violence?

Critical Thinking

4. **Making Connections** If you lived in the early 1900s, which organization would you join to help fight discrimination? Why?

5. **Organizing** Use a diagram like the one below to show the organizations founded by African Americans in the later 1800s.

Booker T. Washington	W.E.B. Du Bois	Maggie Lena

6. **Expository Writing** Read the quotation again in this section from Ida B. Wells's book *A Red Record*. Write a paragraph that answers Wells's question.

Answer the Essential Question

7. How did minority groups react to discrimination?

Business and Politics

Target	Reform
Corrupt politics at all levels of government	• City commissioners • Civil Service Commission
More participation in government	• Seventeenth Amendment • Election reform
Trusts and big business	• Sherman Antitrust Act • Theodore Roosevelt's "Square Deal" • Federal Trade Commission • Clayton Antitrust Act
Railroad oligopoly	• Interstate Commerce Act/Commission
Conservation interests	• U.S. Forest Service • National Conservation Commission
High tariffs	• Sixteenth Amendment • "New Freedom" tariff reform
Banking regulation	• Federal Reserve Act

▲ Yosemite National Park

◄ Educator Booker T. Washington

Prohibition agents dump alcohol ►

Society

Target	Reform
Social problems related to alcohol	• Women's Christian Temperance Union • Anti-Saloon League • Eighteenth Amendment
Unsafe food and medicine	• Meat Inspection Act • Pure Food and Drug Act
Difficult working conditions	• Children's Bureau of Labor Department • Women's Trade Union League • Mine/railroad safety standards • Keating-Owen Act

Gender and Race

Target	Reform
Equal voting rights for women	• Woman suffrage movement • State-by-state voting rights • National Woman's Party • Nineteenth Amendment
Prejudice and discrimination	• Tuskegee Institute • National Negro Business League • Niagara Movement • National Association for the Advancement of Colored People • Society of American Indians • Mexican American *mutualistas*

STUDY TO GO Study anywhere, anytime! Download quizzes and flash cards to your PDA from glencoe.com.

GRADE 8 INTERMEDIATE TEST PRACTICE

TEST-TAKING TIP

Answer the questions you know first and go back to those for which you need more time.

Reviewing Main Ideas

Directions: Choose the best answer for each of the following questions.

1 The Interstate Commerce Act was an attempt to control

(1) the spoils system.

(2) excessive union activity.

(3) railroad oligopoly.

(4) the excessive influence of trusts.

2 For which cause was Carry Nation best known as a crusader?

(1) labor rights

(2) temperance

(3) woman suffrage

(4) immigration reform

3 Grouping trusts into "good" and "bad" ones was a characteristic of

(1) Theodore Roosevelt's first term in office.

(2) William Jennings Bryan's 1908 presidential campaign.

(3) William Howard Taft's administration.

(4) Woodrow Wilson's first term in office.

4 How did W.E.B. Du Bois differ from Booker T. Washington regarding racial discrimination?

(1) Du Bois strongly promoted political involvement by African Americans.

(2) Du Bois put the responsibility on the individual to gain employable skills.

(3) Du Bois called for minorities to use violence against the Ku Klux Klan.

(4) Du Bois encouraged *mutualistas* to help African Americans solve problems.

Short-Answer Question

Directions: Base your answer to question 5 on the excerpt below and on your knowledge of social studies.

> That woman's physical structure and the performance of maternal [motherly] functions place her at a disadvantage in the struggle for subsistence is obvious. This is especially true when the burdens of motherhood are upon her. Even when they are not, . . . continuance for a long time on her feet at work, repeating this from day to day, tends to injurious effects upon the body, and as healthy mothers are essential to vigorous offspring, the physical well-being of woman becomes an object of public interest.
>
> —Supreme Court Justice David J. Brewer, *Muller v. Oregon*, 1908

5 In this opinion, Justice Brewer upholds a law limiting women's workday to 10 hours. What reasons does Justice Brewer give for not striking down the law? Why might some equal-rights feminists have opposed Brewer's decision?

Review the Essential Questions

6 Essay Compare and contrast the role of government with the role of private citizens in the progressive movement.

To help you write your essay, review your answers to the Essential Questions in the section reviews and the chapter Foldables Study Organizer. Your essay should include:

• differences and similarities among progressives, socialists, and muckrakers;

• the role of women in reform;

• the policies and actions of Roosevelt, Taft, and Wilson; and

• attempts of minorities to effect change.

GO ON

History ONLINE

For additional test practice, use **Self-Check Quizzes**—Chapter 21 at glencoe.com.

Document-Based Questions

Directions: Analyze the documents and answer the short-answer questions that follow.

Document 1

In 1916, Theodore Roosevelt stated the following about conservation.

> It is entirely in our power as a nation to preserve large tracts [areas] of wilderness, which are valueless for agricultural purposes and unfit for settlement . . . so that it shall continue to exist for the benefit of all lovers of nature. . . . But this end can only be achieved by wise laws. . . . Lack of such legislation and administration will result in harm to all of us, but most of all in harm to the nature lover who does not possess vast wealth. Already there have sprung up here and there through the country . . . large private preserves.

Source: Theodore Roosevelt, *Outdoor Pastimes of an American Hunter*

7 According to Roosevelt, why should wilderness areas be preserved?

Document 2

George Washington Plunkitt was a powerful state senator in New York. This is what he had to say about the political machine system.

> Have you ever thought what would become of the country if the bosses were put out of business, and their places were taken by a lot of cart-tail orators and college graduates? It would mean chaos. It would be just like takin' a lot of dry-goods clerks and settin' them to run express trains on the New York Central Railroad.

Source: William L. Riordon, *Plunkitt of Tammany Hall*

8 Based on the document, do you think Plunkitt favored or opposed reforms to the political machine system? Explain.

Document 3

This map shows the spread of woman suffrage in the United States from 1890 to 1920.

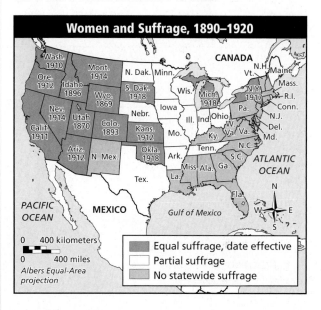

9 Based on the map, which area was most resistant to woman suffrage?

Document 4

This is an excerpt from *The Jungle,* a novel about the meatpacking industry.

> There would be meat that had tumbled out on the floor, in the dirt and sawdust, where the workers had tramped and spit. . . . There would be meat stored in great piles in rooms; . . . and thousands of rats would race about on it.

Source: Upton Sinclair, *The Jungle*

10 Why do you think *The Jungle* was written?

11 **Creative Writing** Using the information from the four documents and your knowledge of social studies, write an essay in which you:
- take on the role of a reformer for a cause of your choice; and
- describe the challenges you face and the tactics you will use to succeed.

Need Extra Help?											
If you missed questions . . .	1	2	3	4	5	6	7	8	9	10	11
Go to page . . .	645	655	657	666–667	651–654	642–668	659	643–644	652–654	647	642–668

Chapter 22

Rise to World Power 1865–1917

When American Commodore Matthew Perry arrived in Tokyo in 1853–54, he presented the Japanese with a miniature steam locomotive.

ANDREW JOHNSON 1865–1869

★ 1867 United States purchases Alaska

ULYSSES S. GRANT 1869–1877

RUTHERFORD B. HAYES 1877–1881

JAMES GARFIELD 1881

CHESTER ARTHUR 1881–1885

GROVER CLEVELAND 1885–1889

PRESIDENTS
U.S. Events
World Events

1865   **1875**   **1885**

★ 1867 Japan ends shogun rule

St. Peter's Basilica in Vatican City ▶

★ 1871 Italian law gives pope possession of Vatican

★ 1875 British take control of Suez Canal

★ 1883 Vietnam becomes French protectorate

Section 1: Expanding Horizons

Essential Question Why did the United States extend its influence to other regions in the late 1800s?

Section 2: Imperialism in the Pacific

Essential Question Why did the United States expand its role in the Pacific?

Section 3: Spanish-American War

Essential Question How did the Spanish-American War help the United States become a world power?

Section 4: Latin American Policies

Essential Question How did the beliefs of the U.S. presidents shape Latin American foreign policies?

FOLDABLES
Study Organizer

Organizing Information
Make this four-tab Foldable to help you learn about how the United States expanded its influence around the world.

Step 1 Fold the sides of three pieces of paper into the middle to make a shutter fold.

Step 2 Cut each flap at the midpoint to form tabs.

Step 3 Label the tabs as shown.

Reading and Writing
As you read the chapter, take notes about the role the United States played in each region. Use your Foldable to help you prepare for assessment.

Alaska and Hawaii | Asia
Latin America | Africa

BENJAMIN HARRISON 1889–1893

GROVER CLEVELAND 1893–1897

★ **1898** Spanish-American War erupts

WILLIAM McKINLEY 1897–1901

THEODORE ROOSEVELT 1901–1909

WILLIAM HOWARD TAFT 1909–1913

WOODROW WILSON 1913–1921

★ **1916** National Park Service established

1895

1905

1915

 ★ **1895** José Martí leads revolt in Cuba

 ★ **1900** Boxer uprising in China

 ★ **1907** Shackleton organizes expedition to Antarctica

 ★ **1911** Qing dynasty overthrown in China

Expanding Horizons

Essential Question

Why did the United States extend its influence to other regions in the late 1800s?

Reading Guide

Content Vocabulary

isolationism (p. 675)   imperialism (p. 676)

expansionism (p. 675)

Academic Vocabulary

communication (p. 676) vision (p. 676)

Key People and Events

Matthew Perry (p. 675)

William H. Seward (p. 676)

Pan-American Union (p. 677)

Reading Strategy

Taking Notes As you read, use a diagram like the one below to describe how the United States was able to expand its influence during the age of imperialism.

U.S. Influence Expands

NEW YORK STANDARDS
The American Journey

U8.I.1 To understand how and why the United States grew during the 19th century

U8.I.3 To describe the reasons for periodizing history in different ways

U8.I.4 To understand the relative importance of United States domestic and foreign policies over time

American Diary

In 1899 Albert J. Beveridge was elected to the U.S. Senate as a Republican from Indiana. A brilliant speaker, Beveridge praised the new strength of the U.S. Navy and called on the country to expand its influence overseas. In a speech in 1900, Beveridge declared: "The Philippines are ours forever. . . . And just beyond the Philippines are China's [vast] markets. We will not retreat from either. . . . The Pacific is our ocean."

—from "In Support of an American Empire"

By the late 1890s, the United States had created a fleet of modern warships.

American Foreign Policy

Main Idea The influence of the United States began to extend to other world regions.

History and You How many products do you own that are made in Japan? Read to learn about the beginning of U.S. trade with Japan.

Senator Albert Beveridge was not alone in his opinions. Many Americans yearned for an empire abroad. This idea greatly differed from earlier attitudes.

In his Farewell Address, George Washington warned Americans to "steer clear of permanent alliances with any portion of the foreign world." This principle guided American foreign policy for about 100 years. Some people, however, interpreted Washington's words differently. They said he supported a policy of **isolationism,** or non-involvement, in world affairs. Others said Washington supported trade with other countries and not complete isolation from the rest of the world.

Americans expanded their territory by moving west and south. This **expansionism** was a driving force in American history. Most of the land between the Atlantic Coast and the Pacific Coast was settled. The American "frontier" had ended.

Americans then looked beyond the nation's borders to frontiers overseas. American merchants already traded with China, but they also wanted to trade with Japan, which had long been isolated from the West.

In 1853 Commodore **Matthew Perry** traveled to Japan. He steamed into Tokyo Bay with four warships and asked the Japanese to open their ports to U.S. ships. He told them he would return in several months for their answer. When Perry returned in 1854, the Japanese signed the Treaty of Kanagawa. They opened two ports to American ships. Perry's mission marked the start of greater U.S. involvement in Asia.

Reading Check **Making Inferences** What effect do you think Perry's warships had on Japan's decision to trade with the United States?

Primary Source / Modern Battleships

A New Navy Moving away from wooden ships powered solely by the wind, the U.S. Navy built steel-hulled ships with steam-powered engines that included sails. One of the U.S. Navy's first armored battleships was the USS *Maine.*

1 Torpedo tubes are devices to launch torpedoes.
2 Steam boilers power the engines.
3 Munitions were stored in the **magazine.**
4 Cowls provided fresh air below deck.

Critical Thinking

Interpreting What do you think Senator Beveridge meant when he said "The Pacific is our ocean"?

Expanding Northward In 1867 Secretary of State William Seward negotiated a treaty to buy Alaska from Russia for $7.2 million. Congress approved his Alaska treaty because it eliminated the Russian presence from North America. Though Seward acquired the vast territory for only two cents per acre, many Americans ridiculed the purchase. Critics at the time called Alaska "a large lump of ice" and "Seward's Folly."

"I can see no good reason for adopting at this time the treaty with Russia for the purchase of 'Alaska,' a country which . . . we know but little about, and judging from its location, doubtful if any of it will . . . induce persons to settle there under a homestead law; and as to minerals, we have little or no reliable information."

—George Miller,
speech in the House of Representatives, July 14, 1868

◄ Seward and the president's Cabinet discussing the Alaska purchase

A gold miner in Alaska ▶

District of Alaska NATIONAL GEOGRAPHIC

Critical Thinking

Identifying Points of View Why did some Americans oppose the purchase of Alaska?

An Age of Imperialism

Main Idea The United States expanded its territory when it bought Alaska and extended its influence in Latin America.

History and You Think about what you have seen on TV and read about Alaska. Read to learn about how Alaska became a territory of the United States.

Other Western nations, in addition to the United States, also began to expand their trade and influence in Asia and other parts of the world. The late 1800s and the early 1900s were called an age of **imperialism.** During this time, powerful European nations created large empires by gaining economic and political control over weaker nations.

The search for materials and markets drove imperialism. The industrial nations of Europe needed raw materials and new markets for the goods they manufactured. This led to competition among European powers for influence in Asia and Africa.

Toward an Empire

After the Civil War, some Americans wanted the nation to build an empire. By annexing new lands, they argued, the United States would join the ranks of the world's great powers. Their country could take its rightful place at the center of power.

Secretary of State **William H. Seward,** appointed by Abraham Lincoln, supported this view. Seward pictured an American empire dominating the Caribbean, Central America, and the Pacific. This vast empire would be connected by a canal across Central America linking the Atlantic and Pacific Oceans, a transcontinental railroad system, and the telegraph, which would provide rapid **communication.**

The Purchase of Alaska

In 1867 Seward moved closer to making his **vision,** or imagined plan, a reality when he bought Alaska from Russia for $7.2 million. It was a great bargain for a territory twice the size of Texas.

Articles and cartoons in American "yellow" newspapers highlighted Spanish atrocities in Cuba. Many Americans wanted to rescue Cuba from the "villainous" Spanish. ▶

▼ The U.S. battleship *Maine* blew up in Havana Harbor on February 15, 1898. The cause of the explosion was a mystery—the Spanish had little motive to destroy a U.S. ship, but Cuban rebels had much to gain by increasing hostilities between the United States and Spain.

In the early morning hours of May 1, Dewey launched a surprise attack on the Spanish fleet in Manila Bay. Dewey destroyed most of the Spanish ships.

American troops arrived in July, and Filipino rebels, led by Emilio Aguinaldo (AH•gee•NAHL•doh), helped the Americans capture the city of Manila. Using American weapons, the rebels then took the main island of Luzon and declared independence. They expected American support, but the United States debated what to do with the islands.

Fighting in Cuba

Meanwhile in the Caribbean, a Spanish fleet entered the harbor of Santiago in Cuba on May 19. American ships soon blockaded the coast, trapping the Spanish in the harbor.

About 17,000 American troops—nearly a quarter of them African American—then came ashore while forces under Cuban general Calixto García drove off the Spanish soldiers. As the Cuban and American forces advanced, heavy fighting followed.

History ONLINE
Student Web Activity Visit glencoe.com and complete the Chapter 22 Web Activity about the Rough Riders.

The Rough Riders

Theodore Roosevelt resigned his position as assistant secretary of the navy to join the fighting in Cuba. He led the First Regiment of U.S. Cavalry Volunteers. The regiment was an assorted group of former cowhands and college students, popularly known as the **Rough Riders.** On July 1, the Rough Riders, with African American soldiers of the Ninth and Tenth Cavalries, joined the **Battle of San Juan Hill.** "I waved my hat and we went up the hill with a rush," Roosevelt wrote later.

The Americans captured San Juan Hill after intense fighting. Two days later the Spanish fleet attempted to break out of the Santiago harbor. In a battle that lasted about four hours, the Spanish fleet was destroyed, ending Spanish resistance in Cuba.

The United States then turned to the Spanish colony of Puerto Rico. American troops landed on Puerto Rico in late July and quickly took control of the island. On August 12, the Spanish signed an **armistice,** or peace agreement, and the war ended.

Losses in the War

Secretary of State John Hay called the Spanish-American War "a splendid little war." The war lasted fewer than four months. About 400 Americans were killed in battle or died from wounds received in the fighting.

Yet the war had other aspects that were not at all "splendid." More than 2,000 Americans died of yellow fever, malaria, and other diseases found in the tropical climate. The African Americans who served during this war faced the additional burden of discrimination. They were placed in segregated units, but they fought alongside the Cuban rebel army, in which African American and white troops fought as equals.

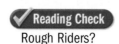 **Reading Check** **Identifying** Who were the Rough Riders?

Uncle Sam's menu includes "Cuba Steak," "Porto Rico Pig," "the Philippine Floating Islands," and "the Sandwich Islands."

1. **Interpreting** What does Uncle Sam's menu represent?

2. **Analyzing** Does the cartoon depict President McKinley as an imperialist or as an anti-imperialist? How do you know?

A. Uncle Sam (United States)
B. President William McKinley C. Menu

"Well, I Hardly Know Which to Take First"

Acquisitions

Main Idea The American empire became a reality after the Spanish-American War.

History and You Think about what it means to be independent. Read to learn how Cuba was ruled after the Spanish-American War.

- -

The United States and Spain signed the Treaty of Paris on December 10, 1898, ending the war. The treaty dissolved most of the Spanish Empire.

Cuba became an American **protectorate.** A protectorate is technically an independent country, but it is under the control of another country. Puerto Rico and Guam became **territories** of the United States. A territory is an area that is completely controlled by another country. Spain also surrendered the Philippines to the United States in exchange for $20 million. The American empire became a reality despite criticism that it was contrary to the democratic values on which the country was based.

Cuban Protectorate

Americans debated what to do about Cuba. Finally, in 1901 the United States granted Cubans full independence, but only if their new constitution included clauses giving the United States certain rights. Known as the **Platt Amendment,** these conditions prohibited Cuba from making treaties with other nations. They gave the United States control of a naval base at Guantanamo Bay. The United States also could intervene in Cuban affairs if the country's independence was threatened.

New Government for Puerto Rico

After the war, Puerto Rico remained under direct military rule. In 1900 the United States set up a new Puerto Rican government under the Foraker Act. The American government controlled the new administration. In 1917 the Jones Act made Puerto Rico a territory of the United States. American citizenship was granted to all Puerto Ricans. Many Puerto Ricans, however, still wanted independence.

Acquiring the Philippines

The United States had gained possession of the Philippines in the treaty that ended the Spanish-American War. Acquisition of the Philippines, however, aroused fierce debate among American citizens.

During the 1890s, the anti-imperialists—people who opposed American foreign expansion—fought approval of the treaty. Some argued that American rule of the Philippines went against the democratic principles on which the United States was founded. Others opposed the large standing army that would be necessary to control the Philippines. Still others feared competition from Filipino laborers. Many Americans—including Andrew Carnegie, Carl Schurz, and Mark Twain—joined the anti-imperialist campaign.

The imperialists, however, led by Senators Henry Cabot Lodge and Albert Beveridge, eventually won out. They emphasized what they believed to be the benefits of taking the islands. Some argued that the Philippines would provide the United States with another Pacific naval base, a stopover on the way to China, and a large market for American goods. Others felt that the Americans had a duty to help "less civilized" peoples. As a result, the Senate ratified the Treaty of Paris on February 6, 1899.

Rebellion in the Philippines

The United States quickly learned that controlling its new empire would not be easy. In February 1899, Emilio Aguinaldo's forces began a fight for independence. This conflict became a gigantic undertaking for the United States. More than 4,000 Americans died. Filipinos suffered far greater casualties—at least 200,000 soldiers and civilians died.

When Aguinaldo was captured in March 1901, many Filipino military officers and soldiers surrendered. Others refused to give up even after Aguinaldo urged them to stop fighting.

In the summer of 1901, the United States transferred authority from a military to a civilian government headed by William Howard Taft. Taft set out to prepare the islands for **eventual,** or later, self-rule. The Philippines gained independence in 1946.

Reading Check **Contrasting** What is the difference between a protectorate and a territory?

Section 3 Review

History ONLINE
Study Central™ To review this section, go to glencoe.com.

Vocabulary

1. Define each of the following terms in a sentence: yellow journalism, trigger, armistice, protectorate, territory, eventual.

Main Ideas

2. **Explaining** How did newspapers contribute to America's declaration of war against Spain in 1898?

3. **Discussing** Why did some Americans oppose empire building by the United States?

Critical Thinking

4. **Summarizing** Use a time line like the one below to summarize the events in the Philippines after the end of Spanish rule in 1898.

1898   1899   1901   1946

Filipino rebels create democratic republic

5. **Creative Writing** Write an account of the Battle of San Juan Hill from the point of view of an African American soldier of the Ninth Cavalry.

6. **Answer the Essential Question** How did the Spanish-American War help the United States become a world power?

Section 4 — Latin American Policies

Essential Question

How did the beliefs of U.S. presidents shape Latin American foreign policies?

Reading Guide

Content Vocabulary

isthmus (p. 691)

anarchy (p. 693)

dollar diplomacy (p. 694)

Academic Vocabulary

eliminate (p. 691)   annual (p. 691)

Key People and Events

Roosevelt Corollary (p. 694)

Francisco "Pancho" Villa (p. 696)

John J. Pershing (p. 696)

Reading Strategy

Taking Notes As you read, use a diagram like the one below to compare the principles on which each American foreign policy was based.

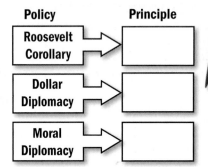

Policy	Principle
Roosevelt Corollary →	
Dollar Diplomacy →	
Moral Diplomacy →	

NEW YORK STANDARDS
The American Journey

U8.I.2 To recognize that American territorial and economic growth had widespread economic, political, and social impacts both at home and abroad

U8.I.4 To understand the relative importance of United States domestic and foreign policies over time

U8.I.5 To analyze the role played by the United States in international politics, past and present

American Diary

On August 15, 1914, the Ancon, a cargo ship, made the first official trip through the Panama Canal. One traveler onboard the Ancon noted: "So quietly did [the ship] pursue [its] way that . . . a strange observer coming suddenly upon the scene would have thought that the canal had always been in operation, and that the Ancon was only doing what thousands of other vessels must have done before [it]."

—quoted in The Path Between the Seas

Since the Ancon's voyage, more than 800,000 ships have passed through the Gaillard (Culebra) Cut, the narrowest channel of the Panama Canal.

Panama

Main Idea The United States negotiated with Panama to build the Panama Canal.

History and You Have you negotiated for better pay for lawn mowing or babysitting services? Read to learn how the United States negotiated in order to build the Panama Canal.

. . . .

The opening of the Panama Canal in 1914 was the fulfillment of a long-held dream. For hundreds of years, Americans and Europeans had wanted to build a canal across Central America to connect the Atlantic and Pacific Oceans. They wanted that connection to **eliminate** the long and dangerous sea voyage around South America. Now that the United States controlled territory in both oceans, it was even more important to have a canal that would allow easier access to American overseas territories.

Panama was an **isthmus**—a narrow strip of land connecting two larger bodies of land—about 50 miles (80 km) wide. Wedged between the Caribbean Sea and the Pacific Ocean, Panama seemed like the perfect site for the canal.

In 1879 a French company acquired a lease from Colombia to build a canal across Colombia's northern province of Panama. French efforts to build a canal failed, however, because of lack of funds and terrible losses from disease among the workers.

The United States had long considered two possible canal sites, one through Nicaragua and one through Panama. The French company eased this choice by offering to sell its rights and property in Panama to the United States.

In 1901 the United States bought the lease from the French for $40 million. Secretary of State John Hay negotiated a treaty with Colombia in 1903 that granted the United States a 99-year lease on a strip of land across Panama. That lease cost the United States a payment of $10 million with an **annual** rent of $250,000.

Revolution in Panama

The Colombian Senate, however, rejected the U.S. offer to lease the strip of land. President Roosevelt then looked for other ways to get land for the canal. He wrote that he would "be delighted if Panama were an independent state."

If You Were There / Working on the Panama Canal

Digging the "Big Ditch" With tropical diseases under control, you and thousands of workers begin digging. In grassy and swampy coastal areas, you struggle against the extreme heat, but your equipment works well. It is difficult work when you reach the rugged inland mountains, though. Heavy rains create mud and landslides. You also have to blast away solid rock with dynamite. After the blasts, giant steam shovels scoop up the rocks and dump them into nearby railroad cars. President Theodore Roosevelt is excited about the project, and he arrives at the site in 1906. He is photographed sitting at the controls of a steam shovel. With such presidential backing, how can you not succeed? In 1913 digging ends at last, and one of the greatest engineering projects of your time is almost complete.

Critical Thinking

Interpreting How does the phrase "The land divided, the world united" reflect the importance of the Panama Canal to the United States and the rest of the world?

The Panamanians had staged a number of revolts against Colombia in the past, but those uprisings had never met with success. This time, however, the Panamanians had reason to believe that the Americans would support them in a revolt against Colombia.

On November 2, 1903, the American warship *Nashville* steamed into the port of Colón on the Caribbean coast of Panama. Encouraged by this show of support, the Panamanians revolted the next day and declared their independence. Colombia sent forces to stop the revolt, but the United States intervened and turned them back.

The Panama Canal

On November 6, the United States recognized Panama's independence. Less than two weeks later, Hay signed a treaty with the new nation of Panama. It gave the United States a 10-mile (16-km) strip of land across the country for the same amount offered earlier to Colombia. The United States now had land to build a canal.

Roosevelt's actions did not meet with praise from everyone, however. Many Latin Americans, some Congress members, and other Americans were angered. The president, however, took great pride in his accomplishment. He later said: "I took the canal zone and let Congress debate, and while the debate goes on, the canal does also."

The United States could now start work on the canal—not an easy undertaking. Disease struck the workers. An English writer described Panama as "a damp, tropical jungle, intensely hot, swarming with mosquitoes." Those mosquitoes carried two deadly diseases—yellow fever and malaria.

The Grand Opening

The Panama Canal opened on August 15, 1914. A cargo ship named the *Ancon* made the first voyage through the new waterway.

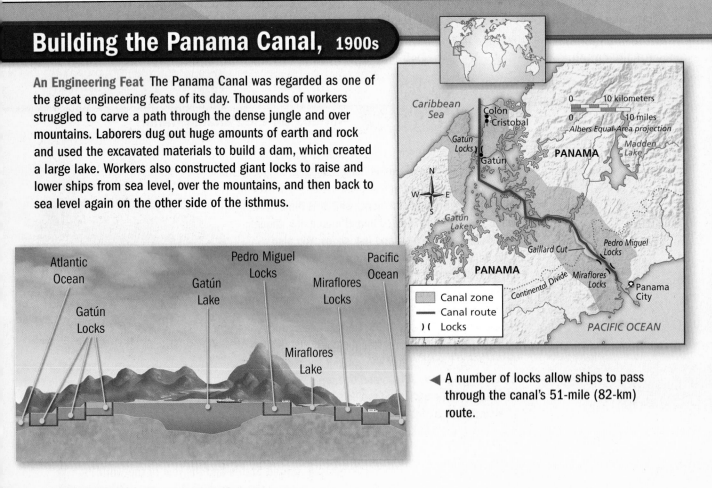

Building the Panama Canal, 1900s

An Engineering Feat The Panama Canal was regarded as one of the great engineering feats of its day. Thousands of workers struggled to carve a path through the dense jungle and over mountains. Laborers dug out huge amounts of earth and rock and used the excavated materials to build a dam, which created a large lake. Workers also constructed giant locks to raise and lower ships from sea level, over the mountains, and then back to sea level again on the other side of the isthmus.

◄ A number of locks allow ships to pass through the canal's 51-mile (82-km) route.

From the start, the canal was a great success. Before the canal opened, ships sailing from New York to San Francisco traveled 12,600 miles (20,277 km) around the treacherous tip of South America. Afterwards, the trip was only 4,900 miles (7,886 km). It could be completed in less than half the time, significantly reducing shipping costs.

The Panama Canal also helped extend American naval power. The U.S. naval fleet could now move freely between the Atlantic and Pacific Oceans. The canal was a valuable property that the United States intended to protect. Thus, it guaranteed that there would be a strong American presence in Latin America. Yet many Latin Americans remained bitter over how the canal land had been acquired. This resentment soured relations between the United States and Latin America for years.

Reading Check **Identifying** What problem faced workers on the canal?

Policing the Western Hemisphere

Main Idea Using its economic and military power, the United States policed the Western Hemisphere.

History and You Have you ever heard the proverb "Speak softly and carry a big stick"? What does that mean? Read to learn about American foreign policies in Latin America.

President Roosevelt often quoted an African proverb, "Speak softly and carry a big stick." He believed the United States should respond to foreign crises not with threats but with military action. Roosevelt became known for his "big stick" approach to foreign affairs.

Roosevelt also believed that America must exercise "an international police power." He felt that this was necessary to preserve order and to prevent the world from falling into **anarchy**—disorder and lawlessness.

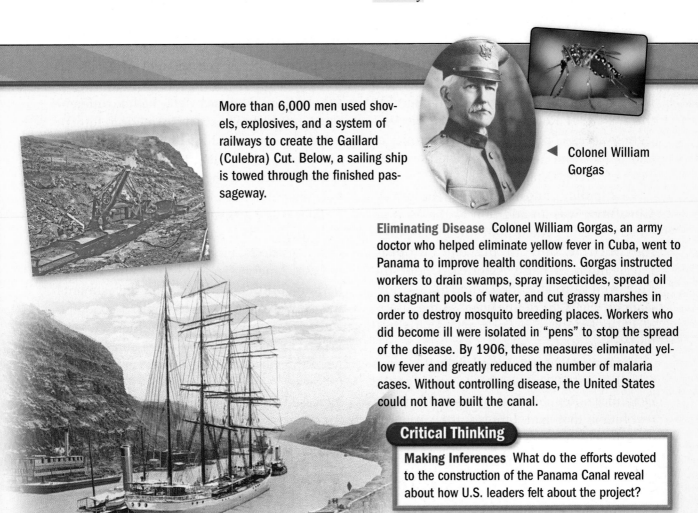

More than 6,000 men used shovels, explosives, and a system of railways to create the Gaillard (Culebra) Cut. Below, a sailing ship is towed through the finished passageway.

◄ Colonel William Gorgas

Eliminating Disease Colonel William Gorgas, an army doctor who helped eliminate yellow fever in Cuba, went to Panama to improve health conditions. Gorgas instructed workers to drain swamps, spray insecticides, spread oil on stagnant pools of water, and cut grassy marshes in order to destroy mosquito breeding places. Workers who did become ill were isolated in "pens" to stop the spread of the disease. By 1906, these measures eliminated yellow fever and greatly reduced the number of malaria cases. Without controlling disease, the United States could not have built the canal.

Critical Thinking

Making Inferences What do the efforts devoted to the construction of the Panama Canal reveal about how U.S. leaders felt about the project?

Primary Sources

INTERPRETING
POLITICAL CARTOONS

When European powers threatened to send warships to the Dominican Republic to collect debts owed them, the United States applied the Roosevelt Corollary to stop them.

1. **Analyzing** How is the Dominican Republic portrayed? What does this suggest about American opinion of Latin Americans?

2. **Interpreting** According to the cartoon, how did the Monroe Doctrine prevent European intervention in Latin America?

A. President Theodore Roosevelt
B. European powers
C. Republic of Santo Domingo (Dominican Republic)

HANDS OFF!

Roosevelt Corollary

Theodore Roosevelt was worried about instability in the Caribbean region. He feared that European powers would try to intervene there. In 1904 Roosevelt asserted America's right to act as a "policeman" in Latin America and to intervene "however reluctantly . . . in cases of wrongdoing."

This policy, known as the **Roosevelt Corollary,** was an addition to the Monroe Doctrine. The United States used the Monroe Doctrine only to prevent European intervention in Latin America. Under the Roosevelt Corollary, the United States now claimed the right to intervene in the affairs of Latin American nations whenever those nations seemed unstable.

The United States first applied the Roosevelt Corollary in 1905 when it took control of the Dominican Republic's finances following a revolution that had toppled the country's government. Then in 1906, the United States used the policy again when troops were sent to Cuba to stop a revolution there.

Dollar Diplomacy

Theodore Roosevelt thought of American power mostly in military terms. His successor, William Howard Taft, had a different view. Taft hoped to change American foreign policy by "substituting dollars for bullets." That is, he was willing to intervene in other nations' affairs if they threatened American business interests.

Taft's policy was known as **dollar diplomacy.** This policy had some positive and some negative effects. First, American investments in Latin America grew. Roads, railroads, and harbors built with American investments helped increase trade and profits. Second, the United States played a stronger role overseas. When U.S. business interests in Latin America were threatened, military intervention often followed. Of course, such action led to increased anti-U.S. feelings throughout Latin America.

Reading Check **Contrasting** How were Taft's views about power different from Roosevelt's?

Relations With Mexico

Main Idea During the early 1900s, the United States and Mexico almost went to war with each other.

History and You Think about a country today that is experiencing a long civil war. Then read about the United States's involvement in the Mexican revolution.

In the early 1900s, Mexico was a poor country. A tiny group of rich landholders controlled the nation. Investors in the United States invested millions of dollars in Mexican oil wells and other businesses.

Then, in 1910, events in Mexico began to threaten American investments. This period also revealed the weaknesses of dollar diplomacy and forced the United States to use military intervention to protect its interests in the area.

In 1911 a popular Mexican reformer named Francisco Madero (muh•DEHR•oh) led a successful revolution. His goal was to overthrow Mexico's brutal dictator, Porfirio Díaz (DEE•ahs). Foreign businesses and some Mexican politicians and landowners prospered under the rule of Díaz. The lives of most Mexicans, however, had grown worse.

Just two years after taking power, Madero was overthrown and killed by General Victoriano Huerta (WEHR•tuh). Like Díaz, Huerta favored the wealthy and foreign interests. President Woodrow Wilson, who had just taken office, refused to recognize Huerta's "government of butchers."

Primary Source — Relations With Mexico

American Troops in Mexico In 1916 Mexican rebel Pancho Villa, angered by American support for a political rival, began attacking Americans. He killed 16 American miners in Mexico, then crossed the U.S. border and burned the town of Columbus, New Mexico, killing even more Americans. American president Woodrow Wilson sent 6,000 soldiers under the leadership of General John Pershing into Mexico to capture Villa. Though Mexican president Carranza also wanted to capture Villa, he opposed the presence of U.S. forces in Mexican territory.

▲ American soldiers used motorcycles, trucks, and horses in their unsuccessful search for Villa.

Pursuing Pancho Villa — NATIONAL GEOGRAPHIC

- Arizona
- New Mexico
- UNITED STATES
- Site of Villa's raid
- Columbus
- El Paso
- Texas
- 30°N
- Pershing's route
- Rio Grande
- Gulf of California
- MEXICO
- 0   200 kilometers
- 0   200 miles
- Albers Equal-Area projection
- 110°W

Bold and ruthless, Villa commanded a strong rebel force in northern Mexico. ▶

"Villa is entirely familiar with every foot of Chihuahua, and the Mexican people, through friendship or fear, have always kept him advised of our every movement. He carries little food, lives off the country, rides his mounts hard and replaces them with fresh stock taken wherever found. Thus he has had the advantage since the end of the first twenty-four hours after the Columbus raid occurred."
—from a report by General John Pershing, April 1916

Critical Thinking

Drawing Conclusions Why do you think U.S. forces failed to capture Pancho Villa?

Wilson's "Moral Diplomacy"

In foreign affairs, Woodrow Wilson hoped to avoid further imperialism by the United States. He sought to promote democracy in other nations as a means of ensuring stability and preventing war and revolution. According to Wilson, the United States had a duty "to teach the South American republics to elect good men." Like Roosevelt and Taft, Wilson recognized the importance of military power and economic interests. Wilson however, wished to base his foreign policy on moral principles.

Wilson's "moral diplomacy" faced a serious challenge in Mexico. After Huerta took power, a civil war broke out in Mexico. Wilson hoped that the Huerta government, without American support, would fall. That did not happen. Wilson then authorized arms sales to Huerta's rival, Venustiano Carranza (kuh•RAN•zuh).

Problems came to a head in April 1914. When Huerta's troops arrested some American sailors, Wilson ordered U.S. troops to seize the port of Veracruz. This show of force strengthened Carranza's position. Huerta was forced to flee in August. Carranza took power, and American troops withdrew.

Francisco "Pancho" Villa

Huerta's departure did not end the civil war. Rebel leader **Francisco "Pancho" Villa** rose up against Carranza. In January 1916, Villa held and shot 16 Americans because of U.S. support for the Carranza government. Villa hoped to damage Mexican-American relations, but the United States did not act against Mexico. Then Villa and his rebels crossed into New Mexico, burning the town of Columbus and killing 18 Americans.

Villa's actions angered the United States. Troops led by General **John J. Pershing** crossed the border into Mexico and pursued Villa for almost a year. Many Mexicans protected Villa from capture. After America's attention turned to the war raging in Europe in 1917, Pershing's troops left Mexico. American actions had brought the countries close to war and led to great resentment in Mexico. As in the Caribbean, America's experience in Mexico showed other nations that the United States would willingly use its power when its interests or its honor was threatened.

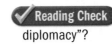 **Reading Check** **Defining** What was "moral diplomacy"?

Section 4 Review

History ONLINE
Study Central™ To review this section, go to glencoe.com.

Vocabulary

1. Define the following terms, using each one in a sentence: eliminate, isthmus, annual, anarchy, dollar diplomacy.

Main Ideas

2. **Identifying** How did the United States benefit from the construction of the Panama Canal? What were the drawbacks?

3. **Explaining** Why did President Roosevelt believe the United States should assert its military power in Latin America?

4. **Discussing** What event prevented an outbreak of war between the United States and Mexico in 1917? What did the United States prove by its actions in Mexico?

Critical Thinking

5. **Evaluating** Use a diagram like the one below to identify the positive and negative effects of Taft's dollar diplomacy in Latin America.

| Positive Effects | ← | Dollar Diplomacy | → | Negative effects |

6. **Creative Writing** You are a follower of Francisco "Pancho" Villa. Write a paragraph explaining why you support him.

Answer the
7. **Essential Question**
How did the beliefs of U.S. presidents shape Latin American foreign policies?

Chapter 22

Visual Summary

Main Idea	Supporting Details
American influence around the world expands in the late 1800s.	• After the closing of the frontier, the U.S. looks overseas to expand its territory. • Matthew Perry's expedition in 1854 opens Japan to U.S. trade. • The U.S. competes with European nations for overseas markets and resources. • Americans seek to spread Christianity and Western culture. • The United States purchases Alaska from Russia and seeks to develop friendly relations with Latin America. • U.S. Navy is strengthened to support overseas territories.
America seeks an empire in the Pacific.	• American sugar planters overthrow Hawaii's Queen Liliuokalani; Hawaii becomes a U.S. territory. • Germany and the United States divide the Samoa Islands. • The Open Door Policy protects and expands American trade in China. • Japan threatens U.S. power in the Pacific.
The Spanish-American War helps the United States become a world power.	• War erupts over concerns about Spanish rule in Cuba; explosion of the USS *Maine*. • U.S. defeats Spain; acquires Puerto Rico, Guam, and the Philippines.
U.S. involvement in Latin America increases in the early 1900s.	• U.S. seeks to build a canal across Central America to ease travel between the oceans. • U.S. supports Panama's revolt against Colombia to gain canal site. • The construction of the Panama Canal guarantees a strong American influence in the region.
The U.S. uses its military and economic power to maintain its interests in Latin America.	• The Roosevelt Corollary supports the use of American military force to prevent instability in Latin America. • Taft's "dollar diplomacy" calls for American intervention to protect U.S. business and economic interests. • Wilson's "moral diplomacy" supports the spread of democracy in Latin America.

▲ Queen Liliuokalani

◄ American troops in Mexico

STUDY TO GO Study anywhere, anytime! Download quizzes and flash cards to your PDA from glencoe.com.

YOU DECIDE

Did the United States Have the Right to Build the Panama Canal?

Building Background

Theodore Roosevelt wanted the United States to be one of the world's great powers. He believed that the citizens of weaker countries were incapable of governing themselves. His beliefs guided him to help Panama secede from Colombia, enabling the United States to build a canal in the area.

Rubén Darío, an influential poet and journalist from Nicaragua, became increasingly concerned about the possibility of U.S. colonization of Latin America. In 1904 Darío wrote a poem entitled "To Roosevelt."

YES

THEODORE ROOSEVELT

I did not lift my finger to incite the revolutionists. . . . I simply ceased to stamp out the different revolutionary fuses that were already burning. . . . We gave to the people of Panama self-government, and freed them from subjection to alien oppressors. . . . When we did act and recognize Panama, Colombia at once acknowledged her own guilt by promptly offering to do what we had demanded, and what she had protested it was not in her power to do. But the offer came too late. . . . It would have necessitated our abandoning the people of Panama, our friends, and turning them over to their and our foes. . . . If, as representing the American people, I had not acted precisely as I did, I would have been an unfaithful or incompetent representative; and inaction at that crisis would have meant not only indefinite delay in building the canal, but also practical admission on our part that we were not fit to play the part on the Isthmus which we had arrogated[1] to ourselves. . . .

I deeply regretted, and now deeply regret, the fact that the Colombian Government [forced] me to take the action I took; but I had no alternative, consistent with the full performance of my duty to my own people, and to the nations of mankind.

---

[1] **arrogated** claimed

698

NO

RUBÉN DARÍO

. . . .

You think that life is fire,
that progress is eruption,
that wherever you shoot
you hit the future.

. . . .

But our America, that has had poets
since the ancient times of Netzahualcoyotl,[2]

. . . .

has lived on light, on fire, on perfume, on love,
America of the great Montezuma, of the Inca,
the fragrant America of Christopher Columbus,
Catholic America, Spanish America,
the America in which noble Cuahtemoc[3] said:
"I'm not in a bed of roses"; that America
that trembles in hurricanes and lives on love,
it lives, you men of Saxon[4] eyes and barbarous soul.
And it dreams. And it loves, and it vibrates, and it is the
daughter of the Sun.
Be careful. Viva Spanish America!
There are a thousand cubs loosed from the Spanish lion.
Roosevelt, one would have to be, through God himself,
the-fearful Rifleman and strong Hunter,
to manage to grab us in your iron claws.

Building the Panama Canal

---

[2] **Netzahualcoyotl** ruler in 1400s Mexico
[3] **Cuahtemoc** last emperor of the Aztecs
[4] **Saxon** a person of English birth or descent

DBQ Document-Based Questions

1. **Interpreting** What did Roosevelt believe was his duty?

2. **Making Inferences** What do you think was more important to Roosevelt: Panamanian independence or the Panama Canal? Why?

3. **Analyzing** According to Darío, what are the differences between the United States and Latin America?

4. **Evaluating** In your opinion, which man made a stronger argument for his position? Explain your answer.

699

GRADE 8 INTERMEDIATE TEST PRACTICE

TEST-TAKING **TIP**

Do not wait until the last minute to prepare for a test. Make sure you ask questions in class after you have studied, but before you take the test.

Reviewing Main Ideas

Directions: Choose the best answer for each of the following questions.

1 Commodore Matthew Perry is most associated with
   (1) the purchase of Alaska.
   (2) improving and expanding U.S. trade.
   (3) ending the Russo-Japanese War.
   (4) the opening of Japanese ports to U.S. ships.

2 What was the Boxer Rebellion?
   (1) a Chinese uprising against foreigners
   (2) a brief skirmish between the United States and Germany over the division of Samoa
   (3) a revolt of sugar planters in Hawaii
   (4) a clash between Japan and Russia

3 Which of the following became U.S. territories or protectorates following America's victory in the Spanish-American War?
   (1) Cuba, Puerto Rico, and Hawaii
   (2) Spain and Cuba
   (3) Cuba, Puerto Rico, and Guam
   (4) the Philippines and Hawaii

4 The Roosevelt Corollary stated that
   (1) all European nations had the right to trade freely in China.
   (2) the U.S. had the right to get involved in Latin America to preserve order.
   (3) the United States was destined to expand from the Atlantic to the Pacific Ocean.
   (4) no European nation should intervene in Latin American affairs.

Short-Answer Question

Directions: Base your answer to question 5 on the excerpt below and on your knowledge of social studies.

> The two great needs of mankind, that all men may be lifted up into the light of the highest Christian civilization, are, first, a pure, spiritual Christianity, and, second, civil liberty. . . . It follows, then, that the Anglo-Saxon, as the great representative of these two ideas, . . . is . . . to be, in a peculiar sense, his brother's keeper.
>
> —Josiah Strong, on imperialism and the Spanish-American War, 1885

5 Based on the document, explain why Josiah Strong supported American imperialism.

Review the Essential Questions

6 **Essay** Which do you believe was the *most important* factor in American imperialism from 1865 to 1914: economic gain, military-strategic interest, or ideology? Explain and defend your answer.

To help you write your essay, review your answers to the Essential Questions in the section reviews and the chapter Foldables Study Organizer. Your essay should include:
   • the actions and ideas of James G. Blaine and Alfred Thayer Mahan;
   • the annexation of Hawaii, division of Samoa, and Open Door policy;
   • events before, during, and after the Spanish-American War;
   • the Panama Canal; and
   • the foreign policies of Roosevelt, Taft, and Wilson.

GO ON

The Germans first used poison gas against Allied troops in April 1915. The gas could kill or seriously injure anyone who breathed it. A British officer said:

PRIMARY SOURCE

"They fought with their terror, running blindly in the gas cloud, and dropping . . . in agony."
—quoted in *Avoiding Armageddon*

The Allies began to use poison gas as well. Soldiers started to carry gas masks.

The armored tank, first used in World War I in January 1916, could cross battle lines and fire on the enemy at close range. By crushing barbed wire, tanks also provided an easier route for advancing troops. After seeing the effectiveness of the Allies' tanks, the Germans produced them, too.

The most dramatic new weapon—the airplane—added a new **dimension**, or magnitude, to fighting in World War I. Both sides used airplanes to watch the movements of enemy troops and bomb targets. Daring pilots waged duels in the skies called "dogfights."

The first fighter planes were **equipped,** or outfitted, only with machine guns fastened to the top wing. The most famous pilots included Germany's Baron von Richthofen—the "Red Baron"—and Eddie Rickenbacker, an American who served in the French air force. The Germans used the zeppelin, or blimp, to bomb Allied cities.

On the Seas

With their land armies deadlocked in western Europe, both sides turned to the sea. Great Britain blockaded all ports under German control, eventually causing severe shortages. Many Germans went without food and other supplies.

Germany had an effective naval weapon of its own: the submarine. Known as **U-boats**—from the German word *Unterseeboot*—submarines sunk ships carrying supplies to Britain. U-boat attacks on ships at sea eventually brought the United States into the war.

Reading Check **Explaining** What did both sides realize after the Battle of the Marne?

Section 1 Review

History ONLINE
Study Central™ To review this section, go to glencoe.com.

Vocabulary

1. Define the following terms in a sentence: nationalism, ethnic group, militarism, alliance system, balance of power, dimension, equip, U-boat.

Main Ideas

2. **Stating** Why did nations form alliances with other nations?

3. **Discussing** Discuss the role of the Slavic nationalist movement in Austria-Hungary in the early 1900s.

4. **Explaining** How did the Central Powers and the Allies try to break the deadlock caused by trench warfare?

Critical Thinking

5. **Organizing** Use a diagram like the one below to identify the Allies and the Central Powers.

6. **Expository Writing** Write a paragraph to explain why the airplane became an important weapon during World War I.

Answer the
7. **Essential Question**
How did militarism contribute to the outbreak of World War I?

World War I and Trench Warfare

The Germans were determined to hold onto the parts of France and Belgium that they still occupied after the Battle of the Marne. They dug trenches for protection from the advancing French and British troops. The Allies could not break through the German trenches and began digging their own. For the next three years, neither side advanced more than a few miles along the line of trenches that became known as the Western Front.

How Did Geography Affect Trench Warfare?

The nature of trench warfare resulted in the development of its own unique form of geography. In the forward zone, traditional methods of transportation such as roads and rail were replaced by a network of trenches and light tramways. Occupying the high ground was critically important. Savage battles were fought just to gain possession of a small hill. Many farmhouses and groves of trees were fought over simply because they were the largest identifiable features of the landscape.

The Western Front

▲ On the Western Front where Allied and German armies faced each other, the troops dug a network of trenches that stretched from the English Channel through parts of France and Germany.

◀ American artist Mal Thompson served in France as a lieutenant with the U.S. Army. After the war, he published a volume of his sketches of war life entitled *In France with the American Expeditionary Forces.*

War Poetry British soldier and poet Wilfred Owen became famous for his realistic verses about life in the trenches. He was killed just one week before the end of the war. This is an excerpt from his poem "Dulce et Decorum Est." The title is taken from a Latin phrase: *Dulce et decorum est pro patria mori* ("How sweet and lovely it is to die for your country").

Gas! Gas! Quick, boys!—An ecstasy of fumbling,
Fitting the clumsy helmets just in time;
But someone still was yelling out and stumbling
And flound'ring like a man in fire or lime . . .
Dim, through the misty panes and thick green light,
As under a green sea, I saw him drowning.

America Enters the War

President Wilson decided that the United States could no longer remain neutral. On the cold, rainy evening of April 2, 1917, he asked Congress for a declaration of war against Germany:

PRIMARY SOURCE

"The world must be made safe for democracy. . . . . . . It is a fearful thing to lead this great, peaceful people into war, into the most terrible and disastrous of all wars. . . . But the right is more precious than peace."

—from *Democracy Today: An American Interpretation*

Congress did not agree at once to a war resolution. In the end, however, most members agreed that the nation must defend its rights if it wished to remain a great world power. As a result, Congress passed a declaration of war, and Wilson signed it on April 6. Fifty-six members of the House and Senate voted against war. One of those 56 was Jeannette Rankin of Montana—the first woman to serve as a representative in Congress.

The United States had to raise an army quickly. On May 18, Congress passed the **Selective Service Act,** setting up a military draft. Men aged 21 to 30 registered by the millions. By war's end, some 24 million men had registered. Of them, about 3 million were called to serve. Another 2 million joined voluntarily. In addition, for the first time, women enlisted in the armed forces. They served in noncombat roles, such as radio operators, clerks, and nurses.

More than 300,000 African Americans joined the armed forces, but they faced discrimination and racism. Most held low-level jobs at military bases. Among the 140,000 African American soldiers sent to Europe, 40,000 fought in combat. Many served with honor, including a regiment that received medals for bravery from France. One of its members, Henry Johnson, was the first American to receive the French Croix de Guerre [Cross of War], a medal for bravery.

Reading Check **Describing** What was the purpose of the Selective Service Act?

Section 2 Review

History ONLINE
Study Central™ To review this section, go to glencoe.com.

Vocabulary

1. Define each of the following terms in a sentence: propaganda, stress, revolution, autocracy.

Main Ideas

2. **Summarizing** Why did many Americans favor the Allies?

3. **Explaining** Why did the revolution in Russia push the United States toward entering the war?

Critical Thinking

4. **Analyzing** How is propaganda used as a "weapon" in war?

5. **Determining Cause and Effect** Use a diagram like the one below to show the consequences of Germany's attacks on various ships.

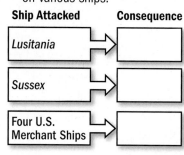

Ship Attacked	Consequence
Lusitania	
Sussex	
Four U.S. Merchant Ships	

6. **Persuasive Writing** Write a letter to President Wilson to persuade him to keep the United States out of the war.

7. **Answer the Essential Question** Why did the United States enter World War I?

Americans Join the Allies

Essential Question ◄

How did the United States help the Allies win the war?

Reading Guide

Content Vocabulary

convoy (p. 719)   kaiser (p. 723)

armistice (p. 723)

Academic Vocabulary

proceed (p. 720)   consent (p. 723)

Key People and Events

Bolsheviks (p. 719)

Vladimir Lenin (p. 719)

Treaty of Brest-Litovsk (p. 720)

John J. Pershing (p. 720)

Reading Strategy

Taking Notes As you read, use a diagram like the one below to describe how the U.S. Navy helped get much-needed supplies to Great Britain.

NEW YORK STANDARDS
The American Journey

U8.II.1 To understand how American relations with other nations developed between the end of the Civil War and the end of World War I

U8.II.3 To understand the relative importance of United States domestic and foreign policies over time

U8.II.4 To analyze the role played by the United States in international politics, past and present

American Diary

"Late one afternoon our captain . . . formed the company and, with great solemnity [seriousness], announced: 'This company is going to France. We are going right away. Is there a man here who does not want to go?' No one replied. He commanded: 'Dismissed.' I have often wondered if that company did not have a pack of silent liars."

—quoted in Doughboy War:The American Expeditionary Force in World War I

A French couple greets U.S. soldiers.

Mobilizing the Nation

Main Idea The United States prepared to fight the war.

History and You If you have a summer job, do you manage the work for someone who is on vacation? Read to learn how the United States had to adjust its workforce during World War I.

- -

After the United States declared war on Germany in 1917, Americans began focusing their energies on getting ready to fight the war. **Mobilization,** or the gathering of resources and the preparation for war, affected almost every part of American life.

To ensure production of vital war materials, the government created the National War Labor Board in April 1918. The board pressured businesses to grant some of the most important demands of workers. As a result, workers won an eight-hour working day. They also received overtime pay, equal pay for women, and the right to form unions. In return, workers agreed not to go on strike.

Workers During the War

To pay for the war, the United States government sold war bonds and increased taxes. Then industries had to expand in order to produce war materials. During this time, however, there was a labor shortage. Millions of men left their jobs to serve in the armed forces. Also, immigration slowed during the war. Fewer immigrants were arriving to take on the jobs.

The labor shortage provided new job opportunities for women. Many women joined the workforce for the first time by taking on jobs previously held by men.

The prospect of finding good jobs also brought hundreds of thousands of African Americans to Northern cities from the rural South. From 1914 to 1920, between 300,000 and 500,000 African Americans left their homes in the rural South to settle in Northern cities and find jobs. This huge population movement was known as the **Great Migration.** In addition, thousands of Mexicans migrated to the United States in search of jobs.

Primary Source | Saving Resources

Make-Do Recipes
The Food Administration enlisted 20 million housewives to promote awareness of the need to follow the rules for conserving food. Eggs, butter, milk, and wheat flour were to be used sparingly so that enough food was available to feed the soldiers. In 1918 the Royal Baking Company even published a book of recipes that identified ingredients that could be substituted for those that were needed for the troops.

Barley or Oat Flour Biscuits

2 cups barley or oat flour

4 teaspoons Royal Baking Powder

1/2 teaspoon salt

1 tablespoon sugar

1 tablespoon shortening

2/3 cup milk

Sift dry ingredients together. Rub in shortening and add enough milk to make a soft dough. Roll out on board to about one-half inch thick and cut with biscuit cutter. Bake in very hot oven 15 to 20 minutes.

Critical Thinking

Analyzing If you lived in the United States during World War I, how could you have contributed to the war effort?

Building Support The Committee on Public Information launched a massive campaign to build support for the war. Posters were an important part of this campaign.

The government sold war bonds to help pay for the cost of the war. ▶

YOU Buy a Liberty **BOND** Lest I Perish!

With millions of men serving in the military, women were needed to take their places in the labor force. ▼

JOIN THE UNITED-STATES SCHOOL GARDEN ARMY
ENLIST NOW
Write to The United States School Garden Army, Bureau of Education, Department of Interior, Washington, D.C.

◀ The Food Administration urged people to observe "Wheatless Mondays," "Meatless Tuesdays," and "Porkless Thursdays," and to add to their own store of food by planting "victory gardens." Slogans such as "Serve Just Enough" and "Use All Leftovers" reminded Americans to conserve food.

▲ James Montgomery Flagg's depiction of Uncle Sam for the U.S. Army is the most famous American wartime poster.

I WANT YOU FOR U.S. ARMY
NEAREST RECRUITING STATION

For EVERY FIGHTER a WOMAN WORKER
CARE for HER through The YWCA
UNITED WAR WORK CAMPAIGN

Critical Thinking

Synthesizing What common message is found in all four posters?

Producing Supplies

The United States had to produce food not only for its own needs but also for the Allies. President Wilson appointed Herbert Hoover to head a new Food Administration. This agency's campaign encouraged American farmers to produce more and persuaded the public to eat less.

The Food Administration also put price controls on many agricultural products to encourage voluntary **rationing,** or the limitation of use. As a result of such efforts, Americans **consumed,** or used, less food, expanded food production, and increased food exports.

Another government agency, the War Industries Board, supervised the nation's industrial production. The board's responsibilities included overseeing the changeover of factories to produce war-related goods and setting prices for key consumer products. Finally, the Fuel Administration managed the nation's coal and oil. To save energy, the

agency introduced daylight savings time and called for "Heatless Mondays."

Mobilizing Support

The federal government also needed to mobilize public support for the war. Antiwar sentiment remained strong even after the United States entered the war. The president appointed journalist George Creel to head the Committee on Public Information. The purpose of the committee was to promote the war as a battle for democracy and freedom.

The Committee on Public Information launched a massive propaganda campaign. The Committee distributed millions of prowar pamphlets, posters, articles, and books, and it provided newspapers with government accounts of the war and advertisements. The committee hired speakers, writers, artists, and actors to build support for the war.

Reading Check **Explaining** Why did the United States face a labor shortage during the early days of World War I?

Public Opinion and the War

Main Idea During World War I, the American government approved legislation to control public opinion.

History and You Have you ever spoken out against a government action? Read to learn how the government tried to stop people from speaking out against the war.

. . . .

World War I helped the American economy. Yet the war had harmful effects on American society. To create a sense of national unity, the government tried to silence opposition. Some Americans became intolerant of those who were different.

Controlling Public Opinion

Even after America entered the war, opposition to it remained strong. Some German Americans and Irish Americans sympathized with the Central Powers. Many **socialists**—people who believe industries should be publicly owned—opposed the war. They thought it would only help rich business owners and hurt working people. **Pacifists**—people who are opposed to the use of violence—were also against the war.

During the war, the Committee on Public Information began trying to silence **dissent.** Dissent is disagreement or opposition. It portrayed people who were against the war as unpatriotic. The **Espionage Act** of 1917 gave the government a new weapon to combat dissent to the war. The law provided stiff penalties for espionage, or spying. People who aided the enemy or interfered with army recruiting also could be penalized.

Congress passed even harsher measures in 1918—the **Sabotage Act** and the **Sedition Act.** These laws made it a crime to say, print, or write any criticism **perceived,** or recognized, as negative about the government. Such acts were considered sabotage—secret action to damage the war effort. Thousands of people were convicted under the laws.

Some people spoke out against these laws and the intolerance they produced. Most Americans, however, believed that in wartime no measure could be "too drastic" toward traitors and disloyal Americans.

Reading Check **Making Inferences** Why do you think Congress passed laws to penalize people who criticized the government?

Section 4 Review

History ONLINE
Study Central™ To review this section, go to glencoe.com.

Vocabulary

1. Define the following terms in a sentence: mobilization, ration, consumed, socialist, pacifist, dissent, perceive.

Main Ideas

2. Identifying How did World War I benefit workers?

3. Explaining For what reasons did some people oppose the U.S. involvement in World War I?

Critical Thinking

4. Organizing Draw a diagram like the one below that explains why each organization was created.

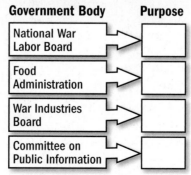

Government Body	Purpose
National War Labor Board	
Food Administration	
War Industries Board	
Committee on Public Information	

5. Persuasive Writing Make a poster to encourage the people in your town to eat less so more food can be given to the Allied troops.

6. **Answer the Essential Question** How did the United States mobilize its resources to fight the war?

Section 5 ★ Searching for Peace

Essential Question ◄
Why did Wilson's Peace Plan fail?

Reading Guide

Content Vocabulary
national self-determination (p. 729)
reparation (p. 730)

Academic Vocabulary
final (p. 730)   achieve (p. 730)

Key People and Events
Fourteen Points (p. 729)
League of Nations (p. 730)
Treaty of Versailles (p. 731)
Henry Cabot Lodge (p. 732)

Reading Strategy
Taking Notes As you read, use a diagram like the one below to list the conditions that Germany agreed to under the Treaty of Versailles.

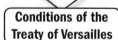

Conditions of the Treaty of Versailles

NEW YORK STANDARDS
The American Journey

U8.II.1 To understand how American relations with other nations developed between the end of the Civil War and the end of World War I

U8.II.3 To understand the relative importance of United States domestic and foreign policies over time

U8.II.4 To analyze the role played by the United States in international politics, past and present

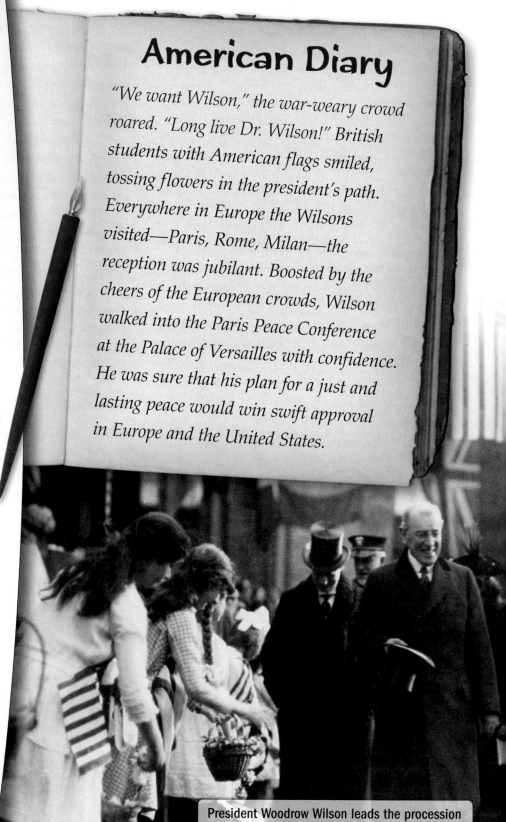

American Diary

"We want Wilson," the war-weary crowd roared. "Long live Dr. Wilson!" British students with American flags smiled, tossing flowers in the president's path. Everywhere in Europe the Wilsons visited—Paris, Rome, Milan—the reception was jubilant. Boosted by the cheers of the European crowds, Wilson walked into the Paris Peace Conference at the Palace of Versailles with confidence. He was sure that his plan for a just and lasting peace would win swift approval in Europe and the United States.

President Woodrow Wilson leads the procession after the signing of the Treaty of Versailles.

Making a Peace

Main Idea World War I ended, but the Allies opposed Wilson's plan for peace.

History and You Think about the destruction caused by war. Read to learn why the Allies wanted to punish Germany.

. . . .

World leaders from 27 nations gathered in Paris, France, in January 1919. They met for the peace conference following World War I. When President Woodrow Wilson arrived in the city, huge crowds cheered him. With great hope, Europeans looked to Wilson to help build a better postwar world, but enormous problems lay ahead.

Europe was in ruins. Its landscape, farms, and towns were destroyed. The human losses were huge. France, Russia, Germany, and Austria-Hungary each lost between 1 million and 2 million people in the fighting. Millions more were wounded. More than 50,000 Americans were killed in battle, while another 60,000 soldiers died from disease. Estimates put the number of soldiers killed worldwide at nearly 9 million. Millions of civilians also lost their lives.

Europe faced social and political turmoil. Millions of people were homeless and hungry, and civil war raged in Russia. Poles, Czechs, and other peoples struggled to form their own nations. The search for peace and stability was difficult.

Wilson's Fourteen Points

Woodrow Wilson had a vision of a just and lasting peace. He outlined his peace plan in the **Fourteen Points.** Several of the proposals dealt with adjusting boundaries in Europe and creating new nations. These points reflected Wilson's belief in **"national self-determination"**—the right of the people to decide how they should be governed.

Wilson also proposed a number of principles for conducting international relations. They included calls for free trade and freedom of the seas.

By the Numbers / The Human Cost of War

Total Mobilized Forces

Allies
42 million

Central Powers
23 million

Military Deaths

Allies
5.1 million

Central Powers
3.4 million

Critical Thinking

Calculating What percent of the Allies' mobilized forces were killed in the war? The Central Powers?

Europe After World War I

The Postwar World

- Treaties changed the boundaries of Europe.
- Allied nations weakened the Central Powers by dividing their land.
- Germany's land area was greatly reduced.
- New nations emerged in Eastern Europe, including Poland, Czechoslovakia, and Yugoslavia.
- Economic depression aided the rise of dictatorships in Europe and Japan.

Map Skills

Regions Which new nations bordered Germany?

Maps In MOtion See StudentWorks™ Plus or glencoe.com.

In addition, Wilson supported an end to secret treaties or agreements among nations. He also called for limits on arms and peaceful settlement of disputes over colonies.

League of Nations

Wilson's **final,** or last, point was the creation of a **League of Nations.** The League's member nations would help preserve peace and prevent future wars. They would respect and protect one another's independence.

At first, many Europeans welcomed Wilson's ideas, but problems developed when nations put their own interests first. Also, some of Wilson's points did not provide clear solutions to difficult questions, such as how to **achieve,** or accomplish, self-determination in regions where different ethnic groups lived closely together.

The Allies Disagree

The Allies did not invite either Germany or Russia to the peace talks. The major participants were called the Big Four. In this group was President Wilson; Prime Minister David Lloyd George of Great Britain; France's premier, Georges Clemenceau; and Italian prime minister Vittorio Orlando.

The European leaders showed little enthusiasm for the Fourteen Points. Wilson opposed punishing the defeated nations. In contrast, the Europeans sought revenge.

Clemenceau wanted to make sure that Germany could never invade France again. He believed that Germany should be broken up into smaller countries. Both he and Lloyd George demanded that Germany make large **reparations,** or payments, for the damage Germans caused in the war. Wilson struggled to uphold the principles of his Fourteen Points at the Paris meeting, yet he was forced to compromise or give in to the demands of the other Allies.

At the same time, the Allies had to decide how to deal with the new Bolshevik government of Russia. Fearing the spread of communism, France, Britain, and the United States supported anti-Bolshevik forces fighting in a civil war for control of Russia. All three countries sent troops to Russia.

The Treaty of Versailles

On June 28, 1919, the Allies and Germany signed the **Treaty of Versailles.** The treaty dealt harshly with the Germans but because they were defeated, they had no choice but to sign. Under the treaty's terms, Germany had to accept full responsibility for the conflict. It had to pay billions of dollars in reparations to the Allies. Also, Germany had to disarm completely and give up its overseas colonies and some territory in Europe.

The treaty carved up the Austro-Hungarian and Russian Empires as well. New nations were created and old nations restored. The new nations fulfilled Wilson's vision of national self-determination. Border disputes, however, would lead to future conflicts.

Wilson succeeded in having the League of Nations included in the treaty. He believed that the League would correct any mistakes in the rest of the treaty.

Reading Check Identifying Cause and Effect Why didn't Great Britain, France, and Italy support Wilson's Fourteen Points?

Opposition at Home

Main Idea The U.S. Senate rejected the Treaty of Versailles and the League of Nations.

History and You Think about how Americans might have felt after World War I. Read to learn how the U.S. Senate reacted to the treaty and the League of Nations.

Wilson presented the Treaty of Versailles to the U.S. Senate for ratification in July 1919. "Dare we reject it and break the heart of the world?" he asked. In spite of Wilson's plea, a difficult struggle lay ahead.

Many Americans had doubts about the treaty. Some thought it dealt too harshly with Germany, while others worried that the League of Nations marked a permanent American commitment to international affairs.

In 1919 the Republicans controlled the Senate, which had to ratify the treaty. Some Republican senators saw the ratification issue as a chance to embarrass President Wilson.

Primary Sources
INTERPRETING POLITICAL CARTOONS

Under the Covenant (constitution) of the League of Nations, members pledged to defend any member nation attacked by any other nation. Many Americans, however, believed the Covenant violated national sovereignty. It would allow other nations to commit American troops to foreign conflicts.

1. **Interpreting** What is the League Covenant trying to do in the cartoon?

2. **Identifying Point of View** Does the cartoon express a view for or against joining the League of Nations? How do you know?

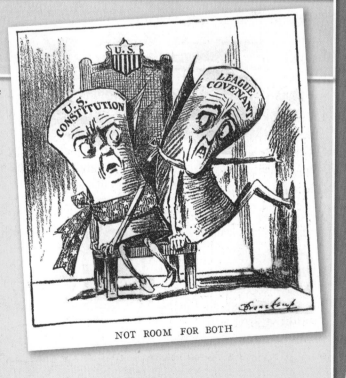

NOT ROOM FOR BOTH

Some Republicans viewed it as an opportunity to weaken the Democratic Party before the upcoming elections of 1920. Other senators had sincere concerns about the treaty, particularly the League of Nations. A few senators opposed signing any treaty.

Lodge vs. Wilson

The most powerful opponent of the treaty was **Henry Cabot Lodge** of Massachusetts. Lodge was head of the Senate Foreign Relations Committee and a longtime foe of President Wilson. Lodge said that membership in the League would mean that:

PRIMARY SOURCE

"American troops and American ships may be ordered to any part of the world by nations other than the United States, and that is a proposition to which I, for one, can never assent."

—from *Vital Forces in Current Events*, 1920

Lodge delayed a vote on the treaty so that opponents could present their cases. He then proposed a number of reservations that would limit America's obligations under the treaty.

Wilson went on a national tour in September to rally support for the treaty and League of Nations. When he returned to Washington, he suffered a stroke. During the president's illness, his wife, Edith Wilson, shielded him from pressures and took a major role in deciding which issues to raise with him.

The Treaty Is Rejected

In the months after Wilson's stroke, opposition to the treaty grew. In March 1920, the Senate voted on the treaty with Lodge's changes. Opposed by most Republicans and deserted by former supporters, the Treaty of Versailles was rejected in the Senate.

Wilson hoped the 1920 election would be a "great and solemn referendum" on the League. He even considered running for a third term. In the end, however, Wilson did not run. In 1921 the United States signed a separate peace treaty with each of the Central Powers. The United States never joined the League of Nations.

Reading Check **Explaining** Why did the Senate reject the Treaty of Versailles?

Section 5 Review

History ONLINE
Study Central™ To review this section, go to glencoe.com.

Vocabulary

1. Define the following terms in a sentence: national self-determination, final, achieve, reparation.

Main Ideas

2. **Explaining** Why did Woodrow Wilson think a lasting peace could be achieved in Europe?

3. **Identifying Cause and Effect** What effect did Wilson's illness have on the ratification of the Treaty of Versailles?

Critical Thinking

4. **Analyzing** Use a diagram like the one below to identify the challenges that the United States and Europe faced after the war.

Challenges Facing U.S. and Europe

5. **Expository Writing** If you were in Paris for the peace talks, do you think you would support Wilson's plan? Why or why not? Write a paragraph that explains your point of view.

Answer the
6. **Essential Question**
Why did Wilson's Peace Plan fail?

Chapter 23 Visual Summary

1914

June Archduke Franz Ferdinand assassinated

July Austria-Hungary declares war on Serbia

Aug. Germany declares war on Russia and France, and invades Belgium; World War I begins

1915

May German U-boat torpedoes the British *Lusitania*, killing 128 Americans

1916

Feb. The Germans launch a major offensive at the Battle of Verdun

July Allies begin their offensive at the Battle of the Somme

Nov. Woodrow Wilson wins presidential reelection

1917

Jan. Germany requests an alliance with Mexico if the U.S. entered the war

March Germany attacks and sinks four American ships

April U.S. Congress declares war against Germany

May Selective Service Act sets up a military draft

Dec. Russia's new Communist government pulls out of the war

1918

March Treaty of Brest-Litovsk shifts German troops to the Western Front

Sept.–Nov. Battle of the Argonne Forest turns war in favor of Allies

Nov. Germany becomes a republic; armistice begins

1919

Jan. World leaders meet at Paris peace conference

June Germany and the Allies sign the Treaty of Versailles

1920

March U.S. Senate rejects the Treaty of Versailles and League of Nations

STUDY TO GO Study anywhere, anytime! Download quizzes and flash cards to your PDA from glencoe.com.

World War I **Chapter 23** 733

TIME NOTEBOOK

What were people's lives like in the past?

These two pages will give you some clues to everyday life in the United States as you step back in time with TIME Notebook.

BETTMANN / CORBIS
FRANK COBB

American Voices

MEETING WITH A TROUBLED PRESIDENT

Just one day before President Wilson appeared before Congress in 1917 to ask for a declaration of war against Germany, he was struggling with whether or not it was the right thing to do. He sent for his friend, **FRANK COBB**, *editor of the* New York World *newspaper. Here is how Cobb remembers that late-night meeting at the White House:*

"[Wilson] was waiting for me sitting in his study. . . . I'd never seen him so worn down. He said he was probably going before Congress the next day to ask a declaration of war, and he'd never been so uncertain about anything in his life as about that decision. For nights, he said, he'd been lying awake going over the whole situation—over the provocation [outrage] given by Germany, over the probable feeling in the United States, over the consequences to the settlement to the world at large if we entered the [war].

"He said he couldn't see any alternative. . . . 'I think I know what war means,' he said, and he added that if there were any possibility of avoiding war he wanted to try it. 'What else can I do?' he asked. 'Is there anything else I can do?'

"I told him his hand had been forced by Germany, that so far as I could see we couldn't keep out."

AMERICAN SCENE
Average Life Spans in 1900

Average life expectancy: **47.3 YEARS**

Male life expectancy: **46.3 YEARS**

Female life expectancy: **48.3 YEARS**

White life expectancy: **47.6 YEARS**

Nonwhite life expectancy: **33.0 YEARS**

0 years 10   20   30   40   50

VERBATIM

WHAT PEOPLE ARE SAYING

❝ The . . . crowds rarely raised a cheer. . . . It was enough to walk . . . with 10,000 strangers, and to realize in that moment of good news not one of them was really a stranger. ❞
AN OBSERVER OF THE ARMISTICE DAY PARADE, *celebrating the end of World War I in New York City, 1918*

❝ I can predict with absolute certainty that within another generation there will be another world war if the nations of the world do not concert [agree on] the method by which to prevent it. ❞
WOODROW WILSON, *1919*

❝ Obey the laws, and wear the gauze; protect your jaws from septic paws. ❞
A PUBLIC SERVICE MESSAGE, *reminding people to wear masks to protect themselves from catching or spreading influenza and pneumonia, which in October 1918 killed about 194,000 people*

❝ Mountains! Look at them! ❞
EDWARD CORSI, *10-year-old Italian immigrant on spotting the high-rise buildings in New York City for the first time in 1907*

❝ Give me your tired, your poor, your huddled masses yearning to breathe free. ❞
WORDS BY EMMA LAZARUS, *engraved on the Statue of Liberty in 1903*

VSTOCK / ALAMY

The Slang Game

Want to express yourself more clearly? Then test your knowledge of the latest slang of the early 1900s! Match the word or phrase with the correct description.

1. Big bug
2. Bully for you
3. Dude
4. Greased lightning
5. Full of grit
6. Into a pucker
7. Schoolmarm
8. Waking snakes

a. Well-dressed person
b. Causing a ruckus
c. Very important person
d. Female teacher
e. Upset
f. Brave
g. Quick speed
h. Good job!

Answers: 1. c; 2. h; 3. a; 4. g; 5. f; 6. e; 7. d; 8. b

MILESTONES

EVENTS AND PEOPLE OF THE TIME

BETTMANN / CORBIS

GRADUATED. Helen Keller from Radcliffe College in 1904. Deaf and blind from a childhood illness, Keller has been assisted by her lifelong friend and teacher, Anne Sullivan. Keller was introduced to Sullivan by none other than Alexander Graham Bell, inventor of the telephone and teacher of the hearing impaired.

NAMED. The "hot dog," after a drawing in 1906 showed a dachshund—a small, long dog—inside a frankfurter bun.

SUNG. The "Star-Spangled Banner" for the first time before a baseball game in 1918. The owner of the Boston Red Sox wanted to honor the many wounded veterans of World War I who were in the stands to watch the Sox take on the Chicago Cubs.

STRUCK. Oil in Spindletop, Texas, in 1901, triggering what many believe will be an oil boom in the American Southwest. Oil companies are springing up quickly as this new fuel is used to heat homes and run trains.

ESTABLISHED. Mother's Day, by President Woodrow Wilson in 1914—after all, it is only fair since Father's Day was created in 1910.

NUMBERS

UNITED STATES AT THE TIME

12 cents
Price of a dozen eggs in 1910

$12 Price of a sewing machine in 1900

$12 Lowest price for a steamship ticket from Italy to America in 1905

$12 Average weekly salary (seven-day weeks/12-hour days) for arriving immigrants in 1907

12 seconds
Air time of Wright brothers' first flight in 1903

BETTMANN / CORBIS

1.2 million
Approximate number of immigrants who entered the United States in 1907

395,000 Approximate number of immigrants in 1908 who gave up on the American dream and returned to their homelands

It Is the Law
Two laws were passed in 1902 to deal with the automobile.

1. Tennessee demands that all drivers give the public a week's notice before they start any trip.
2. Vermont states that an adult waving a red flag has to walk in front of any moving automobile.

CRITICAL THINKING

Creative Writing Write a story about how you would feel arriving in a strange land and starting a new life as an immigrant.

Contrasting Use the graph to determine who had the longest and shortest life expectancies in 1900. What do you think accounts for the differences in life expectancies?

735

GRADE 8 INTERMEDIATE TEST PRACTICE

TEST-TAKING TIP

When reviewing for a test, pay special attention to bold type, questions, and summary paragraphs in your text.

Reviewing Main Ideas

Directions: Choose the best answer for each of the following questions.

1 Nationalism caused much of the tension in Europe that led to World War I. *Nationalism* can best be defined as

(1) the practice of one nation extending its control over another nation.

(2) a feeling of intense loyalty to one's country or group.

(3) a political system based on military strength.

(4) a structure of defense agreements among nations.

2 In 1917 Germany offered Mexico an alliance against the United States in the

(1) Treaty of Brest-Litovsk.

(2) Selective Service Act.

(3) Zimmermann telegram.

(4) Triple Entente.

3 Russia's withdrawal from World War I in December 1917

(1) convinced German military leaders that they had little chance of winning the war.

(2) allowed the Germans to move hundreds of thousands of troops from the Eastern to the Western Front.

(3) eliminated the Allies' need for help from American soldiers.

(4) caused thousands of French and British soldiers to refuse to continue fighting.

Short-Answer Question

Directions Base your answer to question 4 on the excerpt below and on your knowledge of social studies.

In what I have already said about other nations putting us into war I have covered one point of sovereignty [supreme power] which ought never to be yielded—the power to send American soldiers and sailors everywhere, which ought never to be taken from the American people.

—Senator Henry Cabot Lodge, "The League of Nations Must Be Revised," 1919

4 According to the document, why did Senator Lodge oppose U.S. participation in the League of Nations?

Review the Essential Questions

5 Essay When World War I began, many Americans felt torn and personally involved. Why? How did Americans' attitudes toward the war change as the conflict progressed?

To help you write your essay, review your answers to the Essential Questions in the section reviews and the chapter Foldables Study Organizer. Your essay should include:

- the causes and start of World War I;
- American neutrality and the eventual entry of the United States into war;
- the impact of the American military on the war effort;
- mobilization of the war effort at home and the control of public opinion; and
- Wilson's Fourteen Points, the League of Nations, and the Treaty of Versailles.

History ONLINE

For additional test practice, use **Self-Check Quizzes**–Chapter 23 at glencoe.com.

Document-Based Questions

Directions: Analyze the documents and answer the short-answer questions that follow.

Document 1

Theodore Roosevelt wrote the following about the American war effort in 1917.

> The German-language papers carry on a consistent campaign in favor of Germany against England. They should be put out of existence for the period of this war. . . . Every disloyal native-born American should be disfranchised [deprived of rights] and interned [confined]. It is time to strike our enemies at home heavily and quickly.

Source: *The Foes of Our Own Household*

6 How did Roosevelt think disloyal Americans should be treated during the war? Why?

Document 2

This American poster from 1917 was directed toward recent immigrants to the U.S.

Source: The Granger Collection, New York

7 Why does this poster encourage recent immigrants to remember their "first thrill of American liberty"? Name two goals the poster hoped to achieve.

Document 3

The following table shows the number of military deaths by country in World War I.

Country	Number of Deaths
Austria-Hungary	1,200,000
France	1,375,800
Germany	1,773,700
Great Britain	908,371
Italy	650,000
Russia	1,700,000
U.S.	126,000

Source: Susan Everett, *History of World War I*

8 Which two countries had the most deaths? Why were U.S. deaths comparatively low?

Document 4

Sir Harold Nicolson, a British delegate, described the signing of the Treaty of Versailles.

> Through the door at the end appear two huissiers [court officers] with silver chains. . . . After them come four officers of France, Great Britain, America and Italy. And then, isolated and pitiable, come the two German delegates. . . . They keep their eyes fixed away from those two thousand staring eyes [ceremony attendees], fixed upon the ceiling. They are deathly pale. They do not appear as representatives of a brutal militarism.

Source: Harold Nicolson, *Peacemaking 1919*

9 What is the tone of this passage? How does Nicolson seem to feel about events? Explain.

10 Expository Writing Using the information from the four documents and your knowledge of social studies, write an essay in which you:

- discuss the war's most important impact on American society; and

- compare this to its most important impact on Allied and Central Powers.

Need Extra Help?										
If you missed questions. . .	1	2	3	4	5	6	7	8	9	10
Go to page. . .	705	716	720	732	704–732	727	725	728	731	704–732

Unit 8

Change and Conflict
1920–1945

King Kong film poster, 1933

738

"The only thing we have to fear is fear itself."

—Franklin D. Roosevelt

Drought refugees with stalled truck on New Mexico highway, 1937

Reading History

READING SKILL **Questioning**

Learn It!

One way to understand what you are reading is to interact with the text by asking questions.

Practice asking questions by turning headings into questions. For instance, the heading "Government Action" can be turned into the question "What actions did the government take to deal with the Great Depression?"

As you read, you should be able to find the answer in the next paragraph or section.

—*from Chapter 25, p. 777*

Government Action

Eventually Hoover recognized that the federal government had to take steps to combat the Depression. In 1931 he authorized additional federal spending on public works—projects such as highways, parks, and libraries—to create new jobs.

Practice It!

Read the paragraph. Turn the heading into a question and write your answer on another sheet of paper.

—*from Chapter 25, p. 796*

Creating Jobs

Millions of people—20 percent of the workforce—were still unemployed in 1935. In April Congress created the Works Progress Administration (WPA) to give people jobs and help the country. Led by Harry Hopkins, the WPA kept about 2 million people employed between 1935 and 1941. WPA workers built or repaired airports, public buildings, bridges, and roads.

Question

_____

Answer

_____

Academic Vocabulary Preview

Listed below are the academic vocabulary words and their definitions that you will come across as you study Unit 8. Practice It! will help you study the words and definitions.

Academic Vocabulary	Definition	Practice It!
Chapter 24 The Jazz Age		
normal (NAWR · muhl) *p. 745*	typical; average	**Identify** *the term from Chapter 24 that best completes the sentence.*
dynamic (dy · NA · mihk) *p. 747*	active and energetic	1. Mass production _____ led to increased productivity and lower prices.
detect (dih · TEHKT) *p. 752*	to uncover or discover the true character of	2. Businesses hired _____ to help them develop new products.
intervene (IHN · tuhr · VEEN) *p. 753*	to involve oneself in the affairs of another	3. Most people did not want the United States to _____ in the affairs of other countries.
expert (EHK · spuhrt) *p. 755*	a person with advanced knowledge	
technique (tehk · NEEK) *p. 755*	a skillful method	
device (dih · VYS) *p. 759*	an instrument or piece of equipment	
enormous (ih · NAWR · muhs) *p. 760*	huge	
Chapter 25 The Depression and The New Deal		
decline (dih · KLYN) *p. 774*	to descend; drop	**Identify** *the word from Chapter 25 that best matches the underlined term.*
collapse (kuh · LAPS) *p. 775*	to break down	4. When prices <u>fall</u>, many investors sell their stock.
promote (pruh · MOHT) *p. 782*	to help advance	5. President Roosevelt's fireside chats were designed to <u>build</u> people's confidence.
generate (JEH · nuh · RAYT) *p. 782*	to create	
migrate (MY · GRAYT) *p. 788*	to relocate; move	6. Many Dust Bowl families had to leave their homes and <u>move</u> to California in search of work.
advocate (AD · vuh · KAYT) *p. 790*	to support	
scheme (SKEEM) *p. 795*	a plan	
welfare (WEHL · FEHR) *p. 797*	standard care; well-being	
Chapter 26 America and World War II		
obtain (uhb · TAYN) *p. 806*	to gain	**Choose** *the word that best matches the meaning of each vocabulary term listed below.*
unify (YOO · nuh · FY) *p. 807*	to join together	
target (TAHR · guht) *p. 809*	an object of attack	7. **obtain** 9. **tense**
fund (FUHND) *p. 813*	a reserve or source of money	a. select a. anxious
shift (SHIHFT) *p. 815*	to move	b. acquire b. loose
overseas (OH · vuhr · SEEZ) *p. 816*	across the ocean	c. remove c. colorful
concentrate (KAHN · suhn · TRAYT) *p. 821*	to focus	8. **shift** 10. **conflict**
tense (TEHNS) *p. 823*	anxious; nervous	a. delay a. theory
secure (sih · KYUR) *p. 830*	to gain control	b. create b. fight
conflict (KAHN · FLIHKT) *p. 832*	a war; prolonged struggle	c. change c. plan

Chapter 24

The Jazz Age
1920-1929

After World War I, many Americans enjoyed a time of prosperity and confidence.

U.S. Events

World Events

1918

1921

★ **1920**
- Prohibition begins
- Nineteenth Amendment grants woman suffrage

WARREN G. HARDING

★ **1922**
Teapot Dome Scandal

★ **1918**
Flu pandemic kills millions worldwide

Gauze masks were worn to protect against the flu. ▶

★ **1921**
- Ireland becomes an independent country
- Albert Einstein wins Nobel Prize for Physics

Strikes Sweep Country

In September 1919, about 350,000 steelworkers went on strike, demanding an increase in wages and an eight-hour workday. The steel companies accused the strikers of being "Red agitators." This charge cost the strikers public support and forced them to end the strike—but not before 18 strikers died in a riot in Gary, Indiana.

That same month, Boston police officers went on strike for the right to form a union. This strike by public employees angered many Americans, and they applauded when Massachusetts governor **Calvin Coolidge** called out the National Guard. When the strike collapsed, the entire police force was fired.

Many workers did not join labor unions, linking them with radicalism. Distrust of unions, as well as pressure from employers and government, led to a sharp drop in union membership in the 1920s.

Despite the unions' decline, a **dynamic,** or energetic, African American, A. Philip Randolph, started the Brotherhood of Sleeping Car Porters. This union of railroad workers began to grow in the 1930s, when the government began to encourage unions.

Racial Unrest

In 1919 rising racial tensions led to violence. In the South, more than 70 African Americans were lynched. In Chicago a violent riot broke out after a group of whites stoned an African American youth who was swimming in Lake Michigan. The youth drowned and the incident set off rioting. For two weeks African American and white gangs roamed city streets, attacking each other and burning buildings. The riot left 15 whites and 23 African Americans dead and more than 500 people injured.

Many African Americans turned to **Marcus Garvey** for answers. Marcus Garvey was born to a poor family in Jamaica. A powerful leader with a magnetic personality, Garvey opposed integration. Instead he supported a "back-to-Africa" movement, urging African Americans to establish their own country in Africa. Garvey founded the Universal Negro Improvement Association (UNIA) in 1914 to promote African American pride. It also helped African Americans start businesses. Garvey gained a large following.

Reading Check **Explaining** Did Marcus Garvey support or oppose integration? Explain.

Section 1 Review

History ONLINE
Study Central™ To review this section, go to glencoe.com.

Vocabulary

1. Use each of these words in a sentence that explains its meaning: normal, capitalism, anarchist, deport, dynamic.

Main Ideas

2. **Explaining** What was the outcome of the Boston police strike of 1919?

3. **Describing** What was the UNIA? What was its purpose?

Critical Thinking

4. **Analyzing** Why did Americans fear anarchists? What did Americans expect to happen?

5. **Determining Cause and Effect** Create a diagram like the one below to identify reasons why union membership dropped in the 1920s.

Drop in Union Membership

6. **Expository Writing** Write a news summary of the arrest and trial of Sacco and Vanzetti.

Answer the Essential Question

7. How did prejudice and labor strife affect the nation following World War I?

The Great Migration

Before World War I, most African Americans lived in the rural South. Most were farmers or sharecroppers; almost all were poor. Racial barriers kept them from moving into better-paying jobs. Legal racial segregation and frequent harassment were facts of life.

How Did Geography Affect the Great Migration?

Employment opportunities in Northern cities spurred migration. Labor shortages and limits on immigration after World War I prompted Northern factory owners to actively recruit African American workers. By 1920, almost 500,000 African Americans had moved to industrial cities such as Chicago, Detroit, New York, and Philadelphia. Many hoped to escape the racial injustice and economic hardship they faced in the South. This massive population movement, which became known as the Great Migration, radically changed the racial makeup of the entire nation.

◀ Many African American soldiers returning to the United States after World War I settled in the North, seeking better lives for themselves and their families.

The Harlem Renaissance
Painter Jacob Lawrence (1917–2000) moved from the South to Harlem in New York City. He was a member of the movement called the Harlem Renaissance, in which African American writers and artists began creating works grounded in their own experiences and culture. His work included the series of paintings called "The Migration of the Negro" (1940–1941). This panel from the series shows African Americans buying train tickets to Northern cities. ▶

THE NEGRO SPEAKS OF RIVERS

Langston Hughes

I've known rivers:
I've known rivers ancient as the world and older than the
   flow of human blood in human veins.

My soul has grown deep like the rivers.

I bathed in the Euphrates when **dawns** were young.
I built my hut near the Congo and it lulled me to sleep.
I looked upon the Nile and raised the pyramids above it.
I heard the singing of the Mississippi when Abe Lincoln
   went down to New Orleans, and I've seen its muddy
   bosom turn all golden in the sunset.

I've known rivers:
Ancient, **dusky** rivers.

My soul has grown deep like the rivers.

MOTHER TO SON

Langston Hughes

Well, son, I'll tell you:
Life for me ain't been no crystal stair.
It's had tacks in it,
And splinters,
And boards torn up,
And places with no carpet on the floor—
Bare.
But all the time
I'se been a-climbin' on,
And reachin' landin's,
And turnin' corners,
And sometimes goin' in the dark
Where there ain't been no light.
So boy, don't you turn back.
Don't you set down on the steps
'Cause you finds it's kinder hard.
Don't you fall now—
For I'se still goin', honey,
I'se still climbin',
And life for me ain't been no crystal stair.

Analyzing Literature

1. **Respond**
   (a) What is your impression about the lives of African Americans based on these poems?
   (b) What words and phrases in the poems give you that impression?

2. **Recall and Analyze**
   (a) What rivers does Hughes discuss in "The Negro Speaks of Rivers"?
   (b) How does Hughes use the rivers as a symbol for the African American experience?

3. **Evaluate** In what ways are the poems similar? How are they different?

GRADE 8 INTERMEDIATE TEST PRACTICE

TEST-TAKING TIP

If you are stuck on a question, temporarily skip it. Return to the question once you have answered those you are sure about. Come back to the question, and if you are still unsure, take a guess.

Reviewing Main Ideas

Directions: Choose the best answer for each of the following questions.

1 What contributed to the sharp drop in labor union membership in the 1920s?

(1) rising prices

(2) racial tensions

(3) unchanged wages

(4) government pressure

2 Who prospered under Coolidge and his Republican-controlled Congress?

(1) the Ohio Gang

(2) female workers

(3) business interests

(4) American children

3 Ford increased the sales of his automobiles by

(1) building new highways.

(2) establishing labor unions in his factories.

(3) introducing the assembly line.

(4) steadily dropping the price of the Model T.

4 A form of 1920s entertainment that was rooted in African American culture is

(1) jazz.

(2) movies.

(3) football.

(4) speakeasies.

Short-Answer Question

Directions: Base your answer to question 5 on the excerpt below and on your knowledge of social studies.

An ostrich could assimilate a croquet ball or a cobble-stone with about the same ease that America assimilated her newcomers from Central and South-eastern Europe. Most of them seem to have been inoculated [vaccinated] against assimilation before leaving home. Their standard of living in their home countries was as low as any standard of living could possibly be. If it had been any lower, it would have ceased to be a standard, and would have become a hole or socket.

—from *Why Europe Leaves Home*

5 What ideas about immigration are expressed in the above statement?

Review the Essential Questions

6 Essay How did changes after World War I affect American life?

To help you write your essay, review your answers to the Essential Questions in the section review and the chapter Foldables Study Organizer. Your essay should include:

- examples illustrating fear of immigrants and persecution of unions;
- evidence of American support for business and the policy of isolationism;
- factors that led to economic growth;
- changes in the arts; and
- new roles for women and minorities.

GO ON

History ONLINE

For additional test practice, use **Self-Check Quizzes**–Chapter 24 at glencoe.com.

Document-Based Questions

Directions: Analyze the documents and answer the short-answer questions that follow.

Document 1

This excerpt, from a 1920 memoir by Evalyn McLean, talks about the kinds of friendships Warren G. Harding developed during his presidency.

> Unhappily, for many persons [Harding] had become something other than a friend; he was to all of these no less a thing than Opportunity.

Source: Henry Steele Commager, *Witness to America*

7 Based on this document, cite one reason that Harding's administration ended in scandal.

Document 2

First Lady Grace Coolidge describes her role.

> We New England women cling to the old way and being the President's wife isn't going to make me think less about the domestic duties I've always loved.

Source: Carl Sferrazza Anthony, *First Ladies: The Saga of Presidents' Wives and Their Power, 1789–1961*

8 Based on the document, did Grace Coolidge view herself as a liberated woman of the 1920s?

Document 3

This excerpt from *A Farewell to Arms* describes the Italian front during World War I.

> At the start of the winter came the permanent rain and with the rain came the cholera. But it was checked and in the end only seven thousand died of it in the army.

Source: Ernest Hemingway

9 How would you describe the mood of the speaker in Hemingway's story?

Document 4

This political cartoon shows President Coolidge making music while big business dances.

"YES, MR. HE'S MY BABY!"

Source: Picture Research Consultants

10 Based on this cartoon, explain the relationship between government and business during the 1920s.

11 **Persuasive Writing** Using the information from the five documents and your knowledge of social studies, write an essay in which you:

- summarize the needs and goals of most Americans after World War I; and
- convince readers that Harding, Coolidge, and Hoover represented/did not represent most Americans.

Need Extra Help?											
If you missed questions...	1	2	3	4	5	6	7	8	9	10	11
Go to page...	747	752	756–757	760	762–763	754–764	751	752	761	752	745–753

Chapter 25

The Depression and the New Deal 1929-1939

Pickers bring baskets of produce to be weighed.

HERBERT HOOVER

1929
Stock market crashes

1932
Bonus Marchers forced out of Washington, D.C.

FRANKLIN D. ROOSEVELT

PRESIDENTS

U.S. Events

World Events

1928

1931

1934

1930
World population reaches 2 billion

1933
Hitler comes to power in Germany

History ONLINE
Chapter Overview Visit glencoe.com and click on **Chapter 25—Chapter Overviews** to preview chapter information.

Section 1: The Great Depression

Essential Question What were the factors that brought about the Great Depression?

Section 2: Roosevelt's New Deal

Essential Question How did Franklin Roosevelt's leadership bring about change in the U.S. economy?

Section 3: Life During the Depression

Essential Question How did the Great Depression affect the economic and social traditions of Americans, especially minorities?

Section 4: Effects of the New Deal

Essential Question Why did some people support Roosevelt's New Deal and some oppose it?

FOLDABLES
Study Organizer

Organizing Information

Make this Foldable and use it to help you study the chapter vocabulary.

Step 1 Use quarter sheets of binder paper. Fold the sheets in half.

Step 2 Cut a tab along the left side of each sheet.

Step 3 Staple the multiple sections together on the left side. Record the term on the front of each tab.

Relief

Step 4 Record the definitions and examples under each tab.

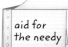

aid for the needy

Reading and Writing Use this Foldable as a self-checking vocabulary study aid by reading the word on the front of the tab, mentally defining the word, and then looking under the tab to check your response.

1935
Social Security Act passes

1936
American Jesse Owens wins four gold medals at Berlin Olympic Games

1937
Court-packing bill defeated

1938
Fair Labor Standards Act passes

1937

1939
World War II begins

1940

Section 1 — The Great Depression

Essential Question ◀

What were the factors that brought about the Great Depression?

Reading Guide

Content Vocabulary

stock exchange (p. 773)   relief (p. 776)

default (p. 775)   public works (p. 777)

Academic Vocabulary

decline (p. 774)   collapse (p. 775)

Key People and Events

"Black Thursday" (p. 774)

Great Depression (p. 774)

Hooverville (p. 776)

Bonus Army (p. 777)

Reading Strategy

Taking Notes Re-create a time line like the one below to record the events that happened in September and October of 1929 that led to the stock market crash.

NEW YORK STANDARDS
The American Journey

U9.II.1 To understand the economic, political, and social impacts of the Great Depression on the United States

U9.II.2 To understand the economic, political, and social changes that took place in the world during the 1930's

U9.II.6 To develop conclusions about economic issues and problems by creating broad statements that summarize findings and solutions

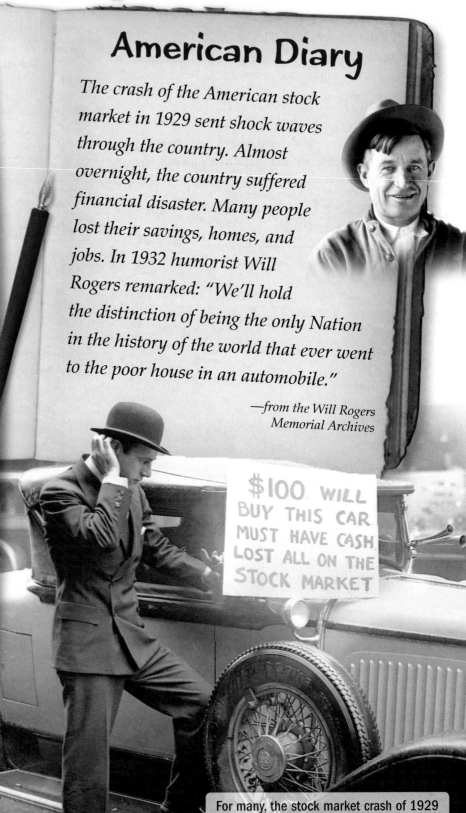

American Diary

The crash of the American stock market in 1929 sent shock waves through the country. Almost overnight, the country suffered financial disaster. Many people lost their savings, homes, and jobs. In 1932 humorist Will Rogers remarked: "We'll hold the distinction of being the only Nation in the history of the world that ever went to the poor house in an automobile."

—from the Will Rogers Memorial Archives

$100. WILL BUY THIS CAR. MUST HAVE CASH. LOST ALL ON THE STOCK MARKET

For many, the stock market crash of 1929 meant bankruptcy.

Roosevelt ordered all banks closed for four days. Congress passed the Emergency Banking Relief Act to help banks reorganize and open again. After a week in office, FDR assured Americans in a radio broadcast "that it is safer to keep your money in a . . . bank than under the mattress."

The president's radio talk was the first of many fireside chats—so called because he sat next to a fireplace in the White House as he spoke. These fireside chats helped FDR gain the public's confidence.

The Hundred Days

During a period that came to be called the **Hundred Days,** Roosevelt's proposals for new economic programs were quickly approved by Congress. It was an amazingly productive time. Optimism swept through the capital. Journalist Thomas Stokes recalled, "The gloom . . . of the closing months of the Hoover administration had vanished."

✔ **Reading Check** **Evaluating** Why did Roosevelt broadcast his fireside chats?

Tennessee Valley Authority

Map Skills

Place Why was the state of Tennessee a prime area to build the Tennessee Valley Authority Project?

Maps In MOtion See StudentWorks™ Plus or glencoe.com.

The New Deal Takes Shape

Main Idea Roosevelt's New Deal affected many areas of American life, including banking, the stock market, industry, agriculture, and welfare.

History and You Has a recent government action had an impact on your life? Read to learn how the New Deal changed the lives of many Americans during the 1930s.

. . . .

The new laws that Congress passed during the Hundred Days—and in the months and years that followed—came to be called the **New Deal.** New Deal laws and regulations affected banking, the stock market, industry, agriculture, public works, relief for the poor, and conservation of resources. These laws changed the face of America dramatically.

Frances Perkins, Roosevelt's secretary of labor, later recalled those early, exciting days of the New Deal:

Primary Source

"In March 1933, the New Deal was not a plan. . . . It was a happy phrase [FDR] had coined during the campaign. . . . It made people feel better, and in that terrible period of depression they needed to feel better."

—from *The Roosevelt I Knew*

Jobs and Relief

Roosevelt gave high priority to creating jobs. He planned to help the unemployed with **work relief** programs, giving needy people government jobs. During his first month in office, FDR asked Congress to create the Civilian Conservation Corps (CCC). Over the next 10 years, the CCC employed about 3 million young people to work on projects that benefited the public, including planting trees to reforest areas, building levees for flood control, and improving national parks.

The president made aid to the poor and suffering another priority. Roosevelt established the Federal Emergency Relief Administration (FERA) to give money to the states for use in helping people in need.

The Depression and the New Deal **Chapter 25** **781**

Primary Sources

INTERPRETING
POLITICAL CARTOONS

This cartoon is a takeoff on the children's nursery rhyme "Ring Around the Rosie." It shows President Roosevelt standing in the middle of a group of children playing the game and singing as they dance around him.

1. **Identifying** What do the letters on the children's clothes represent?

2. **Analyzing Visuals** Why did the cartoonist draw everyone in the picture, including Roosevelt, smiling and laughing?

Roosevelt appointed Harry Hopkins, a New York social worker, to lead the FERA. Hopkins became one of FDR's closest advisers and also became involved in several other New Deal programs.

Roosevelt did not forget agriculture. On May 12, Congress passed the Agricultural Adjustment Act (AAA). The act had two goals: to raise farm prices quickly and to control production so that farm prices would stay up over the long term.

In the AAA's first year, though, the supply of food outstripped demand. The AAA could raise prices only by paying farmers to destroy crops, milk, and livestock. To many, it seemed shocking to throw away food when millions of people went hungry. However, the New Dealers claimed the action was necessary to bring up prices.

To control production and farm prices, the AAA paid farmers to leave some of their land uncultivated. If market prices of key farm products such as wheat and cotton fell below a certain level, the AAA would pay farmers subsidies—grants of money—to make up the difference. In the first three years of the New Deal, farmers' incomes rose by about 50 percent. However, the Supreme Court ruled that the AAA was unconstitutional in *United States v. Butler* (1936) for invading the reserved powers of the states.

Rebuilding a Region

One of the boldest programs launched during the Hundred Days was the **Tennessee Valley Authority** (TVA). The TVA aimed to control flooding, **promote,** or help advance, conservation and development, and bring electricity to rural areas along the Tennessee River. By building new dams and improving others, the TVA ended the region's disastrous floods. And with hydroelectric power **generating,** or creating, affordable electricity, thousands of farms and homes in some Southern states were wired for electricity for the first time.

Some critics charged that funds for the TVA should be used to support programs nationwide. Power companies also attacked the program as unfair and communistic. When the spring rains came in 1937, however, the system worked—the dams prevented the Tennessee River from flooding. In the end, most observers agreed that the TVA was an example of successful social and economic planning.

Helping Business and Labor

On the last day of the Hundred Days, Congress passed the National Industrial Recovery Act (NIRA), which Roosevelt called "the most important and far-reaching legislation" ever passed in the United States. The goal of the NIRA was to boost the economy by helping business regulate itself.

The NIRA created the National Recovery Administration (NRA), which encouraged businesses to set a minimum wage and abolish child labor. The NRA also tried to set up codes governing pricing and other practices for every industry. To promote the agency, its blue eagle symbol and slogan—"We Do Our Part"—soon appeared everywhere.

Another program that the NIRA launched was the Public Works Administration (PWA). Its goal was to stimulate the economy through the building of huge public works projects. The PWA employed many people to work on the construction of roads, shipyards, hospitals, and schools. Many PWA projects—such as New York City's Lincoln Tunnel and Kentucky's Fort Knox—still stand. The PWA spent its funds slowly, though, and the impact on unemployment was not immediate.

To avoid future banking crises, Roosevelt called for reform of the nation's financial system. Congress established the Federal Deposit Insurance Corporation (FDIC) to insure bank deposits. The government guaranteed that money placed in a bank insured by the FDIC would not be lost if the bank failed.

Congress also passed a law regulating the sale of stocks and bonds and created the Securities and Exchange Commission (SEC). This law gave the SEC the power to punish dishonest stockbrokers and speculators.

Assessing the Early New Deal

The New Deal did not cure the nation's ills. The Depression dragged on, and hardships did not cease. Farmers continued to lose their land. Unemployment remained at high levels. Many people still struggled to survive and to make ends meet.

Yet the darkest days had passed. The panic of 1932 and 1933 had receded, and the flurry of activity from the nation's capital had restored some measure of confidence.

✔ **Reading Check** **Describing** What was the goal of the Public Works Administration?

Section 2 Review

History ONLINE
Study Central™ To review this section, go to glencoe.com.

Vocabulary

1. Write a short paragraph using each of the following vocabulary terms: work relief, promote, generate.

Main Ideas

2. **Describing** How did Roosevelt's political experiences prepare him to face the challenges of being president?

3. **Summarizing** What steps did Roosevelt take to restore confidence in banks and in the stock exchange?

4. **Analyzing** Explain how work relief programs benefited the economy.

Critical Thinking

5. **Comparing** Re-create the diagram below to compare the arguments for and against the TVA dam-building project.

TVA Project

For	Against

6. **Descriptive Writing** Write a proposal from the mayor of your city to President Roosevelt that outlines a Public Works Administration project you would like him to authorize. Include specific information about the work as well as how it would benefit your community.

Answer the
7. **Essential Question**
How did Franklin Roosevelt's leadership bring about change in the U.S. economy?

Worker on a WPA project

YOU DECIDE

Was the New Deal an Abuse of Government Power?

Building Background

Roosevelt's New Deal program tried to regulate the American economy to ease the Great Depression. The New Deal differed from the traditional hands-off approach to the economy in American politics.

Herbert Hoover had refused to interfere in the economy. Hungry and jobless Americans blamed the Hoover administration for their suffering. As a result, Roosevelt easily beat Hoover in the 1932 presidential election. Hoover publicly opposed Roosevelt's New Deal. The New Deal was widely supported by Americans, however, because government agencies such as the Works Progress Administration (WPA) reduced the hardships of unemployed workers.

NO

RABBI SIMON COHEN

For about two years now I have been the supervisor of a project . . . under the Works Progress Administration. . . . I wish that those who are opposing such a program could meet these people. I could furnish instance after instance of old people who have worked hard all their lives, only to face desperate need in their old age; of middle-aged workers cast adrift not through their own incapability, but of those who employed them; of young people who have just completed their education and find that the working world has no place for them. I have found some shirkers[1] and cheaters, but they are a very small minority; and the thing that has impressed me is the eagerness with which the unemployed seek for work, even the most difficult, in order that they may do their part in the community.

It goes then without question that I heartily applaud the work that the government has done in this direction and that I feel that it must continue as long as the necessity exists. . . . There is a social need which private business cannot or will not meet, it must be met by the American people as a whole, as a worth-while investment in its own citizens.

—letter to President Roosevelt, October 27, 1935

[1] **shirker** person who avoids his or her responsibility

784

YES

HERBERT HOOVER

You cannot extend the mastery of government over the daily life of a people without somewhere making it master of people's souls and thoughts. . . . Every step in that direction poisons the very roots of liberalism. It poisons political equality, free speech, free press, and equality of opportunity. It is the road not to more liberty but to less liberty. True liberalism is found not in striving to spread bureaucracy,[2] but in striving to set bounds to it. True liberalism seeks all legitimate freedom first in the confident belief that without such freedom the pursuit of other blessings is in vain. . . .

Through four years of experience this New Deal attack upon free institutions has emerged as the transcendent[3] issue in America. . . .

Surely the NRA and the AAA alone, should prove what the New Deal philosophy of government means. . . .

But their illegal invasions of the Constitution are but the minor artillery with which this New Deal philosophy of government is being forced upon us. They are now . . . taking vast sums of the people's money and then manipulating its spending to build up personal power.

—speech given October 30, 1936

---

[2] **bureaucracy** system of government marked by many rules and regulations

[3] **transcendent** most important

DBQ Document-Based Questions

1. **Summarizing** According to Hoover, what is the danger of the New Deal?

2. **Analyzing** Why does Cohen think the Works Progress Administration should continue?

3. **Inferring** How do you think Hoover feels about the Works Progress Administration?

4. **Evaluating** With which position do you agree more? Explain your answer.

Homeless shelters in Seattle, Washington

Section 3 — Life During the Depression

Essential Question

How did the Great Depression affect the economic and social traditions of Americans, especially minorities?

Reading Guide

Content Vocabulary

migrant worker (p. 788)   fascist (p. 790)

Academic Vocabulary

migrate (p. 788)   advocate (p. 790)

Key People and Events

Frances Perkins (p. 787)

Dust Bowl (p. 787)

Ralph Bunche (p. 789)

Mary McLeod Bethune (p. 789)

Indian Reorganization Act (p. 789)

Spanish Civil War (p. 790)

Reading Strategy

Taking Notes Re-create a diagram like the one below to record information about the various groups that were affected during the Depression.

Group	How Affected
Women	

NEW YORK STANDARDS
The American Journey

U9.II.1 To understand the economic, political, and social impacts of the Great Depression on the United States

U9.II.3 To explain how societies and nations attempt to satisfy their basic needs and wants by utilizing scarce capital, natural, and human resources

U9.II.6 To develop conclusions about economic issues and problems by creating broad statements that summarize findings and solutions

American Diary

Dear Mrs. Roosevelt
I am writing to you for some of your old soiled dresses if you have any . . . . I am in the seventh grade in school but I have to stay out of school because I have no books or clothes to ware [wear] . . . . If you have any soiled clothes that you don't want to ware I would be very glad to get them.
Yours Truly

—from **Dear Mrs. Roosevelt**

Organized hunger marches, such as this one in Columbus, Ohio, were common during the years of the Great Depression.

Hard Times in America

Main Idea The Depression was a difficult time because many Americans faced unemployment and the loss of land and other property.

History and You Would you be willing to stay in an area that was damaged by a disaster? Read to find out what happened to people living on the Great Plains and what they did to find a better life.

The letter in the American Diary is one of thousands of letters sent to first lady Eleanor Roosevelt. Many Americans—both young and old—sought relief from the pain brought about by the Depression.

Women Go to Work

Desperation drove a large number of women into the workforce, despite the fact that many people thought that women should not hold jobs as long as men were unemployed. Many families survived on a woman's income—even though American women earned less than men.

Women also worked harder at home to make ends meet. Instead of buying clothes or groceries, they sewed their own clothing, baked their own bread, and canned their own vegetables. Some women started home businesses such as laundries or boardinghouses.

The New Deal era also opened doors for women in public life. President Roosevelt appointed the first woman ever to serve in the cabinet, **Frances Perkins.** He also named more than 100 other women to federal posts. One—Ellen Sullivan Woodward—started a program to provide jobs for women.

Eleanor Roosevelt often acted as her husband's "eyes and ears." She made fact-finding trips for the president because polio had limited his mobility. Mrs. Roosevelt campaigned vigorously for women and families in need.

The Dust Bowl

During the 1930s, while people were struggling to make ends meet, the southern Great Plains suffered an environmental disaster. Hardest hit were western Kansas and Oklahoma, northern Texas, and eastern Colorado and New Mexico—the region dubbed the **Dust Bowl.**

Primary Source / Songs of Sorrow

Music of the Depression Many songs described Americans' feelings during the Great Depression. One of the more famous ballads describes the loss of hope by people who were unemployed.

"Brother Can You Spare a Dime?"

They used to tell me I was building a dream
And so I followed the mob.
When there was earth to plow or guns to bear
I was always there, right on the job.

They used to tell me I was building a dream
With peace and glory ahead.
Why should I be standing in line
Just waiting for bread?

Once I built a railroad, made it run,
Made it race against time.
Once I built a railroad, now it's done,
Brother, can you spare a dime?

Critical Thinking

Drawing Conclusions What do you think is meant by "building a dream" in the song?

Using new technology such as tractors and disc plows, farmers cleared millions of acres of sod for wheat farming. They did not realize that the roots of the grass held the soil in place. When a severe drought struck in 1931, the wheat crops died and the soil dried out. Strong prairie winds blew the soil away.

Each storm stripped away more soil. The drought—and the storms—continued for years. People called the storms "black blizzards" because the blowing dust reduced visibility to near zero. In some areas, sand drifts formed as high as 6 feet (1.8 m), burying roads and vehicles.

Thousands of Dust Bowl farmers went bankrupt and had to give up their farms. About 400,000 farmers **migrated,** or moved, to California and became **migrant workers,** moving from place to place to harvest fruits and vegetables. So many came from Oklahoma that people called them "Okies."

Reading Check **Explaining** Why were dust storms called "black blizzards"?

The Plight of Minorities

Main Idea The Great Depression placed the hardest burden on minority groups. It also led to the growth of radical political movements.

History and You What might it be like to be poor but also to face prejudice? Read to find out about the challenges and gains of African Americans, Native Americans, and Hispanic Americans during the 1930s.

The Depression fell especially hard on the minority groups who were already on the lower rungs of the American economic ladder. These groups included African Americans, Native Americans, and Hispanic Americans.

African Americans

In the South more than half of the African American population had no jobs. African Americans who lived and worked in Southern cities found their jobs taken by white people who had lost theirs. The collapse of farm prices crushed African American farmers.

Primary Source / Voices of the Dust Bowl

In the 1930s the Great Plains got a double dose of catastrophe: the Depression coupled with severe drought and dust storms. This area was labeled the "Dust Bowl." The storms, called "dusters" or "black blizzards," swept across the dry, fine soil of the area, blocking out the sun and burying fences, farm equipment, houses, and even animals.

Lawrence Svobida waited as long as he could for the rains to come to his Kansas wheat farm.

"With my financial resources at last exhausted and my health seriously, if not permanently impaired, I am at last ready to admit defeat and leave the Dust Bowl forever."

—from *An Empire of Dust*

▲ Dust storm in Oklahoma, 1935

◀ Migrant workers in California

Seeking more opportunity, about 400,000 African American men, women, and children migrated to Northern cities during the 1930s. These migrants did not fare much better in the North, however. The jobless rate for African Americans remained high.

However, African Americans did make some social and political gains during the Depression. The National Association for the Advancement of Colored People (NAACP) worked to lessen discrimination in the labor movement. As a result, more than 500,000 African Americans were able to join labor unions. African Americans also won a greater voice in government. President Roosevelt appointed a number of African Americans to federal posts. He had a group of advisers, known as the Black Cabinet, that included Robert Weaver, a college professor, and **Ralph Bunche,** who later played an important role in the civil rights movement. **Mary McLeod Bethune,** who founded Bethune-Cookman College in Florida, also served as an adviser to the president.

African Americans continued to fight against prejudice. In 1939 opera singer Marian Anderson was denied permission to sing in Constitution Hall because she was African American. Mrs. Roosevelt helped arrange for Anderson to give a historic concert at the Lincoln Memorial.

Native Americans

The 1930s did provide some benefits to Native Americans. The head of the Bureau of Indian Affairs, John Collier, introduced a set of reforms known as the Indian New Deal. These changes would help restore Native American culture and heritage.

Collier halted the sale of reservation land, got jobs for 77,000 Native Americans in the Civilian Conservation Corps, and obtained Public Works Administration funds to build new reservation schools. Most importantly, he pushed Congress to pass the **Indian Reorganization Act** of 1934. This law restored traditional tribal government and provided money for land purchases to enlarge some reservations.

Latinos

By 1930, about 2 million people of Latino, or Hispanic, descent lived in the United States, mostly in California and the Southwest. Many had emigrated from Mexico. Some worked as farmers on small pieces of land. Others were laborers in industries or migrant workers, traveling from place to place harvesting crops.

As the Great Depression deepened, resentment against Mexican Americans grew, and many lost their jobs. Politicians and labor unions demanded that Mexican Americans be forced to leave the United States.

The government encouraged Mexican immigrants to return to Mexico. Authorities gave them one-way train tickets to Mexico or simply rounded them up and shipped them south across the border. More than 500,000 Mexican Americans left the United States during the early years of the Depression, often involuntarily.

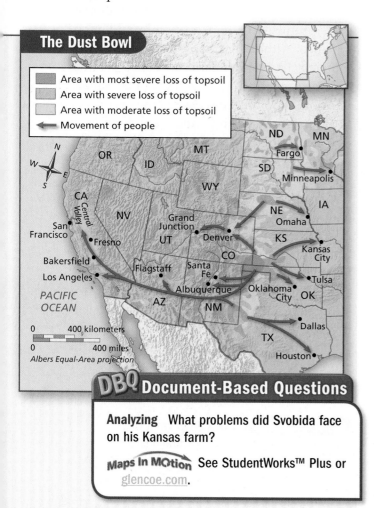

The Dust Bowl

- Area with most severe loss of topsoil
- Area with severe loss of topsoil
- Area with moderate loss of topsoil
- → Movement of people

DBQ Document-Based Questions

Analyzing What problems did Svobida face on his Kansas farm?

Maps In MOtion See StudentWorks™ Plus or glencoe.com.

Riding the Rails During the Depression, at least 250,000 teenagers left home to ride the rails. They crisscrossed the country by hopping freight trains. Many went west to California or south to warmer states in search of jobs, a better life, or just plain adventure. The life of a hobo was often lonely and dangerous. In 1932 alone, nearly 6,000 hoboes were killed or injured when they attempted to jump on or off a train.

Symbol	Meaning
�
_⌐	You can camp here
⊖	Leave quickly
⊗	Good place for food and money
‡ ‡‡	Danger, police
⊡	This water is dangerous to drink

▲ Hoboes developed their own symbols to communicate with other hoboes on the road.

"To be a hobo, you had to know how to get on a train while it is moving. Some hoboes got killed by trying to get on trains that were moving too fast."
—from Luther S. Head, National Heritage Museum

◀ Riding on trains was dangerous but free.

DBQ Document-Based Questions

Speculating How do you think the actions of these teenage hoboes reflected the effects of the Great Depression on American teenagers and families?

Those Mexican Americans who remained in the United States faced continued discrimination. They were kept from getting relief or were offered benefits far below those given to whites. Many hospitals and schools also turned away Mexican Americans. To resist job discrimination, some migrant workers tried to form labor unions, but local food producers and officials cracked down on these organizations.

Radical Political Movements

Hard times helped radical political groups gain ground in the United States during the 1930s. Radical groups **advocate,** or support, extreme and immediate change. Socialists and Communists viewed the Depression not as a temporary economic problem but as the death of a failed system. They proposed sweeping changes.

History ONLINE
Student Web Activity Visit glencoe.com and complete the Chapter 25 Web Activity about The Great Depression and the New Deal.

Communism attracted some Americans with promises to end economic and racial injustice. Although both socialism and communism had significant influence, neither became a political force in the United States.

Another political development was the rise of **fascists** in Germany and Italy. Fascism is a political philosophy that holds the individual second to the nation and advocates government by dictatorship. Although fascism never attracted many Americans, it drew enough attention to make it dangerous. During the Depression, fascists blamed Jews, Communists, and liberals for the country's troubles.

In 1936 the **Spanish Civil War** began. Germany and Italy supported fascists who were trying to take over the Spanish government. Although the United States remained neutral, more than 3,000 Americans went to Spain to fight the fascists.

✓ **Reading Check** **Explaining** What was the purpose of the Indian Reorganization Act?

Entertainment and the Arts

Main Idea The 1930s was a golden age of entertainment, literature, music, and art.

History and You What do you do for entertainment? Read to learn about the ways people sought fun or inspiration during the hard times of the Depression.

The Depression produced two separate trends in entertainment and the arts. One was escapism—light or romantic entertainment that helped people forget about their problems. The other was social criticism—portraits of the injustice and suffering of Depression America.

Radio and the Movies

Radio became enormously popular during the 1930s. "Soap operas" were daytime dramas sponsored by laundry detergents. Adventure programs such as *Dick Tracy* and *Superman* had millions of listeners, as did variety shows featuring comedians George Burns and Gracie Allen and Jack Benny.

Every week about 85 million people went to movie theaters, usually to escape their cares and worries. Walt Disney produced the successful animated film *Snow White and the Seven Dwarfs* in 1937. Two years later, audiences flocked to see *The Wizard of Oz*, a colorful musical that lifted viewers' spirits.

Some movies did explore serious topics. For example, *The Grapes of Wrath* (1940) was a screen version of John Steinbeck's powerful novel about farm families fleeing the Dust Bowl. The 1939 film of Margaret Mitchell's novel *Gone With the Wind*, set in the Civil War era, also portrayed people coping with hard times.

Images of the Times

Many writers and painters portrayed the grim realities of Depression life. Richard Wright's novel *Native Son* told the story of an African American man growing up in Chicago. Writer James Agee and photographer Walker Evans depicted poor Southern farm families in *Let Us Now Praise Famous Men*.

Photographer Margaret Bourke-White also recorded the plight of American farmers, and Dorothea Lange took gripping photographs of migrant workers. Painters such as Grant Wood and Thomas Hart Benton showed ordinary people facing the hardships of Depression life.

Reading Check Analyzing How is social criticism expressed in artwork?

Section 3 Review

History ONLINE
Study Central™ To review this section, go to glencoe.com.

Vocabulary

1. Write a paragraph in which you use all of the following vocabulary terms: migrate, migrant worker, advocate, fascist.

Main Ideas

2. Analyzing What was the Dust Bowl? How did advanced farming technology contribute to it?

3. Identifying What was the Black Cabinet, and why was it important?

4. Making Inferences Why was radio so popular?

Critical Thinking

5. Analyzing In a diagram like the one below, note some examples of social criticism found in 1930s art, movies, and writing.

6. Creative Writing Imagine you are an African American man who moved to a Northern city in 1935 to find work. Write a letter to a Southern relative about your experiences.

Answer the
7. Essential Question
How did the Great Depression affect the economic and social traditions of Americans, especially minorities?

TIME NOTEBOOK

What were people's lives like in the past?

These two pages will give you some clues to everyday life in the United States as you step back in time with TIME Notebook.

Images of Our Nation

PICTURE OF THE PAST

In 1936 photographer **DOROTHEA LANGE** *took a picture called* Migrant Mother, Nipomo, California, *in a camp filled with seasonal agricultural workers. Shooting photos for the Farm Security Administration, Lange was trying to show how government programs might be improving the lives of people in the rural United States. However, Lange found something different from what she expected as she started to snap her photos.*

The woman in the photo was a pea-picker and the mother of seven children —all on the verge of starvation. Lange's photo ran in a San Francisco newspaper, capturing the desperation of the times perfectly. Thanks to the picture, the government immediately sent 20,000 pounds of food to the camp. Here's what Lange had to say about taking the picture:

DOROTHEA LANGE/THE LIBRARY OF CONGRESS

"I approached the hungry mother. She told me her age—that she was 32. She said that they had been living on frozen vegetables from the surrounding fields, and birds that the children killed. There she sat in that lean-to tent with her children huddled around her, and seemed to know that my pictures might help her, and so she helped me.... The pea crop ...had frozen and there was no work for anybody. I did not approach the tents...of other stranded pea-pickers.... I knew I had recorded the essence of my assignment."

HEADLINE FROM THE TIME

Lindbergh Baby Search Still On

Nearly two months have passed since famed flyer Charles Lindbergh and his wife Anne's baby boy was kidnapped in March 1932. A ladder leading up to the baby's window, muddy footprints, and a ransom note demanding $50,000 are the three clues that have been studied by more than 5,000 FBI agents. About 100,000 police and volunteers have combed the country, searching for the baby.

VERBATIM

WHAT PEOPLE ARE SAYING

❝ These storms were like rolling black smoke. We had to keep the lights on all day. We went to school with headlights on and with dust masks on. I saw a woman who thought the world was coming to an end. ❞

A BOY IN TEXAS,
during the devastating dust storms of 1936—with its churning storms called black blizzards that had winds up to 90 miles per hour

❝ While I still have got breath in my lungs, I will tell you what a dandy car you make. I [have driven] Fords exclusively when I could get away with one. ❞

CLYDE BARROW,
(half the team of bank robbers Bonnie and Clyde) in a 1934 letter to Henry Ford

❝ American history shall march along that skyline. ❞

GUTZON BORGLUM,
in 1924, standing near the Black Hills of South Dakota, where work on his Mount Rushmore sculptures would begin three years later

UNDERWOOD & UNDERWOOD / CORBIS

The **Social Security Act** created a tax on workers and employers. That money provided monthly pensions for retired people. Another tax, on employers alone, funded **unemployment insurance** payments to people who lost their jobs. In addition, Social Security helped people with disabilities, the elderly poor, and children of parents who could not support them.

With the Social Security Act, the federal government took responsibility for the **welfare** of all citizens. The act launched the American welfare system.

The Labor Movement

Labor unions grew stronger as workers battled the Depression. In 1937 workers at the General Motors plant in Flint, Michigan, used a new technique—the sit-down strike. Strikers continuously occupied the plant and refused to work until management agreed to negotiate with them about their demands. After 44 days, the Flint strikers won the right to organize their union.

Most unions in the American Federation of Labor (AFL) represented only skilled workers. **John L. Lewis** of the United Mine Workers helped form a new union, the Congress of Industrial Organizations (CIO). The CIO set out to organize unions that included all workers, skilled and unskilled, in a particular industry. By 1938, the CIO had 4 million members, including large numbers of women and African Americans.

Unions found support in the New Deal. The 1935 National Labor Relations Act—also called the Wagner Act after its sponsor, Senator Robert Wagner of New York—guaranteed workers the right to form unions to bargain collectively with employers. In 1938 Congress passed the **Fair Labor Standards Act** (FLSA), which banned child labor and set a minimum wage of 40 cents per hour. The FLSA and the Wagner Act form the basis of American labor rights today.

Reading Check **Comparing** How did the CIO differ from the AFL?

NOW More and more women play important roles in the national government. **Condoleezza Rice** (large image, far left) speaks at the Women of Courage ceremony in 2007. Rice is the first African American female secretary of state. In 1997 **Aída Álvarez** (top right) became the first Latina woman and Puerto Rican to serve in a presidential cabinet. In the 110th Congress beginning in 2007, 16 women serve in the Senate and 74 women serve in the House. **Nancy Pelosi** (sitting at desk) of California is the first woman to serve as Speaker of the House.

Critical Thinking

Analyzing Consider the statement "The number of women in important government positions will continue to grow." Do you agree or disagree? Explain.

The Supreme Court

Main Idea Roosevelt's Second New Deal was challenged by the Supreme Court.

History and You Think about a time when someone questioned what you said or did. How did you answer that person? Read to learn how Roosevelt responded to critics of the New Deal.

Those opposed to the New Deal challenged many of its laws in the courts. Beginning in 1935, the Supreme Court began to declare New Deal legislation unconstitutional. The presidential campaign of 1936 focused on a single issue: Did the American people support FDR and the New Deal? On Election Day, FDR won 61 percent of the popular vote.

Roosevelt's "Court-Packing" Plan

After the election, FDR acted to keep the Supreme Court from undoing the New Deal. He asked Congress to increase the number of Court justices from 9 to 15. FDR planned to fill the six new positions with justices who would uphold the New Deal.

The proposal aroused bitter opposition. Critics accused the president of trying to "pack" the Court and ruin the system of checks and balances. The issue died when the Court ruled in favor of the Wagner Act and the Social Security Act. The New Deal was no longer in serious danger from the Court. The unpopularity of the court-packing plan, however, cost Roosevelt much support.

The End of the New Deal

FDR also ran into trouble with the economy. During 1937, an economic recovery seemed to be in full swing, so FDR cut spending on programs. An economic downturn, known to some as the Roosevelt Recession, took hold and lasted into 1938. Roosevelt helped reverse it with spending on public works. Still, it was clear that the economy had not fully recovered, despite wide-ranging New Deal programs. As the 1930s came to an end, however, dangerous events in Asia and Europe caused Americans to turn their attention from domestic to foreign affairs.

Reading Check **Explaining** Why was FDR's Supreme Court plan criticized?

Section 4 Review

History ONLINE **Study Central™** To review this section, go to glencoe.com.

Vocabulary

1. Use each of these terms in a complete sentence that will explain its meaning: scheme, pension, unemployment insurance, welfare.

Main Ideas

2. **Discussing** Why did many business leaders criticize Roosevelt?

3. **Stating** What was the intended dual purpose of the WPA?

4. **Analyzing** What did the 1936 election say about the public's opinion of the president's policies?

Critical Thinking

5. **Identifying** On a diagram like the one below, list the major labor legislative acts passed by Congress during the Second New Deal.

Labor Legislation

6. **Explaining** What was the Social Security Act of 1935 and why was it a significant act for Congress to pass?

7. **Persuasive Writing** Imagine you were the unemployed head of your family in 1935. Would you have supported President Roosevelt's plan to add six more justices to the Supreme Court? Write a short essay explaining and supporting your view.

Answer the
8. **Essential Question** Why did some people support Roosevelt's New Deal and some oppose it?

Visual Summary

Stock Market Helps Trigger Depression

- Investors buy stocks on margin
- Sharp drop in market prices leaves investors in debt
- International market falters
- Stock market crashes; financial panic

Causes of the Great Depression

- Uneven distribution of income leads to low demand for goods
- Overuse of credit to make purchases
- Supply exceeds demand in industry; leads to large inventories of unsold goods
- Farmers suffer from too much production, low prices, and large debts

Effects

- Businesses lay off workers, close plants
- Millions lose jobs
- Poverty is widespread
- Businesses and banks close
- New Deal legislation enacted
- Despite periods of economic upturn, the Depression remains

STUDY TO GO Study anywhere, anytime! Download quizzes and flash cards to your PDA from glencoe.com.

GRADE 8 INTERMEDIATE TEST PRACTICE

TEST-TAKING TIP

When you take a test, do not answer the questions right away. Look over the test first. How many questions are there? How many different sections? Are some questions worth more points than others? Pace yourself accordingly.

Reviewing Main Ideas

Directions: Choose the best answer for each of the following questions.

1 What hardship did more than 20 percent of Americans face during the Great Depression?

(1) inflation

(2) unemployment

(3) scarcity of goods

(4) high stock prices

2 The National Recovery Administration helped the economy by

(1) providing jobs.

(2) insuring bank deposits.

(3) distributing food and cash.

(4) encouraging businesses to set a minimum wage.

3 Whom did the government encourage to leave the country during the Great Depression?

(1) Native Americans

(2) African Americans

(3) Dust Bowl families

(4) Mexican Americans

4 Conservative critics wanted the Roosevelt administration to

(1) give every American a house.

(2) impose heavy taxes on the wealthy.

(3) play a less active role in the economy.

(4) pay older workers to quit their jobs.

Short-Answer Question

Directions: Base your answer to question 5 on the excerpt below and on your knowledge of social studies.

> Now a lot of people remember [the WPA] as boondoggles and raking leaves. . . . But I can take you to our town and show you things, like a river front that I used to hike through once that was a swamp and is now a beautiful park place built by WPA.
>
> —Ronald Reagan, as quoted in *The New Deal*

5 What were some lasting effects of the New Deal?

Review the Essential Questions

6 Essay Did the New Deal correct the factors that caused the Great Depression? Explain.

To help you write your essay, review your answers to the Essential Questions in the section reviews and the chapter Foldables Study Organizer. Your essay should include:

- factors that caused the Great Depression;
- New Deal programs that addressed these factors;
- changes brought about by New Deal programs; and
- evaluation of the views of supporters and opponents of the New Deal.

GO ON

History ONLINE
For additional test practice, use **Self-Check Quizzes**–Chapter 25 at glencoe.com.

Document-Based Questions

Directions: Analyze the documents and answer the questions that follow.

Document 1

Reverend Reinhold Niebuhr recorded his thoughts about Ford's new model car in 1927.

> The car cost [laid-off] Ford workers at least fifty million in lost wages during the past year. . . . We are now asked to believe that the whole idea of waiting a year after the old car [Model T] stopped selling before bringing out a new one was a great advertising scheme.

Source: Robert Sklar, *The Plastic Age (1917–1930)*

7 What phrases in the excerpt foreshadow the coming of the Great Depression?

Document 2

"Bread Line," a poem by Florence Converse, was first published in 1932.

> What if we should be destroyed
> By our patient unemployed?

Source: David A. Shannon, *The Great Depression*

8 How does the poet think that the unemployed might react to continued hard times?

Document 3

Langston Hughes recorded these observations while in Spain during the Spanish Civil War.

> I've met wide-awake Negroes [African Americans] from various parts of the world—New York, our Middle West . . . all of them here because they know that if Fascism creeps across Spain, across Europe, and then across the world, there will be no more place for intelligent young Negroes at all.

Source: Langston Hughes, "Negroes in Spain"

9 Why did African Americans volunteer in Spain?

Document 4

This cartoon by Cliff Berryman was published in 1938.

Source: Granger Collection

10 Based on the cartoon, explain the economic downturn of the late 1930s and Roosevelt's reaction.

11 **Descriptive Writing** Using the information from the four documents and your knowledge of social studies, write an essay in which you:

- illustrate, with examples, hardships suffered just before and during the Great Depression; and

- describe the feelings these hardships brought out in wealthy, middle-class, and poor Americans.

Need Extra Help?											
If you missed questions. . .	1	2	3	4	5	6	7	8	9	10	11
Go to page. . .	775	783	789	795	794–798	775	790	790	790	796	786–791

America and World War II
1939-1945

American troops land in France, D-Day, June 6, 1944

FRANKLIN DELANO ROOSEVELT

PRESIDENTS

U.S. Events

World Events

★ 1937
Neutrality Act limits trade with warring nations

★ 1940
Selective Training and Service Act passes

1937

1939

★ 1937
Mexico president Lázaro Cárdenas continues land, railroad reform

★ 1939
• Germany invades Austria and Czechoslovakia
• Hitler seizes Poland

History ONLINE
Chapter Overview Visit glencoe.com
and click on Chapter 26—Chapter
Overviews to preview chapter information.

Section 1: The Road to War

Essential Question How did dictators acquire and expand power in Europe in the 1930s?

Section 2: War Begins

Essential Question How did peaceful nations confront foreign aggressors in World War II?

Section 3: On the Home Front

Essential Question In what ways did American men, women, and minorities support the war effort at home?

Section 4: War in Europe and Africa

Essential Question What strategies did the Allies pursue in Europe and Africa to defeat the Axis powers in World War II?

Section 5: War in the Pacific

Essential Question What was the turning point in the war in the Pacific, and what led up to it?

FOLDABLES
Study Organizer

Summarizing Information

Make the following Foldable to help you summarize information about the effects of the war on women and minorities.

Step 1 Collect three sheets of paper and place them on top of each other about an inch apart.

Step 2 Fold up the bottom edges of the paper to form six tabs. This makes all tabs the same size.

Step 3 When all the tabs are the same size, crease the paper to hold the tabs in place, and staple the sheets together. Label each tab as shown.

Women and Minorities in World War II
Women
African Americans
Native Americans
Latinos
Japanese Americans

Reading and Writing As you read the chapter, write details about how the war affected women and minorities.

About 2,000 women were accepted into the Women's Air Force Service Pilots. ▶

FIND YOUR WAR JOB
In Industry – Agriculture – Business
"I've found the job where I fit best!"

★ **1941**
- Lend-Lease Act passes
- U.S. declares war

★ **1942**
- Allies capture North Africa
- U.S. increases war effort on home front

★ **1944**
Supreme Court upholds internment of Japanese American civilians

★ **1945**
U.S. drops atomic bombs on Hiroshima and Nagasaki, Japan

1941   **1943**   **1945**

★ **1940**
- German troops occupy Paris
- Hitler orders bombing of Britain

★ **1941**
- Germany attacks Soviet Union
- Japan bombs Pearl Harbor, Hawaii

★ **1944**
D-Day, Allies invade France

◀ American cemetery, Normandy, France

Section 1 · The Road to War

Essential Question ◄

How did dictators acquire and expand power in Europe in the 1930s?

Reading Guide

Content Vocabulary

dictator (p. 805)   totalitarian (p. 806)
fascism (p. 805)   appeasement (p. 807)
anti-Semitism (p. 806)

Academic Vocabulary

obtain (p. 806)   unify (p. 807)

Key People and Events

Benito Mussolini (p. 805)
Joseph Stalin (p. 806)
Munich Conference (p. 807)

Reading Strategy

Taking Notes Use a chart like the one below to list the dictator and country where each political party originated in the 1930s.

	Nazi Party	Fascist Party	Communist Party
Dictator			
Country			

NEW YORK STANDARDS
The American Journey

U9.II.2 To understand the economic, political, and social changes that took place in the world during the 1930's

U10.I.1 To understand why World War II began and how it changed the lives of millions of people

U10.I.4 To understand the relative importance of United States domestic and foreign policies over time

American Diary

Many people underestimated Adolf Hitler's influence, but not American journalist William Shirer. He described a rally for Hitler at Nuremberg in September 1934: "Like a Roman emperor Hitler rode into this mediæval town. . . . When Hitler finally appeared on the balcony for a moment, . . . [people] looked up at him as if he were a Messiah, their faces transformed into something positively inhuman." The passion of the Nazis shocked Shirer, and soon it would shock the world.

—from **Berlin Diary**

Nazi rally in Nuremberg, Germany

Roosevelt froze all Japanese **funds,** or reserves of money, in U.S. banks. He also stopped the sale of oil, gasoline, and other resources that Japan lacked. The action angered the Japanese.

In October 1941, the Japanese prime minister, Fumimaro Konoye, resigned. Konoye wanted to hold talks with the United States because he believed Japan could not defeat America in a war. The new leader, General Hideki Tōjō, did not share Konoye's views. Still, on November 20, talks began in Washington. Meanwhile, Tōjō's government began planning an attack on the United States.

Attack on Pearl Harbor

At 7:55 A.M. on Sunday, December 7, 1941, Japanese warplanes attacked the American military base at **Pearl Harbor,** Hawaii. Ships there were anchored in a neat row, and airplanes were grouped together on the airfield—easy targets for an air attack.

The attack destroyed many battleships, cruisers, and airplanes. More than 2,300 soldiers, sailors, and civilians were killed. Fortunately, at the time of the attack, the navy's three aircraft carriers were at sea.

The Americans at Pearl Harbor were taken completely by surprise. According to Lieutenant Commander Charles Coe:

PRIMARY SOURCE

"The capsizing of the *Oklahoma* was to me a sight beyond all belief. It was in fact the most awful thing I had ever seen. To watch this big battleship capsize and to see only her bottom sticking up out of the water like the back of a turtle and to realize that U.S. officers and men were still in there—well, I just couldn't believe it. It made me realize . . . that war had come to Hawaii."
—from *December 7, 1941*

The attack on Pearl Harbor united the country. The next day, Roosevelt asked Congress to declare war, calling December 7 "a date which will live in infamy."

On December 11, Germany and Italy—Japan's allies—declared war on the United States. Congress then declared war on them. The United States joined the Allied nations—including Great Britain, France, China, and the Soviet Union—against the Axis Powers—Germany, Italy, and Japan.

Reading Check **Explaining** Why did Japan attack Pearl Harbor?

Section 2 Review

History ONLINE
Study Central™ To review this section, go to glencoe.com.

Vocabulary

1. Use each of these terms in a complete sentence that will help explain its meaning: target, blitzkrieg, disarmament, fund.

Main Ideas

2. **Analyzing** What was the blitzkrieg, and why was it so effective during the war?

3. **Identifying** What was the outcome of the presidential election in 1940?

4. **Analyzing** Explain why the attack on Pearl Harbor was successful.

Critical Thinking

5. **Listing** Re-create a diagram like the one below to list the main goals of the Atlantic Charter.

6. **Creative Writing** You are a teen living in London in September 1940. Write a journal entry explaining what it is like living in a city that is daily bombarded.

Answer the
7. **Essential Question**
How did peaceful nations confront foreign aggressors in World War II?

On the Home Front

Essential Question ◄

In what ways did American men, women, and minorities support the war effort at home?

Reading Guide

Content Vocabulary

mobilization (p. 815) civil defense (p. 817)
ration (p. 817) internment camp (p. 819)

Academic Vocabulary

shift (p. 815) overseas (p. 816)

Key People and Events

WACs (p. 815)
WAVES (p. 815)
Tuskegee Airmen (p. 817)
bracero (p. 819)
Nisei (p. 819)

Reading Strategy

Taking Notes Re-create the diagram below, and describe the new roles adopted by American men and women during World War II.

NEW YORK STANDARDS
The American Journey

U10.I.1 To understand why World War II began and how it changed the lives of millions of people

U10.I.4 To understand the relative importance of United States domestic and foreign policies over time

U10.I.6 To describe historic events through the eyes and experiences of those who were there

American Diary

Sybil Lewis, a riveter for Lockheed Aircraft in Los Angeles, gave this description of her wartime job: "The women worked in pairs. I was the riveter and this big, strong, white girl from a cotton farm in Arkansas worked as the bucker. The riveter used a gun to shoot rivets through the metal and fasten it together. The bucker used a bucking bar on the other side of the metal to smooth out the rivets. Bucking was harder than shooting rivets; it required more muscle. Riveting required more skill."

—from "Rosie the Riveter"

During the war years, women worked at jobs traditionally held by men.

The Holocaust

Main Idea The Nazis increased their persecution of the Jews and set up death camps in an effort to kill all of Europe's Jewish population.

History and You Today many people use the word *Nazi* to mean "someone very evil." The main reason is the Holocaust. Read on to learn about this dark chapter in human history.

⸱⸱⸱⸱⸱⸱⸱⸱⸱⸱⸱⸱⸱⸱⸱⸱⸱⸱⸱⸱⸱⸱⸱⸱⸱⸱⸱⸱⸱⸱⸱⸱⸱⸱⸱⸱⸱

As the Allies freed German-held areas, they discovered numerous instances of Nazi cruelty. During World War II, the Nazis developed what they called "the final solution." Their "solution" was **genocide**—wiping out an entire group of people. About 6 million Jews were killed in what is known as the **Holocaust.** Millions of others—Slavs, Roma (Gypsies), communists, homosexuals, and people with handicaps—were also killed, though Jews were the only group singled out for total extermination.

Persecution of Germany's Jews

Ever since Hitler gained power in 1933, the Nazis had persecuted the Jews of Germany. They first quickly deprived Jews of many rights that all Germans had long taken for granted. In September 1935, the Nuremberg laws removed citizenship from Jewish Germans and banned marriage between Jews and other Germans. Other laws kept Jews from voting, holding public office, and employing non-Jewish Germans. Later, Jews were banned from owning businesses and practicing law and medicine. With no source of income, life became difficult for Jews in Germany.

By the end of the decade, Nazi actions against the Jews became more violent. On the night of November 9, 1938, the Nazis burned Jewish places of worship, destroyed Jewish shops, and killed many Jews. About 30,000 Jewish men were sent to **concentration camps,** large prison camps used to hold people for political reasons.

Numbers	
Allied Forces	**Casualties**
· 15,000 troops (11 divisions)	By the end of the day, 2,500 Allied soldiers were killed.
· 1,500 tanks	
· 5,300 ships and landing craft	
· 12,000 airplanes	D-Day planners had forecast 10,000 dead.
· 20,000 airborne troops	

"I could not swim when we jumped off the [landing craft]. I was tied to my platoon sergeant with a nylon rope. . . . I was too scared to even know my name."
—Dale L. Shrop, 1st Engineer Combat Battalion

Critical Thinking

Speculating What might have happened if the German forces had pushed the Allied forces back when they tried to establish a beachhead at Normandy? How might such an outcome have affected the war?

Primary Source / Young People in the Holocaust

The Final Solution Before and during World War II, many Jewish young people in Europe suffered terrible persecution and eventual death at the hands of the Nazis.

Auschwitz, 1940 At death camps like Auschwitz (right), Jews were the Nazis' main victims. Alexander Ehrmann, a 17-year-old from Czechoslovakia, experienced a nightmarish scene when he reached one of the death camps:

"The doors flung open and we saw strange uniformed men. . . . Sentries and dogs were there, and they yelled at us . . . as they beat us out of the wagon."

—from *Children With A Star*

Hungary, 1944 Thirteen-year-old Èva Heyman described her fears as the Nazis forced her family to leave their home in Hungary:

"We are allowed to take along . . . the clothes on our bodies, and the shoes on our feet. . . . All the while I thought I was just having a bad dream. . . . I have never been so afraid."

—from *We Are Witnesses*

Critical Thinking

Analyzing What was life like for Jewish young people during the years of the Holocaust?

This event became known as *Kristallnacht,* or the "night of the shattered glass," because of the Jewish shop windows that were broken by Nazi mobs.

The Persecution Spreads

During World War II, the Nazis mistreated the Jews in the lands they conquered. They forced Jews to wear a yellow, six-pointed star on their clothing. The mass killing of Jews began when the German army invaded the Soviet Union in 1941. Special Nazi forces carried out these murders. They rounded up thousands of Jews, shooting them and throwing them into mass graves. Josef Perl, who survived a massacre of Czech Jews, wrote of the act:

PRIMARY SOURCE

"We marched into a forest where a huge long ditch was already dug. . . . I could hear . . . a machine gun going . . . . All of a sudden, . . . I saw my mother and four sisters lined up and before I had a chance to say,

'Mother!' they were already dead. Somehow time stands still. . . . But what woke me was the sight of my five nieces and nephews being marched, and the murderers had the audacity to ask them to hold hands. . . . I would have been almost the next one but all of a sudden the bombers came over, we were ordered to lay face downwards, but everyone started running . . . and I . . . ran deep into the forest.

—from *Remembering: Voices of the Holocaust*

Nazi troops crammed thousands more into railroad cars like cattle, depositing them in concentration camps, such as Buchenwald in Germany. Guards took the prisoners' belongings, shaved their heads, and tattooed camp numbers on their arms. Prisoners often had only a crust of bread or watery soup to eat. Thousands became sick and died.

The Final Solution

In January 1942, the Nazis agreed on what they called the "final solution" to destroy the Jews. They built death camps, such as those at Auschwitz and Treblinka in Poland.

At these camps, many people died in poison gas chambers. Others died of starvation. Still others were victims of cruel experiments carried out by Nazi doctors. Of the estimated 1.6 million people who died at Auschwitz, about 1.3 million were Jews.

Upon arrival at a death camp, healthy prisoners were chosen for slave labor. The elderly, disabled, sick, and mothers and children were sent to the gas chambers, after which their bodies were burned in giant furnaces.

Although information about the unfolding Holocaust had reached western leaders well before 1945, Allied forces moving through Germany and Poland after V-E Day saw the unspeakable horrors of the camps firsthand. British soldier Peter Coombs described the condition of the survivors in a camp:

PRIMARY SOURCE

"One has to take a tour round and see their faces, their slow staggering gait and feeble movements. The state of their minds is plainly written on their faces, as starvation had reduced their bodies to skeletons."
—from *The Holocaust*

People around the world were stunned by this terrible result of Nazi tyranny. Allied governments, however, had evidence of the death camps as early as 1942. Historians today debate why and how an event as horrifying as the Holocaust could have occurred. They also discuss why so relatively little was done to stop it.

In Remembrance

The United States Holocaust Memorial Museum is located near the National Mall in Washington, D.C. This memorial provides a national mark of respect for all victims of Nazi persecution.

In 2004 the National World War II Memorial opened on a site on the National Mall. The Memorial is dedicated to the 16 million who served in the military during World War II, the more than 400,000 who died, and the men and women who supported the war effort on the home front.

Reading Check **Identifying** What groups did the Nazi government victimize?

Section 4 Review

History ONLINE
Study Central™ To review this section, go to glencoe.com.

Vocabulary

1. Write a sentence for each of the following terms that explains its meaning: concentrate, siege, tense, genocide, Holocaust, concentration camp.

Main Ideas

2. Explaining When the United States joined the Allies, why did the Allies concentrate first on defeating Hitler?

3. Identifying What was the significance of Operation Overlord?

4. Describing What was the Nazis' "final solution"?

Critical Thinking

5. Determining Cause and Effect Create a cause-and-effect chart like the one below to describe the two fronts fought in Europe to defeat the Nazis.

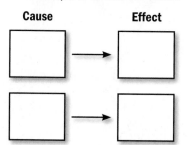

6. Persuasive Writing Take the role of an American relative of a Polish Jew. Write a letter to the editor of your local newspaper explaining what you know about the Nazi persecution of the Jews and urging the United States to take action.

Answer the
7. Essential Question
What strategies did the Allies pursue in Europe and Africa to defeat the Axis Powers in World War II?

Section 5 — War in the Pacific

Essential Question

What was the turning point in the war in the Pacific, and what led up to it?

Reading Guide

Content Vocabulary

island hopping (p. 830)
kamikaze (p. 830)

Academic Vocabulary

secure (p. 830)
conflict (p. 832)

Key People and Events

Douglas MacArthur (p. 829)
Bataan Death March (p. 829)
Battle of Midway (p. 830)
Guadalcanal (p. 830)
Battle of Leyte Gulf (p. 830)
V-J Day (p. 832)

Reading Strategy

Taking Notes On a time line like the one below, track the important events on the Pacific front in 1945.

Mar. 1945   July 1945   Aug. 1945   Sept. 1945

NEW YORK STANDARDS
The American Journey

U10.I.2 To be aware of the much different world left as a legacy of World War II

U10.I.3 To investigate key turning points in New York State and United States history and explain why these events or developments are significant

U10.I.5 To analyze the role played by the United States in international politics, past and present

American Diary

Marine Private Newman Baird was a machine gunner on a tracked landing vehicle. As the Marines hit the beaches on the island of Tarawa, he recalls: "'They [the Japanese] were knocking out [boats] left and right. A tractor'd get hit, stop, and burst into flames, with men jumping out like torches.' Baird's own vehicle was then hit by a shell, . . . killing many of the troops. . . . 'I didn't want to put my head up. The bullets were pouring at us like a sheet of rain.'"

—from Across the Reef

American Marines in battle on the Pacific island of Tarawa, November 21, 1943

The Pacific Front

Main Idea The Allies fought the Japanese for four long years in the Pacific.

History and You Have you ever had to follow a step-by-step plan to finish a project? Read to learn how step-by-step, the Allies pushed back Japan on the Pacific front.

. . . .

On December 7, 1941, the same day Japan attacked Pearl Harbor, Japanese bombers struck American airfields in the Philippines and on the islands of Wake and Guam—key American bases in the Pacific. In the following days, the Japanese intensified their campaign in the Pacific. They invaded Thailand and Malaya and captured Guam, Wake Island, and Hong Kong.

Japanese troops landed in the Philippines in mid-December and had quickly took the capital of Manila. The defending forces—Filipino and American troops commanded by American general **Douglas MacArthur**—were forced to retreat to the rugged Bataan Peninsula west of Manila and the small island fortress of Corregidor.

The Philippines Fall

After months of fierce fighting, the exhausted Allied troops defending Bataan surrendered on April 9, 1942. The forces on Corregidor held out for another month. The Japanese forced their Bataan prisoners—many sick and near starvation—to march to a prison camp more than 60 miles away. About 76,000 prisoners started out, but only about 54,000 of those on the **Bataan Death March** reached the camp. As survivor Marion Lawton recalled:

PRIMARY SOURCE

"We'd march all day, a continuous plodding along, just trying to keep up. I always tried to stay in the middle of the column rather than on the flanks. That way I was further away . . . and might avoid a . . . beating. I don't know how to explain a typical day except that it was brutal, exhausting, hot, and your feet and legs just ached."

—from *Death March: The Survivors of Bataan*

Two months before the surrender, General MacArthur left for Australia to command Allied forces in the Pacific. MacArthur told the Filipinos, "I shall return."

Island Hopping

With Japan's victories, American morale was low. Then in April 1942, 16 American bombers, launched from an aircraft carrier in the Pacific, bombed Tokyo. This daring raid led by James Doolittle had little military importance, but it lifted Americans' spirits.

Primary Source / **Amphibious Warfare**

The LVT "Amphtrac" In the invasion of Tarawa, only one vehicle—the LVT, or amphibious tractor "amphtrac"—was able to cross hazardous coral reefs and deliver troops onto the beaches. The "amphtrac" is like a boat with tank tracks. A true amphibian is capable of movement afloat and ashore.

Critical Thinking

Making Connections How did physical geography affect U.S. military strategy on the Pacific front during the war?

Ⓐ Armor-plated pontoon (float)

Ⓑ Tracks

Ⓒ Machine guns

In May 1942 American warships defeated a Japanese fleet in the Battle of the Coral Sea. An even greater victory followed in June 1942. In the **Battle of Midway,** northwest of Hawaii, the navy destroyed four Japanese aircraft carriers and hundreds of airplanes.

The United States was now ready to go on the offensive against Japan. The commanders—General MacArthur and Admiral Chester Nimitz—adopted a strategy known as **island hopping.** This called for attacking and capturing certain key islands. The United States then used these islands as bases for leapfrogging to others, moving ever closer to the Philippines—and to Japan.

Between August 1942 and February 1943, American forces engaged in a campaign for control of **Guadalcanal,** one of the Solomon Islands. The Japanese put up stiff resistance, but the Americans finally **secured** the island.

In June 1944, American forces captured Guam and other islands nearby. Guam provided a base for launching bombing strikes on Japan. In October, American ships destroyed most of the Japanese fleet at the **Battle of Leyte Gulf** in the Philippines.

The Advance on Japan

American forces then closed in on Japan. In March 1945, they seized the island of Iwo Jima and in June the island of Okinawa. The Japanese fought fiercely to defend these islands so near Japan. Thousands of Americans died in the battles, and many thousands more were wounded.

With most of the Japanese air force and navy destroyed, American bombers pounded Tokyo and other major cities of Japan. In desperation, the Japanese unleashed suicide pilots known as **kamikazes.** They crashed planes loaded with explosives into American ships. Kamikaze pilots sank several destroyers during the battle for Okinawa.

✓ **Reading Check** **Explaining** What is significant about the Battle of Midway?

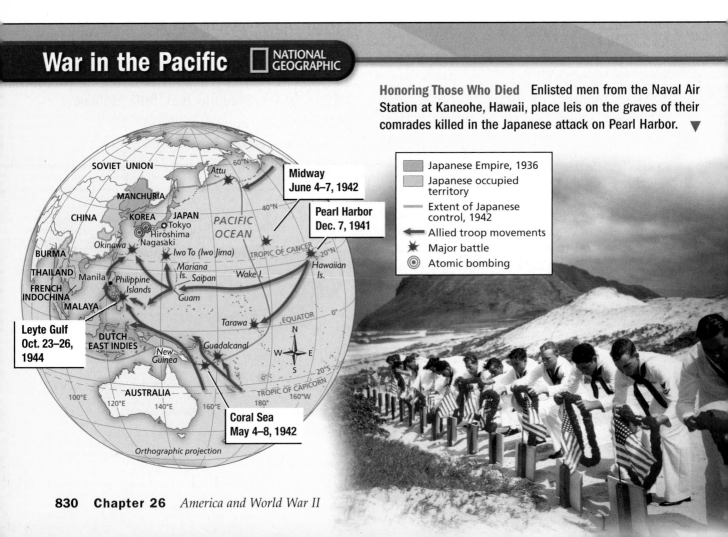

War in the Pacific NATIONAL GEOGRAPHIC

Honoring Those Who Died Enlisted men from the Naval Air Station at Kaneohe, Hawaii, place leis on the graves of their comrades killed in the Japanese attack on Pearl Harbor. ▼

Legend:
- Japanese Empire, 1936
- Japanese occupied territory
- Extent of Japanese control, 1942
- Allied troop movements
- Major battle
- Atomic bombing

Midway June 4–7, 1942
Pearl Harbor Dec. 7, 1941
Leyte Gulf Oct. 23–26, 1944
Coral Sea May 4–8, 1942

Orthographic projection

The End of the War

Main Idea American use of the atomic bomb brought about Japan's surrender in the Pacific conflict.

History and You What challenges in your life have forced you to make changes? Read to find out how Japanese leaders were forced to make changes as a result of a powerful new weapon.

. . . .

Although the Japanese faced certain defeat, they continued to fight. Their refusal to surrender led the United States to use a powerful new weapon: the atomic bomb.

In 1939 the German-born physicist Albert Einstein wrote to President Roosevelt warning him that the Nazis might try to use the energy of the atom to build "extremely powerful bombs." Roosevelt then organized a committee of scientists to study the issue. In 1941, the committee members met with British scientists who already were working on a similar bomb. The Americans were impressed with the British research. They then urged Roosevelt to start a program so that the U.S. could develop its own atomic bomb.

President Roosevelt created a top-secret operation, the Manhattan Project. In 1942 scientists at the University of Chicago built the world's first nuclear reactor, a device that splits apart atoms and releases energy. Later, another team of scientists and engineers built an atomic bomb at a secret laboratory in Los Alamos, New Mexico. On July 16, 1945, the first atomic bomb went off in a test near Alamogordo in the New Mexico desert.

Dropping the Atomic Bomb

Even before the bomb was tested, American officials began to debate how to use it. The final decision rested with President Harry Truman. Truman had taken office after President Roosevelt's death on April 12, 1945. Truman did not know the bomb existed until a few weeks before he had to make the decision to use it.

Pearl Harbor Hero

Doris "Dorie" Miller (1919–1943), Mess attendant, USS *West Virginia*
Doris Miller was one of the first heroes of the war in the Pacific. He was awarded the Navy Cross for his actions during the attack on Pearl Harbor. Less than two years later, Miller was killed when the USS *Liscome Bay* was torpedoed and sunk in the Pacific Ocean. A navy ship, the USS *Miller*, was named in his honor in 1973.

◄ **Raising the Flag at Iwo Jima** Five Marines and one sailor raise the flag on Mount Suribachi on Iwo Jima. For many Americans, the image remains a symbol of courage and patriotism.

Iwo Jima

Ira Hayes (1923–1955), Corporal, 2nd Battalion, 28th Marines
Born and raised on a Pima Indian Reservation in Arizona, Ira Hayes enlisted in the Marine Corps at the age of 19. He was one of the six who raised the flag at Iwo Jima, but Hayes did not feel like a hero:
How could I feel like a hero when only five men in my platoon of 45 survived?

Map Skills

Place What strategic importance does the map show for Iwo Jima and Okinawa?

Maps In MOtion See StudentWorks™ Plus or glencoe.com.

President Truman later wrote that he "regarded the bomb as a military weapon and never had any doubts that it should be used." His advisers warned him to expect large numbers of casualties if American soldiers invaded Japan. Truman believed it was his duty as president to use every weapon available to save American lives.

The Allies then issued the Potsdam Declaration, warning that if Japan did not surrender, it faced "prompt and utter destruction." The Japanese did not surrender, and Truman ordered the use of the bomb.

Japan's Surrender

On August 6, 1945, an American B-29 bomber, the *Enola Gay,* dropped an atomic bomb on the Japanese city of Hiroshima. Three days later, a second bomb was dropped on the city of Nagasaki. The atomic bombs caused immense destruction. The first bomb leveled Hiroshima and killed between 80,000 and 120,000 people; the Nagasaki bomb killed between 35,000 and 74,000. Thousands more were injured, and many died later from burns and radiation sickness.

Faced with such destruction, the Japanese emperor said that "the unendurable must be endured" and ordered his government to surrender. August 15, 1945, was proclaimed **V-J Day** for "Victory over Japan." All around America, people expressed happiness and relief. Japan signed the formal surrender on September 2 aboard the battleship USS *Missouri.* World War II had finally ended.

In the years immediately after the war, Allied authorities put the top Nazi and Japanese leaders on trial. They were accused of war crimes and crimes against humanity. The Allies held the trials in Nuremberg, Germany, and in Tokyo.

The Cost of the War

World War II was the most destructive **conflict** in history. More than 55 million people died during the war; more than half of these were civilians killed by bombing, starvation, disease, torture, and murder. American casualties—about 322,000 dead and 800,000 injured—were high, but light compared with those of other nations. The Soviet Union suffered more than 22 million deaths. Those who survived faced the huge task of trying to rebuild their lives and their countries.

Reading Check **Describing** What was the goal of the Manhattan Project?

Section 5 Review

History ONLINE
Study Central™ To review this section, go to glencoe.com.

Vocabulary

1. Write a sentence for each key term that demonstrates its meaning: island hopping, secure, kamikaze, conflict.

Main Ideas

2. **Explaining** What was the strategy of island hopping, and what was its purpose?

3. **Describing** What was the Manhattan Project?

Critical Thinking

4. **Comparing** Create a chart like the one below in which you note the reasons for and against using the atomic bomb in World War II.

For	Against

5. **Analyzing** Why were the battles on the islands of Iwo Jima and Okinawa important to the Americans?

6. **Evaluating** What was significant about the cost of World War II?

Answer the
7. **Essential Question**
What was the turning point in the war in the Pacific, and what led up to it?

Chapter 26 Visual Summary

1939

Sept. 1 Germany invades Poland.

Sept. 3 Britain and France declare war on Germany.

▼ Japanese American soldiers fighting in Italy

1940

June German troops enter Paris.

July German air force launches Battle of Britain.

Sept. Germany, Japan, and Italy sign a pact.

1941

March U.S. passes the Lend-Lease Act.

June Hitler attacks the Soviet Union.

Dec. 7 Japan bombs Pearl Harbor.

Dec. 11 U.S. and Britain declare war on Japan. Germany and Italy declare war on the U.S.

1942

April Japan captures Bataan, leading to Death March.

May United States defeats Japan in the Battle of Coral Sea.

June U.S. defeats Japan at Midway.

The more WOMEN at work the sooner we WIN!

WOMEN ARE NEEDED ALSO AS:

1943

Feb. Germans are defeated at Stalingrad.

July Allies invade Sicily; Mussolini resigns.

Aug. Women Air Force Service Pilots is formed.

Sept. Allies invade mainland Italy; Italy surrenders.

1944

June 6 D-Day: Allies launch an invasion of Europe.

Aug. Paris is liberated from German control.

1945

Jan. U.S. forces invade Luzon, Philippines.

Feb. U.S. flag is raised over Iwo Jima.

April Franklin Roosevelt dies; Harry Truman becomes president.

May 8 Germany surrenders, victory in Europe.

June U.S. troops capture Okinawa, liberate Philippines.

Aug. Atomic bombs are dropped on Hiroshima and Nagasaki.

Sept. 2 Japan signs unconditional surrender, ending World War II.

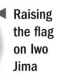

◄ Raising the flag on Iwo Jima

Tuskegee Airmen ►

STUDY TO GO Study anywhere, anytime! Download quizzes and flash cards to your PDA from glencoe.com.

America and World War II **Chapter 26** 833

GRADE 8 INTERMEDIATE TEST PRACTICE

TEST-TAKING TIP

When answering multiple-choice questions, your first answer is usually correct. Do not change the answer unless you are absolutely certain your first answer is wrong.

Reviewing Main Ideas

Directions: Choose the best answer for each of the following questions.

1 One of the factors that contributed to the rise of European dictators was

  (1) American neutrality.

  (2) the Nazi-Soviet pact.

  (3) a policy of appeasement.

  (4) joblessness and resentment.

2 The United States entered World War II because

  (1) the Japanese seized Manchuria.

  (2) German soldiers invaded Poland.

  (3) Japanese planes bombed Pearl Harbor.

  (4) German subs fired on American destroyers.

3 How did the American economy change when the U.S. entered World War II?

  (1) Many women lost their jobs.

  (2) Factories shifted to producing tanks.

  (3) African American workers faced discrimination.

  (4) The military began drafting workers.

4 Who fought the Axis Powers on the Eastern Front?

  (1) Soviets   **(3)** Japanese

  (2) Italians   **(4)** Americans

5 The war with Japan ended when the U.S.

  (1) unleashed suicide pilots.

  (2) imposed an economic blockade.

  (3) offered concessions for surrender.

  (4) dropped atomic bombs on Japanese cities.

Short-Answer Question

Directions: Base your answer to question 6 on the excerpt below and on your knowledge of social studies.

> We Americans will contribute unified production and unified acceptance of sacrifice and of effort. That means a national unity that can know no limitations of race or creed or selfish politics. The American people expect that much from themselves.
>
> —quoted from Roosevelt's fireside chat on February 23, 1942

6 Did the American people live up to Roosevelt's ideals? Give examples to support your answer.

Review the Essential Questions

7 Essay How did the Allies defeat Axis ideas and armies in World War II?

To help you write your essay, review your answers to the Essential Questions in the section reviews and the chapter Foldables Study Organizer. Your essay should include:

- the ideas and acts of aggression by Axis Powers;
- the responses of the Allied Powers to these ideas and acts;
- reasons the Allies were able to cast doubt on fascist ideas and defeat the Axis armies; and
- the costs of the war.

GO ON

History ONLINE

For additional test practice, use **Self-Check Quizzes**–Chapter 26 at glencoe.com.

Document-Based Questions

Directions: Analyze the documents and answer the short-answer questions that follow.

Document 1

Gunnar Myrdal wrote the following excerpt in *American Dilemma: The Negro Problem and Modern Democracy* published in 1944.

> Fascism and nazism . . . came to power by means of racial persecution and oppression.

Source: Ronald Takaki, *A Different Mirror*

8 Give two examples from the chapter that support Myrdal's claim.

Document 2

Jan Karski, a leader in the Polish resistance, gave this report to Roosevelt in 1943.

> Our underground authorities are absolutely sure that the Germans are out to exterminate the entire Jewish population of Europe.

Source: Doris Kearns Goodwin, *No Ordinary Time*

9 What events were occurring in European cities that support this statement?

Document 3

For a full week, Allied planes bombed the German city of Hamburg in 1943. Journalist Gwynne Dyer described what the bombing was like.

> Practically all the apartment blocks in the firestorm area had underground shelters, but nobody who stayed in them survived; those who were not cremated died of carbon monoxide poisoning. But to venture into the streets was to risk being swept by the wind into the very heart of the firestorm.

Gwynne Dyer, *War: The Lethal Custom*

10 How much longer did it take for Allied forces to defeat Hitler's army? Describe the effectiveness of the Allied bombing raids using this quote, as well as other facts, to support your opinion.

Document 4

Pearl Harbor was a naval base in Hawaii. The Japanese attacked it early in the morning on December 7, 1941.

11 Using the information shown on the map, explain how the attack on Pearl Harbor impacted the U.S. Navy and American military readiness.

12 Creative Writing Using the information from the four documents and your knowledge of social studies, write an essay in which you:

- create a fictional character—soldier, pilot, diplomat, or leader—who participated in one or more events described in the documents; and

- include details about the person's hardships and reactions.

Need Extra Help?												
If You Missed Questions. . .	1	2	3	4	5	6	7	8	9	10	11	12
Go to Page. . .	805	813	815–819	811–823	831–832	817–819	807–812	805–806	825–827	822	813	811–832

Unit 9

Challenges at Home and Abroad
1945–1975

Chapter 27
The Cold War Era
1945–1960

Chapter 28
The Civil Rights Era
1954–1974

Chapter 29
The Vietnam Era
1960–1975

VOTE YES OUT NOW VIETNAM REFERENDUM 70

Peace movement button, 1970

provided immediate aid to the Greeks and the Turks. In the long run, the doctrine pledged that the United States would fight the spread of communism worldwide.

The Marshall Plan

In June 1947, George Marshall, the U.S. secretary of state, proposed that the United States give massive economic aid to Western European countries. Their economies were in ruins, and people were starving. After Communists took over the Eastern European country of Czechoslovakia in 1948, Congress approved the plan. From 1948 to 1951, the Marshall Plan pumped $13 billion worth of supplies, machinery, and food into Western Europe. The economic recovery that followed weakened the appeal of communism.

Reading Check **Summarizing** What were the goals of the Truman Doctrine and the Marshall Plan?

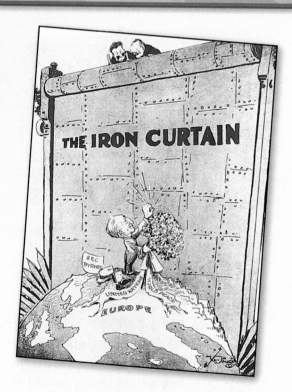

▲ U.S. Secretary of State Byrnes calls on Soviet leader Joseph Stalin and government official Vyacheslav Molotov.

Crisis in Berlin

Main Idea The Western Allies successfully resisted Soviet attempts to halt the Allies' plans for uniting West Germany.

History and You Suppose you are trapped on an island without food or water. How might help reach you? Read to learn how the people of West Berlin were helped by the Western Allies when their city was cut off by the Soviets.

The Allied leaders at Yalta divided Germany into four occupation zones. The Soviet Union controlled the eastern part of the country, while the United States, Britain, and France held zones in the western part. The German capital of Berlin, located deep within Soviet-controlled East Germany, also was divided among the four nations.

President Truman believed that a reunited Germany was essential to the future of Europe. Stalin, on the other hand, feared that a reunited Germany would once again **pose,** or present, a threat to the Soviet Union. He sought to maintain Soviet influence in a divided Germany. Tensions over the German issue led to a serious crisis in 1948.

The Berlin Blockade

On June 7, 1948, the United States, Britain, and France stated their plan to unite their zones to form a new West German republic. Each nation's section of Berlin would be included in this republic as well, even though the city of Berlin lay within Soviet-held East Germany.

The Berlin blockade was Stalin's answer to the West's plans. On June 24, 1948, Soviet troops rushed into position around the edge of West Berlin. Almost overnight they created a blockade, stopping traffic on all highway, rail, and water routes through East Germany to West Berlin. As a result, West Berlin's 2.2 million citizens were cut off from needed supplies. The Soviets hoped this blockade would force the Americans, British, and French to reconsider their plan.

The Berlin Airlift

Believing that the Soviets wanted the West out of the city, President Truman made U.S. intentions clear: "We stay in Berlin, period." The president, however, did not want to risk war by using military force to end the blockade. Instead he organized a large **airlift** to save the city. American and British planes began flying food, fuel, and other supplies into West Berlin.

The airlift continued day and night for more than 10 months, delivering supplies to West Berlin. In May 1949, Stalin finally ended the blockade, realizing that the West was still intent on uniting their zones. Despite the airlift's success, Berlin and Germany remained divided. By the end of 1949, there were two German states—the Federal Republic of Germany (West Germany), allied with the United States, and the German Democratic Republic (East Germany), a Communist state tied to the Soviet Union.

Reading Check **Analyzing** How did the West respond to the blockade of Berlin?

Two Armed Camps

Main Idea The United States and the Soviet Union formed rival alliances, and their competition for influence spread to other parts of the world.

History and You Does your school compete with a nearby school in sports or another activity? Read to learn how the United States and the Soviet Union sought support from other nations in their rivalry with each other.

The Berlin crisis showed that the United States and the Soviet Union were locked in a **cold war**—a war in which the two enemies did not actually fight each other. Instead each side began building up its military forces and arms to intimidate the other.

The United States and other Western democracies agreed that military cooperation was the best way to contain the Soviets. In 1949 the United States, Canada, and 10 Western European nations formed the North Atlantic Treaty Organization. Member states agreed to aid any member that was attacked.

Primary Source / Berlin Airlift

Allied Assistance In June 1948, the Soviet Union stopped all land and water traffic from entering or exiting Western-controlled Berlin. The Soviets wanted the Allies to pull out of Berlin, leaving the entire city under their control. Instead, the Allies took to the air. For more than 10 months, British and U.S. cargo planes flew medicine, food, clothing, and even coal to the city's more than 2 million residents. The Berlin airlift involved some 278,000 flights delivering 2 million tons of supplies. Finally in May 1949, the Soviet Union lifted its blockade. Not only did the airlift succeed in stopping the Soviets' European expansion, it created a new bond between the Americans and Germans.

▲ Berliners watch as sacks of flour are unloaded.

A 15-year-old girl living near one of the airports where a plane landed every three minutes, said,

"The noise of the planes didn't bother us at all. As a matter of fact, we felt secure. As long as we heard those planes flying, we felt like everything was all right."
—from *Berlin in the Balance*

German children wave to a U.S. cargo plane as it flies over Berlin. ▼

Six years later, West Germany was allowed to form an army and join NATO. In response, the Soviets in 1955 set up a military alliance—the Warsaw Pact—with the Communist governments of Eastern Europe. The formation of NATO and the Warsaw Pact divided Europe into two armed camps.

The United States Rearms

After World War II, some of President Truman's foreign policy advisers in the National Security Council (NSC) argued that America could not rely on other nations to contain the Soviets. Unlike the supporters of the containment policy, these NSC advisers believed the United States needed to take a more active stand against communism everywhere—not just in strategic locations.

In 1950 the NSC released a report, known as NSC-68, which said that the United States must actively "foster the seeds of destruction within the Soviet Union" and fight Communist movements wherever they arose. The United States vowed to combat communist expansion everywhere in the world.

Independence Movements

As the Cold War deepened, many nations experienced dramatic change. Many areas broke free of colonial rule and became independent. The Philippines gained independence from the United States in 1946. For years afterward, Filipinos struggled with poverty, government corruption, and civil war. In the late 1940s, the South Asian countries of India, Pakistan, and Burma won freedom from British rule. During the 1950s and 1960s, more than 25 African nations gained independence from European powers. The path to freedom in Africa was often bloody. New nations faced the difficult task of building modern societies.

In the Middle East, Jews and Arabs both claimed Palestine, an area the British had controlled. In 1947 the United Nations divided Palestine into independent Jewish and Arab states. The Jews accepted the plan, but the Arabs did not. After declaring independence, the Jewish state of Israel was attacked by the armies of neighboring Arab countries in the first of six major wars between the Arabs and Israelis.

Communism in China

Meanwhile, significant change came to China, Asia's largest country. In 1949 Communist forces under **Mao Zedong** (MOW DZUH·DUNG) defeated armies led by China's leader Chiang Kai-shek (CHAHNG KY·SHEHK). Mao Zedong formed a new Communist state, the People's Republic of China. Chiang Kai-shek retreated with his forces to the island of Taiwan off the southeastern coast of China. The United States recognized the government in Taiwan as the legitimate government of all China.

With Communists ruling mainland China, the Soviet Union had a powerful ally in Asia. It appeared to many people that the entire continent of Asia was in danger of falling to communism.

Reading Check Evaluating What do you think was the main cause of the cold war? Why?

West Berlin, located in the middle of Soviet-controlled Germany, was isolated when Soviet leader Joseph Stalin blockaded all roads, railways, and waterways into the city. All planes were streamed along one of three 20-mile-wide air corridors. ▼

Critical Thinking

Speculating What might have happened to Germany and other parts of Europe if the Allies had not conducted the airlift?

Primary Sources

INTERPRETING POLITICAL CARTOONS

Cartoonist Herblock comments on the evidence provided by Senator Joe McCarthy for the 1954 Army-McCarthy hearings.

1. **Analyzing Visuals** What does the cartoon imply about McCarthy's tactics?
2. **Evaluating** What were the effects of McCarthyism?

Cold War Fears

Main Idea The Cold War heightened Americans' fears about communism in American society.

History and You Have you ever heard unproven charges made against a friend? How did you react? Read to find out how fear of communism caused some Americans to distrust other Americans in the late 1940s and early 1950s.

The Cold War increased Americans' fears of communist **subversion,** or sabotage. Many Americans worried that Communists—"Reds"—had penetrated all levels of American society and were weakening the government. This Red Scare led to a massive hunt to uncover Communists. In 1947 President Truman ordered an investigation into the loyalty of all federal employees. Although little evidence of **espionage** was found, many federal workers lost their jobs.

Congressional Investigations

During the Red Scare, both houses of Congress set up investigation committees. In 1947 the House Un-American Activities Committee (HUAC) held hearings on alleged, or suspected, Communist influence in the entertainment industry. As a result, several screenwriters and film directors—the "Hollywood Ten"—went to jail for refusing to answer questions about their political beliefs or those of their colleagues. Reacting to pressure, film companies created **blacklists**—lists of individuals whose loyalty was suspect—that kept people from working in films.

In 1950 Congress passed the McCarran Act, which required all Communist groups to register with the government and to provide lists of members. Truman vetoed the act. "In a free country, we punish men for crimes they commit," he said, "but never for the opinions they hold." Congress overrode his veto.

American Spies Revealed

Meanwhile, stories of spies gripped the country. In 1948 Whittaker Chambers, a magazine editor, told the HUAC that he had spied for the Soviets in the 1930s. He accused Alger Hiss, a former government official, of giving him secret documents to pass on to the Soviets. To support this claim, Chambers showed copies of secret information that he said came from Hiss. Investigators could not prosecute Hiss for spying because too much time had passed since the events occurred. He was found guilty, however, of **perjury,** or lying under oath, and sent to prison.

The most dramatic spy case involved the atomic bomb, which the Soviets had acquired by 1949. Julius and Ethel Rosenberg, a New York couple who were Communist Party members, were accused of passing secrets about the atomic bomb to the Soviet Union. The Rosenbergs denied the charges but were sentenced to death for spying. Many people believed that the Rosenbergs were not spies but victims caught up in the Red Scare. Public appeals for mercy failed, however, and the couple was executed in June 1953.

McCarthyism

From 1950 to 1954, the hunt for Communists was led by Republican Senator Joseph McCarthy of Wisconsin. McCarthy claimed that a vast Communist network existed within the government. He called government employees to defend themselves before his committee. His unfounded charges ruined the careers of many innocent Americans. The word "McCarthyism" emerged to describe "the use of unproven charges to discredit people."

Millions of Americans, however, believed McCarthy. As a result, even the most powerful government officials hesitated to oppose him. In 1954 McCarthy made claims that Communists had infiltrated the U.S. Army. In a series of televised hearings, McCarthy hurled wild accusations at highly respected army officials. Toward the end of the hearings, Joseph Welch, an attorney for the army, said to McCarthy: "Until this moment, Senator, I think I never really gauged your cruelty or your recklessness. . . . Have you left no sense of decency?"

Many Americans now came to view McCarthy as a cruel bully who had little basis for his accusations. Congress also turned against McCarthy. In December 1954, the Senate voted to **censure,** or formally criticize, him for "conduct unbecoming a senator."

✔ **Reading Check** **Describing** What claims did McCarthy make against the U.S. Army?

Section 1 Review

History ONLINE
Study Central™ To review this section, go to glencoe.com.

Vocabulary

1. Write a paragraph using each of the following terms: iron curtain, cooperate, containment, pose, airlift, cold war, subversion, espionage, blacklist, perjury, censure.

Main Ideas

2. **Explaining** Who met at Yalta in 1945, and why did they meet?

3. **Analyzing** Was the Berlin airlift in 1948 successful? Explain why or why not.

4. **Determining Cause and Effect** How did the creation of NATO and the Warsaw Pact eventually affect the relations among European nations?

Critical Thinking

5. **Specifying** On a web diagram like the one below, list some of the direct results in America of the Red Scare.

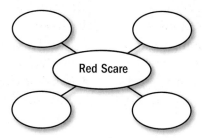

6. **Persuasive Writing** What do you think about the conviction and execution of the Rosenbergs? Write a paragraph that supports your point of view.

Answer the
7. **Essential Question**
How and why did America aid European nations after World War II?

The Cold War Era **Chapter 27** **849**

Section 2

Postwar Politics

Essential Question ◄
What economic, social, and political challenges did Americans face after World War II?

Reading Guide

Content Vocabulary
inflation (p. 851)   desegregate (p. 855)
closed shop (p. 853)

Academic Vocabulary
stable (p. 851)
domestic (p. 852)

Key People and Events
Fair Deal (p. 852)
Taft-Hartley Act (p. 853)

Reading Strategy
Taking Notes Create a diagram to describe social and economic change in postwar America.

NEW YORK STANDARDS
The American Journey

U10.II.3 To understand the relative importance of United States domestic and foreign policies over time

U11.I.1 To understand that the period immediately following World War II was a prolonged period of prosperity with a high level of public confidence in the United States

U11.II.1 To understand the economic, social, and political trends that shaped the end of the 20th century and point to the 21st century

American Diary

When soldiers returned home after World War II, they came back to a nation facing the difficult task of changing from wartime to peacetime. Would the economy collapse again and another depression sweep the country? President Truman was optimistic: "We are having our little troubles now . . . just a blowup after the letdown from war." Public fears, however, forced the nation's leaders into a debate over how best to deal with America's economic problems.

—Harry S. Truman, October 10, 1945

The GI Bill provided many veterans and their families with affordable housing.

The Postwar Economy

Main Idea Americans faced rising prices and labor unrest during the late 1940s.

History and You How difficult is it for you to adjust to major changes? Read to learn about how Americans tried to adjust to a peacetime economy after World War II.

After World War II, the United States had to adjust its economy to peacetime life. Industries shifted from producing war materials to making consumer goods, such as cars and appliances. Defense workers had to be retrained to work in consumer industries, and returning soldiers needed jobs.

During the war, government price controls kept the cost of consumer goods **stable,** or unchanging. When the government lifted these controls, prices began to climb. This rise in prices, or **inflation,** also came from a huge increase in consumer demand and spending. During the war years, Americans saved their money because many consumer goods were unavailable or rationed. Now they were eager for new consumer products and services.

Because of inflation, prices rose much faster than wages. During the war, workers had accepted government controls on wages and agreed not to strike. Now they would no longer be put off. When employers refused to raise wages, labor strikes broke out and disrupted the economy. In 1946 a miners' strike raised fears about fewer coal supplies. Meanwhile, a strike by railroad workers led to a shutdown of the nation's railroads.

Alarmed by the labor unrest, President Truman pressured the striking miners and railroad workers to go back to their jobs. In May 1946, he threatened to draft them into the army if they did not return to work. The president insisted he had the right to take such steps to keep vital industries operating.

President Truman finally forced striking miners back to work. He did this by having the government take over the mines. At the same time, he persuaded mine owners to grant many of the workers' demands. Truman also pressured railroad workers to return to work.

Reading Check **Describing** What happened to prices when demand grew after the war?

Primary Source / The GI Bill

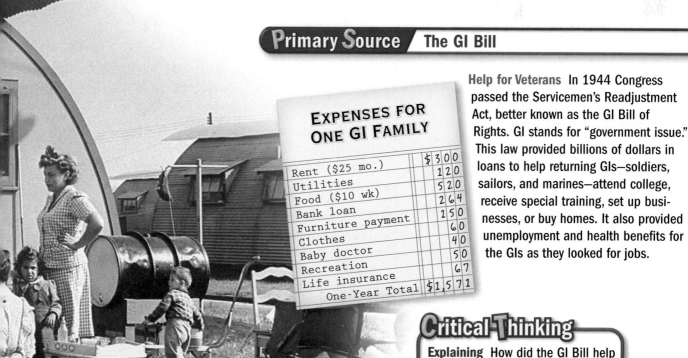

EXPENSES FOR ONE GI FAMILY

Rent ($25 mo.)	$300
Utilities	120
Food ($10 wk)	520
Bank loan	264
Furniture payment	150
Clothes	60
Baby doctor	40
Recreation	50
Life insurance	67
One-Year Total	$1,571

Help for Veterans In 1944 Congress passed the Servicemen's Readjustment Act, better known as the GI Bill of Rights. GI stands for "government issue." This law provided billions of dollars in loans to help returning GIs—soldiers, sailors, and marines—attend college, receive special training, set up businesses, or buy homes. It also provided unemployment and health benefits for the GIs as they looked for jobs.

Critical Thinking
Explaining How did the GI Bill help war veterans?

Truman Faces the Republicans

Main Idea President Truman and the Republican-controlled Congress disagreed over how to solve the nation's economic problems.

History and You Have you ever been at a game in which a team that was predicted to lose won a stunning victory? Read to find out how Truman beat the odds in the 1948 presidential race.

. . . .

In September 1945, President Truman presented a plan of **domestic**—or home-based—reforms aimed at solving some of the nation's economic problems. Truman later called this program the **Fair Deal.**

Truman proposed to raise the minimum wage, expand Social Security benefits, increase federal spending to create jobs, build new public housing, and create a system of national health insurance. However, because of opposition by a coalition of Republicans and Southern Democrats, these measures failed to pass in Congress.

Republicans Control Congress

Many Americans blamed Truman and the Democrats for the nation's problems and called for change. The Republicans seized upon this discontent in the congressional elections of 1946. The slogan "Had Enough?" helped the Republican Party win control of both houses of Congress.

The new Republican Congress set out to limit government spending, control labor unions, and reverse New Deal policies. Conservative Republicans especially favored big business and wanted to limit the power of labor unions.

People IN HISTORY

Hiram Fong
U.S. Senator, Hawaii

On March 12, 1959, Congress voted to admit the territory of Hawaii as a state. One of the two senators elected was Hiram Fong, who had served 14 years in the territorial legislature. As the first person of Chinese descent to hold a seat in the Senate, Fong supported civil rights. He also supported immigration reform that removed discrimination against Asian-Pacific people. Hawaii Senator Daniel Inouye described Fong as *"a legend in his time. He was a patriot . . . a most revered Asian-American leader."*

Margaret Chase Smith
U.S. Senator, Maine

In 1950 Senator Margaret Chase Smith and six other senators issued the Declaration of Conscience condemning "hate and character assassination."

"Those of us who shout the loudest about Americanism . . . are all too frequently those who, by our own words and acts, ignore some of the basic principles of Americanism— The right to criticize. The right to hold unpopular belief. The right to protest. The right of independent thought."

In the spring of 1947, Republican legislators introduced a measure that became known as the **Taft-Hartley Act.** This measure limited the actions workers could take against their employers. It outlawed the **closed shop,** or the practice of forcing business owners to hire only union members.

The Taft-Hartley Act also allowed the government to temporarily stop any strike that endangered public health or safety. This provision was intended to prevent any future strikes like those of the miners and the railroad workers the year before.

Labor unions sharply criticized the Taft-Hartley Act. They claimed that the measure erased many of the gains that labor had made since 1933. Truman, realizing that the Democrats needed the support of labor, vetoed the act. The Republican-controlled Congress, however, overrode Truman's veto.

Dennis Chavez
U.S. Senator, New Mexico

Dennis Chavez represented New Mexico in the U.S. Senate from May 11, 1935, until his death in 1962. He was the first American-born Latino senator. A lifelong supporter of civil rights, he cowrote one of the first Senate bills to stop discrimination in employment. He declared, *"I have been fighting for the so-called underprivileged all my days because I was one of them."*

CRITICAL Thinking

Speculating If Fong, Smith, and Chavez were in the Senate today, what issues do you think they might be addressing? Why?

Government Reorganization

Truman and Congress agreed on improving the efficiency of the federal government, which had grown considerably since the New Deal. In 1947 Congress passed the National Security Act. It unified the armed services under the Department of Defense. The act also set up a permanent Joint Chiefs of Staff, made up of the heads of each of the armed forces, to coordinate military policy. A National Security Council, located within the White House, would advise the president on foreign and military matters.

The National Security Act also set up another institution, the Central Intelligence Agency (CIA). The CIA aids American foreign policy by collecting information about what is going on in other countries, evaluating it, and passing it on to the president and other foreign-policy decision makers.

Many Americans feared that the CIA would be used to spy on American citizens. Truman, however, promised that the new agency would operate only in foreign lands and would not bring "police state methods" into American society.

The Election of 1948

As the 1948 presidential race neared, Truman seemed to have little chance of winning. Continuing economic problems made the president unpopular with many voters. Truman's failure to get U.S. domestic reforms passed made him look weak and ineffective.

Divisions within the Democratic Party also increased the chances of a Republican victory. At the Democratic national convention, two groups left the party altogether. Reacting angrily to Truman's support of civil rights, a group of Southern Democrats formed the States' Rights Democratic Party, or Dixiecrats. They nominated South Carolina's governor Strom Thurmond for president. At the same time, some Democrats left to form the Progressive Party, with Henry Wallace as their nominee for president. Wallace opposed Truman's foreign policy and called for closer American-Soviet ties.

The Election of 1948 — NATIONAL GEOGRAPHIC

Candidate	Electoral Vote	Popular Vote	Political Party
Truman	303	24,105,812	Democrat
Dewey	189	21,970,065	Republican
Thurmond	39	1,169,021	States' Rights

"We were getting good crowds despite the newspaper reports that Mr. Dewey was a 10-to-1 bet to win the election."
—William J. Bray, assistant on the 1948 presidential campaign train

Map Skills

1. **Comparing** From which region did Thurmond receive the most support?
2. **Calculating** By how many electoral votes did Truman win over Dewey?

Maps In MOtion See StudentWorks™ Plus or glencoe.com.

Dewey Leads Polls

With the Democrats badly divided, it looked as though Governor Thomas Dewey of New York, the Republican nominee, would surely win the election. A dignified and popular candidate, Dewey seemed unbeatable. Opinion polls showed him with a huge lead. One pollster remarked: "Mr. Dewey is still so clearly ahead that we might just as well get ready to listen to his inaugural."

Perhaps the only one who gave Truman a chance to win was Truman himself. Ignoring the polls, the determined president poured his efforts into an energetic campaign. Traveling more than 21,000 miles (33,800 km) by train on a "whistle-stop" tour of the country, he gave some 300 speeches along the way. In town after town, he sharply attacked what he called "that do-nothing, good-for-nothing, worst Congress" for rejecting his Fair Deal legislation.

Truman Stages an Upset

On Election Day experts still expected Dewey to win. Expectations for a Republican victory were so great that on the evening of the election—before many votes were counted—the *Chicago Daily Tribune* newspaper issued a special edition announcing "Dewey Defeats Truman."

The nation was in for a great surprise. When all the ballots were counted, Truman had edged out Dewey by more than 2 million votes. The president's narrow victory was based largely on support from workers, African Americans, and farmers. Almost as remarkable as Truman's victory was the new popularity of the Democratic Party. In the election, Democrats regained control of both houses of Congress.

Reading Check **Analyzing** Why was the outcome of the 1948 presidential election a surprise?

Truman and MacArthur Disagree

As the stalemate continued, Truman thought about negotiating an end to the fighting. MacArthur, however, argued that dropping atomic bombs on Chinese bases and supply lines would bring a quick victory. Truman opposed MacArthur's plan, fearing that it would lead to a larger war with China or develop into another world war.

MacArthur publically criticized the president. In a letter to a member of Congress, MacArthur complained that he was being kept from doing his job. "We must win," he wrote. "There is no substitute for victory."

On April 11, 1951, President Truman relieved General MacArthur of his command in Korea. He **concluded,** or decided, that it was the only action he could take and "still be president of the United States." Truman wrote: "If I allowed him to defy the civil authorities in this manner, I myself would be violating my oath to uphold and defend the Constitution."

MacArthur's firing created a storm of protest in the United States. The general was popular, and polls showed that most Americans supported him against the president. Moreover, MacArthur did not go quietly. He returned home to a hero's welcome. MacArthur also delivered a farewell speech before Congress. "Old soldiers never die," he said, "they just fade away."

Ending the Conflict

The two sides in the Korean War began talks in July 1951. A cease-fire agreement ending the fighting was finally signed in July 1953 during the presidency of Dwight D. Eisenhower. It set up a **demilitarized zone**—a region barring military forces—between the two Koreas. The zone stretched along the border near the 38th parallel.

The Korean War ended with no victory for either side and almost no change in territory. More than 36,000 Americans died, and another 103,000 were wounded. Nearly two million Koreans and Chinese were killed.

By fighting in Korea, the United States showed the Soviets that it was willing to use force, if necessary, to block the spread of communism. At the same time, the lack of a clear victory led to uncertainty at home about America's foreign policy.

Reading Check **Comparing** How did Truman's view on Korea differ from General MacArthur's view?

Section 3 Review

History ONLINE
Study Central™ To review this section, go to glencoe.com.

Vocabulary

1. **Explain** the significance of each of these terms: assure, stalemate, conclude, demilitarized zone.

Main Ideas

2. **Explaining** How did the Korean conflict begin?

3. **Discussing** Why did Truman relieve General MacArthur of his command in Korea?

4. **Identifying** What is a demilitarized zone, and where was it located in Korea?

Critical Thinking

5. **Comparing and Contrasting** Re-create a chart like the one below to compare the stalemate solutions of Truman and MacArthur.

6. **Expository Writing** Explain in a paragraph the major events that led directly to the stalemate in Korea.

7. **Answer the Essential Question** How and why did America involve itself in the Korean conflict of the 1950s?

America in the 1950s

Essential Question ◄

How did the American prosperity of the 1950s affect the country's economy and culture?

Reading Guide

Content Vocabulary

surplus (p. 861)   affluence (p. 863)

arms race (p. 862)   materialism (p. 866)

summit (p. 862)

Academic Vocabulary

nuclear (p. 862)   economy (p. 863)

Key People and Events

Dwight D. Eisenhower (p. 861)

Nikita Khrushchev (p. 862)

Reading Strategy

Taking Notes Re-create a diagram like the one below to identify two Cold War crises that occurred in 1956 and how each was resolved.

NEW YORK STANDARDS
The American Journey

U10.II.3 To understand the relative importance of United States domestic and foreign policies over time

U10.II.4 To analyze the role played by the United States in international politics, past and present

U11.I.1 To understand that the period immediately following World War II was a prolonged period of prosperity with a high level of public confidence in the United States

American Diary

"Trust was the bedrock of Ike's presidency," one reporter said, adding, "We knew what was in his heart." These words were used to describe Dwight D. Eisenhower, Republican presidential candidate in 1952. Eisenhower's appeal went far beyond party label. His role in World War II made him an unquestioned hero. Above all, his personality made many people feel safe, comfortable, and confident.

—from Hugh Sidey, TIME *magazine reporter*

Eisenhower supporters in Shreveport, Louisiana, during the 1952 campaign

The Eisenhower Years

Main Idea President Eisenhower promoted policies to maintain prosperity at home and to compete with the Soviets abroad.

History and You Have you ever taken part in an exciting contest to win first prize? Read to learn how the United States and the Soviet Union were rivals in a "contest" for world leadership.

In November 1952, Americans elected **Dwight D. Eisenhower** to the presidency in a landslide victory—the first Republican to win the White House since 1928. Eisenhower collected more than 6 million popular votes over Illinois Governor Adlai E. Stevenson, his Democratic opponent, and carried the electoral college 442 to 89. The Republicans also won control of Congress.

Born in Texas and raised in rural Kansas, Dwight D. Eisenhower rose steadily through the army to become supreme commander of the Allied forces in Europe during World War II. People called him "Ike"—and voters trusted him. He won wide support with his pledge to bring the Korean War to an "early and honorable end."

Domestic Policy

During his two terms in office, Eisenhower followed a moderate, or middle-of-the-road, approach to domestic policy. He avoided ambitious new government programs but resisted the pressure to end popular older ones, and sometimes he even expanded them. As he once told reporters: "I feel pretty good when I'm attacked from both sides. It makes me more certain I'm on the right track."

President Eisenhower wanted to make the federal government "smaller rather than bigger." He backed free enterprise, shifted some financial powers to the states, and cut federal spending. When Eisenhower completed his second term in 1961, the federal budget had a **surplus,** or excess, of $300 million.

The greatest domestic program of the Eisenhower years involved building a network of interstate highways. In 1956 Congress passed the Federal Highway Act. The law funded the building of more than 40,000 miles (64,000 km) of highways that tied the nation together. The highway program spurred economic growth, especially in the automobile and oil industries, while improving military mobility in case of an attack.

Primary Source / Election of 1952

Electoral Vote
- 83% — Dwight D. Eisenhower (R)
- 17% — Adlai E. Stevenson (D)

Popular Vote
- 55.1% — Dwight D. Eisenhower (R)
- 44.4% — Adlai E. Stevenson (D)
- 0.5% (Other)

Critical Thinking

1. **Interpreting** Which candidate won a majority of the popular vote?
2. **Applying** What is a landslide victory? Would you consider Eisenhower's election a landslide? Explain.

United States–Soviet Rivalry

During the 1950s, the United States and the Soviet Union engaged in a nuclear **arms race.** Both sides built more and more **nuclear,** or atomic, warheads and guided missiles that could destroy the other side many times over. With the threat of nuclear destruction so great, the United States and the Soviet Union had to act carefully. A crisis, badly managed, could lead to all-out war.

In 1956 two crises tested the superpowers. First, trouble arose in the Middle East when Egypt's president Gamal Abdel Nasser seized the Suez Canal from its European owners. In October, Britain and France joined Israel in invading Egypt. Britain and France hoped to get rid of Nasser, and Israel wanted to end Egypt's military threat. American and Soviet opposition finally forced the three nations to pull out of Egypt.

The second crisis erupted in Hungary, when students and workers demonstrated to demand changes in the government. A new government called for Soviet troops to withdraw. In early November 1956, Soviet leader **Nikita Khrushchev** (kroosh·CHAWF) ordered Soviet forces to crush the revolt. President Eisenhower condemned the Soviet crackdown but did not intervene.

By the mid-1950s, the superpowers were interested in easing Cold War tensions. In July 1955, Eisenhower, NATO leaders, and Soviet officials met at a summit conference in Geneva, Switzerland. A **summit** is a meeting of heads of government. The leaders discussed major issues, raising hopes for peace.

After the Geneva summit, a policy of peaceful coexistence emerged. This meant the two superpowers would compete but avoid war. For example, the U.S. and the Soviet Union began competing in a space race. In October 1957, the Soviets sent into space the world's first artificial satellite, called *Sputnik*. The United States set up its own space program headed by the National Aeronautics and Space Administration (NASA).

✔ Reading Check **Describing** How did relations between the superpowers change after the Geneva summit?

LINKING PAST TO PRESENT — Computers

THEN In the mid-1940s, the earliest computers were built specifically for scientific calculations in military use. Unveiled in 1946, ENIAC (Electronic Numerical Integrator and Computer) was the first programmable, general-purpose digital computer. It could take workers days, using punch cards, plug boards, and switches, to program the machine for each new task.

★ **1940s** ENIAC
Weight—30 tons
(27 metric tons)
Area—1,800 sq. feet
(167 sq. m)

★ **1977** First preassembled desktop, personal computer with color graphics; called "Apple II"

★ **1990** Microsoft Windows 3.0 software introduced

★ **1991** World Wide Web available to general public

Prosperity and Change

Main Idea A booming economy changed the social and cultural life of Americans during the 1950s.

History and You You probably have heard this expression: "Those were the good old days." For some older Americans, this expression describes the 1950s. Read to find out why the 1950s has this appeal for them.

• •

During the 1950s, the American **economy** —the system of production, distribution, and consumption—grew rapidly. Americans earned higher wages and bought more consumer goods than ever before. As a result, factory production soared. A "baby boom," or increased birthrate, promised even more economic growth in the future.

Many women left the workforce to stay home and raise children. The demand for baby products and services grew. School enrollment soared as the "baby boomers" reached school age, putting a strain on the educational system.

The Consumer Society

Americans of the 1950s went on a buying spree. **Affluence,** the growing variety and quantity of products available, and expanded advertising all played a role in the increased demand for consumer goods. Buying goods became easier, too. Many Americans used credit cards, charge accounts, and easy-payment plans to purchase goods.

Consumers sought the latest products— dishwashers, washing machines, television sets, stereos, and clothes made from synthetic fabrics. The growing market for cars prompted automakers to outdo one another by manufacturing bigger, faster, and flashier cars. New models added stylish features such as chrome-plated bumpers and soaring tail fins.

The advertising and marketing of products on television, on radio, and in magazines created consumer fads and crazes that swept the nation. In the late 1950s, Americans bought millions of hula hoops—large plastic rings they twirled around their waists. Other popular fads included crew cuts for boys, poodle skirts for girls, and a new snack—pizza.

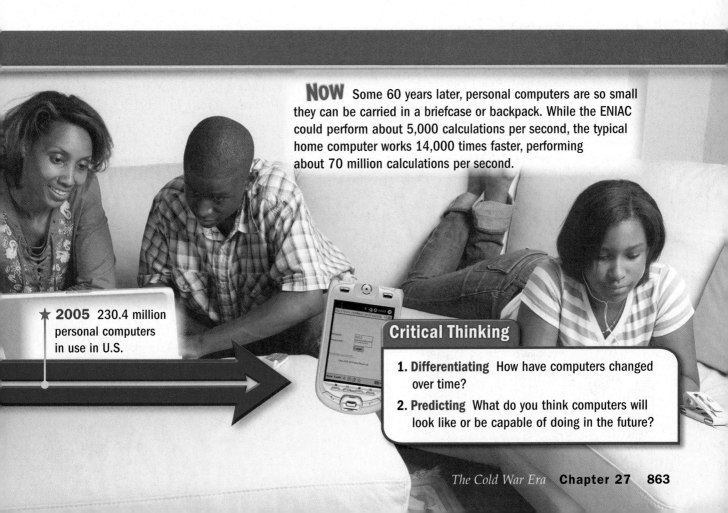

NOW Some 60 years later, personal computers are so small they can be carried in a briefcase or backpack. While the ENIAC could perform about 5,000 calculations per second, the typical home computer works 14,000 times faster, performing about 70 million calculations per second.

★ **2005** 230.4 million personal computers in use in U.S.

Critical Thinking

1. **Differentiating** How have computers changed over time?
2. **Predicting** What do you think computers will look like or be capable of doing in the future?

An American Culture

By 1949 more than 900,000 American households had television sets. The sets, in large wooden cabinets, had small screens that displayed grainy black-and-white images. During the 1950s, an average of 6.5 million sets were produced annually. By the end of the decade, most American families had television.

Television changed American life. It became the main form of entertainment as well as an important source of news and information. Millions of Americans gathered to watch weekly episodes of programs such as *I Love Lucy* and *Father Knows Best*. The images shown in many programs—of happy families in neat, middle-class homes—helped shape Americans' expectations for their own lives.

A new form of music—rock 'n' roll—achieved great popularity among teenagers. Rock 'n' roll grew from the rhythm and blues music that African American musicians cre-ated years before. It often had some elements of country music. In rock 'n' roll, the tempo was quicker, and electrically amplified instruments—mostly guitars—were used.

One of the first rock hits, reaching number one in 1955, was Bill Haley and the Comets' *Rock Around the Clock*. Adapting the style of African American performers such as Chuck Berry and Little Richard, Elvis Presley burst on the national scene in 1956. Presley quickly became an idol to millions of young Americans. Many young men copied his ducktail haircut and swaggering mannerisms.

For teenagers, the shared experience of listening to the music helped forge a common identity. The differing attitudes of the older and younger generations toward music and other forms of popular culture later came to be known as the generation gap.

Reading Check **Analyzing** How did television change American life in the 1950s?

Economics & History

Bread 180 loaves

Oranges 2 crates

Eggs 131 dz.

Food for a Year *How far would a weekly grocery budget of $25 go to feed a family of four in 1951?*

31 Chickens

Milk 698 qts.

Problems in a Time of Plenty

Main Idea Many Americans did not share in the prosperity of the 1950s.

History and You Can you recall hard times in your life? Read on to learn what groups considered the 1950s to be hard times.

In the 1950s, more than 20 percent of Americans lived in poverty. Millions more struggled to survive on incomes that were only slightly above the poverty level. Such poverty marred the landscape of the affluent society.

Many farmers did not share in the prosperity of the 1950s. Business enterprises created large profitable farms that used new technology to produce an abundance of food for American and foreign consumers. Small farms, however, could not compete with large farms, so many small-farm families sold their land and migrated to urban areas. Small farmers who continued to farm struggled.

Rural poverty did not always come from agricultural problems. In Appalachia—a region stretching along the Appalachian Mountains—the decline of the coal industry plunged thousands of rural mountain people into desperate poverty. During the 1950s, about 1.5 million people abandoned Appalachia to seek a better life in the nation's cities.

Urban Poverty

As increasing numbers of middle-class Americans moved to the suburbs in the 1950s, they left the poor behind. The inner cities became islands of poverty. Still, people came to cities looking for work. Continuing their migration from rural areas of the South, more than 3 million African Americans moved to cities in the North and the Midwest between 1940 and 1960. For many, however, life proved to be little better in Northern cities. Many poor Latinos—Puerto Ricans in the East and Mexicans in the Southwest and the West— also moved to American cities.

The migration of poor African Americans and Latinos to Northern cities hastened the departure of whites to the suburbs. This "white flight" turned some areas of cities into ghettos—neighborhoods that were inhabited mainly by poor minority groups.

Few good job opportunities existed for the urban poor. Many factories and businesses relocated to suburban areas. In addition, automation—producing goods using mechanical and electronic devices—reduced jobs in the industries that remained. It became more and more difficult for the urban poor to rise from poverty and improve their lives.

The urban poor struggled not only with poverty but also with racial discrimination in employment, housing, and education. Crime and violence often grew out of inner-city poverty, especially among young people who saw no hope for escape from life in the ghetto.

By the Numbers

1951	Comparing by Cost	2007
$0.92	Milk, per gallon	$3.07
$0.75	Eggs, per dozen	$1.54
$0.15	Loaf of bread	$1.15
$0.49	Oranges, per dozen	$1.09
$0.60	Chicken, per pound	$1.03
$0.03	Cost of first-class postage stamp	$0.41
$0.49	Movie ticket	$6.50
$1.45	Average hourly wage	$17.30
$1,995	Average cost of a new car	$27,800
$3,709	Median income for a family of four	$59,000
$299	Television set, 16-inch screen	$299

—from various sources

Critical Thinking

Calculating What percentage of a family's income in 1951 was needed to buy a new car? In 2007?

History ONLINE
Student Web Activity Visit glencoe.com and complete the Chapter 27 Web Activity about life in the 1950s.

Social Critics

Changes in American society in the 1950s caused some people to question the values that were emerging. Some critics charged that the sameness of corporate and suburban life had a cost—the loss of individuality. Others condemned American **materialism**—a focus on accumulating money and possessions rather than an interest in personal and spiritual matters.

Leading social critics examined the complexity of modern society. Many wrote about its effects on individual behavior. William H. Whyte, Jr., studied American business life in *The Organization Man*. He drew a picture of young executives as "organization men" who "have left home spiritually as well as physically." He concluded that businesses discouraged independent thinking and considered the person with new ideas "a threat." Young executives who abandoned their own views were the ones most likely to fit in.

In his book, *The Affluent Society*, economist John Kenneth Galbraith wrote of the prosperous American society of the 1950s. However, not all Americans shared in this prosperity. Galbraith described a suburban family, comfortably installed in an "air-conditioned, power-steered and power-braked automobile, driven through cities that are badly paved, made hideous by litter, blighted buildings, and billboards." Prosperous Americans, Galbraith claimed, often ignored the hardships faced by the rural and urban poor.

Changing Times

A group of writers called the Beats had even sharper criticism of American society. The term "Beat," said novelist Jack Kerouac, meant "weariness with all forms of the modern industrial state." Many young Americans read the works of Kerouac, poet Allen Ginsberg, and other Beat writers. Some adopted Beat attitudes of rebellion against middle-class America.

With American society changing, women and African Americans began questioning their roles. They became increasingly impatient for change and less willing to accept their status as second-class citizens. In the 1950s both groups launched efforts to gain greater freedom and equality.

Reading Check **Describing** What criticisms were made about American society in the 1950s?

Section 4 Review

History ONLINE
Study Central™ To review this section, go to glencoe.com.

Vocabulary

1. Write each of the terms and a definition of each in your own words: surplus, arms race, nuclear, summit, economy, affluence, materialism.

Main Ideas

2. **Discussing** While president, what was Eisenhower's greatest domestic achievement, and why was it important?

3. **Explaining** What does it mean to say that Americans became a consumer society in the 1950s?

4. **Summarizing** Why did urban poverty increase during the 1950s?

Critical Thinking

5. **Determining Cause and Effect** On a chart like the one below, identify the direct effects of the 1950s baby boom.

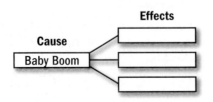

6. **Descriptive Writing** Write a brief description of the types of music that were popular in the 1950s.

7. **Answer the Essential Question** How did the American prosperity of the 1950s affect the country's economy and culture?

The Cold War

- Soviets occupy much of Eastern and Central Europe
- Truman doctrine proposed
- Congress approves Marshall Plan
- Berlin airlift
- With United Nations, U.S. fights in Korea
- Crisis in the Middle East
- Uprising in Hungary
- War in Southeast Asia
- Troubles in Latin America
- Geneva summit encourages peaceful coexistence
- Space race

THE IRON CURTAIN

Berlin airlift (above);
Senator Margaret Chase Smith (right)

Prosperity

- Productivity increases
- Per-capita income and the standard of living increases
- The baby boom increases population
- Suburban housing developments boom
- Car culture grows
- Consumerism grows
- Television viewing increases

Problems and Issues

- Growing competition hurts small farmers
- Decline in coal industry increases poverty in rural areas
- Inner cities decay as businesses and residents relocate
- Social critics question conformity
- Women question their roles in society
- African Americans challenge segregation

Eisenhower's Domestic Policy

- Attempts to limit government spending
- Federal Highway Act
- Extends social programs

◀ Students receive polio vaccine

Whatever the weather
We only reach welfare
together

STUDY TO GO Study anywhere, anytime! Download quizzes and flash cards to your PDA from glencoe.com.

Changing Settlement Patterns

Shortly after World War II, suburbs sprang up around American cities. By 1960 a majority of Americans lived in suburban areas rather than in cities. Meanwhile, many people were moving from older cities in the Northeast and Midwest toward newer centers in the South and West, the so-called Sunbelt. In most cases, people were going to where the jobs were.

How Did Geography Affect Changing Settlement Patterns?

The open spaces of the Sunbelt were well-suited for population growth. The economy of this area expanded as government defense spending created many jobs. A relatively cheap, nonunion workforce also drew industries from other parts of the nation. Additional factors in the Sunbelt's growth were low housing costs, lower taxes, improved public health, and milder climates. Some of the greatest growth occurred in Florida, Texas, and California.

Over the past several decades, population growth has been greatest in Southern and Western states.

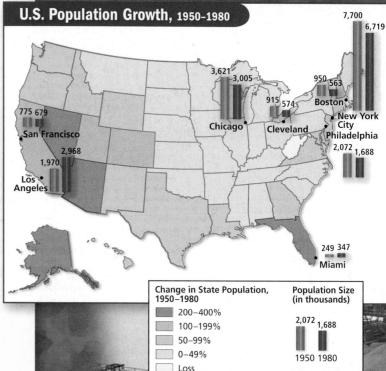

U.S. Population Growth, 1950–1980

San Francisco 775 679
Los Angeles 1,970 2,968
Chicago 3,621 3,005
Cleveland 915 574
Boston 950 563
New York City 7,700 6,719
Philadelphia 2,072 1,688
Miami 249 347

Change in State Population, 1950–1980
- 200–400%
- 100–199%
- 50–99%
- 0–49%
- Loss

Population Size (in thousands)
2,072 (1950) 1,688 (1980)

HISTORIC US 66

Increasing Mobility
Automobiles were essential to the development of the Sunbelt. The Interstate Highway Act of 1956 authorized the construction of a national highway system linking the entire country with roads that were at least four lanes wide. The highways made it easier for Americans to travel west and south.

A Changing Economy In the 1960s, the U.S. economy began to change from a manufacturing-based economy to a service economy or information economy. Many U.S. firms relocated overseas—partly to take advantage of cheaper labor and production costs. Older industrial regions of the Northeast and Midwest started to decline, and these areas came to be known as the Rust Belt, in contrast to the thriving Sunbelt.

Resources As people moved to the dry Southwest, they needed water and electricity. Hoover Dam, on the Colorado River, was built in the 1930s to control flooding and provide electric power. Today, the electricity produced is shared by Arizona, Nevada, and California.

Growing Cities The population of Sunbelt cities such as Las Vegas, Nevada, has exploded in recent decades. Urban sprawl—unplanned development across the landscape— has become common. Destruction of natural habitats and increased traffic and pollution are some effects of urban sprawl. ▼

Analyzing Geography

1. **Movement** Between 1950 and 1980, which states had the largest percentage of population growth?

2. **Human-Environment Interaction** What kinds of challenges do you think the Sunbelt faces as a result of rapid growth?

TEST-TAKING TIP

When answering essay questions, organize your thoughts before you begin writing. This will help reduce the time you need to revise.

Reviewing Main Ideas

Directions: Choose the best answers for each of the following questions.

1 Which group formed to stop the spread of Soviet influence in Western Europe?

(1) United Nations

(2) Warsaw Pact nations

(3) North Atlantic Treaty Organization

(4) House Un-American Activities Committee

2 What proposal was part of Truman's program to solve the nation's economic problems?

(1) the closed shop

(2) the Taft-Hartley Act

(3) abolition of the poll tax

(4) national health insurance

3 Truman tried to contain communism on the Korean Peninsula by

(1) dividing Korea.

(2) attacking China.

(3) defending South Korea.

(4) bombing the Soviet Union.

4 Eisenhower established the National Aeronautics and Space Administration (NASA) to

(1) conduct U.S. space activities.

(2) create jobs for the urban poor.

(3) make the federal government smaller.

(4) increase demand for consumer goods.

Short-Answer Question

Directions: Base your answer to question 5 on the excerpt below and on your knowledge of social studies.

> More than any single action by the government since the end of the war, this one [the interstate highway system] would change the face of America.... Its impact on the American economy—the jobs it would produce in manufacturing and construction, the rural areas it would open up—was beyond calculation.
>
> —Dwight Eisenhower in *Mandate for Change,* *1953–1956*

5 Why did Eisenhower think an interstate highway system was so important to the nation?

Review the Essential Questions

6 Essay How did the economies in the United States and Europe change after World War II?

To help you write your essay, review your answers to the Essential Questions in the section reviews and the chapter Foldables Study Organizer. Your essay should include:

- how and why America gave aid to Europe;
- economic challenges Americans faced;
- how you think the Korean War affected the American economy; and
- how American prosperity affected the economy.

GO ON

History ONLINE
For additional test practice, use Self-Check Quizzes–Chapter 27 at glencoe.com.

Document-Based Questions

Directions: Analyze the documents and answer the short-answer questions that follow.

Document 1

Julius and Ethel Rosenberg were on trial for espionage. The Rosenbergs' lawyer, Emanuel Bloch, made the following plea.

> Through you [Judge Kaufman] the rest of the world will either believe that we are a compassionate nation, a nation built upon the ideals of humanity and justice, or a nation that has been gripped in panic and fear and is embarked upon mad acts.

Source: Emanuel Bloch, NCRRC Letters

7 Was Bloch's plea successful? Explain.

Document 2

President Truman summed up a major economic problem in postwar America during his address to the nation in 1947.

> We all know that recent price increases have denied to many of our workers much of the value of recent wage increases.

Source: Harry S. Truman, *State of the Union Address*

8 What good and bad news did Truman deliver in this excerpt from his speech?

Document 3

President Truman explained why he was relieving General Douglas MacArthur of his command in South Korea.

> The free nations have united their strength in an effort to prevent a third world war. That war can come if the Communist rulers want it to come. This Nation and its allies will not be responsible for its coming.

Source: *Department of State Bulletin*, April 16, 1951

9 What strategy did Truman reject because he thought it could start another world war?

Document 4

This graph shows labor union membership.

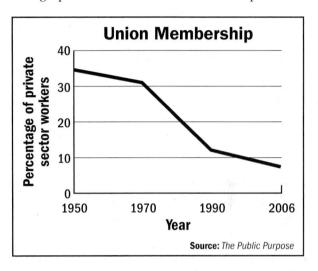

Union Membership

Source: *The Public Purpose*

10 Describe the trend in union membership.

Document 5

This excerpt comes from the novel *On the Road*.

> [T]he only people for me are the mad ones, the ones who are mad to live, mad to talk, mad to be saved, desirous of everything at the same time, the ones who never yawn or say a commonplace thing, but burn, burn, burn like fabulous yellow roman candles.

Source: Jack Kerouac, *On the Road*

11 Kerouac uses the term "mad ones." To whom do you think he is referring?

12 **Expository Writing** Using the information from the five documents and your knowledge of social studies, write an essay in which you:

- describe social and economic changes in the 1950s; and
- describe political changes in the 1950s.

Need Extra Help?												
If you missed questions...	1	2	3	4	5	6	7	8	9	10	11	12
Go to page...	846	852	857	862	861	844–847	849	851	859	852–853	866	845–850

Chapter 28

The Civil Rights Era 1954-1974

March on Washington, August 28, 1963

Section 1: The Civil Rights Movement

Essential Question What were the legal and social challenges to racial segregation in the 1940s and 1950s?

Section 2: Kennedy and Johnson

Essential Question How were Kennedy and Johnson alike and different as presidents of the United States?

Section 3: The Struggle Continues

Essential Question What areas of civil rights did groups try to improve in the 1960s, and what methods did those groups use?

Section 4: Other Groups Seek Rights

Essential Question How did the civil rights movement affect minorities other than African Americans?

FOLDABLES Study Organizer

Organizing Information
Make this Foldable to help organize what you learn about how the courts addressed civil rights issues.

Step 1 Fold a sheet of paper in half from side to side so that the left edge lies about 1/2 inch from the right edge.

Step 2 Cut the top layer only to make four tabs.

Step 3 Label the tab as shown.

Reading and Writing As you read the chapter, list key court decisions about civil rights on the outside of the Foldable. Summarize important details on the inside of the Foldable.

César Chávez was a leading voice for migrant farmworkers. ▶

1968
- Martin Luther King, Jr., assassinated
- Indian Civil Rights Act passes

RICHARD NIXON 1969–1974

1970
Grape workers gain better pay and working conditions

GERALD FORD 1974–1977

1969   **1974**

1967
First heart transplant performed in South Africa

1972
Britain imposes direct rule on Northern Ireland

1972
Terrorists kill Olympic athletes

Section 1 The Civil Rights Movement

Essential Question

What were the legal and social challenges to racial segregation in the 1940s and 1950s?

Reading Guide

Content Vocabulary

segregation (p. 875)
integrate (p. 876)
boycott (p. 878)
civil disobedience (p. 879)

Academic Vocabulary

discriminate (p. 875) civil (p. 875)

Key People and Events

NAACP (p. 875)
Thurgood Marshall (p. 876)
Brown v. Board of Education of Topeka, Kansas (p. 876)
Rosa Parks (p. 878)
Dr. Martin Luther King, Jr. (p. 878)

Reading Strategy

Taking Notes Create a time line like the one below to record important events in the early struggle for equal rights.

1909 1954 1955 1957

NEW YORK STANDARDS
The American Journey

U10.I.6 To describe historic events through the eyes and experiences of those who were there

U10.III.2 To understand the relative importance of United States domestic and foreign policy over time

U11.I.2 To investigate key turning points in New York and United States history and explain why these events or developments are significant

American Diary

Howard Bailey remembers that when the white high school got new textbooks, the old ones would be dropped off at his African American school. "I can remember that occasionally they would shovel the books out of the pickup trucks with coal shovels and just . . . dump them on the ground outside of the school building. So our teachers and principals would . . . gather them up and tape up . . . the books that were in real bad shape."

—Kentucky Civil Rights Oral History Commission

In *Brown v. Board of Education,* the Supreme Court found that segregated classrooms denied children like Linda Brown (first row, far right) equal education.

Equality in Education

Main Idea After World War II, African Americans and other supporters of civil rights challenged discrimination in the nation's public schools.

History and You What might it have been like to be told that you could go only to certain schools because of your racial or ethnic background? Read to learn about the struggle to achieve equal rights for African American students in the 1950s.

. . . .

African Americans had suffered from racism and **discrimination,** or unfair treatment, since colonial times. By the mid-1900s, many African Americans believed that the time had come for them to enjoy an equal place in American life. They fought for equal opportunities in jobs, housing, and education. They also fought against **segregation**—the separation of people of different races.

The Push for Equal Rights

During World War II, African Americans demanded more rights. Their efforts helped end discrimination in factories that held government contracts and increased opportunities for African Americans in the military.

In Chicago in 1942, James Farmer and George Houser founded the Congress of Racial Equality (CORE). A year later, CORE carried out protests against public places that refused to admit or serve African Americans. CORE protesters successfully ended segregation in many restaurants, theaters, and other public places in Chicago, Detroit, Denver, and Syracuse.

When World War II ended, many African American soldiers returned home hopeful that their country would appreciate their loyalty and sacrifice. In the 1950s, when change did not come as quickly as desired, their determination to end injustices in the United States led to protests and marches—and to the rise of the **civil** (meaning, citizens as individuals) rights movement.

The **NAACP** (National Association for the Advancement of Colored People) had worked on behalf of African Americans since its founding in 1909. In the 1950s, NAACP lawyers searched for cases they could use to challenge the laws allowing the segregation of public schools.

When and Where / **School Segregation, 1950**

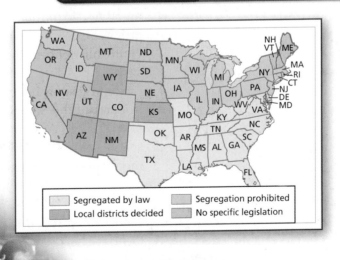

Regional Differences
School segregation was treated differently in various parts of the United States.

Legend:
- Segregated by law
- Local districts decided
- Segregation prohibited
- No specific legislation

Critical Thinking

1. **Identifying** In which category did more states belong: those where the law ordered segregation or those where the law prohibited segregation?
2. **Theorizing** Why do you think segregation was widespread in the South and prohibited in the North?

The *Brown* Decision

The Supreme Court had upheld segregation laws in the past. In 1896 in *Plessy* v. *Ferguson,* it ruled that "separate but equal" public facilities were legal. **Thurgood Marshall,** the chief lawyer for the NAACP, decided to challenge the idea of "separate but equal." Seven-year-old African American Linda Brown was not permitted to attend an all–white elementary school just blocks from her house. She was told to attend an all–African American school across town. The Brown family sued the school system but lost. Marshall and the NAACP appealed the case all the way to the Supreme Court.

The case of ***Brown* v. *Board of Education of Topeka, Kansas,*** combined with similar cases, reached the Supreme Court in December 1952. Marshall argued that segregated schools were not and could not be equal to white schools. Thus segregated schools violated the Fourteenth Amendment.

On May 17, 1954, the Court unanimously ruled in *Brown* v. *Board of Education of Topeka, Kansas,* that it was unconstitutional to separate schoolchildren by race. The *Brown* decision reversed the Court's decision in the earlier *Plessy* v. *Ferguson* case. Chief Justice Earl Warren summed up the Court's new ruling when he wrote:

PRIMARY SOURCE

"In the field of public education, the doctrine of 'separate but equal' has no place. Separate educational facilities are inherently [essentially] unequal."
—from *Brown* v. *Board of Education of Topeka, Kansas*

Integrating the Schools

The Court's decision in *Brown* v. *Board of Education* applied only to public schools. However, it had the much greater effect of threatening the entire system of segregation. The ruling convinced many African Americans that the time had come to oppose other forms of discrimination as well. At the same time, the Court's decision angered many

Primary Source / School Integration

"In these days, it is doubtful that any child may reasonably be expected to succeed in life if he is denied the opportunity of an education. Such an opportunity, . . . must be made available to all on equal terms."

—*Brown* v. *Board of Education*

The Supreme Court ruled in *Brown* v. *Board of Education* that segregation in public schools was unconstitutional. Some segregated school districts integrated their schools quickly and with no incident. Other attempts to integrate led to anger and opposition. Many schools kept their schools segregated for many years.

◄ Linda Brown was at the center of the *Brown* decision.

white Southerners, who became more determined to defend segregation, no matter what the Supreme Court ruled.

In 1955 the Supreme Court followed up its decision in *Brown* v. *Board of Education* with another ruling. It called on school authorities to make plans for **integrating**—bringing races together—in public schools. The Court also ordered that integration was to be carried out "with all deliberate speed"—as fast as reasonably possible.

Some schools integrated quickly. However, in parts of the South, local leaders vowed to keep African American children out of white schools. A clash between the federal government and these states seemed likely.

Confrontation in Little Rock

In 1957 a federal judge ordered all-white Central High School in Little Rock, Arkansas, to admit African American students. Arkansas governor Orval Faubus opposed integration. In September he called out the state's National Guard to prevent African Americans from entering the high school.

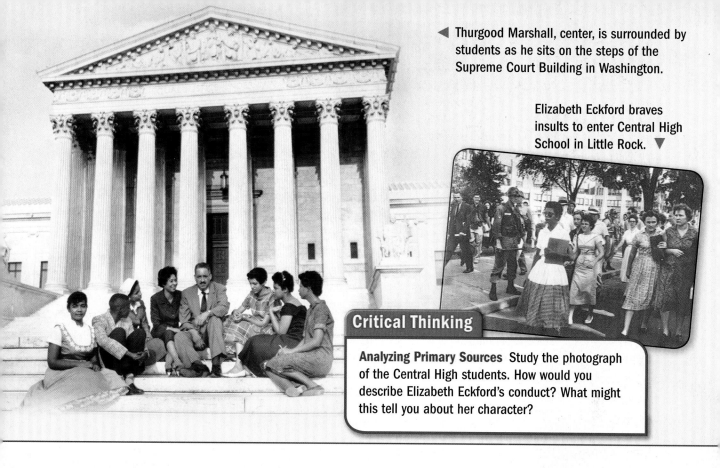

◀ Thurgood Marshall, center, is surrounded by students as he sits on the steps of the Supreme Court Building in Washington.

Elizabeth Eckford braves insults to enter Central High School in Little Rock. ▼

Critical Thinking

Analyzing Primary Sources Study the photograph of the Central High students. How would you describe Elizabeth Eckford's conduct? What might this tell you about her character?

On the first day of classes, armed members of the National Guard blocked the school's entrance and turned away nine African American students. One of them, 15-year-old Elizabeth Eckford, recalled that when she tried to squeeze past a member of the guard, "He raised his bayonet, and then the other guards moved in and raised their bayonets."

For the first time since the Civil War, a Southern state defied the federal government. Although Eisenhower had doubts about the *Brown* decision, he believed he had to enforce the law. The president warned Faubus that if the students were not admitted, the federal government would act.

When a federal judge ruled that the governor had violated the law, Faubus removed the National Guard. Eisenhower sent hundreds of soldiers to Little Rock to patrol the school and protect the students. Shielded by federal troops, the African American students entered the school.

✓ **Reading Check** **Explaining** How had the *Plessy* ruling contributed to segregation?

Gains on Other Fronts

Main Idea The success of the Montgomery bus boycott showed that nonviolent protest could help African Americans secure their rights.

History and You Have you ever tried hard to win over someone to your point of view? Read to learn how African Americans convinced officials in Montgomery, Alabama, to end segregation on city buses.

While school integration continued, African Americans made other advances in securing their rights. More and more took part in a movement dedicated to securing fair and equal treatment. In 1955, events in Montgomery, Alabama, sparked a chain reaction—the beginning of a mass movement that would change American society over the next 20 years.

History ONLINE

Student Web Activity Visit glencoe.com and complete the Chapter 28 Web Activity about school integration.

People IN HISTORY

Rosa Parks

1913-2005
Civil Rights Activist

Parks was a civil rights activist as early as the 1940s, but it was her role in the Montgomery bus boycott that ushered in an era of real change for African Americans. Late in life she said: *"I do the very best I can to look upon life with optimism and hope and looking forward to a better day. . . . [yet] It pains me that there is still a lot of Klan activity and racism."* In 1999 Parks was awarded the highest civilian award in the country, the Congressional Gold Medal.

Dr. Martin Luther King, Jr.

1929-1968
Minister, Civil Rights Activist

In the 1950s, Dr. Martin Luther King, Jr., established himself as one of the main leaders of the civil rights movement. A Baptist minister and stirring speaker, King organized marches, boycotts, and demonstrations that opened many people's eyes to the need for change. In 1964 he was awarded the Nobel Prize for Peace. He said, *"I have the audacity [boldness] to believe that peoples everywhere can have three meals a day for their bodies, education and culture for their minds, and dignity, equality, and freedom for their spirits."* Dr. King was assassinated in 1968 in Memphis, Tennessee.

CRITICAL Thinking

Inferring What do the statements by Parks and King have in common?

The Montgomery Bus Boycott

On the evening of December 1, 1955, **Rosa Parks,** an African American, boarded a bus in downtown Montgomery, Alabama. Parks, a seamstress, was secretary of the local chapter of the NAACP. She found an empty seat in the section reserved for whites.

When white passengers entered the bus, the driver told Parks to move to the rear of the bus. Parks refused. At the next bus stop, she was taken off the bus by police, arrested for breaking the law, and fined $10. The episode could have ended there—but it did not.

Rosa Parks's arrest led African Americans in Montgomery to organize a **boycott**—a refusal to use—the city's buses. The boycott organizers hoped to hurt the city financially and force it to alter its policies. They had strength in numbers—almost 75 percent of the bus company's riders were African American.

At a boycott meeting, a young Baptist minister came forward to speak. Not widely known at the time, **Dr. Martin Luther King, Jr.,** made an impact on the crowd. He declared:

PRIMARY SOURCE

"We are here . . . because first and foremost we are American citizens and we are determined to apply our citizenship to the fullness of its meaning. . . . And you know, . . . there comes a time when people get tired of being trampled over by the iron feet of oppression."
—from *The Papers of Martin Luther King, Jr.*

The boycott upset many people's daily lives, but the African Americans of Montgomery pulled together to make it work.

The Movement Grows

Main Idea New leaders and groups emerged as the civil rights movement took on new causes.

History and You What do you do if you think you are not being treated fairly? How do you speak out? Read on to learn what actions African Americans took in the 1960s to secure their rights.

A new wave of civil rights activity swept across the nation during the Kennedy and Johnson administrations. Early activity targeted segregation in the South. Segregation existed in the North as well.

In Northern urban areas, African Americans and whites often lived in different neighborhoods; as a result, their children often attended different schools. Soon African Americans expanded their goal to fighting discrimination and racism in the North as well as in the South.

High school and college students staged sit-ins in nearly 80 cities. A **sit-in** is the act of protesting by sitting down. Sit-ins were held throughout the nation against stores that practiced segregation. Store managers wanted to end the disturbances and loss of business. Gradually many stores agreed to integrate.

The sit-ins launched a new civil rights group, the Student Nonviolent Coordinating Committee (SNCC). Civil rights activist **Ella Baker** was a guiding spirit behind SNCC and one of its organizers. Earlier, Baker played major roles in both the NAACP and the SCLC. SNCC was a key player in the civil rights cause for several years.

Freedom Rides

The Supreme Court had ruled in 1960 against segregated bus facilities. Another civil rights group, the Congress of Racial Equality (CORE), decided to see if the ruling was being enforced. On May 4, 1961, a group of African Americans and white CORE members left Washington, D.C., on two buses bound for New Orleans. They called themselves Freedom Riders. The trip went smoothly until it reached Alabama, where angry whites stoned and beat the Freedom Riders.

Television and newspapers reported the beatings. The president's brother, **Robert Kennedy,** the United States attorney general, asked CORE to stop the Freedom Rides for a "cooling-off period." CORE leader James Farmer responded: "We have been cooling off for 350 years. If we cool off anymore, we will be in a deep freeze."

Primary Source / **Birth of the SNCC**

Students Organize As the sit-ins spread, student leaders in different states realized they needed to coordinate their efforts. The person who brought them together was Ella Baker, the executive director of the Southern Christian Leadership Conference (SCLC). At a meeting in 1960, Baker urged students to create their own organization instead of joining the NAACP or the SCLC. Baker told them that students had "the right to direct their own affairs and even make their own mistakes." From this beginning was born the Student Nonviolent Coordinating Committee (SNCC).

Ella Baker ▶

Critical Thinking

Explaining What was the purpose of sit-ins?

Violence and Arrests

The Freedom Riders pressed on, only to meet more violence in Birmingham and Montgomery, Alabama. No mobs were waiting for the Freedom Riders in Jackson, Mississippi. However, police, state troopers, and Mississippi National Guard units were everywhere. As the Riders stepped off the bus and tried to enter the whites-only waiting room at the bus station, they were arrested for trespassing and jailed.

Despite the violence and the jail sentences, more Freedom Riders kept coming all summer. In the fall, the Interstate Commerce Commission enforced the Supreme Court ruling, issuing new regulations that banned segregation on **interstate** buses—those that crossed state lines—and in bus stations.

Integrating Universities

African Americans continued to apply pressure to secure their civil rights. They spurred President Kennedy to take a more active role in the civil rights struggle.

In 1962 a federal court ordered the University of Mississippi to enroll its first African American student, **James Meredith.** However, Mississippi Governor Ross Barnett, with the aid of state police, kept Meredith from registering. When President Kennedy sent federal marshals to escort Meredith to the campus, riots erupted. A mob armed with guns and rocks stormed the administration building. The marshals fought back with tear gas and nightsticks. Meredith succeeded in registering, but two people were killed. Federal troops remained at the university to protect him until he graduated in 1963.

Another clash between state and federal power took place in June 1963 in Alabama. Governor **George Wallace** vowed he would "stand in the schoolhouse door" to block the integration of the University of Alabama in Tuscaloosa. President Kennedy, acting on the advice of his brother, Robert, sent the Alabama National Guard to ensure the entry of African Americans to the university. As a result, Wallace backed down.

Birmingham

In the spring of 1963, Dr. Martin Luther King, Jr., and the SCLC targeted Birmingham, Alabama, for a desegregation protest. Police arrested hundreds of demonstrators, including Dr. King, but the demonstrations continued. During Dr. King's two weeks in jail, he wrote the eloquent "Letter from Birmingham Jail," in which he wrote: "We must come to see . . . that justice too long delayed is justice denied."

National television carried vivid pictures of police setting snarling police dogs on unarmed demonstrators and pushing small children across streets with the powerful impact of fire hoses. President Kennedy sent 3,000 troops to restore peace. On June 11, 1963, in Jackson, Mississippi, **Medgar Evers,** the state field secretary for the NAACP, was murdered. The murder and the events in Alabama forced President Kennedy to make a decision. Appearing on national television, Kennedy spoke of the "moral issue" facing the nation:

PRIMARY SOURCE

"It is not enough to pin the blame on others, to say this is a problem of one section of the country or another, or deplore the fact that we face. A great change is at hand, and our task, our obligation, is to make that revolution, that change, peaceful and constructive for all. Those who do nothing are inviting shame as well as violence. Those who act boldly are recognizing right."

—Kennedy's address to the nation, June 1963

Days later, the president introduced new legislation giving all Americans the right to be served in public places and barring discrimination in employment.

March on Washington

To rally support for the civil rights bill, Dr. King and the SCLC organized a massive march on Washington, D.C., on August 28, 1963. More than 200,000 people of all colors and from all over the country arrived to take part in the event.

Visual Summary

African Americans and Civil Rights

Changes brought about by the civil rights movement are still with us.

- *Brown v. Board of Education of Topeka, Kansas* attacks school segregation.
- Rosa Parks inspires Montgomery bus boycott.
- Freedom rides, the Birmingham demonstrations, and the march on Washington help build support for the civil rights movement.
- The Civil Rights Act (1964) outlaws discrimination based on race, gender, and religion, and gives equal access to public facilities.
- The Voting Rights Act (1965) ensures African Americans of the right to vote.

Latino and Native American Advances

Minority groups developed new ways to improve their status in the United States.

- La Raza Unida and the LULAC fight for education, employment, and government participation rights.
- César Chávez leads farm workers to gain better wages and improve working conditions.
- The Indian Civil Rights Act of 1968 recognizes the laws the Native American nations make on their own lands.
- The American Indian Movement works for improved equal rights and living conditions.

Women Fight for Equal Rights

During the 1960s and 1970s, a large number of American women organized to push for greater rights and opportunities.

- Equal Pay Act (1963)
- National Organization for Women (NOW) forms
- Equal Rights Amendment (ERA) proposed but failed to pass

Americans With Disabilities

People with disabilities sought equal rights and treatment in the 1960s and 1970s.

- Gain access to public facilities
- Gain more opportunities in the workplace
- Claim right of children with disabilities to equal education

STUDY TO GO Study anywhere, anytime! Download quizzes and flash cards to your PDA from glencoe.com.

GRADE 8 INTERMEDIATE TEST PRACTICE

TEST-TAKING TIP

Do not wait until the last minute to prepare for a test. Make sure you ask questions in class after you have studied but before you take the test.

Reviewing Main Ideas

Directions: Choose the best answers for each of the following questions.

1 Who argued against "separate but equal" schools before the Supreme Court?

(1) Earl Warren

(2) James Farmer

(3) George Houser

(4) Thurgood Marshall

2 How did Johnson expand on Kennedy's plans to help people with low incomes?

(1) by establishing Medicare

(2) by setting up Model Cities

(3) by introducing the Job Corps

(4) by pushing through the Civil Rights Act

3 What cause did civil rights workers take on during Freedom Summer in 1964?

(1) voter registration in the South

(2) enforcement of bus desegregation

(3) integration of Southern universities

(4) discrimination in employment and housing

4 La Raza Unida was formed to

(1) organize farmworkers.

(2) demand equal pay for equal work.

(3) elect Latinos to government office.

(4) extend voting rights to Spanish speakers.

Short-Answer Question

Directions: Base your answer to question 5 on the graph below and on your knowledge of social studies.

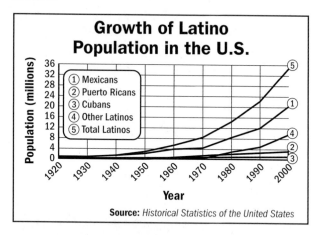

Growth of Latino Population in the U.S.

① Mexicans
② Puerto Ricans
③ Cubans
④ Other Latinos
⑤ Total Latinos

Population (millions) / Year

Source: *Historical Statistics of the United States*

5 Why have Latinos experienced a growing political influence in recent years?

Review the Essential Questions

6 Essay How did political, student, and labor leaders respond to different groups' demands for more rights and opportunities?

To help you write your essay, review your answers to the Essential Questions in the section reviews and the chapter Foldables Study Organizer. Your essay should include:

- names of political, student, and labor leaders during the 1940s, 1950s, and 1960s;
- names of organizations formed to meet the demands of struggling Americans; and
- descriptions of the interaction between leaders and organizations.

GO ON

Document-Based Questions

Directions: Analyze the documents and answer the short-answer questions that follow.

Document 1

James Baldwin wrote about the experiences of African Americans in novels such as *Go Tell It on the Mountain* and *If Beale Street Could Talk.*

> I love America more than any other country in the world, and, exactly for this reason, I insist on the right to criticize her perpetually.

Source: James Baldwin, "Notes of a Native Son"

7 What were two major reasons that Americans like James Baldwin criticized the U.S.?

Document 2

President Kennedy made the following remark in a speech given on May 18, 1963.

> [L]iberty without learning is always in peril, and learning without liberty is always in vain.

Source: John F. Kennedy Presidential Library & Museum

8 Which of Kennedy's proposals for the New Frontier addressed the concerns in this quote?

Document 3

Malcolm X explained his view on racism in a speech entitled, "Prospects for Freedom in 1965."

> [M]y religion makes me against all forms of racism. It keeps me from judging any man by the color of his skin. It teaches me to judge him by his deeds and conscious behavior. And it teaches me to be for the rights of all human beings.

Source: John Bartlett, *Familiar Quotations*

9 Compare the views Malcolm X held before 1965 with the view expressed in the quote.

Document 4

Voter Registration Before and After The Voting Rights Act

> 7% of African American adults registered to vote in Mississippi before passage of the Voting Rights Act of 1965

> 67% of African American adults in Mississippi registered to vote in 1969

> 70% of white adults registered to vote nationwide in 1964

> 90% of white adults registered to vote nationwide in 1969

Source: *TIME* magazine

10 Do you think the Voting Rights Act was strongly enforced in Mississippi? Why or why not?

Document 5

Betty Friedan wrote about the effects of a high birthrate.

> By the end of the fifties, the United States birthrate was overtaking India's. . . . Where once [college women] had two children, now they had four, five, six. Women who had once wanted careers were now making careers out of having babies.

Source: Betty Friedan, *The Feminine Mystique*

11 Did Friedan approve or disapprove of the trend she described in this quote? Explain.

12 Descriptive Writing Using the information from the five documents and your knowledge of social studies, write an essay in which you:

- describe a vision of American life that all the people quoted would approve of; and

- compare this vision with your observations of life in the United States today.

Need Extra Help?												
If you missed questions. . .	1	2	3	4	5	6	7	8	9	10	11	12
Go to page. . .	876	883	888	897	896–897	875–879	875	882	890	889	895	884–898

The Vietnam Era 1960-1975

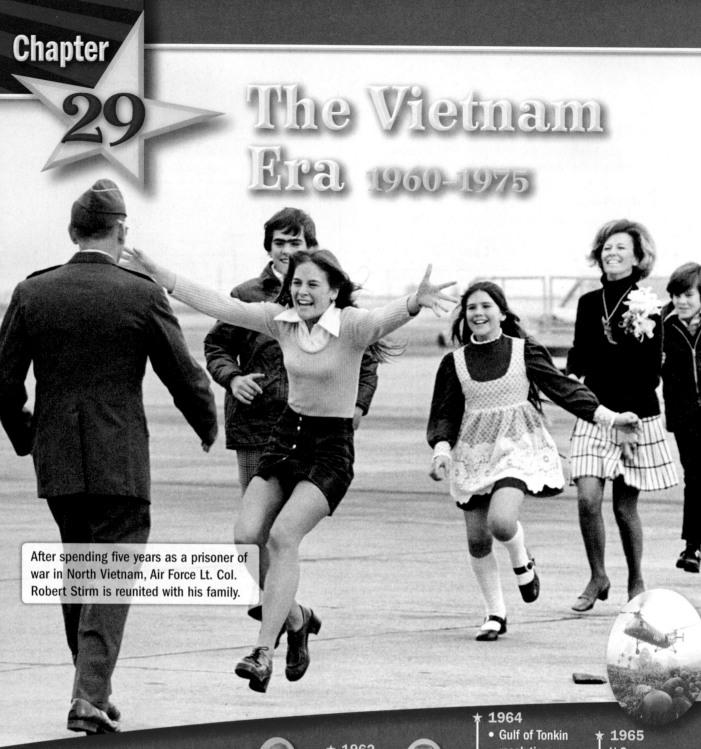

After spending five years as a prisoner of war in North Vietnam, Air Force Lt. Col. Robert Stirm is reunited with his family.

PRESIDENTS

U.S. Events

World Events

1960

1964

JOHN F. KENNEDY

1962
Cuban missile crisis erupts

1961
Berlin Wall erected

LYNDON B. JOHNSON

1964
- Gulf of Tonkin resolution passes
- Johnson elected president

1965
U.S. sends troops to Vietnam

1966
Mao Zedong launches Cultural Revolution

History ONLINE
Chapter Overview Visit glencoe.com
and click on Chapter 29—Chapter
Overviews to preview chapter information.

Section 1: Kennedy's Foreign Policy

Essential Question What were the key foreign policy challenges the United States faced during the Kennedy administration?

Section 2: War in Vietnam

Essential Question How and why did America involve itself in the war in Vietnam?

Section 3: The Vietnam Years at Home

Essential Question How did the Vietnam War affect the political and social climate in the United States?

Section 4: Nixon and Vietnam

Essential Question How did President Nixon remove the United States from the Vietnam War?

FOLDABLES
Study Organizer

Organizing Information

Make this Foldable to help organize what you learn about foreign policy challenges during the Vietnam years.

Step 1 Fold the sides of a piece of paper into the middle to make a shutterfold.

Step 2 Cut each flap at the midpoint to form four tabs.

Step 3 Label the tabs as shown.

Bay of Pigs | Berlin Wall
Cuban Missile Crisis | Vietnam Conflict

Reading and Writing As you read the chapter, list key people, events, and outcomes for each of these foreign policy issues.

American soldier equipped for battle ▶

1968 ★ Martin Luther King, Jr., assassinated

★ 1968 Robert Kennedy assassinated; Nixon elected president

RICHARD M. NIXON

★ 1969 Neil Armstrong becomes first human on the moon

★ 1973 Last U.S. troops leave Vietnam

1968

1972

1976

★ 1967 Arab-Israeli Six-Day War fought

1971 ★ Idi Amin seizes power in Uganda

★ 1972 11 Israeli athletes killed at Munich Olympic Games

★ 1975 Vietnam War ends after fall of Saigon

Section 1 — Kennedy's Foreign Policy

Essential Question

What were the key foreign policy challenges the United States faced during the Kennedy administration?

Reading Guide

Content Vocabulary

guerrilla warfare (p. 905)

flexible response (p. 905)

executive order (p. 906)

blockade (p. 908)

Academic Vocabulary

respond (p. 905)　　occur (p. 907)

Key People and Events

Fidel Castro (p. 906)

Bay of Pigs (p. 907)

Berlin Wall (p. 907)

Cuban missile crisis (p. 908)

Reading Strategy

Taking Notes On a diagram like the one below, note the different areas of work in which Peace Corps volunteers were involved.

Peace Corps Work

NEW YORK STANDARDS
The American Journey

U10.II.2 To appreciate the historical background for the formation of United States foreign policy of this era

U10.II.3 To understand the relative importance of United States domestic and foreign policies over time

U10.II.4 To analyze the role played by the United States in international politics, past and present

U11.I.2 To investigate key turning points in New York State and United States history and explain why these events or developments are significant

American Diary

"In the long history of the world, only a few generations have been granted the role of defending freedom in its hour of maximum danger. I do not shrink from this responsibility—I welcome it." Although President Kennedy talked of approaching this responsibility with "energy" and "devotion," events unfolding around the world—in Cuba, Eastern Europe, and Vietnam—would challenge his determination. The new president and the nation soon faced a series of crises.

—from Kennedy's Inaugural Address

President Kennedy called the green beret worn by one of the nation's special military forces "a symbol of excellence, a badge of courage, a mark of distinction in the fight for freedom."

New Directions

Main Idea President John F. Kennedy sought new ways to deal with the challenges and fears of the Cold War.

History and You Have you ever heard the phrase "winning hearts and minds"? It means convincing people to support you rather than just forcing them to obey. Read on to learn how the United States used "good works" to convince the world's poor countries to reject communism.

. . . .

When Kennedy became president in 1961, America's dangerous rivalry with the Soviets continued to be a major challenge. As a result, the new president had to devote much of his energy in foreign policy to guiding the nation through the deepening Cold War. President Kennedy continued the anti-Communist foreign policy begun under Presidents Truman and Eisenhower. In pursuing that policy, though, Kennedy tried some new approaches.

During the presidential campaign, Kennedy led Americans to believe that the nation had fewer nuclear missiles than the Soviet Union. As president, Kennedy increased spending on nuclear arms. At the same time, he tried to convince Nikita Khrushchev, the Soviet leader, to agree to a ban on nuclear testing.

Strength Through Flexibility

Kennedy also worked to improve America's ability to **respond**—or reply with action—to threats abroad. In certain areas of the world, Communist groups fought to take control of their nations' governments. Many of these groups received aid from the Soviet Union. They employed **guerrilla warfare,** or fighting with small bands of soldiers who use tactics such as sudden ambushes.

The United States needed a new approach for fighting guerrilla wars. Kennedy introduced a plan called **flexible response,** to provide help to nations fighting Communist movements. This plan relied on special military units trained to fight guerrilla wars. One of these units was the Special Forces, known as the Green Berets. The Special Forces provided the president with troops that were ready to fight guerrilla warfare anywhere around the world.

Primary Source / U.S.–Soviet Relations

In a letter to Premier Nikita Khrushchev of the Soviet Union, President Kennedy expressed the need for direct communication between the leaders. "I think we should recognize, in honesty to each other, that there are problems on which we may not be able to agree."

Kennedy suggested a "hot line" to communicate quickly and directly between the United States and the Soviet Union in times of crisis. The original hot line was a teletypewriter. The hot line today uses two satellite systems and an undersea cable link. The American end of the hot line is located in the Pentagon, the headquarters of the U.S. Department of Defense.

Teletype used for hot line ▶

Critical Thinking

Speculating In what ways might use of the hot line lessen a crisis?

Strength Through Aid

President Kennedy understood that the poverty in Latin America, Asia, and Africa made the Communist promises of economic equality seem attractive. He decided to provide aid to countries in those areas to counteract the appeal of communism. For example, to help Latin America's economic growth, Kennedy set up a 10-year development plan called the Alliance for Progress.

In 1961 the president signed an **executive order,** or presidential directive, creating an organization called the Peace Corps. Peace Corps volunteers worked in other countries as teachers, health workers, and advisers in farming, industry, and government. Volunteers spent two years in countries that had asked for assistance. By 1963 some 5,000 volunteers were working in more than 40 countries around the world. Today, the Peace Corps is still active and remains one of Kennedy's most lasting legacies.

Reading Check **Describing** What was the purpose of the Alliance for Progress?

Cold War Confrontations

Main Idea The Kennedy administration responded to Cold War crises in Cuba and Berlin.

History and You How do you think the U.S. government should deal with threats from other countries? Read to learn how the Kennedy administration dealt with Soviet threats in various parts of the world during the early 1960s.

In 1961, just a few months after taking office, President Kennedy had to deal with a foreign policy crisis in Latin America. That same year, tensions between the United States and the Soviet Union arose in Europe.

Cuba

The United States faced a new challenge in Cuba, an island country in the Caribbean Sea. This challenge had begun during the last months of the Eisenhower administration. In January 1959, rebel leader **Fidel Castro** seized power and formed a new Cuban government. He soon set up a Communist dictatorship.

Primary Source **Soviet Influence**

Footholds and Fences The United States began to see the influence of communism spreading around the world. The U.S. tried to shut down the threat closest to home with the invasion of the Bay of Pigs in Cuba. Half a world away, the U.S. could only watch as Communist East Germany isolated Democratic West Berlin with a cinder block and barbed wire wall.

Invasion of Cuba CIA-trained Cuban exiles landed at the Bay of Pigs on April 17, 1961. Within two days, Cuban President Fidel Castro's troops had captured more than 1,000 of the exiles and stopped the attempt at overthrowing his government.

The Berlin Wall ▶

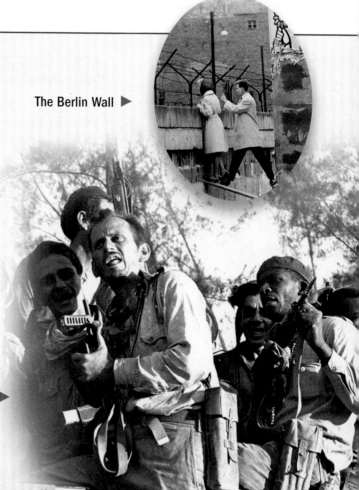

Armed militia of the Castro government ▶

◀ Exiles taken prisoner

Cuba also became an ally of the Soviet Union. These actions worried many Americans because Cuba lies only 90 miles (145 km) south of Florida.

Late in Eisenhower's presidency, the Central Intelligence Agency (CIA) forged a plan to overthrow Castro. The CIA recruited Cuban refugees who had settled in the United States. The plan called for them to land in Cuba and spark an uprising that would overthrow Castro's rule. When Kennedy became president, he learned about the plan and had doubts about it. However, he accepted the advice of military advisers and the CIA and allowed the plan to go forward.

On April 17, 1961, about 1,500 CIA-trained Cuban exiles landed at the **Bay of Pigs** on the south coast of Cuba. Many blunders occurred, and at a crucial moment, Kennedy refused to provide American air support. Within days Cuban forces crushed the invasion and captured the survivors.

The Bay of Pigs embarrassed Kennedy, who took the blame for the failure. The disaster had three effects. First, Kennedy never again completely trusted military and intelligence advice. Second, nations in Latin America lost trust in Kennedy. Third, Soviet premier Khrushchev concluded that Kennedy was not a strong leader and could be bullied.

The Berlin Wall

Although 16 years had passed since the end of World War II, the wartime Allies had still not settled the status of Germany. West Germany became a full member of the Western alliance, and the Soviet Union continued to control East Germany.

The location of Berlin—fully within East Germany—posed special problems. American, British, and French troops still remained in the western part of the city, and they sometimes had difficulty getting into West Berlin and maintaining control there. Meanwhile a steady flow of people fled to West Berlin from Communist East Berlin, hoping to escape economic hardship and find freedom.

At a June 1961 summit conference in Vienna, Austria, Premier Khrushchev told President Kennedy that the West must move out of Berlin, and he insisted on an agreement by the end of the year. Kennedy rejected Khrushchev's demand. To emphasize the West's right to stay in West Berlin, the United States later sent more troops to the city.

Later that summer, a large number of East Germans fled to the West. On August 13, the East German government, with Soviet backing, closed the border between East and West Berlin and built a wall of concrete blocks with barbed wire along it. The Soviets posted armed guards along the wall to stop more East Germans from fleeing to the West. The **Berlin Wall** cut communications between the two parts of the city.

The Western Allies remained in West Berlin. They could do little, however, to stop the building of the wall, which came to symbolize Communist repression.

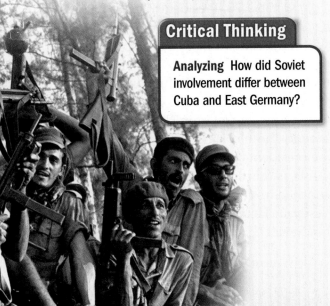

August 1961 To stop the flow of skilled workers, professionals, and intellectuals from leaving East Germany, the Communist country began building the Berlin Wall on August 13. By the 1980s, it had been made taller and wider and stretched 28 miles (45 km) through the middle of Berlin and another 75 miles (120 km) around West Berlin.

Critical Thinking

Analyzing How did Soviet involvement differ between Cuba and East Germany?

Reading Check **Explaining** What kind of government did Fidel Castro establish in Cuba?

What if the Soviets Had Ignored the Blockade?

Just days after President Kennedy ordered a U.S. blockade to prevent Soviet deliveries of missiles to Cuba, Soviet ships abruptly turned away. When the Soviets offered a deal, Kennedy took it. The Soviets would withdraw their missiles in exchange for a U.S. pledge to never invade Cuba. While it seemed like a victory at the time, it left a Communist government intact just miles from the U.S. coastline. The humiliation of giving in also prompted the Soviets to begin the largest peacetime military buildup in history.

Critical Thinking

Theorizing What might have happened if the Soviets had chosen to ignore the blockade and steamed forward to Cuba?

Maps in Motion See StudentWorks™ Plus or glencoe.com.

The Cuban Missile Crisis

Main Idea The United States forced the Soviet Union to withdraw Soviet missiles that had been placed in Cuba.

History and You Have you ever been in a situation that was so scary, you thought that you would never get through it alive? Read to learn how another crisis in Cuba left Americans and people in many other nations wondering whether the world would survive.

. . . .

The most dangerous Cold War dispute between the Americans and Soviets came in 1962. Once again the dispute involved Cuba.

In mid-October 1962, an American spy plane flying over Cuba made a disturbing discovery. Photographs revealed that the Soviets were building launching sites for nuclear missiles. These missiles could easily reach the United States in a matter of minutes.

For the next week, President Kennedy met secretly with advisers to determine how to deal with the **Cuban missile crisis.** They explored several options, including invading Cuba and bombing the missile sites. New spy photographs showed the bases nearing completion much faster than expected. Kennedy and his advisers needed to reach a decision quickly.

On October 22, President Kennedy, speaking on national television, revealed the "secret, swift, and extraordinary buildup" of Soviet missiles in Cuba. Kennedy ordered the navy to **blockade,** or close off, Cuba until the Soviets removed the missiles. He threatened to destroy any Soviet ship that tried to break through the blockade and reach the island. The president declared: "It shall be the policy of this nation to regard any nuclear missile launched from Cuba against any nation in the Western Hemisphere as an attack by the Soviet Union on the United States."

The United States would respond, he warned, with a nuclear attack against the Soviet Union.

As the two superpowers neared the brink of nuclear war, people all over the world waited nervously. After five agonizing days, the Soviet ships turned back. Soviet leaders also agreed to withdraw their missiles from Cuba. The United States agreed not to invade Cuba. Nuclear war had been avoided.

Having come so close to nuclear disaster, the two nations worked to establish better relations. In the summer of 1963, Kennedy and Khrushchev created the hot line between Moscow and Washington to allow the leaders to communicate instantly in times of crisis. That same summer, the two nations signed a treaty banning nuclear tests aboveground and underwater.

Rivalry in Space

Americans and Soviets continued their rivalry in space. In April 1961, Soviet cosmonaut Yuri Gagarin (guh•GAHR•uhn) became the first person to orbit the Earth. One month later, Alan Shepard, Jr., became the first American to make a spaceflight.

Shortly after Shepard's spaceflight, Kennedy committed the nation to the goal of landing a man on the moon by the end of the decade. He asked Congress for more money for NASA (National Aeronautics and Space Administration), which ran the space program. NASA expanded its launching facility in Florida and built a control center in Houston, Texas.

Astronaut John Glenn thrilled the country in February 1962 when he orbited the Earth in a spacecraft, the first American to do so. An even greater triumph for the space program came on July 20, 1969, with the Apollo project. Awestruck television viewers around the world watched the spacecraft *Eagle* land on the surface of the moon.

Hours later, with millions still watching, astronaut Neil Armstrong took the first human step on the moon and announced: "That's one small step for a man, one giant leap for mankind." By the end of the Apollo project in 1972, 10 more Americans had landed on the moon.

Reading Check Explaining How was the Cuban missile crisis resolved?

Section 1 Review

History ONLINE
Study Central™ To review this section, go to glencoe.com.

Vocabulary

1. Write a sentence that explains the meaning of each of the following terms: respond, guerrilla warfare, flexible response, executive order, occur, blockade.

Main Ideas

2. **Describing** What was the relationship between guerrilla warfare and Kennedy's flexible response plan?

3. **Explaining** Why did the Soviet Union build the Berlin Wall?

4. **Summarizing** What was the responsibility of NASA?

Critical Thinking

5. **Analyzing** Re-create the diagram below and identify strategies that the Kennedy administration considered to stop the buildup of missiles in Cuba.

6. **Expository Writing** Take the role of a recruiter for the Peace Corps. Write a speech that describes the creation and mission of the Peace Corps and encourages people to apply.

Answer the
7. **Essential Question**
What were the key foreign policy challenges the United States faced during the Kennedy administration?

Section 2

War in Vietnam

Essential Question

How and why did America involve itself in the war in Vietnam?

Reading Guide

Content Vocabulary

escalate (p. 913)
napalm (p. 914)
search-and-destroy mission (p. 914)
Agent Orange (p. 914)

Academic Vocabulary

trace (p. 911)
regime (p. 912)

Key People and Events

Ho Chi Minh (p. 911)
Vietcong (p. 912)
Gulf of Tonkin Resolution (p. 913)

Reading Strategy

Taking Notes On a chart like the one below, identify each president's main philosophy about America's involvement in Vietnam.

President	Philosophy
Eisenhower	
Kennedy	
Johnson	

NEW YORK STANDARDS
The American Journey

U10.II.2 To appreciate the historical background for the formation of United States foreign policy of this era

U10.II.3 To understand the relative importance of United States domestic and foreign policies over time

U10.II.4 To analyze the role played by the United States in international politics, past and present

American Diary

American efforts to stop the spread of communism led to U.S. involvement in Vietnam. President Eisenhower believed that "the loss of all Vietnam, together with Laos on the west and Cambodia in the southwest, would have meant the surrender to Communist enslavement of millions." In the late 1950s, President Eisenhower sent military supplies and advisers to pro-Western South Vietnam in support of its fight against Communist North Vietnam. President Kennedy continued this policy.

—from American Policy Toward Laos

Vietnamese women work in a rice field.

910

Frustration Grows

The bombing of the Ho Chi Minh Trail and the North did not stop the constant flow of troops and equipment south. Neither did it break the morale of the North Vietnamese. As one of their leaders later said:

PRIMARY SOURCE

"[We survived] because of our courage and determination, together with wisdom, tactics, and intelligence. . . . We had to resort to different measures, some of which are quite simple, like hiding in man-holes and evacuating to the countryside. And we fought back with all our forces and with every kind of weapon."

—from an interview with General Vo Nguyen Giap

The search-and-destroy missions killed thousands of North Vietnamese and Vietcong troops—but the troops always seemed to be replaced. What Ho Chi Minh had said to the French became true again: "You can kill ten of my men for every one I kill of yours. But even at those odds, you will lose and I will win."

American troops advanced into rice paddies, jungles, and small villages and killed scores of Vietcong. Yet the next day, the same area often had to be attacked again. American soldiers grew frustrated. Philip Caputo, a young marine lieutenant, recalled the changing attitude:

PRIMARY SOURCE

"When we marched into the rice paddies on that damp March afternoon, we carried, along with our packs and rifles, the implicit convictions that the Viet Cong would be quickly beaten. . . . We kept the packs and rifles; the convictions, we lost."

—from A Rumor of War

Debate in the White House

Officials in the Johnson administration saw the mounting Communist losses and believed at first that the United States could succeed. As the war dragged on, however, some officials saw a gloomier situation. Secretary of Defense McNamara began to argue that the ground war and the air attacks had failed and that the war could not be won. Outside the nation's capital, opposition to U.S. involvement in Vietnam grew.

✓ **Reading Check** **Identifying** By what means did President Johnson escalate the U.S. presence in Vietnam?

Section 2 Review

History ONLINE
Study Central™ To review this section, go to glencoe.com.

Vocabulary

1. Write a paragraph using each of the following terms: trace, regime, escalate, search-and-destroy mission, napalm, Agent Orange.

Main Ideas

2. **Describing** What was the domino theory, and how did it shape American policy in Vietnam?

3. **Summarizing** How large was the American troop increase in Vietnam between 1963 and the end of 1965?

Critical Thinking

4. **Explaining** What was the Gulf of Tonkin Resolution, and why was it important?

5. **Organizing Information** Recreate the diagram below to show the different warfare techniques used in search-and-destroy missions.

6. **Descriptive Writing** Imagine you are an American soldier arriving in Vietnam. In one or two paragraphs, describe the terrain you find yourself fighting in and how it affects your abilities as a soldier.

7. **Answer the Essential Question** How and why did America involve itself in the war in Vietnam?

YOU DECIDE

Should We Be Fighting the Vietnam War?

Building Background

Government officials urged Americans to support the war's goals of spreading freedom and democracy. President Lyndon B. Johnson responded to criticism of his management of the war by defending the struggle as an idealistic cause.

As U.S. involvement in the war increased, so did opposition to it. The mainstream media, which had tried to remain balanced in their war coverage, now openly criticized the effort. Walter Cronkite, then the nation's most respected newscaster, supported the war effort at first. After traveling to Vietnam to report on the fighting, Cronkite's stories began to include his disappointments with the status of the war.

NO

WALTER CRONKITE,
after the Tet Offensive, February 27, 1968

We have been too often disappointed by the optimism of the American leaders, both in Vietnam and Washington, to have faith any longer in the silver linings they find in the darkest clouds. . . .

To say that we are closer to victory today is to believe, in the face of the evidence, the optimists who have been wrong in the past. To suggest we are on the edge of defeat is to yield to unreasonable pessimism. To say that we are mired[1] in stalemate seems the only realistic, yet unsatisfactory, conclusion. . . . It is increasingly clear to this reporter that the only rational way out then will be to negotiate, not as victors, but as an honorable people who lived up to their pledge to defend democracy, and did the best they could.

Fighting in Saigon during the Tet Offensive, May 1968

[1] **mired** stuck

916

YES

PRESIDENT JOHNSON

Addresses Johns Hopkins University, April 7, 1965

We fight because we must fight if we are to live in a world where every country can shape its own destiny. And only in such a world will our own freedom be finally secure.

This kind of world will never be built by bombs or bullets. Yet the infirmities[2] of man are such that force must often precede reason, and the waste of war, the works of peace. . . .

. . . To abandon this small and brave nation [Vietnam] to its enemies, and to the terror that must follow, would be an unforgivable wrong. . . .

We are also there because there are great stakes in the balance. Let no one think for a moment that retreat from Viet-Nam would bring an end to conflict. The battle would be renewed in one country and then another. The central lesson of our time is that the appetite of aggression is never satisfied.

---

[2] infirmities weaknesses

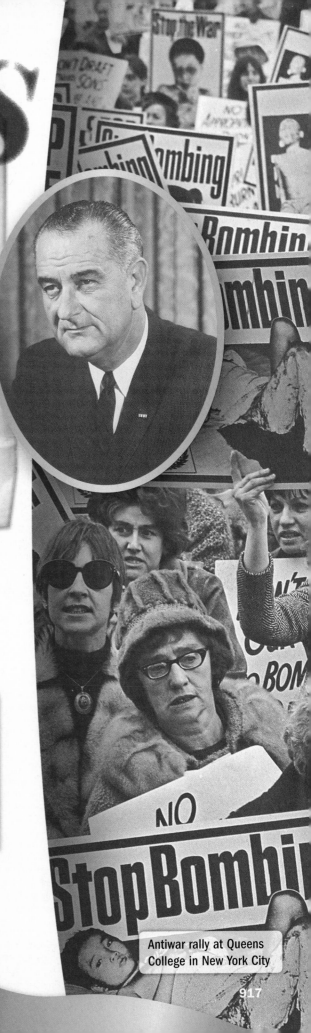

Antiwar rally at Queens College in New York City

DBQ Document-Based Questions

1. **Interpreting** Why does Johnson believe the United States should be fighting the war in Vietnam?

2. **Making Inferences** What does Cronkite believe the result will be if the United States continues fighting in Vietnam?

3. **Analyzing** How do Johnson and Cronkite differ in their views on achieving peace?

4. **Synthesizing** Why might Americans, such as Walter Cronkite, be frustrated with the war?

The Vietnam Years at Home

Essential Question

How did the Vietnam War affect the political and social climate in the United States?

Reading Guide

Content Vocabulary

counterculture (p. 919)

conscientious objector (p. 920)

deferment (p. 920)

credibility gap (p. 921)

Academic Vocabulary

conduct (p. 920)   exclude (p. 923)

Key People and Events

Tet Offensive (p. 921)

Robert F. Kennedy (p. 921)

Dr. Martin Luther King, Jr. (p. 922)

Hubert H. Humphrey (p. 922)

George C. Wallace (p. 923)

Richard M. Nixon (p. 923)

Reading Strategy

Taking Notes On a diagram like the one below, record characteristics of the counterculture in America during the war.

Counterculture

NEW YORK STANDARDS
The American Journey

U10.II.3 To understand the relative importance of United States domestic and foreign policies over time

U11.I.2 To investigate key turning points in New York and United States history and explain why these events or developments are significant

U11.I.3 To compare and contrast different interpretations of key events and issues in New York State and United States history and explain reasons for these different accounts

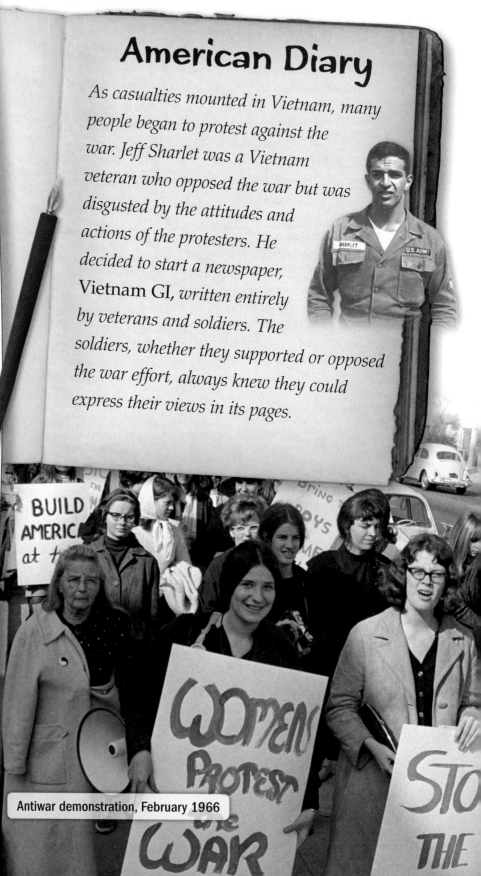

American Diary

As casualties mounted in Vietnam, many people began to protest against the war. Jeff Sharlet was a Vietnam veteran who opposed the war but was disgusted by the attitudes and actions of the protesters. He decided to start a newspaper, *Vietnam GI,* written entirely by veterans and soldiers. The soldiers, whether they supported or opposed the war effort, always knew they could express their views in its pages.

Antiwar demonstration, February 1966

The Democratic Convention

By the time the Democrats held their convention in Chicago, Humphrey seemed to have enough votes to win the nomination. As a supporter of civil rights and labor causes, Humphrey had much backing in the party. As a supporter of Johnson's Vietnam policy, however, Humphrey was linked to the party's pro-war wing. Antiwar Democrats felt angry and **excluded,** or shut out, from the convention.

Meanwhile, thousands of antiwar activists flocked to Chicago to protest Humphrey's almost certain victory. Chicago's mayor, Richard J. Daley, feared violence and had the police out in force. When antiwar protesters tried to march to the convention site, police blocked the marchers, who began to pelt the officers with sticks and bottles. The police threw tear gas and charged in, wielding nightsticks. They pursued those who fled, beating some and arresting many.

Humphrey won the Democratic nomination, but the violence—all shown on television—damaged his candidacy. Humphrey admitted, "Chicago was a catastrophe."

The Election of 1968

Most Americans opposed the violence and longed for a return to law and order. As Election Day neared, third-party candidate Governor **George C. Wallace** of Alabama criticized protesters and efforts to integrate schools by busing. His tough stand on law and order and his appeal to racial fears won many voters. Republican nominee, former vice president **Richard M. Nixon,** claimed to stand for the conservative "silent majority" who wanted law and order and did not protest or demonstrate. He also offered "peace with honor" in Vietnam, but gave no details.

In the election, the popular vote was close. Nixon edged Humphrey by about 500,000 votes. In the electoral vote, however, Nixon won a solid majority—301 votes to Humphrey's 191. Nixon became president with the votes of only 43.4 percent of the people, but he and Wallace together won about 57 percent. It seemed that a sizeable majority of Americans wanted the government to restore order.

✔ **Reading Check** **Identifying** What two popular leaders were assassinated in 1968?

Section 3 Review

History ONLINE
Study Central™ To review this section, go to glencoe.com.

Vocabulary

1. Use each of these terms in a complete sentence that will explain its meaning: counterculture, deferment, conscientious objector, conduct, credibility gap, exclude.

Main Ideas

2. Explaining What were draft deferments, and who received them?

3. Summarizing What was the Tet Offensive? Why was it significant to the course of the war?

4. Analyzing Why did President Lyndon B. Johnson decide not to seek reelection?

Critical Thinking

5. Identifying On a diagram like the one below, list the major points that Nixon campaigned on in 1968.

6. Analyzing Who were the "silent majority," and how did their votes affect the outcome of the 1968 presidential election?

7. Persuasive Writing Write a short essay to convince the reader to agree with your point of view on this question: *Should America use a draft system with the armed services?*

Answer the
8. Essential Question
How did the Vietnam War affect the political and social climate in the United States?

TIME NOTEBOOK

What were people's lives like in the past?

These two pages will give you some clues to everyday life in the United States as you step back in time with TIME Notebook.

NASA

Profile

On July 20, 1969, **NEIL ARMSTRONG** *became the first human to walk on the moon. There he spoke the famous words, "That's one small step for a man, one giant leap for mankind." Later, Armstrong reflected on his voyage and the "spaceship" we call Earth.*

"From our position here on Earth, it is difficult to observe where the Earth is, and where it's going, or what its future course might be. Hopefully by getting a little farther away, both in the real sense and the figurative sense, we'll be able to make some people step back and reconsider their mission in the universe, to think of themselves as a group of people who constitute [make up] the crew of a spaceship going through the universe. If you're going to run a spaceship you've got to be pretty cautious about how you use your resources, how you use your crew, and how you treat your spacecraft."

—*from the book* First on the Moon

The Peace Corps

Established by President Kennedy in 1961, the Peace Corps sends trained Americans as "goodwill ambassadors" to developing nations. Once there, these volunteers help with agriculture, education, and health projects—as well as with small businesses and rural engineering. Here is what one volunteer said about working with the Peace Corps from 1963–1965:

"I was in college when JFK created the Peace Corps, and I thought it was a great idea. I was inspired by his question, 'Ask not what your country can do for you; ask what you can do for your country.' I wanted to travel and experience a different culture, and I admired President Kennedy's idealism, so I applied. Living in another country, I learned to appreciate my own country more."

BETTMANN / CORBIS

African American Firsts

Many African Americans are making a mark on United States history. Match these famous people with their achievements as the first African Americans to hold these positions.

1. Beverly Johnson

2. Arthur Ashe

3. Constance Baker Motley

4. Shirley Chisholm

5. Thurgood Marshall

a. in 1968, elected to Congress, and in 1972, first woman and first African American to run for United States president

b. in 1964, New York state senator who became a federal judge in 1966

c. in 1975, tennis champ at Wimbledon

d. in 1974, cover model on *Vogue* magazine

e. in 1967, sworn in as justice of the United States Supreme Court

(BALL) COMSTOCK / PHOTODISC;

Answers: 1. d; 2. c; 3. b; 4. a; 5. e

MILESTONES

EVENTS OF THE TIME

PUBLISHED. *Silent Spring* by Rachel Carson in 1961, helping to start a new environmental movement in America.

ENROLLED. James Meredith at the University of Mississippi in 1962. The Supreme Court ordered his admission to the previously segregated school.

BROKEN. 25-day fast by César Chávez, labor organizer in 1965. His protest led others to join his nonviolent strike against the grape growers.

TAKEN AWAY. Boxer Muhammad Ali's heavyweight championship title in 1967 after refusing induction into military service. He was found guilty in federal court of violating the Selective Service Act. In 1971 the U.S. Supreme Court overturned his draft conviction.

AIRED. *Sesame Street* for the first time in 1969.

OPENED. Walt Disney World in Orlando, Florida, in 1971.

EVACUATED. The last of American soldiers from Vietnam in 1975.

AL FRENI / TIME LIFE PICTURES / GETTY IMAGES

GIFTED. The Pet Rock was 1975's hot holiday gift. For $3.95 you received a small, obedient "pet" and an owner's manual with housebreaking tips and tricks any rock could learn. A million rocks sold in just a few months.

NUMBERS

WHAT HAPPENED IN 1969

3 Days Duration of the Woodstock Music and Art Fair that attracted hundreds of thousands of young people to a 600-acre (243 ha) farm in New York to celebrate peace and music

7 Baseball player Mickey Mantle's team number, which the Yankees retired when Mantle stopped playing

747 The model number of Boeing's "Jumbo" jet launched this year; the world's largest and heaviest aircraft, it can carry at least 362 passengers, twice as many as an ordinary jet

ANDREAS MANOLIS / REUTERS / CORBIS

250,000 Number of people who marched from the United States Capitol to the Washington Monument in the largest demonstration in Washington's history—all to protest the U.S. involvement in the Vietnam War; President Nixon vowed to ignore the demonstration

CRITICAL THINKING

Making Generalizations How did African Americans who were first in their fields help move the civil rights movement forward?

Speculating What do you think programs such as the Peace Corps and landing a person on the moon did for the image of the United States around the world?

Section 4

Nixon and Vietnam

Essential Question ◄

How did President Nixon remove the United States from the Vietnam War?

Reading Guide

Content Vocabulary
Vietnamization (p. 928)
martial law (p. 929)
MIA (p. 932)

Academic Vocabulary
authority (p. 927)
demonstration (p. 928)

Key People and Events
Henry Kissinger (p. 927)
Pentagon Papers (p. 930)

Reading Strategy
Taking Notes On a diagram like the one below, list the major points of Nixon's "peace with honor" strategy to end the war.

Nixon
Strategy

NEW YORK STANDARDS
The American Journey

U10.III.1 To understand the historic, political, and social context in which United States foreign policy has evolved during the post-Cold War era

U10.III.2 To understand the relative importance of United States domestic and foreign policy over time

U10.III.3 To analyze the role played by the United States in international politics, past and present

U11.I.2 To investigate key turning points in New York State and United States history and explain why these events or developments are significant

American Diary

Speaking to reporters after his election, the new president, Richard Nixon, recalled seeing a young girl carrying a hand-lettered sign at one of his rallies that read: "Bring Us Together Again." This, he promised, would be his chief goal as president. Nixon also vowed to implement his plan to end the Vietnam War. Even though the United States began scaling back its involvement in Vietnam, the American home front remained divided.

Crowds lined the streets for the Inaugural parade following the swearing in of President Richard Nixon, in January 1969.

A New Strategy

Main Idea Nixon took steps to bring American forces home and end the war in Vietnam.

History and You Have you ever worked long and hard on a project and wished that someone could come and replace you so that you could take a rest? Read to find out about a "changing of the guard" during the war in Vietnam.

. . . .

In his Inaugural Address in January 1969, Richard M. Nixon appealed to the American people for calm: "We cannot learn from one another until we stop shouting at one another—until we speak quietly enough so that our words can be heard as well as our voices."

Nixon had campaigned on a pledge of "peace with honor" in Vietnam. Shortly after taking office, Nixon began taking steps to end the nation's involvement in the war. As a first step, the president appointed Harvard professor **Henry Kissinger** as his national security adviser. Kissinger was given wide **authority**—the power to give orders and make decisions—to use his diplomatic skills to end the conflict. Kissinger launched a policy he called "linkage." This policy aimed at improving relations with the Soviet Union and China—suppliers of aid to North Vietnam. Kissinger hoped to persuade the two Communist nations to cut back on their aid and help end the war.

At the same time, Nixon wanted to begin pulling American forces out of Vietnam. However, he did not want American withdrawal to be seen as a sign of defeat. Nixon's strategy of "peace with honor" had three parts—reforming the selective service system, giving South Vietnam more responsibility in fighting the war, and expanding the bombing campaign.

Changes in the Draft

Under President Nixon, the selective service system changed. College students could no longer obtain draft deferments, only 19-year-olds could be called for service in Vietnam, and draftees would be chosen by lottery on the basis of their birthdays. Protests against the draft faded with these reforms because the government began calling up fewer young men and because President Nixon promised to eliminate the selective service in the future.

Primary Source / **A Changing Foreign Policy**

The Nixon Doctrine Nixon and national security adviser Henry Kissinger shared views on many issues. The Nixon Doctrine spelled out a change in the nation's foreign policy. The United States would continue to provide military aid and training to allies. Nixon, however, set limits:

"America cannot—and will not—conceive all the plans, design all the programs, execute all the decisions and undertake all the defense of the free nations of the world."

Critical Thinking

Theorizing Do you think the Nixon Doctrine would change the role of the U.S. in Vietnam? Why or why not?

Troop Withdrawal

Meanwhile, President Nixon cut back the number of American troops in Vietnam. Known as **Vietnamization,** this plan called for the South Vietnamese to take a more active role in fighting—and for Americans to become less involved. As South Vietnamese soldiers took over, American troops would gradually withdraw from the country. In June 1969, Nixon announced the withdrawal of the first 25,000 American soldiers.

Increased Bombing

In the third part of his Vietnam policy, Nixon expanded the bombing campaign. Hoping to relieve pressure on troops in South Vietnam, Nixon ordered the bombing of enemy supply routes and hideouts in neighboring Cambodia and Laos. Although the president announced the changes to the draft and the troop withdrawals, he kept the bombing of Cambodia secret.

Reading Check **Identifying** To what position did President Nixon appoint Henry Kissinger?

Renewed Opposition at Home

Main Idea As Vietnamization moved forward, a new wave of antiwar protests gripped the nation.

History and You What would make you want to write an angry letter to a newspaper editor, join a protest march, or boycott a film producer? Read to learn why protests against the war in Vietnam resumed in 1969.

A new round of antiwar **demonstrations,** or protest marches, began in late 1969, reflecting the growing sentiment for ending the war. In October more than 300,000 people took part in an antiwar protest in Washington, D.C.

The government also tried to end the war through peace talks with North Vietnam. Henry Kissinger, the president's national security adviser, represented the United States in the Paris talks. The United States had launched the bombing campaign to persuade the North Vietnamese to agree to peace terms.

The Vietnam War

Bombers fly more than 2,000 missions against North Vietnam, Dec. 1972

Invasion of Laos, Feb. 8–March 1971

Invasion of Cambodia, May 1–June 29, 1970

My Lai massacre, March 16, 1968

Major U.S. and South Vietnamese troop movement
Major North Vietnamese supply line
U.S. base

An Unpopular War

Americans were sharply divided about U.S. involvement in Vietnam. Failed peace talks and increased bombings sparked antiwar demonstrations across the nation.

Antiwar demonstration in New York City ▼

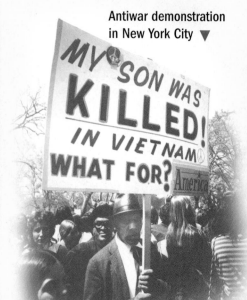

The North Vietnamese, however, adopted a wait-and-see attitude. They believed that the growing strength of the antiwar movement in the United States would force the Americans to withdraw.

The new antiwar protests and North Vietnam's unyielding attitude alarmed President Nixon. In a speech in November, he appealed to the "silent majority" of Americans for support for his policy. "North Vietnam cannot defeat or humiliate the United States," he said. "Only Americans can do that."

Expanding the War

Further conflict gripped Southeast Asia when Cambodia plunged into a civil war between Communist and non-Communist forces. In April 1970, Nixon decided to send American troops to destroy Communist bases in Cambodia.

The attack aroused outrage throughout the nation. By sending U.S. troops to Cambodia, critics charged, Nixon invaded a neutral country and overstepped his constitutional authority as president.

Campus Protests

Many Americans viewed the Cambodian invasion as a widening of the Vietnam War. Nixon's action provoked a storm of antiwar protests on campuses across the nation. Most proceeded peacefully. Two protests, however, ended in tragedy.

At a protest at Kent State University in Kent, Ohio, students burned a military building on campus. Ohio's governor declared **martial law**—emergency military rule—on the campus and ordered 3,000 National Guard troops to Kent State.

At noon on May 4, students gathered for a protest rally on the campus lawn. The National Guard, young, inexperienced, and nervous, told the protesters to leave. When some students threw rocks at Guard members, the troops shot tear gas toward the students, and many students ran.

One National Guard unit chased some students between two buildings. Then—for reasons that are unclear—the troops opened fire. Four students were dead, and at least nine more were wounded.

By the Numbers

United States Troops in Vietnam, 1965–1973

Source: *Statistical Abstract of the United States*

Opposition to the War

Source: *The Gallup Poll: Public Opinion*

Graph Skills

1. **Identifying** What percentage of Americans were against the war in 1965?
2. **Analyzing** In what year was opposition to the war the highest? The lowest? Why?

Violence flared again on May 15 at the nearly all-African American Jackson State University in Mississippi. Following a night of campus protests, two students were shot and killed. Witnesses charged that the police had recklessly blasted a residence hall with gunfire. The police claimed they were protecting themselves from sniper fire. A wave of student strikes followed the tragedies at Kent State and Jackson State. Hundreds of colleges and universities suspended classes.

The Pentagon Papers

In addition to sparking violence on campuses, the Cambodian invasion cost Nixon much support in Congress. Numerous lawmakers expressed outrage over the president's failure to tell them about the action. In December 1970, an angry Congress repealed the Gulf of Tonkin Resolution, which had given the president near-complete power in directing the war in Vietnam.

Support of the war weakened further that year when Daniel Ellsberg, a disillusioned former Defense Department worker, leaked documents to the *New York Times*. These documents, which became known as the **Pentagon Papers,** revealed that many government officials during the Johnson administration privately questioned the war while publicly supporting it.

The documents contained details of decisions that were made by presidents and their advisors without the approval of Congress. They also showed how various administrations acted to deceive Congress, the press, and the public about the situation in Vietnam. The Pentagon Papers backed up what many Americans had long believed: The government had not been honest with them.

Reading Check **Describing** What tragedies occurred at Kent State and Jackson State Universities?

Legacy of the War

A Monument to the Fallen The war took a heavy toll on America's soldiers and their families. Post-Traumatic Stress Disorder, once called "shell shock," caused hallucinations, nightmares, and depression. In 1982 the Vietnam Veterans' Memorial Wall was dedicated in Washington, D.C. The names of those who were killed or missing in the war are engraved into two black granite walls.

United States . . .
- 58,000 American military personnel were killed
- 75,000 were severely disabled
- 2,338 were listed as Missing in Action (MIA) and 766 were Prisoners of War (POW)
- 725,000 Vietnamese resettled in U.S.
- 6.7 million tons of bombs were dropped on Vietnam (compared with 2.7 million tons dropped on Germany during World War II)

"Dear Michael: Your name is here but you are not. I made a rubbing of it, thinking if I rubbed hard enough I would rub your name off the wall. And you would come back to me. I miss you so."
—from an anonymous note left at the Vietnam Veterans' Memorial

Peace and the War's Legacy

Main Idea Peace talks led to the withdrawal of all American forces from Vietnam.

History and You Have you ever visited or seen pictures of the Vietnam War Memorial in Washington, D.C.? What effect did the memorial have on you? Read to find out about the end of the war and its impact on Americans.

. . . .

While antiwar feelings swelled at home— 1971 polls showed that nearly two-thirds of Americans wanted the war to end quickly— the Nixon administration negotiated with representatives of the North Vietnamese government. These talks stalled, however.

In March 1972, the North Vietnamese launched another major offensive in the South. Because the United States had few troops left in Vietnam, Nixon resumed bombing. Nixon ordered American planes to bomb targets near Hanoi, the capital of North Vietnam. He also ordered the navy to plant mines in North Vietnamese harbors.

The president, however, stopped insisting that North Vietnam remove all its troops from South Vietnam before a full American withdrawal. Nixon sent Henry Kissinger to negotiate. In the fall of 1972 an agreement seemed ready, but South Vietnam opposed allowing North Vietnamese forces to remain in its territory. As a result the agreement collapsed.

Paris Peace Accords

After his reelection, Nixon unleashed American airpower against North Vietnam. In December 1972, the heaviest bombardment of the war fell on North Vietnam's cities. Nixon stood firm and North Vietnam returned to the talks. Meanwhile, the Americans pressured the South Vietnamese to accept the peace terms. On January 27, 1973, the negotiators signed the peace agreement.

Vietnam . . .

- 1.5 million Vietnamese soldiers and civilians were killed
- 362,000 were severely disabled
- 800,000 children were orphaned
- at least 1 million people fled the country
- 3.5 million acres of Vietnamese land were sprayed with chemicals that could impact the area for up to 100 years

The effects of the Vietnam War still linger. Since the end of the war, more than 40,000 people in Vietnam have been killed by land mines or bombs that did not explode on impact. Agent Orange, a chemical sprayed by Americans to defoliate forests during the war, has been blamed for many birth defects.

"When the war has ended and
the road is open again,
the same stars will course through the heavens.
Then will I weep for the white bones heaped
    together in desolate graves.
of those who sought military honors for their leaders."
—from the diary of an anonymous North Vietnamese soldier

Critical Thinking

Making Inferences Although the countries and soldiers went into battle for different reasons, what did all people involved in the Vietnam War experience?

The War Ends

The United States agreed to pull its remaining troops out of the country. The North Vietnamese agreed to return all American prisoners of war. American involvement in Vietnam ended, but the conflict did not.

The North Vietnamese never gave up their goal of unifying Vietnam under their rule. In early 1975 they began a major offensive. The weakened South Vietnamese army collapsed on all fronts. Within a few weeks, North Vietnamese tanks approached Saigon. As North Vietnamese forces advanced, the last Americans left the country, some by helicopter from the roof of the U.S. embassy. Thousands of Vietnamese who had supported the Americans also fled to the United States. Many more could not escape. On April 30, 1975, Saigon fell to the Communists. Soon after, South Vietnam surrendered. The long war was over.

The Human Toll

The Vietnam War took a staggering toll. More than one million Vietnamese soldiers and civilians died, and Vietnam lay in ruins with many villages destroyed. More than 58,000 Americans were dead; 300,000 were wounded, many of them permanently disabled. The United States had poured more than $150 billion into the war.

Impact of the War

About 2.7 million Americans had served in Vietnam. Unlike the veterans of World War II, they found no hero's welcome when they returned home. Many Americans simply wanted to forget the war. They paid little attention to those who had fought and sacrificed in Vietnam.

The relatives of the American soldiers who had been classified as missing in action, or as **MIAs,** continued to demand that the government press the Vietnamese for information. The Vietnamese did allow a number of American groups to search the countryside. As the years passed, however, the likelihood of finding anyone alive faded.

Reading Check **Identifying** Who was in control of Vietnam when the war ended?

Section 4 Review

History ONLINE
Study Central™ To review this section, go to glencoe.com.

Vocabulary

1. Write a sentence for each of the following terms, explaining its significance in the Vietnam War era: authority, Vietnamization, demonstration, martial law, MIA.

Main Ideas

2. **Summarizing** What were the results of Nixon's Vietnamization plan?

3. **Explaining** What did Americans realize about the government after the release of the Pentagon Papers?

4. **Discussing** What did the Paris Peace Accords achieve?

Critical Thinking

5. **Categorizing** On a chart like the one below, list the major results from the Vietnam War in each category.

	Numbers of/ Results to
Vietnamese civilians and soldiers killed	
American soldiers killed	
American soldiers wounded	
U.S. cost in dollars	
Vietnamese countryside	

6. **Descriptive Writing** In a paragraph, describe how you feel about Nixon's actions during the Vietnam War and whether they were successful.

Answer the
7. **Essential Question**
How did President Nixon remove the United States from the Vietnam War?

1954–1962

1954

July Geneva Accords divide Vietnam

1957

Oct. Soviet Union launches *Sputnik*

1961

April Bay of Pigs invasion fails

Aug. Berlin Wall is erected

▲ Berlin Wall

1962

Oct. Cuban missile crisis occurs

1963–1967

1963

Nov. John F. Kennedy is assassinated

Nov. Lyndon B. Johnson sworn in as president

1964

Aug. Gulf of Tonkin Resolution passes

1965

Dec. U.S. troop levels reach 180,000

1967

March War protesters march on Pentagon

Vietnamese village ▶

1968–1969

1968

Jan. North Korea captures USS *Pueblo*

Jan. North Vietnamese launch Tet offensive

April Dr. Martin Luther King, Jr., is assassinated

June Robert Kennedy is assassinated

Aug. Violence erupts at Democratic convention in Chicago

Nov. Richard Nixon wins presidency

1969

July Neil Armstrong walks on the moon

◀ Richard M. Nixon

1970–1975

1970

May Nixon sends troops to Cambodia

May Six students killed at Kent State and Jackson State

1973

Jan. Paris peace accords end U.S. involvement in Vietnam

1975

April South Vietnam surrenders to North Vietnam

Vietnam War protest ▼

STUDY TO GO Study anywhere, anytime! Download quizzes and flash cards to your PDA from glencoe.com.

GRADE 8 INTERMEDIATE TEST PRACTICE

TEST-TAKING TIP

To understand the questions better, rewrite them in your own words, if you have time. Be careful not to change the meaning.

Reviewing Main Ideas

Directions: Choose the best answer for each of the following questions.

1 President Kennedy counteracted the appeal of communism in poor areas of Asia, Africa, and Latin America by

  (1) creating the Peace Corps.

  (2) introducing Green Berets.

  (3) employing guerrilla warfare.

  (4) spending more on nuclear arms.

2 Communism took root in South Vietnam because

  (1) President Diem persecuted Buddhists.

  (2) North Vietnam supported the Vietcong.

  (3) Eisenhower sent billions in aid to Diem.

  (4) many Vietnamese lacked land and services.

3 When did President Johnson halt the bombing of North Vietnam's cities?

  (1) after the Tet Offensive

  (2) after Nixon's election

  (3) before the march on the Pentagon

  (4) during the Democratic Convention

4 Nixon provoked protests on campuses by

  (1) leaking the Pentagon Papers.

  (2) sending troops to Cambodia.

  (3) ending draft deferments for students.

  (4) having Kissinger seek a peace settlement.

Short-Answer Question

Directions: Base your answer to question 5 on the excerpt below and on your knowledge of social studies.

> He was now in Ward 1-C with fifty other men who had all been recently wounded in the [Vietnam] war—twenty-year-old blind men and amputees, men without intestines, men who limped, men who were in wheelchairs, men in pain. He noticed they all had strange smiles on their faces and he had one too, he thought. They were men who had played with death and cheated it at a very young age.
>
> —Ron Kovic, *Born on the Fourth of July*

5 What was the human cost of the Vietnam War?

Review the Essential Questions

6 Essay What roles did Presidents Kennedy, Johnson, and Nixon play in the Vietnam War?

To help you write your essay, review your answers to the Essential Questions in the section reviews and the chapter Foldables Study Organizer. Your essay should include:

- why and how Americans became involved in the Vietnam War;
- presidential decisions that kept the war going; and
- how citizen protests influenced Johnson's and Nixon's policies.

GO ON

History ONLINE

For additional test practice, use **Self-Check Quizzes**—Chapter 29 at glencoe.com.

Document-Based Questions

Directions: Analyze the documents and answer the short-answer questions that follow.

Document 1

Four days before the Bay of Pigs invasion, Kennedy responded to press reports of CIA-trained invaders.

> There will not be, under any conditions, any intervention in Cuba by United States armed forces.

Source: Howard Zinn, *A People's History of the United States*

7 Why do you think President Kennedy did not tell reporters about the planned invasion?

Document 2

Madame Nhu, a member of President Diem's family, commented on the monks who protested Diem's policies by setting themselves on fire.

> "Let them burn," she said. "We shall clap our hands."

Source: Stephen Kinzer, *Overthrow*

8 What impact did the monks' protests have on Diem and others?

Document 3

The author of this excerpt talks about the beginning of the Tet Offensive.

> When the assault . . . first began we didn't know what was going on. . . . All the towns of the Delta . . . were full of [Vietcong]. Every town and city in the country was under siege. Every airfield had been hit. Every road cut. They were in the streets of Saigon, in the American embassy. All in one night.

Source: Tobias Wolff, *In Pharoah's Army*

9 Why did Americans criticize the conduct of the war after the Tet Offensive?

Document 4

This political cartoon, titled "Our Position Hasn't Changed At All," appeared in the *Washington Post* on June 17, 1965.

Source: The Herb Block Foundation

10 What does this cartoon say about President Johnson's policy in Vietnam?

Document 5

General James Carroll defended his son's decision to seek conscientious objector status in 1972.

> All I know for sure is this: if human beings don't drastically change the way they resolve their conflicts, we won't survive this century. My son . . . certainly represents a drastic change from the way we were brought up. And that may be just the change we need.

Source: James Carroll, *An American Requiem*

11 What did Carroll's son decide to do? What options did the young man have regarding going to war?

12 Expository Writing Using the information from the five documents and your knowledge of social studies, write an essay in which you:

- explain why the Vietnam War was difficult for Vietnamese and American soldiers and civilians; and
- describe how support for U.S. involvement in Vietnam changed over time.

Need Extra Help?												
If you missed questions. . .	1	2	3	4	5	6	7	8	9	10	11	12
Go to page. . .	906	912	922	929	932	910–932	906–907	913	921	913–922	919–920	910–932

Unit 10

America in a Modern Era
1968 to Present

The iPhone is a multimedia mobile phone.

"We have every right to dream heroic dreams. . . . You can see heroes every day going in and out of factory gates."
—Ronald Reagan

Melissa Etheridge performs at Live Earth, the Concerts for a Climate in Crisis, 2007.

Reading History

READING SKILL

Monitoring and Clarifying

Learn It!

Monitoring is the ability to know whether you understand what you have read. If you do not understand the information, then you must try to identify why you do not understand it. You must *clarify*, or clear up, the parts that are confusing. Read the following paragraph. Use the "Ways to Clarify" column for tips about how you can clarify your reading.

Monitor	Ways to Clarify
Are there any words that are unfamiliar?	Use the glossary, a dictionary, or context clues.
What is the main idea of the paragraph?	Try to summarize the information into one sentence to create a main idea.
Is it helpful to use what I already know about democracy to understand the text?	Think about what you have learned about democracy. Then think about how this relates to Iraq.
What questions do I still have after reading this text?	Write the questions and continue to read to find the answers.

—from Chapter 31, p. 994

The United States set out to create a democracy in Iraq. . . . The United States and its allies trained more Iraqis to serve in the police and the military. They also attempted to provide electricity, clean water, schools, and improved health care for Iraq's people.

Practice It!

Read the following paragraph. Draw a chart like the one below to help you monitor and clarify your reading.

—from Chapter 31, p. 1004

Because pollution crosses international borders, many experts believe that nations have to work together to find solutions. In 1987, for example, 23 nations agreed to ban chemicals suspected of harming the ozone layer— a part of the atmosphere that shields Earth from the sun's radiation.

Monitor	Ways to Clarify
1. _____	1. _____
2. _____	2. _____
3. _____	3. _____

Academic Vocabulary Preview

Listed below are the academic vocabulary words and their definitions that you will come across as you study Unit 10. Practice It! will help you study the words and definitions.

Academic Vocabulary	Definition	Practice It!
Chapter 30 America in the 1970s		
relax (rih · LAKS) *p. 943*	to ease	**Identify** *the term from Chapter 30 that best completes the sentence.*
technology (tehk · NAH · luh · jee) *p. 945*	scientific tools and material	1. Diplomatic negotiations can dramatically _____ tensions and improve relations between countries.
energy (EH · nuhr · jee) *p. 952*	sources of usable power	
controversy (KAHN · truh · vuhr · see) *p. 954*	arguments between opposing viewpoints	2. The Soviet Union hoped détente with the United States would give them access to American _____.
integrity (ihn · TEH · gruh · tee) *p. 959*	moral character	3. The 1973 oil embargo forced Americans to conserve _____.
exceed (ihk · SEED) *p. 959*	to be greater; go beyond	4. A _____ erupted because Nixon would not give White House tapes to the special prosecutors.
		5. Most candidates for public office talk about their personal _____.
Chapter 31 New Challenges		
quote (KWOHT) *p. 973*	to repeat the words of another	**Identify** *the term from Chapter 31 that best matches the underlined term or terms.*
theme (THEEM) *p. 974*	a subject	6. The United States wants to <u>keep</u> its position as a leader in world trade.
retain (rih · TAYN) *p. 977*	to hold on to	
site (SYT) *p. 979*	a location	7. Many scientists believe that changes in weather patterns due to global warming are <u>certain</u>.
adequate (A · dih · kwuht) *p. 983*	enough	
scope (SKOHP) *p. 985*	a range; area	8. Terrorists gave no <u>earlier</u> notice of their attack on the United States.
prior (PRY · uhr) *p. 993*	earlier	
definite (DEH · fuh · niht) *p. 997*	precise; well-defined	**Choose** *the word that best matches the meaning of each vocabulary term listed below.*

decade (DEH · KAYD) *p. 1001*	a period of ten years	9. **quote** 11. **decade**
		   a. comment a. one hundred
		   b. punctuation b. ten
		   c. guess c. lifetime

aware (uh · WEHR) *p. 1003*	to be mindful; have knowledge of	10. **site** 12. **adequate**
		   a. location a. good
		   b. vision b. too much
		   c. spirit c. enough

Chapter 30

America in the 1970s 1968–1981

One goal of space exploration was reached on July 20, 1969, when U.S. astronauts set foot on the moon.

RICHARD NIXON
1969–1974

PRESIDENTS

U.S. Events

World Events

1968

1971

★ 1967
Six-Day
Arab-Israeli
War

★ 1971
People's Republic
of China is admit-
ted to UN

1972
Nixon
visits
Beijing

★ 1972
SALT I is
signed

★ 1973
Watergate
hearings
begin

★ 1973
OPEC
imposes
embargo of
oil to U.S.

History ONLINE
Chapter Overview Visit glencoe.com
and click on **Chapter 30—Chapter
Overviews** to preview chapter information.

Section 1: Nixon's Foreign Policy

Essential Question What were President Nixon's main goals in foreign policy, and how did he work to achieve them?

Section 2: Nixon and Watergate

Essential Question What were President Nixon's major domestic challenges in the 1970s?

Section 3: The Carter Presidency

Essential Question What major foreign affairs issues did President Carter face during his presidency, and how did he deal with them?

American hostages are paraded by their Iranian captors, 1979. ▼

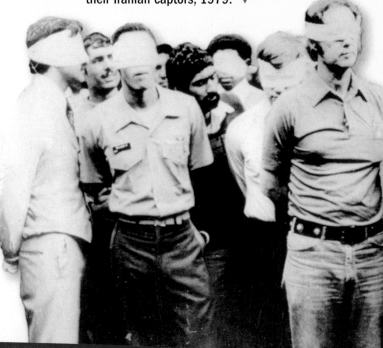

FOLDABLES
Study Organizer

Organizing Information

Make this Foldable to organize what you learn about the presidents and their policies during the 1970s.

Step 1 Fold a 2 1/2 inch tab along the long edge of a sheet of paper.

Step 2 Fold the paper in thirds.

Step 3 Open the paper pocket Foldable. Staple the ends of the pockets together.

Step 4 Label the pockets as shown.

Reading and Writing
As you read the chapter, summarize key facts on note cards or on quarter sheets of notebook paper. Organize your notes by placing them in your pocket Foldable inside the appropriate pockets.

★ **1974**
President Nixon resigns

GERALD FORD
1974–1977

JIMMY CARTER
1977–1981

★ **1979**
Iranians take Americans hostages

★ **1980**
U.S. boycotts Moscow Olympics

★ **1981**
Iranians release U.S. hostages

RONALD REAGAN
1981–1989

1974   **1977**   **1980**

◀ Fluctuating prices and supplies of gas meant long lines at gas pumps.

★ **1979**
Soviet troops invade Afghanistan

★ **1981**
Scientists identify AIDS

Section 1 — Nixon's Foreign Policy

Essential Question

What were President Nixon's main goals in foreign policy, and how did he work to achieve them?

Reading Guide

Content Vocabulary

détente (p. 943)   embargo (p. 946)
balance of power (p. 943)

Academic Vocabulary

relax (p. 943)   technology (p. 945)

Key People

Henry Kissinger (p. 943)
Zhou Enlai (p. 944)
Leonid Brezhnev (p. 945)
Golda Meir (p. 946)
Anwar el-Sadat (p. 946)

Reading Strategy

Taking Notes Re-create a diagram like the one below to show the countries that were the focus of Nixon's foreign policy.

Countries

NEW YORK STANDARDS
The American Journey

U10.II.4 To analyze the role played by the United States in international politics, past and present

U10.III.1 To understand the historic, political, and social context in which United States foreign policy has evolved during the post-Cold War era

U10.III.3 To analyze the role played by the United States in international politics, past and present

U11.I.2 To investigate key turning points in New York and United States history and explain why these events or developments are significant

American Diary

Richard Nixon was long known for his anticommunist views. Thus, many people were surprised when Nixon set out to improve relations with the nation's main rivals—China and the Soviet Union—in the interests of world peace. Nixon announced: "We seek an open world—open to ideas, open to the exchange of goods and people—a world in which no people, great or small, will live in angry isolation."

—from Nixon's Inaugural Address, January 1969

President Nixon's visit to China in 1972 was the first step in establishing better relations between the U.S. and the People's Republic of China.

Easing the Cold War

Main Idea President Nixon sought to ease Cold War tensions by improving relations with the Soviet Union and China.

History and You Have you ever tried to "mend fences" with somebody after a long disagreement? Read to learn about the changing relationships between the United States and Communist nations in the 1970s.

In his Inaugural Address, President Nixon told the American people, "The greatest honor . . . is the title of peacemaker." Many Americans wondered whether Nixon fit the role of peacemaker. During his years in Congress, he gained a reputation as a fierce enemy of communism. Few people imagined that Nixon, the anti-Communist crusader, would introduce policies to improve America's relations with the Communist world.

Behind the Iron Curtain

President Nixon intended to leave his mark on foreign policy. He hoped to build a more stable, peaceful world by reaching out to the Soviet Union and the People's Republic of China. In the summer of 1969, Nixon visited several countries, including Romania—the first time an American president went behind the iron curtain. Nixon wanted to find areas of common interest and cooperation with these Cold War opponents.

Détente

To help him in this task, Nixon appointed **Henry Kissinger,** a Harvard University professor, as his national security adviser. Kissinger and Nixon shared a belief in *realpolitik*—policies based on national interests rather than political beliefs. They believed that peace among nations would come through negotiation rather than through threats or force. Nixon followed a policy of **détente**—attempts at **relaxing,** or easing, international tensions. As détente replaced confrontation, the United States and Communist states could begin working together to resolve issues that divided them.

Nixon realized that détente would work only if a **balance of power** existed. A balance of power is a distribution of power among nations that prevents any one nation from becoming too powerful. "It will be a safer world and a better world," he declared, "if we have a strong, healthy United States, Europe, Soviet Union, China, Japan—each balancing the other, not playing one against the other."

Primary Source / "Ping-Pong" Diplomacy

One of the first steps in improving relationships between China and the United States was the visit of the U.S. table-tennis team to China. *TIME* magazine called it "the ping heard round the world."

Pat Oliphant. *The Denver Post,* 1971.

Critical Thinking

Analyzing Do you think sports can help improve relations between nations? Explain.

Détente in Space

Détente led to the first cooperative space mission between the United States and the Soviet Union. The U.S. *Apollo* and the Soviet *Soyuz* linked up in Earth's orbit on July 17, 1975.

▲ Astronauts and cosmonauts share a meal inside the *Soyuz* mock-up during training at the Johnson Space Center in Houston.

▲ A view of the *Soyuz* space capsule from the *Apollo* command module

China

Détente began with improved American-Chinese relations. Since 1949, when a Communist government came to power in China, the United States had refused to recognize the People's Republic of China. Instead it recognized the anti-Communist Chinese government under Chiang Kai-shek in exile on the island of Taiwan.

By the time of Nixon's presidency, however, each side had good reasons for wanting to improve relations. China distrusted the Soviet Union. Since the 1960s, disagreements had developed between them that divided the Communist world. Chinese and Soviet troops occasionally clashed along their borders. The United States hoped that recognition of China would help end the war in Vietnam and drive a deeper wedge between the two Communist powers.

The winds of change began to blow in the fall of 1970 when Nixon told reporters that he wanted to go to China. Noting this change in tone, the Chinese responded by inviting an American table tennis team to visit the country in April 1971. A week later the United States announced the opening of trade with China.

"Ping-Pong diplomacy" was accompanied by secret talks between American and Chinese officials about forging closer ties between the two nations. After Kissinger made a secret trip to China in July 1971, President Nixon announced that he would visit Beijing, the Chinese capital, "to seek the normalization of relations."

In February 1972, Nixon arrived in China for a weeklong visit. Nixon and China's premier **Zhou Enlai** agreed to allow greater scientific and cultural exchange and to resume trade. Although formal diplomatic relations were not established until 1979, Nixon's trip marked the first formal contact with China in more than 25 years.

What Is Détente?

The Nixon administration developed a policy called détente, or relaxation of tensions, between the United States and the Soviet Union and China.

Goals of Détente
- Reduce risk of nuclear war
- Cut back on military budget
- Forge better relations with rivals

Apollo-Soyuz patch ▲

Détente at Work
- President Nixon visits China, Soviet Union
- 1972 SALT I agreement signed
- U.S.-Soviet joint venture in space
- 1975 Helsinki Accords promote rights, trade

Critical Thinking

Analyzing The *Apollo-Soyuz* mission provided an opportunity for scientific research. According to U.S. pilot Vance Brand, the mission also had another goal: "to open the door a little bit between East and West." What do you think Brand meant?

The Soviet Union

Nixon followed his trip to China with a visit to Moscow, the Soviet capital, in May 1972. The Soviets welcomed a Cold War thaw. They wanted to prevent a Chinese-American alliance. They also hoped to buy United States **technology,** or scientific tools and material. Soviet leader **Leonid Brezhnev** remarked, "There must be room in this world for two great nations with different systems to live together and work together."

While in Moscow, Nixon signed the Strategic Arms Limitation Treaty (SALT I). This treaty restricted the number of certain types of nuclear missiles. The United States and the Soviet Union also agreed to work together in trade and science. Nixon—and the world—hoped that a new era of cooperation would bring greater stability to world affairs.

Reading Check **Identifying** What is détente?

The Middle East

Main Idea Nixon's foreign policy included easing Arab-Israeli tensions in the Middle East.

History and You Do you think that people of very different backgrounds can live together peacefully? Read to find out how the United States set out to achieve peace between the Arabs and the Israelis.

President Nixon's foreign policy aimed to maintain world stability without being drawn into regional disputes. The president stated that the United States would help other nations but would not take "basic responsibility" for the future of those nations. A crisis soon arose in the Middle East that tested this policy.

Arab-Israeli Tensions

Since the founding of the Jewish state of Israel in 1948, the U.S. had supported Israel in its struggles against its Arab neighbors. Tensions between Israel and the Arab states erupted in war in 1948 and 1956.

After Egypt closed a key waterway and massed its troops near Israel's border, Israel bombed Egyptian airfields on June 5, 1967. Within six days, Israel wiped out the air forces of its Arab neighbors. Israeli troops moved west into the Gaza Strip and Egypt's Sinai Peninsula and north into the Golan Heights, which were part of Syria. Israel also captured the old city of Jerusalem and the territory west of the Jordan River that Jordan had absorbed.

The "Six-Day War" of 1967 left Israel in control of these areas. When the fighting ended, the United Nations asked the Israelis to leave the captured territories. It asked the Arab nations to accept Israel's right to exist. Both sides refused.

The 1967 war also increased the number of Arab refugees, or displaced people. Thousands of Palestinians now lived in Israel-held territory, and thousands more lived neighboring Arab states. The Palestinian demand for their own homeland became another source of instability.

Primary Sources

INTERPRETING POLITICAL CARTOONS

The fuel shortages caused by the 1973 oil embargo plunged the nation into a state of emergency. The Department of Energy considered different plans to save fuel. One plan was to close gas stations on Sundays.

1. **Identifying** What is the event or issue that inspired this cartoon?

2. **Analyzing Visuals** What message is the author trying to convey in this cartoon?

"My text this morning is taken from Paragraph 15 of the President's message in regard to Sunday driving."

Yom Kippur War

Tensions remained high between Arabs and Israelis. As a result, war erupted again in 1973. Egypt and Syria attacked Israel to regain land lost in the 1967 War. Because this attack occurred on Yom Kippur, a major Jewish holiday, the conflict became known as the Yom Kippur War.

Egypt's forces attacked Israel, hoping to recapture the Sinai Peninsula. In early battles, many Israeli planes were shot down. Egypt's troops crossed into the Sinai, and Syria moved into the Golan Heights. With an American airlift of weapons, Israel struck back. The fighting raged until the United Nations negotiated a cease-fire. By this time, the Israelis had regained the land lost in the initial Arab advance. Israel also took additional territory from Syria and Egypt.

Angered by the U.S. support of Israel, Arab oil-producing states placed an **embargo**—a ban on shipments—of oil to the United States and other "non-friendly" nations.

The embargo led to an oil shortage in the United States. Long lines of cars formed at gas pumps as gas prices skyrocketed.

Shuttle Diplomacy

President Nixon sent Kissinger, now secretary of state, to the region to gain Arab trust and to negotiate an agreement between Israel and its Arab neighbors. Kissinger engaged in shuttle diplomacy—traveling back and forth among Middle Eastern capitals trying to resolve the oil crisis and forge a lasting peace.

Early in 1974, **Golda Meir,** the prime minister of Israel, and **Anwar el-Sadat,** the president of Egypt, agreed to separate Israeli and Egyptian forces in the Sinai Peninsula. Then in March 1974, Kissinger persuaded the Arab nations to end the oil embargo. Kissinger also improved U.S. ties with Egypt, the most powerful Arab state, by promising large amounts of foreign aid.

History ONLINE

Student Web Activity Visit glencoe.com and complete the Chapter 30 Web Activity about shuttle diplomacy.

Reading Check **Summarizing** What happened in the United States because of the oil embargo?

Latin America

Main Idea The Nixon administration continued the effort to halt the spread of communism in Latin America.

History and You Do you believe one country has the right to interfere in the affairs of another country? Read to find out how concerns about communism shaped the Nixon administration's policies in Latin America.

The Nixon administration sought to prevent the spread of communism in Latin America. In 1970 the country of Chile elected Salvador Allende president. Allende was a follower of Karl Marx, the founder of communism. He became the first Marxist, or supporter of Marx, to rise to power in the Americas through peaceful means.

To boost Chile's economy, Allende's government took over large businesses, gave land to the poor, and raised workers' wages. The economy grew, and the jobless rate declined. Not all of Allende's policies were successful, however. His breakup of large farms led to a decline in food production, which in turn caused food shortages. Also, increased wages led businesses to raise prices.

More important, Allende's policies made him enemies. Wealthy Chileans, frightened by Allende's Marxist views, took their money out of the country and invested it abroad. The United States, angered by Allende's takeover of American companies, decided to undermine the Allende government. It gave money to Allende's political opponents and promoted strikes. It also convinced foreign investors to stop loaning money to Chile. By 1972, Chile's economy was near collapse.

In 1973 Chile's military decided to take action. With the backing of the Central Intelligence Agency (CIA), a group of Chilean military leaders under General Augusto Pinochet overthrew the government and killed Allende. The United States immediately recognized the new military dictatorship and restored foreign aid to Chile.

Reading Check **Explaining** Why did the United States oppose Salvador Allende?

Section 1 Review

History ONLINE
Study Central™ To review this section, go to glencoe.com.

Vocabulary

1. Use each of the following terms in a paragraph about U.S. foreign policy: détente, relax, balance of power, technology, embargo.

Main Ideas

2. **Analyzing** What did the United States hope recognition of China would achieve?

3. **Discussing** What was the purpose of shuttle diplomacy?

4. **Explaining** How did the United States combat President Allende in Chile?

Critical Thinking

5. **Determining Cause and Effect** On a chart like the one below, list a major effect in each country caused by Nixon's foreign policy.

6. **Expository Writing** In a short essay, discuss Kissinger's achievements during the crisis in the Middle East.

Answer the
7. **Essential Question**
What were President Nixon's main goals in foreign policy, and how did he work to achieve them?

Nixon and Watergate

Essential Question

What were President Nixon's major domestic challenges in the 1970s?

Reading Guide

Content Vocabulary

revenue sharing (p. 949)

executive privilege (p. 953)

affirmative action (p. 950)

impeach (p. 953)

tight money policy (p. 950)

amnesty (p. 954)

deficit (p. 951)

Academic Vocabulary

energy (p. 952)　　controversy (p. 954)

Key People and Events

New Federalism (p. 949)

Watergate (p. 952)

Sam Ervin (p. 953)

Gerald R. Ford (p. 953)

Reading Strategy

Taking Notes On a diagram like the one below, record the factors that led to stagflation.

NEW YORK STANDARDS
The American Journey

U10.III.2 To understand the relative importance of United States domestic and foreign policy over time

U11.I.2 To investigate key turning points in New York and United States history and explain why these events or developments are significant

U11.I.3 To compare and contrast different interpretations of key events and issues in New York State and United States history and explain reasons for these different accounts

American Diary

President Nixon believed that the national government had grown cumbersome and inefficient, and that too many people were dependent on it. In August 1969, he announced a policy called "New Federalism" in a speech to the nation: "After a third of a century of power flowing from the people and the States to Washington it is time for a New Federalism in which power, funds, and responsibility will flow from Washington to the States and to the people."

—Richard Nixon's address to the nation, August 8, 1969

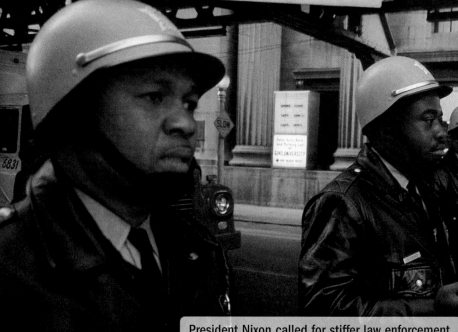

President Nixon called for stiffer law enforcement measures and more aid for state and local law enforcement agencies.

Columbus Junior High was a **stucco** group of pink and green buildings and a track the color of rust. The grass, like the grass at other schools, was mostly brown. The trash cans were buckled, but no candy wrappers or potato-chip bags scuttled across the campus. . . .

The kids dressed stylishly. When they smiled, their teeth gleamed with braces. It would never enter their minds to shop at K-mart or tote a bologna sandwich in a twice-used paper bag. Lincoln **opted** to live a simple life. His bologna sandwich, along with an apple and some chips, sat in his backpack, crushed between his geography and math books.

His mother **harangued** him about his clothes, but he wore jeans, busted at the knees, and his coat was a hand-me-down from an uncle. The front of Lincoln's shirt was **splotched** blue where he once let his Bic pen ride in the pocket during a wash.

Lincoln sighed and entered the school grounds. Just two more days to the weekend. . . .

At lunch he ate alone, scribbling out his homework for English, which was mostly recognizing the parts of speech. He thought it was funny how the teacher, Mrs. Baker, said the same things over and over. "A chair is a noun; a beach umbrella is a noun. . . ."

Lincoln bit into his sandwich roughly. He opened his geography book and once again the guy on the camel was smiling his lined face at him. He's like me, Lincoln thought. Brown as earth and no one knows his name. He closed the book when a basketball play came to his mind. . . .

He took another bite of his bologna sandwich and looked up to see James with a girl. Lincoln wiped his mouth, cleared his throat, and said to James, "Hey, homes." To the girl, he said, "Hi." . . .

He's like me, Lincoln thought.
Brown as earth
and no one knows his name.

James said, "This is Monica Torres. Monica, this is Lincoln, ah, let me see. What's your last name, Linc?"

"Mendoza."

"That's right, Linc Mendoza, star basketball player."

Monica smiled as she sat down. "James said you went to Franklin. I used to go there."

"Really?" Lincoln asked, curious, his eyebrows raised. "I don't remember you."

"Well, I did, for two months," she said. "But we moved here. My dad didn't like me going to school in the city."

"But your dad didn't have to go to school."

"It's true. But you know how Franklin is."

"You mean nasty."

"That's one way of putting it."

"That's the only way of putting it."

Lincoln wanted to tell her about the Franklin he knew, but how could he keep the conversation polite?

Analyzing Literature

1. **Respond** With which of Lincoln's experiences do you identify?

2. **Recall and Analyze** In what ways is Columbus Junior High different from Franklin?

3. **Evaluate** Lincoln says the man on the camel is like him: "Brown as earth and no one knows his name." What is Lincoln's view of himself?

GRADE 8 INTERMEDIATE TEST PRACTICE

TEST-TAKING TIP

On a multiple-choice test, remember that you are looking for the best, or most accurate, answer. It might not necessarily be the only answer that applies.

Reviewing Main Ideas

Directions: Choose the best answer for each of the following questions.

1 Nixon improved U.S. relations with China by

(1) promising aid.

(2) resuming trade.

(3) signing SALT I.

(4) sharing technology.

2 What was an outcome of the 1967 Six-Day War?

(1) more Arab refugees

(2) long lines at U.S. gas pumps

(3) improved U.S. relations with Egypt

(4) Egyptian control of the Sinai Peninsula

3 Nixon reduced the involvement of the federal government in people's lives by

(1) introducing revenue sharing.

(2) promoting affirmative action.

(3) approving the creation of the EPA.

(4) enforcing orders to integrate schools.

4 Why were the Ayatollah Khomeini and his supporters hostile to the United States?

(1) Carter ordered sanctions against Iran.

(2) U.S. policies were based on human rights.

(3) American leaders supported the shah.

(4) Carter condemned the practice of apartheid.

Short-Answer Question

Directions: Base your answer to question 5 on the excerpt below and on your knowledge of social studies.

> Finally, I feel that Richard Nixon and his loved ones have suffered enough and will continue to suffer, no matter what I do, no matter what we, as a great and good nation, can do together to make his goal of peace come true.
>
> —President Gerald R. Ford, September 8, 1974

5 Do you think this is a valid reason for pardoning President Nixon? Explain.

Review the Essential Questions

6 Essay Compare and contrast U.S.-Soviet relations in the Nixon and Carter administrations.

To help you write your essay, review your answers to the Essential Questions in the section reviews and the chapter Foldables Study Organizer. Your essay should include:

- an analysis of Nixon's relationship with the Soviets;
- an analysis of Carter's relationship with the Soviets; and
- similarities and differences in the leadership roles the presidents played in an international setting.

GO ON

Document-Based Questions

Directions: Analyze the documents and answer the short-answer questions that follow.

Document 1

Kissinger made this comment about the U.S. role in the overthrow of Chile's elected leader.

> I don't see why we need to stand by and watch a country go communist due to the irresponsibility of its own people.

Source: Tarak Barkawi, *War Inside the Free World*

7 What can you infer about Kissinger's attitude toward communism?

Document 2

In a 1977 interview, former President Nixon was asked about his views on the presidency and the law.

> Well, when the president does it that means that it is not illegal.

Source: Richard Nixon, from an interview with David Frost

8 What does Nixon's statement reflect about how he views the relationship of the president to the laws of the United States?

Document 3

In the following statement, Carter criticized the rise in oil imports during the Ford administration.

> We now import about 44 percent of our oil. . . . We need to shift very strongly toward solar energy and have strict conservation measures.

Source: The First Carter-Ford Presidential Debate, 1976

9 Why was the rise in oil imports a campaign issue in 1976?

Document 4

The graph shows President Nixon's approval rating during parts of 1973 and 1974.

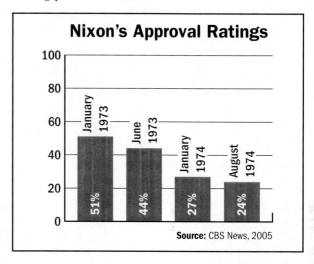

Nixon's Approval Ratings

January 1973: 51%
June 1973: 44%
January 1974: 27%
August 1974: 24%

Source: CBS News, 2005

10 What was Nixon's approval rating before he resigned in August 1974? What was the rating in January of that year?

Document 5

Senator William Proxmire objected to billions in military aid authorized by the Camp David Accords.

> The notion that we must provide military assistance to [these] nations . . . is precisely what has led us down this long and bloody and reprehensible road of providing the weapons of death and destruction in the name of peace.

Source: Barbara Hinckley, *Less Than Meets the Eye*

11 What does Senator Proxmire suggest Carter used to persuade Begin and Sadat to sign a peace treaty?

12 **Expository Writing** Using the information from the five documents and your knowledge of social studies, write an essay in which you:
- discuss the goals of federal policies in the 1970s; and
- discuss how the Watergate scandal affected Americans' view of the presidency.

Need Extra Help?												
If you missed questions. . .	1	2	3	4	5	6	7	8	9	10	11	12
Go to page. . .	944	945	949	962	952	943–962	943	953	960	953	961	943–955

New Challenges
1981 to Present

Students take part in a team effort to clean up area near Long Beach, California.

PRESIDENTS

RONALD REAGAN

1983
U.S. troops invade Grenada

1986
Space shuttle *Challenger* explodes

GEORGE H.W. BUSH

1990
Americans with Disabilities Act passes

U.S. Events

1980

1987

World Events

1981
Egypt's president Anwar el-Sadat assassinated

1985
Mikhail Gorbachev becomes leader of Soviet Union

1989
Students protest in Tiananmen Square, China

1990
Nelson Mandela released from South African prison

Section 1: The Reagan Presidency

Essential Question How was President Reagan's attitude about communism reflected in his actions and policies?

Section 2: The Bush Presidency

Essential Question How did President Bush deal with the domestic challenges facing his presidency?

Section 3: A New Century

Essential Question How did the Clinton presidency change the U.S. domestic scene in the 1990s?

Section 4: The War on Terror

Essential Question How has the war on terror changed the way Americans live?

Section 5: Challenges Ahead

Essential Question How have economic and environmental developments led to the world's nations becoming more interdependent?

FOLDABLES Study Organizer

Organizing Information

Make this Foldable to organize what you learn about the challenges faced by the United States.

Step 1 Place three sheets of paper on top of one another about 1 inch apart.

Step 2 Fold the papers to form six equal tabs.

Step 3 Staple the sheets and label each tab as shown.

New Challenges 1981–Present
The Reagan Presidency
The Bush Presidency
A New Century
The War on Terror
Challenges Ahead

Reading and Writing As you read the chapter, record notes, collect terms, note important dates and events, and answer the Essential Questions beneath the tabs.

A family in Mississippi is rescued from flood waters caused by Hurricane Katrina. ▶

BILL CLINTON

★ **1995** Bomb kills 168 at Oklahoma City federal building

★ **1998** President Clinton impeached

GEORGE W. BUSH

★ **2001** War on terror begins

★ **2005** Hurricane Katrina strikes Louisiana and Mississippi

★ **2007** Nancy Pelosi becomes first female Speaker of the House

1994 — **2001** — **2008**

★ **1991**
• Operation Desert Storm
• Breakup of Soviet Union

★ **1994** U.S., Mexico, and Canada found NAFTA

★ **2004** Tsunami devastates Indonesia and surrounding regions

★ **2005** Terrorists bomb London subway system

Woman surveys destruction after hurricane. ▶

The Reagan Presidency

Essential Question ◀

How was President Reagan's attitude about communism reflected in his actions and policies?

Reading Guide

Content Vocabulary
deregulation *(p. 972)*   federal debt *(p. 973)*
supply-side economics *(p. 972)*

Academic Vocabulary
quote *(p. 973)*   theme *(p. 974)*

Key People and Events
Sandra Day O'Connor *(p. 972)*
George H.W. Bush *(p. 974)*
Geraldine Ferraro *(p. 974)*
Mikhail Gorbachev *(p. 975)*

Reading Strategy
Taking Notes On a diagram like the one below, identify the building blocks of President Reagan's conservative federal government.

Reagan Conservatism

NEW YORK STANDARDS
The American Journey

U10.III.1 To understand the historic, political, and social context in which United States foreign policy has evolved during the post-Cold War era

U10.III.2 To understand the relative importance of United States domestic and foreign policy over time

U11.II.1 To understand the economic, social, and political trends that shaped the end of the 20th century and point to the 21st century

American Diary

On March 30, 1981, President Ronald Reagan left a Washington, D.C., hotel after giving a speech. As he passed press photographers and TV cameras, six gunshots rang out. Secret Service agents rushed the president into his limousine and sped toward the hospital. A bullet had punctured his lung and lodged just an inch from his heart. Despite the seriousness of the situation, the president joked on the way into the operating room, telling his doctors, "I hope you're all Republicans."

President Reagan waves to the crowd moments before the assassination attempt.

The Reagan Revolution

Main Idea President Reagan brought a new conservative approach to government.

History and You What are principles? What principles do you live by? Read to discover the principles that guided the policies of the Reagan presidency.

Ronald Reagan's election to the presidency in 1980 marked a significant conservative shift in America. During the 1970s, the conservative movement had grown throughout the country, most particularly in the South and Southwest.

Many Americans now wanted a return to what Ronald Reagan, a former actor with Illinois small-town roots, called "traditional American values"—an emphasis on family life, hard work, respect for law, and patriotism. They shared the conservative view that the federal government made too many rules, collected too much in taxes, and spent too much money on social programs.

Reagan believed that the key to restoring America's strength and influence was to get Americans to believe in themselves again. He expressed this idea in his Inaugural Address:

PRIMARY SOURCE

"We have every right to dream heroic dreams. . . . You can see heroes every day going in and out of factory gates. Others, a handful in number, produce enough food to feed all of us. . . . You meet heroes across a counter. . . . Their patriotism is quiet, but deep. Their values sustain our national life."
—*Ronald Reagan's First Inaugural Address, January 1981*

Air Traffic Controllers' Strike

A few months after Ronald Reagan became president, the nation's air traffic controllers went on strike. They refused to go back to work despite the president's orders to do so. President Reagan acted at once, firing the controllers and ordering military staff to oversee air traffic while new controllers were trained to do the work.

Critics of former president Carter felt he lacked leadership and was indecisive. With this action, Ronald Reagan showed that he would stand firm and use his presidency to carry out the policies in which he believed.

Primary Source / The Great Communicator

In His Own Words Ronald W. Reagan was nicknamed "the Great Communicator" because of his extraordinary skill as an orator. He appeared in more than 50 films as a Hollywood actor, which helped him polish his speaking skills.

"Honey, I forgot to duck."
—March 30, 1981, from www.pbs.org (said to Nancy Reagan when she arrived at the hospital following the assassination attempt)

"I've always believed that a lot of the trouble in the world would disappear if we were talking to each other instead of about each other."
—April 11, 1984, from www.reaganfoundation.org

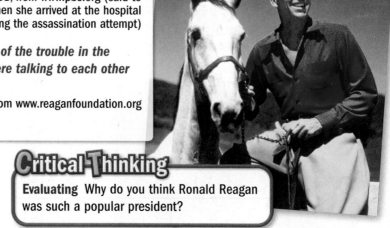

Critical Thinking

Evaluating Why do you think Ronald Reagan was such a popular president?

Deregulation

As part of his promise to reduce government and "get the government off the backs of the American people," Reagan pursued a policy of **deregulation.** This meant cutting the rules and regulations that government agencies placed on businesses. The Department of Transportation, for example, wrote new rules for automobile exhaust systems and safety measures that were easier for car manufacturers to meet.

The Supreme Court

Reagan also put a conservative stamp on the Supreme Court by naming justices to the Court who shared his views. He wanted justices who favored a stricter interpretation of the Constitution. When the president appointed **Sandra Day O'Connor** in 1981, she became the first woman ever appointed to the Court. Reagan later appointed Antonin Scalia and Anthony Kennedy as Supreme Court justices.

Reaganomics

Economic policy formed the core of the "Reagan Revolution." The president believed that lower taxes would allow individuals and corporations to invest in new businesses. Because a tax cut would mean less government income, Reagan also called for less government spending.

Supporters called President Reagan's policy **supply-side economics** because it aimed to boost the economy by increasing the supply of goods and services. Critics labeled the policy "Reaganomics." They held that Reagan's policy would help corporations and wealthy Americans, while only a little prosperity would "trickle down" to average Americans.

In 1981 Congress lowered taxes and reduced federal programs such as student aid, welfare, and low-income housing. Supporters argued that Reaganomics would stimulate the economy, helping everybody in the long run.

People IN HISTORY

Sally Kristen Ride

First American woman in space

In 1983 Sally Ride became the first American woman in space when she orbited the Earth aboard the space shuttle *Challenger.* A strong advocate for improved science education, Ride has written several books for young readers. She says, *"Our future lies with today's kids and tomorrow's space exploration."*

Sandra Day O'Connor

First woman to serve on the Supreme Court

When a Supreme Court vacancy opened in 1981, President Reagan decided to fulfill his campaign promise to name the first woman justice. He chose Sandra Day O'Connor, an Arizona appeals court judge. O'Connor served until 2006. In an interview, she discussed the increased opportunities for women: *"When I went to law school, about 1 percent of all law students were women. And last year, over 50 percent were."*

loan associations (S&Ls)—financial institutions that specialized in making loans to home buyers.

Banking Crisis

The new laws allowed S&Ls to pay very high interest rates to attract deposits and to make far too many risky loans and investments. When many borrowers could not repay their loans and real estate values declined, S&Ls lost millions of dollars. Individual S&L deposits were insured by the government, which now had to pay out billions of dollars to customers of failed S&Ls. To limit the crisis, the government bailed out other struggling S&Ls, a move costing taxpayers almost $500 billion.

Economic Downturn

The heavy borrowing of the 1980s brought trouble to the economy. As the federal debt reached new highs, business and personal debt grew. In 1990 the economy slowed to a recession, partly caused by the end of the Cold War. Cuts in military spending led to job losses in defense-related businesses.

Companies also began to **downsize**—lay off workers—to become more efficient. The nation's debt burden made the recession worse. Individuals and businesses had borrowed heavily and now could not meet loan payments. Some had to declare **bankruptcy**, selling off what they owned to pay debts.

Many people urged the government to stimulate the economy. President Bush refused to increase federal spending. He did agree to extend benefits to the jobless, but he opposed further government involvement.

Accomplishments

Despite disagreements, the president and Congress cooperated on updating the Clean Air Act and pushing forward on civil rights. The Americans with Disabilities Act of 1990 banned job discrimination against people with disabilities. It also opened ways for disabled people to gain easier access to workplaces, transportation, and housing.

Bush also carried out a war on illegal drugs. In 1989 President Bush created the Office of National Drug Control Policy. This department oversees more than 50 federal agencies involved in the war on drugs.

Reading Check **Analyzing** Why did so many S&Ls fail in the 1980s?

Section 2 Review

History ONLINE
Study Central™ To review this section, go to glencoe.com.

Vocabulary

1. Use each of these terms correctly in a sentence: retain, coalition, site, downsize, bankruptcy.

Main Ideas

2. **Analyzing** Why was START so important?

3. **Explaining** What action did Bush take in Panama using U.S. troops?

4. **Discussing** Why did the government lose so much money through the failure of S&L banks?

Critical Thinking

5. **Sequencing** Using a diagram like the one below, generally sequence the events that led to the country's deep recession during the 1990s.

6. **Creative Writing** Take a stand on how you feel about U.S. participation in Operation Desert Storm. Write a short protest or support song about your feelings.

Answer the

7. **Essential Question**
How did President Bush deal with the domestic challenges facing his presidency?

Section 3

A New Century

Essential Question

How did the Clinton presidency change the U.S. domestic scene in the 1990s?

Reading Guide

Content Vocabulary

grassroots movement (p. 983)

deficit spending (p. 983)

budget deficit (p. 983)

gross domestic product (p. 985)

perjury (p. 985)

Academic Vocabulary

adequate (p. 983)   scope (p. 985)

Key People and Events

Bill Clinton (p. 983)

Al Gore (p. 983)

George W. Bush (p. 987)

Richard Cheney (p. 987)

Condoleezza Rice (p. 989)

Reading Strategy

Taking Notes On a diagram like the one below, identify early Clinton-sponsored legislation that passed into law.

Clinton Legislation

NEW YORK STANDARDS
The American Journey

U10.III.2 To understand the relative importance of United States domestic and foreign policy over time

U10.III.3 To analyze the role played by the United States in international politics, past and present

U11.II.1 To understand the economic, social, and political trends that shaped the end of the 20th century and point to the 21st century

American Diary

At 16 years old, Bill Clinton heard the "I Have a Dream" speech by Dr. Martin Luther King, Jr., for the first time. It inspired him to find common ground in politics for the benefit of all citizens. After becoming president in 1993, he still held his vision of people working together for the common good. He said, "We have got to move beyond division and resentment to common ground. We've got to go beyond cynicism to a sense of possibility."

—from Remarks at Georgetown University, July 1995

Candidate Bill Clinton greets supporters at a campaign rally in 1992.

982

The Clinton Administration

Main Idea President Clinton struggled with Republicans in Congress and faced impeachment, but he achieved several major economic and social reforms.

History and You Have you ever visited our closest neighbors—Canada and Mexico? Read to find out how the United States and these two nations drew closer together in the 1990s.

After victory in the Persian Gulf War, President Bush's popularity with Americans soared. A troubled economy, however, hurt Bush's reelection chances for 1992 and encouraged challengers to enter the presidential race. The Democrats nominated Arkansas governor **Bill Clinton** to run against President Bush. Clinton chose Tennessee senator **Al Gore** as his running mate. The Clinton campaign focused on the economy and the high unemployment rate.

Unhappy with "politics as usual," many Americans did not want to vote for either Bush or Clinton. A **grassroots movement**—people around the nation organizing at the local level—put Texas business leader H. Ross Perot on the ballot as a third-party candidate.

Perot called for an end to the government's **deficit spending,** or spending more money than it takes in.

Voters elected Clinton, the first president born after World War II. Clinton received 43 percent of the popular vote, Bush 38 percent, and Perot 19 percent. Clinton received less than a majority of the votes because of Perot's strong showing, the highest percentage of popular votes for any third-party candidate since Theodore Roosevelt in 1912.

Domestic Program

One of the new president's goals was reducing the **budget deficit**—the amount by which spending exceeds revenue. Clinton proposed cutting government spending, raising taxes for middle-and upper-income Americans, and providing tax credits to the poorest. Most Republicans in Congress opposed this plan, but it narrowly passed.

Clinton faced even stronger opposition to his plan for health-care reform. His goal was to control rising health-care costs and provide **adequate,** or enough, health insurance for every American. The president named the First Lady, Hillary Rodham Clinton, to head the task force.

By the Numbers / The 1992 Election

Popular Vote

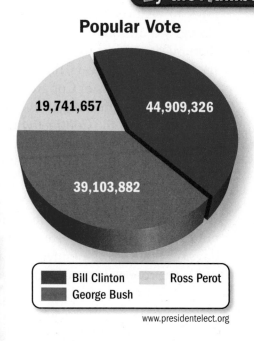

- Bill Clinton
- George Bush
- Ross Perot

19,741,657
44,909,326
39,103,882

www.presidentelect.org

Three-Way Race Democratic candidate Bill Clinton won the electoral vote by more than a 2-to-1 margin over incumbent President George H.W. Bush. Clinton, however, did not win a majority of the nation's popular vote, but he did beat Bush by six percentage points.

Critical Thinking

Evaluating How can a third-party candidate for the presidency like Perot affect an election?

Voting for Impeachment The House of Representatives accused President Clinton of lying under oath and obstructing justice, and voted to impeach him. Now it was up to the Senate to convict and remove him from office. Passionate voices cried out for and against conviction.

For Conviction *"As the youngest member of this body, I believe we must hold firm to the oldest truths. . . . I vote as I do because I will not stand for the proposition that a President can, with premeditation and deliberation, obstruct justice and commit perjury before a grand jury. It cannot be."*

Senator Peter Fitzgerald (R–Illinois) ▲

	GUILTY	NOT GUILTY
GOP	30	3
DEM	0	31
TOTAL	30	34

CLINTON ACQUITTED

SENATE VOTE
67 VOTES TO CONVICT
IMPEACHMENT ARTICLE 2
OBSTRUCTION OF JUSTICE
LIEBERMAN D

Against Conviction *"Impeachment is a power singularly lacking any of the checks and balances on which the Framers depended. It is solely a power of the Congress. Do not doubt that it could bring radical instability to American government."*

▲ Senator Daniel Moynihan (D–New York)

Congress rejected the Clinton plan, calling it too expensive and too reliant on government control. Later, Congress did pass measures that provided more health-care protection for the elderly, children, and other groups that were not previously covered.

During his first term, President Clinton won some legislative battles. Despite strong opposition, the president succeeded in passing the Brady Bill of 1993. The law imposed a waiting period and background checks for handgun purchases. The 1994 crime bill banned 19 kinds of assault weapons and provided for 100,000 new police officers.

Another Clinton proposal that became law was the Family and Medical Leave Act of 1993. It permitted workers to take time off from their jobs for special family situations.

Contract With America

Before the 1994 mid-term elections, House Republicans led by Newt Gingrich of Georgia created a new plan. Known as the Contract with America, it called for a "return to the basic values that had built the country: work and family and the recognition of a higher moral authority."

In the contract, the Republicans promised to reduce the federal government, balance the budget, lower taxes, and reform how Congress operates. They also pledged to pass laws to reduce crime, reform welfare, and strengthen the family. The result was a strong Republican victory in the 1994 elections. For the first time in 40 years, the Republicans controlled both houses of Congress. In their first hundred days in office, the Republicans passed much of the Contract with America.

In 1995, however, the Republicans lost ground when they clashed with President Clinton over the new federal budget. This dispute caused the federal government to run out of money. The government shut down nonessential services twice for a total of 27 days. Congress and the president recognized that compromise was needed.

The Power to Impeach If a majority of the House votes to impeach, the Senate then has the power to try the official. Only two presidents have been impeached: Andrew Johnson in 1868 and Bill Clinton in 1998. Both were tried by the Senate and acquitted (not removed from office).

Critical Thinking

1. **Analyzing** Why did Senator Fitzgerald believe that the president should be removed from office?

2. **Explaining** What reasons does Senator Moynihan give for his vote not to remove President Clinton from office?

Soon afterward, the Republicans in Congress and President Clinton reached an agreement to balance the budget. The president pushed for an increase in the minimum wage and supported a welfare reform act. This measure set a work requirement for people receiving benefits and put a five-year time limit on benefits.

Clinton Wins a Second Term

The Republicans hoped to regain the White House in 1996. However, the economy was healthy and unemployment was at a 30-year low. President Clinton easily won reelection, beating the Republican candidate, former Senate majority leader Robert Dole.

During Clinton's second term, the economy continued to grow. One measure of economic growth is the **gross domestic product** (GDP), the value of all the goods and services produced in a nation in a year. In 1996 and 1997, the GDP grew by about 4 percent per year—one of the highest rates of growth since the post-World War II boom.

The economy's growth increased the amount of tax money the government received. At the same time, the president and Congress cut back the size of the federal budget. The federal budget is prepared for a fiscal year—a 12-month planning period. The 1998 fiscal year ended with a federal budget surplus—the amount of money remaining after all expenditures—of about $80 billion, the first surplus in three decades.

Scandals and Impeachment

The strong economy kept Clinton's popularity high, but scandals threatened his presidency. Clinton was accused of arranging illegal loans for a real estate company while he was governor of Arkansas. Former judge Kenneth Starr led the investigation. A new scandal emerged involving a personal relationship between the president and a White House intern. Evidence suggested that the president may have committed **perjury,** or lied under oath, about the relationship. Starr widened the **scope,** or range, of the investigation. In September 1998, Starr sent a report to Congress claiming that President Clinton had committed perjury and obstructed justice.

The House of Representatives then began hearings to decide whether to impeach the president. To impeach is to make a formal accusation of wrongdoing against a public official. Despite general agreement that the president had lied, the House was split over whether his actions justified impeachment. Clinton's supporters argued that his offenses did not qualify as "high crimes and misdemeanors," as stated in the Constitution. Clinton's accusers insisted that the president was accountable if his actions were illegal.

In December 1998, the House passed two impeachment articles—for perjury and for obstruction of justice. The case moved to the Senate for trial. A two-thirds majority vote is needed to convict and remove a president from office. In February 1999, the Senate acquitted the president of both charges.

New Challenges **Chapter 31 985**

Foreign Policy

Even as the nation struggled with domestic issues, foreign affairs presented new challenges. Important decisions faced American policy makers on defining the nation's role in the post–Cold War world.

In 1993 Clinton persuaded Congress to ratify the North American Free Trade Agreement, or NAFTA. Under NAFTA the United States, Canada, and Mexico agreed to eliminate trade barriers among the three nations. NAFTA opponents feared a loss of U.S. jobs. Farmers also feared NAFTA, saying that low-priced Mexican produce would undercut American goods. Supporters argued that the treaty would lower prices for American consumers and expand markets.

The Middle East was also a major concern. In September 1993, President Clinton invited Israeli prime minister Yitzhak Rabin and Yassir Arafat, head of the Palestine Liberation Organization (PLO), to the White House for the signing of a historic agreement between the two leaders. Israel recognized the PLO as the representative of the Palestinians, and the PLO recognized Israel's right to exist. The agreement created a plan for limited Palestinian self-government in certain areas.

Opposition to the plan emerged on both sides, and violence in the area continued. In 1995 an Israeli extremist assassinated Prime Minister Rabin. During the remainder of his term, Clinton continued peace efforts, but little success was achieved.

As you read in Section 2, civil war had erupted in the former Yugoslavia. In Bosnia, Serbs engaged in ethnic cleansing—forcibly removing or killing members—of the Muslim population. In 1998 Serbian leader Slobodan Milošević tried to drive Muslims out of the Kosovo region. U.S. and NATO air strikes against Serbia finally forced the Serbs to leave Kosovo and agree to negotiate. Clinton then led peace talks, which produced the Dayton Accords in late 1995.

✔ **Reading Check** **Identifying** What major trade agreement did Clinton make in 1993?

National Defense, Selected Nations

Defense Spending, 2006 (% of world total)

Britain 5.1
France 4.6
China 4.3
Japan 3.8
Germany 3.2
Russia 3.0
India 2.1
U.S. 45.7
Rest of world 28.3

Total: $1.2 trillion

Sources: Stockholm International Peace Research Institute (SIPRI); Center for Strategic and Budgetary Assessments; International Institute for Strategic Studies

U.S. Defense Spending as % of GDP

GDP, or Gross Domestic Product, is the market value of goods and services produced by a country. The graph compares spending for defense with the GDP.

Years

A New President for a New Century

Main Idea As the 2000s began, the United States enjoyed economic prosperity but was deeply divided politically.

History and You Have you seen or taken part in a race in which the outcome was so close that it was difficult to declare a winner? Read to find out how the winner of the 2000 presidential race—one of the closest in American history—was determined.

As Clinton prepared to leave office, his legacy was uncertain. He had balanced the budget and succeeded in turning around the nation's economy. The impeachment trial during Clinton's second term, however, had left the country divided. Many Americans were pleased with his accomplishments but were disappointed with the president's personal conduct. As the 2000 election approached, the major parties looked for candidates who appealed to a wide cross section of voters.

Comparing the Military, Selected Nations The U.S. military has about 1.5 million personnel on active duty. An additional 1.3 million men and women serve in the reserves.

	Armed forces* in millions	Nuclear warheads, est.	Aircraft carriers
U.S.	1.5	5,163	12
Britain	0.2	200	3
China	2.3	400	0
France	0.3	350	2
India	1.3	50	1
Japan	0.2	0	0
Russia	1.0	5,830	1

*Not including reservists

Graph Skills

Analyzing Explain any trends apparent in U.S. defense spending as a percentage of GDP. *Graphs In Motion*

The Candidates

The Democrats nominated Vice President Al Gore for president, hoping that the popularity of Clinton's policies would mean votes for Gore. The large Republican field eventually came down to two men: Governor **George W. Bush** of Texas and Senator John McCain of Arizona. Ultimately, the Republicans chose Bush, the son of former President George H.W. Bush, as their nominee.

Gore made history by naming Senator Joseph Lieberman, from Connecticut, as his running mate. This marked the first time in U.S. history that a Jewish American ran on a national ticket. George W. Bush chose **Richard Cheney** as his running mate. Cheney had served as chief of staff to President Gerald Ford and defense secretary to former President Bush in 1989.

During the campaign, Gore stressed protecting the environment and improving education. Bush also supported educational reform. Calling himself a "compassionate conservative," Bush favored local "grassroots" efforts to help the disadvantaged without large and costly government programs. A major campaign issue was what to do with the budget surplus. Gore and Bush agreed that Social Security and Medicare needed reform, but they disagreed on the details. Both also supported tax cuts and plans to help seniors pay for prescription drugs.

Claiming that there was little difference between Bush and Gore, activist Ralph Nader entered the race. Noting that "too much power in the hands of the few has further weakened our democracy," Nader ran as the nominee of the Green Party, which was known for its strong environmental views.

The Election of 2000

The 2000 election was extraordinarily close between Bush and Gore. For five weeks after the race, the outcome remained undecided. The key state was Florida, where Bush had a slim lead. Without Florida's 25 electoral votes, neither Bush nor Gore had the 270 electoral votes needed to win.

Election of 2000

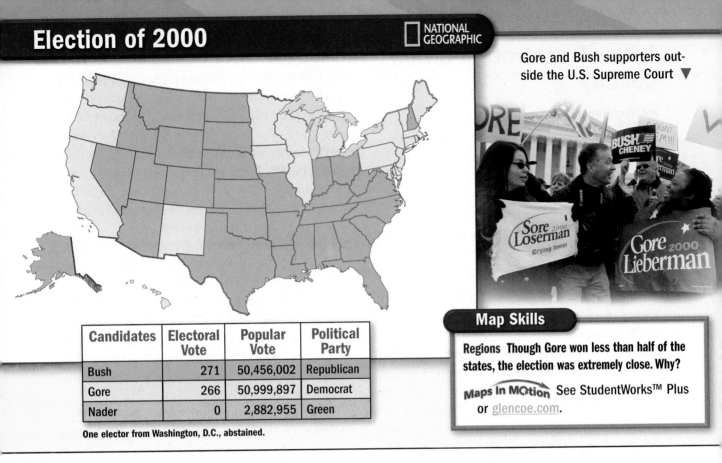

Gore and Bush supporters outside the U.S. Supreme Court ▼

Candidates	Electoral Vote	Popular Vote	Political Party
Bush	271	50,456,002	Republican
Gore	266	50,999,897	Democrat
Nader	0	2,882,955	Green

One elector from Washington, D.C., abstained.

Map Skills

Regions Though Gore won less than half of the states, the election was extremely close. Why?

Maps In Motion See StudentWorks™ Plus or glencoe.com.

Because the results in Florida were so close, state law required a recount of the ballots using vote-counting machines. Gore also asked for hand recounts in several counties, and a battle began over whether and how to conduct them. Lawsuits were filed in state and federal courts. The issue ultimately reached the U.S. Supreme Court.

On December 12, in *Bush* v. *Gore,* the Court ruled that the hand recounts of selected votes in Florida ordered by the Florida Supreme Court violated the equal protection clause of the Constitution. It further held that there was not enough time to conduct a recount that would pass constitutional standards. This ruling left Bush the winner in Florida. The next day, Gore conceded the election.

Bush Becomes President

On January 20, 2001, Bush became the 43rd president of the United States. In his Inaugural Address, President Bush called for "inclusion, not division," saying that America should be united. The need for unity and cooperation was important in Congress as well. After the election the Senate was evenly split—50 Republicans and 50 Democrats.

In May 2001 Vermont senator James Jeffords left the Republican Party and became an independent. This led to a historic switch in power, transferring control to the Democrats in mid-session. However, in the midterm elections of 2002, the Republicans regained control of the Senate and increased their majority in the House.

When assembling his cabinet, President Bush sought people from different career backgrounds. He appointed popular retired Army general Colin Powell as secretary of state. He also named Donald Rumsfeld as secretary of defense. Rumsfeld previously served as secretary of defense during the Ford adminstration. The Bush cabinet also reflected much of the country's diversity, including three African Americans, two Asians, and one Latino.

In addition, five women served in President Bush's cabinet. Elaine Chao, the secretary of labor, was the first Asian American woman to serve in a president's cabinet.

Other women played leading roles in the new administration. **Condoleezza Rice,** the first woman in history to hold the job of national security adviser, was instrumental in shaping foreign policy. First Lady Laura Bush promoted education. She called attention to the need for recruiting more teachers and improving reading skills.

Domestic Policy

Once in office, President Bush focused on his domestic plans: cutting taxes, improving public education, reforming Social Security and Medicare, and strengthening the nation's defenses. Bush's first task was to carry out his campaign pledge to cut taxes. Some politicians argued that the tax money lost could be used more responsibly, for example, to pay off the national debt. Supporters claimed the cut would help the economy, which had gone into a slump during the election campaign. In June 2001, Congress passed and Bush signed into law the 10-year, $1.3 trillion tax-cut bill.

After passage of the tax-cut plan, Bush proposed reforms in education. He called for public schools to hold yearly tests to measure student performance. He also wanted to allow parents to use federal funds to pay for private schools if their public schools were doing a poor job. Congress refused to give federal funds to private schools, but it did vote in favor of annual testing in public schools for grades 3 to 8. This law became known as the No Child Left Behind Act.

Foreign Policy

In foreign affairs, Bush pushed for new military programs. One was a National Missile Defense System designed to shoot down incoming missiles before they reached the United States. The president argued that missile defense was needed because many hostile nations were developing long-range missiles.

Meanwhile, a horrifying event took place on September 11, 2001, that changed everything. A stunned nation realized that it was not immune to the dangers of a violent world. A new kind of war had begun.

Reading Check **Summarizing** What was George W. Bush's policy on education?

Section 3 Review

History ONLINE
Study Central™ To review this section, go to glencoe.com.

Vocabulary

1. Write a sentence using each of the following terms correctly: grassroots movement, deficit spending, budget deficit, adequate, gross domestic product, perjury, scope.

Main Ideas

2. **Analyzing** What was Clinton's plan for health-care reform, and who did he name to administer it?

3. **Explaining** What were the main goals of the Contract with America?

4. **Discussing** What caused the confusion over the outcome of the 2000 presidential election?

Critical Thinking

5. **Interpreting** What did George W. Bush mean when he called himself a compassionate conservative?

6. **Identifying** On a diagram like the one below, identify the main goals in Bush's domestic plans.

Bush Domestic Plans

7. **Persuasive Writing** Decide the answer to this question: *Should a president be protected from impeachment because the presidency is the highest office in America?* Write a one-page persuasive paper describing your opinion on this topic.

Answer the
8. **Essential Question**
How did the Clinton presidency change the U.S. domestic scene in the 1990s?

Section 4 ★ The War on Terror

Essential Question ◄

How has the war on terror changed the way Americans live?

Reading Guide

Content Vocabulary

terrorism (p. 991)
fundamentalist (p. 992)
counterterrorism (p. 993)
insurgent (p. 994)
levee (p. 997)

Academic Vocabulary

prior (p. 993)
definite (p. 997)

Key People and Events

Osama bin Laden (p. 991)
USA Patriot Act (p. 993)
Hurricane Katrina (p. 997)
Nancy Pelosi (p. 997)

Reading Strategy

Taking Notes On a diagram like the one below, identify the American sites of the September 11 terrorist attacks.

September 11 Sites

NEW YORK STANDARDS
The American Journey

U11.I.3 To compare and contrast different interpretations of key events and issues in New York State and United States history and explain reasons for these different accounts

U11.II.1 To understand the economic, social, and political trends that shaped the end of the 20th century and point to the 21st century

U11.II.2 To investigate problems and opportunities the United States faces in its immediate future

American Diary

On September 11, New York City firefighter John Breen had orders to search for trapped people on the top floor of a hotel, nestled between the towers of the World Trade Center. Once inside, Breen felt the hotel begin to sway as the first tower collapsed. "I heard it getting louder and louder like an approaching train. You could hear the floors one on top of each other like dominoes." After the second tower collapsed, it was reported that at least 41 firefighters had been killed inside the hotel.

—*from* Firehouse Magazine

A man walks amid the rubble of the World Trade Center looking for victims to help.

Hurricane Katrina

A major natural disaster as well as political storms affected Bush's second term. On August 29, 2005, **Hurricane Katrina** struck the Gulf of Mexico coast. Storm conditions raged from Florida to Louisiana. The hurricane destroyed buildings, roads, and electrical lines. Thousands of people were left homeless, and at least 1,800 people died.

The city of New Orleans suffered extensive damage. After the hurricane had passed, rising waters broke through the **levees,** or high walls, that protected the low-lying city. As water flooded neighborhoods, residents who stayed behind during the hurricane were forced to await rescue or to flee. Many waited for days without much food, clean water, or information. Eventually troops and transportation arrived and moved flood survivors to other cities.

News broadcasts of the disaster, however, caused many Americans to wonder why national, state, and local governments were failing to respond more quickly. President Bush fired the head of the federal government's emergency relief agency. He also pledged federal funds to rebuild the city.

The 2006 Midterm Elections

American voters expressed their unhappiness with Bush administration policies in the 2006 mid-term elections. The Democrats won control of both houses of Congress for the first time since 1992. House Democrats then elected **Nancy Pelosi** to be the first female Speaker of the House of Representatives.

The day after the election, Secretary of Defense Donald Rumsfeld—a chief planner of the Iraq war—resigned. Bush chose Robert Gates to replace Rumsfeld and put a new commander—General David Patraeus—in charge of the forces in Iraq. The president then announced a "surge," or rapid increase, of some 20,000 more troops to Iraq.

House Democrats criticized the president's plan. They called for the president to set a **definite,** or precise, timetable for pulling U.S. troops out of Iraq. Whether or not the surge could work was unclear. However, by the autumn of 2007, what was clear was that Americans were divided over the Iraq war and that its outcome remained uncertain.

Reading Check **Summarizing** What did the Supreme Court rule in *Hamdan v. Rumsfeld*?

Section 4 Review

History ONLINE
Study Central™ To review this section, go to glencoe.com.

Vocabulary

1. Use each of these terms correctly in a sentence: terrorism, fundamentalist, counterterrorism, prior, insurgent, levee, definite.

Main Ideas

2. **Describing** How did Osama bin Laden become so strong in Afghanistan?

3. **Explaining** What powers did the USA Patriot Act give to federal officers?

4. **Analyzing** Why was the Supreme Court ruling in *Rasul v.Bush* important?

Critical Thinking

5. **Sequencing** On a time line like the one below, name the events in the war on terror that took place on these dates:

| Sept. 2001 | Oct. 2001 | June 2002 | March 2003 |

6. **Descriptive Writing** In a paragraph, describe how Hurricane Katrina affected specific areas as well as the entire United States.

Answer the
7. **Essential Question**
How has the war on terror changed the way Americans live?

YOU DECIDE

Should the Patriot Act Be Reauthorized?

Building Background

The USA Patriot Act gave federal law officials the power to track personal communications and check personal records. Federal officials can tap telephones and computers and get legal access to voice mail and e-mail messages. They could also obtain personal medical, financial, educational, and even library records without proof that a crime has been committed.

Congress passed the USA Patriot Act in 2001 and renewed it in 2006. Americans who supported it said it was an important part of the war on terror. Others, however, argued that the act represents a threat to civil liberties and privacy.

NO

CONGRESSWOMAN LOUISE McINTOSH SLAUGHTER

Mr. Speaker, I rise today in defense of nothing less than our national security, but national security is not just about protecting our borders. It is also about protecting our freedoms.

All of my colleagues understand that the PATRIOT Act has provided the law enforcement agencies with many valuable tools which facilitate[1] their work in the struggle against terrorism. But with these new tools comes a very real danger that the liberty we seek to protect could be easily compromised. . . .

We have evidence which suggests, in contrast to information coming out of the Justice Department, that many of these measures have resulted in the violation of the civil liberties of American citizens. In addition, we understand that some of the extended search and seizure powers used by the law enforcement are apparently not being used for their intended purpose, which is strictly to fight terrorism, and that is unacceptable.

Public protests of the Patriot Act

---

[1] **facilitate** to make easy

998

YES

ATTORNEY GENERAL JOHN ASHCROFT

Our responsibility was to reorganize our justice system from a backward-looking system focused on prosecution,[2] to a forward-looking system first focused on prevention. Our response was to track down and dismantle highly compartmentalized[3] terrorist networks. To forge new relationships of cooperation with other nations. To mobilize a frightened citizenry. To fight for new and needed tools for law enforcement. To do anything and everything we could under the Constitution to prevent further acts of terrorism. . . .

Congress provided these tools in the USA Patriot Act, . . . and while our job is not finished, we have used the tools provided in the Patriot Act to fulfill our first responsibility to protect the American people. We have used these tools to prevent terrorists from unleashing more death and destruction on our soil. We have used these tools to save innocent American lives. We have used these tools to provide the security that ensures liberty. . . .

America MUST remember. It is my commitment to you that we WILL remember. In the war against terror, we will not falter and we will not fail.

Firefighter in New York City on September 11, 2001

---

[2] **prosecution** the pursuit of legal action

[3] **compartmentalized** divided into separate sections

DBQ Document-Based Questions

1. **Interpreting** What does Ashcroft mean when he states, "We have used these tools to provide the security that ensures liberty"?

2. **Analyzing** What do Ashcroft and Slaughter agree about?

3. **Analyzing** What do Ashcroft and Slaughter disagree about?

4. **Evaluating** Who do you think makes the stronger argument: Ashcroft or Slaughter? Explain your answer.

Section 5 — Challenges Ahead

Essential Question ◄

How have economic and environmental developments led to the world's nations becoming more interdependent?

Reading Guide

Content Vocabulary

interdependent (p. 1001)

acid rain (p. 1003)

globalism (p. 1001)

global warming (p. 1004)

trade deficit (p. 1002)

deport (p. 1005)

free trade (p. 1002)

amnesty (p. 1005)

urban sprawl (p. 1003)

Academic Vocabulary

decade (p. 1001)   aware (p. 1003)

Reading Strategy

Taking Notes Complete a diagram like the one below by identifying three global challenges. Then explain why each of these is a problem.

NEW YORK STANDARDS
The American Journey

U11.I.2 To investigate key turning points in New York and United States history and explain why these events or developments are significant

U11.II.1 To understand the economic, social, and political trends that shaped the end of the 20th century and point to the 21st century

U11.II.2 To investigate problems and opportunities the United States faces in its immediate future

American Diary

In the 1960s, educator Marshall McLuhan used the phrase "the global village" to express the idea that electronic communication would unite the world. The Internet, for example, allows us to communicate with one another regardless of distance. Soon half the people of the world will access the Web, many through wireless devices. Already, more than 25 billion e-mails are sent internationally each day—that adds up to more than 9 trillion e-mails each year!

Students with learning disabilities in Brooklyn, New York, use laptop computers to work on reading skills.

The New Global Economy

Main Idea Advances in technology now link the United States to a global economy.

History and You Describe something you know about the way people live in another part of the world. How do you know what you know? Read to find out why the world has become more connected during the last 30 years.

. . . .

In recent years, the United States and other nations of the world have developed a global economy. This means that they are **interdependent,** or rely on one another for raw materials to make goods and for markets in which to sell goods. When the economies of countries are linked, a drought or a war in one region can cause price increases or shortages in another region far away.

The Technology Revolution

A major reason for the rise of the global economy is the technology revolution. Today we take for granted computers, cell phones, cable television, and compact discs. A few **decades**—periods of 10 years—ago, these things had either not been invented or were not widely available.

The invention that drives this revolution is the computer. In the 1960s, scientists developed the integrated circuit, a small electronic device. A decade later, more powerful circuits called microprocessors were developed. They made it possible to make smaller, faster computers that could store a lot of information.

Through their personal computers, people are now able to go on the Internet. This is a huge web of linked computer networks. The Internet has made global communications almost instantaneous.

Global Trade and the U.S.

The technology revolution has tied together people and nations more closely than before. It has contributed to the rise of **globalism.** This is the idea that the world's economies and societies are all part of one big system. Interaction is no longer limited by physical distance.

The United States is a key player in the global economy. Its large, productive economy, based on the free enterprise system, has made it a leader in world trade. The United States exports chemicals, farm products, and manufactured goods, as well as raw materials such as metals and cotton fiber.

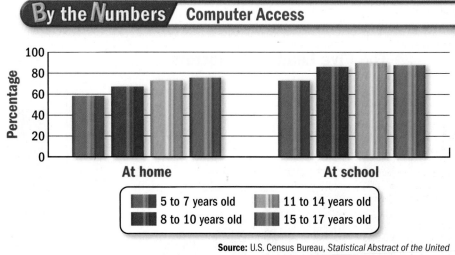

By the Numbers — Computer Access

Legend:
- 5 to 7 years old
- 8 to 10 years old
- 11 to 14 years old
- 15 to 17 years old

Source: U.S. Census Bureau, *Statistical Abstract of the United States*: 2006; U.S. National Center for Education Statistics

Critical Thinking

Calculating Which age group has the highest percentage of computer use at home? At school?

The nation imports most of its energy resources, however. The suppliers include Canada, Mexico, Saudi Arabia, and Nigeria.

The United States also buys many additional products from other countries. In fact, the United States spends hundreds of billions of dollars more on imports than it earns from exports. The result is a massive **trade deficit.** A trade deficit occurs when a country spends more on imports than it earns from exports. A trade deficit that lasts over a long period can cause economic troubles for a country.

Therefore, selling American-made goods has long been important to the prosperity of the United States. To further American economic growth, Republican and Democratic administrations since World War II have supported **free trade.** This means the removal of trade barriers so that goods flow freely among countries. In 2001 President Bush called for a world trading system that is dramatically open and more free:

PRIMARY SOURCE

"We know that nations that open their economies to the benefits of trade are more successful in climbing out of poverty. . . . We also know that free trade encourages the habits of liberty that sustain freedom."
—President George W. Bush in a speech to the World Bank

Since its formation in 1995, the World Trade Organization (WTO) has arranged numerous trade agreements and settled trade disputes among the nations of the world. Today, the WTO has more than 140 member countries.

Debate on Free Trade

As the world economy becomes more interconnected, Americans debate whether ending trade barriers helps or hinders the United States. Supporters claim that free trade generally helps the American economy. Those supporters say that American businesses make money selling more goods around the world.

Economics & History

The United States imports many manufactured goods from Japan. Automobiles are the largest single category. ▶

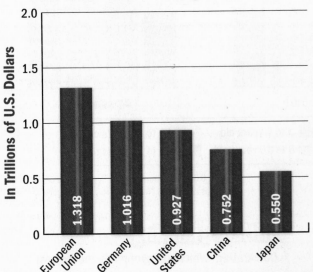

The Five Leading Exporters

In Trillions of U.S. Dollars

Country	Value
European Union	1.318
Germany	1.016
United States	0.927
China	0.752
Japan	0.550

Source: CIA World Factbook, 2006

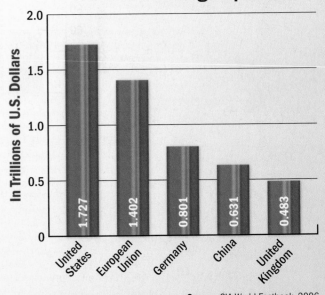

The Five Leading Importers

In Trillions of U.S. Dollars

Country	Value
United States	1.727
European Union	1.402
Germany	0.801
China	0.631
United Kingdom	0.483

Source: CIA World Factbook, 2006

They also claim that American consumers benefit by being able to buy foreign goods that are less expensive than those made in the United States. Supporters of free trade also state that importing low-cost goods keeps inflation and interest rates low.

Opponents, however, charge that free trade has caused manufacturing jobs to move from the United States to nations where wages are low and where there are fewer regulations. They state that having cheap imports available to buy does not help those Americans who can no longer find work because their industries have moved overseas. This transfer of work to other countries is called outsourcing. Because free trade affects jobs—and votes—the debate between supporters and opponents of free trade has become an important part of American politics.

Reading Check **Explaining** What does the World Trade Organization (WTO) do?

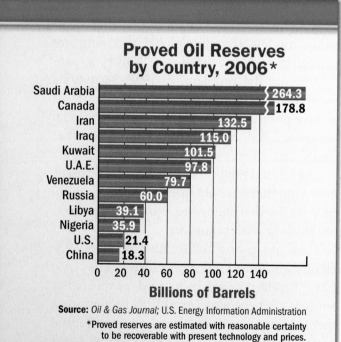

Proved Oil Reserves by Country, 2006*

Country	Billions of Barrels
Saudi Arabia	264.3
Canada	178.8
Iran	132.5
Iraq	115.0
Kuwait	101.5
U.A.E.	97.8
Venezuela	79.7
Russia	60.0
Libya	39.1
Nigeria	35.9
U.S.	21.4
China	18.3

Billions of Barrels

Source: *Oil & Gas Journal;* U.S. Energy Information Administration

*Proved reserves are estimated with reasonable certainty to be recoverable with present technology and prices.

Graph Skills

1. **Calculating** What is the difference in dollar amounts between U.S. exports and U.S. imports?

2. **Classifying** Which of the 12 nations shown on this graph are in South America? In Africa?

The Environment

Main Idea Concern about the environment has become a serious political issue in recent years.

History and You Have you seen instances of air or water pollution in your area? Read to learn about challenges to the nation's environment.

Globalism has made people **aware,** or mindful, of issues that affect the world as a whole. In recent years, people have become aware of dangers to the world environment. For example, many people fear that the Earth's resources will soon be unable to support a rapidly rising world population, especially in cities.

Urban sprawl, or the spread of human settlements into natural areas, has created many problems. Urban growth leads to the loss of farmland and wilderness areas. The building of homes and roadways also can produce traffic jams and increase air pollution. Growing populations put strains on water supplies, food supplies, and other resources as well. People in some areas that are growing rapidly want to slow the rate of growth. They fear that having too many people will destroy the wide-open spaces and scenery that attracted them.

Air and Water Pollution

The United States faces several environmental challenges. Air and water pollution remains a problem. Americans burn coal, oil, and natural gas to power their factories and run their cars. Burning these fossil fuels pollutes the air. The pollution mixes with water vapor in the air to make **acid rain,** or rain containing high amounts of chemical pollutants. Acid rain damages trees and harms rivers, lakes, and the stone used in buildings. The United States has acted to reduce the amount of chemicals that are released into the air. Climate experts are particularly concerned about damage to some areas in the eastern United States.

How Much Do We Recycle?

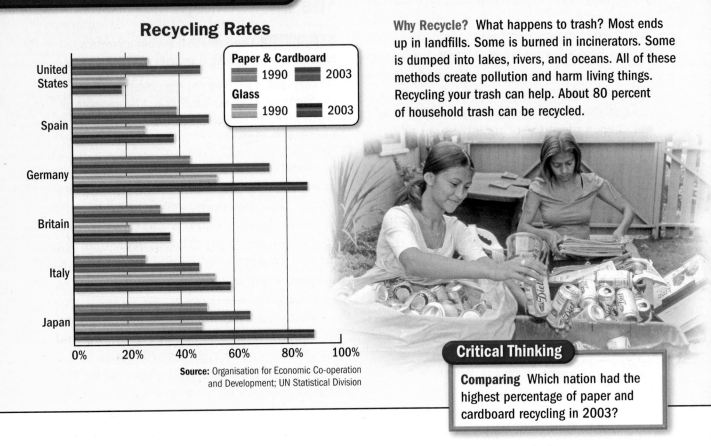

Recycling Rates

Paper & Cardboard: 1990, 2003
Glass: 1990, 2003

United States, Spain, Germany, Britain, Italy, Japan

0% 20% 40% 60% 80% 100%

Source: Organisation for Economic Co-operation and Development; UN Statistical Division

Why Recycle? What happens to trash? Most ends up in landfills. Some is burned in incinerators. Some is dumped into lakes, rivers, and oceans. All of these methods create pollution and harm living things. Recycling your trash can help. About 80 percent of household trash can be recycled.

Critical Thinking

Comparing Which nation had the highest percentage of paper and cardboard recycling in 2003?

Because pollution crosses international borders, many experts believe that nations have to work together to find solutions. In 1987, for example, 23 nations agreed to ban chemicals suspected of harming the ozone layer—a part of the atmosphere that shields Earth from the sun's radiation.

Global Warming

Many scientists also think that Earth is getting warmer and are worried that this might be caused by pollution. They claim that the increased burning of coal, oil, and natural gas has released more gases into the atmosphere. These gases have trapped more of the sun's heat near the Earth's surface, raising temperatures around the planet.

Such **global warming,** these scientists claim, will lead to changing weather patterns. For example, a warmer climate could lead to drought conditions in some areas and could melt the polar ice caps. Melting would raise ocean levels and flood low-lying coasts.

The issue of global warming has become very controversial. Critics argue that computer models showing global warming are unrealistic. Many nations, however, are addressing the problem. In 1997, 38 nations signed the Kyoto Protocol promising to reduce pollution that might be causing global warming, but few countries have put the treaty into effect.

The United States has not signed the treaty, believing that it would hurt economic growth. Still, the United States and many other nations are dealing with pollution.

They are trying to use energy more efficiently and burn coal more cleanly. They also have funded research to find new energy sources that are less harmful to the environment. Many countries already have adopted nonpolluting forms of energy such as wind and solar power.

Reading Check **Describing** How does acid rain affect the environment?

A Changing Society

Main Idea As the 2000s begin, immigrants and the elderly make up a larger share of the American population.

History and You Do you remember the reasons why some Americans objected to immigration in the 1800s? Read to find out how the debate on immigration continues today.

. . . .

As America enters the twenty-first century, its population is changing significantly. The number of older Americans has risen. Ways of living and working have changed as a result of new technologies. Above all, changes in U.S. laws and unstable conditions worldwide have led to a dramatic rise in the number of immigrants to the United States.

By 2007, nearly half of all the country's immigrants came from Latin America and Canada, and another third from various parts of Asia. Less than 15 percent came from Europe, the place of origin of most immigrants throughout U.S. history.

Illegal Immigration

Many immigrants have entered the United States legally, but an estimated 12 million of them have arrived without official permission. Today, most Americans view this illegal immigration as a serious challenge to the country. However, people are deeply divided about how to solve the problem.

Some Americans believe that letting illegal immigrants stay in the country undermines respect for the rule of law. They often call for illegal immigrants to be **deported,** or sent out of the country. Others are willing to grant **amnesty,** or a pardon, to people who are already here illegally so that they can take steps toward becoming citizens. To stop further illegal immigration, some people favor allowing potential immigrants to apply for temporary work permits and earn permanent residence if they learn English, pay back taxes, and have no criminal record.

Many Americans on both sides of the issue agree on the need for more border patrols. Some propose building a continuous wall from Texas to California.

U.S. Foreign-Born Population, 1850–2005

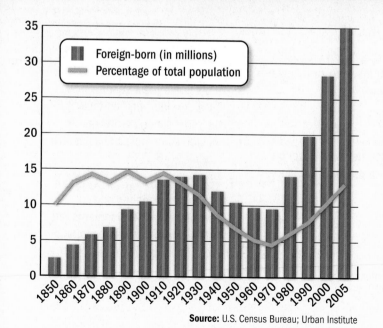

Legend:
- Foreign-born (in millions)
- Percentage of total population

(bar chart with years 1850, 1860, 1870, 1880, 1890, 1900, 1910, 1920, 1930, 1940, 1950, 1960, 1970, 1980, 1990, 2000, 2005; y-axis 0 to 35)

Source: U.S. Census Bureau; Urban Institute

Three generations of the Solano family from San Antonio, Texas ▶

Graph Skills

1. **Identifying** In what year did the foreign-born population reach its all-time high?

2. **Calculating** In what year did the foreign-born population reach its all-time numeric high? Percentage high?

Graphs In Motion See StudentWorks™ Plus or glencoe.com.

New Challenges **Chapter 31 1005**

They believe the wall is needed to prevent illegal immigration from Mexico. Critics of the wall-building proposal, however, claim that this would not stop people who are determined to enter the country illegally. Instead, it would force them to take more dangerous risks.

Health Issues

Immigration contributes to population growth. Another factor is natural population increase, or the surplus of births over deaths. Today, the United States has a larger percentage of young people than do other developed countries. Yet, the overall population of the country is aging. This aging is due to a rising birthrate and a declining death rate as well as to the effects of better health care.

Despite health advances, the rates of cancer have risen. Today, cancer and heart disease are the leading causes of death in the United States. This is because of an aging population, pollution, and the unhealthy lifestyle of many Americans who eat high-fat foods and do not exercise enough.

The United States devotes many resources to health care. Still, many Americans are unable to buy health insurance, and others cannot afford health care even with insurance. The high cost of health care also places a burden on businesses that provide health care to employees.

America on the Move

Being mobile, or moving from place to place, has always been a characteristic of American life. Widespread use of the automobile has given people a greater choice of where to live and work.

In recent decades, most of the nation's population growth has taken place in the West and South. These two regions attract residents because of their mild climates and growing industries. Meanwhile, areas of the North, East, and Midwest have lost population. There, heavy manufacturing has declined, although efforts are being made to build more high-tech businesses.

Reading Check **Summarizing** What factors have led to population growth?

Section 5 Review

History ONLINE
Study Central™ To review this section, go to glencoe.com.

Vocabulary

1. Use each of the following terms correctly in a sentence: interdependent, decade, globalism, trade deficit, free trade, aware, urban sprawl, acid rain, global warming, deport, amnesty.

Main Ideas

2. Analyzing How did international trade change the world economy?

3. Explaining What is the goal of the Kyoto Protocol?

4. Summarizing What proposals have been made to stop illegal immigration?

Critical Thinking

5. Organizing Complete a diagram like the one below to describe the characteristics of the global economy.

6. Expository Writing Identify the issue of global concern that you think is the most serious. In an essay, explain why you think it is the most serious problem. Include some possible solutions.

Answer the
7. Essential Question
How have economic and environmental developments led to the world's nations becoming more interdependent?

Reagan's Agenda

- Supply-side economics to boost the economy
- Military buildup to fight communism
- Treaty with Soviets to reduce nuclear arms

World Change

- Communism collapses in Eastern Europe and the Soviet Union
- Persian Gulf War/Operation Desert Storm
- Economic recession weakens President Bush's reelection campaign

The Clinton Years

- Clinton and Congress cut spending; reform welfare and health care
- U.S. economy grows; federal budget is balanced
- Scandal and impeachment tarnish the Clinton administration

Bush Takes Office

- Supreme Court resolves 2000 election results dispute; George W. Bush becomes president
- Bush focuses on cutting taxes and reforming education
- Terrorists destroy the World Trade Center and attack the Pentagon
- Bush launches war on terror

Toward the Future

- World trade plays major part in global interdependence
- Global community faces serious environmental problems
- Population increases due to immigration and aging Americans

▲ First section of Berlin Wall torn down, November 10, 1989

Presidential candidate Bill Clinton at campaign rally ▼

California teens clean up trash and litter ▼

▲ Worker walks through the rubble of the World Trade Center, September 11, 2001

STUDY TO GO — Study anywhere, anytime! Download quizzes and flash cards to your PDA from glencoe.com.

New Challenges **Chapter 31 1007**

Immigration

The United States is undergoing its fourth great period of immigration. According to the Census Bureau, the number of foreign-born in the United States increased from 19.8 million in 1990 to 31.1 million in 2000. Never before have so many people immigrated to America.

How Does Geography Affect Immigration?

In recent years, most immigrants to the United States have come from Latin America and Asia. By far the greatest number is from Mexico. While immigration has increased, its effects have not been felt in equal measure throughout the country. Immigrants have tended to settle in the more densely populated areas of the United States: California, Florida, Texas, and the Northeast. The foreign-born population of the United States is growing four times faster than the native-born population. Over the next 50 years, immigrants will account for two-thirds of U.S. population growth.

▼ Mexican American celebration

U.S. Immigration: Place of Origin, 2004

0   4,000 kilometers
0   4,000 miles
Miller Cylindrical projection

Percentage of Population Immigrating to the U.S.

| >15% | 3–4.9% | <1% |
| 5–15% | 1–2.9% | |

California road signs in English and Spanish ▼

DANGER
STAY OUT / STAY ALIVE
216
LIVES LOST IN KERN RIVER SINCE 1968

PELIGRO
POR FAVOR / NO NADE
216
VIDAS PERDIDAS EN EL RIO KERN DESDE 1968

◄ **Becoming Citizens**
Immigrants to America can apply to become U.S. citizens. Applicants must offer proof of residence; evidence of good moral character; and knowledge of the history and government of the United States. In most cases, applicants must have a basic knowledge of the English language.

Asian seafood shop in New York City's Chinatown ▶

U.S. Foreign-Born Population

Foreign-born population as a percentage of county population, 2000

- 23.4–50%
- 11.2–23.3%
- 7.1–11.1%
- 3.0–7.0%
- 0–2.9%

▲ Sign in English and Arabic urging people to vote

Illegal Immigration

Americans are divided over what to do about the illegal population living in the United States. Solutions have ranged from finding and deporting all illegals, to granting various forms of legalization and naturalization, to building a wall along the 2,000-mile (3,219 km) border with Mexico.

As recently as 1960, almost three-quarters of all immigrants to America came from Europe. Today, eight of every ten immigrants to the U.S. come from Asia or Latin America. ▶

Foreign-Born Population by Region of Birth

1960

- 5%
- 10%
- 1%
- 1%
- 9%
- 74%

2000

- 3%
- 3%
- 26%
- 16%
- 52%

- Europe
- Latin America
- Asia
- Northern America
- Other regions (Oceania and Africa)
- Not reported

Source: Migration Policy Institute

Analyzing Geography

1. **Location** Use the map on the previous page to identify the part of the world that provided the most U.S. immigrants.
2. **Movement** How do you think the United States will be different in 2050 because of current immigration patterns? Explain.

GRADE 8 INTERMEDIATE TEST PRACTICE

TEST-TAKING TIP

Answer the questions you know first and go back to those for which you need more time.

Reviewing Main Ideas

Directions: Choose the best answers for each of the following questions.

1 One result of Reagan's approach to government was

   (1) safe, environmentally friendly cars.

   (2) more housing for low-income families.

   (3) a tripling of the 1980 federal debt.

   (4) a reduction in troop levels.

2 How did the federal government deal with the failures of S&Ls during the late 1980s?

   (1) bailouts

   (2) deregulation

   (3) spending cuts

   (4) supply-side economics

3 Which of Clinton's goals went unrealized?

   (1) stricter gun control

   (2) a federal budget surplus

   (3) family leave for workers

   (4) health care for all Americans

4 A major result of George W. Bush's presidency was

   (1) a more conservative Supreme Court.

   (2) the expansion of U.S. citizens' rights.

   (3) federal budget surpluses.

   (4) improved relations with the Middle East.

5 Which pair of environmental terms has a cause-and-effect relationship?

   (1) chemicals and urban sprawl

   (2) acid rain and solar radiation

   (3) global warming and rising seas

   (4) water pollution and the ozone layer

Short-Answer Question

Directions: Base your answer to question 6 on the excerpt below and on your knowledge of social studies.

> A few months ago I told the American people I did not trade arms for hostages. My heart and my best intentions still tell me that's true, but the facts and the evidence tell me it is not. . . . [N]o one kept proper records of meetings or decisions. This led to my failure to recollect whether I approved an arms shipment before or after the fact. I did approve it; I just can't say specifically when.
>
> —from President Reagan's address to the nation about Iran-Contra

6 Why do you think the Iran-Contra hearings never produced any proof of the president's involvement?

Review the Essential Questions

7 **Essay** How are the U.S. economy and environment today linked to the policies of Reagan, Clinton, and the Bushes?

To help you write your essay, review your answers to the Essential Questions in the section reviews and the chapter Foldables Study Organizer. Your essay should include:

- the effects of military spending on the economy;
- the effects of deregulation on the environment;
- the effects of NAFTA on American jobs; and
- the effects of spending on the war in Iraq on the economy.

GO ON

Drawing Inferences and Conclusions

Why Learn This Skill?

When you make an *inference*, you "read between the lines," or use clues to figure something out that is not stated directly in the text. A *conclusion* is a logical understanding that you reach based on details or facts that you read or hear. By drawing inferences and conclusions you can formulate ideas and make decisions.

Jefferson Davis ▶

 Learn It!

Follow these steps to draw inferences and conclusions:

1. Read carefully for facts and ideas, and list them.

2. Summarize the information.

3. Consider what you may already know about the topic.

4. Use your knowledge and insight to develop some logical conclusions based on the facts.

> *There can be but little rivalry between ours and any manufacturing or navigating community, such as the Northeastern States of the American Union. It must follow, therefore, that a mutual interest would invite good will and kind offices. If, however, passion or the lust of dominion [power] should cloud the judgment or inflame the ambition of those States, we must prepare to meet the emergency and to maintain, by the final [deciding power] of the sword, the position which we have assumed among the nations of the earth. We have entered upon the career of independence, and it must be inflexibly pursued. . . . As a necessity, not a choice, we have resorted to the remedy of separation; and henceforth our energies must be directed to the conduct of our own affairs, and the [lasting life] of the Confederacy which we have formed.*
>
> —Jefferson Davis's inaugural speech,
> February 18, 1861

 Practice It!

After reading the passage above, answer the following questions:

1. What points does the author make?
2. Which point does your experience contradict?
3. What inference can you make about the Confederate states' reasons for declaring their independence?
4. What conclusions can you draw about Davis' beliefs about a possible war?

 Apply It!

Read an editorial printed in today's newspaper. What can you infer about the importance of the topic being addressed? Can you tell how the writer feels about the topic? Explain your answer.

Writing a Paragraph

Why Learn This Skill?

Paragraphs are the building blocks of an essay or other composition. Each paragraph is a unit—a group of sentences about a single topic or idea.

Washington observes Von Steuben drilling troops at Valley Forge ▶

1 Learn It!

Most well-written paragraphs share four characteristics:

At first glance the British had an overwhelming advantage in the war. They had the strongest navy in the world. They also had an experienced, well-trained army and the wealth of a worldwide empire. Britain also had a much larger population than the United States. There were over 8 million people in Britain, compared with only 2.5 million in the United States.

1. A paragraph expresses one main idea or is about one subject. A topic sentence states the main idea, and may be located at the beginning, middle, or end of the paragraph.

2. The rest of the sentences support the main idea. The main idea may be developed by facts, examples, or reasons.

3. The sentences are arranged in a logical order.

4. Transitional words link sentences within the paragraph. Examples include *next, then, finally, also, because, however,* and *as a result.*

2 Practice It!

Use the following sentences to build a paragraph containing a topic sentence and other sentences that give supporting details. Put the sentences in a logical order and add transitional words if you need to. Underline your topic sentence.

1. They were forced to ship soldiers and supplies thousands of miles across the Atlantic.

2. They were fighting on their own ground and fought with great determination to protect it.

3. The Americans possessed some advantages.

4. The British, in contrast, had to wage war in a faraway land.

3 Apply It!

Choose a topic from the era of the Revolutionary War and write a paragraph about it. Then rewrite the paragraph with its sentences out of order. Exchange papers with a classmate. Can he or she find the topic sentence? Does it read logically?

Taking Notes and Outlining

Why Learn This Skill?

Taking notes and outlining are ways of recording important information about what you read. Both methods also help you recall information. Writing down information in a brief and orderly form helps you remember key points and makes it easier to study.

Outlining is similar to sketching a scene. First, you draw the rough shape, or outline, of the picture. Then you fill in the details. Outlining helps you identify main ideas and group related facts.

 Learn It!

To learn how to take notes, use the following steps:

1. **Identify** the subject and write it at the top of your page.

2. **Select** specific details that support the main subject and include them in your notes. Look for topic sentences of paragraphs and words in bold or italics.

3. **Paraphrase** the information. Putting it in your own words helps you understand the meaning of the information.

4. **Condense** words into a personal shorthand, such as dropping vowels ("develop" becomes "dvlp"), and use symbols ("and" becomes "+") to save time.

*In 1776 the Second Continental Congress appointed a committee to draw up a plan for a new government. After much debate the Congress adopted the **Articles of Confederation** in November 1777. The Articles, America's first constitution, provided for a new central government under which the states kept most of their power. For the states, the Articles of Confederation were "a firm league of friendship" in which each state retained "its sovereignty, freedom and independence." Under the Articles of Confederation, Congress had the authority to conduct foreign affairs, maintain armed forces, borrow money, and issue currency.*

 Practice It!

Read the excerpt above. Then, on a separate sheet of paper, take notes on the paragraph. Be sure to consider the following questions.

1. What is the subject of the paragraph?
2. What is the main point of the paragraph?
3. What details are especially important to write down?

 Apply It!

Read a short article from a local newspaper about a governmental issue. Outline the important information. Write a short summary of the article using only your outline.

Summarizing Information

Why Learn This Skill?

Imagine you have been assigned a long chapter to read. How can you remember the important facts? Summarizing information means that you reduce large amounts of information to a few key phrases. Being able to summarize can help you remember the main ideas and key details.

Statue of Liberty ▶

 Learn It!

To summarize information, follow these guidelines when you read:

1. Read through the selection. Determine the main idea and the most important supporting details.

2. A summary can be a sentence or a short paragraph that includes the main ideas. In your summary, restate the text using your own words. Be brief—do not include many supporting details.

3. For the first paragraph, a summary statement might be: By the early 1900s, immigration patterns were changing and most new immigrants came from southern and eastern Europe.

In the mid-1880s, the pattern of immigration started to change. Large groups of "new" immigrants arrived from eastern and southern Europe. Greeks, Russians, Hungarians, Italians, Turks, and Poles were among the newcomers. At the same time, the number of "old" immigrants from northern and western Europe started to decrease. By 1907, 80 percent of immigrants came from southern and eastern Europe.

Many of these newcomers were Catholics or Jews. Few spoke English. Because of this, they did not blend into American society as easily as the "old" immigrants had. Often, they clustered together in neighborhoods made up of people of the same nationality.

 Practice It!

After reading the excerpt above, answer the following questions:

1. In a summary of the first paragraph, would you include the statement, "The number of 'old' immigrants decreased"? Why or why not?

2. Write a summary statement for the second paragraph.

 Apply It!

Read the section titled "Citizen Participation" of the Constitution Handbook of this book. Summarize the information in two or three sentences.

Reading a Time Line

Why Learn This Skill?

Knowing the relationship of time to events is important in studying history. A time line is a visual way to show the flow of dates and events in the correct order that they occurred. On many time lines, the years are evenly spaced. For example, a time line showing 1,000 years might be divided into ten 100-year intervals. Each event on a time line is described beside the date when the event took place.

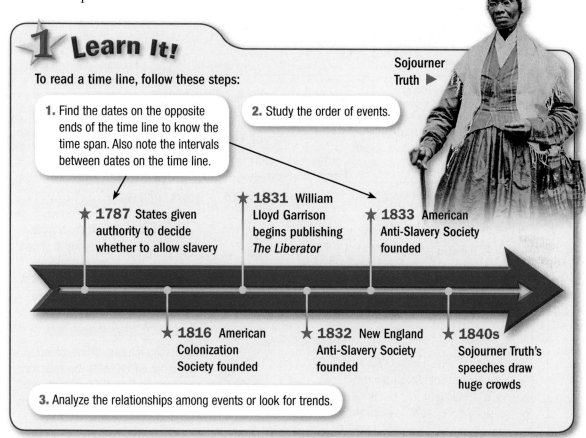

Learn It!

To read a time line, follow these steps:

Sojourner Truth ►

1. Find the dates on the opposite ends of the time line to know the time span. Also note the intervals between dates on the time line.

2. Study the order of events.

★ **1787** States given authority to decide whether to allow slavery

★ **1831** William Lloyd Garrison begins publishing *The Liberator*

★ **1833** American Anti-Slavery Society founded

★ **1816** American Colonization Society founded

★ **1832** New England Anti-Slavery Society founded

★ **1840s** Sojourner Truth's speeches draw huge crowds

3. Analyze the relationships among events or look for trends.

Practice It!

Analyze the time line about the Abolition movement. Use it to answer the questions that follow.

1. What time span is represented?

2. Which occurred first: the founding of the American Colonization Society or the founding of the American Anti-Slavery Society?

3. How many years after states were allowed to decide the issue of slavery did William Lloyd Garrison begin publishing *The Liberator*?

Apply It!

List 10 key events that have occurred in your life and the dates on which these events occurred. Write the events in chronological order on a time line.

Understanding Parts of a Map

Why Learn This Skill?

Maps can direct you down the street or around the world. There are as many different kinds of maps as there are uses for them. Being able to read a map begins with learning about its parts.

1 Learn It!

To understand the parts of a map, follow these steps:

The French and Indian War, 1754–1763

1. Locate the map key, which explains the meaning of special colors, symbols, and lines used on the map.

2. Find the compass rose, which shows the cardinal directions of north, south, east, and west.

3. Look for a measuring line, called a scale bar, which helps you estimate distance on a map. Example: 1 inch (2.54 cm) on the map may represent 100 miles (160.9 cm) on the Earth.

2 Practice It!

The map above shows the territories held by Great Britain and France in North America, as well as the battles between these two countries in their quests to control the North American continent. Look at the parts of the map and then answer the following questions:

1. What color shows the disputed territory?

2. Which direction would you travel to go from Fort Oswego to Boston?

3. About how many miles was it from New York City to Fort Ticonderoga?

4. Who won the battle in Quebec?

3 Apply It!

Create a mental image of your house. Draw a map showing the location of various areas. Include a map key to explain any symbols or colors you use, as well as a scale bar to explain the size of your map compared to the real area. Finally, add a compass rose and title to your map.

Recognizing Historical Perspectives

Why Learn This Skill?

As you study historical events or read primary sources from the past, you may be surprised by the actions taking place or the beliefs being expressed. To accurately evaluate the event or statement, you must carefully consider the time period and the experiences and viewpoints of the people involved.

1 Learn It!

To learn how to recognize historical perspectives, ask yourself these questions:

1. When was the statement made? To what event or time does the statement refer, and what other related events had occurred before or were occurring at the time?

2. Who is the author or speaker of the statement? What past experiences or current considerations might influence that person's viewpoint?

3. Why is it important to think critically about historical perspectives?

An 1868 treaty was supposed to bring peace, but tensions remained and erupted in more fighting. This time the conflict arose over the Black Hills of the Dakotas. The government had promised that "No white person or persons shall be permitted" to settle on the Black Hills. However, the hills were rumored to contain gold, and white prospectors swarmed into the area.

The Sioux protested against the trespassers. Instead of protecting the Sioux's rights, the government tried to buy the hills. Sitting Bull, an important leader of the Lakota Sioux, refused. "I do not want to sell any land. Not even this much," he said, holding a pinch of dust.

2 Practice It!

Read the excerpt above and answer the following questions:

1. What conflict is being discussed in the excerpt above?

2. What past events and beliefs may have influenced Sitting Bull's statement? How did white and Native American beliefs about land differ at that time?

3. How does recognizing historical perspectives help you better understand the events and statements related to a historical period?

3 Apply It!

Look in a current newspaper or news-magazine to find an example of a conflict between two or more groups of people. Write a short summary of how their perspectives of each other have determined their historical and current relationships.

Analyzing News Media

Why Learn This Skill?

Every citizen needs to be aware of current issues and events to make good decisions when exercising citizenship rights. To get an accurate profile of current events, you must learn to think critically about the news.

Herbert Hoover ▶

1 Learn It!

The following steps will help you think critically:

1. Think about the source of the news story. Reports that reveal sources are more reliable than those that do not. If you know the sources, you can evaluate them for reliability and bias.

2. Many news stories also interpret events. Such analyses may reflect a reporter's biases. Look for biases as you read or listen to news stories.

3. Ask yourself whether the news is even-handed and thorough. Is it reported on the scene or secondhand? Does it represent both sides of an issue?

AIM TO PACK COURT, DECLARES HOOVER

President Roosevelt's message to Congress asking for authority to appoint new Federal judges whenever existing ones were over 70 years old was characterized last night by Herbert Hoover, his predecessor in the White House, as a proposal for "packing" the Supreme Court to get through New Deal measures. . . .

"The Supreme Court has proved many of the New Deal proposals as unconstitutional. Instead of the ample alternatives of the Constitution by which these proposals could be submitted to the people through constitutional amendment, it is now proposed to make changes by 'packing' the Supreme Court. It has the implication of subordination of the court to the personal power of the Executive."

2 Practice It!

The excerpt above is from the *New York Times* newspaper of February 6, 1937. Read the passage; then answer the following questions:

1. What point is the article trying to make?
2. Is the article reporting something on the scene or secondhand?
3. Does the article reflect bias or strong opinion about the issue?
4. Is only one side of the issue presented? Explain.

3 Apply It!

Think of a current issue in the news that is controversial or in which public opinion is divided. Read newspaper features and editorials and watch television reports on the issue. Can you identify biases? Which reports more fairly represent the issue and the solutions? Which reports are the most reliable?

Analyzing Primary and Secondary Sources

Why Learn This Skill?

To determine what happened in the past, historians do some detective work. They comb through bits of written and illustrated evidence from the past to reconstruct events. These bits of evidence are called *primary sources.* They are records of events made by people who witnessed them. Primary sources include letters, diaries, photographs, newspaper articles, and legal documents.

This textbook, like many other history books, is a secondary source. It was written by using primary sources to explain the topics covered. The value of a secondary source depends on how well the author has used primary sources. Learning to analyze secondary sources will help you figure out whether they are presenting topics completely and accurately.

Dr. Martin Luther King, Jr. ▶

 Learn It!

To analyze a **primary source,** follow these steps:

We have waited for more than 340 years for our constitutional and God-given rights . . . [W]e still creep at horse and buggy pace toward gaining a cup of coffee at a lunch counter. Perhaps it is easy for those who have never felt the stinging darts of segregation to say, 'Wait.'. . . Let us all hope that the dark clouds of racial prejudice will soon pass away.

—Dr. Martin Luther King, Jr.
Letter from Birmingham Jail, April 1963

1. Identify the author, the publication, or the document.

2. Determine when and where the document was written or illustrated.

3. Read the document or study the illustration for its content. Try to answer the five "W" questions:
Whom is it about?
What is it about?
When did it happen?
Where did it happen?
Why did it happen?

 Practice It!

The primary source above is a small part of a letter written by civil rights leader Dr. Martin Luther King, Jr., while he was in an Alabama jail.

1. When was the letter written?

2. To whom do you think the letter was written?

3. Why do you think Dr. King wrote the letter?

4. How do you know this is a primary source and not a secondary source?

 Apply It!

Find a primary source and a secondary source related to a single historical topic. In several paragraphs, compare and contrast the information presented in the two sources.

Analyzing Historical Maps

Why Learn This Skill?

Historical maps show a portion of the world at a specific time in history. These maps can show physical, political, economic, climatic, or cultural information as it relates to that time period. They are useful because of the concise, visual way they present information.

1 Learn It!

To read a historical map, follow these steps:

1. Read the title to see what topic is illustrated. The specific time period is often referenced in the title.

2. Read the legend and any other text.

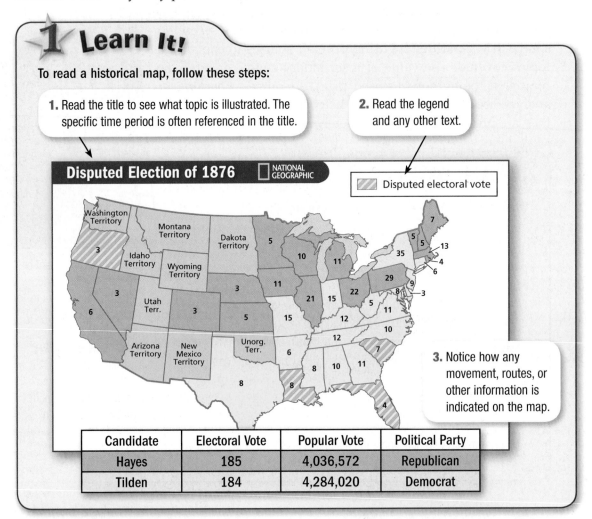

Disputed Election of 1876 — NATIONAL GEOGRAPHIC

Disputed electoral vote

3. Notice how any movement, routes, or other information is indicated on the map.

Candidate	Electoral Vote	Popular Vote	Political Party
Hayes	185	4,036,572	Republican
Tilden	184	4,284,020	Democrat

2 Practice It!

Answer the following questions about the map above:

1. What event and time in history does the map cover?

2. For whom did most Northern states vote?

3. In which states were the electoral votes disputed?

4. Why are there no numbers for electoral votes in the territories?

3 Apply It!

Study the United States Territorial Growth maps on pages Ref 10–Ref 11 in the front of your textbook. Then answer these questions:

1. In which general direction did growth take place?

2. What time period is covered in the last map?

Researching on the Internet

Why Learn This Skill?

Imagine that your teacher has sent you to the Internet to research and write a report about the current makeup of the United States Congress. Knowing how to locate and choose sources that contain accurate and current information will help save you time. You will also be able to write a better and more accurate report.

Joint meeting of Congress ▶

 Learn It!

Information on the Internet varies widely in its relevance and quality. Not all sources will be useful for your report on members of the Senate and House of Representatives. After choosing a search engine and typing in your topic, follow these steps to help you evaluate and select Internet resources:

1. Locate the author of the Web site and assess his/her qualifications. Is the person or organization credible and legitimate?

2. Evaluate the accuracy of the information. Are the facts on the site documented? Does the site contain a bibliography?

3. Judge whether the information is biased. Does the author present only one point of view?

4. Determine how the information is presented. Are there helpful visuals? Does the text skim the surface or offer in-depth details?

5. Review when the site was last updated. Is the information current?

6. Look for a list of links to other useful resources. Is the information on those sites appropriate and reliable?

 Practice It!

Look at the following list of sources. Which would be most helpful in writing a report on the United States Congress? Explain your choices.

1. An online encyclopedia written by anyone who wants to contribute

2. www.senate.gov, the home page for the U.S. Senate

3. A student's notes on the Internet about a family trip to Washington, D.C.

4. A government site on Congressional documents drawn up between 1774 and 1785

 Apply It!

Log onto the Internet to create a bibliography of six sources you might use to write your report. Explain why you would choose each source. Make sure you include information about both the House of Representatives and the Senate, including a breakdown of the membership of each.

Interpreting a Political Cartoon

Why Learn This Skill?

Political cartoons express opinions through art. The cartoons appear in newspapers, magazines, books, and on the Internet. Political cartoons usually focus on public figures, political events, or economic or social conditions. This type of art can give you a summary of an event or circumstance, along with the artist's opinion in an entertaining way.

1 Learn It!

Follow these steps to interpret a political cartoon:

1. Read the title, caption, or conversation balloons. They help you identify the subject of the cartoon.

2. Identify the characters, people, or symbols shown. Symbols are objects that stand for something else.

3. Examine the actions in the cartoon. Ask yourself: What is happening and why?

4. Identify the cartoonist's purpose; is it to persuade, criticize, or just make people think? What statement or idea is he or she trying to express?

SECESSIONISTS LEAVING THE UNION

2 Practice It!

Study the cartoon above. Then answer these questions:

1. What is the subject of the cartoon?
2. What words give clues to the meaning of the cartoon?
3. What is happening in the cartoon?
4. What message do you think the cartoonist is trying to send?

3 Apply It!

Bring a newsmagazine to class. With a partner, analyze the message in each political cartoon you find.

Writing a Case Study

Why Learn This Skill?

Have you ever wondered what can be done to help keep your community clean? A case study on environmental clean-up and recycling would help define the issue and propose various solutions to the problem.

A case study is an in-depth analysis of a particular situation or problem that could apply to a broader field. It involves thorough research and interviews to gain a better understanding of a problem and to suggest solutions. In this example, a case study might be done on the placement of recycling bins for aluminum cans to determine that action's effect on the community. This type of research tool can help both the writer and reader gain a more extensive understanding of a situation.

 Learn It!

To learn how to write a case study, follow these steps:

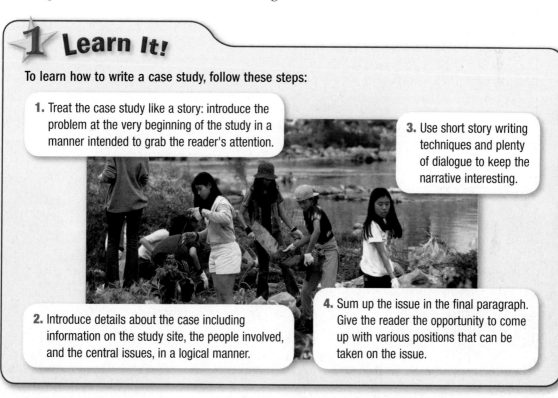

1. Treat the case study like a story: introduce the problem at the very beginning of the study in a manner intended to grab the reader's attention.

2. Introduce details about the case including information on the study site, the people involved, and the central issues, in a logical manner.

3. Use short story writing techniques and plenty of dialogue to keep the narrative interesting.

4. Sum up the issue in the final paragraph. Give the reader the opportunity to come up with various positions that can be taken on the issue.

Practice It!

Identify a situation or event described in this book that you think could be investigated as a case study. Write a case study in which you answer the following questions:

1. Is there a problem/issue that could apply to a broader group of people?

2. What are the major issues, and who is involved?

3. What solutions have been attempted and what others could be tried?

 Apply It!

Research to find two sources of information on the topic of banning teenagers from using cell phones while driving. Create fictional characters that might be affected by a law like this. Use your sources and your imagination to write a one-page case study on the topic.

Presidents of the United States

In this resource, you will find portraits of the individuals who served as presidents of the United States, along with their occupations, political party affiliations, and other interesting facts.

George Washington 1

Presidential term: 1789–1797
Lived: 1732–1799
Born in: Virginia
Elected from: Virginia
Occupations: Soldier, Planter
Party: None
Vice President: John Adams

John Adams 2

Presidential term: 1797–1801
Lived: 1735–1826
Born in: Massachusetts
Elected from: Massachusetts
Occupations: Teacher, Lawyer
Party: Federalist
Vice President: Thomas Jefferson

Thomas Jefferson 3

Presidential term: 1801–1809
Lived: 1743–1826
Born in: Virginia
Elected from: Virginia
Occupations: Planter, Lawyer
Party: Republican**
Vice Presidents: Aaron Burr,
George Clinton

James Madison 4

Presidential term: 1809–1817
Lived: 1751–1836
Born in: Virginia
Elected from: Virginia
Occupation: Planter
Party: Republican**
Vice Presidents: George Clinton,
Elbridge Gerry

James Monroe 5

Presidential term: 1817–1825
Lived: 1758–1831
Born in: Virginia
Elected from: Virginia
Occupation: Lawyer
Party: Republican**
Vice President: Daniel D. Tompkins

John Quincy Adams 6

Presidential term: 1825–1829
Lived: 1767–1848
Born in: Massachusetts
Elected from: Massachusetts
Occupation: Lawyer
Party: Republican**
Vice President: John C. Calhoun

Andrew Jackson 7

Presidential term: 1829–1837
Lived: 1767–1845
Born in: South Carolina
Elected from: Tennessee
Occupations: Lawyer, Soldier
Party: Democratic
Vice Presidents: John C. Calhoun,
Martin Van Buren

Martin Van Buren 8

Presidential term: 1837–1841
Lived: 1782–1862
Born in: New York
Elected from: New York
Occupation: Lawyer
Party: Democratic
Vice President: Richard M.
Johnson

William H. Harrison 9

Presidential term: 1841
Lived: 1773–1841
Born in: Virginia
Elected from: Ohio
Occupations: Soldier, Planter
Party: Whig
Vice President: John Tyler

** *The Republican Party during this period developed into today's Democratic Party. Today's Republican Party originated in 1854.*

Presidents of the United States

John Tyler 10

Presidential term: 1841–1845
Lived: 1790–1862
Born in: Virginia
Elected as V.P. from: Virginia
Succeeded Harrison
Occupation: Lawyer
Party: Whig
Vice President: None

James K. Polk 11

Presidential term: 1845–1849
Lived: 1795–1849
Born in: North Carolina
Elected from: Tennessee
Occupation: Lawyer
Party: Democratic
Vice President: George M. Dallas

Zachary Taylor 12

Presidential term: 1849–1850
Lived: 1784–1850
Born in: Virginia
Elected from: Louisiana
Occupation: Soldier
Party: Whig
Vice President: Millard Fillmore

Millard Fillmore 13

Presidential term: 1850–1853
Lived: 1800–1874
Born in: New York
Elected as V.P. from: New York
Succeeded Taylor
Occupation: Lawyer
Party: Whig
Vice President: None

Franklin Pierce 14

Presidential term: 1853–1857
Lived: 1804–1869
Born in: New Hampshire
Elected from: New Hampshire
Occupation: Lawyer
Party: Democratic
Vice President: William R. King

James Buchanan 15

Presidential term: 1857–1861
Lived: 1791–1868
Born in: Pennsylvania
Elected from: Pennsylvania
Occupation: Lawyer
Party: Democratic
Vice President: John C. Breckinridge

Abraham Lincoln 16

Presidential term: 1861–1865
Lived: 1809–1865
Born in: Kentucky
Elected from: Illinois
Occupation: Lawyer
Party: Republican
Vice Presidents: Hannibal Hamlin, Andrew Johnson

Andrew Johnson 17

Presidential term: 1865–1869
Lived: 1808–1875
Born in: North Carolina
Elected as V.P. from: Tennessee
Succeeded Lincoln
Occupation: Tailor
Party: Republican
Vice President: None

Ulysses S. Grant 18

Presidential term: 1869–1877
Lived: 1822–1885
Born in: Ohio
Elected from: Illinois
Occupations: Farmer, Soldier
Party: Republican
Vice Presidents: Schuyler Colfax, Henry Wilson

Rutherford B. Hayes 19

Presidential term: 1877–1881
Lived: 1822–1893
Born in: Ohio
Elected from: Ohio
Occupation: Lawyer
Party: Republican
Vice President: William A. Wheeler

James A. Garfield 20

Presidential term: 1881
Lived: 1831–1881
Born in: Ohio
Elected from: Ohio
Occupations: Laborer, Professor
Party: Republican
Vice President: Chester A. Arthur

Chester A. Arthur 21

Presidential term: 1881–1885
Lived: 1830–1886
Born in: Vermont
Elected as V.P. from: New York
Succeeded Garfield
Occupations: Teacher, Lawyer
Party: Republican
Vice President: None

Grover Cleveland 22

Presidential term: 1885–1889
Lived: 1837–1908
Born in: New Jersey
Elected from: New York
Occupation: Lawyer
Party: Democratic
Vice President: Thomas A. Hendricks

Benjamin Harrison 23

Presidential term: 1889–1893
Lived: 1833–1901
Born in: Ohio
Elected from: Indiana
Occupation: Lawyer
Party: Republican
Vice President: Levi P. Morton

Grover Cleveland 24

Presidential term: 1893–1897
Lived: 1837–1908
Born in: New Jersey
Elected from: New York
Occupation: Lawyer
Party: Democratic
Vice President: Adlai E. Stevenson

William McKinley 25

Presidential term: 1897–1901
Lived: 1843–1901
Born in: Ohio
Elected from: Ohio
Occupations: Teacher, Lawyer
Party: Republican
Vice Presidents: Garret Hobart, Theodore Roosevelt

Theodore Roosevelt 26

Presidential term: 1901–1909
Lived: 1858–1919
Born in: New York
Elected as V.P. from: New York
Succeeded McKinley
Occupations: Historian, Rancher
Party: Republican
Vice President: Charles W. Fairbanks

William H. Taft 27

Presidential term: 1909–1913
Lived: 1857–1930
Born in: Ohio
Elected from: Ohio
Occupation: Lawyer
Party: Republican
Vice President: James S. Sherman

Woodrow Wilson 28

Presidential term: 1913–1921
Lived: 1856–1924
Born in: Virginia
Elected from: New Jersey
Occupation: College Professor
Party: Democratic
Vice President: Thomas R. Marshall

Warren G. Harding 29

Presidential term: 1921–1923
Lived: 1865–1923
Born in: Ohio
Elected from: Ohio
Occupations: Newspaper Editor, Publisher
Party: Republican
Vice President: Calvin Coolidge

Calvin Coolidge 30

Presidential term: 1923–1929
Lived: 1872–1933
Born in: Vermont
Elected as V.P. from: Massachusetts; succeeded Harding
Occupation: Lawyer
Party: Republican
Vice President: Charles G. Dawes

Herbert C. Hoover 31

Presidential term: 1929–1933
Lived: 1874–1964
Born in: Iowa
Elected from: California
Occupation: Engineer
Party: Republican
Vice President: Charles Curtis

Franklin D. Roosevelt 32

Presidential term: 1933–1945
Lived: 1882–1945
Born in: New York
Elected from: New York
Occupation: Lawyer
Party: Democratic
Vice Presidents: John N. Garner, Henry A. Wallace, Harry S. Truman

Harry S. Truman 33

Presidential term: 1945–1953
Lived: 1884–1972
Born in: Missouri
Elected as V.P. from: Missouri Succeeded Roosevelt
Occupations: Clerk, Farmer
Party: Democratic
Vice President: Alben W. Barkley

Dwight D. Eisenhower 34

Presidential term: 1953–1961
Lived: 1890–1969
Born in: Texas
Elected from: New York
Occupation: Soldier
Party: Republican
Vice President: Richard M. Nixon

John F. Kennedy 35

Presidential term: 1961–1963
Lived: 1917–1963
Born in: Massachusetts
Elected from: Massachusetts
Occupations: Author, Reporter
Party: Democratic
Vice President: Lyndon B. Johnson

Lyndon B. Johnson 36

Presidential term: 1963–1969
Lived: 1908–1973
Born in: Texas
Elected as V.P. from: Texas Succeeded Kennedy
Occupation: Teacher
Party: Democratic
Vice President: Hubert H. Humphrey

Richard M. Nixon 37

Presidential term: 1969–1974
Lived: 1913–1994
Born in: California
Elected from: New York
Occupation: Lawyer
Party: Republican
Vice Presidents: Spiro T. Agnew, Gerald R. Ford

Gerald R. Ford 38

Presidential term: 1974–1977
Lived: 1913–2006
Born in: Nebraska
Appointed as V.P. upon Agnew's resignation; succeeded Nixon
Occupation: Lawyer
Party: Republican
Vice President: Nelson A. Rockefeller

James E. Carter, Jr. 39

Presidential term: 1977–1981
Lived: 1924–
Born in: Georgia
Elected from: Georgia
Occupations: Business, Farmer
Party: Democratic
Vice President: Walter F. Mondale

Ronald W. Reagan 40

Presidential term: 1981–1989
Lived: 1911–2004
Born in: Illinois
Elected from: California
Occupations: Actor, Lecturer
Party: Republican
Vice President: George H.W. Bush

George H.W. Bush 41

Presidential term: 1989–1993
Lived: 1924–
Born in: Massachusetts
Elected from: Texas
Occupation: Business
Party: Republican
Vice President: J. Danforth Quayle

William J. Clinton 42

Presidential term: 1993–2001
Lived: 1946–
Born in: Arkansas
Elected from: Arkansas
Occupation: Lawyer
Party: Democratic
Vice President: Albert Gore, Jr.

George W. Bush 43

Presidential term: 2001–
Lived: 1946–
Born in: Connecticut
Elected from: Texas
Occupation: Business
Party: Republican
Vice President: Richard B. Cheney

Supreme Court Case Summaries

CONTENTS

Alphabetical
Brown v. Board of Education
Bush v. Gore
Dred Scott v. Sandford
Furman v. Georgia
Gibbons v. Ogden
Gideon v. Wainwright
Hamdan v. Rumsfeld
Korematsu v. United States
Marbury v. Madison
McCulloch v. Maryland
Minnesota v. Mille Lacs Band of Chippewa Indians
Miranda v. Arizona
New York Times v. United States
Plessy v. Ferguson
Roe v. Wade
Tinker v. Des Moines School District
United States v. Nixon
Worcester v. Georgia

Chronological
Marbury v. Madison (1803)
McCulloch v. Maryland (1819)
Gibbons v. Ogden (1824)
Worcester v. Georgia (1832)
Dred Scott v. Sandford (1857)
Plessy v. Ferguson (1896)
Korematsu v. United States (1944)
Brown v. Board of Education (1954)
Gideon v. Wainwright (1963)
Miranda v. Arizona (1966)
Tinker v. Des Moines School District (1969)
New York Times v. United States (1971)
Furman v. Georgia (1972)
Roe v. Wade (1973)
United States v. Nixon (1974)
Minnesota v. Mille Lacs Band of Chippewa Indians (1999)
Bush v. Gore (2000)
Hamdan v. Rumsfeld (2006)

Brown v. Board of Education
1954

In *Brown* v. *Board of Education of Topeka, Kansas,* the Supreme Court overruled *Plessy* v. *Ferguson* (1896) making the separate-but-equal doctrine in public schools unconstitutional. The Supreme Court rejected the idea that truly equal but separate schools for African American and white students would be constitutional. The Court explained that the Fourteenth Amendment's requirement that all persons be guaranteed equal protection of the law is not met simply by ensuring that African American and white schools "have been equalized . . . with respect to buildings, curricula, qualifications and salaries, and other tangible factors."

The Court then ruled that racial segregation in public schools violates the Equal Protection Clause of the Constitution because it is inherently unequal. In other words, the very fact of separation marks the separated race as inferior. The Court's decision has been extended beyond public education to virtually all public facilities and activities.

George E.C. Hayes, Thurgood Marshall, and James Nabrit, Jr., were attorneys who argued the case against segregation in *Brown* v. *Board of Education.*

Bush v. Gore
2000

The 2000 presidential election was hanging in the balance as the state of Florida recounted their disputed ballots. Candidates George W. Bush, Republican, and Al Gore, Democrat, were so close in the polls that there was a manual recount of the votes.

Bush went to the Court to stop the recount, stating that it violated the Fourteenth Amendment. The Court ruled that since the manual recount had no uniform way to judge each disputed vote equally, it did violate the Constitution and had to be stopped. As a result, Bush won Florida's electoral votes and became president.

Dred Scott v. Sandford
1857

Dred Scott was taken by slaveholder John Sanford to the free state of Illinois and to the Wisconsin Territory, which had also banned slavery. Later they returned to Missouri, a slave state. Several years later, Scott sued for his freedom under the Missouri legal principle of "once free, always free." In other words, under Missouri law enslaved people were entitled to freedom if they had lived in a free state at any time. Missouri courts ruled against Scott, but he appealed the case all the way to the United States Supreme Court.

The Supreme Court decided this case before the Fourteenth Amendment was added to the Constitution. (The Fourteenth Amendment provides that anyone born or naturalized in the United States is a citizen of the nation and of his or her state of residence.) The Court held that enslaved African Americans were property, not citizens, and thus had no rights under the Constitution. The decision also overturned the Missouri Compromise of 1820, which

Dred Scott

had outlawed slavery in territories north of 36° 30' latitude. Many people in the North were outraged by the decision, which moved the nation closer to civil war.

Furman v. Georgia
1972

This decision put a halt to the application of the death penalty under state laws then in effect. For the first time, the Supreme Court ruled that the death penalty amounted to cruel and unusual punishment, which is outlawed in the Constitution. The Court explained that existing death penalty laws did not give juries enough guidance in deciding whether or not to impose the death penalty. As a result, the death penalty in many cases was imposed arbitrarily, that is, without a reasonable basis in the facts and circumstances of the offender or the crime.

The *Furman* decision halted all executions in the 39 states that had death penalty laws at that time. Since the decision, 38 states have rewritten death penalty laws to meet the requirements established in the *Furman* case.

Gibbons v. Ogden
1824

Thomas Gibbons had a federal license to operate a steamboat along the coast, but he did not have a license from the state of New York to travel on New York waters. He wanted to run a steamboat line between Manhattan and New Jersey that would compete with Aaron Ogden's company. Ogden had a New York license. Gibbons sued for the freedom to use his federal license to compete against Ogden on New York waters.

Gibbons won the case. The Supreme Court made it clear that the authority of Congress to regulate interstate commerce (among states) includes the authority to regulate intrastate commerce (within a single state) that bears on, or relates to, interstate commerce.

Before this decision, it was thought a state could close its borders to interstate commerce. The Court affirmed, however, that a state can regulate purely internal commerce, but only Congress can regulate commerce having both intrastate and interstate dimensions.

Gideon v. Wainwright
1963

After being accused of robbery, Clarence Gideon, a poor man, could not afford to hire a lawyer. Gideon defended himself in a Florida court because the judge in the case refused to appoint a free lawyer. The jury found Gideon guilty. Eventually, Gideon appealed his conviction to the United States Supreme Court, claiming that, by failing to appoint a lawyer, the lower court had violated his rights under the Sixth and Fourteenth Amendments.

The Supreme Court agreed with Gideon. In *Gideon* v. *Wainwright* the Supreme Court held for the first time that poor defendants in criminal cases have the right to a state-paid attorney under the Sixth Amendment. The rule announced in this case has been refined to apply whenever the defendant, if convicted, can be sentenced to more than six months in jail or prison.

Hamdan v. Rumsfeld
2006

In 2004 the Bush administration began holding captured terrorist suspects at the American military base in Guantanamo Bay, Cuba. It insisted that these prisoners, as illegal enemy fighters, did not have the right of appeal to American courts. Instead, the president as commander in chief would create special military courts to hear their cases.

In 2006 the Supreme Court struck down this plan in *Hamdan* v. *Rumsfeld*. It argued that Bush's military courts, as they stood, violated both U.S. military law and international law regarding the treatment of prisoners of war. President Bush then asked Congress to pass legislation setting up military courts that met the Court's objections. Prisoners would have the right to see evidence against them, and any evidence obtained by torture would not be accepted in court. However, prisoners could be held indefinitely without trial if the military courts had determined they were being lawfully held.

In 1988 Congress officially apologized for the internment of Fred Korematsu (center) and other Japanese Americans.

Korematsu v. United States
1944

After the Japanese bombing of Pearl Harbor in 1941, thousands of Japanese Americans on the West Coast were forced to abandon their homes and businesses, and they were moved to internment camps in California, Idaho, Utah, Arizona, Wyoming, Colorado, and Arkansas. The prison-like camps offered poor food and cramped quarters.

The Supreme Court's decision in *Korematsu* v. *United States* upheld the authority of the federal government to move Japanese Americans, many of whom were citizens, from designated military areas that included almost the entire West Coast. The government defended the so-called exclusion orders as a necessary response to Japan's attack on Pearl Harbor. Only after his reelection in 1944 did President Franklin Roosevelt rescind the evacuation orders, and by the end of 1945 the camps were closed.

Marbury v. Madison
1803

During his last days in office, President John Adams commissioned William Marbury and several other men as judges. This action by Federalist president Adams angered the incoming Democratic-Republican president Thomas Jefferson. Jefferson then ordered James Madison, his secretary of state, not to deliver the commissions, thus blocking the appointments. William Marbury sued, asking the Supreme Court to order Madison to deliver the commission that would make him a judge.

The Court ruled that the Judiciary Act—the law that gave Marbury his appointment—was unconstitutional. More importantly, the *Marbury* decision established one of the significant principles of American constitutional law. The Supreme Court held that it is the Court itself that has the final say on what the Constitution means. The Court had secured for itself the power to review acts of Congress—the power of judicial review. It is also the Supreme Court that has the final say in whether or not an act of government—legislative or executive at the federal, state, or local level—violates the Constitution.

McCulloch v. Maryland
1819

Following the War of 1812, the United States experienced years of high inflation and general economic turmoil. In an attempt to stabilize the economy, the United States Congress chartered a Second Bank of the United States in 1816. Maryland and several other states, however, opposed the competition that the new national bank created and passed laws taxing its branches. In 1818 James McCulloch, head of the Baltimore branch of the Second Bank of the United States, refused to pay the tax to the state of Maryland. The case worked its way through the Maryland state courts all the way to the United States Supreme Court.

The Supreme Court declared the Maryland tax unconstitutional and void. More importantly, the decision established the foundation for expanded congressional authority. The Court held that the necessary and proper clause of the Constitution allows Congress to do more than the Constitution expressly authorizes it to do. The decision allows Congress to enact nearly any law that will help it achieve any of its duties as set forth in the Constitution. For example, Congress has the express authority to regulate interstate commerce. The necessary and proper clause permits Congress to do so in ways not actually specified in the Constitution.

Minnesota v. Mille Lacs Band of Chippewa Indians
1999

An 1855 Treaty with the United States set aside lands in present-day Minnesota and Wisconsin to several Chippewa bands as reservations at Mille Lacs but made no mention of, among other things, whether it abolished rights guaranteed by previous treaties. Minnesota was admitted to the Union in 1858. In 1990 the Mille Lacs Band and several members sued Minnesota, its Department of Natural Resources, and state officials (collectively State), seeking, among other things, a declaratory judgment that they retained their ownership rights to the land without state interference. The District Court ultimately concluded that the Chippewa retained their claim under the 1837 Treaty and resolved several resource allocation and regulation issues. The State's argument under the "equal footing doctrine," that Minnesota's entrance into the Union in 1855 extinguished any Indian treaty rights, was considered void. The Supreme Court ruled in favor of the Chippewa and the existing 1837 treaty.

In 1963 the arrest of Ernesto Miranda (left) led to a landmark decision.

Miranda v. Arizona
1966

In 1963 police in Arizona arrested Ernesto Miranda for kidnapping. The court found Miranda guilty on the basis of a signed confession. The police admitted that neither before nor during the questioning had Miranda been advised of his right to consult with an attorney before answering any questions or of his right to have an attorney present during the interrogation. Miranda appealed his conviction, claiming that police had violated his right against self-incrimination under the Fifth Amendment by not informing him of his legal rights during questioning.

Miranda won the case. The Supreme Court held that a person in police custody cannot be questioned unless told that he or she has: 1) the right to remain silent, 2) the right to an attorney (at government expense if the accused is unable to pay), and 3) that anything the person says after stating that he or she understands these rights can be used as evidence of guilt at trial. These rights have come to be called the Miranda warning. They are intended to ensure that an accused person in custody will not unknowingly give up the Fifth Amendment's protection against self-incrimination.

New York Times v. United States
1971

In June 1971, the *New York Times* published its first installment of the "Pentagon Papers," a classified document about government actions in the Vietnam War era. The secret document had been leaked to the *Times* by antiwar activist Daniel Ellsberg, who had previously worked in national security for the government. President Richard Nixon went to court to block further publication of the Pentagon Papers. The *New York Times* appealed to the Supreme Court to allow it to continue publishing without government interference.

The Supreme Court's ruling in this case upheld earlier decisions establishing the doctrine of prior restraint. This doctrine protects the press (broadly defined to include newspapers, television and radio, filmmakers and distributors, etc.) from government attempts to block publication. Except in extraordinary circumstances, the press must be allowed to publish.

Plessy v. Ferguson
1896

In the late 1800s, railroad companies in Louisiana were required by state law to provide "separate-but-equal" cars for white and African American passengers. In 1890 a group of citizens in New Orleans selected Homer Plessy to challenge that law. In 1892 Plessy boarded a whites-only car and refused to move. He was arrested. Plessy appealed to the Supreme Court, arguing that the Louisiana separate-but-equal law violated his right to equal protection under the Fourteenth Amendment.

Homer Plessy lost the case. The *Plessy* decision upheld the separate-but-equal doctrine used by Southern states to perpetuate segregation following the Civil War. The court ruled that the Fourteenth Amendment's equal protection clause required only equal public facilities for the two races, not equal access to the same facilities. This decision was overruled in 1954 by *Brown* v. *Board of Education of Topeka, Kansas* (discussed previously).

Roe v. Wade
1973

Roe v. *Wade* challenged restrictive abortion laws in both Texas and Georgia. The suit was brought in the name of Jane Roe, an alias used to protect the privacy of the plaintiff.

In this decision, the Supreme Court ruled that females have a constitutional right under various provisions of the Constitution—most notably, the due process clause—to decide whether or not to terminate a pregnancy. The Supreme Court's decision in this case was the most significant in a long line of decisions over a period of 50 years that recognized a constitutional right of privacy, even though the word "privacy" is not found in the Constitution.

Tinker v. Des Moines School District
1969

During the Vietnam War, some students in Des Moines, Iowa, wore black armbands to school to protest American involvement in the conflict. Two days earlier, school officials had adopted a policy banning the wearing of armbands to school. When the students arrived at school wearing armbands, they were suspended

The Monroe Doctrine

In 1823 President James Monroe proclaimed the Monroe Doctrine. Designed to end European influence in the Western Hemisphere, it became a cornerstone of United States foreign policy.

. . . With the existing colonies or dependencies of any European power we have not interfered and shall not interfere. But with the Governments who have declared their independence and maintained it, and whose independence we have, on great consideration and on just principles, acknowledged, we could not view any interposition for the purpose of oppressing them, or controlling in any other manner their destiny, by any European power in any other light than as the manifestation of any unfriendly disposition toward the United States. . . .

James Monroe

Our policy in regard to Europe, which was adopted at an early stage of the wars which have so long agitated that quarter of the globe, nevertheless remains the same, which is, not to interfere in the internal concerns of any of its powers; to consider the government de facto as the legitimate government for us; to cultivate friendly relations with it, and to preserve those relations by a frank, firm, and manly policy, meeting in all instances the just claims of every power, submitting to injuries from none. . . .

Memorial of the Cherokee Nation

The Indian Removal Act of 1830 called for the relocation of Native Americans to territory west of the Mississippi River. Cherokee leaders protested the policy.

We are aware that some persons suppose it will be for our advantage to remove beyond the Mississippi. We think otherwise. Our people universally think otherwise. . . .

We wish to remain on the land of our fathers. We have a perfect and original right to remain without interruption or molestation. The treaties with us, and laws of the United States made in pursuance of treaties, guaranty our residence and our privileges, and secure us against intruders. Our only request is, that these treaties may be fulfilled, and these laws executed. . . .

. . . We have been called a poor, ignorant, and degraded people. We certainly are not rich; nor have we ever boasted of our knowledge, or our moral or intellectual elevation. But there is not a man within our limits so ignorant as not to know that he has a right to live on the land of his fathers, in the possession of his immemorial privileges, and that this right has been acknowledged by the United States; nor is there a man so degraded as not to feel a keen sense of injury, on being deprived of his right and driven into exile. . . .

The Seneca Falls Declaration

One of the first documents to express the desire for equal rights for women is the Declaration of Sentiments and Resolutions, issued in 1848 at the Seneca Falls Convention in Seneca Falls, New York. Led by Lucretia Mott and Elizabeth Cady Stanton, the delegates adopted a set of resolutions that called for woman suffrage and opportunities for women in employment and education. Excerpts from the Declaration follow.

When, in the course of human events, it becomes necessary for one portion of the family of man to assume among the people of the earth a position different from that which they have hitherto occupied, but one to which the laws of nature and of nature's God entitle them, a decent respect to the opinions of mankind requires that they should declare the causes that impel them to such a course.

We hold these truths to be self-evident: that all men and women are created equal; that they are endowed by their Creator with certain inalienable rights; that among these are life, liberty, and the pursuit of happiness; that to secure these rights governments are instituted, deriving their just powers from the consent of the governed. Whenever any form of government becomes destructive of these ends, it is the right of those who suffer from it to refuse allegiance to it, and to insist upon the institution of a new government, laying its foundation on such principles, and organizing its powers in such form as to them shall seem most likely to effect their safety and happiness. Prudence, indeed, will dictate that governments long established should not be changed for light and transient causes; . . . But when a long train of abuses and usurpations, pursuing invariably the same object, evinces a design to reduce them under absolute despotism, it is their duty to throw off such government, and to provide new guards for their future security. . . .

The history of mankind is a history of repeated injuries and usurpations on the part of man toward woman, having in direct object the establishment of an absolute tyranny over her. To prove this, let facts be submitted to a candid world. . . .

Now, in view of the entire disfranchisement of one-half the people of this country, their social and religious degradation—in view of the unjust laws above mentioned, and because women do feel themselves aggrieved, oppressed, and fraudulently deprived of their most sacred rights, we insist that they have immediate admission to all the rights and privileges which belong to them as citizens of these United States. . . .

Elizabeth Cady Stanton

The Emancipation Proclamation

On January 1, 1863, President Abraham Lincoln issued the Emancipation Proclamation, which freed all enslaved people in states under Confederate control. The Proclamation was a step toward the Thirteenth Amendment (1865), which ended slavery in all of the United States.

. . . That on the 1st day of January, in the year of our Lord 1863, all persons held as slaves within any state or designated part of a state, the people whereof shall then be in rebellion against the United States, shall be then, thenceforward, and forever free; and the Executive Government of the United States, including the military and naval authority thereof, will recognize and maintain the freedom of such persons, and will do no act or acts to repress such persons, or any of them, in any efforts they may make for their actual freedom.

That the Executive will, on the 1st day of January aforesaid, by proclamation, designate the states and parts of states, if any, in which the people thereof, respectively, shall then be in rebellion against the United States; and the fact that any state, or the people thereof, shall on that day be in good faith represented in the Congress of the United States, by members chosen thereto at elections wherein a majority of the qualified voters of such states shall have participated, shall, in the absence of strong countervailing testimony, be deemed conclusive evidence that such state, and the people thereof, are not then in rebellion against the United States. . . .

And, by virtue of the power and for the purpose aforesaid, I do order and declare that all persons held as slaves within said designated states and parts of states are, and henceforward shall be, free; and that the Executive Government of the United States, including the military and naval authorities thereof, will recognize and maintain the freedom of said persons.

And I hereby enjoin upon the people so declared to be free to abstain from all violence, unless in necessary self-defense; and I recommend to them that, all cases when allowed, they labor faithfully for reasonable wages.

And I further declare and make known that such persons, of suitable condition, will be received into the armed service of the United States. . . .

And upon this act, sincerely believed to be an act of justice, warranted by the Constitution upon military necessity, I invoke the considerate judgement of mankind and the gracious favor of Almighty God. . . .

Abraham Lincoln

The Gettysburg Address

On November 19, 1863, President Abraham Lincoln gave a short speech at the dedication of a national cemetery on the battlefield of Gettysburg. His simple yet eloquent words expressed his hopes for a nation divided by civil war.

Four score and seven years ago our fathers brought forth on this continent a new nation, conceived in liberty, and dedicated to the proposition that all men are created equal.

Now we are engaged in a great civil war, testing whether that nation, or any nation so conceived and so dedicated, can long endure. We are met on a great battlefield of that war. We have come to dedicate a portion of that field as a final resting place for those who here gave their lives that that nation might live. It is altogether fitting and proper that we should do this.

But, in a larger sense, we can not dedicate—we can not consecrate—we can not hallow—this ground. The brave men, living and dead, who struggled here, have consecrated it far above our poor power to add or detract. The world will little note nor long remember what we say here, but it can never forget what they did here. It is for us, the living, rather, to be dedicated here to the unfinished work which they who fought here have thus far so nobly advanced. It is rather for us to be here dedicated to the great task remaining before us—that from these honored dead we take increased devotion to that cause for which they gave the last full measure of devotion; that we here highly resolve that these dead shall not have died in vain; that this nation, under God, shall have a new birth of freedom; and that government of the people, by the people, for the people, shall not perish from the earth.

Current day photo of Gettysburg battlefield

I Will Fight No More

In 1877 the Nez Perce fought the government's attempt to move them to a smaller reservation. After a remarkable attempt to escape to Canada, Chief Joseph realized that resistance was hopeless and advised his people to surrender.

Tell General Howard I know his heart. What he told me before I have in my heart.

I am tired of fighting. . . . The old men are all dead. It is the young men who say yes or no. He who led the young men is dead. It is cold and we have no blankets. The little children are freezing to death. My people, some of them have run away to the hills, and have no blankets, no food; no one knows where they are—perhaps freezing to death. I want to have time to look for my children and see how many of them I can find. Maybe I shall find them among the dead. Hear me, my chiefs.

I am tired; my heart is sick and sad. From where the sun now stands I will fight no more forever.

Cheyenne shield

The Pledge of Allegiance

In 1892 the nation celebrated the 400th anniversary of Columbus's landing in America. In connection with this celebration, Francis Bellamy, a magazine editor, wrote and published the Pledge of Allegiance. The words "under God" were added by Congress in 1954 at the urging of President Dwight D. Eisenhower.

I pledge allegiance to the Flag of the United States of America and to the Republic for which it stands, one Nation under God, indivisible, with liberty and justice for all.

Students in a New York City school recite the Pledge of Allegiance.

The American's Creed

William Tyler Page of Friendship Heights, Maryland, wrote The American's Creed. This statement of political faith summarizes the true meaning of freedom available to all Americans. The U.S. House of Representatives adopted the creed on behalf of the American people on April 3, 1918.

I believe in the United States of America as a Government of the people, by the people, for the people; whose just powers are derived from the consent of the governed; a democracy in a republic; a sovereign Nation of many sovereign States; a perfect union, one and inseparable; established upon those principles of freedom, equality, justice, and humanity for which American patriots sacrificed their lives and fortunes.

I therefore believe it is my duty to my Country to love it, to support its Constitution, to obey its laws, to respect its flag, and to defend it against all enemies.

The Fourteen Points

On January 8, 1918, President Woodrow Wilson went before Congress to offer a statement of aims called the Fourteen Points. Wilson's plan called for freedom of the seas in peace and war, an end to secret alliances, and equal trading rights for all countries. The excerpt that follows is taken from the president's message.

. . . We entered this war because violations of right had occurred which touched us to the quick and made the life of our own people impossible unless they were corrected and the world secured once for all against their recurrence. What we demand in this war, therefore, is nothing peculiar to ourselves. It is that the world be made fit and safe to live in; and particularly that it be made safe for every peace-loving nation which, like our own, wishes to live its own life, determine its own institutions, be assured of justice and fair dealing by the other peoples of the world as against force and selfish aggression. All the peoples of the world are in effect partners in this interest, and for our own part we see very clearly that unless justice be done to others it will not be done to us. The program of the world's peace, therefore, is our program; and that program, the only possible program, as we see it, is this:

I. Open covenants of peace, openly arrived at, after which there shall be no private international understandings of any kind but diplomacy shall proceed always frankly and in the public view.

II. Absolute freedom of navigation upon the seas, outside territorial waters, alike in peace and in war, except as the seas may be closed in whole or in part by international action for the enforcement of international covenants.

XIV. A general association of nations must be formed under specific covenants for the purpose of affording mutual guarantees of political independence and territorial integrity to great and small states alike. . . .

alliance a close association of nations or other groups, formed to advance common interests or causes (p. 109)

alliance system defense agreements among nations (p. 706)

*alter to change (p. 40)

ambush a surprise attack (p. 178)

*amend to alter; improve (pp. 199, 218)

amendment an addition to a formal document such as the Constitution (p. 210)

American System policies devised by Henry Clay to stimulate the growth of industry (p. 323)

amnesty the granting of pardon to a large number of persons; protection from prosecution for an illegal act (pp. 519, 954, 1005)

anarchist person who believes that there should be no government (p. 745)

anarchy disorder and lawlessness (p. 693)

annex to add a territory to one's own territory (p. 371)

*annual yearly (p. 691)

anti-Semitism hostility toward or discrimination against Jews (p. 806)

apartheid racial separation and economic and political discrimination against nonwhites, a policy formerly practiced in the Republic of South Africa (p. 960)

appeasement accepting demands in order to avoid conflict (p. 807)

*approach move toward (p. 135)

arbitration settling a dispute by agreeing to accept the decision of an impartial outsider (p. 658)

archaeology the study of ancient peoples (p. 7)

armistice a temporary peace agreement to end fighting (pp. 687, 723)

arms race the competition between the United States and the Soviet Union to build more and more weapons in an effort to surpass the other's military strength (p. 862)

arsenal a storage place for weapons and ammunition (p. 461)

artifact an item left behind by early people that represents their culture (p. 7)

*aspect category, feature, or part (p. 895)

alianza asociación estrecha de las naciones u otros grupos, formada para fomentar intereses o causas comunes (pág. 109)

sistema de alianza acuerdos de defensa entre las naciones (pág. 706)

*alterar modificar (pág. 40)

emboscada ataque sorpresa (pág. 178)

*enmendar modificar; mejorar (págs. 199, 218)

enmienda adición a un documento formal como la Constitución (pág. 210)

Sistema estadounidense políticas creadas por Henry Clay para estimular el crecimiento de la industria (pág. 323)

amnistía otorgamiento del perdón a un gran número de personas; protección para no ser procesado por un acto ilegal (págs. 519, 954, 1005)

anarquista persona que considera que no deberían existir los gobiernos (pág. 745)

anarquía desorden y falta de normas (pág. 693)

anexar agregar un territorio al territorio propio (pág. 371)

*anual cada año (pág. 691)

antisemitismo hostilidad o discriminación hacia los judíos (pág. 806)

apartheid separación racial y discriminación política y económica contra las personas de color, política que se practicaba anteriormente en la República de Sudáfrica (pág. 960)

pacificación aceptación de las exigencias para evitar conflictos (pág. 807)

*acercarse dirigirse hacia (pág. 135)

arbitraje resolver una disputa acordando aceptar la decisión de una persona imparcial (pág. 658)

arqueología el estudio de pueblos antiguos (pág. 7)

armisticio acuerdo de paz temporal para poner fin a las guerras (págs. 687, 723)

carrera armamentista competencia entre Estados Unidos y la Unión Soviética para construir cada vez más armas con el fin de superar la fortaleza militar de la otra nación (pág. 862)

arsenal lugar para el almacenaje de armas y municiones (pág. 461)

artefacto artículos provenientes de antiguas civilizaciones que representan su cultura (pág. 7)

*aspecto categoría, característica o componente (pág. 895)

Glossary/Glosario

assembly line a system with machines and workers arranged so that each person performs an assigned task again and again as items pass before him or her (p. 593)

línea de ensamblaje sistema con maquinaria y trabajadores dispuestos de tal manera que cada persona realiza una tarea asignada una y otra vez a medida que pasan los artículos frente a ellos (pág. 593)

*__assign__ appoint (p. 881)

*__asignar__ designar (pág. 881)

assimilate to absorb a group into the culture of a larger population (p. 616)

asimilar absorber a un grupo dentro de la cultura de una población más grande (pág. 616)

*__assure__ to promise (p. 858)

*__garantizar__ prometer (pág. 858)

astrolabe an instrument used by sailors to observe positions of stars (p. 31)

astrolabio instrumento usado por los marineros para observar las posiciones de las estrellas (pág. 31)

attitude way of thinking and acting (p.617)

actitud forma de pensar o actuar (pág. 617)

*__author__ writer (p. 421)

*__autor__ escritor (pág. 421)

*__authority__ power to decide; power to give orders and make decisions (pp. 283, 927)

*__autoridad__ poder para decidir; poder para dar órdenes y tomar decisiones (págs. 283, 927)

autocracy government in which one person has unlimited power (p. 716)

autocracia gobierno en el que todo el poder se concentra en una persona (pág. 716)

*__aware__ mindful; to have knowledge of (p. 1003)

*__conciente__ atento; tener conocimiento de (pág. 1003)

B

backcountry a region of hills and forests west of the Tidewater (p. 94)

zona rural región de colinas y bosques al oeste de Tidewater (pág. 94)

balance of power the distribution of power among nations so that no single nation can dominate or interfere with another (pp. 706, 943)

equilibrio de poderes distribución de poderes entre las naciones de tal manera que ninguna de las naciones pueda dominar a otra o interferir entre sí (págs. 706, 943)

bankruptcy the condition of being unable to pay one's debts; one's property is managed or sold to pay those to whom one owes money (p. 981)

bancarrota condición en la que una persona no puede pagar sus deudas; la propiedad de una persona se vende o administra con el fin de pagar a las personas a las que le debe dinero (pág. 981)

barrio a Spanish-speaking neighborhood in a city (p. 668)

barrio vecindario de habla hispana en una ciudad (pág. 668)

*__behalf__ in the interest of (p. 646)

*__en nombre de__ en beneficio de (pág. 646)

*__bias__ prejudice; unbalanced view or consideration (p. 665)

*__parcialidad__ prejuicio; punto de vista o consideración tendenciosa (pág. 665)

bicameral consisting of two houses, or chambers, especially in a legislature (p. 187)

bicameral que consiste en dos cámaras, en especial en una asamblea legislativa (pág. 187)

black codes laws passed in the South just after the Civil War aimed at controlling freedmen and enabling plantation owners to exploit African American workers (p. 523)

códigos negros leyes aprobadas en el Sur después de la Guerra Civil que apuntaban al control de los libertos y permitían que los dueños de plantaciones explotaran a los trabajadores afroamericanos (pág. 523)

blacklist list of persons who are disapproved of and are punished, such as by being refused jobs (p. 848)

lista negra lista de personas a las que se rechazaba y castigaba, por ejemplo, al negarles empleos (pág. 848)

blitzkrieg name given to the sudden, violent offensive attacks the Germans used during World War II; "lightning war" (p. 809)

blitzkrieg nombre que se da a los ataques repentinos, violentos y ofensivos que los alemanes realizaban durante la Segunda Guerra Mundial; "guerra relámpago" (pág. 809)

Glossary/Glosario

blockade cut off an area by means of troops or warships to stop supplies or people from coming in or going out; to close off a country's ports (pp. 170, 477, 908)

bond a note issued by the government, which promises to pay off a loan with interest (p. 256)

boomtown a community experiencing a sudden growth in business or population (p. 379)

border ruffian Missourian who traveled in armed groups to vote in Kansas's election during the mid-1850s (p. 455)

border state state between the North and the South that was divided over whether to stay in the Union or join the Confederacy (p. 475)

bounty money given as a reward, such as to encourage enlistment in the army (p. 496)

boycott to refuse to buy items from a particular country (p. 125); to refuse to use in order to show disapproval or force acceptance of one's terms (p. 878)

*brief short in duration (p. 410)

budget deficit the amount by which government spending exceeds revenue (p. 983)

burgess elected representative to an assembly (p. 61)

bloqueo aislamiento de un área por medio de tropas o barcos de guerra para impedir el ingreso o el egreso de suministros o personas; cierre de los puertos de un país (págs. 170, 477, 908)

bono título emitido por el gobierno con la promesa de pagar un préstamo con intereses (pág. 256)

pueblo en bonanza comunidad que experimenta un crecimiento repentino en los negocios o la población (pág. 379)

rufianes fronterizos hombres de Missouri que viajaban en grupos armados para votar en las elecciones de Kansas a mediados de la década de 1850 (pág. 455)

estado fronterizo estado ubicado entre el Norte y el Sur dividido teniendo en cuenta si formaba parte de la Unión o de la Confederación (pág. 475)

recompensa dinero otorgado como premio, por ejemplo, para incentivar el enrolamiento en el ejército (pág. 496)

boicot negarse a comprar artículos de un país en particular (pág. 125); negarse a usar algo con el fin de demostrar desaprobación o imponer aceptación de los términos de una persona (pág. 878)

*breve de duración corta (pág. 410)

déficit presupuestario monto por el cual el gasto del gobierno excede los ingresos (pág. 983)

representante electo representante electo de una asamblea (pág. 61)

C

cabinet a group of advisers to the president (p. 253)

Californio Mexican who was one of the original settlers of California (p. 376)

canal an artificial waterway (p. 315)

*capable having the necessary abilities (p. 437)

capital money for investment (pp. 307, 403)

capitalism an economic system based on private property and free enterprise (pp. 307, 745)

carbon dating a scientific method used to determine the age of an artifact (p. 9)

carpetbagger northerner who moved to the South after the Civil War (p. 530)

cash crop farm crop raised to be sold for money (pp. 92, 539)

gabinete grupo de consejeros del presidente (pág. 253)

californio mexicano que fue uno de los primeros pobladores de California (pág. 376)

canal vía artificial de agua (pág. 315)

*capaz tener las habilidades necesarias (pág. 437)

capital dinero disponible para inversiones (págs. 307, 403)

capitalismo sistema económico basado en la propiedad privada y en la libre empresa (págs. 307, 745)

datación por carbono método científico usado para determinar la antigüedad de un artefacto (pág. 9)

carpetbagger norteño que se trasladó al Sur después de la Guerra Civil (pág. 530)

cultivo comercial producto agrícola que se vende por dinero (págs. 92, 539)

Glossary/Glosario

casualty a military person killed, wounded, or captured (p. 483)

caucus a meeting held by a political party to choose their party's candidate for president or decide policy (pp. 268, 340)

cede to give up by treaty (p. 377)

censure to express formal disapproval of some action (p. 849)

census official count of a population (p. 313)

*challenge demanding situation (pp. 261, 479)

*channel a trench or groove to allow the passage of water (p. 17)

*chart to map (p. 51)

charter a document that gives the holder the right to organize settlements in an area (p. 60)

charter colony colony established by a group of settlers who had been given a formal document allowing them to settle (p. 101)

checks and balances the system in which each branch of government has a check on the other two branches so that no one branch becomes too powerful (p. 208)

circumnavigate to sail around the world (p. 41)

*civil relating to citizens as individuals (p. 875)

civil defense protective measures taken in case of attack (p. 817)

civil disobedience refusal to obey laws that are considered unjust as a nonviolent way to press for changes (pp. 421, 879)

civilization a highly developed culture, usually with organized religions and laws (p. 11)

civil war conflict between citizens of the same country (p. 455)

clan a group united by a common interest or characteristic (p. 22)

classical relating to ancient Greece and Rome (p. 30)

*clause a condition added to a document (p. 191)

clipper ship a fast sailing ship with slender lines, tall masts, and large square sails (p. 390)

closed shop a workplace in which the employer by agreement hires only union members (p. 853)

coalition a group united for action (p. 979)

---

víctima persona del ejército asesinada, herida o capturada (pág. 483)

caucus reunión celebrada por un partido político para elegir el candidato presidencial de su partido o definir una política (págs. 268, 340)

ceder renunciar por tratado (pág. 377)

censurar expresar la desaprobación formal de alguna acción (pág. 849)

censo registro oficial de una población (pág. 313)

*desafiar situación difícil (págs. 261, 479)

*canal fosa marina o surco para permitir el pasaje de agua (pág. 17)

*trazar un mapa hacer un mapa (pág. 51)

carta de privilegio documento que le otorga al poseedor el derecho de organizar los asentamientos en un área (pág. 60)

colonia con carta de privilegio colonia formada por un grupo de colonos que recibieron un documento formal que establece que pueden establecerse (pág. 101)

controles y balances sistema en que cada rama del gobierno controla a las otras dos ramas, de manera que ninguna de éstas pueda adquirir demasiado poder (pág. 208)

circunnavegar navegar por el mundo (pág. 41)

*civil relativo a ciudadanos como individuos (pág. 875)

defensa civil medidas protectoras que se toman en caso de ataques (pág. 817)

desobediencia civil rehusarse a obedecer las leyes que se consideran injustas, forma no violenta de exigir cambios (págs. 421, 879)

civilización cultura muy evolucionada, generalmente con leyes y religiones organizadas (pág. 11)

guerra civil conflicto entre ciudadanos de un mismo país (pág. 455)

clan grupo unificado por un interés o una característica en común (pág. 22)

clásico relativo a las antiguas Grecia y Roma (pág. 30)

*cláusula condición anexada a un documento (pág. 191)

velero barco de vela rápido con líneas delgadas, mástiles altos y amplias velas cuadradas (pág. 390)

empresa cerrada lugar de trabajo en el que el empleador contrata, por acuerdo, sólo a miembros del sindicato (pág. 853)

coalición grupo unificado para la acción (pág. 979)

Glossary/Glosario

coeducation the teaching of male and female students together (p. 437)

cold war a struggle over political differences between nations carried on by methods short of war (p. 846)

*collapse break down (p. 775)

collective bargaining discussion between an employer and union representatives of workers over wages, hours, and working conditions (p. 605)

Columbian Exchange exchange of goods, ideas, and people between Europe and the Americas (p. 51)

commence to begin (p. 375)

*commission a group of persons directed to perform some duty (p. 536)

committee of correspondence an organization that spread political ideas through the colonies (p. 128)

*communication process of exchanging information (p. 676)

*community group of people living in a particular place (p. 396)

*complex complicated; highly detailed (p. 11)

compromise agreement between two or more sides in which each side gives up some of what it wants (p. 200)

*concentrate to focus one's effort on something (p. 821)

concentration camps prison camps used to hold people for political reasons (p. 825)

*conclude decide (p. 859)

concurrent powers powers shared by the states and the federal government (p. 216)

*conduct to direct the course of (p. 920)

Conestoga wagon large, broad-wheeled, canvas-covered wagon used by western settlers (p. 281)

*conflict disagreement (p. 279); war or prolonged struggle (p. 832)

conquistador Spanish explorer in the Americas in the 1500s (p. 43)

conscientious objector person who refuses military service on the basis of moral or religious beliefs (p. 920)

*consent agree to (p. 723)

*consequence result or effect of (p. 402)

coeducación enseñanza conjunta de hombres y mujeres (pág. 437)

guerra fría lucha por diferencias políticas entre las naciones llevada a cabo a través de métodos no bélicos (pág. 846)

*colapsar derrumbar (pág. 775)

negociación colectiva discusión entre un empleador y los representantes del sindicato de los trabajadores acerca de los sueldos, las horas y las condiciones de trabajo (pág. 605)

Intercambio Colombino intercambio de mercancías, ideas y gente entre Europa y las Américas (pág. 51)

comenzar empenzar (pág. 375)

*comisión grupo de personas dirigidas para realizar tareas (pág. 536)

comité de correspondencia organización que divulga ideas políticas a través de las colonias (pág. 128)

*comunicación proceso de intercambio de información (pág. 676)

*comunidad grupo de personas que viven en un lugar en particular (pág. 396)

*complejo complicado; sumamente detallado (pág. 11)

compromiso acuerdo entre dos o más partes en el que cada una de ellas renuncia a algo de lo que desea (pág. 200)

*concentrar dirigir los esfuerzos a algo (pág. 821)

campos de concentración campos de prisión usados para retener a las personas por razones políticas (pág. 825)

*llegar a una conclusión decidir (pág. 859)

poderes concurrentes poderes compartidos por los estados y el gobierno federal (pág. 216)

*conducir dirigir el curso de (pág. 920)

carreta Conestoga carreta grande de ruedas anchas, cubierta con lona que usaban los colonos del oeste (pág. 281)

*conflicto desacuerdo (pág. 279); guerra o lucha prolongada (pág. 832)

conquistador explorador español en las Américas en los años 1500 (pág. 43)

objetor de conciencia persona que se rehúsa al servicio militar por creencias religiosas o morales (pág. 920)

*consentir aceptar (pág. 723)

*consecuencia resultado o efecto de (pág. 402)

Glossary/Glosario

conservation the protection and preservation of natural resources (p. 659)

*consist make up of (p. 883)

consolidation the practice of combining separate companies into one (p. 585)

constitution a list of fundamental laws to support a government (pp. 79, 187, 380)

*consult to seek opinions or information from (p. 681)

*consume to use (p. 726)

containment the policy or process of preventing the expansion of a hostile power (p. 844)

*contrast large degree of difference (p. 476)

*contribute help to cause an event or situation (p. 305)

*controversy arguments between opposing viewpoints (p. 954)

*convention formal meeting (p. 198)

*convert change religious beliefs (p. 105)

*convince to persuade (someone) that something is true (p. 523)

convoy a group that travels with something, such as a ship, to protect it (p. 719)

*cooperate work together (p. 844)

cooperative store where farmers bought products from each other; an enterprise owned and operated by those who use its services (p. 575)

corporation a business in which investors own shares (p. 596)

corruption dishonest or illegal actions (p. 530)

cotton gin a machine that removed seeds from cotton fiber (pp. 306, 401)

counterculture a social movement whose values go against those of established society (p. 919)

counterterrorism military or political activities intended to combat terrorism (p. 993)

coureur de bois French trapper living among Native Americans (p. 52)

*create to form; to make (p. 575)

credibility gap lack of belief; a term used to describe the lack of trust in the Johnson administration's statements about the Vietnam War (p. 921)

*credit a form of loan; ability to buy goods based on future payment (p. 530)

conservación protección y preservación de los recursos naturales (pág. 659)

*consistir estar compuesto de (pág. 883)

consolidación práctica de combinar diferentes compañías en una (pág. 585)

constitución lista de leyes fundamentales para sostener un gobierno (págs. 79, 187, 380)

*consultar buscar opiniones o infor mación de (pág. 681)

*consumir usar (pág. 726)

contención política o proceso de prevención de la expansión de un poder hostil (pág. 844)

*contraste amplio grado de diferencia (pág. 476)

*contribuir ayudar a provocar un evento o una situación (pág. 305)

*controversia argumentos entre puntos de vista opuestos (pág. 954)

*convención reunión formal (pág. 198)

*convertir cambiar de creencias religiosas (pág. 105)

*convencer persuadir (a alguien) de que algo es verdadero (pág. 523)

convoy grupo que viaja con algo, como un barco, para protegerlo (pág. 719)

*cooperar trabajar en conjunto (pág. 844)

cooperativa tienda en la que los agricultores compraban productos entre sí; empresa que es propiedad de aquellos que utilizan sus servicios y es operada por ellos (pág. 575)

corporación empresa en la que los inversores tienen acciones (pág. 596)

corrupción acciones ilegales o deshonestas (pág. 530)

desmotadora de algodón máquina que sacaba las semillas de las fibras de algodón (págs. 306, 401)

contracultura movimiento social cuyos valores van en contra de aquellos establecidos por la sociedad (pág. 919)

contraterrorismo actividades políticas o militares dirigidas a combatir el terrorismo (pág. 993)

coureur de bois cazador francés que vivía entre nativoamericanos (pág. 52)

*crear construir; confeccionar (pág. 575)

brecha de credibilidad falta de creencias; término utilizado para describir la falta de confianza en las declaraciones de la administración de Johnson acerca de la Guerra de Vietnam (pág. 921)

*crédito una forma de préstamo; capacidad de comprar bienes en función de un pago futuro (pág. 530)

culture a way of life of a group of people who share similar beliefs and customs (p. 9)

*currency metal coins and paper notes used as money (p. 577)

customs duty tax on foreign imported goods (p. 278)

cultura estilo de vida de un grupo de personas que comparten creencias y costumbres similares (pág. 9)

*moneda monedas de metal y billetes usados como dinero (pág. 577)

derecho aduanero impuesto sobre los productos extranjeros importados (pág. 278)

*debate discussion by opposing points of view (p. 141)

debtor person or country that owes money (p. 80)

*decade a period of ten years (p. 1001)

*decline descend (p. 774)

decree an order given by one in authority (p. 368)

default to fail to meet an obligation, especially a financial one (p. 775)

deferment an excuse, issued by the draft board, that lets a person be excused from military service for various reasons (p. 920)

deficit the shortage that occurs when spending is greater than income (p. 951)

deficit spending the government spending more money than it takes in (p. 983)

*definite precise or well-defined (p. 997)

demilitarized zone a region where no military forces or weapons are permitted (p. 859)

*demonstration a protest march (p. 928)

*deny not allow access to (p. 664)

deport to send out of a country aliens who are considered dangerous (pp. 745, 1005)

depreciate to fall in value (p. 191)

depression a period of low economic activity and widespread unemployment (pp. 195, 350)

deregulation the act of cutting the restrictions and regulations that government places on business (p. 972)

desegregate to end the practice of separating or isolating people of different races (p. 855)

desert to leave without permission (p. 162)

*design a plan or course of action (p. 106)

*debate discusión al oponer puntos de vista (pág. 141)

deudor persona o país que debe dinero (pág. 80)

*década período de diez años (pág. 1001)

*decaer declinar (pág. 774)

decreto orden otorgada por una autoridad (pág. 368)

incumplimiento no cumplir con una obligación, especialmente del tipo financiero (pág. 775)

prórroga excusa, emitida por la junta de reclutamietno que le permite a una persona excusarse del servicio militar por diferentes motivos (pág. 920)

déficit carencia que se produce cuando el gasto es mayor que el ingreso (pág. 951)

gastos déficitarios el gobierno gasta más dinero que el que tiene (pág. 983)

*definitivo decisivo o bien definido (pág. 997)

zona desmilitarizada región donde se prohíben fuerzas o armas militares (pág. 859)

*demonstración una marcha de protesta (pág. 928)

*negar no permitir el acceso a (pág. 664)

deportar sacar del país a los extranjeros que son considerados peligrosos (págs. 745, 1005)

desvalorizar reducir el valor (pág. 191)

depresión período de actividad económica baja y desempleo generalizado (págs. 195, 350)

desregulación acción de reducir las restricciones y las regulaciones que el gobierno impone en el comercio (pág. 972)

abolicir de la segregación terminar de la práctica separarción o aislamiento de personas de diferentes razas (pág. 855)

desertar abandonar sin permiso (pág. 162)

*diseño plan o instrucciones para realizar algo (pág. 106)

Glossary/Glosario

*detect uncover or discover the true character of (p. 752)

détente a policy which attempts to relax or ease tensions between nations (p. 943)

*device instrument or piece of equipment (p. 759)

*devote to commit by a solemn act (p. 39)

dictator a leader who rules with total authority, often in a cruel or brutal manner (p. 805)

*dimension aspect; one element or factor among many (p. 709)

*diminish to lessen the authority, dignity, or reputation of (p. 223)

disarmament removal of weapons (p. 812)

*discriminate to treat unfairly (p. 875)

discrimination unfair treatment of a group; unequal treatment because of a person's race, religion, ethnic background, or place of birth (pp. 396, 663, 875)

dissent disagreement with or opposition to an opinion (pp. 65, 727)

*distribute give out (p. 493)

*diverse differing from one another (p. 896)

dividend a stockholder's share of a company's profits, usually as a cash payment (p. 596)

dollar diplomacy a policy of joining the business interests of a country with its diplomatic interests abroad (p. 694)

*domestic home-based, internal (p. 852)

downsize the practice of companies laying off workers to become more efficient and to increase their earnings (p. 981)

draft the selection of persons for military service (p. 496)

dry farming a way of farming dry land in which seeds are planted deep in ground where there is some moisture (p. 565)

*dynamic active and energetic (p. 747)

*detectar revelar o descubrir el carácter real de (pág. 752)

détente política que se dirige a distender o aliviar las tensiones entre las naciones (pág. 943)

*dispositivo instrumento o pieza de un equipo (pág. 759)

*dedicarse comprometerse por un acto solemne (pág. 39)

dictador líder que gobierna con autoridad total, en general de forma atroz y cruel (pág. 805)

*dimensión aspecto; elemento o factor entre varios (pág. 709)

*aminorar disminuir la autoridad, la dignidad o la reputación de (pág. 223)

desarme eliminación de las armas (pág. 812)

*discriminar tratar injustamente (pág. 875)

discriminación trato injusto de un grupo; trato desigual debido a la raza, la religión, el origen étnico o el lugar de nacimiento de una persona (págs. 396, 663, 875)

disentimiento desacuerdo con una opinión u oposición a ésta (págs. 65, 727)

*distribuir repartir (pág. 493)

*diverso que difieren entre sí (pág. 896)

dividendo parte de las ganancias de una empresa de un accionista, en general en forma de pago en efectivo (pág. 596)

diplomacia del dólar política que une los intereses comerciales de un país con sus intereses diplomáticos en el extranjero (pág. 694)

*nacional hecho en el país, interno (pág. 852)

reducción de personal práctica de las compañías que despiden trabajadores para aumentar su eficacia y sus ganancias (pág. 981)

llamamiento a filas selección de personas para el servicio militar (pág. 496)

agricultura de secano método de cultivar la tierra seca con el que se plantan las semillas en la profundidad de la tierra, donde reciben humedad (pág. 565)

*dinámico activo y vigoroso (pág. 747)

E

*economy system of production, distribution, and consumption (p. 863)

effigy rag figure representing an unpopular individual (p. 125)

*economía sistema de producción, distribución y consumo (pág. 863)

efigie figura que representa a un individuo impopular (pág. 125)

Glossary/Glosario

Electoral College a special group of voters selected by their state's voters to vote for the president and vice president (p. 207)

*element one part of a larger whole (p. 307)

*eliminate to remove; to eradicate; to end (p. 691)

embargo an order prohibiting trade with another country (pp. 290, 946)

*emerge to rise up (p. 890)

emigrant a person who leaves a country or region to live elsewhere (p. 362)

emigrate to leave one's place of residence or country to live somewhere else (p. 613)

empresario a person who arranged for the settlement of land in Texas during the 1800s (p. 367)

encomienda system of rewarding conquistadors with tracts of land and the right to tax and demand labor from Native Americans who lived on the land (p. 47)

*encounter to come upon; meet (pp. 127, 502)

*energy source of usable power (p. 952)

*enormous huge (p. 760)

*ensure make certain (p. 567)

entrenched occupying a strong defensive position (p. 499)

enumerated powers powers belonging only to the federal government (p. 216)

*environment the complex of physical, chemical, and biotic factors that surround living organisms (p. 605)

*equip furnish; provide with (p. 709)

escalate to increase or expand (p. 913)

espionage spying (p. 848)

*establish to set up (p. 367)

*estate property; land (p. 77)

*estimate approximate number (p. 9)

*ethnic pertaining to a group sharing a common culture (p. 74)

ethnic group a minority that speaks a different language or follows different customs than the majority of people in a country (p. 614); people who share a common language and traditions (p. 705)

*eventual occurring later (pp. 374, 689)

evolution the scientific theory that humans and other living things have evolved over time (p. 763)

Colegio Electoral grupo especial de votantes seleccionados por los votantes de su estado para elegir al presidente y al vicepresidente (pág. 207)

*elemento parte de un entero (pág. 307)

*eliminar sacar; erradicar; terminar (pág. 691)

embargo una orden que prohíbe el comercio con otro país (págs. 290, 946)

*surgir aflorar (pág. 890)

emigrante persona que abandona un país o región para vivir en otro país (pág. 362)

emigrar dejar el lugar de residencia o el país para vivir en otro lugar (pág. 613)

empresario persona que disponía el asentamiento de la tierra en Texas durante los años 1800 (pág. 367)

encomienda sistema de recompensa a los conquistadores con extensiones de tierra y el derecho de cobrar impuestos y exigir trabajo de los nativoamericanos que vivían en el territorio (pág. 47)

*encuentro topar con; reunirse con (págs. 127, 502)

*energía fuente de alimentación útil (pág. 952)

*enorme inmenso (pág. 760)

*asegurar garantizar (pág. 567)

atrincherado que ocupa una fuerte posición defensiva (pág. 499)

poderes enumerados poderes que pertenecen sólo al gobierno federal (pág. 216)

*medio ambiente complejo de factores físicos, químicos y bióticos que rodean a los organismos vivos (pág. 605)

*equipar abastecer; ofrecer (pág. 709)

escalar aumentar o expandir (pág. 913)

espionaje infiltración (pág. 848)

*establecer instalar (pág. 367)

*propiedad finca, tierra (pág. 77)

*estimación número aproximado (pág. 9)

*étnico que pertenece a un grupo que comparte una cultura en común (pág. 74)

grupo étnico minoría que habla un idioma diferente o sigue diferentes costumbres que la mayoría de las personas en un país (pág. 614); personas con un idioma y tradiciones en común (pág. 705)

*final que ocurre después (págs. 374, 689)

evolución teoría científica que sostiene que los seres humanos y otras formas de vida evolucionaron con el paso del tiempo (pág. 763)

Glossary/Glosario

*exceed to be greater; to go beyond (p. 959)

*exclude shut out (p. 923)

executive branch the branch of government, headed by the president, that carries out the nation's laws and policies (p. 207)

executive order a rule issued by a chief executive that has the force of law (p. 906)

executive privilege President Nixon's belief that all White House conversations should be kept secret to protect national security (p. 953)

*expand to increase in size or scope (p. 61)

expansionism a policy that calls for expanding a nation's boundaries (p. 675)

expatriate a person who gives up his or her home country and chooses to live in another country (p. 761)

*expert person with advanced knowledge on a particular subject (p. 755)

*exploit to make use of meanly or unjustly for one's own advantage (p. 682)

export to sell goods abroad (pp. 99, 477)

*extract to remove, usually by force (p. 553)

*exceder sobrepasar; ir más allá (pág. 959)

*excluir negar la entrada (pág. 923)

poder ejecutivo rama del gobierno, encabezada por el presidente, que maneja las leyes y las políticas de la nación (pág. 207)

orden ejecutiva regla establecida por un jefe ejecutivo con fuerza de ley (pág. 906)

privilegio ejecutivo creencia del Presidente Nixon acerca de que las conversaciones de la Casa Blanca debían mantenerse en secreto para proteger la seguridad nacional (pág. 953)

*expandir aumentar en tamaño o alcance (pág. 61)

expansionismo política que solicita la expansión de las fronteras de una nación (pág. 675)

expatriado persona que se retira de su país de origen y decide vivir en otro país (pág. 761)

*experto persona con conocimientos avanzados sobre un tema particular (pág. 755)

*explotar hacer uso mezquino o injusto de las cosas para el beneficio propio (pág. 682)

exportar vender bienes en el exterior (págs. 99, 477)

*extraer quitar, en general por la fuerza (pág. 553)

*factor contributing circumstance (p. 563)

factory system system bringing manufacturing steps together in one place to increase efficiency (p. 306)

famine an extreme shortage of food (p. 398)

fascism a political system, headed by a dictator, that calls for extreme nationalism and racism and no tolerance of opposition (p. 805)

fascist a person with extremely nationalistic views (p. 790)

*federal the national or central governing authority (p. 343)

federal debt the amount of money owed by the government (p. 973)

federalism the sharing of power between federal and state governments (pp. 206, 216)

federation a type of government that links different groups together (p. 21)

feminist a person who advocates or is active in promoting women's rights (p. 895)

final last, ultimate (p. 730)

*factor circunstancia que contribuye (pág. 563)

sistema de fábrica sistema que reúne las categorías de fabricación en un solo lugar para aumentar la eficiencia (pág. 306)

hambre escasez extrema de alimentos (pág. 398)

fascismo sistema político, encabezado por un dictador, que establece nacionalismo y racismo extremos sin permitir la oposición (pág. 805)

fascista persona con puntos de vista extremadamente nacionalistas (pág. 790)

*federal autoridad del gobierno nacional o central (pág. 343)

deuda federal cantidad de dinero que debe un gobierno (pág. 973)

federalismo posesión conjunta del poder entre los gobiernos centrales y estatales (págs. 206, 216)

federación tipo de gobierno que une a diferentes grupos (pág. 21)

feminista persona que defiende los derechos de la mujer o participa en su promoción (pág. 895)

final último (pág. 730)

flapper a young woman of the 1920s who defied conventions in her behavior and dress (p. 759)

flexible response a plan that used special military units to fight guerrilla wars (p. 905)

forty-niner person who went to California during the gold rush of 1849 (p. 379)

*found establish or set up (p. 46)

free enterprise the freedom of private businesses to operate competitively for profit with minimal government regulation (p. 307)

free trade the absence of trade barriers so that goods flow freely among countries (p. 1002)

frigate small warship (p. 296)

fugitive running away or trying to run away (p. 451)

*function operate (p. 75)

*fund source of money (p. 813)

fundamentalist a person who believes in the literal meaning of religious texts and follows strict obedience to religious laws (pp. 962, 992)

Fundamental Orders of Connecticut the first written plan for a government in America (p. 68)

joven moderna mujer joven de la década de 1920 que desafiaba las convenciones en su conducta y forma de vestir (pág. 759)

respuesta flexible plan que usaba unidades militares especiales para pelear en guerras de guerrillas (pág. 905)

hombres del cuarenta y nueve persona que se trasladó a California durante la Fiebre del Oro de 1849 (pág. 379)

*fundar instaurar o establecer (pág. 46)

libre empresa libertad de los negocios privados de operar de forma competitiva para obtener ganancias con regulación gubernamental mínima (pág. 307)

libre comercio ausencia de barreras comerciales de modo que los bienes circulan libremente entre los países (pág. 1002)

fragata buque de guerra pequeño (pág. 296)

fugitivo que se fuga o está tratando de fugarse (pág. 451)

*funcionar operar (pág. 75)

*fondo fuente de dinero (pág. 813)

*fundamentalista persona que cree en el significado literal de los textos religiosos y obedece estrictamente las leyes religiosas (págs. 962, 992)

Órdenes Fundamentales de Connecticut primer plan escrito para un gobierno de Estados Unidos (pág. 68)

G

*generate create (p. 782)

genocide the deliberate destruction of a racial, political, or cultural group (p. 825)

globalism the idea that the world's economies and societies are all part of one big system (p. 1001)

global warming a steady increase in average world temperatures (p. 1004)

*globe the planet Earth (p. 51)

*goal aim or purpose (p. 297)

grandfather clause a clause that allowed individuals who did not pass the literacy test to vote if their fathers or grandfathers had voted before Reconstruction began; an exception to a law based on preexisting circumstances (p. 539)

*grant special privilege or authority (p. 43)

grassroots movement people at the local level organizing for political action (p. 983)

*generar crear (pág. 782)

genocidio destrucción deliberada de un grupo racial, político o cultural (pág. 825)

globalismo idea de que las economías y las sociedades de todo el mundo forman parte de un gran sistema (pág. 1001)

calentamiento global aumento continuo de las temperaturas promedio en el mundo (pág. 1004)

*mundo planeta Tierra (pág. 51)

*meta objetivo o propósito (pág. 297)

cláusula del abuelo cláusula que permitía que los individuos que no aprobaban la prueba de alfabetización pudieran votar si sus padres o abuelos habían votado antes de que se iniciara la Reconstrucción; una excepción a la ley basada en circunstancias preexistentes (pág. 539)

*concesión privilegio o autoridad especial (pág. 43)

movimiento de las bases personas en una comunidad que se organizan para la acción política (pág. 983)

Glossary/Glosario

greenback a piece of U.S. paper money first issued by the North during the Civil War (p. 497)

verdes billete estadounidense emitido por primera vez por el Norte durante la Guerra Civil (pág. 497)

gross domestic product the value of all the goods and services produced in a nation during a one-year period (p. 985)

producto interno bruto valor de todos los bienes y servicios producidos por una nación en un año (pág. 985)

gross national product the total value of all goods and services produced by a nation's residents during a year, regardless of where production takes place (p. 755)

producto nacional bruto valor total de bienes y servicios producidos por los residentes de una nación en un año, independientemente del lugar donde se realiza la producción (pág. 755)

guerrilla tactics referring to surprise attacks or raids rather than organized warfare (p. 347)

tácticas de guerrilla se refiere a ataques sorpresa en lugar de técnicas militares organizadas (pág. 347)

guerrilla warfare a hit-and-run technique used in fighting a war; fighting by small bands of warriors using tactics such as sudden ambushes (pp. 172, 905)

guerra de guerrillas técnica de golpear y huir que se usaba para pelear una guerra; lucha de pequeños grupos de guerreros que usaban tácticas como emboscadas repentinas (págs. 172, 905)

habeas corpus a legal order for an inquiry to determine whether a person has been lawfully imprisoned (p. 495)

hábeas corpus orden legal para una indagación con el fin de determinar si una persona ha sido arrestada injustamente (pág. 495)

headright a 50-acre grant of land given to colonial settlers who paid their own way (p. 61)

interés concesión de 50 acres de tierra que se les dio a los colonos que pagaron a su manera (pág. 61)

hieroglyphics an ancient form of writing using symbols and pictures to represent words, sounds, and concepts (p. 12)

jeroglíficos forma antigua de escritura con el uso de símbolos e imágenes para representar palabras, sonidos y conceptos (pág. 12)

Holocaust the name given to the mass slaughter of Jews and other groups by the Nazis during World War II (p. 825)

holocausto nombre que se le dio a la masacre de judíos y otros grupos por parte de los nazis durante la Segunda Guerra Mundial (pág. 825)

homestead to acquire a piece of U.S. public land by living on and cultivating it (p. 563)

cesión de tierras adquirir una porción de tierra pública de Estados Unidos al habitarla o cultivarla (pág. 563)

Hull House settlement house founded by Jane Addams in Chicago in 1889 (p. 623)

Hull House casa de asistencia social fundada por Jane Addams en Chicago en 1889 (pág. 623)

human rights rights regarded as belonging to all persons, such as freedom from unlawful imprisonment, torture, and execution (p. 960)

derechos humanos derechos que pertenecen a todas las personas, como la libertad de arresto injusto, tortura y ejecución (pág. 960)

*identify recognize (p. 604)

*identificar reconocer (pág. 604)

*impact effect or influence (pp. 171, 487)

*impacto efecto o influencia (págs. 171, 487)

impeach to formally charge a public official with misconduct in office (pp. 527, 953)

impugnar denunciar formalmente a un funcionario público por mala conducta en el desempeño de su cargo (págs. 527, 953)

imperialism the actions used by one nation to exercise political or economic control over smaller or weaker nations (p. 676)

imperialismo medidas tomadas por una nación para ejercer el control político o económico sobre una nación más pequeña o más débil (pág. 676)

implied powers powers not specifically mentioned in the Constitution (pp. 219, 266)

poderes implícitos poderes no mencionados específicamente en la Constitución (págs. 219, 266)

Glossary/Glosario

import to buy goods from foreign markets (p. 99)

*impose to establish or imply by authority (p. 32)

impressment forcing people into service, as in the navy (pp. 263, 289)

*incorporate to include (p. 382)

indentured servant laborer who agreed to work without pay for a certain period of time in exchange for passage to America (p. 77)

*individual person (p. 585)

*inevitable unavoidable (p. 455)

inflation a continuous rise in the price of goods and services (pp. 164, 497, 851)

initiative the right of citizens to place a measure or issue before the voters or the legislature for approval (p. 647)

injunction a court order to stop an action, such as a strike (p. 606)

*innovation introduce something new (p. 389)

inspect to examine carefully (p. 658)

installment buying a system of paying for goods in which customers promise to pay small, regular amounts over a period of time (p. 756)

*institution an organization (p. 349)

insurgent a person who revolts against civil authority; rebel (p. 994)

integrate to end separation of different races and bring into equal membership in society (pp. 531, 876)

*integrity moral character (p. 959)

*intelligence the ability to understand and use knowledge (p. 651)

*intense exhibiting strong feeling (p. 322)

interchangeable parts uniform pieces that can be made in large quantities to replace other identical pieces (p. 306)

interdependent rely on one another (p. 1001)

*internal within a location such as a nation or state (p. 322)

internment camp detention center where Japanese Americans were moved to and confined during World War II (p. 819)

*interpret to explain the meaning of (p. 509)

interstate across state lines; connecting or existing between two or more states (p. 886)

importar comprar bienes de los mercados extranjeros (pág. 99)

*imponer establecer o inculpar por autoridad (pág. 32)

requisición captura de personas para el servicio militar, como en la armada naval (págs. 263, 289)

*incorporar incluir (pág. 382)

sirviente por contrato trabajador que acepta trabajar sin que le paguen durante un período a cambio del pasaje a Estados Unidos (pág. 77)

*individuo persona (pág. 585)

*inevitable ineludible (pág. 455)

inflación aumento continuo en el precio de los bienes y los servicios (págs. 164, 497, 851)

iniciativa derecho de los ciudadanos de presentar una medida o un problema ante los votantes o la asamblea legislativa para su aprobación (pág. 647)

prohibición judicial orden judicial para detener una acción, como una huelga (pág. 606)

*innovación introducción de algo nuevo (pág. 389)

inspeccionar examinar cuidadosamente (pág. 658)

compra a plazos sistema de pago de bienes en el que los clientes prometen pagar pequeños montos en forma regular durante un período (pág. 756)

*institución organización (pág. 349)

insurgente persona que inicia una rebelión contra la autoridad civil; rebelde (pág. 994)

integrar terminar la separación de diferentes razas e implantar la pertenencia igualitaria en la sociedad (págs. 531, 876)

*integridad carácter moral (pág. 959)

*inteligencia capacidad de comprender y aprovechar el conocimiento (pág. 651)

*intenso que expresa sentimientos fuertes (pág. 322)

partes intercambiables partes uniformes que pueden fabricarse en grandes cantidades para reemplazar otras partes idénticas (pág. 306)

interdependientes que confían unos en otros (pág. 1001)

*interno dentro de un lugar, como una nación o un estado (pág. 322)

campo de internamiento centro de detención donde los estadounidenses japoneses fueron trasladados y confinados durante la Segunda Guerra Mundial (pág. 819)

*interpretar explicar el significado de (pág. 509)

interestatal a lo largo de las líneas estatales; que conecta dos o más estados o se encuentra entre ellos (pág. 886)

Glossary/Glosario

intervene to involve oneself in the affairs of another (p. 753)

involve include (p. 221)

iron curtain the political and military barrier that isolated Soviet-controlled countries of Eastern Europe after World War II (p. 844)

ironclad armored naval vessel (p. 483)

Iroquois Confederacy a powerful group of Native Americans in the eastern part of the United States made up of five nations: the Mohawk, Seneca, Cayuga, Onondaga, and Oneida (p. 105)

island hopping a strategy used during World War II that called for attacking and capturing certain key islands and using these islands as bases to leapfrog to others (p. 830)

isolate cut off or separate (p. 628)

isolationism a national policy of avoiding involvement in world affairs (pp. 675, 753)

issue point or matter of discussion (p. 165)

isthmus a narrow strip of land connecting two larger land areas (p. 691)

intervenir involucrarse en los asuntos de otros (pág. 753)

implicar incluir (pág. 221)

cortina de hierro barrera política y militar que aislaba a los países controlados por la Unión Soviética de Europa Oriental después de la Segunda Guerra Mundial (pág. 844)

acorazado barco naval blindado (pág. 483)

Confederación Iroquesa grupo poderoso de nativoamericanos en la parte este de Estados Unidos compuesto de cinco naciones: mohawk, seneca, cayuga, onondaga y oneida (pág. 105)

ir de isla en isla estrategia usada durante la Segunda Guerra Mundial que consistía en el ataque y la captura de ciertas islas clave y el uso de estas islas como bases para pasar por encima a otras (pág. 830)

aislar apartar o separar (pág. 628)

aislacionismo política nacional de evitar la participación en asuntos mundiales (págs. 675, 753)

asunto punto o tema de discusión (pág. 165)

istmo franja angosta de tierra que conecta a dos superficies más grandes (pág. 691)

jazz American music developed from ragtime and blues with African rhythms (p. 632)

joint occupation the possession and settling of an area shared by two or more countries (p. 359)

joint-stock company a company in which investors buy stock in the company in return for a share of its future profits (p. 60)

judicial branch the branch of government, including the federal court system, that interprets the nation's laws (p. 208)

judicial review the right of the Supreme Court to determine if a law violates the Constitution (p. 279)

justify find reason to support (p. 464)

jazz música estadounidense desarrollada a partir del ragtime y el blues con ritmos africanos (pág. 632)

ocupación en común posesión y asentamiento de un área compartida por dos o más países (pág. 359)

sociedad por acciones compañía en la que los inversores compran acciones en la compañía a cambio de una parte de sus ganancias futuras (pág. 60)

poder judicial rama del gobierno, incluido el sistema de tribunales federales, que interpreta las leyes de una nación (pág. 208)

revisión judicial derecho de la Corte Suprema a determinar si una ley viola la Constitución (pág. 279)

justificar encontrar razones para apoyar (pág. 464)

kaiser emperor; the leader of Germany from 1871 to 1918 (p. 723)

kamikaze during World War II, a Japanese suicide pilot whose mission was to crash into his target (p. 830)

káiser emperador; líder de Alemania de 1871 a 1918 (pág. 723)

kamikaze en la Segunda Guerra Mundial, piloto suicida japonés cuya misión consistía en estrellarse contra su objetivo (pág. 830)

Glossary/Glosario

L

*labor to work (p. 585)

laissez-faire policy that government should interfere as little as possible in the nation's economy (pp. 278, 351)

land-grant college originally, an agricultural college established as a result of the 1862 Morrill Act that gave states large amounts of federal land that could be sold to raise money for education (p. 628)

Latino American who has come to the United States from or is descended from people who came from Latin America or Spain (p. 896)

lease to hand over property in return for rent (p. 751)

*lecture talk or speech given to an individual or a group for education or as a gentle scolding (p. 419)

*legal permitted by law (p. 409)

legislative branch the branch of government that makes the nation's laws (p. 207)

levee high walls or an embankment to prevent flooding in low-lying areas (p. 997)

*license to grant official authority (p. 397)

line of demarcation an imaginary line running down the middle of the Atlantic Ocean from the North Pole to the South Pole dividing the Americas between Spain and Portugal (p. 41)

*link join or connect (p. 13)

literacy ability to read and write (p. 412)

literacy test a method used to prevent African Americans from voting by requiring prospective voters to read and write at a specified level (p. 539)

*locate establish (p. 561)

lock in a canal, an enclosure with gates at each end used in raising or lowering boats as they pass from level to level (p. 316)

Long Drive the herding of cattle for 1,000 miles or more to meet the railroad (p. 561)

Loyalists American colonists who remained loyal to Britain and opposed the war for independence (p. 137)

lynching putting to death a person by the illegal action of a mob (p. 540)

*trabajar obrar (pág. 585)

laissez-faire (dejar hacer) política que establece que el gobierno no debe interferir en la economía de una nación (págs. 278, 351)

universidad con dotación de tierras federales originalmente, una universidad de agricultura fundada como resultado de la Ley de Morrill de 1862 que le otorgó a los estados grandes cantidades de tierras federales que podían venderse con el fin de reunir dinero para la educación (pág. 628)

latino americano que se trasladó a los Estados Unidos y que es descendiente de personas que provienen de América Latina o España (pág. 896)

alquilar entregar una propiedad a cambio de una paga (pág. 751)

*sermón charla o discurso dirigido a un individuo o grupo con fines educativos o como reprimenda gentil (pág. 419)

*legal permitido por ley (pág. 409)

poder legislativo rama del gobierno que dicta las leyes de una nación (pág. 207)

dique muros altos o terraplén para evitar inundaciones en áreas de baja altura (pág. 997)

*autorizar otorgar autoridad oficial (pág. 397)

línea de demarcación línea imaginaria a lo largo del océano Atlántico desde el Polo Norte al Polo Sur que divide a las Américas entre España y Portugal (pág. 41)

*vincular unir o conectar (pág. 13)

alfabetización capacidad de leer y escribir (pág. 412)

prueba de alfabetización método usado para impedir que los afroamericanos votaran al exigirles a los votantes futuros un nivel específico de lectura y escritura (pág. 539)

*ubicar situar (pág. 561)

esclusa en un canal, un cercamiento con puertas en cada extremo usadas para elevar o bajar barcos al pasar de un nivel a otro (pág. 316)

larga marcha pastoreo de ganado durante 1,000 millas o más hasta llegar al ferrocarril (pág. 561)

partidarios colonos americanos que permanecieron leales a Gran Bretaña y se opusieron a la guerra por la independencia (pág. 137)

linchamiento muerte de una persona por la acción ilegal de una banda (pág. 540)

Glossary/Glosario

*maintain keep or uphold (p. 261)

maize an early form of corn grown by Native Americans (p. 9)

*major greater in size, extent, or importance (p. 621)

majority more than half (p. 337)

Manifest Destiny the idea popular in the United States during the 1800s that the country must expand its boundaries to the Pacific (p. 363)

manumission the freeing of some enslaved persons (p. 197)

martial law the law applied by military forces in occupied territory or in an emergency (p. 929)

martyr a person who sacrifices his or her life for a principle or cause (p. 461)

mass media types of communication that reach large numbers of people, such as newspapers, radio, and television (p. 759)

mass production the production of large quantities of goods using machinery and often an assembly line (p. 593)

materialism attaching too much importance to physical possessions and comforts (p. 866)

Mayflower Compact a formal document, written in 1620, that provided law and order to the Plymouth colony (p. 66)

*mechanism mechanical device (p. 592)

Medicaid a social program that gives the states money to help those who cannot afford to pay for their hospital bills (p. 883)

*medical health; pertaining to the practice of medicine (p. 431)

Medicare a social program that helps pay for medical care for the elderly (p. 883)

mercantilism the theory that a state's or nation's power depended on its wealth (p. 50)

mercenary paid soldier who serves in the army of a foreign country (p. 155)

merger the combining of two or more businesses into one (p. 599)

MIAs soldiers classified as missing in action (p. 932)

*mantener conservar o preservar (pág. 261)

millo forma antigua de grano que cultivaban los nativoamericanos (pág. 9)

*principal de mayor tamaño, grado o importancia (pág. 621)

mayoría más de la mitad (pág. 337)

Destino Manifiesto idea popular en Estados Unidos durante los años 1800 que establecía que el país debía extender sus fronteras al Pacífico (pág. 363)

manumisión liberación de algunos esclavos (pág. 197)

ley marcial ley aplicada por las fuerzas militares en un territorio ocupado o en un caso de emergencia (pág. 929)

mártir persona que sacrifica su vida por un principio o una causa (pág. 461)

medios masivos de información tipos de comunicación que llegan a un gran número de personas, como los periódicos, la radio y la televisión (pág. 759)

producción en serie producción de grandes cantidades de bienes usando maquinaria y a veces una línea de montaje (pág. 593)

materialismo otorgarle mucha importancia a posesiones físicas y comodidades (pág. 866)

Convenio de Mayflower documento formal, redactado en 1620, que le otorgó ley y orden a la colonia de Plymouth (pág. 66)

*mecanismo dispositivo mecánico (pág. 592)

Medicaid programa social que le otorga al estado dinero para ayudar a las personas que no pueden pagar sus gastos hospitalarios (pág. 883)

*médico salud; perteneciente a la práctica de la medicina (pág. 431)

Medicare programa social que ayuda a pagar la atención médica de los ancianos (pág. 883)

mercantilismo teoría que sostiene que el poder de una nación o un estado depende de su riqueza (pág. 50)

mercenario soldado pago que presta sus servicios en el ejército de un país extranjero (pág. 155)

fusión empresarial combinación de dos o más negocios en uno (pág. 599)

MIAs (Desaparecidos en Acción) soldados clasificados como desaparecidos en acción (pág. 932)

Glossary/Glosario

Middle Passage a part of the Triangular trade when enslaved Africans were shipped to the West Indies (p. 91)

migrant worker a person who moves from place to place to find work harvesting fruits and vegetables (p. 788)

*****migrate** relocate (p. 788)

migration a movement of a large number of people into a new homeland (p. 8)

militarism a buildup of military strength within a country (p. 706)

militia a group of civilians trained to fight in emergencies (pp. 107, 133)

*****ministry** the office, duties, or functions of a minister (p. 438)

*****minor** lesser in size, extent, or importance (p. 623)

minutemen companies of civilian soldiers who boasted that they were ready to fight on a minute's notice (p. 134)

mission religious settlement (pp. 46, 82)

mobilization gathering resources and preparing for war (pp. 725, 815)

Model T America's first mass production car made by the Ford Motor Company (p. 593)

monopoly total control of a type of industry by one person or one company (p. 597)

Morse code a system for transmitting messages that uses a series of dots and dashes to represent the letters of the alphabet, numbers, and punctuation (p. 392)

mosque a Muslim house of worship (p. 33)

mountain man a frontiersman living in the mountain wilderness (p. 360)

muckraker a journalist who uncovers abuses and corruption in a society (p. 647)

mutualista Mexican American self-defense group (p. 668)

Travesía intermedia parte del comercio triangular cuando los esclavos africanos se embarcaban hacia las Antillas (pág. 91)

trabajador migratorio persona que se traslada de un lugar a otro para buscar trabajo en el cultivo de frutas y vegetales (pág. 788)

*****migrar** cambiar de sitio (pág. 788)

migración traslado de un gran número de personas a una nueva tierra (pág. 8)

militarismo creación de fortaleza militar en un país (pág. 706)

milicia grupo de civiles entrenados para luchar en emergencias (págs. 107, 133)

*****clerecía** oficio, deberes o funciones de un pastor (pág. 438)

*****inferior** de menor tamaño, grado o importancia (pág. 623)

minutemen compañías de soldados civiles que se jactaban de estar listos para pelear de un momento a otro (pág. 134)

misión asentamiento religioso (págs. 46, 82)

movilización reunión de recursos y preparación para la guerra (págs. 725, 815)

Modelo T primer automóvil estadounidense de producción masiva fabricado por la Ford Motor Company (pág. 593)

monopolio control total de un tipo de industria por una persona o una compañía (pág. 597)

código Morse sistema de transmisión de mensajes que utiliza una serie de puntos y rayas para representar letras del alfabeto, números y puntuación (pág. 392)

mezquita casa de culto musulmana (pág. 33)

hombre montañés colonizador que vive en áreas montañosas naturales (pág. 360)

sensacionalista periodista que revela abusos y corrupción en una sociedad (pág. 647)

mutualista grupo de autodefensa mexicano-estadounidense (pág. 668)

napalm an explosive material dropped from airplanes during the Vietnam War (p. 914)

national debt the amount of money a national government owes to other governments or its people (p. 255)

napalm material explosivo arrojado desde los aviones durante la Guerra de Vietnam (pág. 914)

deuda nacional cantidad de dinero que un gobierno nacional debe a otros gobiernos o a su población (pág. 255)

National Grange the first farmers' organization in the United States (p. 575)

nationalism intense loyalty to one's nation or group and promotion of its interests above all others (pp. 293, 705)

national self-determination the right of people to decide how they should be governed (p. 729)

nativism the belief that those born in a country are superior to immigrants (p. 762)

nativist a person who favors those born in his country and is opposed to immigrants (p. 399)

*__network__ an interconnected system of people or things (p. 453)

neutral rights the right to sail the seas and not take sides in a war (p. 289)

neutrality a position of not taking sides in a conflict (p. 262)

*__nevertheless__ however (p. 501)

nomad person who moves from place to place in search of food or grazing land (p. 8)

nomadic moving from place to place with no permanent home (p. 567)

nominating convention system in which delegates from the states selected the party's presidential candidate (p. 340)

nonimportation the act of not importing or using certain goods (p. 125)

*__normal__ typical or average (p. 745)

normal school a two-year school for training high school graduates as teachers (p. 420)

Northwest Passage water route to Asia through North America sought by European explorers (p. 51)

*__nuclear__ atomic (p. 862)

nullify to cancel or make ineffective (pp. 270, 341)

Agricultores Nacionales primera organización de agricultores en Estados Unidos (pág. 575)

nacionalismo lealtad intensa a una nación o a un grupo y promoción de los intereses por encima de todos (págs. 293, 705)

autodeterminación nacional derecho de las personas a decidir cómo deben ser gobernadas (pág. 729)

nativismo creencia acerca de que las personas nacidas en un país son superiores a los inmigrantes (pág. 762)

nativista persona que apoya a las personas nacidas en su país y que se opone a los inmigrantes (pág. 399)

*__red__ sistema interconectado de personas o cosas (pág. 453)

derechos neutrales derecho a navegar en el mar sin tomar partido en una guerra (pág. 289)

neutralidad no tomar partido en un conflicto (pág. 262)

*__no obstante__ sin embargo (pág. 501)

nómada persona que se traslada de un lugar a otro en búsqueda de alimentos o tierras para pastoreo (pág. 8)

nómada trasladarse de un lugar a otro sin hogar fijo (pág. 567)

convención nominadora sistema en el que los delegados de los estados seleccionaban el candidato presidencial del partido (pág. 340)

no importación no importar o usar ciertos bienes (pág. 125)

*__normal__ típico o promedio (pág. 745)

escuela normal escuela de dos años para capacitar a los graduados de preparatoria par ser maestros (pág. 420)

Pasaje del Noroeste ruta marítima a Asia a través de América del Norte que buscaban los exploradores europeos (pág. 51)

*__nuclear__ atómico (pág. 862)

anular cancelar o hacer inefectivo (págs. 270, 341)

O

*__obtain__ to gain (p. 806)

*__occupy__ to control (p. 127)

*__occur__ to take place (p. 907)

oligopoly market in which a few large companies control prices for an industry (p. 645)

*__obtener__ lograr (pág. 806)

*__ocupar__ controlar (pág. 127)

*__suceder__ que tiene lugar (pág. 907)

oligopolio mercado en el que unas pocas compañías grandes controlan los precios para una industria (pág. 645)

ordinance a law or regulation (p. 190)

*outcome result (p. 536)

override to overturn or defeat, as a bill proposed in Congress (p. 524)

*overseas across the ocean (p. 816)

overseer person who supervises a large operation or its workers (pp. 94, 408)

ordenanza ley o regulación (pág. 190)

*resultado desenlace (pág. 536)

anular revocar o derrotar, como un proyecto de ley propuesto en el Congreso (pág. 524)

*extranjero del otro lado del océano (pág. 816)

capataz persona que supervisa una operación importante o a sus trabajadores (págs. 94, 408)

pacifist person opposed to the use of war or violence to settle disputes (pp. 75, 727)

*participate take part in (p. 340)

partisan favoring one side of an issue (p. 265)

*partner associate who agrees to operate a business with another (p. 597)

patent a document that gives an inventor the sole legal right to an invention for a period of time (p. 306)

Patriot American colonist who favored American independence (p. 137)

patroon landowner in the Dutch colonies who ruled like a king over large areas of land (p. 73)

pension a sum paid regularly to a person, usually after retirement (p. 795)

*perceive to recognize; understand (p. 727)

perjury lying when one has sworn an oath to tell the truth (pp. 849, 985)

petition a formal request (pp. 140, 190)

*philosophy a set of ideas and beliefs (p. 627)

Pilgrim Separatist who journeyed to the colonies during the 1600s for a religious purpose (p. 65)

pilgrimage a journey to a holy place (p. 33)

plantation a large estate run by an owner or manager and farmed by laborers who lived there (p. 47)

plurality largest single share (p. 337)

*plus in addition (p. 359)

*policy plan of action (p. 68)

poll tax a tax of a fixed amount per person that had to be paid before the person could vote (p. 539)

pacifista persona que se opone al uso de guerras o violencia para solucionar conflictos (págs. 75, 727)

*participar formar parte de (pág. 340)

partidista favorece un punto de vista de un asunto (pág. 265)

*socio persona que acepta operar un negocio con otra (pág. 597)

patente documento que le otorga al inventor el derecho exclusivo legal de una invención durante un período determinado (pág. 306)

patriota colono americano a favor de la independencia de Estados Unidos (pág. 137)

patroon terrateniente en las colonias holandesas que gobernaba como un rey en grandes extensiones de tierra (pág. 73)

pensión monto pagado a una persona de forma regular, en general después de su retiro (pág. 795)

*percibir reparar; entender (pág. 727)

perjurio mentir cuando se juró decir la verdad (págs. 849, 985)

petición solicitud formal (págs. 140, 190)

*filosofía conjunto de ideas y creencias (pág. 627)

peregrino separatista que visitó las colonias durante los años 1600 para un propósito religioso (pág. 65)

peregrinación viaje a un lugar sagrado (pág. 33)

plantación propiedad extensa dirigida por un propietario o un administrador y cultivada por los trabajadores que vivían allí (pág. 47)

pluralidad parte mayor (pág. 337)

*más en suma (pág. 359)

*política plan de acción (pág. 68)

impuesto de votación impuesto de una cantidad fija por persona que debía pagarse para que una persona pudiera votar (pág. 539)

pool a group sharing in some activity, for example, among railroad barons who made secret agreements and set rates among themselves (p. 587)

popular sovereignty political theory that government is subject to the will of the people (p. 215); before the Civil War, the idea that people living in a territory had the right to decide by voting if slavery would be allowed there (p. 454)

populism appeal to the common people (p. 577)

*****pose** to present (p. 845)

poverty line a level of personal or family income below which one is classified as poor according to government standards (p. 883)

prairie schooner a covered wagon used by pioneers in cross-country travel (p. 362)

preamble the introduction to a formal document, especially the Constitution (pp. 142, 215)

precedent a tradition (p. 253)

prejudice an unfair opinion not based on facts (p. 396)

*****previous** earlier, coming before (p. 155)

*****primary** an election in which voters choose their party's candidates (p. 660)

*****principal** most important (p. 93)

*****principle** basic or fundamental reason, truth, or law (p. 270)

*****prior** earlier or before (p. 993)

privateer armed private ship licensed to attack merchant ships (pp. 170, 296)

*****proceed** continue on (p. 720)

*****process** prepare (p. 402)

productivity how much work each worker does (p. 755)

*****professional** occupations requiring special knowledge or education (p. 651)

*****prohibit** stop; disallow (p. 123)

Prohibition the nationwide ban on the manufacture, sale, and transportation of liquor in the United States that went into effect when the Eighteenth Amendment was ratified in 1919 (pp. 655, 761)

*****promote** to help advance (p. 782)

propaganda ideas or information designed and spread to influence opinion (pp. 127, 713)

conjunto grupo que comparte una actividad, por ejemplo, los barones ferroviarios que establecían acuerdos secretos y fijaban sus propias tarifas (pág. 587)

soberanía popular teoría política acerca de que el gobierno está sujeto a la voluntad de las personas (pág. 215); antes de la Guerra Civil, la idea de que las personas que vivían en un territorio tenían el derecho de decidir por votación si se permitiría la esclavitud en dicho lugar (pág. 454)

populismo atractivo para la gente común (pág. 577)

*****plantear** presentar (pág. 845)

línea de pobreza un nivel de ingreso personal o familiar por debajo de lo que la clasificación es pobre de acuerdo con los estándares del gobierno (pág. 883)

goleta de pradera una carreta cubierta usada por los pioneros en los viajes por el país (pág. 362)

preámbulo introducción a un documento formal, especialmente la Constitución (págs. 142, 215)

precedente tradición (pág. 253)

prejuicio opinión injusta no basada en los hechos (pág. 396)

*****previo** anterior, que antecede (pág. 155)

*****primarias** elección en la que los votantes eligen los candidatos de su partido (pág. 660)

*****principal** más importante (pág. 93)

*****principio** razón básica o fundamental, verdad o ley (pág. 270)

*****previo** anterior o antes (pág. 993)

corsario buque privado armado autorizados a atacar a barcos mercantes (págs. 170, 296)

*****proseguir** continuar (pág. 720)

*****procesar** preparar (pág. 402)

productividad cantidad de trabajo que realiza un trabajador (pág. 755)

*****profesional** ocupaciones que requieren conocimiento o educación especial (pág. 651)

*****prohibir** detener; desaprobar (pág. 123)

prohibición proscripción nacional en la fabricación, venta, y transporte de licor en Estados Unidos que entró en vigencia cuando la Decimoctava Enmienda fue ratificada en 1919 (págs. 655, 761)

*****promover** contribuir al avance (pág. 782)

propaganda ideas o información diseñadas y difundidas para influenciar la opinión (págs. 127, 713)

proportional to be the same as or corresponding to (p. 199)

proprietary colony colony run by individuals or groups to whom land was granted (pp. 74, 101)

*****prospect** chance for success; outlook (p. 110)

protectorate a country that is technically independent, but is actually under the control of another country (p. 688)

provisional government temporary government (p. 680)

public works projects such as highways, parks, and libraries built with public funds for public use (p. 777)

pueblo home or community of homes built by Native Americans (pp. 17, 46)

*****purchase** something bought and paid for (p. 283)

Puritans Protestants who, during the 1600s, wanted to reform the Anglican Church (p. 65)

*****pursue** to continue (p. 177)

proporcional ser lo mismo que o corresponder a (pág. 199)

colonia propietaria colonia dirigida por personas o grupos que recibían las tierras (págs. 74, 101)

*****perspectiva** oportunidad de éxito; visión (pág. 110)

protectorado país teóricamente independiente, pero que en realidad está bajo el control de otro país (pág. 688)

gobierno provisional gobierno temporal (pág. 680)

obras públicas proyectos como autopistas, parques y bibliotecas construidos con fondos públicos para uso público (pág. 777)

pueblo casa o comunidad de casas construidas por nativoamericanos (págs. 17, 46)

*****compra** algo adquirido y pagado (pág. 283)

puritanos protestantes que, durante los años 1600, deseaban reformar la Iglesia Anglicana (pág. 65)

*****perseguir** perseverar (pág. 177)

Quechua language spoken by the Inca (p. 15)

quipu calculating device developed by the Inca (p. 15)

*****quote** to repeat the words of another (p. 973)

quota system an arrangement placing a limit on the number of immigrants from each country (p. 762)

Quran the book composed of sacred writings accepted by Muslims as revelations made to Muhammad by Allah through the angel Gabriel (p. 33)

quechua idioma hablado por los incas (pág. 15)

kipu dispositivo para calcular diseñado por los incas (pág. 15)

*****citar** reproducir las palabras de otra persona (pág. 973)

sistema de cupos un acuerdo que fija un límite en el número de inmigrantes de cada país (pág. 762)

Corán libro compuesto de escrituras sagradas aceptadas por los musulmanes como revelaciones hechas a Mahoma por Alá a través del ángel Gabriel (pág. 33)

*****radical** extreme (p. 520)

ragtime a type of music with a strong rhythm and a lively melody with accented notes, which was popular in early 1900s (p. 632)

railroad barons powerful and aggressive businessmen who controlled the nation's railroads (p. 585)

ranchero Mexican ranch owner (p. 374)

rancho huge properties for raising livestock set up by Mexican settlers in California (p. 374)

ratify to give official approval to (p. 177)

*****radical** extremo (pág. 520)

ragtime tipo de música con un ritmo intenso y una melodía animada con notas acentuadas, que era popular a principios de los años 1900 (pág. 632)

barones ferroviarios empresarios poderosos y agresivos que controlaban los ferrocarriles de la nación (pág. 585)

ranchero dueño de un rancho mexicano (pág. 374)

rancho vastas propiedades para la cría de ganado establecidas por pobladores mexicanos en California (pág. 374)

ratificar otorgar aprobación oficial a (pág. 177)

Glossary/Glosario

ration to give out scarce items on a limited basis (pp. 726, 817)

ración producir artículos escasos en un período limitado (págs. 726, 817)

*react respond (p. 289)

*reaccionar responder (pág. 289)

realism an approach to literature and the arts that shows things as they really are (p. 629)

realismo enfoque a la literatura y las artes que muestra las cosas como realmente son (pág. 629)

rebate discount or return of part of a payment (p. 587)

reembolso descuento o devolución de parte de un pago (pág. 587)

recall the right that enables voters to remove elected officials from office (p. 647)

llamar a elecciones derecho que le permite a los votantes destituir a los funcionarios electos de sus puestos (pág. 647)

recession a downward turn in business activity (p. 755)

recesión giro descendiente en la actividad comercial (pág. 755)

Reconstruction the reorganization and rebuilding of the former Confederate states after the Civil War (p. 519)

reconstrucción reorganización y reconstrucción de los antiguos estados de la Confederación después de la Guerra Civil (pág. 519)

recruit to enlist soldiers in the army (p. 155)

reclutar enrolar soldados al ejército (pág. 155)

referendum the practice of letting voters accept or reject measures proposed by the legislature (p. 647)

referéndum práctica que consiste en permitir que los votantes acepten o rechacen medidas propuestas por la asamblea legislativa (pág. 647)

*regime governing authority (p. 912)

*régimen autoridad del gobierno (pág. 912)

*region an area inside a larger area (p. 314)

*región área dentro de un área más amplia (pág. 314)

regionalism art or literature focused on a particular region of the country (p. 629)

regionalismo arte o literatura que se centra en una región particular de un país (pág. 629)

*register to enroll (p. 889)

*registrarse inscribirse (pág. 889)

*regulate to control (p. 450)

*regular controlar (pág. 450)

*reject refuse to accept (p. 464)

*rechazar negarse a aceptar (pág. 464)

*relax to ease (p. 943)

*relajar aliviar (pág. 943)

relief aid for the needy; welfare (p. 776)

alivio ayuda para los necesitados; bienestar (pág. 776)

relocate to force a person or group of people to move (p. 343)

trasladar obligar a una persona o grupo de personas a trasladarse (pág. 343)

*rely depend (p. 89)

*confiar depender (pág. 89)

*remove take away (p. 368)

*quitar arrebatar (pág. 368)

rendezvous a meeting (p. 360)

encuentro reunión (pág. 360)

reparations payment by a defeated aggressor nation for damages caused by war (p. 730)

reparaciones pago realizado por una nación agresora derrotada por los daños causados por la guerra (pág. 730)

repeal to cancel an act or law (p. 125)

revocar cancelar una ley (pág. 125)

republic a government in which citizens rule through elected representatives (p. 188)

república gobierno en que los ciudadanos gobiernan a través de representantes electos (pág. 188)

republicanism favoring a republic, or representative democracy, as the best form of government (p. 215)

republicanismo a favor de un república, o democracia representativa, como mejor forma de gobierno (pág. 215)

reservation an area of public lands set aside for Native Americans (p. 568)

reservación área de tierras públicas reservadas para los nativoamericanos (pág. 568)

reserved powers powers retained by the states (p. 216)

poderes reservados poderes conservados por los estados (pág. 216)

*reside to exist or live within (p. 208)

*residir existir o vivir dentro (pág. 208)

*resistance an opposing force (p. 509)

resolution a formal expression of opinion (p. 125)

*resolve bring to an end (p. 269)

*resource something used by people (p. 374)

*respond to reply (p. 905)

*restriction limitation (p. 291)

*retain hold onto (p. 977)

*reveal show something that was hidden (p. 313)

revenue incoming money (p. 123)

revenue sharing money raised from federal taxes and given to the states for use at the state and local levels (p. 949)

revival a series of meetings conducted by a preacher to arouse religious emotions (p. 419)

*revolution a war to overthrow a government (p. 716)

*rigid firm and inflexible (p. 458)

*route line of travel (p. 430)

royal colony colony run by a governor and a council appointed by the king or queen (p. 101)

*resistencia fuerza opuesta (pág. 509)

resolución expresión formal de opinión (pág. 125)

*resolver poner fin (pág. 269)

*recurso algo usado por la gente (pág. 374)

*responder contestar (pág. 905)

*restricción limitación (pág. 291)

*retener quedarse con (pág. 977)

*revelar mostrar algo que estaba oculto (pág. 313)

ingresos dinero entrante (pág. 123)

participación en los ingresos dinero recolectado de los impuestos federales y otorgado a los estados para gastos estatales y locales (pág. 949)

renacimiento religioso serie de reuniones dirigidas por un predicador para incitar emociones religiosas (pág. 419)

*revolución guerra para revocar un gobierno (pág. 716)

*rígido firme e inflexible (pág. 458)

*ruta línea de viaje (pág. 430)

colonia real colonia dirigida por el gobernador y un consejo designado por el rey o la reina (pág. 101)

S

saga a long detailed story (p. 38)

scalawags name given by former Confederates to Southern whites who supported Republican Reconstruction of the South (p. 529)

*scheme a plan (p. 795)

*scope range or area (p. 985)

search-and-destroy mission a strategy used in Vietnam in which American forces sought Vietcong and North Vietnamese units to destroy them (p. 914)

secede to leave or withdraw (pp. 285, 341, 451)

secession withdrawal from the Union (p. 463)

sectionalism loyalty to a region (pp. 322, 449)

*secure gain control (p. 830)

sedition activities aimed at weakening established government (p. 270)

segregation the separation or isolation of a race, class, or group (pp. 540, 875)

*select choose (p. 337)

Separatists Protestants who, during the 1600s, wanted to leave the Anglican Church in order to found their own churches (p. 65)

saga historia larga y detallada (pág. 38)

scalawags nombre otorgado por los primeros confederados a los blancos del Sur que apoyaban la Reconstrucción Republicana del Sur (pág. 529)

*esquema plan (pág. 795)

*alcance rango o área (pág. 985)

misión de búsqueda y destrucción estrategia usada en Vietnam en la que las fuerzas estadounidenses buscaban unidades vietnamitas y vietcong para destruirlas (pág. 914)

separarse abandonar o retirarse (págs. 285, 341, 451)

secesión retiro de la Unión (pág. 463)

seccionalismo lealtad a una región (págs. 322, 449)

*seguro que tiene el control (pág. 830)

sedición actividades dirigidas a debilitar un gobierno establecido (pág. 270)

segregación separación o aislamiento de una raza, clase o grupo (págs. 540, 875)

*seleccionar elegir (pág. 337)

separatistas protestantes que, durante los años 1600, deseaban dejar la Iglesia Anglicana para fundar sus propias iglesias (pág. 65)

Glossary/Glosario

series a number of events coming in order (p. 507)

settlement house institution located in a poor neighborhood that provided numerous community services such as medical care, child care, libraries, and classes in English (p. 623)

sharecropping system of farming in which a farmer works land for an owner who provides equipment and seeds and receives a share of the crop (p. 531)

shareholder a person who invests in a corporation by buying stock and is a partial owner (p. 596)

*__shift__ to move (p. 815)

siege military blockade (pp. 505, 822)

*__similar__ having common qualities (p. 278)

*__site__ location (p. 979)

sit-in the act of occupying seats or sitting down on the floor of an establishment as a form of organized protest (p. 885)

skyscraper a very tall building (p. 624)

slave codes laws passed in the Southern states that controlled and restricted enslaved people (pp. 94, 410)

slum poor, crowded, and run-down urban neighborhoods (p. 622)

socialist person who believes industries should be publicly owned and run by the government rather than by private individuals (p. 727)

sodbuster a name given to the Plains farmer (p. 565)

*__source__ a supply (p. 8)

spectator sport sporting event that draws a crowd (p. 631)

speculator person who risks money in order to make a large profit (p. 112)

sphere of influence section of a country where one foreign nation enjoys special rights and powers (p. 682)

spiritual an African American religious folk song (p. 409)

spoils system practice of handing out government jobs to supporters; replacing government employees with the winning candidate's supporters (p. 340)

square deal Theodore Roosevelt's promise of fair and equal treatment for all (p. 658)

*__stable__ unchanging (p. 851)

serie un número de eventos que van en orden (pág. 507)

casa de beneficencia institución ubicada en un barrio pobre que brindaba diferentes servicios comunitarios como atención médica, atención infantil, bibliotecas, y clases de inglés (pág. 623)

aparcería sistema de agricultura en el que el agricultor trabaja la tierra para un propietario que aporta el equipo y las semillas y recibe una parte de los cultivos (pág. 531)

accionista persona que invierte en una sociedad anónima mediante la compra de acciones y es propietario parcial (pág. 596)

*__cambiar__ transferir (pág. 815)

sitio bloqueo militar (págs. 505, 822)

*__similar__ con las mismas cualidades (pág. 278)

sitio ubicación (pág. 979)

sentada acción de ocupar asientos o sentarse en el piso de un establecimiento como forma de protesta organizada (pág. 885)

rascacielos en edificio muy alto (pág. 624)

códigos de esclavitud leyes aprobadas en los estados sureños que controlaban y clasificaban a los esclavos (págs. 94, 410)

barrio pobre barrios urbanos pobres, superpoblados y destartalados (pág. 622)

socialista persona que cree que las industrias deben ser públicas y estar dirigidas por el gobierno y no por particulares (pág. 727)

rompedor de cesped nombre otorgado al agricultor de Planicies (pág. 565)

*__fuente__ un suministro (pág. 8)

deporte espectáculo evento deportivo que atrae a una gran multitud (pág. 631)

especulador persona que arriesga dinero para obtener grandes ganancias (pág. 112)

esfera de influencia sección de un país donde una nación extranjera goza de derechos y poderes especiales (pág. 682)

espiritual canción popular religiosa afroamericana (pág. 409)

sistema de despojo práctica de repartir puestos gubernamentales a los defensores; reemplazo de empleados del gobierno con defensores del candidato triunfador (pág. 340)

trato justo promesa de Theodore Roosevelt de un trato igualitario y justo para todos (pág. 658)

*__estable__ que no se modifica (pág. 851)

Glossary/Glosario

Stamp Act Not found!

stalemate a situation during a conflict when action stops because both sides are equally powerful and neither will give in (p. 858)

standard gauge the uniform width of 4 feet, 8.5 inches for railroad tracks, adopted during the 1880s (p. 586)

states' rights rights and powers independent of the federal government that are reserved for the states by the Constitution (p. 270); the belief that states' rights supersede federal rights and law (p. 464)

state sovereignty the concept that states have the right to govern themselves independent of the federal government (p. 322)

*****status** rank or position (p. 142)

steerage cramped quarters on a ship's lower decks for passengers paying the lowest fares (p. 614)

stock shares of ownership a company sells in its business which often carry voting power (p. 596)

stock exchange a place where shares in corporations are bought and sold through an organized system (p. 773)

strait a narrow passageway connecting two larger bodies of water (p. 41)

*****strategy** plan of action (p. 175)

*****stress** call particular attention to; emphasize (p. 713)

strike a stopping of work by workers to force an employer to meet demands (p. 396)

strikebreaker person hired to replace a striking worker in order to break up a strike (p. 606)

*****structure** something that is constructed or built (p. 17)

subsidy grant of money from the government to a person or a company for an action intended to benefit the public (p. 555)

subsistence farming farming in which only enough food to feed one's family is produced (p. 89)

*****substitute** replacement (p. 496)

suburbs residential areas that sprang up close to or surrounding cities as a result of improvements in transportation (p. 622)

subversion an attempt to overthrow a government by persons working secretly from within (p. 848)

estancamiento situación durante un conflicto en la que una acción se detiene porque ambos lados son igualmente poderosos y ninguno se rendirá (pág. 858)

medida estándar ancho uniforme de 4 pies, 8.5 pulgadas para los ferrocarriles durante la década de 1880 (pág. 586)

derechos estatales derechos y poderes independientes del gobierno federal que se reservan para los estados a través de la Constitución (pág. 270); creencia acerca de que los derechos de los estados superan los derechos y las leyes federales (pág. 464)

soberanía estatal concepto acerca de que los estados tienen derecho a gobernarse independientemente del gobierno federal (pág. 322)

*****estatus** rango o posición (pág. 142)

bodega espacio estrecho en la cubierta inferior de un barco para pasajeros que pagan la tarifa más baja (pág. 614)

acciones participaciones de la propiedad de una compañía que en general cuentan con poder de votación (pág. 596)

bolsa de valores lugar donde las acciones en las sociedades anónimas se compran y se venden a través de un sistema organizado (pág. 773)

estrecho pasadizo estrecho que conecta dos masas de agua mayores (pág. 41)

*****estrategia** plan de acción (pág. 175)

*****resaltar** poner especial atención en; enfatizar (pág. 713)

huelga cese laboral de los trabajadores para imponerle a un empleador el cumplimiento de las exigencias (pág. 396)

rompehuelgas persona contratada para reemplazar a un trabajador en huelga con el fin de detener la huelga (pág. 606)

*****estructura** algo construido o fabricado (pág. 17)

subsidio préstamo de dinero del gobierno a una persona o compañía por una acción cuya intención es beneficiar al público (pág. 555)

agricultura de subsistencia agricultura en la que sólo se producen alimentos suficientes para abastecer a una familia (pág. 89)

*****sustituto** reemplazo (pág. 496)

suburbios áreas residenciales que se extienden cerca o alrededor de las ciudades como resultado de mejoras en el transporte (pág. 622)

subversión intento de derrocar a un gobierno por parte de las personas que trabajan en secreto desde adentro (pág. 848)

Glossary/Glosario

*successor one who follows another in order (p. 99)

suffrage the right to vote (p. 435)

suffragist a man or woman who fought for a woman's right to vote (p. 652)

*sum amount or total (p. 553)

summit a meeting of heads of government (p. 862)

supply-side economics an economic theory that proposes tax cuts as a means of stimulating the economy to produce more goods and services (p. 972)

surplus excess; amount left over after necessary expenses are paid (pp. 93, 861)

*survive continue to live (p. 347)

*suspend to prevent or bar from carrying out official duties (p. 526)

*sustain to suffer or experience (p. 173)

sweatshop a shop or factory where workers work long hours at low wages under unhealthy conditions (pp. 603, 615)

*symbol an object that represents something else (p. 352)

*sucesor persona que sigue a otra en orden (pág. 99)

sufragio derecho a votar (pág. 435)

sufragista hombre o mujer que lucha por los derechos de las mujeres a votar (pág. 652)

*suma monto o total (pág. 553)

cumbre reunión de los líderes gubernamentales (pág. 862)

economía del lado de la oferta teoría económica que propone recortes impositivos para estimular la economía con el fin de producir más bienes y servicios (pág. 972)

superávit exceso; cantidad que queda después de pagar los gastos necesarios (págs. 93, 861)

*sobrevivir continuar con vida (pág. 347)

*suspender detener o prohibir la continuidad de las tareas de un funcionario (pág. 526)

*sufrir experimentar o sobrellevar (pág. 173)

fábrica donde se explota a los obreros tienda o fábrica donde los empleados trabajan muchas horas por salarios bajos y en condiciones insalubres (págs. 603, 615)

*símbolo objeto que representa una cosa (pág. 352)

*target an object of attack (p. 809)

tariff a tax on imports or exports (pp. 257, 341)

*technique skillful method (p. 755)

*technology the use of science in commerce and industry (pp. 31, 945)

Tejano a Mexican who claims Texas as his home (p. 367)

telegraph a device or system that uses electric signals to transmit messages by a code over wires (p. 391)

temperance the use of little or no alcoholic drink (p. 419)

*temporary not lasting (p. 449)

tenant farmer farmer who works land owned by another and pays rent either in cash or crops (pp. 81, 407)

tenement a building in which several families rent rooms or apartments, often with little sanitation or safety (p. 622)

*tense anxious or nervous (p. 823)

*objetivo objeto de ataque (pág. 809)

arancel impuesto sobre las importaciones o las exportaciones (págs. 257, 341)

*técnica método especializado (pág. 755)

*tecnología uso de ciencia en el comercio y la industria (págs. 31, 945)

tejano mejicano que reclama Texas como su patria (pág. 367)

telégrafo dispositivo o sistema que usa señales eléctricas para transmitir mensajes mediante códigos y cableado (pág. 391)

templanza consumo de pocas bebidas alcohólicas o ninguna (pág. 419)

*temporal que no dura (pág. 449)

arrendatario agricultor que trabaja la tierra de otra persona y paga un alquiler en efectivo o mediante cultivos (págs. 81, 407)

inquilinato construcción en la que varias familias alquilan habitaciones o departamentos, en general con escaso saneamiento y seguridad (pág. 622)

*tenso ansioso o nervioso (pág. 823)

terrace a raised piece of land with the top leveled off to promote farming (p. 15)

territory an area that is completely controlled by another country as a colonial possession (p. 688)

terrorism the use of violence by groups against civilians to achieve a political goal (p. 991)

*theme a subject or topic of a work (p. 974)

theocracy a form of government in which the society is ruled by religious leaders (p. 12)

Tidewater a region of flat, low-lying plains along the seacoast (p. 94)

tight money policy the practice of raising interest rates to slow personal spending (p. 950)

time zone a geographical region within which the same standard of time is used (p. 557)

*topic subject of discussion (p. 460)

total war war on all aspects of the enemy's life (p. 507)

totalitarian a political system in which the government suppresses all opposition and controls most aspects of people's lives (p. 806)

*trace follow back to (p. 911)

trade deficit the situation when the value of a country's foreign imports exceeds the value of its exports (pp. 959, 1002)

trade union organization of workers with the same trade or skill (pp. 396, 604)

*tradition cultural beliefs and practices (p. 205)

transcendentalist any of a group of New England writers who stressed the relationship between human beings and nature, spiritual things over material things, and the importance of the individual conscience (p. 421)

transcontinental extending across a continent (p. 555)

*transfer to move from one place to another (p. 155)

*transform to change (p. 391)

*transmit send from one place to another (p. 589)

*trend general direction (p. 599)

triangular trade a trade route that exchanged goods between the West Indies, the American colonies, and West Africa (p. 90)

tributary a smaller river that flows into a larger river (p. 482)

tribute money paid for protection (p. 287)

terraza terreno elevado con el extremo superior nivelado para promover la agricultura (pág. 15)

territorio área controlada completamente por otro país como posesión colonial (pág. 688)

terrorismo uso de violencia contra los civiles por parte de grupos para lograr una meta política (pág. 991)

*tema asunto o temática de un trabajo (pág. 974)

teocracia forma de gobierno en la que la sociedad es gobernada por líderes religiosos (pág. 12)

Tidewater región de llanuras planas de baja altura a lo largo de la costa marina (pág. 94)

política monetaria restrictiva práctica de aumentar las tasas de interés para bajar el gasto personal (pág. 950)

huso horario región geográfica en la que se usa la misma hora estándar (pág. 557)

*tema objeto de discusión (pág. 460)

guerra total guerra en todos los aspectos de la vida del enemigo (pág. 507)

totalitarismo sistema político en el que el gobierno reprime la oposición y controla la mayoría de los aspectos de las vidas de las personas (pág. 806)

*rastrear perseguir (pág. 911)

déficit comercial situación en la que el valor de las importaciones extranjeras de un país exceden el valor de sus exportaciones (págs. 959, 1002)

gremio organización de trabajadores con el mismo oficio o destreza (págs. 396, 604)

*tradición creencias y prácticas culturales (pág. 205)

transcendentalista cualquier grupo de escritores de Nueva Inglaterra que enfatizaba la relación entre los seres humanos y la naturaleza, las cosas espirituales en lugar de las cosas materiales; y la importancia de la conciencia del individuo (pág. 421)

transcontinental que se extiende a lo largo de un continente (pág. 555)

*transferir llevar de un lugar a otro (pág. 155)

*transformar modificar (pág. 391)

*transmitir enviar de un lugar a otro (pág. 589)

*tendencia dirección general (pág. 599)

comercio triangular ruta comercial que intercambia bienes entre las Antillas, las colonias estadounidenses, y África Occidental (pág. 90)

afluente un río más pequeño que desemboca en un río más grande (pág. 482)

tributo dinero que se paga a cambio de protección (pág. 287)

Glossary/Glosario

*trigger to start (p. 686)

trust a combination of firms or corporations formed by a legal agreement, especially to reduce competition (p. 597)

trustbuster someone who breaks up a trust into smaller companies (p. 657)

turnpike a road that one must pay to use; the money is used to pay for the road (p. 313)

*desencadenar iniciar (pág. 686)

sindicación combinación de compañías o sociedades anónimas formadas por un acuerdo legal, en especial para reducir la competencia (pág. 597)

destructor de monopolios persona que divide la empresa en compañías más pequeñas (pág. 657)

autopista ruta cuyo uso debe pagarse; el dinero se utiliza para pagar la ruta (pág. 313)

U-boat German submarine in World Wars I and II (p. 709)

unconstitutional not agreeing or consistent with the Constitution (p. 257)

*underestimate misjudge; disbelieve the abilities of others (p. 295)

Underground Railroad a system that helped enslaved African Americans follow a network of escape routes out of the South to freedom in the North (p. 430)

unemployment insurance payments by the government for a limited period of time to people who have lost their jobs (p. 797)

*uniform identical; unchanging (p. 255)

*unify to join together (p. 807)

urban sprawl the spread of human settlements into natural areas (p. 1003)

utopia community based on a vision of a perfect society sought by reformers (p. 419)

U-boat (submarino) submarino alemán en la Primera y Segunda Guerra Mundial (pág. 709)

inconstitucional que no concuerda ni concuerda con la Constitución (pág. 257)

*subestimar juzgar mal; desacreditar las capacidades de otros (pág. 295)

Ferrocarril Subterráneo sistema que ayudó a los esclavos afroamericanos a seguir una red de rutas de escape del Sur para obtener libertad en el Norte (pág. 430)

seguro de desempleo pagos del gobierno durante un período limitado a las personas que perdieron sus empleos (pág. 797)

*uniforme que es idéntico; no se modifica (pág. 255)

unificar poner juntos (pág. 807)

expansión urbana expansión de los asentamientos humanos en áreas naturales (pág. 1003)

utopía comunidad basada en una visión de la sociedad perfecta deseada por los reformadores (pág. 419)

vaquero Hispanic ranch hand (p. 562)

vaudeville stage entertainment made up of various acts, such as dancing, singing, comedy, and magic shows (p. 631)

veto to reject a bill and prevent it from becoming a law (p. 349)

Vietnamization Nixon's policy that called for South Vietnam to take a more active role in fighting the war and for Americans to become less involved (p. 928)

vigilantes people who take the law into their own hands (pp. 380, 553)

*violate disturb or disregard (p. 124)

vaquero dueño de un rancho hispano (pág. 562)

vodevil entretenimiento en un escenario que consta de varios actos, como danza, cantos, comedia y espectáculos de magia (pág. 631)

veto rechazar un proyecto de ley y evitar que se convierta en ley (pág. 349)

vietnamización política de Nixon que sostenía que Vietnam del Sur debía tener un papel más activo en la guerra y que Estados Unidos debía involucrarse menos (pág. 928)

vigilantes personas que toman la ley en sus propias manos (págs. 380, 553)

*violar alterar o hacer caso omiso (pág. 124)

*__vision__ an imagined plan (p. 676)

*__volunteer__ willingly step forward (p. 136)

*__visión__ plan imaginado (pág. 676)

*__voluntario__ que tiene voluntad de avanzar (pág. 136)

*__welfare__ standard care; well-being (p. 797)

*__widespread__ far-reaching (p. 569)

__work relief__ programs that gave needy people government jobs (p. 781)

__writ of assistance__ legal document that enabled officers to search homes and warehouses for goods that might be smuggled (p. 123)

*__bienestar__ atención estándar; saludable (pág. 797)

*__generalizado__ trascendental (pág. 569)

__alivio laboral__ programas en los que se repartieron empleos del gobierno a las personas necesitadas (pág. 781)

__escritos de asistencia__ documento legal que le permitía a los funcionarios buscar casas y depósitos para almacenar los posibles productos de contrabando (pág. 123)

__yellow journalism__ writing which exaggerates sensational, dramatic, and gruesome events to attract readers, named for stories that were popular during the late 1800s (p. 630); a type of sensational, biased, and often false reporting (p. 686)

__yeoman__ Southern owner of a small farm who did not have enslaved people (p. 407)

__periodismo amarillo__ escrito que exagera eventos sensacionalistas, dramáticos y atroces para atraer la atención de los lectores, su nombre proviene de las historias populares a fines de los años 1800 (pág. 630); un tipo de información sensacionalista, parcial, y, en general, falsa (pág. 686)

__terrateniente menor__ propietario sureño de una pequeña granja que no tuvo esclavos (pág. 407)

The following abbreviations are used in the index: m=map, c=chart, p=photograph or picture, g=graph, crt=cartoon, ptg=painting, q=quote.

AAA. *See* Agricultural Adjustment Act (AAA)

Abbott, E.C., *q560*

Abbott, Robert Sengstacke, 746, *p746, q746*

Abernethy, R.L., *q497*

Abilene, Kansas, 560, 561

abolitionists, 424–31, 452; American Anti-Slavery Society, 425, 428; bleeding Kansas, 455; Confederacy, opinions of, *q464*; early work of, 425–26; Harper's Ferry, 460, 461; increased momentum of, 426–31; leaders of, 426–30; Massachusetts Anti-Slavery Society, 428; reactions against, 430–31; women's rights movement and, 435, 652. *See also* anti-slavery movement

Abu Ghraib prison, 995

ACLU. *See* American Civil Liberties Union (ACLU)

Acoma, the, 20

Act of Toleration, 78

Adams, Abigail, 141, 164, *p164, q164,* 165, *q165, q166,* 321

Adams, John, *p186, p226, p251, p302, 1035, p1035,* 1042; 1796 election, 268; 1800 election, 277–78; American Revolution, 132, *q132, q145,* 153, *q153;* Continental Congress, 133; Declaration of Independence, *q139,* 141, *p141, q141;* federal court system, 279; France, relations with, 269–70; Great Britain, relations with, 193; James Monroe visit to, 321; Second Continental Congress, 139, 186, *q186;* Spain, relations with, 326; Treaty of Paris, 177; as vice president, 253

Adams, John Quincy, *p303, p334, p356, p386,* 1035, *p1035;* 1824 election, 336, 337–38, 356; 1828 election, 337, 338, *crt339;* Manifest Destiny, 363, *q363;* as secretary of state, 325, 326, 359

Adams-Onís Treaty, 326, 359, 367

Adams, Samuel, *p136;* American Revolution, 135, *q135,* 136, *q136;* Boston Massacre, 127–28; Boston Tea Party, *q128;* Continental Congress, 133; Second Continental Congress, 139; Shays's Rebellion, *q196;* Sons of Liberty, 125

Adams, Samuel Hopkins, 646, *q646*

Addams, Jane, 619, 623, *p623, q623,* 651, 653

Adena Mound Builders, 18

Adovasio, James, 6, *p6, q6*

Adventures of Huckleberry Finn (Twain), 629

Adventures of Tom Sawyer, The (Twain), 629

AEF. *See* American Expeditionary Force (AEF)

affirmative action, 950

Affluent Society, The (Galbraith), 866

Afghanistan, 992–93; Soviet invasion of, 961

AFL. *See* American Federation of Labor (AFL)

Africa: aid to, 906; American Colonization Society and, 425–26; Barbary Coast states, 287; British colonies, 154; Columbian Exchange, 51; Columbus's first voyage, 39; early kingdoms of, 32–33; European colonies in, 705; exploration of, 31; influence in, 676–77; Islam in, 29; Liberia, 426; slave trade, 90–91; Songhai Empire, 26; trade route around, 35–37, 284; trading kingdoms of, *m32;* World War II, 821–22

African Americans: 1948 election, 854; 1976 election, 959; abolitionists, 428–30; American Revolution, 154, 157, 165, 172; Black Codes, 523–24; Christianity, 409–10, 529; in the Civil War, 478, 479, 500, *g500, p500–01;* cowboys, 561, *p561;* cultural traditions of, 409; discrimination against, 198, 420, 539, 662, 663–67, 717, 721, 818, 875–79; draft riots, 496; education of, 627, 628; equal rights for, 666–68; exploration by, 284, 360; factory workers, 396; farmers, 576; Fifteenth Amendment, 240, 516, 527, *c536,* 539, 652; Freedmen's Bank, 531; Freedmen's Bureau, 520, 523–24, 531; Freedmen's schools, 520, *p520,* 523, *p523;* free, in the South, 412; in government, 988; Great Depression, 788–89, 796; Great Migration, 725, 746; Harlem Renaissance, 760–61; Jim Crow Laws, 540; labor unions and, 604, 797; Lincoln assassination, 521; in military, 875; Native Americans and, 347; newspapers, 630; plantation system, 407–08; population of, in colonial America, 89; Populist Party, 578; prejudice against, 664, 789; railroad workers, 556; Reconstruction, 527, 529; rights of, 523–25, 530, 536–37, 762, 875–79; Sherman's March the Sea, 510; Spanish-American War, 687; in Texas Revolution, 369; urban migration of, *p528–29,* 621, 818, 865; in Virginia, 197; voting rights of, 101, 187, 196, 200, 340, 396, 524, 526, 528, 578, 855, 889; western settlers, 562, 564; women's clubs, 652; in World War I, *p636–37,* 717, 721, *p721;* in World War II, 817–18, *p817;* writers, 630. *See also* civil rights movement; slavery; slave trade

Agee, James, 791

Agent Orange, 914

Age of Innocence, The **(Wharton),** 629

Agnew, Spiro, 953

Agricultural Adjustment Act (AAA), 782

agriculture: after American Revolution, 257; California Gold Rush, 379; colonial, 66, 79–80; dry farming, 565; during Great Depression, 782; Industrial Revolution, 307–08; in Mali, 33; move away from, 595; of Native Americans, 5, 9, 11, 12, 15, 20–21, 22; new methods of, 565; products introduced from Europe, 51; railroads and, 557; Southern, 401–02, 407–08, 538, *g539;* technology effect on, 392–93, 621. *See also* farmers

Aguinaldo, Emilio, 687, 689

AIM. *See* American Indian Movement (AIM)

airplanes: Boeing jets, 925; first powered flight, 583, 590–91; Lindbergh flight, 758, 759; in World War I, 708, *p708;* in World War II, *p808–09*

Alabama, 923, 951; civil rights movement in, 885–86; Native Americans in, 22, 343; readmission to Union, 526; secession, 464; statehood, 317; steel industry in, 538

Alamo, Battle of the, 368, 369

Alamogordo, New Mexico, 831

Alaska, 7, *m676;* oil resources in, 952; purchase of, 516, 676–77

Albania, 805

Albany, New York: Dutch settlement of, 52; Erie Canal, 316; exploration of Hudson River, 51; Revolutionary War, 158–59; steamboat travel, 314–15

Albany Plan of Union, *crt97, crt106,* 107, 112

Alcatraz Island, 898

alcohol: temperance movement, 419, *crt420,* 654, 655, 665, 761; Eighteenth Amendment, 240–41, 654, 655, 761; Prohibition, 242; Twenty-first Amendment, 242, 762

Aldrin, Edwin "Buzz," *q591*

Alexander VI, Pope, 41

Alger, Horatio, 630

Algeria, 356; World War II, 821

Algiers, 287

Algonquin, the, 21–22, 49

Alianza Hispano-Americo **(Hispanic-American Alliance),** 667, 668

Alien Act, 745

Alien and Sedition Acts, 251, 269–70

Ali, Muhammad, *q924,* 925

Alito, Samuel Jr., 996

Allegheny River, 107

Allende, Salvador, 947

Allen, Ethan, 136

Allen, Frederick Lewis, 773, *q773*

Allen, Gracie, 791

Bush, George H.W., 976, *p976, p977,* 1039, *p1039;* 1984 election, 974; 1988 election, 977; 1992 election, 983; domestic policy of, 980–81; foreign policy of, 979–80; Persian Gulf War, 979, *q979,* 983; Soviet Union, relations with, 977, *q977*

Bush, George W., *p253, q992,* 1039, *p1039;* 2000 election, 987–88, 1041; cabinet of, 988; domestic policy of, 989; foreign policy of, 989; Hurricane Katrina, 997; Inaugural Address, 988, *q988;* Iraq war, 994; war on terror, 990–97, *q993;* world trade, 1002, *q1002*

Bush, Laura, 989

Bush v. Gore, 524, 988, *p988,* 1041

business: advertising for, 756; capitalism, 307; corporations, 308–09; deregulation, 972; foreign competition in, 951; free enterprise, 307; government, cooperation with, 764; high-tech, 1006; management of, 755; monopolies, 595, 597, 599, 645, 657; Republican Party, 852–53; stock, 596; trusts, 599, 645, 657, 659, 661. *See also* capitalism; labor unions

Butler, Andrew P., 455

Butler, Pierce, 199

Cabeza de Vaca, Álvar Núñez, 45–46

cabinet: creation of, 231; of George Washington, 265; of George W. Bush, 988; of Harding, 751; of president, 253; of Roosevelt, Franklin Delano, 787, 789

Cabot, John, 26, *m40,* 51

Cabral, Pedro Álvares, 37, *m40*

Cabrini, Mother, 651

Cahokia Mound Builder settlement, 18–19, *p19,* 172

Calhoun, John C., *q318, p340;* Compromise of 1850, opposition to, 450, 451; Nullification Act, 341; state sovereignty, support of, 322–23, *p322, q322,* 339; War Hawks, 293

Calicut, India, 37

California, 457, 795, 922, 962; anti-Asian policies in, 664; Bear Flag Republic, 375, 376–77; Gold Rush, 378, *p378–79,* 379–80, *c379, m379, crt380,* 387, 423, 553; immigration to, 615, 683, 1005; internment camps in, 1042; Manifest Destiny, 378–82; Mexico, war with, 375–76, 450; migrant workers in, 788, *p788;* Native Americans in, 20; railroads, 585; Spanish influence in, 82, 372, 374, 789; statehood, 374, 380, 451; women's rights movement in, 438

California Trail, 361

Californios, 376–77

Call of the Wild, The **(London),** 629

Calvert, Cecilius, 77–78, *c79*

Calvert, Sir George, 77

Calvin, John, 49

Cambodia, 911, 914, 928–30

Cambridge, Massachusetts, 103

Camden, South Carolina, 171, 173

Camp David Accords, 961

Canada: African American immigration to, 428, 430; African Americans, free in, 154; American fishing rights, 177; American Revolution, 140, 158; energy resources of, 1002; French and Indian War, 109, 111; fur traders, 291; immigrants from, 763, 1005; NAFTA, 986; Native Americans, 21, 570; North Atlantic Treaty Organization, 846; Rush-Bagot Treaty, 325; Seven Years' War, 110; War of 1812, 293, 295, 297; World War II, 824

canals, *p302–303,* 303, 316, 390, 690–93

Canary Islands, 39

Cape Breton Island, 105

Cape Cod, Massachusetts, 64, 66

Cape Fear, North Carolina, 40

Cape of Good Hope, 36–37

capitalism: Communism, threat to, 745; Industrial Revolution, 307; welfare capitalism, 755. *See also* business; economy; industry; labor unions; trade unions

Capitol, The, Washington D.C., *c187,* 251, 257, *p276–77,* 293, 296–97, 302, 371, 391; burning of in 1814, *p294–95*

Capone, Al, 762

Caputo, Philip, *q915*

Caribbean Islands, 34, 40–41, 82, 110, 178, 282, 676, *m686,* 974

Carmichael, Stokely, 890

Carnegie, Andrew, 598–99, *p600, q600,* 606, 629, *crt645,* 689

Carnegie Hall, 599

Carnegie Steel Company, 599

carpetbaggers, 530

Carranza, Venustiano, 695, 696

Carroll, Daniel, 199

Carson, Kit, 361, 376–77

Carson, Rachel, 925

Carson River, 553

Carteret, Sir George, *c79*

Carter, James E. Jr., *q956,* 1039, *p1039;* 1976 election, *p958–59,* 959, *g959, m959;* 1980 election, 962; criticism of, 971; energy crisis, *crt946, c960, p960;* foreign policy, 960–62, 973; human rights, 960–61; presidency of, 958–62, 974

Carter, Rosalynn, *p958–59*

Cartier, Jacques, *m40,* 51, *q51*

Carver, George Washington, 628, 668

Carver, John, *c79*

Cascade Mountains, 20

Cassatt, Mary, 632

Cass, Lewis: 1848 election, 450

Castillo San Marcos, 45, *p45*

Castro, Fidel, 897, 906–07, 961

Catholics: 1960 election, 880, 881; discrimination against, 664, *crt664;* explorers, 49; first presidential nomination of, 764; immigrants, 399; Maryland, settlement of, 77–78; in Mexico, 367; Native Americans, conversion to, 81; prejudice against, 663, 664, 762; Protestants, conflict with, 50, 59, 65, 397, 763; in Vietnam, 913; in western Europe, 29

Catt, Carrie Chapman, 652–53, *q653*

cattle industry, 560–65; cattle kingdom, end of, 562; long drive, 561, *m562;* Native Americans and, 567; railroads and, 561; Spanish influence on, 561–62

Caulkins, Nehemiah, *q410*

Cavelier, René-Robert, Sieur de La Salle, 81

Cayuga, the, 21, 106

Cayuse, the, 361–62, *p361*

CCC. *See* Civilian Conservation Corps (CCC)

census, 313; of 1890, 565, 763; of 2000, 957

Central America: American empire in, 676; canal across, 691–93; early civilizations of, 5, 11, *m12,* 18; exploration of, 40–41; slave trade and, *c93;* Spanish control of, 82

Central Intelligence Agency (CIA), 853, 907, 947

Central Pacific Company, 556, 585

Central Park, New York, 625

Central Powers, 727; World War I, 707, 713–14, 732

Chamberlain, Neville, 807

Chambers, Whittaker, 848

Champlain, Samuel de, 52

Chancellorsville, Battle of, 485, *g485,* 498, *p498–99,* 499–500, 502

Chao, Elaine, 988

Chapin, John, *q532*

Charles I, king of England, 67, 73, 77

Charles II, king of England, 73, 74, 75, 79, 99

Charleston Mercury, the, 462

Charleston, South Carolina, *c96, p98–99,* 408, *p430, p456–57,* 466

Charles Town (Charleston), South Carolina, 79, 89, 171, 177

Charlottesville, Virginia, 274

charter colonies, 101

Charter of Liberties, 75

Charter of Privileges, 75

Chase, Lucy, *q520*

Chase, Sarah, *q520*

Château-Thierry, France, 721

Chattanooga, Tennessee: Civil War, 507; growth of, 412

Chávez, César, *p873,* 896, *p896,* 925

Chavez, Dennis, 853, *p853, q853*

checks and balances, 206, 208, 953; Franklin D. Roosevelt and, 798

Cheney, Richard, 987

"Cherokee Rose, A" (Brown), 342

Cherokee, the, 21, 22, 169, 335, 342, 343, 344, 423, 1045; athletes, *p626–27;* Trail of Tears, 345–46

Chesapeake Bay, 61, 175, 296

Chesnut, Mary, *q509*

Cheyenne, the, 568, 569, 570, 1053

Chiang Kai-shek, 847, 944

Chicage Defender, 746

Chicago, Illinois, 618, *p620–21;* African Americans in, 791; cattle industry, 563, 621; civil rights movement, 875; Coffey School of Aeronautics, 759; Democratic Conventions, 923; fire in, 550; gangsters, 762; growth of, 390, 398; Haymarket Riot, *p601,* 606; Hull House, 517, 619, 623, *p623,* 651; immigrants in, 616, 621; lynchings, 747; meatpacking industry, 647; Republican Conventions in, *p462–63,* 660, 750, 779; steel industry in, 598; tenement houses in, 622; World's Fair in, 625

Index

Chicago Tribune, 505
Chickasaw, the, 22, 343
child labor laws, 603, 654, 661, 752, 783, 797
Child, Lydia Maria, 520
Chile, 14, 325, 326, 947
China: communism in, 847, 979; compass, invention from, 31; fur trade with, 287, 360; Geneva Accords and, 911; Great Wall of, 4, *p4*; immigrants from, 379, 556, 613, 616, 617, 664, 665, 763; Japanese control of, 812; Korean War and, 858–59; Marco Polo's journey to, 28, 29, *m29*; Ming dynasty of, 5; Nixon's visit to, 940, *p942–43*, 943, 944–45; Open Door policy towards, 682; Opium War and, 357; ping-pong diplomacy with, 943, *crt943*, 944; relations with, 955; trade with, 675, 689; Vietnam War and, 927
Chinese Americans: in California, 379; Chinese Exclusion Act and, 551; prejudice against, 664, 762; railroad workers, 556
Chinese Exclusion Act, 551, 617, 664
Chinook, the, 20
Chippewa, the, 1043
Chisholm, Shirley, 925
Chisholm Trail, 561
Chivington, John, 569
Christianity, 36, 39, 381; Crusades, the, 29; Hawaii, missionaries in, 680; imperialism and, 677; Native Americans' conversion to, 46, 374; Protestant Reformation, 49; slavery and, 165, 409–10. *See also* Great Awakening; individual religious groups
Churchill, Winston, 821, *q844;* Atlantic Charter, 812; Battle of Britain, 810, *q810;* Iron Curtain, 844; Yalta, 842, *p842–43,* 843
Church of England, 49
Church of Jesus Christ of Latter-day Saints. *See* Mormons
CIA. *See* Central Intelligence Agency (CIA)
Cigar Makers' Union, 605
Cincinnati, Ohio, 396; growth of, 309, 390, 398; steamboats, 315, *p390*
CIO. *See* Congress of Industrial Organizations (CIO)
cities, *p620–21;* changes in late 1800s, 620–25; in crisis, 623; of early civilizations, 5, 10–15; Industrial Revolution, growth of, 309, 397–99; life in industrial, 412
citizenship: to African Americans, 524; U.S. Constitution, views of, 208; duties and responsibilities of, 222–23, *c222*
civil disobedience, 879
"Civil Disobedience" (Thoreau), 453
Civilian Conservation Corps (CCC), *p780,* 781, 789
civil liberties, 805, 995
Civil Rights Act of 1866, 523–24, *c536*
Civil Rights Act of 1875, *c536*
Civil Rights Act of 1964, 746, 872, 883, 889
civil rights movement, *c536,* 666, 855; era of, 872–901; march on Washington

D.C. for, *p836–37, p872–73,* 886, 888; Nixon administration and, 950; nonviolent protest, 879
Civil Service Commission, 644
Civil War (1861-1865), *p442–43;* African Americans in, 478, 479, 500, *p500–01;* Anaconda Plan and, 477; army salaries during, *c477;* beginning of, 95, 427, 430, 447, 464–65; border states during, 475, 501; costs of, *g507, g511,* 512; effect of disease during, 494; early stages of, 480–87; in the East, 484–86, *m484;* end of, 473; events leading to, 197, 446–71; final stages of, 506–12, *m510, m511;* Hispanic soldiers in, 479, 509; life during, 490–97, *p490–91;* North, invasion of, 485–86; resources in North and South, *g476;* Southern production during, 403; strain of, 498–505; two sides, comparing, 474–79, *g475;* in the West, 482, *m482;* women in, 492–93
Civil War: First at Vicksburg **(McBarron),** *ptg472–73*
Clark, George Rogers, 169, 172
Clark, William, 281, 283–85, *q284*
Clay, Henry, *p323;* 1824 election, 337–38; 1828 election, *crt339;* 1832 election, 349, 350; 1844 election, 352, 363; Compromise of 1850, 451, 453; Missouri Compromise and, 323, *q323,* 449; Treaty of New Echota, opposition to, 345; War Hawks, support for, 293
Clayton Antitrust Act, 661
Clayton, Frances Louisa, 492, *p492*
Clean Air Act, 981
Clemenceau, Georges, 730
Clemens, Samuel. *See* Twain, Mark
Clemente, Roberto, 897
Clement VII, pope, 49
Clerisseau, Charles-Louis, 278
Cleveland, Grover, 619, 1037, *p1037;* 1893 election, 645; Cuba, relations with, 685; Hawaii, annexation of, 681; overthrow of Hawaiian monarchy, opposition to, 679; Pullman Strike and, 606; Statue of Liberty, *q615*
Cleveland, Ohio, 588, 597, 598
climate: 15,000 years ago, 8; Arctic, 19; of California, 374; effect of, on Native Americans, 19; global warming effect on, 1004; of North America's West Coast, 19–20
Clinton, DeWitt, 315, *q316*
Clinton, Henry, 159, 171, 173, 175, 176, 316
Clinton, Hillary Rodham, 983
Clinton, William J., 982, *p982, q982, p985,* 1039, *p1039;* 1992 election, *p982–83,* 983; 1996 election, 985; domestic policy, 983–84; foreign policy, 986, *g986, c987;* impeachment of, 969, 984, 985, 987
clipper ship, 391, *p391*
Clymer, George, 199
coal industry: 1920s, difficulties during, 757; in Pennsylvania, 305; railroads and, 557, 586; Southern, 538; worker strikes in, 657–58, 851
Cobb, Frank, 734, *q734*
Cobb, Jerrie, 894, *p894*
Coe, Charles, *q813*

Coercive Acts, 129
Cohen, Simon, *q784*
Cold Harbor, Battle of, 507–08
Cold War, 840–71, 905–09, 973; Berlin, crisis in, 845–47; causes of, 842–49; Cuba, crisis in, 906–07, *m908;* easing of, 943; end of, 977–78, 981; Red Scare and, 848–49
Coleman, Bessie, 759, *p759*
College of William and Mary, *p101*
colleges, 420, 428, 437, 438, 628, 886
Collier, John, 789
Collier's, 646
Colman, Samuel, 246–47
Colombia, 14, 325, 326, 691–92
colonies. *See* Dutch colonies; English colonies; French colonies; Spanish colonies
Colorado: Dust Bowl in, 787; exploration of, 285; gold in, 552, *p552–53,* 569; internment camps in, 1042; Native Americans in, 17–18, 569; New Mexico Territory, 373; statehood, 554; western settlers, 563
Colorado River, 46
Colored Farmers' National Alliance, 576
Columbian Exchange, *m50,* 51
Columbia River, 20, 359, 362
Columbus, Christopher, *p39;* Columbian Exchange and, *m50,* 51; voyages of, 26, 29, *p34, q34,* 35, 38–40, *q39, m40, q40, c54*
Columbus, Georgia, *p950*
Columbus, New Mexico, 695, 696
Columbus, Ohio, *p786*
Comanche, the, 16, 17, 21, 347, 367, 567
Commerce, Illinois, 381
Committee on Public Information, 726
committees of correspondence, 128
Common Sense **(Paine),** 138, 140
communication: electronic, *p936,* 1000; global, 1001; improvements in, 391–92, 589–90, 676; mass media, 759
Communism: 1920s, fears of, 744, *p744–45,* 745; criticism of, 795; in Cuba, 897; during Great Depression, opinion of, 790; in Korea, 857–59; in Latin America, 947, 973–74; resistance to, 977; in Russia, 719, 730, 806; in Southeast Asia, 911; spread of, 843–47
companies. *See* corporations
compass, 31
Compromise of 1850, 450–51, 453, 454, *m454*
Compromise of 1877, 536–37
Comstock, Henry, 553
Comstock Lode, 553
concentration camps, 825
"Concord Hymn, The" (Emerson), 135
Concord, Massachusetts, 134–35, *m134, p135,* 136, 157
concurrent powers, 216
Conestoga wagon, 281, 282, *p282*
Coney Island, New York, *p588–89*
Confederacy: formation of, 464–66; strategies of, 476
Confederate States of America. *See* Confederacy
Confederation Congress: Articles of Confederation, 188–89; land policies, 190

Congress of Industrial Organizations (CIO), 797
Congress of Racial Equality (CORE), 875, 885
Congress of Vienna, 275
Congress, U.S., 219–20, 256, 268; 1800 election, 277; 1876 election, 536; Bank of the United States, creation of, 257, 266; checks and balances, 206, 208; Force Bill, 341; how bill becomes law, c220; Indian Territory and, 344; Liberia, creation of, 426; Mexico, declaration of war against, 375; Missouri Compromise, and, 448, 449; national bank and, 349, 351; Reconstruction and, 519–20, 523–24; Smithsonian Institution, creation of, 446; trade, regulation of, 266. *See also* House of Representatives, U.S.; Senate, U.S.
Connecticut, 987; colonial, 68–69, 73, c79, 101, 136, 154, 156, 162; Constitution ratification, 187; Hartford Convention, 298; slavery, prohibition of, 196
Connecticut River valley, 68
conservationism, 656, 659
constitution: of California, 380; defined, 79; Fundamental Orders of Connecticut, 68; of Iraq, 994; of Iroquois, 22, 24; of Mexico (1824), 368, 370; state, 188. *See also* Constitution of the United States (1787)
Constitutional Convention (1787), p184–85, 188, 197–99; approving the new constitution, p198, 201; New Jersey Plan and, 199; slavery issue and, 425; Three-Fifths Compromise and, 200–01; Virginia Plan and, 199
Constitutional Union Party, 463
Constitution of the United States (1787), 194–201, 204–10, p204–05, 224–45, crt265; amendment process, 218, 234, 254 (*See also* specific amendments by number); Articles of Confederation compared to, 206, 207; Bill of Rights, 201, 205–06, 255; checks and balances, 206–07, 216, g217; concurrent powers, 214, 216; elastic clause, 218–19; enumerated powers, 214, 216; federal court system established by, 207; federalism, 216; first president under, 253; framers of, g195; implied powers, 257, 267–68; individual rights, 217; limited government, 215, 216, 217; national bank, 324, 348; new territory and, 283; political parties, 265; popular sovereignty, 215; preamble to, 214, 215; ratification of, 202–03, crt208, 235, 266; Republicanism, 215; reserved powers, 214, 216; right to secede under, 464; roots of, 205–07; separation of powers, 216; slavery and, 322, 459, 509; states' rights, 270; supremacy clause of, 207. *See also* federal government; state government
Constitution, USS, 287, p287
consumer economy, 756
Continental Army, 139, 140, 152, 154, 156–57, 158, 162–63, p163, 170, 173, 175, 177, 188, 195
Continental Congress (1774), 133

Continental Congress, Second, 177; Continental Army, creation of, 139–40, 155, 157, 160; Declaration of Independence, creation of, p138–39, 141, 321; Philadelphia, flee from, 159, 186; plan for new government, 187, 188; Revolutionary War, debt from, 164, 191–92; warships, creation of, 170–71
Contract with America, 984
Convention of 1818, 325
Cooke, Jay, 536
Coolidge, Calvin, crt752, q754, 1038, p1038; 1920 election, 751, p751; 1928 election, 764; Boston police officers' strike and, 747; business, support of, 754; foreign policy of, 753; presidency of, 752, q752
cooperatives, 575–76
Cooper, Peter, 390
Copperheads, 495, crt496
copper mining: in Africa, 32
Coral Sea, Battle of the, 830
Corbin, Margaret, 155
CORE. *See* Congress of Racial Equality (CORE)
Corinth, Mississippi, 483
Cornish, Samuel, 396, 428
Cornwallis, Charles, 158, 171, 173, p174–75, 176, 177
Coronado, Francisco Vázquez de, m44, 46
corporations: development of, 308–09; downsizing, 981; growth of, 596, 599; horizontal integration, 597, 598, p598; mergers, 599; vertical integration, 598, p598, 599
corruption: in business, 645; Grant administration, 535, 536; Harding administration, 751–52; in local governments, 643–44; in Reconstruction governments, 530, 535–36; Watergate scandal, 940, 951–53, 954, 958, 959
Corsi, Edward, q734
Cortés, Hernán, 14, 27, 42, p42–43, q42, 43–44
cost of living: early 1900s, 603, c603
cotton gin, 306, 308, 400, 401
cotton industry: during 1920s, difficulties of, 757; Civil War and, 476, 477, 502; decline of, 539; growth of, 305–06, 426; Panic of 1837, effect on, 350–51; Southern, 307–08, 400–03, m401, c402, 408, 538; textiles and, 389
Coughlin, Charles, 795
Counting on Grace (Winthrop), 648–49
court system, federal, 253, 255
Cowpens, South Carolina, 173
Cox, James, 751
Crane, Stephen, 488–89, p488, 629
Crawford, William H., 337–38
Crazy Horse, chief, 569, 570
Creek, the, 22, 296, 339, 343
Creel, George, 726
Creoles, the, 172
Cresswell, Nicholas, q158
critical thinking skills: analyzing and interpreting information, 1019; classifying and categorizing information, 1016; distinguishing fact from opinion,

1020; drawing inferences and conclusions, 1021; making comparisons, 1017; predicting consequences, 1018; understanding cause and effect
Crittenden, John, 463, q463, 477
Croatia, 980; immigrants from, 613
Croatoan Island, North Carolina, 60
Crockett, Davy, 369
Cromwell, Oliver, 73
Cronkite, Walter, p916, q916
Crow, the, 566
Crusades, the, 5, 29
Cuba, 819; American protectorate, 688; American Revolution, aid during, 163, 172; communism in, 973; exploration of, 40, 42; immigrants from, 897; imperialism and, crt688; missile crisis in, 902, 908–09; Roosevelt Corollary in, 694; Spanish control of, 686–87
Cuban Americans, 897, 961
Cubría, Mercedes, 818–19
culture(s): 1800s, changes in, 626–32; 1920s, changes in, 759–60; 1950s, changes in, 864; 1820s American, 421; American music, 408–09; Aztec, 5; clash of, 761–63; colonial, 98–103; counterculture, 919; of immigrants, 399, 616; Native American, 4, 9, 17–22, m20, 668
Cumberland, Maryland, 314
Cumberland River, 482
Cumming, Kate, 492, q492
currency. *See* money
Currier, Nathaniel, crt420
Curtis, Christoper Paul, 892–93, p892
Custer, George, p569, 570
Cuzco, 14–15
Czechoslovakia: communism in, 845; independence of, 722–23; World War II, 807

Dade, Francis, 347
Dade Massacre, 347
da Gama, Vasco, m36, 37
Dakota, the, 21
Daley, Richard J., 923
Da Nang, South Vietnam, 913
Dare, Virginia, 59
Darío, Rubén, p699, q699
Darrah, Lydia, p154
Darrow, Clarence, 763
Daugherty, Harry, 750, q750
Daughters of Liberty, 125, 129
Davis, Benjamin Jr., 817
Davis, Benjamin Sr., 817
Davis, Jefferson, p465, p469; Inaugural Address, p469; president of Confederacy, 464, 466, q469, 485, 496, 510–11
Davis, John W., 752
Dawes Act, 571
Dawes, William, 135
Day of Tears (Lester), 404–05
Dayton Accords, 980
Dayton, Jonathan, 199
Dayton, Ohio, 590
Dayton, Tennessee, 763
Dayton, William L., p458

Index

Elections (Congressional): of 1812, 323; of 1842, 460; of 1846, 460; of 1848, 451; of 1854, 457; of 1858, 460; of 1866, 525; of 1870, 528, 529; of 1874, 529, 536; of 1890, 577; of 1894, 578; of 1900, 674; of 1918, 716; of 1932, 780; of 1940, 716; of 1946, 852, 881; of 1952, 861; of 1958, 881; of 1988, 977; of 1994, 984; of 2000, 988; of 2006, 997

Elections (Presidential): of 1796, 268; of 1800, 270, 277–78, $m277$, 285; of 1804, 288; of 1808, 290; of 1816, 321; of 1820, 321; of 1824, 336, 337–38, $c337$; of 1828, 298, $c337$, 338–39, $crt339$; of 1832, 349–50; of 1836, 350; of 1840, 351; of 1844, 352, 363, 371, 450; of 1848, 450; of 1856, 457–58, $m458$; of 1860, 463; of 1864, 509; of 1868, 527; of 1872, 535; of 1876, 536, $c537$, $m537$; of 1884, 677; of 1892, 577–78, 645; of 1896, $m576$, 578, 685; of 1900, 657; of 1904, 658; of 1908, 659; of 1912, 660–61; of 1916, 715; of 1920, 654, 732, 750, 751, 779; of 1924, 752; of 1928, 764; of 1932, $q779$, 780; of 1936, 798; of 1940, 811; of 1948, 853–54, $m854$; of 1952, 860, p860–61, 861, $g861$; of 1960, 880, 881–82, $m881$; of 1968, 921–23, $m922$, 949; of 1972, 951–52; of 1976, 958, 959, $g959$, $m959$; of 1980, $m961$, 962, 971; of 1984, 974–75; of 1988, 977; of 1992, 983, $g983$; of 2000, 524, 987–88, $m988$; of 2004, 995

Electoral College, 207; 1796 election, 268; 1800 election, 277; 1808 election, 290; 1820 election, 321; 1824 election, 336, 337, 338; 1828 election, 337, 338; 1856 election, 458; 1864 election, 509; 1876 election, 536; 1912 election, 661; 1952 election, 861; 1960 election, 881, 882; 1968 election, 922, 923; 1972 election, 952; 1976 election, 959; 1980 election, 962; 1984 election, 975; 1988 election, 977; 2000 election, 987

electricity, p588–89

Electronic Numerical Integrator and Computer (ENIAC), 862–63, p862

Elementary and Secondary Education Act of 1965, 883

Eleventh Amendment, 237

El Fronterizo, 667

Elizabeth I, queen of England, 50, 59

Elk Hills, California, 751

Ellington, Duke, 760

Ellis Island, New York Harbor, 611, p611, p612–13, 614, 615

Ellsberg, Daniel, 930

Elmira, New York, 493

Emancipation Proclamation (1863), 473, 486, 496, 500, 1051

Embargo Act, 290, crt290

Emergency Banking Relief Act, 781

Emergency Quota Act, 762–63

Emerson, Ralph Waldo, 135, 335, 421

England, 30, 51; American Revolution and, 150–83; civil war in, 73, 99; Confederation government, conflict with, 193; exploration by, 51–52; France, war with, 57, 82, 87, 104–12, 184, 274, 283, 287, 288, 289; Holland, war with, 151; Magna Carta of, 5;

Protestant Reformation in, 49–50; religious persecution in, 65, 67–68, 74; Spain, war with, 151, 161; Spanish Armada, conflict with, 27, 56, 59–60. *See also* English colonies; Great Britain

English Bill of Rights, 87, 99, 205–06

English colonies, p86, p122–23; British government, conflict with, 122–42; growth of, 86–115; Middle colonies, 72–75; Native Americans, relations with, p56; New England colonies, 64–69; settlement of, 50, 58–61, c79; slave trade and, c93; Southern colonies, 76–82. *See also* England; New England colonies; specific colonies

English settlements, the first, 58–61

ENIAC. *See* Electronic Numerical Integrator and Computer (ENIAC)

Enlightenment, 103, 205–06

Enola Gay, 832

enslaved persons. *See* slavery

Enterprise, **USS,** 288, p288

entertainment: communist influence in, 848; during Great Depression, 791; movie industry, 738, 759–60, 791; radio, 779, 791; television, p840, 864; vaudeville and movies, 631–32. *See also* music; sports

enumerated powers, 216

environment, the: air and water pollution, 1003–04; changes in, 8; conservationism, 656, 659; effect of, on Native Americans, 19; global warming, 1004; Green Party, 987; recycling, 1004, g1004, p1004

Environmental Protection Agency (EPA), 950

EPA. *See* Environmental Protection Agency (EPA)

Equal Pay Act, 895

Equal Rights Amendment (ERA), 895

Equiano, Olaudah, 91, q91

ERA. *See* Equal Rights Amendment (ERA)

Era of Good Feelings, 321

Erie Canal, p302–03, 303, 316, 319, 391

Eriksson, Leif, 4, 38

Ervin, Sam, 953, 954, p954, q954

Espionage Act, 727

Estevanico, 45

Estonia, 809

Etheridge, Melissa, p936–37

Ethiopia, 805

ethnic groups, 614, 705

E.T., the Extra-Terrestrial, 957

Europe: after World War II, m844; clash with Native Americans, 36; colonization by, 48–52; Columbian Exchange, effect of, 51; early exploration by, 7, 11, 14, 22, 26–55, m40; early maps of, 35; farm exports to, 51, c51; immigrants from, 80, 379, 613, 664, 1005; slave trade and, c93

Evanston, Illinois, 618

Evans, Walker, 791

Everett, Edward, 505

Evers, Medgar, 886

executive branch, 220–21, 253; checks and balances, 206, 208; creation of, 207, 230; departments of, 207, 220,

221; powers of, 220, 221; terms of office, 217. *See also* presidency

Exeter, New Hampshire, 69

Exodusters, 564

expansionism, 675. *See also* Manifest Destiny

exploration: of the Americas, 26–55. *See also* specific countries

factories: assembly lines, 611, 755, 756, p756; closing of, 955; during Great Depression, 775; growth of, 306, p306; immigrant workers, 398, 615; mass production, 755; in the North, mid-1800s, 389; women workers, 435, 615; working conditions in, 431, 602, 603. *See also* labor unions

factors of production, 595–96, p596

Fair Deal, 852, 855

Fair Labor Standards Act (FLSA), 771, 797

Fall, Albert, 751

Fallen Timbers, Battle of, 262

families: Civil War, 477; European colonies, 89, 102; of immigrants, c634; western settlement, 317; enslaved persons, 409; smaller, 651

Family and Medical Leave Act of 1993, 984

Farmer, James, 875, 885, q885

farmers: during 1920s, difficulties of, 757; 1948 election and, 854; during 1950s, difficulties of, 865; African American, 576; American Revolution and, 195, 196, 266; Andrew Jackson and, 339; Civil War and, 497; colonial, 79–80, 89, 92, 93–94, 102; Dust Bowl, effect on, 787–88; Farmer's Alliances, 576; during Great Depression, 774, 782; on Great Plains, 563; hard times for, g575; Industrial Revolution, effect on, 309; Irish immigrant, 398; migrant workers, 788, p788, 896–97; Mormon, 382; National Grange for, 575–76; Native American, 18; in Oregon Country, 362; Panic of 1837, 350–51; protests of, 574–78; railroads, conflict with, 575–77, 587; during Reconstruction, 531; sodbusters, 565; in the South, 407–08, 575; tenant, 539; in the West, 564, 567, p574–75, 575; Whiskey Rebellion, 260, 261

Farmer's Alliances, 576, 577

Farragut, David, 484, 509, q509, 819

fascism, 790, 805

Fascist Party, 805

Father Knows Best, 864

Faubus, Orval, 876–77

Fauset, Jessie Redmon, 760, p760, q760

FDIC. *See* Federal Deposit Insurance Corporation (FDIC)

Federal Convention of 1787, 195

Federal Deposit Insurance Corporation (FDIC), 783

Federal Emergency Relief Administration (FERA), 781–82

Index

Index

Gadsden Purchase, 377
Gagarin, Yuri, 909
Gage, Sir Thomas, 134
Gage, Thomas, *q134*
Galbraith, John Kenneth, 866, *q866*
Galilei, Galileo, 86
Gallatin, Albert, 278
Gallaudet, Thomas, 319, 420
Gall, chief, 569, *p569*
Galveston, Texas, 644, *p644*
Gálvez, Bernardo de, 161, 172
Gamin **(Savage),** 761
Gandhi, Mohandas, 879
García, Calixto, 687
Garfield, James A., *q618*, 1037, *p1037*; spoils system, 644
Garrison, William Lloyd, 425, 426–27, *q427*, 429, 431
Garvey, Marcus, 747
Gary, Indiana, 747
Gates, Horatio, 159, 171, 177
Gates, Robert, 997
Gay, Martha, 358, *q358*
General Motors Company, 756–57, 773, 797
General Trades Union of New York, 396
Genêt, Edmond, 263
Geneva Accords, 911
Geneva College, 438
Geneva, Switzerland, 49, 862, 911
Genoa, Italy, 29, 38
genocide, 825–27
George III, king of England, 128, 129, 134, 140, 152, *q166*, 207, *crt290*
George, David Lloyd, 730
Georgia, 337, 958, 984; colonial, 79–80, *c79*, 94, 101, 133, 154; Constitution ratification, 187; economy of, 401; Ku Klux Klan in, 664; land policies, 190; Native Americans in, 22, 343, 344; readmission to Union, 526; Reconstruction, 531; secession, 464; slavery in, 196
German Americans, 727
German Democratic Republic (East Germany), 846
Germantown, Pennsylvania, 159
Germany: American Revolution, 150, 155; China, influence in, 682; divided, 843, 845–46; fascism in, 790; Hawaii, trading rights to, 681; under Hitler, 807, 809–13, 821–22, 823–26; Holocaust, 825–27; immigrants from, 92, *g395*, 398–99, 713; Protestantism, 49; Treaty of Versailles, 731; World War I, 705–09, 714–16, 718–23, 725, 729, 730; World War II, 805–06
Geronimo, *q547*, 551, *p551*, 570, *p570*, *q570*, 571
Gerry, Elbridge, 201
Gettysburg Address, 504, 505, 1052
Gettysburg, Battle of, 485, *g485*, 502–03, *m503, p1052*
Ghana, 32, *m32*, 33
Gharnātī, Abū Hāmid al-, *q32*
Ghent, Belgium, 298

Ghost Dance, 571
Gibbons, Floyd, *q720*
Gibbons, Thomas, 1041
Gibbons **v.** *Ogden,* 279, 324, 1041
GI Bill, *p850–51*, 851
Gideon, Clarence, 524, *p524*, 1042
Gideon **v.** *Wainwright,* 524, 1042
Gila River valley, 17
Gilbert, Sir Humphrey, 59
Gilded Age, 622
Gilman, Nicholas, 199
Gingrich, Newt, 984
Giuliani, Rudy, *q992*
Gleig, George Robert, *q294*
Glen, James, *q114*
Glenn, John, 909
Global Positioning System (GPS), 30, *p31*
global warming. *See* environment
Glorious Revolution, 99
GNP. *See* gross national product (GNP)
Gobi, 28
Golan Heights, 945–46
gold: in Africa, 32, 33, 35–36; in America, 60; in California, 378, *p378–79*, 379–80, *m379, crt380*, 387; in Colorado, 553, 569; in Montana, 569; in South Dakota, 570; in the West, 554
Gold Coast, 36, 38
golf, 631, 957
Goliad, Texas, 370
Gompers, Samuel, 605, *p605, q605, q608*
Gone With the Wind **(Mitchell),** 791, 793
Gorbachev, Mikhail, 975, 977–78, *p977*
Gore, Al, 1041; 1992 election, 983; 2000 election, 987–88
Gorgas, William, 693, *p693*
Gorges, Ferdinando, *c79*
Gorham, Nathaniel, 199
government: bicameral legislature, 187; business, concurrent powers, 216; cooperation with, 764; checks and balances, 206, 208; colonial, 98–103; democracy, 363; enumerated powers, 216; limited, 100–01; popular sovereignty, 215; representative, 68, 74, 100, 267; republic, 187, 188; reserved powers, 216; separation of powers, 216; spoils system, 644. *See also* cities; federal government; state government; states' rights
GPS. *See* Global Positioning System
Grady, Henry, 538
Graff, Frederick, 319
Grand Council, 22
grandfather clause, 539
Grandy, Moses, *q411*
Grant, Ulysses S., 473, 509, *p509, q509*, 535, 1036, *p1036*; 1868 election, 527; 1872 election, 535; 1876 election, 536; Battle of Shiloh, 483; Reconstruction, 534, 535; unconditional surrender, 482, *q482*; Union strategy, 507–09, *q507, q508*, 510–11, 512, *q512*; Vicksburg Siege, 503–05
Grapes of Wrath, The **(Steinbeck),** 791
Grasse, François de, 175, 176
Gray, Robert, 359
Gray, Thomas, 411
Great Awakening, 87, 102, 419

Great Basin, 20
Great Britain: American Civil War and, 476, 487, 502–03; Berlin Crisis and, 845–46; China, influence in, 682; Constitution, influence on, 209, 266; Egypt, invasion of, 862; Five-Power Treaty, signing of, 753; France, conflict with, 261–63, *crt268*; Geneva Accords and, 911; Hawaii, trading rights to, 681; immigrants from, 80; Industrial Revolution, beginning of, 305; Iraq war and, 994; John Adams, ambassador to, 269; Opium War and, 357; Oregon Country and, 359; rules colonial America, 99–101; World War I and, 705–09, 714, 718–21, 730; World War II and, 807, 809–13, 821. *See also* England; French and Indian War
Great Compromise, the, 200, 207
Great Depression, 770–801; causes of, 773–75; Hoover's policies during, 776–77; Hoovervilles, 776, *p776*; unemployment during, *g773*, 775, 781–83, 796–97
Great Lakes, 106, 109, 193, 315, 325, 390, 398, 585
Great Migration, 67–68, 362, 725, 746
Great Peace, 21
Great Plains, 285, 343, 362, 392; Dust Bowl in, 787–88; life on, 562; Native Americans of, 17, 567; settlement of, 563, 568
Great Salt Lake, Utah, 382
Great Serpent Mound, *p18*
Great Society, 883, 949
Great Wall of China, 4, *p4*
Greece, 844–45; immigrants from, 613
Greeley, Horace, 487, 535
Green Berets, *p904–05*, 905, 912
Greene, Nathanael, 173
Greenhow, Rose O'Neal, 493
Greenland, 38
Green Mountain Boys, 136, 159
Green Party: 2000 election, 987
Green River, 360
Greensboro, North Carolina, 173, 884, *p884–85*
Greenwich, Massachusetts, 195
Gregg, William, 403
Grenada, 974
Grenville, George, 123
Griffith, D.W., 665
Grimké, Angelina, 427, *q427*
Grimké, Sarah, 427
gross national product (GNP), 755
Guadalcanal, 830
Guam, 688; World War II, 829–30
Guantanamo Bay, Cuba, 995, 1042; naval base at, 688
Guatemala, 11
Guilford Courthouse, North Carolina, 173
Gulf of Mexico, 19, 81, 178, 297, 997
Gulf of Tonkin Resolution, 902, 913, 930
Gutenberg, Johannes, 26

habeas corpus, writ of, 495–96
Haida, the, 20

613; from Hungary, 613; from Ireland, *g395*, 398–99, *crt398*, 496, 556, 622, 665, 713; from Italy, 613, 616, 746; from Japan, 664, 683, 763; Jewish, 616, 622, 663; journey to America, 614; labor unions, discrimination by, 604; from Latin America, 1005; from Mexico, 613, 725, 763, 865; from Poland, 613, 616; population (1820, 1860), *c397*; prejudice against, 664, 762; from Puerto Rico, 865, 897; from Russia, 613; from Scandinavia, 564; from Scotland, 598; from Serbia, 613; from southern and eastern Europe, 664, 702, 762; from Sweden, 613; tenements, 622, *p622*; from Turkey, 613; western settlers, 563

immigration: to California, 615, 683; Chinese Exclusion Act, 551, 617, 664; Ellis Island, 611, *p611, p612–13*; Emergency Quota Act, 762–63; to English colonies, 89; foreign-born population, *g1005*; illegal, 1005–06; Immigration Act of 1917, 617; limits to, *crt616*; mid-1800s, *g395*; National Origins Act, 763; Nativism, 397; Northern cities, growth of, 397–99; response to, 613

Immigration Act of 1917, 617

impeachment, 226; of Andrew Johnson, 527, 985; of Bill Clinton, 969, 984, 987; of Richard Nixon, 953

imperialism: age of, 676–77, *m681*; opposition to, 689; in the Pacific, 678–83, *crt688*

Inaugural Address: of Abraham Lincoln, first, 465, *p468*; of Abraham Lincoln, second, 514, *q526*; of George Washington, 253; of George W. Bush, 988, *q988*; of James Monroe, *q320*; of Jefferson Davis, *p469*; of John F. Kennedy, 882, 1056; of Richard Nixon, 927, *q927*, 943, *q943*; of Ronald Reagan, 971, *q971*; of Rutherford B. Hayes, 537, *q537*; of Thomas Jefferson, 276, 278

Incas, the, 5, 14–15, *m14, p14*, 44–45

Inch'ŏn, South Korea, 857

income tax, 659–60, 661; creation of, 577–78; history of, 660, *c660*; lowering of, 752

indentured servants, 77, 101, 102

Independence Day, *p141*, 153, *p320–21*, 321, 428

Independence Hall, Philadelphia, Pennsylvania, 153, *p202*

Independence, Missouri, 362, 373

India, 35–37, 51, 110, 287, 387, 847, 879

Indiana, *m313*, 460, 674; 1856 election, 458; Civil War, 495; population of, *c313*; railroads, 391; statehood, 317; women's rights movement in, 438

Indianapolis Journal, 422

Indiana Territory, 292

Indian Civil Rights Act of 1968, 873, 897

Indian New Deal, 789

Indian Peace Commission, 568

Indian Removal Act, 334, 343

Indian Reorganization Act, 789

Indians. *See Native Americans; individual Native American nations*

Indian Territory, 344

Indochina, *m911*

Industrial Revolution: in Great Britain, start of, 305; in New England, 305; technology of, 306, *m306*

industry, 600–01; after World War II, 851; agricultural equipment, 587, 621; Civil War, 497; development of, 255; economy of, 595; Era of Good Feelings, 321; foreign competition in, 950; during Great Depression, 774; Industrial Revolution, 305–06; Midwestern, 391; in New England, 393; protective tariffs, 256, 322; regulation of, 646; Southern, growth of, 538; Southern, mid-1800s, 402–03; technology and, 755; during World War II, 816. *See also* factories; labor unions

INF. *See* Intermediate-Range Nuclear Forces Treaty (INF)

Ingersoll, Jared, 199

Inglis, Charles, 140, *p140, q140*

Inouye, Daniel, *q852*

Intermediate-Range Nuclear Forces Treaty (INF), 975

Internal Revenue Service (IRS), 951

International Ladies' Garment Workers Union (ILGWU), 605, 615

Internet, 1000

internment camps, 803, 819

Interstate Commerce Act, 645

Interstate Commerce Commission (ICC), 645, 886

Intolerable Acts, 129

Inuit, the, 19

inventions: of 1800s, 423; of 1920s, 755; by African Americans, 592; communication, 589–90; by Edison, 591

Iowa, 392, 454; Native Americans, 346

Iran-Contra scandal, 975

Iran hostage crisis, 941, *p941*, 962

Iraq, 979; war in, 994

Ireland: immigrants from, 316, *g395*, 398–99, *crt398*, 496, 556, 665, 713; World War I, 714

Irish Americans, 727

Iron Curtain, 844, *crt845*

iron industry, 92; Civil War, during, 403; impact of, 305; railroads and, 586; Southern, 538; strikes, 583

Iroquois Confederacy, the, 86, 105–06, 107

Iroquois, the, 21–22, *p86*

IRS. *See* Internal Revenue Service (IRS)

Isabella, queen of Spain, 39, *p39, q39*, 40

Islam, 29, 32, 33, 39, 962

isolationism, 675, 753, 811–12

Israel, 29, 847, 862, 945–46, 961, 986, 992

Italy, 753; exploration by, 28; fascism in, 790, 805; immigrants from, 613, 616, 746; ports of, 29, 31; the Renaissance in, 29, 30; World War I, 705–07, 730; World War II, 805–06, 810, 812, 813, 822

I Will Fight No More **(Chief Joseph),** 1053

Iwo Jima, Japan, 830, 831, *p831*

Jackson, Andrew, *p297*, 334–55, *p336, crt339, p340, q340, q344, crt349, q350*, 1035, *p1035;* 1824 election, 337–38; 1828 election, 298, 337, 338; Bank of the United States, opposition to, 348–52; *Hermitage, p348–49;* inauguration of, *p336–37;* national bank and, *crt350*, 351; Native Americans, relocation of, 296, 342–47, 1045, *q1045;* Nullification Act and, 341, *q341;* political beliefs, 336–41; Spain, relations with, 325–26; spoils system and, 644; statehood of Texas, 371; voting rights and, 339–40; War of 1812 and, 337, 339

Jackson, Jesse, *q776*

Jackson, Mississippi, 886

Jackson, Rachel Donelson, 338, *p338*

Jackson State University, 930

Jackson, Thomas "Stonewall," *q498;* Battle of Chancellorsville, *p498–99*, 499–500; First Battle of Bull Run, 481–82; leadership of, 485, 499

Jackson, William, 199

Jamaica, 40, 747

James II, king of England, 99

James I, king of England, 60–61

James River, 61, 76

Jamestown settlement, 56, 58, 59, 60–61, 65, 78

Janney, Eli H., 587

Japan: China, influence in, 682; Five-Power Treaty, 753; immigrants from, 664, 683, 763; Indochina, capture of, 911; Korea, control of, 683; Open Door policy, opposition to, 683; trade with, 675; World War I and, 707; World War II and, 806, 810, 812–13, 821, 828–32, 843

Japanese Americans: internment of, 803, 819; World War II, service in, 818, *p818*

Jay, John, *p251;* as chief justice, 251, 255, 263; Constitution, support of, 209; Continental Congress, 133; Jay's Treaty, 263; Treaty of Paris, 177

Jay's Treaty, 263, 269

jazz: age of, 742–69

Jazz Singer, The, 759

Jefferson, Thomas, *q278*, 448, *q448*, 1035, *p1035*, 1042; 1796 election, 268; 1800 election, 277; 1804 election, 288; Alexander Hamilton, conflicts with, 265; Constitution, support for, 209, *q209;* Declaration of Independence, writing of, 139, 141, *p141*, 142, *q142*, *q321;* Democratic-Republican Party, support of, 266–68, *p266, q266;* embargo, use of, 290, *crt290;* federal courts and, 279; France, relations with, 282; freedom of religion and, *q218;* Inaugural Address of, 276, *q276*, 278; Kentucky and Virginia Resolutions and, 270; laissez-faire and, 658; Lewis and Clark expedition and, 283–85; Louisiana Purchase and, 280–85; *Monticello, p274–75;* national bank and, 257; Missouri Compromise and, *q324;* Pike's expedition and, 285; policies of, 278–79; Revolutionary War and, 173; as secretary of state, 253, 268; Shays's Rebellion and, 196, *q196;* Tripoli, war with, 287–88; George Washington, relations with, 265, *crt265*, 268; Whiskey Rebellion and, 261

Jeffords, James, 988

Jenifer, Daniel, 199
Jenney, William LeBaron, 624
Jennison, Edwin Francis, *p478*
Jerked Down (Russell), *ptg560–61*
Jerusalem, Israel, 945
Jews/Jewish Americans: in colonial America, 68, 74, 80, 89; in government, 987; immigrants, 616; newspapers of, 630; persecution of, 614, 795, 806, 825–27; prejudice against, 663, 664, 762
Jim Crow Laws, 540
Joan of Arc, 26
Job Corps, 883
John II, king of Portugal, 36
John, king of England, 5, 101
Johnson, Andrew, *p526*, *p985*, 1036, *p1036*; 1866 election, 525; impeachment of, 527, 985; Reconstruction, 521, *q521*, 523–24; Tenure of Office Act, 526–27
Johnson, Anthony, 76, *q76*, 77
Johnson, Beverly, 925
Johnson, Charles F., 522
Johnson, James Weldon, 760
Johnson, Lyndon B., 1038, *p1038*; 1964 election, 902; civil rights, *q882*, 885, 888–89, *q889*, 891; Great Society, 883, 949; Kennedy assasination, 882; Vietnam War, 913, *q913*, 915, *p917*, *q917*, 919, 921, *q922*, 923, 930
Johnson, William Samuel, 199
Johnston, Albert Sidney, 483
Joliet, Louis, 81
Jones Act, 688
Jones, John Paul, *q166*, 170, *p170*, *q170*
Jones, Mary Harris, 605, *p605*, *q605*, *q618*
Joplin, Scott, 632
Jordan, 945
Jordan, Barbara, q219, 954, *p954*, *q954*
Joseph, Chief, 1053
journalism: muckrakers, 642, 646, 646–47; World War II, 821; yellow journalism, 630, 685–86
Journal of William Thomas Emerson: A Revolutionary War Patriot, The (Denenberg), 130–31
Journal, the, 685
Joyce, Diane, 950, *p950*
Judaism. *See* Jews/Jewish Americans
judicial branch, 221; checks and balances, 206, 208; creation of, 232. *See also* Supreme Court, U.S.
Judiciary Act of 1789, 250, 253, 255
Judiciary Act of 1801, 279
Jungle, The (Sinclair), 647, 671

Kamehameha I, king of Hawaii, 679
kamikazes, 830
Kaneohe, Hawaii, 830
Kansas, 46, 861, 959; bleeding Kansas, 460; Dust Bowl in, 787; Exodusters, 564; western settlers, 552, 575
Kansas City, Kansas: cattle industry, 621
Kansas-Nebraska Act, 447, 454, *m454*, 457, 458
Kansas Pacific Railroad, 560
Kansas Territory, 454

Kaskaskia, Illinois, 169, 172
Kearny, Stephen Watts, 376, 377
Keating-Owen Act, 661
Keller, Helen, 735, *p735*
Kellogg-Briand Pact, 753
Kellogg, John Harvey, *q618*
Kennan, George F., 844
Kennedy, Anthony, 972
Kennedy, Jacqueline, 882, *q924*
Kennedy, John F., *p880–81*, *q880*, 1038, *p1038*; 1960 election, 880, 881–82, *q881*; assassination of, 882, 913; civil rights, *q882*, 885, 886, *q886*, 888; Cuban missile crisis, 908–09, *q908*; domestic policy, 882; foreign policy of, 904–09, *q904*, *q905*; Inaugural Address of, 882, 1056, *p1056*; Peace Corps, 924
Kennedy, Robert F., 885, 886, 903, 922, *p922*; 1968 election, 921–22
Kent State University, 929–30
Kentucky, 293, 323, 337, 351, 453, 460, 463, 477; Civil War, border state during, 475; farming in, 392; Fort Knox, 783; public education in, 412; secession, 465; settling of, 281; statehood, 317
Kenya, 992
Kerner Commission, 891
Kerouac, Jack, 866, *q871*
Kerry, John: 2004 election, 995
Key, Francis Scott, 297, 303, 319
Khomeini, Ayatollah, 962
Khrushchev, Nikita, 862, 905, 907, 909
Kiel, Germany, 723
Kinghts of Labor, 604
King Lear (Shakespeare), 56
King, Martin Luther Jr., *p836–37*, *p878*, *q924*, *p1057*; assassination of, 873, 891, 903, 922; civil rights leader, 878, *q878*, 886, *q886*, *q888*, *q891*; "I Have a Dream" speech, 889, 1057; *Letter from Birmingham Jail*, 887, *p887*
King Philip's War, 57, 69
King, Rufus, 199, *p324*
Kings Mountain, Battle of, 173
Kiowa, the, 347, 367
Kissinger, Henry, 927–28, *p927*, 931, 943–44, 946, 955
Kitty Hawk, North Carolina, 590
Know-Nothing Party, 397, 399, 458
Kodiak Island, Alaska, 185
Korea: Japan, control of, 683
Korean War, 856–59, *p856–57*, *m857*; beginning of, 857–58; end of, 859, 861
Korematsu, Fred, 1042, *p1042*
Korematsu v. United States, 819, 1042
Kosciusko, Thaddeus, 163
Kosovo, 986
Kristallnacht, 826
Kublai Khan, 29
Ku Klux Klan: in 1900s, 664–65, *c665*, *p665*; 1920s, revival of, 762; during Reconstruction, 530, 535
Kuwait, 979
Kyoto Protocol, 1004

labor unions: 1972 election and, 952; after World War II, 851; collective bargain-

ing and, 605; criticism of, 600–01, 795; discrimination by, 604; during Great Depression, 797; growth of, 604–06; Lowell Female Labor Reform Organization and, 397; Republican Party, opposition from, 852–53; Sherman Antitrust Act and, 645; women, members of, 605; World War I, during, 725. *See also* trade unions
Ladies' Home Journal, 630
Lafayette, Marquis de, *p162*, 163, 173
Lafitte, Jean, 297, *p297*
La Follette, Robert, 647, 752
La Grande, Orgeon, *p584–85*
Lahaina, Hawaii, 679
laissez-faire, 278, 351, 658, 752
Lake Champlain, 52, 136
Lake Champlain, Battle of, 297
Lake Erie, 295, 315–16
Lake George, 110
Lake Michigan, 747
Lake Ontario, 110, 111, 158
Lake Texcoco, 13
Lakota, the, 567, 570
Lamar, Mirabeau, 371
Lancaster, Pennsylvania, *c187*, 282
land bridge, 7, 19
Landing of the Pilgrims, The (Bartoll), *ptg1*
Land Law of 1851, 379
land policies, 190–91
Langdon, John, 199
Lange, Dorothea, 791, *q792*
Langley, Virginia, *p490–91*
L'Anse aux Meadows, 38
Laos, 911, 914, 928
La Raza Unida, 897
Larcom, Lucy, *q304*, 305
Las Casas, Bartolomé de, *q1*, 46, *p46*, *q46*, 47
Last of the Mohicans, The (Cooper), 386
Latimer, Lewis Howard, 589, *p589*, 592
Latin America, 290; aid to, 906; communism in, 947, 973–74; immigrants from, 1005; involvement in, 753; Monroe Doctrine and, 325, 677; policies toward, 690–96. *See also* individual countries
Latinos. *See* Cuban Americans; Hispanic Americans; Mexican Americans
Latvia: World War II, 809
law: under Articles of Confederation, 189; colonial, 74, 99–101; emergence in Europe, 30; English colonial, 61, 66, 67, 129; Spanish colonial, 46–47; under United States Constitution, 207
Lawrence, Kansas, 455
Lawton, Marion, *q829*
Lazarus, Emma, 614, *q614*, *q637*, *q734*
League of Armed Neutrality, 184
League of Nations, 703, 730–32, *crt731*, 753, 805–06, 806
League of United Latin American Citizens (LULAC), 897
Leaves of Grass (Whitman), 421
Lebanon, 974, 975
Lee, Richard Henry, 133, 139, 141, *q141*, 188, *p188*, *q188*, 190, *q190*
Lee, Robert E., *p472*, *p502*, 508, *p508*, *q508*; Battle of Antietam, 486; Battle

Index

Index

Index

money: Civil War, *p228;* coins, *p230;* Continentals, 191–92, *p192;* currency, after Revolution, 185, 189; free silver, 578; greenbacks, 497; seven-dollar bill, 1776, *p116;* United States Constitution, 206

Monks Mound, 19

Monongahela River, 107

monopolies, 595, *crt595,* 597, 657; prohibition of, 599, 645

Monroe Doctrine, 326, 334, 677, *crt694,* *q694,* 716, 1049

Monroe, James, *p320, p334,* 1035, *p1035, p1049;* 1816 election, 321; 1824 election, 337; France, representative to, 283; Inaugural Address, *q320;* Monroe Doctrine, 325, *p325,* 326, *q328*

Montana, 717, 796; gold in, 569; Native Americans, 570; statehood, 554

Montcalm, Marquis de, 109, *p109, q109*

Monterey, California, 82, 377

Monterrey, Mexico, 376

Montesquieu, Baron de, 87, 206, 207

Montezuma, Carlos, 668

Montezuma (Moctezuma), 43

Montgomery, Alabama: bus boycott, 872; civil rights movement in, 872, 877–78, 886; growth of, 412

Montgomery, Bernard, 822

Montgomery Ward, 593

Monticello, *p274–75,* 278

Monticello, John Holmes, 448

Montreal, Canada, 51, 111, 140, 589

Moore's Creek, Battle of, 171

Morehouse College, 531

Morgan, Barbara, *p973*

Morgan, Daniel, 173

Mormons, 381–82, *p381,* 419

Mormon Trail, 382

Morning Journal, 630

Morocco, 33, 287; World War II, 821

Morrill Act, 628

Morris, Elias Campbell, 529, *q529*

Morris, Gouverneur, 198, 199, *c205, p205*

Morrison, Toni, 628

Morris, Robert, 192, 199

Morse code, 589

Morse, Samuel, 391, *q391,* 392, *p392, q392, q422,* 589

Moscow, Russia, 823, 909, 945, 962, *p976–77*

Moses, Robert, *q111*

"Mother to Son" (Hughes), 766–67

Motley, Constance Baker, 925

Mott, Lucretia, 435, *q435*

Mound Builders, the, 17, 18–19, *m18*

mountain men, *p358–59,* 360–61, *m360,* 374

Mount Holyoke Female Seminary, *p434–35,* 435, 437, 438

Mount Vernon, Virginia, *q177*

Moynihan, Daniel, 984, *p984, q984*

Mozart, Amadeus, 167

Muhammad, Askìya, 33

Muller v. Oregon, 670

Munich Conference, 807

Munich, Germany, 807

Murphy, Audie, 823, *p823, q823*

Murray, Judith Sargeant, 165

Mūsā, Mansa, 33

music: African American, 409, 864; American, roots of, 408–09; counterculture, 919; country, 864; Great Depression, 787; jazz, 760; late 1800s, 631; patriotic, 685, *p685;* rock 'n' roll, 864

Muskie, Edmund, 951–52

Muslims. *See* Islam

Mussolini, Benito, 805, 812, 822

NAACP. *See* National Association for the Advancement of Colored People (NAACP)

Nabrit, James Jr., *p1040*

NACW. *See* National Association of Colored Women (NACW)

Nader, Ralph: 2000 election, 987

NAFTA. *See* North American Free Trade Agreement (NAFTA)

Nagasaki, Japan, 803, 832

Naismith, James, 631

Narraganset, the, 68, 69

Narrative of the Life and Adventures of Venture, A **(Smith),** 96

Narrative of the Life of Frederick Douglass **(Douglass),** 408, 423

Narváez, Pánfilo de, 45

NASA. *See* National Aeronautics and Space Administration (NASA)

Nashville, Tennessee, 348, 483

Nasser, Gamal Abdel, 862

Nast, Thomas, 533, *q642,* 644

Natchez, Mississippi, 161, 172, 315

Natchez, the, 19

National Aeronautics and Space Administration (NASA), 862, 909

National American Woman Suffrage Association, 652–53

National Association for the Advancement of Colored People (NAACP), 641, 667, 789, 875–76, 878, 885, 886, 890

National Association of Colored Women (NACW), 652, 667

national bank: creation of, 323; regional conflict over, 322, 323

National Child Labor Committee, 646

National Congress of American Indians (NCAI), 897

National Conservation Commission, 659

National Energy Plan, 959–60

National Gazette, 266

National Grange, 575–76

National Industrial Recovery Act (NIRA), 783

nationalism: after War of 1812, 325; prior to World War I, 705; sectionalism and, 322–24

National Labor Relations Act, 797

National Liberation Front (NLF), 912. *See also* Vietcong

National Missile Defense System, 989

National Municipal League, 644

National Negro Business League, 666

National Negro Committee, 663

National Organization for Women (NOW), 895

National Origins Act, 763

National Park System, *g659*

National Recovery Administration (NRA), 783

National Republican Party: 1824 election, 338–39; 1836 election, 350

National Road, 246, 313–14, 315

National Security Act, 853

National Security Council (NSC), 847, 853, 975

National Socialist Party, 806. *See also* Nazi Party

National War Labor Board, 703, 725, 816

National Women's Party, 653

National World War II Memorial, 827

Nation, Carry, 655

Nation of Islam, 890

Native Americans, *p49;* American expansion, resistance to, *m262,* 291–92; American Revolution and, 159, 168, *p168–69,* 169, 172; Christianity, conversion to, 48, 50, 81, 82, 105, 361, 374; citizenship of, 525; culture of, 4, 60, 571; Dawes Act and, 571; discrimination against, 198; disease, effect on, 50; early civilizations of, 5, 7–9, 10–15, 16–22; economy of, 192; education of, 628; English colonists, relations with, *p56,* 58, 61, 66, 68, 69, 75, 78, 112, 123, 124, 139; equal rights for, 666–68; European treatment of, 39, 46, 47, 82; French and Indian War and, 105–06, 108–12; French trade with, 52; during Great Depression, 788–89, 796; Indian Removal Act, 334, 343; Indian Territory, 344; language of, 49; Lewis and Clark expedition, relations with, 281, 284; in Mexico, 367; mountain men and, 360; New Mexico Territory and, 373; population decline of, 568; prejudice against, 668; railroad lands and, 555; relocation of, 343–47, *g343, m344;* relocation, resistance to, 346–47; rights of, 895, 897–98; Spanish colonies and, 41–47; Trail of Tears, *p334–35,* 342, *p342–43,* 345–46, 423; voting rights of, 340; War of 1812 and, 295; western settlers, conflict with, 566–71, *m568;* World War II and, 818. *See also* individual Native American nations

Native Son **(Wright),** 791

Nativists, 397, 399, 617; 1920s, revival of, 762–63, 764; Immigration Act of 1917, 617

NATO. *See* North Atlantic Treaty Organization (NATO)

Naturalization Act, 269

"Nature" (Emerson), 335

Nauvoo, Illinois, 381

Navajo, the, 21, 568, 818

Navigation Acts, 86, 100

navy: British, 153, 170; expansion of, 674, 677, 679, 811

Nazi Party, 805, 806, 812, 825–27, 832

NCAI. *See* National Congress of American Indians (NCAI)

Nebraska Territory, 454

Index

Index

Index

Pinckney, Charles: 1796 election, 268; 1808 election, 290; Constitution, signing of, 199
Pinckney, Charles Cotesworth, 199
Pinckney, Eliza Lucas, 80, 81, *q81,* 98, *q98,* 99
Pinckney's Treaty, 263
Pinckney, Thomas, 263
Pinochet, Augusto, 947
Pisa, Italy, 29
Pitcher, Molly, 155, 164, *p164, q164*
Pittsburgh, Pennsylvania, 7, 107; growth of, 309, 313, 397–98; railroads, 390–91; steel industry, 598, 615, 621
Pittsburg Landing, Mississippi, 483
Pitt, William, 110–11
Pizarro, Francisco, 44
Plains of Abraham, 111
plantation system, 47, *p76–77,* 77, 91, 94–95, *p94, p98–99,* 99, 195, 196, 266, 308, 407–08, *p429,* 539
Platt Amendment, 688
Platte River, 362
Plattsburgh, New York, 297
Pledge of Allegiance, 1053
Plessy, Homer, 1044
Plessy v. Ferguson, 540, 664, 876, 1044
PLO. *See* Palestine Liberation Organization (PLO)
Plymouth settlement, 56, *p64–65,* 65, 67
Pocahontas, 58, *p58,* 59, 61
Poindexter, John, 975
Poland: German invasion of, 807, 809; immigrants from, 613, 616; independence of, 722–23; Solidarity, 977; Soviet invasion of, 302; World War II, 824, 826–27
polio vaccination, *p841*
political machines, 643–44, 647
political parties: forming of, 265
Polk, James K., 1036, *p1036;* 1844 election, 352, 363, 450; Mexico, war with, 375–77; statehood of Texas, 371
poll tax: abolishment of, 855; after Reconstruction, 539
pollution. *See* environment
Polo, Marco, 28, *p28,* 29, *m29,* 31
polygraph, 278
Pompeii, Italy, 274
Ponce de León, Juan, 45
Pontiac's War, 112
Pope, John, 485
popular sovereignty, 215
population: California, Gold Rush, 378; census, first, 313; of English colonies, 89; foreign-born, *g1005;* of Great Britain, during American Revolution, 153; growth of (1800–1840), *g308;* of Inca Empire, 15; Native American, decline of, 12–13; of New York colony, 74; railroads impact on, 587; of the South (1860), 407, *g407;* United States (1820), *m308;* urban and rural growth, late 1800s, *g621;* Urban, increase in, 397–99; west of Appalachians (1800), 317
Populist Party, 551, 577–78
Port Hudson, Louisiana, 505
Portolá, Gaspar de, 374
Portsmouth, New Hampshire, 683

Portugal, 30, *m36;* exploration by, 31, 32, 35–37, 38–41, 51
Posey, Alexander Lawrence, *q346*
Post, Wiley, 793
Potomac River, 257, 314, 483
Potsdam Declaration, 832
Pottawatomie Creek, 455
Powderly, Terence V., 604
Powell, Colin, 979, 988
Powell, Lewis, 949
Powhatan, the, 58, 61
Powhattan confederacy, 69
Preamble to the Constitution, 215
Preble, Edward, 288, *p288*
prejudice: against African Americans, 535, 664, 789; against Asian Americans, 664, 762; against Catholics, 663, 664, 762; against immigrants, 664, 762; against Jews, 663, 664, 762; against Mexican Americans, 668; against Native Americans, 668; progressivism and, 665–66; against Europeans, 762. *See also* discrimination; lynchings; racism
Prescott, William, 137
presidency: cabinet of, 253, 526; checks and balances, 206, 208, 953; commander in chief, 207, 220; election to, 208; executive branch, authority over, 207, 220; limit to terms, 242, 577; powers of, 232; roles of, 207, 220, 221; State of the Union Address, 220; veto by, 208, 217
Presley, Elvis, 864
press, freedom of, 103
Prevost, Sir George, 297
Pride and Prejudice **(Austen),** 303
Priestly, Joseph, 150, *p150*
Princeton, Battle of, *m156,* 157–58
Princeton, New Jersey, *c187*
Princeton University, 631
Princip, Gavrilo, 706
printing press, 100, *p100*
Proclamation of 1763, 87, 112, 123, *m124*
Proclamation of Neutrality, 263
Progressive Party, 660–61, 752, 853–54
progressivism: business and government reforms, 642–47; prejudice and, 665–66; presidential policies of, 656–61; women's involvement in, 650–55
Prohibition, 242; Eighteenth Amendment, 655, 742, 761–62, 764; repeal of, 762
propaganda, 713–14, 726, *p726*
Prophetstown, Indiana, 292
proprietary colonies, 101
protective tariffs, 256, *g256,* 257
Protestant Reformation, 27, 49
Protestants: Catholics, conflict with, 50, 59, 65, 397, 663, 763–64; Maryland, settlement of, 78; spread of, 49
Providence, Rhode Island, 68
Prussia, 57, 163; Monroe Doctrine, 326
Ptolemy, 38
Public Works Administration (PWA), 783, 789
Pueblo Bonito, 17
Pueblo, the, 46
Puerto Rico, 819; immigrants from, 865, 897; imperialism and, 687, *crt688;*

becomes territory of United States, 688
Pulaski, Casimir, 163
Pulitzer, Joseph, 630, 685
Pullman, George M., 586, 587, 606
Pullman Strike, *p604,* 606
Pure Food and Drug Act (1906), 646, 647, 658
Puritans, 56, 65, 67–68, 69, 73, 103; slavery, criticism of, 95
Pusan, South Korea, 857
PWA. *See* Public Works Administration (PWA)
Pyle, Ernie, *q810,* 820, *q820,* 821

Quadruple Alliance, 326
Quakers, 75, 103; American Revolution, neutrality in, 153; movement of, 74; slavery, criticism of, 95, 167, 196, 425, 429, 435, 437
Quebec Act, 129
Quebec, Battle of, 109, 111
Quebec, Canada, 48, 49, 52, 81, 108, *p108–09,* 140
Quechua, 15
Quin, Percy E., 712, *q712*
Quran, 33

Rabin, Yitzhak, 986
racism: against African Americans, 717; after Reconstruction, 535, 539; fight against, 885; slavery defense and, 431. *See also* prejudice
Radcliffe College, 735
Radical Republicans, 520, 523–24, 525–27
radio, *p778–79,* 779, *m779,* 791
railroads: agriculture, impact on, 391, 392–93; buffalo and, 550; cattle industry and, 561, 562; Civil War and, 497, 509, 510; competition among companies, 587; consolidation of companies, 585, 586; corporations, formation of, 596; economy, impact on, 391, 586–87; expansion of, 388, *p388–89,* 389, *c389, m389,* 538, 584–87, *g585, m586,* 621; farmers, conflict with, 575–77, 587; first, 386; hoboes on, 790, *p790;* improvement of, 586–87; monopolies, 657; Native Americans and, 567; network of, 390–91; oligopoly, 645; safety in, 659; in the South, 403, 412; steam locomotive, 555, *p555;* steel industry and, 598–99; transcontinental, 554–56, *m556,* 582, 619, 676; western expansion and, 563; workers on, 398, *p602–03,* 747, 757, 851
Raleigh, Sir Walter, 59
Rama I, king of Siam, 184
Randolph, A. Philip, 746, *p746, q746,* 747, 818, 879
Randolph, Edmund, 194, *q194,* 199, *p200,* 201, 253
Randolph, James Madison, 319

Index

Ross, John, 345, *p345, q345*
Ross, Nellie Tayloe, 752
Roughing It **(Twain),** 558–59
Rough Riders, *ptg684–85, q684,* 685, 687
Rowe, John, *p126, q126,* 127
royal colonies, 101
rugby, 631
Rules of Civility & Decent Behaviour in Company and Conversation **(Washington),** 97
Rumsey, James, 314
Rumsfeld, Donald, 988, 997
Rush-Bagot Treaty, 325
Rush, Benjamin, 177, *p177, q177*
Russell, Charles, 560
Russia: Alaska, purchased from, 359, 676–77; China, influence in, 682; civil war in, 729, 730; immigrants from, 613; Japan, war with, 683; Monroe Doctrine and, 326; Poland, invasion of, 302; revolution in, 716, 745; World War I and, 706–08, 718–21, 729, 730, 731
Russo-Japanese War, 683
Russwurm, John B., 396, 428
Rutgers University, 631
Ruth, Babe, 743
Rutledge, John, 199

S

Sabotage Act, 727
Sacagawea, 284, *p284*
Sacco, Nicola, 746
Sacramento, California, 556
Sadat, Anwar el-, 946, 961
Sahara Desert, 32
Saigon, South Vietnam, 912, *p916,* 921, 932
Saint Domingue, 178
Saint-Mihiel, France, 721
Salem, Peter, 157
Salem Provincial Congress, *c133*
SALT. *See* Strategic Arms Limitation Treaty (SALT)
Salt Lake City, Utah, *p381*
Salt River valley, 17
Samoa Islands, 681
Samoset, 66
Sampson, Deborah, 155
San Antonio, Texas, 82, 369
Sanford, John, 1041
San Diego, California, 57, 82, 374 377
Sandwich Islands, *crt688*
San Felipe, Texas, 366
San Francisco, California, 391, 693; American Indian Movement, in 898; earthquake of 1906 in, 611; growth of, 379; immigrants in, 616; Mexico, war with, 376–77; Populist Party forms in, 551; seaport, role of, 621
San Jacinto, Battle of, 371
San Juan Hill, Battle of, 684, 687
San Martín, José de, 325, *p325,* 326
San Salvador, 34, 40
Santa Anna, Antonio López de, 368–71, *p368, q368*
Santa Fe, New Mexico, 82, *p374,* 376
Santa Fe Trail, 361, 373, 374, *m374,* 376, 379

Santo Domingo, 282, 283
Sarajevo, Bosnia, 705
Saratoga, Battle of, 150, 158–59, 160, 161, 177
Saudi Arabia, 991, 1002
Sauk, the, 346
Savage, Augusta Christine, 761
Savannah, Georgia, 80, 89, 171, 177, 321; slavery in, *p424–25*
scalawags, 529
Scalia, Antonin, 972
Scandinavia, 564
Schlafly, Phyllis, 895
Schurz, Carl, 689
Schwarzkopf, Norman, 979
SCLC. *See* Southern Christian Leadership Conference (SCLC)
Scopes, John, 763
Scotland, 49, 590, 598
Scott, Dred, 458–59, 1041, *p1041*
Scott, Winfield, 345, *q345,* 377, 477
SDI. *See* Strategic Defense Initiative (SDI)
search and seizure, unreasonable, 254
Sears Roebuck, 593
Seattle, Washington, 745, *p785*
Sea Wolf, The **(London),** 629
SEC. *See* Securities and Exchange Commission (SEC)
secession, 462–66, *crt464, m465,* 468–69; ribbon supporting, *p463*
Second Amendment, 236
Second Great Awakening, 419
sectionalism: Missouri Compromise, 449; slavery issue, 322, 454
Securities and Exchange Commission (SEC), 783
Sedition Act, 727
segregation: of African Americans, 524, 539, 540, 561, 664, 817, 875–79, 885; banned, 889; in schools, 531, 627, 683, *p874–75, m875,* 950
selective service, 702, 717, 802, 811, 815, 919–20, 927
Selma, Alabama, 889
Seminole, the, 325, 343, 346
Senate, U.S., 253, 278, 323; creation of, 200, 207; direct election of, 647; Jay's Treaty, 263; national bank, 348; Treaty of New Echota, 345
Seneca Falls Convention, 435–36
Seneca Falls Declaration, 435, 436, 1050
Seneca, the, 21, 106
Seoul, South Korea, 857–58
separatists, 65
Sepoy Rebellion, 387
September 11, 2001, 989, 990, 991–94, *c993, p999*
Sequoyah, 346, *p346,* 416
Serbia, 613; World War I, 706–07
Serra, Junípero, 82, 374
Servicemen's Readjustment Act. *See* GI Bill
Sesame Street, 925
Seton, Elizabeth Ann, 356
settlement houses, 623, 651, 654
Seven Cities of Cibola, 45–46
Seven Days' Battle, 485
Seventeenth Amendment, 240, 647
Seventh Amendment, 237

Seven Years' War, 110
Seward, William H., 676–77, *p676,* 679
Seymour, Horatio, 527
Shakespeare, William, 56, 631
sharecroppers, 538, *p538,* 539
Sharlet, Jeff, 918, *p918*
Sharpsburg, Maryland, 486
Shaw, Anna Howard, 652
Shawnee, the, 262, 291
Shays, Daniel, 195–96
Shays's Rebellion, 185, 195–96, 198
Shenandoah Valley, 493
Shepard, Alan Jr., 909
Sherman Antitrust Act, 583, 599, 645, 657, 661
Sherman, Roger, 139, 199, 200
Sherman, William Tecumseh, 473, *p473, p483, q483,* 506, *p506, q506,* 507, 509; March to the Sea, 510
Shiloh, Battle of, 479, 482–83, 483, *p483,* 484, 493, 507
shipbuilding: colonial, 90
ships, 41; American, French attack on, 269–70; American merchant, 287; American Revolution, *p170; Ancon,* 690, *p690–91,* 692; *Boston,* 681; caravel, 31, 37, *p37; Chesapeake,* 289, 290; of Christopher Columbus, *p35,* 39; *Clermont,* 314–15, 390, *p390;* clipper, 391, *p391;* colonial trade, 90; *Constitution,* USS, 287, *p287,* 296; Dutch, 52; *Empress of China,* 287; *Enterprise,* USS, 288, *p288;* Great White Fleet, 682, *p682,* 683; of Henry Hudson, 51–52; ironclad, 481, 482–83, 503, *p513; Leopard,* 289; *Liscome Bay,* USS, *p831; Maine,* USS, 687; *Mayflower,* the, 65–66, *p66,* 67; *Merrimack,* 480, *p480–81,* 481, 483, *p513; Miller,* USS, *p831; Missouri,* USS, 832; *Monitor,* 480, *p480–81,* 483; *Nashville,* USS, 692; *Philadelphia,* 288; *Tripoli,* 288; used in slave trade, 92, *p92;* Viking, *p38; Virginia,* 481, 483, *p513;* warships, *p674–75,* 675, *p675;* whaling, 90, *p90*
Ships of the Plains **(Colman),** *ptg246–47*
Shogunate, Tokugawa, 86
Sholes, Christopher, 590
Shoshone, the, 20, 284
Shreveport, Louisiana, *p860–61*
Shrop, Dale L., *q825*
Siam, 184
Siberia, 7, 19
Sicily, Italy, 822
Sidisin, Ruth, *q920*
Sidey, Hugh, *q860*
Sierra Leone, 154
Sierra Nevada Mountains, 20
Sikorsky, Igor, 793
Silent Spring **(Carson),** 925
silver mining, 553–54, 578
Sinai Peninsula, 945–46
Sinclair, Upton, 647, 671
Sioux, the, 566, 567, 568, 569, 570, 571, 619, 898
sit-ins, 884, *p884–85,* 885, 888, *p888*
Sitting Bull, chief, 570, *p570, q570,* 571
Six-Day War, 945
Six Nations, 106

adoption of, 187, 210; electoral college, 207; federal government, sharing powers with, 206–07, 216, c216; federal powers compared to, 187–210, 214–223; powers of, 207, 216

states' rights: Confederacy, formation of, 464–65; *Gibbons* v. *Ogden*, 279, 324, 1041; Kentucky and Virginia resolutions, 270; *McCulloch* v. *Maryland*, 279, 324, 349; nullification right, 341; regional conflict over, 322, 323; state sovereignty, 322; John C. Calhoun, supporter of, 322–23

States' Rights Democratic Party: 1948 election, 853, c854

Statue of Liberty, 551, 614, p614, p615, 619

St. Augustine, Florida, 45, p45, 399

St. Clair, Arthur, 261

steamboats, 318, p318, 390, p390, p448–49

steel industry: railroads and, 556, 586, 598–99, 621; Southern, 538; strikes, 583, 606, 747; working conditions in, 603, 615

Steffens, Lincoln, 647

Steinbeck, John, 791

Steiner, Edward A., q612

Stein, Gertrude, 761, q761

Stephens, John Lloyd, 10, 11

Steuben, Friedrich von, 162, 163, p163, 167

Stevens, John, 681

Stevenson, Adlai E.: 1952 election, 861, c861

Stevenson, Robert Louis, 610

Stevens, Thaddeus, 520, q520, 535

Stirm, Robert, p902–03

St. Lawrence River, 51, 81, 109, 111

St. Leger, Barry, 158, 159

St. Louis, Missouri, 281, 284, 315, 397–98, p448–49, p459, 625

St. Louis Post-Dispatch, 752

St. Luke Penny Savings Bank, 668

stock market: 1929 crash of, 770, 772, p772–73, 773–74

stock, of corporations, 596

Stokes, Thomas, q781

Stone, Kate, q478

Stone, Lucy, 434

Stone, William, 478

Stowe, Harriet Beecher, 421, 427, p427, q427

Strategic Arms Limitation Treaty (SALT), 945, 961

Strategic Arms Reduction Treaty (START), 977

Strategic Defense Initiative (SDI), 973

Strauss, Levi, 380

streetcars, 625

strikes, 605–06, 746–47

Strong, Josiah, 677

Stryker, George A., p478

Stuart, Robert, 360

Student Nonviolent Coordinating Committee (SNCC), 885, 890

Stumpe, Ella May, 724, q724

Stuyvesant, Peter, 72, p72–73, q72

submarine, 274, 709, 714, p714, 715

suburbs, 622, 865–66

subways, 625

Sudetenland: German annexation of, 807

Suffolk Resolves, 133–34

suffrage, p640–41, 641, 651, 652–54, 742; opposition to, 653

Sugar Act, 123–24

Sullivan, Anne, 735

Sullivan, Louis, 624

Summers, Alison, q992

Sumner, Charles, 455

Superman, 791

Supreme Court, U.S., 255, 263; 1876 election, 536; creation of, 208, 233; judicial review, 274. *See also* individual court cases

Sussex, the, 715

Sutter, John, 378

Svobida, Lawrence, q788

sweatshops, 615

Sweden: immigrants from, 92

Swift, Gustavus, 587

Switzerland: World War II, 809

Syracuse, New York, 875

Syria, 945–46

Taft-Hartley Act, 853

Taft, William Howard, 1037, p1037; 1908 election, 659; 1912 election, 660–61; dollar diplomacy, 694, q694; military power and, 696; Philippine Islands, independence of, 689; progressive policies of, 660

Taiwan, 847

Taking Sides (Soto), 964–65

Taliban, 992–93

Talleyrand, Charles, 283

Taney, Roger B., 459, p459, q459

Tanner, Henry, 632

Tanzania, 992

Taos, New Mexico, 374

Tarawa, p828–29

Tarbell, Ida M., 594, 647

tariffs: of 1816, 323; Coolidge administration, 752; Era of Good Feelings, 321; during Great Depression, 775; on Hawaiian sugar, 680; Nullification Proclamation, 340; Nullification Act, 341; protective, 256, 257; reforms of, 645, 660, 661; regional conflict over, 322

taxation: under Articles of Confederation, 188, 189, 191, 192; colonial, 74, 101; customs duties, 278; emerges in Europe, 30; during Great Depression, 795; income tax, 577–78, 659–60, c660, 661, 752; in Mormon communities, 382; protective tariffs, 256, g256, 257, 368; revenue sharing, 949; in Songhai Empire, 33; Three-Fifths Compromise, 200–01; unemployment insurance, 797; under United States Constitution, 206–07; voting rights and, 187; without representation, 122–25, 142; during World War II, 816

Taylor, Bayard, q554

Taylor, E.W., q430

Taylor, Maxwell, 911, q911

Taylor, Zachary, 375–76, q375, 450–51, 1036, p1036

Tea Act, 128

Teapot Dome Scandal, 742, 751

technology: adding machine, 590; advances in, 7, 26; agriculture, 392–93; camera, 590; communication, 391–92, 630; computers, 862–63, 1001, g1001; defined, 31; gramaphone, p546; impact on exploration, 31; Industrial Revolution and, 305, 306; industry and, 389, 755; lightbulb, 582, 589; railroads, 389–91, 587; Soviet interest in, 945; steamboats, 390; telegraph, 589, 610, 676; telephone, 582, 589, 590; television, 1001; typewriter, 590; vacuum cleaner, 590; of World War I, 708–09, p708

Tecumseh, 275, 291, 292, q292, 293, 295, 296, q318, 351

Tejanos, 367, 369

telegraph, 589, 610, 676

telephone, 582, 589, 590

television, p840, 864

temperance movement, 419, crt420, 654, 655, 665, 761

tenant farmers, 539

tenements, 622, p622, 643

Tennessee, 735, 983; Civil War, 484; readmission to Union, 519, 525; Reconstruction, 531; secession, 465–66; settlement of, 281; statehood, 317

Tennessee River, 482–83, 782

Tennessee Valley Authority (TVA), m781, 782

tennis, 631

Tenochtitlán, 5, 13, 14, p42–43, 43–44

Tenskwatawa, 292, p292

Tenth Amendment, 237, 254, 255

Tenure of Office Act, 526

Terrell, Mary Church, 652, p652, q652

terrorism, 991–96, m994

Terry, Peggy, q776

Texas, 45, 373, 403, 861, 983; 1825 cost of land, c367; annexation of, 357, 450; cattle industry in, 560, 561; Civil War and, 482, 505; in Deep South, 401; Dust Bowl in, 787; exploration of, 285; female governor of, 743, 752; immigration into, 1005; independence of, 366–71; Mexican War and, 375–76; readmission to Union, 521, 526; Republic of, 369–71; secession of, 464; settlement of, 366, p366–67, 367–68, 561; Spanish in, 82, 326; war for independence, m370

Texas Revolution, 369

textile industry: 1920s, difficulties for, 757; British inventions for, 305; cotton, demand for, 307; Lowell, Massachusetts and, 396, p396; New England factories, 389; in the South, 403, 538; trade unions, 396; working conditions of, 395

Thailand: World War II, 829

Thames, Battle of the, 292, p292, 295, 296

Their Eyes Were Watching God (Hurston), 760

There Is Confusion (Fauset), 760

"The Stars and Stripes Forever" (Sousa), 632

Third Amendment, 236

Index

Index

Whitefield, George, 102
White House, *p1034*
White, John, 59–60, *q60*
Whitman, Marcus, 361–62
Whitman Mission, 361–62, *p361*
Whitman, Narcissa, 361–62, *p361, q361*
Whitman, Walt, 421
Whitney, Eli, 302, 306, 401–02
Whittier, John Greenleaf, *q428*
Whyte, William H. Jr., 866, *q866*
Wicks, Hamilton S., *q564*
Wigfall, Louis, *q403*
Wilderness, Battle of, 507–08
Willard, Emma Hart, 437–38
Willard, Frances, 654, *p654*, 655
William and Mary College, 103
William III, king of England, 99
Williamson, Hugh, 199
Williams, Roger, 68–69, *q68, c79*
Willkie, Wendell L.: 1940 election, 811
Wilmington, North Carolina, 171
Wilmot, David, 450
Wilmot Proviso, 450
Wilson, Edith, 732
Wilson, James, 199, *p203, q203, c205*
Wilson, Woodrow, 734, *q734*, 735, 1038,
p1038; 1912 election, 661; 1916 elec-
tion, 715; Fourteen Points and, 729–30;
League of Nations, 730–32; Mexico,
relations with, 695–96, *q696*; neutrality
policies of, 713–15, *q713*; Nobel Peace
Prize of, 703; Pancho Villa, pursuit of,
695; suffrage, 653; tariff reforms, 661;
Treaty of Versailles, *p728–29*, 731–32,
q731; World War I, armistice of, 723,
q723; World War I, beginning of, 704,
716–17, *q717*; World War I, support
for, 726
Windsor, Connecticut, 68
Winesburg, Ohio (Anderson), 761
Winfrey, Oprah, 956
Winslow, Edward, 64, *p64, q64*
Winthrop, Elizabeth, 648–49
Winthrop, John, 67, 68, *q68, c79*
Wisconsin, 587, 752; reform of electoral
system, 647; women's rights move-
ment in, 438
Wisconsin Territory, 458
Witch of Blackbird Pond, The
(Speare), 70–71
Wizard of Oz, The, 791
Wolfe, James, 108, 109, *p109*, 111
Woman's Christian Temperance Union
(WCTU), 654
women: African American, 667; American
Revolution, 154, *p154*, 155, 164–65;
Civil War (1861–1865), 492–93; colo-
nial, 102–03; discrimination against,
198, 397, 420; education of, 420, 651;
factory workers, 603, 605, 615; first
member of Congress, 715, *p715, q715*,
717; in government, 796, 797, 988;
Harlem Renaissance, 760–61; higher
education of, 628, 651; immigrants,
616; Industrial Revolution and, *ptg304–
05, p305*, 306; labor unions and, 604,
605, 797; in late 1800s, 621, *p650–51*;
Lowell girls, 396, *p396*; in military,
155, *p155*, 815; Native American, 567;
pioneer, 317; rights of, 894, 895; roles,

changing of, 651–52; unequal pay,
895, *g895*; voting rights of, 101, 102,
340, 435–37, 636, 742, 751, 759; wages
of, 752; western settlers, 553, 563, 564;
in workforce, 787; World War I, 724,
p724–25, 725; World War II, *p814–15*,
815, 816, *p816*, 817. *See also* women's
rights movement
Women Appointed for Volunteer
Emergency Service (WAVES), 815
Women's Army Corps (WACs), 815, 819
Women's Peace Party, *p712–13*
women's rights movement, 434–38;
beginning of, 431; education, 438;
leaders, 424, 429; progress in, 437. *See
also* women
Women's Trade Union League
(WTUL), 655
Wood, Grant, 791
Woods, Granville, 592
Woods, Tiger, 957
Woodstock, New York, 925
Woodward, Ellen Sullivan, 787, *q794*
Wool, John, 345
Woolworth Building, 593, 624
Woolworth, F.W., 593
Worcester, Massachusetts, 142, 435
Worcester v. Georgia, 344, 1045
Work and Win (Alger), 630
Works Progress Administration
(WPA), *p784*, 794, *p794–95, c795*, 796
World, the, 630, 685
World Trade Center, 990, *p990–91*,
991–92, *p991*
World Trade Organization (WTO), 1002
World War I, 704–09; *m720*; alliance sys-
tem prior to, 705, 706; American neu-
trality, 713–17; armies, size of, *g713*;
beginning of, 707–09; *m707*; Europe
after, *m730*; Germany's involvement
in, *p704–05*; imperialism and, 705–06;
military buildup, 706; military deaths
in, *g729*; nationalism prior to, 705;
reparations from, 730; sea, on the, 709;
Western Front, 720, 722
World War I, U.S. involvement, 702,
p702; events leading to, 712–17;
propaganda for, 713–14, 726, *p726*;
public opinion of, 727; rationing during, 726; resources for, 725; support
for, 726; workers during, 725
World War II, 802–35; American neutrality, 806; beginning of, 808–11; cost of,
832; dictators, rise of prior to, 805–06;
Europe after, *m844*; in Europe and
Africa, 820–27, *m822*; events leading
to, 804–07; military increases prior to,
809, *c809, g809*; in the Pacific, 828–32,
m830; Tuskegee airmen, 759, 818,
p818; western front, 809
World War II, U.S. involvement:
events leading to, 811–13; minorities, effect on, 817–19; war economy,
815–16; wartime hardships of, 816–17;
women, effect on, 817
Wounded Knee, South Dakota, 569,
571, 619, 898
WPA. *See* Works Progress Administration
(WPA)
Wright, Orville, 590–91, *p590*

Wright, Richard, 791
Wright, Wilbur, 590–91, *p590, p591*
writs of assistance, 123
writ of habeas corpus, 495–96
WTUL. *See* Women's Trade Union League
(WTUL)
WTO. *See* World Trade Organization (WTO)
Wyoming: exploration of, 360; female
governor of, 743, 752; internment
camps in, 1042; New Mexico Territory,
373; statehood, 554; western settlers,
563; women's suffrage in, 437, 653
Wyoming Valley, Pennsylvania, *p168–69*

XYZ affair, 251, 269

Yakima, the, 20
Yalta, 842, *p842–43*, 843, 845
Yank, Billy, *q479*
"Yankee Doodle," 175, 176
yellow journalism, 630, 685–86, 687
Yellow Kid, The (Outcault), 619
Yellowstone National Park, 658
Yeltsin, Boris, 978, *q978*
Yemen, 992
Yom Kippur War, 946
York, 284
York, Alvin, 722
York, Duke of, 74
York, Pennsylvania, 186, *c187*
Yorktown, Battle of, 151, 174, *p174–75*,
175, 176, *p176*, 177, 178
Yorktown, Virginia, 173, 175, 176
Young, Brigham, 381, *p381, q381*, 382
Yuba River, 379
Yucatán peninsula, 57
Yugoslavia, 980, 986
Yung Cheng, 87

Zenger, John Peter, 103
Zhou Enlai, 944
Zimmermann, Arthur, 716
Zimmermann telegram, 702, 716
Zuni, the, 20, 46

Index

Acknowledgments

Text Acknowledgments

Grateful acknowledgement is given authors, publishers, and agents for permission to reprint the following copyrighted material. Every effort has been made to determine copyright owners. In case of any omissions, the Publisher will be pleased to make suitable acknowledgments in future editions.

70 Excerpt from *The Witch of Blackbird Pond* by Elizabeth George Speare. Copyright © 1958, renewed 1986 by Elizabeth George Speare. Reprinted by permission of Houghton Mifflin Company. All rights reserved.; **130** From *My Name is America: The Journal of William Thomas Emerson—A Revolutionary War Patriot* by Barry Denenberg. Copyright © 1998 by Barry Denenberg. Reprinted by permission of Scholastic, Inc.; **310** Reprinted by permission of Simon & Schuster Books for Young Readers, an imprint of Simon & Schuster's Publishing Division, from *Fever, 1793* by Laurie Halse Anderson. Copyright © 2000 by Laurie Halse Anderson.; **404** From *Day of Tears* by Julius Lester. Copyright © 2005 by Julius Lester. Reprinted by permission of Hyperion Books for children. All rights reserved.; **421** "Hope is the thing with feathers" reprinted by permissions of the publishers and the Trustees of Amherst College from *The Poems of Emily Dickinson*, Thomas J. Johnson, ed., Cambridge, Mass.: The Belknap Press of Harvard University Press, copyright © 1951, 1955, 1979, 1983 by the President and Fellows of Harvard College.; **648** From *Counting on Grace* by Elizabeth Winthrop, copyright © 2006 by Elizabeth Winthrop. Used by permission of Wendy Lamb Books, an imprint of Random House Children's Books, a division of Random House, Inc.; **767** "The Negro Speaks of Rivers," from *The Collected Poems of Langston Hughes* by Langston Hughes, copyright © 1994 by The Estate of Langston Hughes. Used by permission of Alfred A. Knopf, a division of Random House, Inc.; **767** "Mother to Son," from *The Collected Poems of Langston Hughes* by Langston Hughes, copyright © 1994 by The Estate of Langston Hughes. Used by permission of Alfred A. Knopf, a division of Random House, Inc.; **892** From *The Watsons Go to Birmingham—1963* by Christopher Paul Curtis. Copyright © 1995 by Christopher Paul Curtis. Used by permission of Doubleday, a division of Random House, Inc.; **964** Excerpt from *Taking Sides*, copyright © 1991 by Gary Soto, reprinted by permission of Harcourt, Inc.

Glencoe would like to acknowledge the artists and agencies who participated in illustrating this program: SettingPace; American Artists Reps Inc.; GeoNova LLC.

Photo Credits

Cover (t)Rubberball/JupiterImages, (b)Museum of the City of New York/CORBIS; **iv** (bl)Bettmann/CORBIS; **v** (tl)Francis G. Mayer/CORBIS; (tr)Tom Grill/CORBIS; **vi** (bl)Smithsonian American Art Museum, Washington, D.C./Art Resource, NY, (br)Royalty-Free/CORBIS; **vii** (tr)The Granger Collection, New York; **viii** (c)David J. & Janice L. Frent Collection/CORBIS, (others)Flip Schulke/CORBIS; **ix** (t)Shannon Stapleton/Reuters/CORBIS; **x** (tc)Getty Images, (tcr)The New York Public Library, New York, NY, USA/Art Resource, NY, (tr)Brand X/CORBIS, (bl)The Granger Collection, New York, (bc)The British Museum/HIP/The Image Works; **xi** (tr)Hulton-Deutsch Collection/CORBIS; **xii** Library of Congress; **xiii** (tr)North Wind Picture Archives, (br)The Granger Collection, New York; **0** (bl)Pilgrim Hall Museum; **0–1** (l to r, t to b)Peabody Essex USA/The Bridgeman Art Library; **4** (bkgd)Frank Lukasseck/CORBIS; **5** (cr)The British Museum/Heritage-Images/The Image Works, (bl)The British Library/HIP/The Image Works, (bl)Werner Forman/Topham/The Image Works, (br)Indianapolis Museum of Art, USA/Bridgeman Art Library; **6–7** Kenneth Garrett; **8** Gianni Dagli Orti/CORBIS; **10–11** (bkgd)Jon Davison/Lonely Planet Images, Werner Forman/Topham/The Image Works; **12** Scala/Art Resource, NY; **13** Archivo Iconografico, S.A./CORBIS; **14** (l)Craig Lovell/Eagle Visions Photography/Alamy Images, (r)Danita Delimont/Alamy Images; **16** Liu Jianmin/Panorama/The Image Works; **17** (bkgd)The Art Archive/Musée du Nouveau Monde La Rochelle/Dagli Orti, (r)Peabody Essex Museum, Salem, Massachusetts, USA/The Bridgeman Art Library International; **18–19** (bkgd)Richard A. Cooke/CORBIS; **19** (t)Werner Forman/Topham/The Image Works, (c)Werner Forman/Art Resource, NY, (br)Michael S. Lewis/CORBIS; **20–21** (bkgd)Stock Montage, Inc./Alamy Images; **21** (br)The Art Archive/Buffalo Bill Historical Center Cody Wyoming/Mireille Vautier, (others)Werner Forman/Topham/The Image Works; **23** The British Museum/Heritage-Images/The Image Works; **26** (c)Bettmann/CORBIS, (b)Kazuyoshi Nomachi/CORBIS, (bc)Bildarchiv Steffens/The Bridgeman Art Library; **27** (c)© National Library of Australia, Canberra, Australia/The Bridgeman Art Library, (r)Bettmann/CORBIS, (bl)Tim Davis/CORBIS, (bl)P.H/Art Resource, NY; **28** (tr)Roger-Viollet/The Image Works, (br)Bruno Morandi/Getty Images; **30** (bl)The Art Archive/Marine Museum Lisbon/Dagli Orti, (bc)AKG Images, (br)Lockheed Martin; **31** Comstock/Superstock; **32** (tr)Private Collection, Photo © Heini Schneebeli/The Bridgeman Art Library, (tr)David Morris/Alamy; **34–35** Bettmann/CORBIS; **35** (c)CORBIS; **36** Jack Sullivan/Alamy; **38** (tl)Bettmann/CORBIS, (others)Werner Forman/Art Resource, NY; **39** (bcl)The Art Archive/General Archive of the Indies Seville/Dagli Orti, (br)Bridgeman-Giraudon/Art Resource, NY; **42–43** Ned Seidler/National Geographic Image Collection; **43** (br)George H. H. Huey/CORBIS; **45** (tl)World History Archive/Alamy, (tcl)Schomburg Center/Art Resource, NY, (tr)The Granger Collection, New York, (tr)Wendell Metzen/Index Stock; **46** (cr)The Art Archive/National Palace Mexico City/Dagli Orti, (bl)North Wind/North Wind Pictures; **47** White House Historical Association; **48–49** Musée des Ursulines de Québec, collection of the Monastère des Ursulines de Québec; **49** (t)Hudson's Bay Company Archives, Provincial Archives of Manitoba; **50** (cr br)C Squared Studios/Getty Images; **50–51** (br)Pixtal/age fotostock; **56** (t c)The Granger Collection, New York, (tc)Darrell Gulin/CORBIS, (bc)Musée de l'Armée/Dist. Réunion des Musées Nationaux/Art Resource, NY; **57** Werner Forman/Art Resource, NY; **58** (tl)MPI/Getty Images; **58–59** Private Collection/The Bridgeman Art Library International; **60** (tl)North Wind/North Wind Picture Archives, (others)The Granger Collection, New York; **62–63** David Muench/CORBIS; **63** (bl)The Granger Collection, New York; **64** (tr)Mary Evans Picture Library; **64–65** Swerve/Alamy; **65** (b)Collection of the New York Historical Society, USA/The Bridgeman Art Library International; **66–67 68** The Granger Collection, New York; **70** Bettmann/CORBIS; **72** (tr)Stapleton Collection/CORBIS; **72–73** (br)Library of Congress, Prints & Photographs Division; **73** (bc)Henry Francis Dupont Winterthur Museum, Delaware/Bridgeman Art Library; **74** (tc)The Granger Collection, New York, (tr)Art Resource, NY; **76–77** The Granger Collection, New York; **77** (b)CORBIS; **78** (tr)StockBrazil/Alamy, (tr)The Granger Collection, New York; **79** The Granger Collection, New York; **80** (bl)Schlesinger Library, Radcliffe Institute, Harvard University/The Bridgeman Art Library, (br)Louis S. Glanzman/National Geographic Image Collection; **81** akg–images; **83** Collection of the New York Historical Society, USA/The Bridgeman Art Library International; **86** (tc)Superstock, (cl)The Art Archive/Lucien Biton Collection Paris/Dagli Orti, (bc)SSPL/The Image Works; **87** (c)National Portrait Gallery, London, UK/The Bridgeman Art Library, (bcl)The Granger Collection, New York; **88–89** (bc)Collection of the New York Historical Society, USA/The Bridgeman Art Library International; **89** (bc)James Leynse/CORBIS; **90** (tc)Collection of the New York Historical Society, USA/The Bridgeman Art Library, (tc)SSPL/The Image Works, (tr)North Wind Pic-

ture Archive; **92** (bcl)Mary Evans Picture Library/The Image Works; **92–93** Superstock; **93** (cr)Chicago History Museum, USA/The Bridgeman Art Library; **94** The Granger Collection, New York; **96** (bl)North Wind Picture Archives/Alamy, (br)Mary Evans Picture Library/Alamy; **97** (tc)North Wind Picture Archives/Alamy, (c)CORBIS, (cr)Jack Carey/Alamy; **98–99** © age fotostock/SuperStock; **99** (bc)The Colonial Williamsburg Foundation; **100–101** The Granger Collection, New York; **100** (bl)Courtesy American Antiquarian Society, (others)The Granger Collection, New York; **102** Topham/The Image Works; **104–105** (br)Artist Robert Griffing/Paramount Press Inc.; **104** (tr)Bettmann/CORBIS; **106** The Art Archive; **108–109** (br)The Art Archive/General Wolfe Museum Quebec House/Eileen Tweedy; **109** (bcr)The Granger Collection, New York, (br)Stapleton Collection/CORBIS; **110** (cr)Geography & Map Division/Library of Congress; **110–111** (b)Superstock; **111** (bcl)National Gallery of Canada, Ottawa, Ontario, Canada/The Bridgeman Art Library International; **113** (bcl)Collection of the New York Historical Society, USA/The Bridgeman Art Library, (br)Geography & Map Division/Library of Congress, (others)The Granger Collection, New York; **116** (cl)The National Archives/HIP/The Image Works; **116–117** Superstock; **120** (bl br)The Granger Collection, New York, (br)Ironbridge Gorge Museum, Telford, Shropshire, UK/Bridgeman Art Library, (bkgd)Superstock; **121** (l)Massachusetts Historical Society, Boston, MA, USA/The Bridgeman Art Library, (t)Maya Barnes Johansen/The Image Works, (r)Kevin Fleming/CORBIS, (b)Réunion des Musées Nationaux/Art Resource, NY; **122–123 126** (t)Courtesy of the Massachusetts Historical Society; **126–127** (bkgd)Historic New England, Boston, Massachusetts, USA/The Bridgeman Art Library International; **127** (bc)Bettmann/CORBIS; **128** (t)Bettmann/CORBIS, (r)Massachusetts Historical Society, Boston, MA, USA/The Bridgeman Art Library; **130** (cr)Library of Congress, (cr)Private Collection/Bridgeman Art Library; **132–133** North Carolina Museum of Art/CORBIS; **133** (bc)Kevin Fleming/CORBIS; **134** Nichipor Collection, Courtesy Minuteman National Historical Park/Rob Huntley/Lightstream; **135** (t)Geoffrey Clements/CORBIS, (t)Kevin Fleming/CORBIS, (br)Bettmann/CORBIS; **136** (tl)National Portrait Gallery, Smithsonian Institution/Art Resource, NY, (r)Collection of the New York Historical Society, USA/The Bridgeman Art Library; **138–139** Francis G. Mayer/CORBIS; **139** (bc)CORBIS; **140** (t)American Antiquarian Society, Worcester, Massachusetts, USA/The Bridgeman Art Library, (b)National Portrait Gallery, London; **141** (l)Collection of the New York Historical Society, USA/The Bridgeman Art Library, (r)Superstock, (bc)Bridgeman Art Library; **145** The Art Archive; **147** CORBIS; **149** (r)Bettmann/CORBIS, (b)CORBIS; **150** (c)American Illustrators Gallery, NYC/The Bridgeman Art Library, (bl)Blanc Kunstverlag/SV-Bilderdienst/The Image Works, (bc)Collection of the New York Historical Society, USA/The Bridgeman Art Library; **151** (c)Painting by Don Troiani, photo courtesy Historical Art Prints, Ltd., (br)Former Grandidier collection Musée national des Arts asiatiques-Guimet G 956/Thierry Ollivier/RMN/Art Resource, NY; **152–153** (b)The Granger Collection, New York; **153** (bc)Bob Krist/CORBIS; **154** The Granger Collection, New York; **155** Drew Crawford/The Image Works; **156** Bettmann/CORBIS; **157** The Granger Collection, New York; **158** Superstock; **161** (bl)SuperStock, Inc./SuperStock, (bc)The Metropolitan Museum of Art/Art Resource, NY; **162** (bl)Superstock, (br)Collection of the New York Historical Society, USA/The Bridgeman Art Library; **163** (cl)JG Photography/Alamy Images, (br)Superstock; **164** Bettmann/CORBIS; **166** (cr)Stock Montage, Inc./Getty Images, (bl)TIME; **167** (bl)Lebrecht Music and Arts Photo Library/Alamy, (br)Old Paper Studios/Alamy; **168** National Gallery of Canada, Ottawa, Ontario, Canada/The Bridgeman Art Library International; **169** (bl)Painting by Don Troiani, Military & Historical Image Bank, (bc)The Granger Collection, New York; **170** (cr)Bettmann/CORBIS, (bl)Guardian Royal Exchange Insurance Collection/The Bridgeman Art Library, (br)National Trust Photographic Library/David Levenson/The Image Works; **171** The Granger Collection, New York; **172** Superstock; **174–175** SuperStock, Inc./SuperStock; **175** (br)Library of Congress Prints and Photographs Division; **176** (cr)Art Media/HIP/The Image Works, (bl)Yale University Art Gallery/Art Resource, NY, (bc)Ann Ronan Picture Library/HIP/The Image Works; **177** Stapleton Collection/CORBIS; **179** The Granger Collection, New York; **180** (bl)Visual Arts Library, London/Alamy, (bl)Atwater Kent Museum of Philadelphia/Courtesy of Historical Society of Pennsylvania Collection/Bridgeman Art Library, (bl)Krause, Johansen/Archivo Iconografico, SA/CORBIS; **181** (c)Visual Arts Library, London/Alamy, (b)North Wind/North Wind Picture Archives; **184** (tc)Private Collection/The Bridgeman Art Library, (br)Mervyn Rees/Alamy; **185** (c)Joseph Sohm; Visions of America/CORBIS, (br)Bridgeman-Giraudon/Art Resource, NY, (others)The Granger Collection, New York; **186** (cr)Courtesy of the Massachusetts Historical Society; **186–187** (b)The Granger Collection, New York; **187** (br)Tom Grill/CORBIS; **188 189** The Granger Collection, New York; **190–191** NorthWind Picture Archive; **191** (cr)The Granger Collection, New York; **192** (tl)Atwater Kent Museum of Philadelphia, Courtesy of Historical Society of Pennsylvania Collection/Bridgeman Art Library, (tcr)StockBrazil/Alamy, (tr)The Granger Collection, New York, (cl)The British Museum/HIP/The Image Works, (c)M Stock/Alamy; **194–195** Stock Montage/Getty Images; **196** (tl)NPS, (r)The Granger Collection, New York; **197** Museum of the City of New York/CORBIS; **198–200** The Granger Collection, New York; **202** (l)Maya Barnes Johansen/The Image Works, (cl)Bettmann/CORBIS; **203** (tr)Smithsonian American Art Museum, Washington, D.C./Art Resource, NY, (r)Joe Sohm/The Image Works; **204** (tr)SuperStock, Inc./SuperStock; **204–205** (b)Michael Ventura/PhotoEdit; **205** (br)The Granger Collection, New York; **206** (bl)Getty Images, (bcr)The Granger Collection, New York; **207** Brand X/CORBIS; **208** The Granger Collection, New York; **209** (bc)Réunion des Musées Nationaux/Art Resource, NY, (br)The Granger Collection, New York; **211** (tcl)The Granger Collection, New York, (tcr)Tom Grill/CORBIS, (cr)Joseph Sohm; Visions of America/CORBIS; **214** (c)PhotoDisc/Getty Images; **214–215** (b)Steve Allen/Brand X Pictures/JupiterImages; **215** (cl)Mark Wilson/Getty Images; **218** Private Collection, Peter Newark American Pictures/The Bridgeman Art Library International; **219** (bl)Library of Congress, (br)Hassan Ammar/AFP/Getty Images; **221** Matthew Cavanaugh/epa/CORBIS; **224** (tr)Bettmann/CORBIS; (c)Joe Sohm/Pan America/Jupiter Images, (b)Comstock/PunchStock; **227** Herminio Rodriguez/AP Images; **228** Bettmann/CORBIS; **230** Boltin Picture Library; **244** Dennis Brack/Black Star/Time Life Pictures/Getty Images; **245** Sandy Schaeffer/Mai/Mai/Time Life Pictures/Getty Images; **246** (cl)Jeff Greenberg/The Image Works; **246–247** Superstock; **250** (c)Superstock, (bcr)AKG London, (br)The Granger Collection, New York; **251** (tl)Hulton-Deutsch Collection/CORBIS, (cl)The Granger Collection, New York, (c)Roy Ooms/Masterfile, (bl)Free Agents Limited/CORBIS, (br)The Gallery Collection/CORBIS; **252–253** The Granger Collection, New York; **253** (c)Charles Dharapak/AP Images; **254** The Granger Collection, New York; **256** Peabody Essex Museum, Salem, Massachusetts, USA/The Bridgeman Art Library; **258** (tr)North Wind Picture Archives/Alamy, (c bl)The Granger Collection, New York, (b)Private Collection/The Stapleton Collection/The Bridgeman Art Library, (bl)CORBIS; **259** (tc)Uyen Le/Alamy Images, (cr)Julia Robertson/Aero Imaging Inc., (br)The New York Public Library, New York, NY, USA/Art Resource, NY; **260–261** Metropolitan Museum of Art, New York, USA, Lauros/Giraudon/The Bridgeman Art Library International; **261** (br)The Granger Collection, New York; **262** The Granger Collection, New York; **264–265** (b)The New York Public Library/Art Resource, NY; **265** (bc)Bettmann/CORBIS; **266** The Granger Collection, New York; **267** (bcl)The Granger Collection, New York, (br)Christie's Images/SuperStock; **268** Library of Congress; **269** American

1116 *Acknowledgments*